BUSINESS COMM.

2/6

8⁹⁵

HANDBOOK OF
BUSINESS LETTERS

BY THE SAME AUTHOR

This Way Up
Smooth Sailing Letters
Real Estate Salesman's Handbook
How to Write Better Business Letters
Effective Credit and Collection Letters
Fundamentals of Real Estate Practice (co-author)

HANDBOOK

OF

BUSINESS

LETTERS

REVISED EDITION

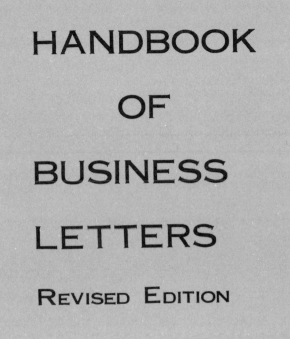

BY **L. E. FRAILEY**

PRENTICE-HALL, INC., Englewood Cliffs, N.J.

PRINTED IN THE UNITED STATES OF AMERICA
37597—B & P

A WORD ABOUT THE REVISED EDITION

Scores of new and revised sample letters form the heart of this Revised Edition of L. E. Frailey's standard work in the business letter writing field. Many of the illustrative letters appearing in the previous edition have been revised or replaced by new letters, while others have stood the test of time and remain effective models.

Among the companies cooperating in the presentation of this edition are such leaders in business and industry as Bankers Life Company, Equitable Life Assurance Society, Plaza Hotel in New York City, Revlon, Inc., Armco Steel Corporation, Minute Maid Company, and Continental Can Company, Inc. These and other important contributions represent successful and profitable letterwriting in action.

New illustrations showing current styles in letterhead design, and a Company Better Letter Program based largely on the program of New York Life Insurance Company are other added features. The prime purpose of this revised edition has been to broaden the applications to types of letters, situations, and industries that did not exist when the first edition was published in 1948, and to retain to the fullest extent the direct and simple approach of the author with its emphasis on short words and brief sentences that has been so phenomenally useful in creating business-getting letters for large and small businesses in every type of industry.

AUTHOR'S PREFACE TO THE FIRST EDITION

Let's talk five minutes about this Handbook!

Twenty-five years ago, I was just as much interested in letters, and what they could be made to do for business, as I am now. Even then I dreamed of one complete book which would give any executive and his secretary a simple, easy-to-read explanation of common-sense principles, and all the reference data needed to settle any questionable point with respect to letter mechanics.

The book I pictured would be concise and practical, but long enough to cover every kind of business correspondence; it would be helpful to sales managers, credit men, personnel directors, chief executives, secretarial workers, and all the clerks who had to "talk on paper" or "take a letter." I wanted very much to write it then, but I realized that first must come years of experience and study, of actual testing for results . . . the accumulation of a great mass of case material. To be of any real value, the writing of such a book would take a long, long time.

Like Topsy, the book just had to *grow*.

Nevertheless, knowing that someday I meant to do the job, I began away back then to keep my eyes open for anything that might help to make the various sections of this Handbook interesting and valuable. Fortunately, all through these years it has been my privilege to know many business executives, to work with many companies, and to gain a down-to-earth view of letter uses and problems. You see, I was *exposed* in a very practical way to the things that had to be known if my book were to become a reality.

Often, it has seemed that Providence was bringing me in contact with the people who could—and did—supply the practical, tested material which you will find on these pages. From business men and women who had to endure my lectures, from those enrolled in the Business Letter Clinics conducted in many cities, from workers in the companies where I reviewed correspondence, from subscribers to the Dartnell Letter Service, from students in my classes at Northwestern University, from the letter-experts with whom I became pleasantly acquainted . . . from all these and many other sources, a flood of letter-contributions came my way. Thus, "Topsy" had many friends—she gained weight steadily.

The above explains why I do not regard myself as the sole author of this Handbook of Business Letters. On the contrary, thousands of generous business friends have helped to make it possible, and to them you and I owe a little bow of appreciation. They have helped to present you with information and suggestions based on practice, not theory. The things talked about are not what I *think* or *assume* about business letters; they represent the actual *experience* of many others like yourself who are constantly trying to make their letters do the best possible job.

The recorded results of experience . . . this I believe to be the only safe guide for one who dares to write a business book. Hence, I would not presume to talk to you about sales unless I myself had been a salesman; or about sales letters unless I myself had written successful sales letters. I would not presume to talk about credit problems unless I myself had wet my feet in trying to solve them. What right would I have to tell you, the head of a company, how to conduct a Better Letter Program unless I had practiced what I preached?

Yes, this is a practical book. There is nothing in it which will not hold water. For a quarter of a century I have been finding out why some letters pull and others flop. If that sounds like blowing my own horn, it is not so intended. It is simply that I have discovered many FACTS that you need to know about business letters, and you'll find them all in this volume.

The majority of the letters, the bulletins and opinions were sent to me with permission to use them as I pleased. For others, permission was secured during the book's preparation. There are a few cases, however, where it has not been possible to identify the writer of the letter, or the company from which it originated. This is regrettable, but I did not believe that any business person would want a letter omitted which might help others to improve their dictation. Certainly, I have tried hard to render unto Caesar what is Caesar's due, and I ask the indulgence of anyone who has been inadvertently overlooked.

L. E. FRAILEY

CONTENTS

HOW LETTERS SERVE BUSINESS

1

HOW LETTERS
SERVE BUSINESS

1. WHY LETTERS MUST BE USED

To take the place of personal contacts. Why should anyone complain about the letters he is forced to write in business? These fast-moving messengers who wear the five-cent armband do a job which no individual could do for himself. You pay what it takes to get them into the mailbox, and that is all. They get no salary, and turn in no expense account.

If you are a credit manager, by using letters you can talk to a hundred, or a thousand, customers who owe your company money—on the same day, and without leaving your desk. If you are a sales manager, you can dictate one interesting form letter that will tell all your distributors about a new product—just the same as if you appeared personally on the same day in their stores. Letters conserve your time, and multiply your efforts, by taking the place of personal contacts. Letters are a great boon to business. They help to get things done.

More necessary as business expands. The bigger the company, and the wider the area which it serves, the greater is the need for letters. The man who operates a neighborhood shoe-store may be able to handle almost everything personally, although he could use sales letters to develop new customers. But the owner of a large chain of shoe-stores, operating in various cities and states, could hardly get along without some device to substitute for personal contacts. Oh, he might depend entirely on telegrams and telephone calls, which have their place in the sun, but he couldn't long compete with others on such a wasteful basis. Yes, we must admit that letters, more than any other part of business, help to make possible growth and expansion. Letters conquer space. Letters make one minute do the work of many. Letters deserve more respect than they have had in business.

Not like the early days. There was a time, of course, and not too far

3

back, when letters were not so necessary or important. Remember how Abe Lincoln, the postmaster, carried what letters he received in his hatband? That was the story we were told in grade-school. There is no reason to doubt it. But those were the days of the small stores—the cobbler, the grocer, the tailor, doing business only in their own restricted areas—each serving a limited number of people who could come in or send someone else for what they wanted.

Getting a letter in those days was an exciting event. It didn't matter particularly how the letter was written. It was passed around, and always got attention. The only rule that seemed to prevail for letter-writing in those days was that it should be written in the dryest possible manner, and in a language so stiff and formal that the true personality of the writer was completely hidden. Unfortunately, that rule was never abolished, and even now there are some who foolishly cling to it.

The awareness of change—the appreciation of up-to-date ways of doing business—are most important to anyone who aspires to become a successful letter-writer. We gain nothing by imitating the past. Like living customs and working conditions, the standards for a business letter have changed for the better. Why should any businessman who drives a modern automobile, tunes in to a television program originating in Europe, or takes a jet from New York to Paris, use the same style for writing a letter as did his great-grandfather?

These are *modern* times! Many letters to write! Much to learn about HOW to write them!

2. THE MAJOR USES OF LETTERS

To handle routine matters. A large part of the correspondence which passes back and forth in business is routine in nature. Letters of this type are usually short, and nobody expects them to be especially interesting or persuasive. In other words, routine letters don't try to influence human behavior, as would one to a salesman whose orders have fallen off, or as would another to a customer who has neglected too long the payment of a bill. There is no problem involved in the dictating of a routine letter, and for that reason the job is comparatively easy. For example, it requires no special skill to confirm an order. That is a routine matter which can be handled courteously in a few words. But if you must decline the order, and the customer is likely to be angry about it, then the letter situation is a problem far above routine level, and great skill is required to write the letter which will say "no" and still retain the goodwill of the customer.

The very simplicity of the job of dashing out a batch of routine letters also tends to set up a trap into which the writer may easily fall. The letters are sometimes too curt—too cold. They become contacts without a smile. They *could* help to win or hold goodwill, but they *don't*.

This tendency to serve the meat without the seasoning can represent a great loss to the company where it prevails. Since every friendly contact helps to maintain the right relationship between the company and the public it must serve to stay in business, why should any chance, no matter how small, to add fuel to the fire be disregarded? The letter-writer most valuable to his company is the person who makes *every* letter, routine or otherwise, a friendly, human message seasoned with a genuine will to serve. No letter can be considered so unimportant as to justify an indifferent job.

To sell products and services. If any one type of letter were to be selected as most valuable in business, the *sales letter* probably would get the nod. Certainly, with the possible exception of some adjustment letters, it is the most difficult to write. As the name obviously implies, the object of the sales letter is to *sell*. If, for example, the letter is mailed to one thousand customers or prospects, its merit can be measured by the percentage of favorable replies.

Too many sales managers and executives still seem unaware of the fact that certain specific principles must be applied in the construction of a good sales letter, and that the percentage of "pull" will invariably depend on the writer's understanding of those principles, plus his ability to put them to work. The successful sales letter is neither the result of genius nor an act of Providence. There are *skills to master*, as will be explained later in this Handbook.

Since sales letters are used to develop orders, and thus have direct relation to profit, it must be the obligation of the sales manager, and even of the president, to make sure they are prepared in the way most likely to be effective. Any ignorance with respect to sales letter construction—any haste or carelessness in doing the job—will mean orders *lost* that might have been *gained*, and thus, a direct waste of possible profit dollars.

There are, of course, as shown in Section 7 and 8, numerous kinds of sales letters—from those that come out at the end and ask for the order, to the more subtle ones that break the ice for future business. In every case, you are writing to a human being, seeking to impel a certain reaction, whether it be to sign and return the enclosed order-blank, or merely to make him say, "I like the way this fellow writes to me—he must work for a good company."

Although the number of sales letters mailed every year is truly enormous, a great many more could still be used to increase business. The smaller merchants, and some of the larger ones, too, usually neglect this opportunity to keep people informed about the mechandise they have in stock. Except for the rare announcement of a bargain-sale, or of some special event such as moving to new quarters, you seldom get letters from the retailers serving your neighborhood. And yet, if used intelligently, sales letters will increase business for the average local merchant. This has been proved in many localities.

To establish credit and collect money. Very few companies keep collectors in the field, and it is not generally considered wise to place any collection burden on the shoulders of salesmen. Hence, a very large percentage of credit and collection problems are solved by the use of letters. On rare occasions, when a large amount of money is involved, the credit manager or an associate may seek a personal interview, but the great bulk of the work necessary to establish credit ratings, to refuse special terms or privileges, and to collect slow accounts, is handled by correspondence.

Here again, a handicap exists for many credit men because they disregard tested principles which would make their letters more effective. The best credit men are both goodwill builders and money collectors. They work with the sales department and often find the way to place a sales "twist" in a letter about some credit situation. They are students of psychology, and expert letter-craftsmen. From the letter-courses sponsored by their National Association, credit men in various cities have gained a fair concept of the principles of letter carpentry, and we are seeing less and less of old time collection methods where the credit man started by calling the wayward customer a dead beat, and then "worked up" to the point where he threatened the delinquent with legal action.

In the section of the Handbook devoted to credit and collections, you will find many fine letters to prove that credit men in general are holding their own in comparison with those in other fields of business; but there are still too many money-collectors who believe, as in days of old, that a collection letter which sizzles with abuse is better than one which reasons man-to-man with the customer.

To adjust complaints and misunderstandings. Even in the best-managed company, where the customer relations policy is "fairplay and good manners," it is impossible to avoid an occasional tangle in the threads of business. No matter where the fault may rest, the company with long-pull vision will do everything possible to satisfy the customer. If the adjustment cannot be in the nature of a "yes," at least the effort is made to save face for the customer by making the "no" as gentle and painless as the adjustment manager can devise. The art of being able to smooth the ruffled feathers of a customer, of changing a frown to a smile, is one that seems better adapted to letters than to personal contacts. This, to be sure, is only a general statement, because there are exceptional cases where no letter could do the job.

The advantage of the letter adjustment over the personal one is that the writer can very carefully state his case from start to finish without the danger of an interruption which may take the argument off on a tangent, result in heated words back and forth, and conclude with the customer even more disturbed than before. The letter affords a better chance to place all the cards face-up on the table, and if the facts are stated in a friendly-game fashion, it is often surprising how neatly and completely the meeting of two minds can be reached. This job is not done so easily in a personal conversation.

Thus, we see that adjustments by letter not only save a lot of time, but also tend to eliminate the bickering which so often ends in the losing of the customer's goodwill. The aim, of course, is to assign the responsibility of handling complaints to a man of good judgment who has the knack of writing friendly letters. Irrespective of whether he gives all, gives a part, or gives not at all, his letter still carries a tone of consideration for the customer's point of view, and a sincere appreciation of his business.

To win and hold goodwill. Naturally, it might be asked, "Why mention only goodwill letters as apart from all the other types? Isn't that one of the objectives in *any* business letter?" Quite true. Just as in one sense every employee of a company is a member of the sales department, so, in the same way, every letter should be a messenger of goodwill. But there are also those letters in business which are written for *no other purpose* than to make the customer feel he is important to the company, to show that a human relationship exists just as one man may be the friend of another. Such a letter is nothing more than the waving of a hand to someone across the street, and a "Hello there! How are you doing? We are interested in you and your business."

You could call these goodwill builders "unnecessary letters," and that's what they are if you think of business as a cold and formal thing in which there is no place or time for those little courtesies which help to make it warm and personal. Many executives hold a different opinion, however. They realize that competition is keen and that companies other than their own are often shooting for their customers. They think the time and effort well spent in sowing seeds of goodwill which may help to keep old customers in the fold and may round up some new ones.

In Section 10 of this Handbook, you will find many of these "unnecessary" goodwill letters—messages of appreciation, of congratulation, of condolence—and you may judge for yourself how *you* would react to them. Certainly, if written at all, they must originate in a friendly company where the spirit of service is strong and genuine.

Whether or not you believe these goodwill letters are worthwhile, the fact remains that many of our leading companies use them to continue building their businesses. Investigate the sales progress of any company committed to a letter-program for building customer goodwill, and you will surely find it a step in front of its competitors.

3. Letters as Part of Public Relations

Not as pigs are pigs. Perhaps because adept correspondence is one of the newer skills developed for use in business, there are still many executives, and others of the rank and file, who think a letter is a letter as a pig is a pig. Businessmen who realize that the preparation of a good sales letter is just as exacting as the preparation of a good sales talk are forced to endure a period of transition, during which the importance of letters, and the need of *trained* writers, must overcome the idea held by many other executives that their own letters are good because they have been writing them for years.

This condition is both confusing and lamentable. You see companies willing to spend large sums of money on intensive training programs for salesmen, but reluctant to spend a dime to improve letters. Yet the same customers and prospects, day in and day out, are contacted by both salesmen and letter-writers, and often with the same objectives. This, of course, is both costly and destructive to business. Often the good accomplished by the highly trained salesman is nullified by a letter-writer who has had no training at all. The salesman works hard to get a new customer for the company. A correspondent comes along with a tactless letter, and the customer is lost. Examples like these are countless, and they all result from the idea that a personal contact is different from one made by letter. That's all nonsense; words written are just as important as words spoken.

A letter is *not* a letter as a pig is a pig. Letter-writing, unless it is of the lowest routine variety, is a psychological process. It involves the mastery of principles which are known and tested. When those principles are applied, success follows. The trained letter-writer is an asset to his company. The man who scorns the training, and thinks he knows it all without investigation of the facts, is just as much a liability.

One man talking to another. Aside from the principles that must be understood is the fact that a letter—a *good* letter—reflects the personality of the writer, which (needless to say) should be pleasing to the reader. In a good letter, *one man talks to another.* The reader must be made to forget that he is *reading* a letter. Instead, the writer has traveled on a piece of paper to *talk* to him—in exactly the same way that he would if he had appeared in person.

A letter is a personal contact. Never forget that. Why should it be anything else? There's a customer in California whose account is lagging. You can't go that far to talk about it, but you can call your secretary, or use your dictating machine, and ask him in a friendly way for a check. You can put the same smile in the words on paper that you would put in your voice if the customer were there in the same room with you.

There are many angles to the construction of various types of business letters, and it takes time and practice to master them. If your own letters have been dry and commonplace, you can add new life and vitality to the next batch by just trying to *talk* to the folks who are going to read what you have to say. Make them see your personality between the lines.

Your readers are human beings. After all, these folks—your readers—are not just *names.* They are *people.* They walk, talk, sleep, eat, gossip, worship, love, hate—just as you do.

Business consists of a multitude of human contacts—the clashing of opinions, the unity of desires—and making the sum total pleasant is the object of what we call "Public Relations." If the nature of these contacts determines the degree of goodwill earned and held by your company, then how can letters be ignored? Letters are part of public relations, and that means *human* relations. Two human beings with their heads together—you and your reader—that's all a letter is. At least, all it *should* be.

"The most effective letters," says a bulletin issued by the Household Finance Corporation, "are frank statements—messages from real people to other real people. They should be easy to read and easy to understand. They must be friendly and courteous. The often-stressed point that business letters should develop goodwill is not 'bunkum' but a principle of vital significance. Every letter involves a problem, and every problem has at least two sides: the customer's point of view, and that of the writer. It sometimes seems that these are opposed to each other, yet they usually are in harmony, because good business transactions are mutually profitable to the parties involved."

What L. A. Downs thought of goodwill. The idea that every contact in business tends to help or hurt in the molding of public relations was ably expressed in a letter written by the late L. A. Downs, then president of the Illinois Central Railroad. He said:

> Cultivation of goodwill is not a departmental activity, but the work of the entire organization. Friends are made, or can be alienated, by the operator who answers the telephone, the person who writes a letter, the clerk who sells a ticket or accepts a shipment; or, even through what is done or left undone by some member of the organization who does not come in direct contact with the public. *Every member of our company is a public relations worker,* and our reputation depends upon the skill with which each one does his part of the common task.

Speaking more directly of letters, Mr. Charles Kell, then personnel director of the General American Life Insurance Company, St. Louis, said in one of his training bulletins: "Business letters, like water, have a tendency to seek the lowest level unless there is a system of pump pressure to direct the flow. It is foolish and wasteful for any organization to build at great expense a high type sales organization, and be indifferent to the counteraction resulting from letters that fail to follow through."

Routine letter that sold Illinois Central. There is no reason why a routine letter, if written by someone properly motivated toward the company, cannot *sell* as well as *tell*. In the author's collection of good letters is one which aptly illustrates this fact. It came from the secretary of Mr. Downs, and handled a situation which every secretary encounters frequently.

> Dear Mr. Frailey:
>
> It will remind you that Illinois Central service extends far beyond our own rails when I tell you that Mr. Downs is calling on some of our shippers this week in California. As soon as he returns, I will show him your letter—and, of course, he will be glad to reply.

The situation was simple. All the secretary *had* to do was to explain why there would be a delay in the answer to my letter. Mr. Downs was out of town. And that is exactly what the average secretary will tell you under the same circumstances. But this one was above average. She saw in this routine letter a chance to be a *salesman* for Illinois Central.

A letter about Movement 26402627X. In contrast with the above example of sales co-operation, consider the story of a friend who inherited an old-style watch. It had been his great-grandfather's, and, of course, was big and amusing to see in these days of thin and elegant watches. But my friend soon discovered that this ancient time-piece faithfully kept on the job. So he said: "This is a remarkable watch. It may look old-fashioned, but the old boy still keeps perfect time. I am going to write to the company that made this watch, and give them the number. Maybe they can tell me how old it really is. Besides, they will be glad to know that one of their watches is still doing a good job."

There was a routine situation to excite anybody with an ounce of sales blood. The clerk who answered that letter had a lot more to work with than did the secretary whose boss was out of town. He had the chance to say, "Thanks for telling us about your old watch. It is still good for many years of perfect service. You see, that's the way our watches always have been made—to last throughout the years, and never cause any trouble."

But, my friend's letter fell into the hands of a—well, judge for yourself. He had all the chance in the world to *sell* as well as *tell*. But here is what he wrote:

> In response to your kind inquiry regarding *Movement* 26402627X, we wish to advise that our records show date of manufacture was July, 1886. We note your appreciation of our *product,* and trust this information will be of some interest to you.

What a travesty on public relations, that such a letter could have been written! Not only was the language full of "whiskers" (see Section 2 of this Handbook) but the writer evidently didn't realize that his company sold *watches.* My friend had inherited a "Movement"—not a watch; and then it became a "product." What about *your* wrist-movement? Does it keep good time?

The greatest fault of the letter, however, appears at the end—"and trust this information will be of some interest to *you.*" Of interest to *him?* Why not of interest to the *company?*

Have we been too severe in our judgment of the clerk who wrote this routine letter? Well, perhaps so. Every day in business, thousands of other clerks are writing routine letters with no better realization of how they could create friendly contacts—winning goodwill for the companies where they originate, and helping to *sell* their services. Yes, the fault rests more with the company than with the individual. We cannot expect the employees on these lower, routine jobs to make the most of letter opportunities unless they are *taught* and motivated. Perhaps Mr. Downs had talked to his secretary about the importance of the letters that she wrote; perhaps, from his own dynamic personality, she had absorbed some of his sales enthusiasm. Perhaps nobody at the watch company had ever pointed the right letter-way to the clerk who wrote so dully about "Movement 26402627X." After all, it is the responsibility of leadership to *lead.* Somebody must make the letter-writers in

American business see the importance of what they are doing. Somebody must train—motivate—them.

Yes, letter contacts are part of the Public Relations Program. But this fact has little meaning until those who write the letters are conscious of it.

4. Letters Need Executive Attention

Progress begins at the top. Almost without exception it is true that the best letters are being written, consistently, and throughout all departments, in those companies where a major executive takes an active interest in the program. Preferably, this major executive should be the president.

Since the president is usually the most respected individual in the company, his word has great weight. When the employees know he has "gone all out" for a project, they are influenced to follow his example and to accept his suggestions without grumbling. Obviously, then, the first and most important step in the initiation of a better-letter program is a message from the president in which he gives his wholehearted approval. This message has more teeth if the president makes it plain that he expects complete co-operation—even from the top ranking executives, who may themselves need letter-instruction just as much or more than the other employees. It is an unhappy condition when the majority of the letter writers in a company are trying hard to write in the easy, natural, modern style, and letters of 1776 vintage continue to roll out of the executive offices.

This need of executive co-operation is so urgent that no competent letter consultant will accept an assignment to establish a better-letter program until he is assured that all those who write letters in the company, from top to bottom, are ready to do their part.

The check of carbon copies. It is hardly possible that any executive can be absolutely sure what kind of a letter-job is being done in his company unless he takes an occasional inventory. This can best be done by asking that an extra carbon copy be made of each letter written on a certain day or during a longer period. An examination of these carbon copies will quickly reveal the weaknesses and strong points of the various letter-writers. In smaller companies where the number of dictators is not too numerous, this check-up can well be made by the president. In larger companies, it can be delegated to a vice-president, the personnel director, the office manager, or to some other high-ranking official. Needless to say, one requisite for the person chosen to take the inventory is that he must already be thoroughly trained in the principles of good letter construction. Otherwise you would face the unhappy condition of the kettle calling the pot black—and the pot could not be expected to co-operate.

How the program can be carried out after the initial check of carbon copies is discussed in Section 6, but obviously the better informed the chief executive is at the start with respect to what needs to be done, the better equipped he is to ask co-operation from those who look to him for their bread and butter.

To secure maximum return per dollar cost. A very substantial reason for executive interest in the quality of the letters mailed from his organization is that they represent a major cost in the operation of the business. Because the average person tends to think of a letter in terms of a five-cent postage stamp, a piece of paper, and an envelope, there often exists an astonishing indifference to the total yearly cost of sending out the necessary letters. As a result, many an executive has no control over this expense, although he may be extremely cautious in approving other expenditures not nearly as large.

As in the operation of any other phase of the business, the chief executive has the right to insist that the cost of company letters be no higher than is necessary to secure the desired results. He cannot be sure of that when the total has not been determined, and little or no curiosity has been shown about it by those who budget annual expense.

Thus, a strange situation exists in many a company. The cost of the personal calls made by salesmen is measured down to a split penny, and every effort is made to hold it down. Dependent upon the type of business and the nature of the product, this cost per personal contact may run from one dollar up to many dollars. Furthermore, the sum varies for each individual according to his ability, persistence, and the territory where he works. Yes, a lot of time is spent checking these items—but in how many companies is the cost known for letter-calls? It is usually considered a part of the overhead, and hardly an item worth worrying about. The executive who feels that way is indeed headed for the surprise of his life—if and when he finally gets the facts. Letters cost money—plenty of money—more than you might think.

What is the average cost of a business letter? Fortunately, a number of intelligent surveys have been made to answer this question, and although the answer varies according to prevailing labor and material costs, it still remains an interesting, and perhaps surprising figure. Considering the dictator's time, stenographic cost, nonproductive labor, fixed charges, materials, mailing cost and filing cost, the average cost for a letter is approximately $2.00.

How savings can be made. By initiating an intelligent cost-cutting campaign, about 50 cents can be saved on each letter. How can this be done?

• by inaugurating a campaign to make letters shorter; equipping executives with dictating machines and form paragraph indexes.

• by centralizing the stenographic and typing departments; using photocopying and transcription machines; installing electric typewriters, efficiency desks and chairs; instituting a bonus (incentive) plan.

• by utilizing efficient equipment to reduce the number of employees needed, with matching reduction in nonproductive time.

• by savings in floor space through centralization of correspondence departments; labor-saving devices cut employees' needs for compensation insurance.

• by using better quality paper, with smaller sizes where possible; gang printing of inter-office letterheads, with other forms done on office printing equipment.

• by use of modern sealing and stamping machines, not only to save labor but also to reduce losses due to pilfering of stamps.

• by centralizing all files and filing operations; modernizing filing equipment and methods.

"When Frailey wore diapers." Assuming that everything possible has been done to hold down letter costs, there still remains the major saving achieved when letters are made to do a better job. This brings us back again to the stern necessity of making sure that every letter-writer understands and *applies* the known principles of good letter construction. Hence, the company must maintain a program through which these principles are *taught,* and follow a system of control that will offset the tendency of letter-writers to slip back into old habits or to become careless and indifferent when little or no attention is given to their handiwork. Lighting the fire which motivates letter-writers to do a better job is a sure step forward, but throughout the year someone must keep the fire burning.

As in the accomplishment of any other objective in business, a program for better letters will succeed in proportion to how completely it gains, in practice and spirit, the co-operation of *all* who write letters. A few old-timers, with minds closed to the possibility that their own letters might be improved, and outspoken in their criticism of the company program, may prove to be a serious obstruction to progress.

Your author well remembers Mr. B., a sales manager in a large company where a concerted effort was being made to improve correspondence. Mr. B. wrote letters that were long, windy, and tiresome. Because of his lengthy service and high position, however, nobody felt qualified to step on his toes, or to suggest that he, too, might benefit by taking advantage of the company's better-letter program. Finally, the problem of Mr. B. was dumped in the lap of the president. The latter waited until he had a particularly bad example of Mr. B.'s letter-writing—a verbose sales letter which had failed to produce any business—then the following conversation took place:

> President: Mr. B., why don't you talk to Frailey about your next sales letter?
> Mr. B.: Who, *me*?
> President: Yes, why not? He has helped some of the other sales managers with their letters. Two heads are sometimes better than one, you know.
> Mr. B.: Huh, that's ridiculous. Why *I* was writing letters *when Frailey wore diapers.*

It makes no difference how *long* a man has been writing business letters. The point is, does he know *how* to put punch and pull in them? There are principles to master. This Handbook seeks to explain and illustrate what they are—and how you can use them.

There are many firms who have tackled the problem with persistence and have achieved gratifying results. Among those that can be mentioned are Montgomery Ward, the Gates Rubber Company, Jewel Tea Company, Monarch Life Insurance Company, the Household Finance Corporation, and numerous others of equal rank. There is no question but that in those organizations where the value of better letters has been recognized, and where an honest attempt has been made to motivate and train those who write them, the gain has far exceeded any imagined loss in time and cost.

The tragic toll of indifference. When we turn to those companies that continue to permit their letter-writers to shift for themselves, the picture is both dismal and discouraging. We know the cost of writing letters in business. We wonder how executives can continue to be indifferent to sales letters that do not sell, collection letters that do not collect, and adjustment letters that do not adjust. The principles of letter-writing are not difficult to master. Indifference to them takes a tragic toll which could very easily be avoided. The reaction to a business letter, as to a personal contact, may often persist throughout the years. You never know when a poor letter may rise from the grave to haunt you or someone else who then becomes the victim of its misguided approach.

There's the memory of a young man who years ago was trying to sell rice for a Texas mill. It was the end of a hard week, and the orders had been scant. Ever hopeful, he went late one afternoon into the buyer's office of a grocery jobber. The buyer was cordial, and he poked his finger with interest into the various sample boxes. Finally he selected certain numbers and began to assemble the specifications for a carload of rice. The young man's heart beat faster. It was satisfying to know that he could send a good order to his company that night, instead of relaying the usual excuses.

Until that moment, the buyer had not been concerned with the name of the mill. Then he frowned. Leaving his office, he returned in a few minutes with a letter which was yellow and brittle with age. It had been written thirty years before, as the young man soon found out, by the credit manager of the mill he represented. And this is what the buyer said: "Young man, I am sorry, but you may tear up that order. Here is a letter which I received thirty years ago from your company. I have been in business a long time, and this is the most insulting letter that I ever had to read. I was a little pressed for cash at the time, but I wasn't a dead beat or a thief. In Texas, an unpaid bill is not an excuse for discourtesy. I wouldn't care to deal with your mill, sir. Please don't call on me again."

The young man learned the hard way how important a business letter can be. You see, this is a true story. The young man wrote this Handbook.

5. The Personal Value of Knowing How

Importance to the individual. Knowing how to write good business letters is an asset in any career. With the increasing importance of letters, and the growing recognition that they help or hurt company objectives, it may even be said that the individual who lacks a thorough knowledge of letter-principles is seriously handicapped in the building of his own career. Other qualities being equal, the capable letter-writer is more likely to win promotion than someone in his department who has neglected to acquire the same knowledge and skill. More and more in the future, the man who can "talk on paper" to a customer or prospect in a friendly, forceful way will be marked as extremely valuable to his company, and his progress will be accelerated accordingly.

If this be true, and it is, then why should any person who hopes to advance in business be indifferent to the importance of letters, or fail to utilize any and every opportunity to become an expert letter-carpenter? If the company provides this opportunity, the problem is simple. If not, the individual himself may create it—there are night schools to attend, books to read, and others to study who have already mastered the art. The road is not barred to anyone who has an adequate knowledge of language and its usage.

College education not required. Unlike many other fields of human endeavor—medicine, law, engineering, chemistry—where advanced education is necessary, you do not need to be a college graduate to master the principles of letter-writing. Average intelligence, common sense, and the right mental attitude—plus the willingness to accept and apply the suggestions offered in this and other books—are the chief essentials. Once you know *what* you are trying to do, and *how* it should be done, the rest is accomplished by on-the-job practice.

Out of your own experience, you begin to compare results. You thought sales letters A and B were equally good. You prepared them carefully, using the formula of the Star, the Chain, and the Hook (Section 3). But when results were counted, letter A proved to be top notch and letter B only mediocre. Why? When you are able to spot the reason, you are a more seasoned letter-writer. You grow in skill as you play the game.

The news gets around. The individual who masters the art of writing a good letter does not remain unnoticed for long. His skill is respected, and you hear it said of him, "John Doe can help with that letter...see John Doe ...John Doe writes the best letters in the company." The news gets around, and soon John Doe's ability reaches executive ears. He is tagged as one worth watching. His chances for promotion are enhanced.

Needs of a good letter-man. Almost any individual in business can learn to write better-than-average letters. The slogan for success (see Section 2) is "Relax...be natural...just talk." Beyond this capacity for letting your hair down and being your everyday natural self, however, there are certain skills and qualities which are needed in the preparation of effective business letters. Although these are discussed more fully in later chapters, a preview will do no harm:

1. You cannot very well dictate a good letter unless you can put words together into correct sentences; that skill involves a workable knowledge of grammar, and a vocabulary sufficiently large to express any thought you wish to convey.

2. It cannot be stated too often—there are certain tested principles which must be mastered, both for general letter-writing and for specific types such as sales, collection, and adjustment. There is nothing about the learning of these principles to frighten anybody—but you *must know them.*

3. No man can successfully serve a company with his head but not with his heart. Loyalty breeds an enthusiasm which is reflected in the letters that you dictate. In plain words, unless you like your company and your job you should quit.

4. The more you know about the products of your company and the

nature of the services rendered, the better you are equipped to talk about them in a letter. This is especially true of situations where sales and complaints are involved. The good letter-writer does not sit in a vacuum and remain indifferent to what goes on about him. Instead, he knows how the company's products are made and why they are good. Consequently, he can write with enthusiasm about them—and that gives him *power* which otherwise he would lack.

5. A genuine liking for people is a "must" that seems to require little comment. If the objective is to make every letter a cordial contact, then the writer must *feel* cordial. Any insincere friendliness would instantly be sensed by the reader. A liking for people leads to an understanding of human nature. You understand their problems and their point of view, and because you "talk their language" you are accepted as a friend even when you must say "no."

6. Imagination is a valuable asset to the letter-writer. Many think of it as a vague "something" which one must be born with. This is not strictly true, although certain people seem more endowed than others. Imagination is basically the taking of images (memories of experiences) from the mind where they have been stored, and creating from them new combinations or mental pictures. Thus, in a practical sense, and that's as far as we need to go, the businessman is using imagination when he *looks ahead*. Perhaps a new building is to be erected. He imagines first of all the uses to which it may be put, and then considers how it should be designed to achieve these uses. Another man thinks of the company's radio or television program under preparation. He imagines the folks who will be listening or watching —their habits and desires—then he seeks to slant the program to fit the mental picture he has formed. Imagination gives color and life to a letter. It can be cultivated more easily than you think.

7. Whether a sense of humor is inherited, acquired, or both, can be left to the psychologists. Certainly, it may be described as a mental attitude which enables one to take the good and bad of life not too seriously; in that sense it would seem worthy of cultivation. Humor in a letter is desirable when not overdone. No reader, for example, wants to feel that his problem has not been taken seriously, nor does he want to be the *object* of the fun. On the other hand, it has been proved frequently that a dash of humor can improve a letter's pull. Later in this Handbook you will encounter many successful letters in which there is a smile or even a guffaw. You, too, will enjoy them, as surely as did the original readers.

8. Even though the mention of another quality essential to success as a letter-writer might seem to come from the pulpit rather than the desk of

a businessman, the fact remains that moral stability is necessary in the handling of all forms of public relations. Letters reflect the character of the writers. The customer or prospect is placed in the mood for favorable reaction when he feels he is reading the words of an honest, impartial, dependable man. Of course, in business there are always some who think they are smart enough to pull the wool over the customer's eyes. Such writers fool only themselves. Good letter-men place their cards face-up on the table. They play the game fairly; they practice the Golden Rule.

BUSINESS LETTER LANGUAGE

5. OTHER LANGUAGE FAULTS

BUSINESS LETTER LANGUAGE

1. A HUMAN CONTACT ACROSS SPACE

Accomplished by putting words on paper. As explained in the previous section, an effective business letter is a personal contact between two human beings. To save time and to cross space quickly, the writer of the letter puts on paper a message which otherwise he would prefer to deliver in person; thus a conversation begins. The writer has "first say," but he may, and often does, invite the reader to reply. As the letters pass back and forth, the two persons *talk* to each other until there is a meeting of minds, or, for lack of it, the conversation ends.

The man who writes with a sense of personal contact has a better chance to make what he says interesting and convincing than the one who feels he is "writing letters." The good dictator says to his secretary, "Bring your book, I want to talk to this man about paying his bill." The poor dictator is more likely to say, "Bring your book, I must write a letter about this delinquent account." Both dictate for the same purpose, but the first is mentally stepping into the shoes of the fellow who later will be reading what he says, while the other stays in his own office, physically *and* mentally.

If you want to write successful letters, always keep in mind that you are going to talk across space. In reality, you put your thoughts on paper, then you jump into an envelope and travel to where the reader lives or works. Out you pop with a friendly handclasp, ready to tell him why he should give you an order, or pay his past-due bill, or merely that you like him a lot as a customer, and will continue to serve him the best that you can. No matter what you talk *about,* the language you use is the same as if you had met him on the street, in his home, or at his office.

No special language of business. Contrary to what some may believe, as revealed by their colorless and tiresome letters, there is no special

23

language for business—unless "special" means making an extra effort to be natural, so that the reader will be warmed by your friendly personality and feel that a likable human being has paused to chat with him. True, you want your sentences to be grammatically correct and free from slang or profanity—you are not on the golf course, or riding to work—nevertheless you are not using a *different* language. You are only dressing it up a little bit.

Of course, you do get letters in which the writers seem to think they are "on parade." Maybe they are thinking about the "dignity of business," or perhaps they have been taught that letters should be cold and formal— cold as an oyster, formal as a Park Avenue butler. People who feel like that about letters are more to be pitied than blamed. They haven't an equal chance in competition with other letter-writers who practice the rule, "Relax...be natural...just talk." They are hopelessly handicapped by their stiff or stilted language. They can't possibly be accepted as friendly human beings or win favor by what they say. The reader simply yawns, and walks away.

One of the family. The president of your company doesn't want letter contacts to be cold and formal. He knows that the most loyal customer is the one who feels like "one of the family." The following letter, amusing though it may be, illustrates the point. It was mailed by a lady in Michigan to an employee of Montgomery Ward in Chicago.

> Ever since receiving your letter, and the enclosed refund check, I have worn a grin like that of the Cheshire cat. Perhaps you'll see the joke if I tell you.
>
> A number of years ago, I visited a friend in Illinois. One day we came home to find her landlady dressed all in black, with her nose all red from weeping. She could hardly control her grief as she read us an item in the paper. Her friend, her *personal* friend (sob), one of the firm, one of the head officers of Montgomery Ward, was *dead*.
>
> No, she had never seen him. But he did (sob) write her the loveliest letters! Ever since that time that a mistake had been made in one of her orders, and she had written about it! He (sob) had answered *personally,* and he had made them correct the mistake, and he had told her that he would attend to her letters and orders *himself!* And now (sob-sob) he was *dead*.
>
> And did we think it would be all right if she sent some flowers? She had some lovely marigolds and zinnias in her garden.
>
> And now *I've* got a "personal friend." I can picture him as that old lady did *her* friend, trotting around from department to department, giving his "personal attention" to the selection of a

paper of pins, measuring off two yards of tatting, and picking out the largest quart cup in the store!

Please don't die, Mr. R. What should I do without you? And I have no marigolds or zinnias.

Yes, we can smile at the little old lady pictured in the letter. And so did the lady from Michigan! But beneath the story is a fact important to the success of any business. When a man can write letters in such a cordial way that the customer feels a "personal friend" is speaking, then a great good has been accomplished for the company. The relationship may often endure throughout the years and spread to friends and relatives, so that many, many sales are developed—and all from a few friendly letters.

When language habits are barriers. Since the language used in a business letter largely determines how successfully a human contact is made with the reader, common sense tells us that we should examine our letters carefully to make sure that we have no language habits hindering the effectiveness of the contact. Bad habits in word usage do exist, and any one of them may be a barrier that tends to hold writer and reader apart.

Unfortunately, some of the guilty letter-writers, usually older men long established in business, meet with a cold eye any suggestion that their style could be improved. Indignantly they reply, "This is the way we've always done it"—a condition of mental obsolescence for which there is no cure—and they keep on dictating letters that confuse or repel their readers. For example, here is a monstrosity in words which was actually mailed from the head office of an insurance company to a policyholder in North Carolina.

> Surrender of the policy is permissible only within the days attendant the grace period, in compliance with the citation relevant options accruing to the policy. We are estopped from acquiescing to a surrender prior to the policy's anniversary date.
>
> We are confident that an investigation relevant the incorporation of this feature will substantiate that the policies are not at variance with policies of other insurance companies.

Fine letter, isn't it? So easy to read—a friendly contact with a customer! Can't you see the smiling face of the writer between the lines? How pleased that North Carolina mountaineer must have been! That insurance company was fortunate to have on hand a letter-expert who knew how to hold the goodwill of a policyholder.

You think so? Nonsense! Of course you do not. Could there be a poorer attempt to contact a policyholder? By what strange and distorted concept was the writer driven? Where did he get the idea that a business letter should display as many big words as possible? Was he just a beginner trying to show his wisdom, or an old fuddy-duddy who believed heart and soul in the "dignity" of business?

Apparently, the policyholder had written to the company, and requested the surrender of his policy. The answer was "No." A little word with two letters would have done the job, but what did the insurance man say? "We are estopped from acquiescing"—how much more impressive! Say those words aloud—"estopped from acquiescing"! Maybe they sound pretty but they certainly don't belong in a business letter. How *could* any human being talk to another in such a strange lingo? Perhaps he swallowed a bumblebee just before he started to dictate.

You see, the writer of that letter had formed one of the bad language habits which become barriers between writer and reader. His fault was "goozling." We will hear more about it later in this section of the Handbook.

2. The Old-Time Whiskers

Word combinations of ancient vintage. Because in the early days of our nation letters were mostly used for formal purposes, the language was very cold and stilted. Those were the days when you might have ended a letter with, "Your obedient servant," or, "We beg to remain, dear Sirs, Faithfully yours." And of course the whole of your letter would have contained many other equally stilted phrases. Such word combinations are a long way removed from the natural, informal language which adds interest and personality to the modern letter.

However, before you criticize too severely the writers of these early letters, you must remember that the social customs of the upper class were much more formal than they are today. The language which seems so amusing to us now was actually *used* in high society. You see, they were partly, at least, following our modern rule for letter-writing—*Write as you talk*. The people of the middle and lower classes had little necessity for letters, and their use in business was the exception rather than the rule.

Today, many of the old customs have vanished. Men no longer wear knee pants, silver buckles on their shoes, or powdered wigs. Women no longer favor hoop-skirts, tightly drawn corsets, or high-buttoned shoes. These are modern times of careless informality—of sport shirts, sweaters, slacks, and two-piece bathing suits—and a host of inventions which have also tended to break down class distinctions and bring people together on a basis of free and easy living. Yes, men still wear white tie and tails for certain formal occasions but they grumble at the idea. Women have their evening gowns, too, but these are cut to reveal more charm than when a party dress called for several petticoats and perhaps a bustle. The modern tempo is to be *natural*—in dress, in speech, in all other human relationships.

The "whiskers" linger on. With all these changes from the old days to the new, you would scarcely expect to find some business-men still using the language of 1776 in their letters. For some strange, unexplainable reason, however, the stilted phrases of yesterday are frequently encountered, although they make impossible that friendly personal contact which, as we have seen, is the aim of any good business letter. For example, here are some sentences taken from the carbon copies of letters mailed recently from the home office of an insurance company:

> We *herewith take the liberty* of acknowledging your letter *of recent date.*
> *Attached hereto,* you will *please find same.*
> *Thanking you very kindly,* we *beg to remain,*
> In reply to your letter of *the 21st instant, we would wish to state,*
> *Trusting you will be in a position* to do *same, we are,*
> *Your favor has duly come to hand,* and *we beg to advise,*

The italicized phrases are *not* the language of modern speech. They are throwbacks—as obsolete and old-fashioned as candle-light or the pump in the village square. The most serious charge against them is that such phrases tend to destroy rather than help the chances of a business letter to succeed. The writer cannot possibly talk in a friendly, natural way with such stiff-shirt language. His true personality is hidden just as his face might be with a two-week-old beard. And that's why your author calls them "Whiskers"—colorless word combinations, embalmed with cold formality—barriers which keep writer and reader utterly apart.

But call them what you will—whiskers, rubber-stamps, stilted phrases—they are taboo in business letters. They make the job hard that should be easy. They throttle personality. They destroy goodwill. They *lessen results.* For this last reason, if for no other, there is nothing good that can be said for Whiskers. Common sense tells us we should do nothing to interfere with the chief objectives of business, namely, to win public acceptance, cultivate goodwill, sell goods, and make a profit. Whiskers obstruct these objectives. Why should any businessman cling to them?

Three examples. If you think that a mountain is being made out of a molehill, and that actually very few whiskers are found in modern business correspondence, you are as wrong as wrong can be. Look at the morning mail which comes to any office and you will find a certain percentage of letters done in the style and spirit of quill-pen days. Here are three, taken from thousands that the writer has collected.

Answering your esteemed favor of recent date, which has been duly received and contents noted, we wish to kindly advise that according to our records, your policy went forth in your direction on the 28th instant.

Pursuant to your question about premiums, we would wish to state that the writer has referred same to our Mr. Jones, who will write to you in due course of time or in the very near future.

Trusting this letter will come to hand, we beg to remain,

.   .   .   .   .

We regret to learn from your esteemed communication that you were unable to favor us with your recent order on which we had the pleasure of quoting, inasmuch as you found it to your advantage to place your order elsewhere at this time.

However, we appreciate your kind indulgence, and trust when you are again in the market that we will have the pleasure of receiving your valued inquiry. At that time, we will endeavor to submit prices and samples to merit our receiving your valued order.

Thanking you for the courtesies extended Mr. Black, and awaiting your further commands at all times with interest, we remain,

.   .   .   .   .

Esteemed Policy-Holder:

Acknowledging with grateful appreciation, receipt of your esteemed favor of the 3rd instant, and to express the hope for the esteemed continuance of your esteemed patronage, we are,

Obediently yours,

No doubt the writers of those three letters are pleasant young men. At home, in the office, they may attract others to them by the warmth of their personalities. But from the way they have written, we have the right to picture three very old men, severe-eyed and white-bearded, clothed in the attire of the last century, seated on high stools, and laboriously writing with quill pens. As full of language freaks as these letters are, perhaps the prize of all is the statement in the first of them—"Your policy went forth in your direction." What a blessing, at least, that it was headed toward the reader.

Nobody talks that way. Can you imagine yourself, or any other human being of our times, *talking* the language of those letters? Would any lover say on the telephone to his sweetheart, "Darling, I wish to state, I'll be over at eight"? Or, later in the evening (perhaps, morning) when seated on the davenport would he say, "I beg to advise, it's time to arise"?

On leaving home this morning, did Mr. Businessman say to his wife as he kissed her good-bye (we hope), "With respect to the information duly received that you will serve corned-beef and cabbage tonight, I take great pleasure in advising that I will be on hand to partake of same"?

What if your company had received a request that a salesman call with information about a certain product? Would the salesman begin his interview as follows: "In reply to your kind request of recent date, I hand you herewith a sample of the product you mentioned. We will appreciate your kind indulgence in giving same your esteemed consideration." No, you have never heard whisker-talk from a salesman. It wouldn't get him any orders.

If people do not use these moth-eaten old phrases in speech, why *do* they use them in their letters? That is a sixty-four dollar question. Can anybody answer it?

Good until the bottom drops out. A truly remarkable example of what Whiskers can do to a letter is the following application for a job. The young man who wrote it was resourceful. He had read William H. Danforth's famous book, *I Dare You,* the theme of which is that we set our own ceilings in life—and can go as far as we dare to think we can. This young man made a clever attempt to dare the author who had dared *him.* Here is his letter:

> Dear Mr. Danforth:
>
> I have just finished reading your wonderful book, *I Dare You,* and so I am daring myself to write you this letter.
>
> I am nineteen years old, and have had only one year in high school, but I am trying to make up for that by studying at night. Right now, I am making fifty dollars a week in a grocery store. My dad is out of work, and I am trying to help support him and my sister, but fifty dollars doesn't go very far.
>
> Now, Mr. Danforth, that is my story, and I DARE YOU to give me a better job, and if you have no opening for me in your company, then I DARE YOU to find one.
>
> Thanking you very kindly, and hoping to hear from you in the near future, I remain,
>
> Yours very truly,

As you read that letter, you can't help but feel the personality of a nice young chap who seems to be made of good stuff, and is worthy of the job he is after. The language most of the way is natural. You can almost hear the young fellow *talking.* And then the bottom drops out!

Had he stopped without the last paragraph, the ending would have been strong and impelling. You could hardly devise a better close than, "Then I DARE YOU to find one."

But what happened? Who knows? Perhaps the youngster had written his letter and then handed it to some older person, perhaps his father. "Do you think this letter will get me the job?" he probably asked.

If we are guessing right, the father handed the letter back with this comment, "Well, son, it needs a better ending—something more businesslike —I'll show you what I mean."

No matter why the letter happened to end so sourly, you will agree that the whole effect was spoiled by the bromides in the closing sentence. Until then, we heard the voice of an ambitious young man, fighting to lift himself by the bootstraps. Then his voice is gone, and we have instead some hidebound old fellow who speaks from the musty past.

A device for lazy thinkers. When some folks call the obsolete phrases "rubber-stamps" they doubtless are thinking of the ease with which they may be used. It takes very little thought to dictate a letter when one's mind is merely a file for clichés. Without any effort, the dictator can say, "We have your letter of," or "Thanking you in advance, we remain." These and similar canned expressions can be used over and over again. It's the lazy way to write, but like anything else that comes too easily, the result is nothing to brag about. Canned letters lack the tang and flavor of those served fresh for each occasion.

Example cited by McQueen. Fortunately, there are in America many letter-men who are fighting to eliminate the formal language which still appears in business correspondence and eventually this united effort may win. We can only hope for the best. One of the crusaders, Harold P. McQueen of Chicago, has cited the following example in which "Squibbs," the bookkeeper, had received a large check in full payment for a purchase made by a new customer. Squibbs rightly felt that the situation deserved a letter of thanks, and this is the one he wrote:

> We beg to acknowledge receipt of your check No. 3433 in the amount of $5,550 in payment of our invoice dated June 7th, for which please accept our thanks.
>
> Enclosed please find receipted bill for your files.
>
> Trusting we may be favored with your future orders, we remain,

The facts in this case were no different from those in thousands of others. The bookkeeper was really grateful for the check. A genuine glow of appreciation warmed his heart. His intentions were good. He wanted to thank the customer, and no doubt thought his letter did a fine job. In the words of Mr. McQueen, however, "it was too much like throwing a cold blanket over the whole pleasant transaction." Too much whisker-talk!

So this was the revision which made the mailbag:

Of course we are always glad to get checks in the mail, but with yours, received this morning, came an added satisfaction. We take it to be a very tangible expression on your part that you are satisfied.

Your attitude made the execution of our work a pleasure, and this letter expresses the sentiments of those of us who had the pleasure of meeting you and working with you.

If one hundred new customers were asked which of these two letters pleased them more, how do you suppose they would vote?

Whiskers here, there, everywhere. It would be incorrect to say that old-time, shopworn phrases are used more frequently in certain types of business and professions, and that other occupations are practically immune to whiskers. Although we know of no surveys that point to such a conclusion, offhand it seems—and this is only an opinion—you do encounter more whiskers in the letters of politicians, lawyers, traffic clerks, government employees, and purchasing agents, than in the letters of sales managers, personnel directors, advertising managers, credit men, and executives. In general, women in business seem to be less hidebound as letter-writers than men, but this, too, is merely an impression. As you would expect, older men with twenty, thirty, or forty years' service are more likely to use stilted language than are younger men who have not been subjected to the habits and traditions of earlier days in business. In companies where better-letter programs have been operating for a number of years, much progress has been made, with the result that only a few die-hards continue to use cut-and-dried canned lingo.

In general, though, whiskers may be found here, there, and everywhere that letters are written. Why this foolish and wasteful language habit is so difficult to eradicate is impossible to explain. In hundreds of books, magazine articles, and speeches, businessmen have been told why they should make their letters personal, human, and natural. They nod their heads in assent, then later dictate sentences like these:

We wish to advise consideration would not be in order at the present time. We crave your indulgence in this respect, and regret our inability to authorize gratis replacement in this instance. (From the desk of an executive in the automobile industry)

.   .   .   .   .

We beg to acknowledge receipt of your favor of the 21st instant, and in replying have pleasure in begging to advise your order has been duly shipped. (Signed by the vice-president of a large corporation)

· · · · ·

We beg to acknowledge receipt of your communication, and under separate cover we are forwarding forthwith additional copies. We trust this action has your esteemed approval and beg to remain, (Dictated by an advertising manager)

· · · · ·

Anticipating our thanks for a reply at your earliest convenience, which we trust will be soon in our hands, we are, (A president was father to this one)

· · · · ·

In compliance with your request of the 24th instant, I transmit herewith a blank voucher for pension due you. (United States Pension Agent)

· · · · ·

We have, therefore, checked and approved same and are returning herewith one copy to you, and are retaining the other and oblige. (A purchasing agent claims it)

You have seen how whisker-talk tends to hide personality and mechanize letters. The sentences just quoted are from the letters of six businessmen, but read them aloud, and you would swear that they were dictated by one man. How could such language, under any circumstances, create the illusion of *personal* contact? The reader is chilled by a conglomeration of words which sound more as if they came from robot than from man.

So much for the worn-out, hackneyed expressions so often seen in business letters—whiskers, rubber-stamps, chestnuts, call them what you please. They are sleeping pills which defeat the aim of making every letter a warm, *personal contact* with the reader.

The following list includes most of these bromides; make sure you avoid them:

You Don't Talk This Way
(Letter-Whiskers)

according to our records	anticipating your reply
acknowledge receipt of	as captioned above
acknowledge with pleasure	as per
acknowledging yours of	as regards
advise (meaning to tell)	as stated above
and oblige	assuring you of
answering yours of	as to your favor
anticipating your advice	as to your esteemed favor
anticipating your favor	at all times
anticipating your order	at an early date

at hand
at the present time
at the present writing
at this time
at your convenience
attached hereto
attached herewith
attached please find
awaiting your further wishes
awaiting your order
awaiting your reply

beg to acknowledge
beg to advise
beg to assure
beg to call your attention
beg to confirm
beg (begging) to remain
beg to state
beg to suggest

carefully noted
check to cover
complying with your favor of
complying with your request
concerning yours of
contents noted
contents duly noted
continued patronage

deem (for think)
desire to state
due to the fact
duly noted

enclosed find
enclosed herewith
enclosed please find
esteemed favor
esteemed order
esteemed request
even date

favor (for letter)
favor us with your order
favor us with your reply
for your files

for your information

hand you herewith
has come to hand
have before us
have your kind favor
hereby advise
hereby insist
herewith enclose
herewith find
herewith please find
hoping for your favor
hoping for your order
hoping to receive

I am (ending last sentence)
I beg to advise
I have your letter of
I trust
in accordance with
in answer to same
in answer to yours
in conclusion would state
in connection therewith
in due course
in due course of time
in re
in reference to
in receipt of
in reply to your favor
in reply would advise
in reply would wish
in response to yours
in response to your favor
in the amount of
in the near future
in this connection
instant (inst.)

kind favor
kind indulgence
kind order
kindly advise
kindly be advised
kindly confirm same

looking forward to

may we suggest
may we hope to receive
meets your approval

of above date
order has gone forward
our Mr. ——
our line
our records show

past favor
per
permit us to remind
please accept
please advise (be advised)
please find herewith
please find enclosed
please note
please rest assured
please return same
pleasure of a reply
proximo (prox.)
pursuant to

re
recent date
recent favor
referring to yours of
regarding the matter
regarding the above
regarding said order
regarding yours
regret to advise
regret to inform
regret to state
replying to your favor of

said (the said regulation)
same (regarding same)
soliciting your advice
soliciting your indulgence
soliciting your patronage

take pleasure in
take the liberty of
thank you kindly
thanking you in anticipation

thanking you in advance
thanking you kindly
the writer
this is to acknowledge
this is to advise
trusting to have
trusting to receive same

ultimo (ult.)
under separate cover
up to this writing

valued favor
valued order
valued patronage

we are (ending last sentence)
we are pleased to advise
we are pleased to note
we have before us
we remain (ending last
sentence)
we take pleasure in advising
we trust
wish to advise
wish to state
with kindest regards
with reference to
with respect to your favor
with your kind permission
would advise
would state
would wish to

your esteemed favor
your esteemed order
your favor has come to hand
your future patronage
your kind indulgence
your letter of even date
your letter of recent date
your Mr. ——
your valued favor
your valued patronage
yours of even date
yours of recent date
yours duly received

yours kindly   yours with respect to same
yours with regard to above

3. THE FOLLY OF BIG WORDS

Gentle art of "goozling." Remembering that the aim of a business letter is to make a personal contact in the simplest way possible—using the words of everyday speech, and just *talking* to the reader—it can readily be understood how the purpose is defeated when the writer allows himself to be pompous or verbose. The gentle art of "goozling" may please the vanity of the man who is good at it, but it retards rather than speeds the effectiveness of his letters.

Do you ever "goozle"? Don't reply too quickly, as did a man in Kansas City who was attending a Letter-Clinic. He said: "You bet, I love to guzzle." "Goozle" is the word, not guzzle. You won't find it in the dictionary, but since it was invented by a college professor in Boston, its social standing is very good. New words, you know, are constantly forcing their way into our language, and we predict that "goozling" is here to stay. Certainly, it seems to describe a serious letter-writing fault as neatly as *any* word could.

"Goozling" is the language-habit of a "goozler." And what, you may ask, is he?

Definition. A "goozler" is one who never uses a short word if he knows a long one of the same or similar meaning. You encounter "goozlers" in all walks of life—politicians, preachers, novelists, commentators, toastmasters— yes, and *letter-writers.* He is harmless and often means well, but others consider him an awful bore. Perhaps "goozling" is an obsession—a little bit of it leads to more and more. When the habit is in advanced stages, the "goozler" may be so proficient in the use of imposing words that he, and he alone, can understand what he has tried to say. Even when the meaning is still vaguely discernible, the "goozler" has made such a spectacle of himself that few take him seriously.

Put this down as a truth for the writing of any kind of copy that seeks to influence human behavior—letters, advertisements, editorials, and all the rest—simple, *short* words do the best job. It may be great sport to "goozle," but it is not a pastime that gets results.

For example, not long ago an "ad" in one of the most popular magazines aimed to arouse interest in hats for men. At the top was the picture of a man and a girl in a flashy sportscar. That was okay. The picture got attention, and, of course, the man was wearing one of the good-looking hats. He was glancing in the rear view mirror, and the first line of copy read: "Is that trooper following us with arresting intent?"

Do you ever call a traffic policeman a "trooper"? No, you might call him an "officer," but the chances are you would say, "cop." And if you feared that soon you would be halted at the curb, with a ticket coming up, would you ask the girl with you, "Are we being followed with *arresting intent*"? You would not. And do you think that artificial jargon would ever help to sell hats?

"Goozling" in business letters. Strange, isn't it, how folks can distort the King's English, once their minds are set to the job? Consider the following extracts from business letters—word for word as actually dictated and mailed:

> "We have now heard from your doctor, and the condition which *necessitated operative procedure . . .*" Credit for this choice bit of "goozling" goes to the Claim Examiner of a big insurance company. Probably he meant the lady needed an operation.

> "Realizing the obvious advantages of personal intercourse over this inadequate correspondence form, and truly conscientious in the belief that association would result in mutual benefit . . ." It seems that this applicant for a job was trying to say it would be much better to get together and talk things over."

> "May we express satisfaction in our confidence that your own experience leads you to agree that at this holiday season, we all have a very real basis for the traditional spirit of happiness and goodwill—a more genuine basis and more nearly up to par, than for several years past . . . especially in view of still better things in store."
> "We hope that the enclosed is excusably appropriate, in connection with the sentiments we express . . . Certainly it connotes a substantial contribution to the efficiency now requisite for prosperity."
> "But regardless of anything else, please accept our most sincere wishes for a prosperous and satisfactory year."

In the above light and merry holiday message, there is one sentence which stands out like a sore thumb. The writer deserves at least an "Oscar" for superlative "goozling." Read it again—"It connotes a substantial contribution to the efficiency now requisite for prosperity." Ho, hum!

Sales letter that flopped. One more example of "goozling" and then you may turn to a more cheerful subject. The paragraph below opened a sales letter mailed to several thousand potential buyers. The writer had high hopes of getting some business with the letter. It produced not a single reply. Since then, no doubt, he has been very bitter about sales letters—probably he thinks they are "for the birds." We could give you the entire letter, but there is no point in punishing you unnecessarily. Anyway, it is hardly possible that any of the original readers went beyond the first paragraph.

Okay! Here it is—the start of a sales letter, done in the very best "goozle."

> From conversations with our clients in diversified lines of business, we have assimilated the impression that buying has reduced existing inventories to the point that their replacement cannot long be deferred, and that the enhancement of grain accumulations has corrected conditions in territories of the commonwealth where for an extensive buying period buying power has been greatly restricted, and the restoration of which is about to be reflected in the acceleration of trade activity.

Now, there *is* a mouthful of choice "goozling." It is doubtful if at the first reading you know what the writer had on his mind; the result is confusion—chaos—in your own. But we wouldn't for the world ask that you read again such a mumble-jumble of words. If you dug *deep* into that long sentence of overweight language, you would find that the writer was trying to say, "In my opinion, this is the time to buy."

The best writers use short words. Here is an experiment you will find most enlightening. Buy two magazines: one of the cheap, lurid variety, and the other of top rank. Remember that those who write for the cheap magazine are paid very little for a story, while those able to sell their efforts to the good magazine receive a high reward. Now, examine the language used in the two periodicals. Do you find any difference? Yes, indeed. The writer who gets very little for his efforts is the one who takes a wild fling with big words. The good writer is more discreet. Occasionally he may use a big word for a special effect, but on the whole he writes very simply. You see, the best writers know the power of short words—and this is true of all kinds of copy—speeches, advertising, and letters.

This statement is made with no thought of slighting the value of a large vocabulary. Words are the writer's tools. The more he has of them in his kit, the better equipped he is to express various shades of meaning, but he never uses a word of many syllables unless there is a *reason* for it. He knows that he is talking to a human being—he wants his message to be easily understood, so he makes it just as simple as he possibly can without the loss of vitality and interest. He is trying to place *thoughts* in the reader's mind, and avoid any confusion in their reception.

Lincoln's Gettysburg Address. You know how high in literature ranks the address made by Abraham Lincoln at Gettysburg. It has been printed in all the major languages of the world, and many scholars say it is the most eloquent speech even made by a President of the United States. And why? Well, not only is this address remarkable for its brevity, but it contains a great truth for those who aspire to influence human behavior or thought by the written or spoken word. Mr. Lincoln had a message to give to his audience. He wanted to make it as simple and direct as possible. He knew that the message would not be enhanced by spectacular phrases or empty-sounding words. He wanted those who were there that day to remember what he had said.

The address contained just 268 words. That alone should put to shame some of our modern politicians who love to break forth with long outbursts of "sweet wind," but of even greater significance is the fact that 196 of those words contained just one syllable. Furthermore, only 20 words in the speech had more than two syllables. In short, on that day Mr. Lincoln's percentage of one-syllable words was seventy-three plus—almost three words out of every four.

Here is the lesson for letter-writers in that speech—keep *high* the percentage of one-syllable words.

What about the letters Lincoln wrote? Perhaps you are saying that nothing can be proved with only one example. You are wondering what the result would be if the same test were applied to Mr. Lincoln's correspondence. Well, that's a good question. Let's see. Following are quotations from his letters written during the Civil War years. In analyzing the percentage of one-syllable words we will not count the names of people or places.

> *To General McClellan:* Shield's division has got so terribly out of shape, out at elbows, and out at toes, that it will require a long time to get it in again.
>
> (80% one-syllable words)
>
> *To General Hooker:* If the head of Lee's army is at Martinsburg and the tail of it on the plank road between Fredericksburg and Chancellorsville, the animal must be slim somewhere. Could you not break him?
>
> (86% one-syllable words)
>
> *To General Meade:* Do not lean a hair's breadth against your own feelings, or your judgement of the public service, on the idea of gratifying me.
>
> (69% one-syllable words)
>
> *To General Grant:* General Sheridan says, "If the thing be

pressed I think that Lee will surrender." Let the thing be pressed.

(93% one-syllable words)

To Secretary of War: On this day Mrs. —— called upon me. She is the wife of Major —— of the regular army. She wants her husband made a brigadier-general. She is a saucy little woman and I think she will torment me until I have to do it.

(72% one-syllable words)

Not counting the proper nouns, since Mr. Lincoln had no control over them, there are a total of 138 words in the above quotations from his letters. One hundred and nine are one-syllable words. Hence, a percentage of 78.9 is the "batting average," several points higher than that of the Gettysburg Address. Abraham Lincoln knew the power of simplicity. He *used short words*—and where in the record of human correspondence can you find letters of greater weight?

Three letters in five words. An amusing example of what short words can be made to do is filed at one of the large insurance companies. It seems that a policyholder had allowed his policy to lapse, so he got the form letter which endeavors to recover lost sheep. Being a polite fellow, but perhaps a busy one, the policyholder took a red pencil and answered the form letter with one word—"NO."

Entering in to the spirit of the game, the dictator for the insurance company went back with two words—"WHY NOT?"

Once more the former policyholder rose to the occasion—"NEW PLAN."

No...Why not?...New Plan—three letters with a total of five words. Who can produce a better evidence of simplicity? Was it not Alexander Pope who wrote: "Words are like leaves; and where they most abound much fruit of sense beneath is rarely found"?

The old-timer had the answer. In the Beloit Daily News there once appeared an editorial which many a letter-writer could well afford to read twice. Here it is, in part:

> They tell a story around newspaper offices of a very young and enthusiastic reporter who once dashed back to the city room after covering a spectacular fire.
>
> He crouched over his typewriter, tense, prepared to turn himself loose with everything he had, almost overcome by the excitement which he was about to transmit to his expectant readers.
>
> Feverishly, he rapped out a couple of words on the typewriter.

He scowled at them, shook his head, and crossed them out. He tapped out two or three words on a fresh sheet, scowled again, and made a third start. He was fairly quivering with the excitement of this grand and dazzling story he had to write, and he was on the point of exploding because he could not seem to turn it into a narrative worthy of the occasion.

There sat watching him an old-timer, who had been writing big stories ever since the battleship Maine blew up in Havana harbor; and this old-timer presently came over to the eager cub and touched him on the shoulder.

"Just put down ONE LITTLE WORD AFTER ANOTHER," he advised.

"One little word after another!" There you have it—the secret which the most effective letter-writers have kept to themselves. At least, it must seem so, or why is this simple but sure-fire formula so often ignored? The big-word complex is still with us, and thousands and thousands of business letters continue to pay the penalty of lessened results.

Your percentage of one-syllable words. What if your letters were put under the microscope, as was done a moment ago with the address and letters of Abraham Lincoln? What is YOUR percentage of one-syllable words? Probably you cannot answer that question because you never have thought to make the test, but it is extremely important that you do find out.

Take ten letters you have dictated recently. Make a random selection rather than one which might help to produce a favorable figure. You want to know the truth. Carefully count all the words, skipping only the proper names. Go back a second time, and count all the one-syllable words. Divide the larger sum (all the words) into the smaller sum (those of one syllable) and there you have it—your percentage.

This analysis may take a couple of hours—depending on the length of your ten letters—but it will give you a tangible idea of whether or not your letter-language is simple or "goozled." There is no way of saying what the *exact* dividing line should be, but an analysis of many, many letters makes it reasonable to conclude that 70 per cent is close to the right figure. Letters with that percentage of one-syllable words, or higher, if not carried to the extreme, are usually easy to understand, and their chances of success enhanced. Letters with a lower percentage tend to be heavy and ineffective. Certainly, if your own test produces a figure of sixty or lower, you have a bad language-habit, and it is imperative that you begin to correct it. Your letters simply will not do the best job if handicapped with a cumbersome load of big words.

The finest letter-writers are critics of their own work. They take time off now and then to review the carbon copies of their own letters. They want to be sure that what they say is simple and direct. Moreover, they have a friendly, curious eye on the letters that pass over their desk. They keep folders of letters for various purposes—just as some people collect postage stamps or coins. They are often able to draw an idea from their collection to use in their own dictation. Letter-writing becomes a hobby as well as daily business—something vital and interesting rather than a necessary chore to be done.

This, perhaps, was the thought of the late newspaper man, Don Marquis, when he composed the rhyme:

> Webster has the words and I
> Pick them up from where they lie;
> Here a word and there a word—
> It's so easy, 'tis absurd;
> I merely range them in a row,
> Webster's done the work you know;
> Word follows word, till, inch by inch,
> I have a column. What a cinch!
> I take the words that Webster penned
> And merely lay them end to end.

Newspaper writers generally lean on short words. You don't have to read a newspaper story twice to get the meaning. Do you suppose short words help to give this little rhyme zest and "oomph"? Let's give it the one-syllable-word-percentage test. Omitting "Webster," a proper noun, we have 63 other words, and only 6 are words of more than one syllable. 90 per cent is the answer. Once again we see it doesn't take a sledge hammer to drive a tack.

Beware of long sentences. Since the object of your business letter is to present your thoughts to the reader in a way that can be easily understood, common sense tells you that long and complicated sentences will defeat that purpose. Periods are like resting places spotted at frequent intervals on a difficult mountain path. They allow the reader to pause and grasp what *has* been said before he is asked to absorb something more. Sentences that run on like a babbling brook soon confuse the reader, and the confusion increases until at the end he cannot remember the beginning. Read the following sentence at normal speed, and judge if you clearly understand the thought when you finally reach the period.

> We are willing to consider an extension of the arrangement to cover the other branches, but feel that such an arrangement should be made with the Doe organization, similar to the one at Reading, or if the Smith Grocery Company can suggest any defi-

nite ways in which they can give us special support and a substantial increase on their outside jobbing business, then we might be able to justify considering a joint arrangement to be made with the Doe organization and the Smith Company based on total purchases of the two combines, the agreement to be based on our being given distribution in all Doe stores, special push by store managers and employees, displays of our products in the stores, special featuring of them in the Doe newspaper advertising, and also special pushing and support by the Smith Company, including a showing of substantial increase in volume at each point over the corresponding period for the previous year, in return for which after the end of the year, we would remit to each branch giving us such support and showing such increase 5% on the net amount of their purchases.

This is not a sample merely constructed to prove a point. It was actually dictated one day by a businessman who must have had great faith in the psychic power of the reader. To understand what the sentence says, an ordinary person would have to go back and take it apart, piece by piece. Finally, by dint of much effort, he might emerge with the meaning, but what right has any writer to impose such a task on the reader of his letter? Unless the reader were a member of the same organization, and *had* to decipher the puzzle, the letter would surely be filed promptly, and with disgust, in the wastebasket.

If you think the above could never happen again, consider another sentence lifted from an actual business letter.

Now the item of October 21, which you show as the balance due you, is in order, but there is a reason for holding it up, and you are fully aware of the fact that this shipment of printing was prepared without our instructions and shipped to the customer, and you admitted that it was an error in your manufacturing department in getting these out before you had authority to proceed, and you will recall that the customer cancelled this order and sent us a new order, but unfortunately, you had already shipped it, and we have been trying to get the customer's permission to bill it and get him to use the order ever since shipment was made, and now we are passing the invoice through, giving the customer December 1 dating in order to get him to use the order, and we are dating your invoice as of December 1, which we trust is satisfactory and will take care of the item mentioned.

You see, once again there has been an attempt to cram into one stretch of thinking far more than the average human mind can take. Instead of inserting periods now and then so that the reader might consolidate what had been said, this businessman wrote "and" ... "and" ... "and." Now, notice what these periods would have done.

> The item of October 21, which you show as the balance due you is correct, but there is a reason for holding it up. You are fully aware that this printing was prepared and shipped to the customer without our instructions. You admitted that it was an error in your manufacturing department in getting the printing out before you had authority to proceed.
>
> You will also recall that the customer cancelled the order, and sent us a new one. Ever since the shipment was made, we have been trying to get the customer's permission to bill it. Now we are giving him December 1 dating in order to get him to use the order. Hence, we are also dating your invoice December 1. This we think should be satisfactory to you.

A few minor changes in wording and the periods have made the copy much easier to understand. The language is still more weighty than need be, but at least the reader has been given a fair chance of meeting the writer halfway. "The period," says Professor Robert Ray Aurner, Wisconsin University letter-master, "is the stop sign in the traffic control of thought. Learn to respect it exactly as you would a stoplight in traffic."*

Neither of the two extremes. Although you are told that long sentences, in proportion to their number and length, tend to reduce the effectiveness of a business letter, you should not be inspired to run amuck in the opposite direction, either. Sentences can be chopped up so drastically that a letter full of them moves along haltingly in a series of "huffs and puffs." Though you should not impose on the intelligence of your reader with sentences that run on and on like Old Man River, neither is it suggested that you approach your reader as if he were a moron. You frequently encounter business letters done in the style of a fourth-grade language book—an experience which is both dull and irritating. Furthermore, it must be remembered that some writers can compose long sentences which take the reader to the end with no confusion or loss of meaning.

After all is said and done, you must accept the suggestions in this Handbook with common sense, and avoid both extremes. You know that simplicity carries great power. You may attain it without the loss of color and personality which makes one letter stand out above the rest. What you are after is a certain "flow" of language which will carry your reader along *smoothly*, as a boat is carried by the current of a swift-moving stream. "Smoothly," is the key word. It is accomplished neither by sentences so

---

* From Professor Aurner's book, *Effective Business Correspondence;* copyrighted 1939 by the South-Western Publishing Company, Inc.

short that the reader is jerked from one thought to another, nor by long spasms of expression which leave him without a clear understanding of the meaning.

4. Use of Unnecessary Words

When the "sweet wind" blows. For at least two reasons, it is foolish to use more words than are needed to convey the thought of a business letter. First, you know that letters cost money. It is pure waste to make them longer than they need to be—more words to dictate, more words to type, more wear on equipment. Second, verbose language is "sweet wind" that makes a letter spineless and ineffective. Many letter-writers blissfully waste words and know it not. Let us examine some of the more common forms of verbosity, so that you will not fall into the same traps. Read the following letter:

> Will you please let us take this opportunity to congratulate you upon the opening of your new drug store. We wish it every possible measure of success, and we believe that with your unusual experience, integrity, reputation and business ability, it will even surpass your highest expectations.
>
> It is also our desire to use this letter as an entering wedge, bringing to your attention the sixty or more well-known and effective remedies of this company which have been on the market for thirty years and which have proven their merit. We want to serve you through your favored jobber, and if you have not already stocked many of the Doe remedies, we shall be glad to make it to your advantage to do so. Give us the name of your wholesaler or jobber and we shall lend every effort toward serving you in the very best possible manner.
>
> It gives us a great deal of pleasure to point out that Lone Wolf and Little Bear products are the best sellers, being especially good in meeting consumer requirements in each and every instance, and enjoying a ready sale. We beg to suggest that you take advantage of the ready sale of these items.
>
> We are taking the liberty of enclosing our latest price list which gives you all the information you will require in ordering this profitable merchandise, and we assure you that at all times we hold ourselves in readiness to be of real service to you. We hope to be favored with your business.
>
> When you have time to take a few minutes from the daily rush of business and its exacting requirements, we shall be glad to know how the store is progressing. May we call attention to the fact that your orders will receive our prompt and very best attention.

Perhaps at first reading even you did not realize how much this letter is padded with unnecessary words. The following revision is not changed in sequence of thought, and nothing of importance is left out. But the "sweet wind" has been red-penciled.

> We congratulate you on the opening of your new drug store. We believe that with your experience and business ability, it will pass your highest expectations.
>
> The sixty well-known and effective remedies of this company have been on the market for thirty years, and have proved their merit. If you already have not stocked many of the Doe remedies, we shall be glad to make it to your advantage to do so. Give us the name of your jobber, and we shall lend every effort toward serving you.
>
> Lone Wolf and Little Bear products are the best sellers, being especially good in meeting consumer requirements. We suggest that you take advantage of their ready sale.
>
> We are enclosing our latest price list which gives you all the information required in ordering this profitable merchandise. We ask to be favored with your business.
>
> We shall be glad to know how the store is progressing. Your orders will receive our very best attention.

To be sure, the diluted version is still not a good sales letter, if you measure it as directed in Section 7. Nothing has been changed or added to make it good, but most of the useless padding is gone. The two copies do the same job, poor as it may be—but there is one striking difference. The original letter contains 313 words, as compared to 162 words in the revised form. Thus, 151 words are blotted out as unnecessary—"sweet wind."

The same letter at half the cost. Always a leader in the fight for better letters in American business has been the Dartnell Corporation of Chicago. In one of the Dartnell bulletins appeared this very fine example of how a windy letter may be trimmed to do a better job. First, you will read the original, which the bulletin calls, "a good biography, but a costly letter to produce," and then the revision made by Cameron McPherson—"the same idea, better stated, in fewer words, at half the cost."

> Dear Mr. Doe:
>
> Please excuse me for writing you personally. It has been my experience that there are mighty few difficulties that cannot be overcome, mighty few differences that cannot be adjusted when the two parties sit down and talk things over.
>
> I would love to walk into your store this morning and have a chat with you. I know you would greet me courteously and

treat me fairly, but since I can't see you personally, let's talk it over.

What I want to talk about is your account with the Eastern Specialty Company of $125.00. Before I do so, however, excuse me please, while I talk for just a little bit about myself. I am living in New York but I am not a New Yorker. I am from "Down South" myself. I have traveled in every Southern state; yes, I guess I have been in every Southern county. I have made my home in the South, I have even followed a mule, plowing corn on an Alabama plantation. I have managed a commissary, have owned and operated my own retail business, in fact I have done pretty much the same thing you are doing, I know your business problems and your local conditions.

When your order was received, it was I who put O. K. on it— I have always insisted that the folks down South were sometimes poor, sometimes a little slow, but always honest.

Now I am in bad. The Company has sent you statements, they have written you letters, but so far they don't seem to be getting very far in collecting your account. Just what is the matter? Can't we get together? The Company wants to do the right thing by you, and I wish you would look on me as your friend and believe me when I tell you that if there is anything you want done that is fair to good business principles, I am here to help you.

I would be mighty well pleased if you would send me a check by the next mail. If you can't pay all your account, send a part payment and see if we can't get everything fixed up. We will advertise for you if your goods aren't selling well; we will make an exchange for you if you have something that doesn't sell as well as some other item.

I am counting on your reply and I am sure you won't disappoint me.

> Cordially yours,

Your first reaction to this long letter may not be unfavorable. The language is natural, and the approach of one southerner to another has some merit. But before you pass final judgment, compare the letter with Mr. McPherson's revision.

Dear Mr. Doe:

I am writing you personally because it has been my experience that there are mighty few difficulties that can't be adjusted when the two parties sit down and talk things over.

What I want to talk about is your account with the Eastern Specialty Company for $125. It so happens that I am from

"Down South" myself, and when your order came in, I put my O. K. on it without a minute's hesitation, because I know that the people down there are all right.

But now I am in bad because the company tells me that you haven't paid any attention to our statements and letters.

Let's get together on this. We'll meet you halfway. If your goods aren't selling, we will advertise for you or make an exchange if you have some slow sellers.

At any rate, send me your check for $50 by the 15th, if you can't send the full amount. Then we will see what we can do to help you get the rest.

Cordially yours,

There is just as much "meat" in the second letter as in the first, but the unnecessary trimmings have been scrapped. The Southerner-to-Southerner approach is still used, but without all the gory details. Moreover, because of its restraint, the second letter seems to carry a tone of sincerity which the first one lacked.

Another example of "sweet wind." There is no end to the verbose letters that could be cited to prove that they are far too common in business correspondence. Here's another of the same dreary vintage. The words in italics are those which pad the letter for no good reason.

Dear Mr. Doe:

Naturally we, *just as any other progressive manufacturer, strive for and much* prefer bouquets *and encomiums* to censure. But we *welcome frank statements, such as you have made and* thank you for telling us exactly what you think of Egyptian quality.

Particularly do we consider, *seriously,* your comments, because we know *that your schooling and reputation have been of such high standard that you could justifiably be and probably are recognized as an art critic of proved repute and renown. As we understand it,* you have designed *and created* for the most prominent New York producers *and have engaged in other masterful creative and designing works,* too numerous to mention.

It would be unnatural then, if your ideas in design were not of the highest possible expectancy. Incidentally, you have dealt with moneyed clients, where price was no object and was quite secondary to the creation of, and the desire to have and own something so different from the usual that even the ordinary layman would, at a casual glance appreciate the difference in cost and value.

But Egyptian Lamps are *manufactured and* designed to occupy a place in the home of the man where price must of *necessity* be considered first, *last, and all times. There is a vast potential and found market for Egyptians as evidenced by sales, testimonials and statistics on average income.* We could not claim, *however,* that Egyptian Lamps would add to the *setting and* beauty of the Rockefeller, Morgan or Whitney mansions. *They would, we admit, be out of place.*

So, far be it from us to attempt *in any way* to sell you on the sales *and customer satisfaction* possibilities of Egyptians in your Miami Beach or New York studios. Neither can it be said that *our sales policy was high pressured or that* we made claims which were *exaggerated and* unfounded. . . . The only thing we can offer *at all* is that you return the Egyptians to our factory, *even though we have always been strict advocates of a non-consignment policy.*

Very truly yours,

Every day, in America, business letters are written that go around and around the mulberry bush, but this one really makes the circle so completely it is wondered the writer did not perish of exhaustion. How much of the letter remains if we omit the italicized words?

Dear Mr. Doe:

Naturally, we prefer bouquets to censure. But we thank you for telling us exactly what you think of Egyptian quality.

Particularly do we consider your comments because we know you have designed for the most prominent New York producers, too numerous to mention.

But Egyptian Lamps are designed to occupy a place in the home of the man where price must be considered first. We could not claim that Egyptian Lamps would add to the beauty of the Rockefeller, Morgan, or Whitney mansions.

So, far be it from us to attempt to sell you on the sales possibilities of Egyptians in your Miami Beach or New York studios. Neither can it be said that we made claims which were unfounded. The only thing we can offer is that you return the Egyptians to our factory.

Very truly yours,

Remarkable, isn't it, how that very poor letter becomes almost a good one, when we simply remove the excess weight? Nothing was changed—nothing removed except a lot of excess words. The thought remains the same, but in a form much easier to take.

Padded phrases used in business letters. It is surprising how many overstuffed phrases you will find in business correspondence, once you start to look for them. The cause may be the monkey-see, monkey-do tendency of the human race to form little language habits which are shared by all—a simple device to avoid original thinking.

Why should a letter-writer speak of "*past* experience," or "*final* completion," or "the *month* of July"? The italicized words are *totally* unnecessary. All experience from which we form judgments is *past*. The completion of a project must be *final*. July is a *month*, and can be nothing else. Things unnecessary must be *totally* so.

And here are some more of the padded phrases so often used in business letters:

> It came *at a time* when we were busy.
> Leather depreciates *in value* slowly.
> During *the year of* 1964.
> It will cost *the sum of* one hundred dollars.
> At a meeting *held* in Philadelphia.
> We will ship these shoes *at a* later *date*.
> In about two weeks' *time*.
> The mistake *first* began due to a misunderstanding.
> A *certain* person by the name of Bill Jones.
> The *close* proximity of these two incidents.
> It happened at *the hour of* noon.
> We see some good in both *of them*.
> In *the city of* Columbus.
> The body is made *out* of steel.
> During the *course of the* campaign.
> *Perhaps* it may be that you are reluctant.
> Our uniform *and invariable* rule is.
> Somebody *or other* must be responsible.
> We are now *engaged in* building a new plant.
> By *means of* this device we are able.
> The radio sells for *a price of* $200.

Read the preceding lines without the italicized words—nothing has been lost in meaning or effectiveness. Hence, those words must be unnecessary. On and on we could go with similar examples—overstuffed phrases which have become habitual in oral and written speech.

The inelegant habit of "doubling." Remember the story of the man who read the directions given by his doctor, "Take one pill every three hours"? He promptly doubled the dose on the assumption that if one pill was good for him, two would be twice as beneficial. Perhaps it is the same reasoning that impels some writers to "double" in their letters. They think that if one word does the job, two should do it better. So they dictate, "it is *evident* and *apparent* that our position is *just* and *fair*," or "we *insist* and *demand* that this bill be paid." In their minds, the use of the *two* words gains added emphasis, but the truth is that they drag out the thought and tend to make it *less* effective.

This practice of "doubling" can do no good in any kind of writing. The man who aims to make his letters simple, direct, and persuasive should avoid a habit so easily acquired and so hard to break. Consider the following New Year's letter.

My dear Mr. Smith:

Out of the fullness of a warm heart . . . I want to extend to you and yours my *sincere* and *earnest* good wishes for a Happy and Prosperous New Year.

The last few years have taught us many lessons . . . the *first* and *foremost* being a new understanding of life's values . . . to *appraise* and *determine* what, after all, are really worthwhile things.

Topping the list on such an inventory are our friends . . . acquired through *experiences together* and *contacts* in a civic, business and a social way . . . with a record in review of their *deeds, actions* and human qualities.

I am happy to have your name on my list of such friends.

May I express the hope that you, like many others, are approaching the New Year with a feeling of *optimism* and *encouragement*.

Cordially yours,

Strange, isn't it, how the writer "doubled" in a vain effort to stress his sentiments?

Sincere and earnest.	Experiences together and contacts.
First and foremost.	Deeds and actions.
Appraise and determine.	Optimism and encouragement.

But before you condemn this one man too severely—he may have let the spirit of the New Year inflate his letter-language—examine the correspondence that comes over your desk. You will surely find thousands of similar examples.

How long should a letter be? In urging the use of concise language in your business letters, there has been no intention of setting up any exact limitation with respect to the length of the conversation you may have with your reader. When Abraham Lincoln was asked how long a man's legs should be, he replied "long enough to reach the ground." If you should ask how long a business letter should be, the answer is "long enough to do the job." The use of unnecessary words is pure waste. The inflation of a letter with "sweet wind" is another form of lost motion. Every letter problem has its own set of facts and conditions. To omit anything which might help a letter to accomplish its purpose is obviously a mistake; to drag a letter out longer than it needs to be is just as unwise.

Brevity is commendable if your letter covers all of the ground that needs to be covered. Just what that ground is, you must decide, remembering that a lengthy letter tends to increase the hazard that the reader may become tired and leave you "waiting at the church."

In some companies the false notion exists that no letter should be longer than one page. Sometimes that limitation is even made obligatory. You will agree that the notion is absurd. Certain sales letters, for example, could not possibly do a good job in one page. The only safe rule to follow is that you handle your subject with restraint and caution, and resist the temptation to run wild with points of no real importance to your reader. As you will discover in the next section of this Handbook, a letter of any consequence deserves analysis of the facts which make it necessary—the selection of those points that should be treated, and *how* it is best to present them. Good letters are *planned* before they are written. And if that plan can be carried out in a short letter, fine! If it takes several pages, then let your letter be long. *Do the job.* Do it *right.* The length is inconsequential.

A friend once wrote to the Radio and TV Editor of a Chicago newspaper. He delivered a long tirade against something the editor had written. Promptly, he received this reply, "Sorry! We'll try to do better." That was a very short letter which did the job neatly.

The president of an oil company in Texas wrote a letter to one of our large corporations, complaining about what he thought to be an unfair sales practice. The reply came back, signed by an official of the corporation, "You have been misinformed. We do not sell as you have outlined in your letter." That short letter did a very poor job. The president of the oil company resented the curt dismissal of his complaint. He deserved a more detailed explanation presented in a more courteous manner. He was a potential customer of the corporation but his goodwill was lost.

A letter soliciting subscriptions to Fortune magazine ran four pages. Another of the same length tried to interest young men in taking a correspondence course in hotel management. Both of these letters did a complete sales job. They were four pages long because they *had* to be. After all, the length of your letter depends on the nature of the particular problem. You can be too brief—you can be too "windy." Good judgment determines what must be said. Certainly there are language faults that stretch a letter longer than is necessary. You have seen what some of them are. Avoid them.

5. OTHER LANGUAGE FAULTS

Use of word pets. Letter-writers, like other craftsmen, must guard constantly against falling into ruts. There is always the danger of growing stale, so that what you write lacks the desired color and originality. Nothing contributes more to such a lamentable condition than the adoption of a number of word pets—words that you use over and over again until they become so habitual that you do not realize how cut-and-dried your writing appears. Mention this fault to almost any secretary, and her eyes will twinkle as she thinks of certain words and phrases which she types day after day in the letters of her "boss."

To be sure, it may be unimportant that the girl who types the letters is bored by these repetitions, but customers, too, may feel their deadly monotony.

He was still "glad to say." The above brings to mind the rather amusing case of a clerk who wrote many letters daily for one of our large shoe manufacturers. Somewhere in his business career he had been impressed with the fact that every letter should start on a cheerful note, so he had fallen into the habit of leading off with, "We are happy to tell you." This was bad enough even in those letters where the introduction jibed with the rest, but it was especially vicious when the news that followed was unwelcome. A check of his carbon copies one day brought to light the following rather startling assertions:

> We are happy to tell you that the shoes you ordered for your Easter Sale will not be ready to ship until a month later.

> We are happy to tell you that we cannot allow credit for the shoes you returned.

You can imagine how the customers getting these two letters must have exploded—to meet with such glee over their bad luck. A more extensive check of the clerk's correspondence revealed that "We are happy to tell you," was a language pet he never failed to take for a walk. Good news or bad news got the same introduction—he was always happy to hand it out.

Word pets in an insurance company. A review of letters used by an insurance company also brought to light word pets not so destructive as the shoe man's pride and joy, but just as tiresome to read. One of them was "out of suspense" and another, "held in abeyance." It was surprising how many things—claims, policies, letters—were either coming out, or still held in. Files, too, were beloved in this company. Here is one of the letters:

We are trying to close as many of our pending *files* as we can.
If the above case is now closed, we would appreciate your returning the *file* so that we may close our pending *file,* or bring before us such information as will place our *file* up-to-date.

"Our records" and "your records" also got a great play in the letters of that insurance company. "According to our records, the grace period will expire next Monday," one letter would say, and the next, "The enclosed copy is for your records." But "records" are necessary in any company, and why can't they be taken for granted? Wouldn't the job be done just as well, or much better, by simply saying, "The grace period will expire next Monday," or "The enclosed copy is yours"? Customers have no special interest in the records you keep—but they are interested in the information supplied from them.

"We await your advice, with every good intention," was the ancient language pet of another writer. Every letter to which a reply was expected closed in the same dismal way. Another benevolent correspondent was very fond of signing off with, "Thanking you kindly, and with best wishes," even though the part that came before was quite often blunt and domineering.

A lawyer favors time. Of course we understand that lawyers are trained to speak with caution. But this one in Wisconsin seems especially diffident as he leads his "pet" by the leash.

> I sincerely regret to advise that I do not feel that I am in just the position at the *present time* to make you the report as to the enclosed, for certain reasons. However, it may be at some *future time* I may be in the position to make such a report, and as aforesaid, I regret indeed just at the *present time* I really do not feel in the position to give you the requested information for certain reasons, that I would prefer not to state, just at the *present time.*

You might call that lawyer "time-minded," from the way he toys with the word. He also has another favorite word combination, "in the position."

This one should end, "Splittingly yours." From a company in New York, you get the following example of word repetition.

> We are sorry that the roll is not satisfactory for the reason that it *splits.*
>
> In this connection, we examined the sample, and find that same *splits.* On this heavy weight it is impossible to guarantee it not to *split to some extent.* We can ship you another roll, but it is possible that it would *split* too. The reason is that it is so thick and has a tendency to *split.*

However, it may be that another roll may not *split*. Does the entire roll *split?* You may of course return the roll if you find this *split* throughout.

This writer had a little pet named Split.

Word pets may indicate limited vocabulary. Many writers use the same words or combinations forever because they are in a rut and are too lazy to climb out of it. Others have slipped into the groove without realizing it. Certain writers are forced into the habit by a limited vocabulary. Members of this last group may know only one word for various shades of meaning, whereas you might have a separate word to match each shade.

For example, you know that *flowers* have *fragrance,* that *cigars* have *aroma,* that *perfumes* have *scent,* that *gases* have *odor*—but to the man whose vocabulary is small, all of these things might simply *smell.* If he wanted to describe an especially disagreeable odor, you know the word he would use. Yes, it "stinks." Sometimes, you hear people of great education and social standing use the same word to describe a play, or a book, or a song, but it seems a pity that those who know better should be so careless.

It is the man with the limited vocabulary to whom lips are *ruby,* teeth are like *pearls,* and the party a *howling* success. If he is a businessman, he may write about the *cordial* invitation, the *stirring* speech, or the *painstaking* effort to improve a product. You can't very well criticize folks who do the best they can with what they have, nor should you expect their letters to be as colorful and interesting as are the letters of those who can draw on a comfortable vocabulary account.

A limited vocabulary is *not* a hopeless handicap, however. If you feel that yours is too small, you *can* make it bigger. Fifteen to thirty minutes a day devoted to vocabulary building will produce amazing results in a year. For reference, any good dictionary will do, and Roget's Thesaurus will serve as a textbook. Reading books, magazines, and newspapers, with an eye for any word which you do not understand, is also very helpful. Once you have mastered the meaning and spelling of a new word, *use* it a sufficient number of times to make it a permanent part of your vocabulary. This may sound like a lot of work, but nothing worthwhile comes easy. When you see your word-chest filling up, the study will become more of a pleasure than a chore. Your letters will take on new life and vitality. Just as a carpenter would be handicapped without an adequate number of tools, so will you always be hindered without an ample and flexible vocabulary.

Avoid red-pepper words. The power of a single word to ruin a business letter is well known to the experts. Sometimes, the trouble-maker is obviously ill-chosen—as when a collection letter insinuates the reader is a dead beat or a chiseler—but often it may appear innocent until the psychology of its use is understood. The collection letter might say, "So far you have ignored our bills and letters." That doesn't appear at first thought to be a tactless statement, but it does carry the insinuation that the reader is one who *ignores* his obligations. In the same way, "We have not had the *courtesy* of a reply," insinuates that the reader is discourteous. Either of the two words is humiliating in inverse proportion to the thickness of the customer's skin. Why disparage a man when trying to appeal to his better self?

Even the harmless little word "should" may arouse an undesirable reaction in your reader's mind. As children, most of us have been told thousands of times what we *should* or *should not* do. Our parents and our teachers have used the word to imply that we were falling short of the expected standard of performance. "Johnny," said the customer's mother, "you *should* know better than to track mud into the house"—and then years later you come along and say to the same man, "John Doe, you should know better than to ask for this unearned discount."

There are many similar words—okay if used cautiously, but little atomic bombs when they tend to irritate through some thoughtless insinuation. Always remember in your letter-writing—never use a word that might humiliate or belittle the reader.

Examples from business letters. We couldn't begin to list all of these red-pepper words. You must constantly be on guard against them, as they have a way of sneaking into a letter, and then popping up to cause trouble. Here are a few more examples taken from actual business letters:

> "We do not understand your *failure* to pay this bill." The insinuation is that the customer cannot be trusted to meet his obligations. Moreover, "failure" is a negative word. We want our name and actions associated with success.
>
> .　　　.　　　.　　　.　　　.
>
> "Your *complaint* about the damaged shipment of flour will have our careful attention." Thus, you say the reader is one who "complains." He dislikes the insinuation. This word should be banned from business letters. There need be no Complaint Department; "Adjustment" Department is better. "Customers' Service" Department is tops.
>
> .　　　.　　　.　　　.　　　.
>
> "We have your letter in which you *claim* two cases of spoiled peas were included in the shipment." When you use "claim" in this sense, you are really insinuating, "You say it is so, but we have our doubts."
>
> .　　　.　　　.　　　.　　　.
>
> "Frankly, we are *surprised* to see you take this attitude after we have tried so hard to please you." You feel very much

abused, and the customer is a "son of a sea-cook." Of course, your "surprise" is humiliating.

.   .   .   .   .

"It seems *strange* that no other customer has mentioned this fault in our product." You are implying that this one customer is unreasonable, or he would climb on the band wagon with all the others.

.   .   .   .   .

"We didn't think you were the *type* to misunderstand our intentions." You mean you didn't think so before, but you do now. Who wants to be a "type" anyway?

.   .   .   .   .

"There will always be leaders and *plodders* on our sales force, although I would much rather see every man a big success, and making lots of money." That's sweet of you, Mr. Salesmanager, but the salesman who read your letter was far down the line—one of the "plodders."

.   .   .   .   .

"You can't *fairly* blame us for the railroad's carelessness." His letter did blame you. He said your shipping cases were too light. Therefore, you have called him "unfair."

.   .   .   .   .

"Certainly, you *know* that we did not offer you any such concession." Well, he told you that you did. He must be a "baldfaced liar."

.   .   .   .   .

"This corrects the *mistake you made* in the amount of the check due us." Why remind anyone of his "mistake"? Help him save face with, "This balances your account, and thanks for your cooperation."

.   .   .   .   .

"In years past, you *used to be* one of our most loyal customers." The good old days are gone; if he "used to be" loyal, then he isn't any more.

.   .   .   .   .

"At *least,* we think we are entitled to know why you have stopped buying." Get out your crying towel. The customer isn't treating you right. The very least he could do would be to explain his peculiar conduct.

.   .   .   .   .

"It appears that you are *disgruntled* about the remark made by our clerk, but surely *you can't expect* us to know what goes on every minute in our store." Your customer is easily disgruntled. He should be more considerate, the old bear!

"*Please understand,* that *we* are still willing to meet you half-way." Not only are you "bossy" with "please understand," but you also insinuate the customer is not a good sport. *We* are still willing (see the pretty halo), but he is not.

* * * * *

"*Others* continue to buy and make money on our goods, while you still *procrastinate.*" The comparison does not favor the prospect. "Others" are smart, but he is dumb. What could be expected of one who puts things off—a "procrastinator"?

* * * * *

"Come, let's end this *childish* argument." A fighting word. You will never end an argument by calling the other fellow "childish."

* * * * *

"Your order was shipped in twenty-four hours. We try to give the same fast service to a *small* buyer, as we would to a large one." What a lucky peewee he is to be served by a company so big-hearted. The insinuation is that the customer's business doesn't amount to much.

* * * * *

"Although we could *ethically* deny your request, you may return the goods." A humiliating sentence—"ethically" is the stinger. The implication is that he was *not* ethical in making the request.

* * * * *

"Do you *fumble* the sales inquiries that come your way?" Who admires a "fumbler"? The question is insulting.

* * * * *

"We have the answer to your heating *problem.*" This is a common beginning in sales letters, and a bad one. Taking for granted that he *has* a "problem" is irritating.

* * * * *

"You can't keep up with competition, using *antiquated* methods and equipment." The company using this letter sold only equipment but the writer for good measure included methods in the slam. You may think a customer is "antiquated" but keep the secret to yourself.

The above examples which show how to destroy goodwill by one or two words are by no means exceptional; you see them frequently in business letters. They are not intentional, but they bore deep, and never fail to irritate.

One word spoils this letter. The tone of the following letter is not bad. The writer is trying to remain friendly, even though the debt is old. But there is one insinuating word—a thoughtless dash of red-pepper.

Supposing a man owed you a few dollars, and they were long past due. What would you do about it?

Would you threaten to sue him? Would you assume he was a dead beat? Would you put him on your blacklist, so that hereafter all orders would be shipped C.O.D.?

I don't know what to do about your account, because when one gets as old as yours, some action has to be taken.

You've been a mighty good customer of ours, so we don't want to do anything drastic; at least, until we hear from you. But we must ask that you do something about clearing up this balance at once.

If there is a red-pepper word in that letter, you would expect to find a quick reference to it in the customer's reply. And that was the first sentence! "Surely by this time you must know that we are NOT *dead beats.*" Yes, out popped that provoking term—and there was trouble.

When "policy" is used as an excuse. Probably the word most frequently used in denying requests is "policy." It is literally worked to death. "We regret to advise that it is not our policy to ship in less than case lots"... "Please excuse us, but a policy of long standing in our company makes it impossible to go along with you"..."Our policy is well understood by the trade, and we can make no exceptions." Some businessmen take this easy way of hiding, behind a word.

Policy means nothing to a customer unless the *reason* for it is understood. Merely to say that you cannot do something because a policy prevents it is both irritating and inadequate. Although policy may be logical, your reader is entitled to an explanation. This involves more thought in writing the letter, but there is no other way to satisfy the reader and retain his goodwill. If the policy won't stand explanation, it is only a subterfuge—as the reader will think when you hide behind it.

The problem of avoiding these red-pepper words is largely psychological. The best solution is to put yourself in the place of the reader, and to contemplate his possible reactions in the light of what your own would be. The letter-writer who holds to the Golden Rule will seldom use an irritating word.

Should slang be used in business letters? You can ask, "How much is two times two?" and the answer is "four." It is the only answer, final and absolute. But ask, "Is slang permissible in business letters?" and the answer is, "It all depends,"—which is no more satisfactory than to call a girl on the telephone, ask for a date, and get the same reply.

Webster defines slang as: "Originally, cant of thieves, gypsies, beggars, etc.; now, language consisting either of new words or phrases, often of the vagrant or illiterate classes, or of ordinary words or phrases in arbitrary senses, and having a conventional but vulgar or inelegant use; also, the jargon of a particular class."

That slang was originally the "cant of thieves, gypsies, and beggars," is interesting, if not complimentary. In modern times, however, the use has spread in far wider circles; slang is now encountered in the speech and writing of all classes. When used with discretion and good taste, it may often add color and interest. Only when writers *lean* on slang for the lack of an adequate vocabulary, or when they use it in a misguided effort to be clever, does it become objectionable. Moreover, since our language is alive and constantly growing, a slang word of today may be found in the dictionaries of tomorrow.

Opinion of an expert. James C. Fernald, author of several books on grammar, had this to say about slang.*

> It should be said that among the multitude of slang words and phrases, there are in each generation a few that meet a real need of the language, and win their way to acceptance. Dean Swift, in 1750, objected to the words *sham, banter, bubble, mob,* and *shuffle,* all of which have become approved English....
>
> When a slang word or phrase is vigorous and expressive, when it meets a real need of the language, it will gradually be adopted by the educated classes; at first in quotation marks, or with some saving clause, such as "to use a common phrase," "so to speak," or the like. Then at length, with all marks of quotation or apology removed, it will take its place as accepted English. Because our language is alive, it is susceptible of change. It is only the dead languages, like the Latin or the classic Greek, that are fixed and unchangeable.
>
> But the burden of proof is always against the slang expression. Let it be put on probation before it is admitted into good society. Make sure that there is a real need for that word or phrase. If it has genuine merit, it will not be hurt by objection and criticism, while our caution will save our language from the inroad of a host of worthless adventurers.
>
> The safe rule is this: slang is never to be used except with care and intent, knowing it to be slang, believing it to be expressive for the immediate purpose, and when no better word or phrase equally forcible can be substituted.

---

* Reprinted by permission from *Expressive English* by James C. Fernald, copyrighted by Funk & Wagnalls Company, New York.

So there you have the "pro and con" for slang, about as well as it could
be stated. If you think a slang word or phrase—not vulgar or inane—will
help your letter, go ahead, use it. But watch carefully that the practice does
not become a habit in which you spread slang all over the page. An overdose
of slang makes many a letter a joke, and a nincompoop of the writer.

Some slang expressions are better than others. You will agree that
there are many breeds of slang, and they don't all rate the same kennel.
Phrases like "on the spot," or "out on a limb," or "take my hair down," are
both useful and natural.

> "Joe, I am sorry if this report puts you *on the spot,* but we just
> must have it by Tuesday."
>
> "It's this way, Mr. Graham. I personally O.K.'d an open ship-
> ment of this order, and now with the bill still unpaid, I am
> *out on a limb."*
>
> "John, there is no need of kidding ourselves about your sales
> record this year. But in the past, you were always a winner.
> So, why don't you *take your hair down* and tell me what's
> wrong?"

Each of those slang phrases helped to make the language more interesting and natural. They are phrases commonly used in speech, and thus they
tend to create the man-to-man effect you are after. They are not vulgar or
inelegant. These words stir the imagination and create a mental picture
which formal language could not achieve in so few words.

But, there are slang words which make a business letter sound like a
schoolboy's note to a friend.

> You failed us, and, by golly, we had so much faith in you too!
> We were sure and confident that YOU, of all people, would keep
> your word.
>
> To be perfectly frank, we feel "kinda" blue about it. And that's
> why we are writing this personal letter, so you will understand
> how we feel.
>
> But you can cheer us up—and here's how: Send your remit-
> tance NOW.
>
> .   .   .   .   .
>
> I'll be a holy Pink Toe'd Prophet if I don't believe you have
> forgotten me entirely.
>
> Gosh! I surely would be happy if you'd send me a little change
> to sort of renew your account and relieve me of a few financial
> burdens. Honest, I need some help, so be a good sport and loosen
> up a bit.

The entire amount is $15.40. All or any will help. Thanks. Can I have it right away, please?

In both of these letters, the writers were trying for a tone of personal cordiality. Like the golfers who press for distance and dub their shots, they tried too hard. Words such as "Golly" and "Gosh" just don't seem to belong in the vocabulary of grown-ups, especially of businessmen. A prophet with pink toes may be a spectacular fellow, but you would expect to find him in a storybook for children, not in a business letter. Equally distasteful are such distortions as "kinda," "sorta," and "wotta"—which we had better hand back to the thieves, the gypsies, and the beggars, in case they could ever use them.

Samples of the more inelegant slang words are "lousy," "nuts," and "guts." These may have a place in a sales manager's letter to his men, or in a letter to a friendly dealer who favors that kind of talk. Usually such slang is dangerous, because you never know whom it may offend. Thus, you are better off not to use it. As Mr. Fernald wrote, "The burden of proof is always against the slang expression." Keep to the safe side. Use slang cautiously; when in doubt—*don't*.

Profanity out in business letters. It is hardly possible to think of any situation where profanity will improve a business letter. This is so obvious that the question of its use needs no discussion. The answer is No! Admitting there may be many times when you *feel* the need of a healthy cuss-word in writing to a cantankerous customer or a lazy salesman, you can't afford to yield to the temptation. Let's keep our letters clean.

Perhaps worse than the cuss-words are the attempts to soften their shock that we see in business correspondence—*"Wotinhel"* for *"What in hell,"* or *"Heluva"* for *"Hell of a,"* or others of the same breed. This is a childish way of fooling nobody.

Taboo profanity. There are plenty of chances for it—without putting it into your letters.

BUSINESS LETTER CARPENTRY

BUSINESS LETTER CARPENTRY

1. CHARTING THE FLIGHT

Before the letter comes the plan. Anything worthwhile in life or business deserves to be planned before it is done. As one popular sales slogan goes, "Plan the work, then work the plan." Certainly, a leap in the dark seldom lands you on the desired spot. It is much better to *see* first where you are leaping.

Only routine, repetitive actions can be carried out without a plan, and even they required intelligent direction in the beginning. The reward for repetitive work is usually meager. The bonus is found where there are problems to solve, and is awarded to those able to think them through. Everything important to business must be planned. Advertising is planned. Products are planned. Sales are planned. Production is planned. Policies are planned. And letters, too, are planned in those companies where an honest effort is being made to avoid waste, and to gain the best possible results.

Not like the grasshopper. Unfortunately, there are still men in business who are "too busy" to do an intelligent letter job. Their chief aim is to dictate as much as possible in a given period of time. You hear one of them say proudly, "I got rid of one hundred letters today." He does not realize that he might better have served his company by writing fifty letters with more thought about their purpose and how to accomplish results. These slam-bang letter-writers are like grasshoppers—good on distance but hell on direction. It is much more commendable to plan and write ten collection letters that bring back four thousand dollars, than to dash off twenty collection letters that bring back only two thousand dollars. Which is more valuable to your company, a sales letter that pulls twenty per cent in orders, even if you took a day to plan and write it, or a sales letter dashed off in fifteen minutes that pulls only two per cent?

65

What if you were a sales manager and had to announce a cut in commission rate? By hard thinking, you might be able to write the letter which would satisfy your salesmen that the cut was necessary and fair to them; or you could just hand out the bad news with no regard for their point of view, and let them figure out for themselves why the cut had been made. The second letter would take less time to write, but would it be better? No; a salesmanager always has the problem of keeping morale at a high pitch. He would surely take time to write the letter that might cushion the shock.

Relation of time to importance. Often when a group of businessmen are reminded that letters must be planned, one of them will exclaim, "That may be true theoretically, but it wouldn't work for me. If I took time to plan every letter I dictate, I couldn't do anything else." This fellow is really not thinking very straight. Nobody intends that he should go into mental contortions over every letter that he writes. Many of the situations handled by correspondence are so similar that one approach serves for all. Others are so simple that they present no real problem. It takes very little planning to write to a customer, thanking him for his order, and telling when it will be shipped. Of course, you might think of something else to add that would warm the customer's heart, and lead to another order—and the extra planning would surely be worthwhile. Even when letter-problems are more complicated, experience is a big help. The planning of one successful letter develops a certain skill and understanding that carries over to the next. Thus, if each day you take time to *think* before you write, the job tends to be less and less difficult. You grow in power. Eventually, you become a letter-craftsman, and the steps you take to plan your letters are not nearly so hard as they were when you were still struggling to master the art.

The time one can afford to give to planning a letter depends, basically, on the nature of the problem, and how important it is to the company that the perfect solution be found. For example, the promotion manager of a Western corporation recently mailed a sales letter that in a very short time brought in orders amounting to over three hundred thousand dollars. When complimented, he said: "It was no miracle. I simply had to sweat blood on the letter to get every word right. I did nothing else for ten days but work on it—couldn't sleep for thinking about it. You see, I *took time to make sure* the letter would do the job."

The letter-writer just quoted is one of America's best. He works as deftly as a surgeon and his output of copy is far above average, for he dictates very rapidly. In preparing that one sales message, however, he made no attempt to hurry. Instead, he was willing to sweat blood for ten days—

"to make sure the letter would do the job." Each of those days spent in planning paid back to his company more than thirty thousand dollars' worth of new business.

Learn to regulate your pace. Give each letter-problem the time and attention it deserves. A little planning for little problems! Big planning for big problems! But plan...plan...plan.

The first step. Knowing exactly what you mean to accomplish is the first step in planning a business letter. Obviously, unless this *purpose* is crystal-clear in the writer's mind, it will certainly not be clear in the reader's. Confusion breeds nothing more orderly than itself.

No doubt you have received letters that read well enough, but when you got to the end, you said, "Well, so what?" And that's a good name for letters that take you no place—"So what" letters. Reading them is like holding the bag in a snipe-hunt—nothing happens. Millions of dollars are wasted every year by letters that seem to have no clearly defined purpose. Apparently, nothing is expected of the readers—at least, nothing is asked. A good example is the one which follows. It was intended to be a sales letter, probably, but no order was requested. Or was the thought merely to keep the company name before the reader? We don't know. Maybe the writer was just as nonplussed.

Dear Sir:

It may be hot—

when you read this letter, so we'll make it short and comfortable. We won't omit sending it, because that would be just like missing a friendly call.

Maybe you'll be "in conference" when this letter reaches you. Along about this time of the year, many big businessmen are. But if you stick around long enough, you'll find them coming back with a bag of clubs.

Which is perfectly all right! American businessmen have found it pays to play—as well as work. It's a good habit, although it would have been frowned on fifty years ago when this business of making boxes was first founded.

Times do change. And habits too. But the fundamental principles of success don't.

A good product—in our case, Boxes—Cartons—Containers—a sincere Service, and courtesy to the customer always—insures Success.

We've found it so!

Cordially yours,

The letter has a few points in its favor. The language is natural—no "whiskers." The words are short, so that the flow is fast—no "goozling." The mention and approval of golf as the businessman's relaxation may rub a "soft spot" and thus tend to bring reader and writer together. There's a very gentle plug for the boxes and service, but just when you would expect a request for reader action, the writer signs off.

"We've found it so," says the writer.

"So what?" asks the reader.

Another "so what" letter. As you will discover later in this section, a good story may help to get a letter off to a good start. It serves as an appetizer, and whets the reader's taste for the "meat" which is to follow. But here's a letter which is *all* appetizer—no soup, no meat, no vegetables, no salad, no dessert. True, the writer finally slaps on a postscript in which there is a very mild request for business. Was that the primary purpose he had in mind, or was it merely to amuse his customer? If the latter, the story might backfire, for puzzles can be irritating unless they are easily solved by the customer.

Dear Mr. Doe:

There were three men on their way to a Kentucky Derby named Taylor, King, and Jones, who are an attorney, a salesman, and an adjustor, but not respectively.

On the train with them were three credit men: a Mr. Taylor, a Mr. King, and a Mr. Jones.

CONSIDER THE FOLLOWING:

1. Mr. King lives in New York.
2. The attorney lives halfway between Chicago and New York.
3. Mr. Jones earns $11,000 a year.
4. Taylor beat the salesman at poker.
5. The attorney's nearest neighbor, one of the credit men, earns exactly three times as much as the attorney who earns $10,000 a year.
6. The credit man whose name is the same as the attorney's lives in Chicago.

Now then, WHO IS THE ADJUSTOR?

Very cordially yours,

P.S. If you can't find the solution . . . or want a confirmation . . . drop me a memo. If you have a claim to place for collection . . . call on the ——— Co.

In somewhat amusing contrast (to us, if not to the writer) is a letter from a man sentenced to liquidation, and with only one last hope. There is little doubt of the writer's purpose. He wanted action, and he wanted it quickly. "Dear Governor," he wrote, "They are fixin' to hang me on Thursday—and here it is Tuesday."

How to handle your mail. If you read and mark a letter correctly, the purpose of the reply is more easily established. Many business correspondents make the mistake of taking a quick peep at the morning mail, and then shoving it aside for later handling. This involves a second reading, which often could be avoided. The most efficient letter-men reduce their letter-writing as much as possible to a one-time operation.

Each letter is read thoroughly, and the points that must be covered in the reply are marked with a red pencil. In many cases, where the facts are already known, the reply can be dictated immediately. No time is lost, and the marked passages establish purpose. Even when it is necessary to defer the reply for the lack of needed information, a second careful reading of the letter is not required. The writer simply picks it up and looks at the red marks.

This use of a red pencil as you read your mail, and the immediate reply to as many letters as possible, are two habits that will save time and also enhance your reputation as a writer who gets things done without fuss or bother.

Declare the purpose to yourself. It is hardly possible that anyone would question the first step in planning a business letter, or for that matter, any other kind of a letter. When you know the "why" of any task, you proceed without lost motion to the "how" it may best be done. It is seldom necessary to rewrite a letter when your purpose is clearly understood at the start. Only scatterbrains are forced to do things over; hence, the smart dictator has another habit that helps him to shoot his arrows straight. He mentally surveys the letter-job he is about to do, and *to himself declares the purpose,* "I am writing this letter...

> to make this dealer understand that the goods substituted were superior in quality to those he ordered—that we were trying to do him a favor so that he would not be caught short of merchandise during his sale.
>
> to prove to this salesman that the new territory he has been asked to take is better than the old one—that the change is a promotion and not unfair as he now thinks.
>
> to explain that we cannot grant a concession to one buyer unless it were available to the rest—to deny his request in such a way that he will respect us all the more.
>
> to show this customer why he should pay this bill before it is placed in the hands of the lawyers—to talk to him as a friend, even though he must be told we will wait only ten days longer.

to find out why this customer stopped buying from us six months ago—to make him feel we really appreciated his business, and sincerely want the privilege of serving him again.

to thank this prospect for the time he gave our salesman, even though he didn't buy—to win goodwill for the company, and a better reception for the salesman on his next call.

to tell this merchant whose store was destroyed by fire not to worry about his account with us—to ask him how we may help to re-establish his business.

to refuse the request of this minister that we contribute goods for the church bazaar—to make him understand the reason, and to keep his friendship.

to acknowledge our mistake in filling the order and to say we are sorry—to do this without using a crying-towel, or attempting to give any excuses or alibis.

It doesn't matter what the situation is—how simple or complicated it may be. The declaration of purpose before you begin to dictate will help immensely to clarify your thinking, and to produce the letter that moves straight to the intended objective.

Second step, get all the facts. To write a business letter, knowing you are not fully informed but thinking you may bluff it through, is both foolish and unpardonable. No only is "face" lost with the reader, but the chances are he will come back for a better explanation. You have to get the facts anyway, and then you have written two letters where one would have sufficed.

When a man talks across space to his reader, surely and positively, because he knows what he is talking about, his words carry power and conviction. We all respect facts. We quickly lose confidence in anyone who, through ignorance or laziness, seems unsure of his own ground.

Fortunately, most of the facts needed to handle business correspondence are easily available. If a clerk in the credit department is about to write about a past-due bill, he can review the copies of previous letters to the same customer. If someone in the sales department is asked a technical question about a new product or a piece of machinery, he can get the answer from the director of research or the chief engineer. Practically everything done in a company is a matter of record. The correspondent who aims for the top will inform himself with respect to the methods, products, and policies of his organization. The facts we need to know are seldom withheld from us. And the greater your knowledge, the greater your power as a letter-writer!

"How to play chess," in two paragraphs. Perhaps you do not know how to play chess. You have heard that it is a very difficult game, to be mastered only after years of study. Well, now you can easily become an expert. In two short paragraphs, the following letter tells you how to play—"through to the finer points." It was written by a clerk in one of the big mail-order houses. The customer, living in North Dakota, was a farmer's wife who had purchased a set of chessmen, and then had written for instructions for playing the game. Here is what Miss Whataguesser told her:

> Dear Madam:
>
> We do not have any special directions printed for playing chess, but I would suggest that you take one chessman and move it from the bottom to the center, following the game through to the finer points.
>
> The first party that fills in the top of the board wins the game. We assure you, that if you follow these instructions carefully, you will be able to play the game to your full satisfaction.
>
> > Very truly yours,

Could such a letter be genuine? Yes, indeed. It was dictated and typed, but fortunately a supervisor in the mail-order house caught the rascal before it got into the mail bag. The clerk perhaps thought she was smart to be able to write something about which she knew absolutely nothing. Smart enough, no doubt, to lose her job!

How lack of facts defeats the letter's purpose. It has been mentioned how the abuse of facts, or the lack of them, tends to destroy reader confidence. It does more than that. Usually, the letter fails utterly to accomplish its purpose. Examine the opening and closing paragraphs of a letter mailed to an alumnus of a Big Ten University by the circulation manager of the campus newspaper.

> We are in the midst of the football season again—that most glamorous time of the entire college year. . . .
>
> Don't pass up this intensely interesting period. Follow the teams from day to day in the columns of the Daily ———.

The parts of the letter omitted were neither too good nor too bad, but whoever approved the mailing overlooked one important fact. "We are in the midst of the football season—follow the teams from day to day," appealed the circulation manager. Had he declared the purpose of his letter, no doubt it would have been "to convince this alumnus that he should keep in touch with the football team this fall by subscribing to our student newspaper."

But—and it's a sad *but*—the letter was dated November 29, and the last football game of the season had been played the week before. The thrills used as bait for the reader's money had ceased to exist until another year— a simple fact that made the letter worthless.

This failure to change with the calendar is no rare accident in the business world. It is easy to prepare a form letter, start it going, check results for a while, and then continue sending it long after the things it talks about have ended or lost their appeal.

From the president of one of Chicago's Michigan Avenue hotels came a nicely worded Christmas letter to a friend. The use of a rubber stamp for the president's signature contradicted the personal tone of the copy, yet the recipient was graciously thanked for the many times he had stopped at the hotel, and heartily invited to make it his Chicago home on every future visit. The letter would have made a fine impression, except for one fact that didn't hold water. The reader had *never* been a guest of that hotel. This made everything in the letter sound insincere.

"Scratching the wrong back" in business correspondence is always a dangerous practice. The reader knows he is getting a letter meant for somebody else, or at least not for him. His opinion of the company goes down instead of up. After a few similar experiences, he becomes suspicious of all goodwill letters.

A very beautiful letter of condolence once came to Mrs. L. E. Frailey. The writer's choice of words was magnificent, and the whole effect would have been quite comforting, had it not been for one error. You see, the purpose of the letter, as revealed toward the end, was to sell the lady a tombstone for her husband's grave—a purpose which the latter deemed absolutely unnecessary and somewhat belittling.

Another letter equally wide of its mark, and thus only a waste of effort and postage, was one that began, "You do not need to be bald any longer." This would have been good news, perhaps, to one whose head was smooth, but not to the recipient. Gray hair, yes! But bald—what an unfounded suggestion!

Know what you are talking about, and shoot at the right target; otherwise, the backfire can be terrific.

When right and left hands work apart. Another form of factual inaccuracy in letters is that caused by lack of co-ordination between men or departments in the same company. For example, the promotion manager of a publishing house writes, "I am really disturbed that we have not heard from you concerning your renewal." Then he sweeps into a long, and somewhat windy exposition of the fine features which the former subscriber has been missing. The close is an urge for immediate action—"You surely cannot afford to delay any longer. We will expect and appreciate your renewal this week."

The letter so far is not too weak, but there follows a startling postscript "If you *have* renewed," it says, "please disregard this letter." The writer admits lack of teamwork between himself and the keeper of records—or else he is just too lazy to find out whether or not the renewal has been received. In either event, he is taking advantage of the reader's time by asking him to wade through a long letter, only to confess it may have been unnecessary.

A somewhat more obliging fellow is the president of a mail-order house. He, too, is shooting in the dark, but he admits it in the first paragraph.

> We have been mighty busy lately, and have not had time to check up your name with our order list to see if you have sent us your order, but we expect to do so soon. If you already have sent us your order, you do not need to pay any attention to this letter.

Evidently, the confession of ignorance weighs heavily in this executive's mind, for toward the end of his letter, he again returns to the subject.

> I am sorry we have not had time to check up your name with our order list, as you probably have sent us your order already, or expect to do so soon. If you haven't, let us hear from you promptly.

The reaction to such a flabby excuse for inefficiency could scarcely be good. Twice the president says he has been "too busy" to "check up" (why *up?*) the reader's name. What he really admits is ignorance of a fact needed, and obtainable, before the letter was written.

The American public has been led to expect efficient performance in big business. Anything short of that is a confession of weakness that undermines faith and interferes with progress. To plan a successful business letter, it is necessary to have or to *get* all facts related to the subject. Facts win respect. Facts build confidence. Be sure you have them.

Third step is to visualize the reader. Know your purpose, know the facts, know your reader. When this third step is taken, the letter is beginning to "jell" in your mind. You can now think of what may be said in terms of the man or woman who is going to read it. The point that might be most persuasive to reader Jones might fall far short if presented to reader Smith. Certain groups of people, bound together by similar living habits, occupations, and cultural levels, will tend to be receptive to the same suggestions—

and that fact is important in planning a form letter—but the psychologists tell us no two individuals are exactly alike, or susceptible to the same arguments or reasons. Hence, the best letter will always be the one that is custom-built to fit the particular reader.

This seeking to approach the reader where he may be vulnerable, this rubbing of his "soft spots," is fundamental in the planning of a business letter. The expert learns to *look through the reader's eyes,* to understand his likes and dislikes, and to share his emotions. "It is a rare and priceless asset," says a famous copy-writer, "when a man dictating a letter can *project* himself two or three days hence and imagine he is just now reading his own letter." When you are able to do that, your own opinions and valuations fade into the background. It is what the reader thinks, or wants, or likes, that counts. He is the one that must be pleased. And the more you know about him, the better are your chances of gaining a favorable reaction.

How to form the mental image. The business correspondent about to dictate a batch of letters will, of course, encounter various degrees of difficulty in visualizing the readers. If he happens to know dealer Brown personally, the problem is comparatively easy. His success then depends on his knowledge of human nature, and his understanding of Brown's personality; but he must still see through Brown's eyes rather than his own. Some men are better judges of human nature than others. They are the "mixers" who get along well with all kinds of people. They make friends with common folks as easily as with "bigwigs," and this is a valuable asset to a letter-writer.

Dealer Martin, next on the list, may be only the name of a customer to the dictator, but certain facts about Martin are learned indirectly. He must be progressive and up-to-date or he would not stand near the top in sales among the several hundred dealers. The correspondence file reveals that Martin pays his bills promptly, that his relations with the sales department always have been friendly, that one of his sons went to Yale, that he was once mayor of his city. Gradually, the mental image of dealer Martin begins to form. His letters, too, are revealing. They indicate a sense of humor, a capacity for seeing both sides of a moot question, but also a well-defined stubbornness once Martin has declared his point of view. His letters frequently mention seeing a football game, playing golf, or something about his bowling average. It is plain he is the athletic type, at least he is keenly interested in sports.

You might ask, "Who would take time to study previous correspondence just to answer one letter?" The truthful answer is that many letter-writers *never* do it, some because they are "too busy," and others because they are too lazy. No one is recommending that such a plan be followed in answering *all* letters. But if you sat at your desk one morning, with a letter from dealer Martin in your hand, wondering what to say because a situation has developed which may break the business relationship—if that were true, wouldn't you want to get from Martin's file all of the help it might give you? The people who push aside any plan that involves a little extra effort are those unable to differentiate between a routine situation and one in which there is a real problem to solve. You cannot take all of the principles of letter-writing too literally—they are to be applied when and if they are necessary.

There can be no question, however, about the advantage of visualizing your reader. Even if the mental image is not perfect or complete, it seems to place the two of you in the same room. He is not just a name, but a human being. You can *talk* to him as you would in person. And you know from previous sections of this Handbook, that *talking* is the secret of writing an effective letter. The mediocre letter-man says, "I must clean up this correspondence today." The good letter-man says, "Now I must talk with all these people."

Visualizing the stranger. Of course, many business letters go to unknown persons—a man in some distant state wants to know about a product, a London broker inquires about sales possibilities in England, a lady doesn't like a radio program because it frightens her children. In such cases the mental images are bound to be vague, although an individual may often reveal things about himself in his letter. Beyond those hints, when they are present, the dictator has only his knowledge of human nature and of certain group characteristics.

A letter to a merchant in Vermont would probably differ from one covering the same subject to a merchant in New Orleans. You would not expect, either, the same language or appeals in letters to prospects in New York City, Farmer, Ohio, and Albuquerque, New Mexico. In the same way, a sales letter to a Methodist minister would differ from one mailed to a manufacturer of slot-machines. There are many of these well-understood factors—geographical, racial, occupational—that influence the letters of experienced letter-writers.

An equally difficult task in forming the right mental image is the preparation of the form letter that may be sent to thousands of people in all parts of the country. Here, the writer can only set up in his mind what appears to be the typical reader, and then plan his message for that composite individual. He knows he cannot influence everybody on his list favorably, but he aims for a favorable reaction from the largest possible number. When the list is occupational, such as schoolteachers, lawyers, or funeral directors, the image of the typical reader is more readily formed. This is also true when those who will receive the form letter have allied interests—society women, club members, labor groups, golf fans, and all the others you can recall.

Fourth step, choosing the ammunition. Down the fairway goes the professional golfer to the place where the next shot is to be made. The caddy is waiting with the usual big bag of clubs. To one who has never played the game, it looks foolish to carry so many, but the caddy doesn't complain. He knows every one of those clubs has a purpose, and the winning of the purse might well depend on the selection of the right one for a particular shot. He wants his man to win.

So now the shot must be made. The "pro" surveys the position of the ball, the distance to the green, and the obstacles to be avoided. Finally, his mind is made up. "Four iron," he says. The caddy looks worried, for the green looks far away, but he knows better than to blink an eyelid. "Crack!" The head of the club cuts a path through the sod and lifts the ball on its course. Just over the trap—the caddy holds his breath! Up toward the cup rolls the ball, and stops short only a few inches.

Down the fairway they go again, the boy and his hero. "Wish I could hit a shot like that," the former exclaims. "Wasn't me," the "pro" replies. "I just happened to take the right club."

The explanation of the golfer could just as well be that of the letter-writer who has received a favorable reply. "Wasn't *me,*" he might say, "I just happened to select the right appeal." You see, the first three steps in planning a letter all contribute to the fourth.

First, know the purpose—that's wanting to reach the green in one shot. Second, know the facts—that's studying the position of the ball, the distance, the obstacles. Third, visualize the reader—that's the mental image of the ball in flight. Fourth, choose the best appeal—that's taking the right club from the bag. Each step is important, but they all co-operate to produce the desired result.

The situations to be handled in golf or letter-writing are never quite the same. To reach other greens no farther away, the golfer may one time take a spoon because he needs loft to clear some trees, or another time he may take a jigger for a bullet-shot under the branches. To gain a reply with an order, the letter-writer may one time use "economy" to overcome the resistance of a tight-fisted prospect, and another time he may use "style" to whet the desire of a playboy who counts not the cost.

For every reader or prospect, you are likely to find a different combination of "soft spots"—the things or benefits or reasons to which *he* is most vulnerable. Knowing *what* to say to *whom* and *when* is part of the planning of a business letter.

How letter-writers probe for "soft spots." Most business correspondents take this fourth step in letter-planning, even though they often seem to ignore the others. You seldom read a sales letter, for example, without noting how the writer appears to be trying to "cash in" on what he thinks to be some point of vulnerability in his reader. Examine the following quotations:

> You know, the Irish are an impulsive race. Take me for an example. I was born on the 14th of March. Now if I hadn't been in such a hurry to see what was goin' on in the world I could have waited three days longer. Then I could have shared the 17th with St. Patrick. And that would have been a great honor for both of us.
>
> (The Irish cling together as a race. They love their saint. The appeal is strong as a door-opener for the letter, but only when mailed to an Irishman.)

> Did you know that twenty years ago there were four Sealyham champions in one litter? This is a record unsurpassed by any other breed except Springer Spaniels.
>
> (Sent to a man who had seven Sealyhams, the letter obviously hits a "soft spot," and, of course, the appeal would be even greater to a lover of Springer Spaniels.)

> Sometimes we get a steak that's a little tough, but we like steak, and there isn't any better steak available—so we take a firm grip on the knife and fork and bear down.
>
> Business is sometimes like that. Conditions are not always the best, but it's beyond us to change them. Still, we can get some of that business if we take hold of the knife and fork, and really cut in.
>
> (Probably steak is a magic word to most men. Thus, the letter gets off to a good start. It would backfire, though, in the hands of one who did not eat steak.)

> A young telegraph operator had no money, and his salary was so small he could hardly make ends meet. But he decided that he had to risk some of that scant salary if ever he was to get anywhere. So he bought $5 worth of postage stamps, and in his spare time penned letters to other telegraphers along the line, telling them about a low-priced watch he could get for them at a low price.

Soon he began to get orders, and as each one came in, he sent part of the money to a watch factory with orders to deliver the watch direct to the buyer, and then he put the rest of the money into more postage stamps. Before many months, he was making so much money selling watches that he gave up his job to build a business by mail. That telegraph operator's name was Sears, and you know the business he founded as Sears, Roebuck and Co.

(The appeal, and it runs throughout the letter, is to the desire for more money—leading the reader to wonder if he, too, might become another Sears.)

Here is a letter that seeks to create business for a landscape gardener. For lack of any request for action at the end, it might be called a "so what" letter, were you not told it was one of a series sent to the same man. Thus, the purpose was to remind rather than to sell.

Dear Mr. Doe:

Let's talk your language for a moment.

In a certain room in your factory is a hide. Sooner or later it will be placed in the show-window of a high class store, in the form of a pair of shoes. Master craftsmen will have transformed it into a pair of the finest shoes made—Doe shoes.

A thousand things have happened to it—things it has taken a lifetime to learn. Cheaper shoes are made—but none that are less expensive—for you tell me they will outlast two ordinary pairs. They are the best—made for the "man who cares."

The grounds around your new home are like that hide.

And like that hide, some master craftsman is going to change them into surroundings—simple, useful, attractive. A thousand things are going to happen to them—things that have taken a lifetime to learn. They must turn out to be the best—because they, too, belong to the "man who cares!"

Durability — snugness — elegance — poise — smoothness — these things are bound up in every pair of Doe shoes.

And those same things will make your grounds entirely satisfactory.

Sincerely yours,

The appeal in that letter is to pride. Harold McQueen, the writer, is saying, "You make the best shoes, and we do the best landscape gardening. Birds of a feather should get together."

The appeal to home-town pride. The fellow who first said, "There is no place like home," may have had an idea, one it would pay letter-writers to adopt more often than they do. There seems to be a streak of loyalty in the average human being that makes him stand up for his home town, though it be as humble as Dogpatch or Toonerville. Thus, when the writer of a business letter is able, without exaggeration, to work in a "plug" for the reader's place of abode, he is using an old appeal that helps to break the ice. For example:

Dear Mr. Doe:

Boston once held a tea party. There was objection to an exorbitant tax on a cargo of tea, you will remember, so it was dumped overboard.

Is Boston today less quick to throw overboard anything that carries too high a tax?

Waste is a form of tax. If there is a way to dump that tax, naturally you are for it.

Paper-carded belt hooks are from 10% to 25% wasteful. That waste tax is avoided by the use of improved Safety Belt Hooks, with Steel Binder Bars, to which there is NO WASTE. Safety Belt Hooks also make smoother, longer-lived joints.

The literature and notebook enclosed tell the story. You can get Safety Belt Hooks and Lacers from the Boston dealers named below. If there are others you prefer to deal with, any one of them will get Safety products for you.

Very truly yours,

Evidently, in the above letter, H. H. Stalker was not using the hometown appeal by accident, for it appears in his messages to prospects and dealers in other cities.

Dear Mr. Brown:

Here is the information requested, and we think something is about ready to explode down there in your fine town in the way of orders.

We say fine town, not as a bit of flattery, but because the writer remembers vividly spending a week in Houston during the International Rotary Convention. If your sales punch down in Houston matches your hospitality, you should decidedly go places with Safety Hooks and Lacers.

There is . . .

.   .   .   .   .

Dear Mr. Black:

A Philadelphian, one Benjamin Franklin by name, had more to say about waste than perhaps any other man who ever lived in Philadelphia, or elsewhere.

With such a tradition, the folks of Philadelphia ought to be about as thrifty as folks come anywhere. If we are right, then you will be very much interested in the next paragraph.

Paper-carded belt hooks are from 10% to 25% wasteful. That waste is . . .

The sincerity of plain talking. The next letter is one in which there is no beating of bushes or sounding of trumpets. The writer uses plain speech that is both convincing and refreshing. The appeal is, "We will treat you right," and you feel it is sincere.

Dear Mr. Doe:

We don't give rare coins but there's more than one way to get your money's worth out of a used car.

The idea that a certain dealer is about to sprout wings, and make things heavenly for used car buyers has been going the rounds so long that it rattles. The reason we give our customers their money's worth isn't because we are so big-hearted we can't help it. If you want to know the reason, it is because we want to stay in business.

The Mrs. has her mind set on sending our boy, Charlie, to college. If he is like I am, it will be wasted, but the Mrs. says he isn't and that's that.

I haven't enough money to retire on and I can't stand to loaf when anybody is looking; and we have such big show windows that people are always looking. So, for those reasons, I figure my best bet is to treat buyers right so they will come back, and tell others they got a good deal from Jimmy Davies.

Right now, I have some cars that are worth looking into. You won't find any rare dimes under the cushions—I look for them myself—but you will get all you bargain for.

I'd like to show you the Dodge Charlie Brooks traded in last week—$495 takes it and you cannot take as long as you like to pay for it. No terms beyond 20 months go here.

Cordially yours,

Buys Car for $150; Finds a Dime in It Worth $450

Alliance, O., April 1.—Mrs. W. H. Shaw of Alliance reported that her cousin, Roy Koontz of Bloomington, Ind., bought a used car in Cleveland for $150. When he cleaned the antique he found a dime dated 1821 under a seat cushion. A coin expert offered him $450 for the dime.

As we recall, this letter was lathed by letter carpenter Vic Knight. Whether or not it sold the Dodge is not recorded. Nevertheless, the appeal is strong to those who are tired of high-sounding but empty promises.

A letter that tickles the funny bone. Appealing to the reader's sense of humor is a device often used to win acceptance for a business letter. The following example was used by The Plaza, a New York City hotel. It really does a double job; it entertains the reader while putting across a sales message.

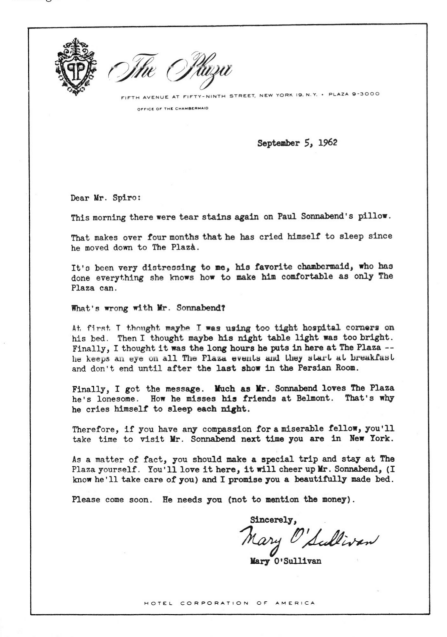

The Plaza

FIFTH AVENUE AT FIFTY-NINTH STREET, NEW YORK 19, N.Y. · PLAZA 9-3000

OFFICE OF THE CHAMBERMAID

September 5, 1962

Dear Mr. Spiro:

This morning there were tear stains again on Paul Sonnabend's pillow.

That makes over four months that he has cried himself to sleep since he moved down to The Plaza.

It's been very distressing to me, his favorite chambermaid, who has done everything she knows how to make him comfortable as only The Plaza can.

What's wrong with Mr. Sonnabend?

At first I thought maybe I was using too tight hospital corners on his bed. Then I thought maybe his night table light was too bright. Finally, I thought it was the long hours he puts in here at The Plaza -- he keeps an eye on all The Plaza events and they start at breakfast and don't end until after the last show in the Persian Room.

Finally, I got the message. Much as Mr. Sonnabend loves The Plaza he's lonesome. How he misses his friends at Belmont. That's why he cries himself to sleep each night.

Therefore, if you have any compassion for a miserable fellow, you'll take time to visit Mr. Sonnabend next time you are in New York.

As a matter of fact, you should make a special trip and stay at The Plaza yourself. You'll love it here, it will cheer up Mr. Sonnabend, (I know he'll take care of you) and I promise you a beautifully made bed.

Please come soon. He needs you (not to mention the money).

Sincerely,

Mary O'Sullivan

Mary O'Sullivan

HOTEL CORPORATION OF AMERICA

Use of "scare copy" as appeal for action. One of the major motives for human behavior is fear. People buy many things to protect themselves against hazards that may be real or imaginary. Hence, the use of "scare copy" is frequently seen in advertising and sales. A picture of some horrible automobile accident, with a description of all the gory details, may influence you to buy tires with a patented safety tread, or an insurance policy that would pay your hospital bills. A story about head-colds, and how they may lead to pneumonia and death, may be used to frighten you into the acquisition of nose-drops or vitamins. Check your own buying habits, and you will be surprised to find how many of them are the result of the desire to protect yourself against poverty, sickness, and other forms of catastrophe. Check the letters that you get, and you will be surprised to find how many of them use fear as the major appeal.

Perhaps there is no emotion more universally shared than the dread of old age, particularly the fear that it may catch us unprepared to live without the aid of charity. To be sure, this is a fear that may vary in degree among different individuals and groups, but few of us are entirely free from it. Lady schoolteachers, never rewarded adequately for their efforts, and hard put to lay aside a nest egg, seem especially susceptible to the fear of old age, and the hardships it may bring upon them. That is the assumption which must have prompted the following sales letter.

Dear Miss Doe:

It was Thursday evening—the School Board was in session. There had been a lot of spirited discussion during the evening, and all items had been disposed of—except one. Down at the bottom of the president's memo were but two words—"Miss Meridith."

To the School Board, it was merely another item of business routine, but to Miss Meridith it was a matter which affected her entire future.

The Board quickly decided: "She has served faithfully and well, but we need younger blood. She always has proved very capable, but she's getting a bit too old to teach. Her health isn't the best, and much as we regret it, she will have to be replaced."

The above incident is tragic, but not unusual. In fact, it is a typical experience which might be multiplied many times daily. And in all cases, the fate of the teacher hangs in the balance.

One of these days, perhaps, *your* name will be scrawled on the president's memo.

Right now, Miss Doe, that day seems far removed, but come it will, as it finally must to all in the teaching profession. Just how will the decision of the Board affect you?

With your earnings reduced, or perhaps cut off entirely, how will you live? Will you be compelled to throw yourself on the charity of friends or relatives—or will you mark the day as the beginning of a new era, bringing release from classroom duties, the thrills of a trip around the world, the opportunity to pursue a hobby, a future free from money worries?

Thousands of teachers already have adopted the Income Reserve Plan. Perhaps, it may appeal to you. But first we suggest you send for the free booklet, "Money for the Wonderful Things All Women Crave."

The card will bring it to you quickly.

Sincerely yours,

Is there anything unethical in the appeal to the fear of old age as used in the above letter? Certainly not! Even though the purpose is to sell an insurance plan, the result may be the solution of the schoolteacher's problem. In that sense, it offers an economic blessing.

Varying the appeal to find vulnerability. The approach just cited is obviously not the only one that could be used in a sales letter to teachers. If you were planning such a letter, your analysis of the individual or group might lead you to shoot from an entirely different angle—or, you might decide to test several appeals whose strength appeared about equal. Here, for example, are the opening paragraphs of three letters, mailed for the same purpose, but each probing a different possible soft spot.

Dear Miss Blank:

There's a little story of Joseph Conrad that every schoolteacher will appreciate.

Long ago, when Conrad was a boy, he sat gazing at a map of the world. Suddenly, thrusting a grimy finger upon a colorful speck, the youngster exclaimed, "Some day I'm going there." "Some day I'm going there!"

I wonder if there is a teacher in all the world, who hasn't said those very words! In teaching some bit of history or geography, you've felt an impelling desire to cast the book aside, and set forth on a joyous journey.

Hidden away in our hearts, we all have that dream of some day visiting those storied countries beyond the sea.

(*Appeal to the desire for travel*)

. . . . .

Dear Miss Blank:

A dear old teacher I used to know, confided to me her fondest dream—to end her days in a cozy little cottage just over the hill from the schoolhouse, where she could hear the cheery ding-dong of the bell . . . and never have to answer it at all.

She loved teaching, of course. And she had given to it the best years of her life. But to each of us there will come a time when we want to retire from active life, and take a well-earned rest. To solve that problem, we have devised a wonderful policy, just for you. It will assure your vine-clad cottage, with happy days for rest and relaxation.

(Appeal to desire to get away from it all)

.   .   .   .   .

Dear Miss Blank:

In that last quarter of an hour, after the scholars have gone home, and you are alone in the schoolroom, straightening up your desk. . . .

. . . don't you sometimes stop and wonder what the future holds for you? Things are running pretty smoothly now. You really are enjoying your work. But what about the declining years of life? Will you have to drudge along at the same old humdrum routine, just as so many elderly teachers of your acquaintance are doing?

Or will you be able to enjoy life, and make your cherished dreams come true?

Now—today—you have an opportunity to decide.

(Appeal to desire for freedom in later years)

Just as the quarterback of a football team may use different plays to test for soft spots in the opposing line, so is it often necessary for the letter-writer to try various appeals before he can be sure which is most effective. This can never safely be determined by opinion or guess. The only sure way to *know* is to test, and then test again.

An appeal to superstition. The soft spot you are seeking when you plan a business letter may not always be of the conventional variety. Instead, by mere intuition—or is it the help of Providence?—you may hit upon an unusual appeal that does the perfect job. A certain young man—you may guess his identity—once sat in his St. Louis office, quite glum and dis-couraged. He was thumbing idly through the card file of customers, wonder-ing what he might do to bring rain where there had been so much drought, when he happened to notice that an out-of-town order had been received several months previously on a Friday, the thirteenth. The calendar on the wall said that this very day was the second and only other Friday the thirteenth of the year. Had the young chap been wiser in the ways of the business world, he would have scorned the idea that the coincidence might develop an order. But he didn't know any better, so he hand-pecked on his typewriter the following "foolish" sales letter:

Dear Mr. Doe:

I am not superstitious, but ...

There are only two Friday, the thirteenths, appearing on this year's calendar.

On Friday, January the thirteenth, you gave me an order for a carload of Fancy Blue Rose Rice. I appreciated that order more than you knew, for it happened to be my first sale to an out-of-town jobber.

Now, here we are again at Friday the thirteenth, and I can't resist wondering if you are not ready to book another carload. I think I can persuade one of our mills to give you a price of 4¢ on the Fancy, and 3⅞¢ on the Choice, f.o.b. mill, of course. And in the car could be placed a little Fancy Head Rice at about 6¼¢!

The prices are right. Give me the specifications, and I *will* be superstitious all the rest of my life.

Gratefully yours,

Many of the young man's friends have laughed at that letter, and when reminded that the only true test of a letter is whether or not it does the job, they have promptly replied, "Luck, my boy, just luck." Some have said "it couldn't happen," which may be true, except that it *did*.

Dear friend Frailey:

The writer's birthday was Friday, January the thirteenth.

While I have a stock of rice and a car in transit from Texas, I am going to give you an order for a car, for I know I can depend on you for QUALITY. So enter me 225 bags Fancy Blue Rose, 75 bags Fancy Head, at prices you mentioned, and would prefer Texas; but that is up to you for quality.

I might say in passing that it is a pleasure for me to send you this order, for from your letter, I know it will be appreciated and happily executed.

Very sincerely yours,

Perhaps you may call the success of that letter a stroke of pure luck; but at least it proves that, contrary to popular thought, there *is* sentiment in business. The man who wrote the letter had the reputation of being a smart buyer, the last to let his heart influence his head. He was vulnerable to appreciation, though. He sensed that the young man needed the order, and he gladly came across. Did the birthday help? Maybe—let's not split hairs.

Be sure the appeal will not backfire. Sometimes a business letter may have the opposite effect from that intended. Basically, the appeal may be good, but it is handled in such a way that the reader is irritated rather than pleased. Consider this sales letter which presents a very necessary service, but not in the most tactful manner.

> Dear Sir:
>
> When you decided on a midnight snack the other night and turned on the kitchen light only to find a few hundred roaches had the same idea—did you cuss under your breath, and say to yourself, "We've got to get rid of these ***!!! roaches"?
>
> Maybe, you forgot the next morning, maybe it was too much trouble—maybe you didn't like the thought of a truck covered with signs such as "WE KILL BEDBUGS" rolling up in front of your house, so that your neighbors would know your troubles.
>
> Now, through our personalized service, we not only rid your home of these obnoxious night prowlers, but we completely moth-proof all clothes closets, furniture, rugs, or garments that show signs of moth attack. Our service also eliminates water-bugs, ants, silverfish, etc., with no fuss, no muss—you and the insects are the only ones who will know we have been around—and the insects won't know it for long.
>
> It is not necessary to leave your home. Our neat, well-trained men will call, do the work, and leave your premises spick-and-span. Our Home Service System is safe, non-contaminating to food, and is non-injurious to humans or animals.
>
> Our price? Well, you will be amazed at the low cost.
>
> Just mail the enclosed card, or 'phone CH ——, and a courteous representative will call with absolutely no obligation on your part.
>
> Sincerely yours,

Fundamentally, the appeal in this letter is sound. Roaches and other insects are not welcome in any home. If you happened to have any of these pests as uninvited guests, you certainly would be glad to know they could be eliminated so easily and so cheaply. The confidential treatment is also a good point. Roaches or bedbugs are nothing to be proud of, and you wouldn't want your neighbors to know they had moved in with you.

But the *backfire* comes from the way the writer of the letter over-played his hand. He starts with the downright assumption that the prospect's kitchen is inhabited by roaches—not a few of them, but *hundreds*. He uses the appeal as a *fact* rather than a *possibility*. Hence, the prospect and his wife, if she read the letter, are humiliated. Particularly obnoxious is the reference later to "bedbugs"—the most hated insect of them all. They are not mentioned as a fact, as were the roaches, but just the same there is an unpleasant insinuation that they, too, might be one of the prospect's "troubles."

The more tactful approach would have been to *start easy and work up*. Instead of the outright assertion that when the lights went on a few hundred roaches were there in the grandstand, ready to root for the home-team, only the *possibility* of their being present should have been mentioned—and even then, not such vast assembly of the pests. A woman looks upon a roach as evidence of uncleanliness, and thus a reflection on her care of the home. A few roaches are bad enough, she figures—she could never stand an army of them. The letter should have started something like this:

> This is the time of the year when the war against roaches and other pests increases in fury. Where these little devils come from, nobody seems to know. When least expected, they appear in the most immaculate homes.
>
> Perhaps, so far, none of these unwelcome guests have moved in on you. And that's fine! You are lucky. But if, by chance, you have some of them around your house, you naturally want to get rid of them before they multiply and become even a greater nuisance.
>
> And that's where we come to the rescue. Not even your closest neighbor will know about it, but quickly, completely, we will liquidate the rascals.

In that introduction, there is nothing to offend or humiliate the readers. They are tactfully told that roaches and other pests (that would include the unmentionable bedbugs) often appear in the most immaculate homes. The rest of the letter could be in the original form. Result? Success—much business!

Remember! *You can't win by insulting your reader.*

Avoid all possible irritants. There's an old and very wise saying, especially pertinent to letter-writers, "When in doubt, *don't*." Unless you know your reader like a book, you run the chance of building your letter around an appeal that may offend rather than please him.

It is dangerous to mention politics, religion or race. A very good story might poke what seems to be innocent fun at the members of a certain faith, and what if it lands in the home of one of them? You might quote a saying of a Mexican, an Irishman, or an Italian, and have any one of those nationalities take it in the wrong way. It is far wiser not to take these chances in business letters. When in doubt, *don't.*

Even the reference to a physical attribute may rub salt in raw flesh. You have a laughable story about a bald-headed man. But it may not be so funny to one who is bald. You refer to a man who resembles a "bag of bones" and the reader has always been sensitive about being so thin. You write about the fat woman who wants to reduce but can't resist her pound of chocolates every day—and the letter is read by a lady in exactly the same plight.

You skate on thin ice when you voice a decided opinion on a controversial subject. You may detest rent control, but your reader thinks it is a fine plan. You may not like the wife of a President who frequently appears in public, but your reader may think she is wonderful. Reading the comics in the newspapers may seem a childish pastime to you, but what if your reader enjoys it? The purpose of your letter is to gain a meeting of minds. Why say anything that might interfere with that result?

Make the reader feel important. Contrary to the irritants just mentioned, it is often possible to "scratch the reader's back" by casual reference to some fact that he considers complimentary to himself. Of course, this cannot be done when writing to a total stranger. For example, any of the following phrases, or similar ones, might help to make the reader feel important.

> "The research that made this product possible started back in the days when *you were playing football at Illinois.*"
>
> "*Your article in Sales Management* makes me sure that your mind is open to any idea which might help to motivate your salesmen."
>
> "The credit report on you and your business was *so outstanding* that we are puzzled not to receive your check."
>
> "We don't think these obstacles are going to get you down, for we think you are *made of the same stuff as that boy of yours* who flew so many missions in Europe."
>
> "Because of *your leadership in civic activities,* we lean heavily on your opinion, which we know will be unbiased."
>
> "Many men, *like yourself,* serve others so generously that they overlook the protection which would take the sting out of old age."
>
> "Any man who has *served three terms as mayor of his city* must be an *enterprising merchant,* and the kind who wins friends by selling only quality products."
>
> "We understand it is useless to talk business to anyone in Columbus during the week of a championship game, but now that

the *Buckeyes have finished the season undefeated,* perhaps you can find time to tell us how you liked the samples."

"For me to have a *daughter like yours,* able to make the pictures in Hollywood, would be a biological miracle, but I do appreciate beauty in design, and I can't help being enthusiastic about our new dresses for summer wear."

"Surely, as men *of good judgment,* you and your partner do not always buy on the lowest price, *nor can you be fooled* by a product which looks better than it really is."

The compliments implied in the above passages are based on *facts* and could be offered *sincerely.* They are not to be confused with the silly flattery so often seen in business letters—those attempts to curry favor which the readers quickly resent.

The fifth step in planning a letter. Now the five steps to be taken in planning an important business letter can be listed. Please remember that the time devoted to them depends on the nature of the problem, and that many routine letter-situations may be "taken in stride," just as you mount and ride a bicycle, once the art is mastered.

1. Know your PURPOSE
2. Get all the FACTS
3. VISUALIZE your reader
4. Choose the best APPEAL
5. CO-ORDINATE the attack

To co-ordinate means putting your points together in the order or combination to gain the best possible effect. In other words, you decide how to play your cards to win the most tricks. You are like the general who is planning to attack a section of the enemy's line. The commanding officer knows that he will use infantry, planes, tanks, rockets, mortars, heavy guns, and other units, but he must co-ordinate them perfectly to achieve the break-through. In less serious measure, this is the letter-man's problem, too. He has decided what the general letter-appeal shall be, and has decided what links to place in the Chain (see page 96), but he still must put the links together in the one best combination to provide the most strength.

As the lawyer arranges his plea. We doubt if the average letter-writer gives much thought to the *arrangement* of his points, and yet it is highly important that he should. He knows that he wants (1) to mention price because his figure is somewhat lower than his competitor's, (2) to talk about quality because it is at least equal to the best, (3) to emphasize style because he has a new design that he thinks will have great popular appeal. Price—quality—style! Those are his three aces, but what does it matter—in what order they are presented to the reader?

By asking that question the letter-writer has displayed an ignorance of psychological principles which go a long way in determining the final reaction—depending, of course, on how well they are understood and applied. One principle is that, in order to gain reader-attention, a very strong point should be used *first*. Another is that, when exposed to a number of items, we tend to remember the last one most vividly. Thus, the most convincing and action-impelling point should be offered *last*.

However, it is also true that at no place in the letter must the reader's interest be allowed to lag. This indicates that weak points, even when preceded and followed by strong ones, are *dangerous*. It is much better not to use them *at all* than to risk the reader's throwing the letter in the waste-basket and turning to something more interesting.

You see now, that the position of the man who is planning a letter is much the same as that of the lawyer who is planning his plea. The lawyer knows he must start with a strong point to get favorable interest, and that he must end with the hammer blow which may obtain the right verdict. He is also faced with the problem of keeping the jury awake throughout his argument. He knows, too, that a few strong points, forcefully presented, will have a better effect than a long list of points that tend to compete with each other in the listener's mind with the result—a little of everything, and nothing much of anything, is remembered. These are the facts that the letter-man also must understand!

If you ever have studied the formula for debate, you recognize its similarity to the above reasoning. When there are three speakers on a team, the arguments are reduced to three, each one strong and difficult to refute. These arguments are then assigned in the following order: the strongest to the last speaker, the second-strongest to the first speaker, and the second speaker gets what's left. Sometimes a very strong point is reserved for use in the last rebuttal, the thought being that it will impress the mind of each judge, even if earlier portions of the argument have been forgotten.

A case example. To understand how the capable letter-writer plans a co-ordinated attack to break down reader-resistance, consider the following hypothetical situation:

Jasper Jones, a real estate man, has been asked to sell a small suburban property. Based on the present market, the owner's price is a little high, but the home has many advantages that may offset this one objection. Mr. Jones reviews these sales points in his own mind (Step Two, Get the Facts), and makes a list of them on his memo pad.

> Easy transportation—a bus to the city every hour—four-lane express highway for automobiles.

Restricted neighborhood of first-class homes—served by all the utilities—free from smoke and dirt of sections closer in.

Beautiful site—more than one acre of land—large oak trees, many shrubs, ravine.

House designed by nationally known architect—plans won first prize in contest conducted by popular magazine—small and compact, with all modern conveniences.

Brick walls and tile roof, insulated—low cost for repair and maintenance—built by contractor with reputation for quality construction.

Two-car garage, with one room and lavatory overhead—detached from the house.

Kennel for dogs, with three runs, at rear of the lot—disguised by brick wall which has climbing roses.

Rock garden, fish pool, and open-air oven.

House features large studio living room, two tiled baths, ultra-modern kitchen, and basement recreation room with bar. Wood-burning fireplace.

Priced high at $30,000, but owner will accept low down-payment, and a long-term mortgage at only 5% interest.

School one of the best in the area—special bus service for children.

Healthier place to live than in city—cooler in summer—always a nice breeze.

Five miles from 18 hole golf course—within walking distance of community shopping center.

Now the telephone rings. Cy Jerkins has heard about the suburban home. No, he isn't ready to look at it. His wife isn't too keen about living out there. No, he doesn't want to talk to Jasper. "Just give me the dope in a letter," says Mr. Jerkins, "and make it short—I'll let you know if we are interested."

Matching needs and benefits. Okay! Jasper Jones has a nibble, but it isn't a bite. What should he say in his letter to lure Mr. and Mrs. Jerkins to an inspection of the property? He begins to think about them (Step Three, Visualize the Reader) and what *they,* as apart from all other prospects, might want in a home (Step Four, Choose the Best Appeal).

It's all very simple. "I *sold* him today," boasts salesman Doe, but he didn't, really. A sale is nothing more than *matching needs and benefits.* When you can do that, the sale is inevitable.

Jasper Jones knows a lot about Jerkins and his wife. That will save him time. However, if they had been strangers, he would still need information about them before he writes his letter. How else could he select those advantages of the home that seem to fit the pattern of their peculiar needs? Well, what *does* he know about them?

Mr. and Mrs. Jerkins are renting a rather expensive apartment in the city. They are the type who spend most or all of their income. He is a consultant on advertising and sales problems, and writes for both business and fiction magazines. Their only child is married and lives in the East. Mrs. J. has quite a reputation as a bridge player. They both play golf—and, yes—they belong to the club only five miles from the Oak Ridge home. Dogs? Of course! Didn't Jasper read something in the paper last year about one of their Scotties winning "best in show"?

All right! Now Jasper has the two mental pictures—of the home and all its advantages, and—of the prospects and their possible soft spots. He is ready to make the blend. "And make it short," Cy Jerkins had said. Obviously, Jasper's problem is to choose carefully a few of the points most likely to strike fire—and he knows that is the most effective plan for *all* sales letters.

Easy transportation? Not important. Both Mr. and Mrs. Jerkins have their own automobiles.

Restricted neighborhood? Well, yes and no. Mrs. Jerkins is socially minded. But everybody knows Oak Ridge is first class. Skip it.

Beautiful site? Yes, they are the kind to whom that will appeal. *Plans won first prize?* Yes, indeed, Mrs. Jerkins at least will love that point.

Quality construction? No. They will probably take it for granted.

Two-car garage? A necessary point, but not worth emphasis. What's that? Wait a moment. Maybe that room over the garage would be a swell place for Cy Jerkins to write. Yes—use that.

Kennel? Wonderful. They show dogs.

Rock garden, pool, oven? No, she is not the kind to stay home with her flowers.

Large studio living room? Good for her bridge parties. *Recreation room with bar?* Fine! He especially will like that. What man wouldn't?

Low down-payment? Yes. The price will appeal to their vanity, so long as they can swing the deal. Their monthly income is ample to meet the mortgage payments.

School bus? No. Their only child is an adult.

Healthier place to live? Doubtful. They are not old enough to be seriously health-minded. The breeze might appeal. No. "When in doubt, *don't.*"

Golf course near? Yes, strong point. *Shopping center?* No. If anyone walks there, it will be the maid.

There you are. Jasper Jones has completed Steps Three and Four. From all the points that *could* be used, he has chosen the following as most likely to please Mr. and Mrs. Cy Jerkins:

1. Beautiful site
2. Plans won first prize
3. Room over garage
4. Kennel
5. Large studio living room
6. Recreation room with bar
7. Low down-payment and easy terms
8. Close to their golf club

Co-ordination for best effect. Is Jasper Jones now ready to write his letter? No, not yet. Step Five has not been taken. He could just start with point number one at the head of the list and go right through to number eight, but only by sheer luck could that be the *best* combination.

Which of the eight points is the strongest? Not just for *any* prospect, but for Mr. and Mrs. Cy Jerkins? The decision calls for judgment, and you might not agree, but Jasper's choice is number *seven*—low down payment and easy monthly terms. He thinks that if the other points can make the Jerkins family want the home, they might ask themselves, "How can we possibly afford it?" Jasper knows how, so he saves the answer to their question for a "clincher" at the end.

Okay! Which of the remaining points ranks next to number seven in strength of appeal? To Cy Jerkins alone, it might be number three. Perhaps for years he has dreamed of a hide-away place to work and write. Since Jasper isn't sure about it, he can't afford to take a chance. No, he wants to start his letter with a point that will gain immediate acceptance from *both* husband and wife. He finally decides to appeal to their pride—combination of number one and number two. Also, he thinks he may be able to work number eight into the first paragraph.

Thus, for the middle of his letter, Jasper has left only the room over the garage, the kennel, the studio living room, and the recreation room. He decides on the combination 5–6–4–3. At last—J. J. is ready to write.

His plan has been carefully devised. Within the scope of his ability, he has prepared what seems to be the attack most likely to succeed.

> Prize winner on beautiful site, close to golf club
> Large studio living room
> Recreation room with bar
> Room over garage
> Kennel
> Low down-payment and easy terms

Perhaps you are scowling. You say, "Who would take so much time and trouble, just to plan *one* business letter?" Well, the answer is "Who *wouldn't?*"—with so much at stake. The commission which Jasper Jones earns on a sale of property is 5 per cent, and the price of this one is $30,000. How about it now? Wouldn't *you* gladly spend an hour, a day, or a week, if a commission of $1,500 depended on the success of that one letter? Remember, the time you can afford to spend on one letter is determined by the nature of the problem, and the importance of getting it solved.

The letter that sold the home. So Jasper Jones writes the letter. He wonders if it should be mailed to the office of Cy Jerkins, or to his home; the latter seems best. He wants both husband and wife to read it together. He knows, too, that when homes are bought the man may *think* he has made the decision, but the one who *really* does it is the woman who lets him have that pleasure.

So much for this hypothetical example of planning a business letter. But what's a story without an end? Did the letter develop a sale? Well, we think it was mailed one morning and delivered that afternoon. At eight o'clock in the evening, Jasper Jones reached the promised land. Came a voice over the wire, "Thanks for your letter...Mrs. Jerkins and I are not much interested...but we'll meet you there at ten in the morning."

No, not much interested, but the following afternoon the contract was signed. Good news for all—even the pups.

What did Jasper say in his letter? Well, you have his outline of points. Why don't you write it—something like this:

> Dear Mr. and Mrs. Jerkins:
>
> I don't sell real estate. It's a lot more fun to find a perfect home, and then the people who *belong* in it—just as you folks surely do belong in the Oak Ridge home Mr. Jerkins asked me about.
>
> When John Boardman, the famous architect, designed this prize-winning home—the one not far from your golf course—he must

have visualized it set in an acre of trees and shrubs as it is now —and folks like you who would love it as much as he did when drawing the plans.

Mr. Jerkins said I must make this letter short, so I can't begin to explain all the charm of this magnificent little home. You'll have to see it to appreciate what I mean.

You, Mrs. Jerkins, will be delighted with the studio living room with its huge fireplace—plenty of space for a dozen bridge tables without crowding. And you, Mr. Jerkins, would surely be a proud host in the tiled recreation room with its unusual bar. Then over the garage—this is a secret—is the perfect place for you to write your stories. If you are like me, you always have wanted a hide-away. Every man needs one, and especially a writer like you.

Maybe, too, Mr. Boardman was thinking of folks like you—or he just loved dogs and couldn't imagine a real home without them—when he designed the kennel so cleverly hidden behind a brick wall covered with climbing roses.

Of course, there is always one thing that comes up in finding a home—the price and terms. They may not be important to you, but the owner will accept a very low down-payment, and a mortgage for the balance with interest of only 5%.

Will you do me a favor? When you read this letter—perhaps at dinner tonight—multiply many, many times in your mental image of this home the few things I have said about it. Then call me tonight, and say when you'll have the thrill of seeing it.

I've got the keys, and can meet you there any time tomorrow. Please do call me—MAIN 3343—as I'll wait until you do.

Sincerely yours,

Think before you write. Nothing worthwhile yields to human effort without a PLAN. The actual saying is easy. It's the planning *what* to say and *how* that determines how good your letter will be. When Abraham Lincoln was asked how he would write a speech if he had just fifteen minutes for the job, he replied, "Well, I would spend at least ten of the fifteen minutes planning what to write, and then I would use the last five minutes to write it."

Maybe it was a similar plan that the Reverend George Washington Abraham Lee used so successfully in getting so many converts for his church. Rival ministers witnessed his results with mingled jealousy and admiration. When questioned about the secret of his success, he said—"Fust ah tell 'em wut ah's gwine to tell 'em—den ah tells 'em—den ah tells 'em wut ah dun tole 'em." Amen, Parson Lee. You work with a PLAN.

2. BLUEPRINTS FOR LETTER-BUILDING

One skeleton that they all possess. In spite of the million and one variations in the blueprints from which business letters are constructed, there is one basic formula that all letters must follow, or else they are almost certainly doomed to fail. True, a writer may now and then risk another plan, but it rarely succeeds, and is then only the exception which proves the rule. Letters, like human beings, are built on a skeleton that has a striking similarity of form, although in "flesh and other attributes" they may seem totally unlike. No matter what kind of letters you write—sales, collection, or any of the others—you must always recognize the necessity of this "skeleton," and make sure it is there.

Many experts in the letter-world have devised figures of speech to describe this formula, skeleton, or whatever you may choose to call it. Even your grade-school teacher, when you were first being exposed to English Composition, had the formula in mind without a name for it, when she said that what you were trying to write must start with an Introduction, continue with a Body, and end with a Conclusion. She may or may not have made plain to you the "why" of these three parts, but it is improbable that you understood then the psychological purpose of each part, or the connection of the whole procedure with the influencing of human behavior.

Dr. Dignan had a name for it. The names for the three steps in letter-construction which seem to have persisted the longest, and for that reason may be the best, were invented years ago by Dr. Frank W. Dignan. He was one of the pioneers who taught that letters should be simple, friendly, and natural, and was a master who helped to inspire this Handbook.

Dr. Dignan said that every letter needed first a "Star"—something to be said in the beginning that would quickly capture the attention of the reader. If this could be accomplished, he reasoned, then the reader would be willing to go on to find out what else the letter had to tell him. Without the Star, unless the reader had a personal reason for wanting to continue, the letter would be pushed aside and no matter how interesting the rest of it might be, it would never be read.

The second of the three parts, and the one which did the major job, Dr. Dignan called the "Chain,"—a series of facts that would change the reader's casual attention to a real and sustained interest. This meant, of course, that each link—each fact—in the Chain had to be strong, for interest also can easily be interrupted, and when that happened, the reader would be gone.

Finally, said the old master, a letter needs something to impel the desired action—a final urge that would make the reader send the check or buy the goods. This he called the "Hook." A hook grabs and holds fast. The reader no longer can escape the issue. As he read through the Chain there was always the danger that he might stop before the story had been told, but now he knows what you want. He can still decide either way, but if the Hook is strong, he is inclined to say "Yes."

"The Star, the Chain, and the Hook"—easy to remember, isn't it? Just like a watch-chain, with the watch on one end and a pocket-knife on the other!

> First, get the reader's favorable *attention*. Do it deliberately with an opening paragraph which is bright and brisk—the *Star*.
>
> Second, follow quickly with a flow of facts, reasons, benefits, all selected and placed in the best order to transform attention to real *interest*, and finally to *desire*—that's the *Chain*.
>
> Third, suggest *action*, and make it as easy as possible—the *Hook*.

Attention...interest...desire...action! There are the four psychological reactions in the mind of your reader, and they happen *in that order* as he takes your letter from the envelope, begins to read, continues through the several paragraphs, and finally arrives at the last period. Obviously, it is a *progressive* process, each step paving the way for the next. Attention increases until it blends into interest. Interest deepens until desire is aroused. Desire, when strong and bold, leads to action. Hence, your letter is planned to stimulate those mental reactions, and each part does a *separate* job. If the Star does get favorable attention, nothing more should be expected of it. Developing interest and desire is the job of the Chain, but it does not reach for action. You still have a player on the bench with an eagle eye, and you use him to shoot the last winning basket. He is the Hook.

So you see the co-ordination between your efforts and the mental response of the reader. Cold, lukewarm, warm, hot—attention, interest, desire, action! The steps *must* be in that order.

Using the Star, the Chain, and the Hook. Although they deal with different situations, and have little affinity in either content or style, the following letters are all built on similar "skeletons." In each example, you can see how the writer has tried to lead the reader from attention→to interest→to desire→to ACTION. The first is a sales letter mailed by the Pangborn Corporation, Hagerstown, Maryland.

IT'S THE LITTLE THINGS IN LIFE THAT COUNT
And We Don't
Mean *Maybe!*

A cinder in the eye...

Gets more attention than a coal barge on the Ohio River. And a tiny pebble in his boot will cause a hunter more grief than a big bear.

Yes—it's the little things in life that count—that are important—that.bring quickest reactions. (End of the Star.)

Take the blast cleaning division of a company, for instance. What could be more important than the operator's safety helmet, the air blast hose he uses, the nozzles, and the steel shot and grit? Yet these items are small—the "accessories" to the blast cleaning machines.

Yet in June, July and August, when the temperature reaches 92 degrees in the shade, what could be more important than the comfort, weight, and fresh air feed of your operator's blast helmet? Or the long wearing life of a GOOD blast cleaning nozzle? Or the extra thickness of the rubber lining in the air blast hose? Or the reliability of size, and the toughness and strength of the steel abrasives?

These are some of the little things in blast cleaning life that really count—that pay a tremendous return in satisfaction and production and profit, when they are RIGHT—and just as you want them. (End of the Chain.)

That's why we ask you to "come to Pangborn" now. For over forty years, we have specialized in providing the BEST BLAST CLEANING EQUIPMENT AND SUPPLIES—and we will be happy to serve your needs now—promptly and carefully. Just drop us a note *today*. (End of Hook.)

                                        Very truly yours,

(Signed by Victor F. Stine, Vice-President in charge of Sales)

The following letter was used to revive inactive customers. The Star supplies the theme for the whole message, and since the readers already knew about the products and services of the company, the Chain plays a minor role.

Gentlemen:

I feel just like the Irishman who dashed up to a hotel desk one evening—hat gone, and clothes all streaked with dirt.

"I want room thirty-siven," he shouted.

"But I can't give you room thirty-seven," said the clerk, after looking at the board.

"I tell you, I want room thirty-seven," was the rising reply.

"But room thirty-seven is taken. Mr. Murphy has that room."

"Don't I know it? I'm Murphy. I jist feel out av the winder, and I want to git back in again." (End of Star.)

Yes, I feel something like that, and I want to get back in the room, where you give out your orders for printing.

It's been a mighty long time since we've had the pleasure of serving you, Mr. Doe, and it certainly would make us happy to see your name back on our books.

Our equipment is modern and complete. We have both the facilities for doing good printing, and the will to give you the best of service. (End of Chain.)

There's a blotter enclosed with our telephone number on it in nice bold figures. Why not do unto us as you would unto Murphy. Give us a ring when you need your next printing job. (End of Hook.)

Cordially yours,

Collection letters, too, contain the Star, the Chain, and the Hook— first, something to put the reader in a good mood, then the reasons why he should pay, and last, either a request for the money, or a statement of what will happen if he doesn't pay. The emphasis on the three steps varies considerably in collection letters—depending on the age of the unpaid account, and what the company intends to do about it.

Even short, routine letters can easily be fitted to the Star, the Chain, and the Hook, as is the following "reminder." The bill is not old, and there is no reason for a long letter. However, it starts gaily, states the necessary facts, and ends with a gentle request for action.

The Star to capture ATTENTION	The letter S is made up, as you know, of curved lines, but look what a straight and narrow path does for it . . . $.
The Chain to state the FACTS	And good old Uncle Sam will bring your check for $58.00, in payment of our January 31 invoice, straight to our door.
A Hook to ask ACTION	Why not send it along, and then we'll all be happy.

There are only fifty-seven words in the above letter, but some credit men would still insist it is far too long. They would ask one question—"Will you please send us your check for $58.00, in payment of your invoice of January 31?"—and call it a good job. Others, more reckless with their time, might add "Thank you," but nothing more. The difference in the effectiveness of the two letters could only be measured by *results*. If each of the two letters were sent to identical groups of one hundred customers, which would pull the highest percentage of checks, and in the shortest time? Personally, we vote for the longer one, because it is the more interesting.

Relation of length to difficulty. "Long enough to do the job," is how long a business letter should be (Section 2), but certainly the problem of holding reader-interest becomes more difficult as the length increases. Irrespective of how many pages a letter may run, the Star and the Hook tend to remain short. The burden of keeping interest alive falls upon the Chain. Every point added is another link, and the letter-writer is ever reminded of the adage, "A chain is only as strong as its weakest link." He hates to omit a point that might help his cause, and yet he knows that when the reader is bored, the cause is lost.

Some of the best *longer letters* seen in business correspondence are those that seek to obtain magazine subscriptions. The writers probably wish they could do the job in a few short paragraphs, but they know that mention of one or two points about a magazine will not heat the water to a boil. They are forced to tell a longer story, even at the risk of letting the fire go out. That hazard, of course, they fight hard and cleverly to avoid.

The Hook to impel action. Some letters in business ask for no reply, and are purely routine in nature—acknowledgments of orders, carriers of checks, expressions of goodwill, answers containing requested information, and others. Most of the important ones—those written to sell, or collect, or adjust—do reach out for a favorable response. No matter how interesting and convincing such a letter may be, you will agree it is wasted unless the desired reader-reaction is attained. Many letters, like race horses, get away from the post beautifully, lead most of the way, but falter coming down the stretch. The cause of their failure is the weakness of the Hook.

There is an old saying, often heard in sales meetings, that "the way to get an order is to *ask* for it." This thought neatly fits all business letters in which an attempt is made to influence human behavior. To get action, you must *ask* for it. Furthermore, you must ask with the implied confidence that a favorable reply is expected. The end of your letter is not the place for timidity or lack of faith. Assuming that you *believe* what has been said in the Chain, and that what you are asking is to the benefit of the reader, why should anything else but the desired reaction be expected?

The situation at the end of the letter is quite different from what it was at the beginning. First, you had to get the reader's attention. He was cold, indifferent. You had to pull something out of the bag that would quicken his pulse, make him willing to continue. Then you presented fact after fact (link after link) to arouse interest and build desire. Hence, if the Chain was strong and convincing, the reader is thinking as you think when it comes time for the Hook. He is ready to go along with you, and does not resent being "told" as he would have earlier in the letter. Often, he stands on top of the fence, but needs a little "push" to make him jump in the right direction. That's your job, and the "how" of it is to be explained later in this section.

Which is the most important? Sometimes, the question is asked, "Which is the most important in writing a successful business letter—the Star, the Chain, or the Hook?" Well, which does you the most good— breakfast, luncheon, or dinner? The difficulty in rating the comparative importance of the three parts is that each does a *separate* job, and each must be judged by a separate set of standards. If one of the three parts is poorly constructed, then the whole letter is a failure. The three parts team together to score the touchdown; one opens a hole in the line, one blocks, and the other carries the ball. *All* are important.

To be sure, the *first* job is to open the hole in the line. That's done by the Star. Unless the hole is there, the blocker and the ball-carrier are stopped. But if the blocker fails to get his man, or if the ball is fumbled, the play still fails. So you see why the Star, the Chain, and the Hook cannot be rated comparatively. Each part is an independent function that contributes to the success of the whole.

Other comparisons. We have chosen the figure of speech used by Dr. Dignan as the one that best describes the three parts of a business letter. There are others with which you may wish to be familiar, however. One of the experts compares the writing of an effective letter to a successful flight in an airplane. First comes the take-off—getting the reader's attention. Once in the air, the pilot follows his course as swiftly as possible—the time when interest is quickened, and desire awakened. Finally, comes the landing, end of the flight—request for action. The analogy is good, because each of the three operations is quite different from the others—just as the three parts of a business letter are different in function, and in the skills needed to complete them.

In the Dartnell publication, *American Business*, the writing of a business letter was once compared to setting off a giant firecracker. The description was as follows:

The flame of the match is the opening paragraph. It gets the reader's attention—makes him want to see what is going to happen next. Once lit, the fuse should burn steadily. The flame is carried along to that exciting moment when it reaches the powder.

Well, so must the interest of the reader be carried along to the end of the letter. Back in the days when we were kids, you can remember the suspense of those few seconds while the fuse was burning. There must be the same suspense in a letter. A defective fuse means that the flame stops burning. Sometimes, in the middle of a letter, the reader's interest is also extinguished.

And finally, the cracker is fired. Bang! It is the climax of an interesting experience. But the crackers don't always explode. Some fizzle and sputter—others are complete duds. So it is with the closing paragraphs of a business letter. They either go off with a bang, or they fizzle. The reader is sold, or he is lost.

Flame—fuse—fire! Those are the three steps in writing a business letter.

Another comparison, more applicable to sales letters than to the others, is the one of the five "P's." The idea is that the writer of a business letter must in the following order—please, picture, prove, promise, and push. This conforms very well with the other comparisons.

Please} . . . . get **Attention**
Picture ⎫   **Interest**
Prove ⎬ . . . .   to
Promise⎭   **Desire**
Push . . . . **Action**

Okay! You have seen that there are three parts in a business letter; that all combine to do the job, but that each is quite different in function and the manner of execution. Naturally, your mind now turns to "HOW." *How* is attention gained? *How* are interest and desire developed? *How* is action impelled?

3. How to Get Reader's Attention

Value of the first impression. One of America's leading letter authorities, Frank H. Roy, in his capacity as Correspondence Supervisor for Montgomery Ward & Co., wrote this in a bulletin to Montgomery Ward letter-writers: "A letter to the reader is a great deal like a conversation. A letter drags just like a conversation that is dull unless there is some spirit and life in the opening paragraph. The question with most of us is—'How can I liven up my starting paragraph? What appeal can I use that will be so interesting the reader wants to go on?' The first impression your reader gets from your letter is very important. You can open the door graciously or you can slam it in his face, and all you can say in your remaining paragraphs will be of little value."

Mr. Roy is absolutely on the beam. First impressions, by personal contact or by letter, are extremely important. You are introduced to a stranger, and before he utters a word, an impression has been formed which will tend to persist as long as you know him. You pull a letter out of an envelope, and before a line has been read, you have formed an impression of its general appearance which may influence, favorably or otherwise, your final reaction. Then, that first quick impression is strengthened or weakened by what you read in the first paragraph.

There are many factors that contribute to the appearance of a business letter—the quality of the paper, the design and printing of the letterhead, the way it is typed, the signature—but they will be explained in Section 4. What we want to know now is *in what ways, in the beginning of a letter, can attention be captured?*

"Get off to a flying start." This is the advice of William H. Butterfield, the author of numerous books on business correspondence. In one of them, *Goodwill Letters that Build Business,** he writes: "If all the preliminary steps have been handled effectively, the reader approaches the first sentence with at least a spark of casual interest. The opening sentence applies the fuel that either ignites the spark or smothers it. The application must be immediate, too, for the average reader allows a letter only a few seconds in which to prove its interest to him. This means that the lead-off sentence must "click.' "

In the book, *Modern Business English,* by Babenroth and Parkhurst,** we read: "The purpose of the first sentence is to win the reader's attention. Upon its power to interest him depends his willingness to read further.... The attention-getter must be brief, attractive, and appropriate. Because a long paragraph is heavy and uninviting, the first paragraph should always be short."

There is hardly a person who will throw a letter away without reading a word, *unless* he recognizes the letterhead, guesses what it is about, and from previous correspondence is utterly indifferent to the content. Usually there is an element of curiosity that forces him to take at least a quick peep at the opening paragraph. If he finds something there of interest to *him,* he is quite likely to continue. If not, another letter has died in infancy—another postage stamp has been used in vain. As Butterfield says, only a few seconds will decide what happens. You get him quick, or you get him not at all.

A poor place for whiskers. In view of this necessity for a fast start—

---

* Englewood Cliffs, N. J.: Prentice-Hall, Inc.

something to change casual attention to at least a small degree of interest —it must be apparent that whiskers, as you saw them in Section 2, are strictly taboo in the Star of a business letter. Who would not yawn on reading, "Your kind favor of recent date has duly come to hand," or "With reference to your esteemed communication, we would wish to state"? Who would go a word further?

> "We have your favored epistle of the 21st instant, and have read same with considerable embarrassment."
>
> "I have just read your letter—and is my face red!"

Which of those two opening sentences would arouse the most interest? Which would be most likely to spur the reader on? If you have no special design for capturing interest, at least be sure to remember the slogan— "Relax...be natural...just talk."

Taking advantage of previous contacts. In those cases where you know your reader, or have had previous contacts with him by letter or in person, there may often be a mutual interest that tends to get the letter off to a good start. "It doesn't seem possible that two years have passed since we took time off at the Milwaukee convention to bowl together—but I still remember how you pinned my ears back." A sentence like that would be sure to get you off to a flying start, but it wouldn't have been so good had the reader's ears been pinned instead of yours. Nevertheless, any contact which has been pleasant is quite useful as an attention-winner.

> Your letters always make good reading—that last one was a whangdoodle.
>
> .   .   .   .   .
>
> Hello, Mr. Gordon. Remember me? We met last week at the University Club, and you told me about your dogs, and all the ribbons they have won.
>
> .   .   .   .   .
>
> Our mutual friend, George Davis, wants the three of us to play golf together soon. In the meantime, I need your opinion on a problem in our business.
>
> .   .   .   .   .
>
> Last summer, when I camped near Nisswa, in Minnesota, your son was my guide on several fishing trips. I have never seen anyone cast as well as he does. One day we were talking about your business and mine. Bob thought we should get together.

To be sure, it requires no particular skill to start a letter, when the gate is already wide open. On the other hand, when these personal contacts are available, it would be foolish not to take advantage of them.

A tip from newspaper reporters. When you know your letter is going to an individual or group that should be interested in the contents—if time is taken to digest them—newspaper reporters have a plan which you could well afford to copy. In the first paragraph of most news stories an effort is made to summarize all that is to follow. This is called the "lead" and it contains the five "W's"—Who, What, When, Where, and Why. Thus, the lead is really a preview of the story, and the reader goes on to get the details.

> This morning at nine o'clock (WHEN), crazed with jealousy (WHY), John Doe, local dentist (WHO), returned to his former home at 1010 West Broad Street (WHERE), and killed his divorced wife with a hatchet (WHAT).

That's newspaper style, and it can be very effective in starting certain kinds of business letters. Say the head of a retail organization wants to announce a sale in a letter to customers. He believes the values are outstanding, and that any reader is sure to be interested if he takes time to read about them. To assure that happy circumstance, it seems best to hand out the good news just as quickly as possible.

> Beginning next Monday morning, and as long as they last (WHEN), in order to clear our shelves for summer stock (WHY), the Carlson Company (WHO), at all of our six stores in the Twin Cities (WHERE), will sell all remaining winter shoes at exactly half-price (WHAT).

Details about the sale, that it was only for old customers who brought the letter with them, and something about the types and brands available, could follow later. The biggest inducement—Half-Price—can be counted on to arouse interest, especially in old customers who have been buying shoes at the Carlson stores and know their quality.

Use of a question. There is something about a question that seems to demand an answer. This fact is well known to speakers and schoolteachers. When they see a yawn coming up, they simply ask the offender a question. In that way, he is quickly brought back to the world of reality. It's an old, old method of getting attention, and it works just as well for the letter-writer.

Of course, there are questions and questions, and like everything else pertaining to business letters, they need to be used with intelligence and discretion. Merely to ask a question, tell a story, or state an interesting fact, knowing there is little or no connection between what you are saying and the "meat" of the letter, is an insult to the reader. You are then merely a trickster, and even if you gain momentary attention, it will surely be lost when the reader discovers you have "taken him for a ride."

But when appropriate to the subject matter, in keeping with good taste, and not "wild and woolly," a question can capture immediate attention, and help to hold it as the meaning develops. Here are a few "stoppers" that might induce you to keep on reading. They are all taken from successful business letters:

"People do the darndest things, don't they?"...Yes, you agree, but just what in particular does he mean?

"Do you know that if you were to take one penny, and double your money each day for thirty days, you would then have more than five million dollars?"...No, you probably didn't, but the thought is pleasant. You may even start figuring to see if it is true.

"Can you keep a secret for $500?"...You bet, but he had better not be kidding. I'll read on to find out.

"Can fish tell one color from another?"...Well, if not, why do fishermen carry all those colored flies and gadgets?

"Would you think a man could make a million dollars selling onion plants by mail?"...No. I wouldn't, but maybe this fellow had a secret for getting rich that I should know.

"Do you know what a dozen eggs, a bottle of milk, or a loaf of bread will cost next month, next year, or in half a century?" ...No, but if this fellow does, you would like to be cut in on the secret.

"Wouldn't you like, with our compliments, to have a new road map which tells you in a jiffy the best routes between thousands of cities in the United States and Canada?"...Yes, I would. I'll read on to find how to get one.

Probably all of those questions got favorable attention, but you couldn't tell whether or not there was an appropriate connection with what followed. On the next page is the whole of the letter which started with the rather vague but interesting question, "People do the darndest things, don't they?" Stop, and read that letter now.

Dear Mr. Kamprath:

People do the darndest things, don't they?

We know of a man who hadn't kissed his wife in five years. . . and then shot another fellow who did.

A few days ago I overheard two business men grousing because their customers were so disloyal. . . persisted in switching their orders to competing houses. Yet neither one of those men had ever taken the trouble to thank a customer for his business, or wish him "Merry Christmas".

Maybe loyalty and friendship are supposed to work only one way. But I always figured that a person couldn't expect to receive friendship unless he gave friendship in return.

That's why I feel that a warm, personal, whole-hearted message to customers at Christmas-time is one of the best investments any firm can make. The Holidays are one time of the year when the average man drops his guard a little. He's a bit more susceptible to overtures of friendship. He's more inclined to take the wish for what it is. . . a sincere expression of good will and appreciation.

In the last few years, our organization has helped hundreds of business men plan and prepare Christmas greetings to customers. . . individual messages as friendly as a Newfoundland pup at a picnic. Greetings that stand out in the mind of the people who receive them, long after other greetings are forgotten.

This year your customers will appreciate knowing that you look upon them as something more than just animated dollar signs. Let us help you prepare a really outstanding Christmas message to them. We are ready to start any time that you give us the word. Just call 333-4457, or drop the enclosed card in the mail.

Cordially yours,
BURGESS-BECKWITH, Inc.

MCBurgess:ev

BURGESS-BECKWITH, INC., 426 South Sixth Street, Minneapolis, Minnesota

All right, what's the verdict? Is there a logical tie-up between the Star and what followed? Well, yes, but you have to reason it out. The man shot another fellow for kissing his wife, although he had neglected that goodwill gesture for five years. In the same way, the two business executives were angry at the disloyal customers who also had been neglected. Really, you are supposed to think, neither wife nor customer was very much to blame. If you feel inclined to call the connection far-fetched, don't overlook the fact that the letter *did* do a successful job.

There was one question among those quoted which had a double pull —"Can fish tell one color from another?" Fishermen are great fellows to talk about their favorite sport, and in the hands of one of them, the letter would be sure to arouse interest.

An interesting fact. One of the most deep-seated traits of human nature is curiosity. It is often said that a reporter must have a nose for news. In our opinion, all people have it. They especially like to hear about facts they did not know before—unusual facts—anything to relieve what might otherwise be the monotony of everyday existence. If this were not so, why are the gossip purveyors in newspapers and on radio programs so popular? Why do people flock to the museums, read travel books about strange places, go miles out of their way to see a two-headed calf, or pay to see the freaks in the circus side-show? Yes, we all have a bump of curiosity big as a mountain, if only it could be seen.

It is this thirst to be informed, to pry into things we do not understand, that has lifted man above the level of other animals. The cow doesn't seem to care what other cows are doing. She chews her cud complacently all day long and is no wiser at the end than at the beginning. The sow wallows in the mud, and is content to stay there. Man looks about for new worlds to conquer. He is never quite so happy as when he contemplates something out of the ordinary, or when he reflects about some choice bit of information that later he can proudly pass on to others.

If you agree that the above is true, then you understand why letter-writers so often begin their messages with a few bizarre notes—statements of unusual or not commonly known facts to satisfy the instinctive craving for news which they know is shared by all their readers. Sometimes, the fact is offered plain and without sauce, sometimes it takes the form of a story, but, either way, the effect is to gain reader-interest. He may feel pleased to have had such a choice piece of information. He returns the favor by going on with the letter. But woe to the writer if the fact used as bait is *not* new to the reader, or *not* interesting. Then he is bored, as from the ninety-ninth telling of Uncle Ezra's First World War story, and his opinion of the writer promptly falls below zero.

Here are some Stars of the factual type. You may judge from your own reading how interesting they may have been to those who originally received the letters.

"Is Sing, the fish dealer, crazy?" an American asked a Chinese friend, when he saw Sing carrying a lighted lantern in broad daylight.

"No, that is only the custom," was the reply. "It means Sing has not been able to pay his debts. Chinese New Year began a week ago, but he may exchange no New Year's greetings until he has settled—and until then, he must carry the lantern."

(This was a good story when first used several years ago. By now, it has probably lost its punch.)

.   .   .   .   .

Ebbinghaus, one of the first to study the antics of the human mind, gave us his famous "Chart of Forgetting." Briefly, it is this:

Thirty minutes after we have read something, we forget at least half of the subject matter. In eight hours, two-thirds is forgotten. And what is more surprising, we forget more in the first thirty minutes than in the next thirty days.

(This is interesting, but is it true? We will have to consult the most up-to-date psychologists. Surely no statement *should* be quoted until it has been verified.)

.   .   .   .   .

We once heard about a man in China called "I" and of another fellow whose last name is "Hurrizzissteizzii." That's going from one extreme to the other.   ,

(Interesting. Again, could it be true?)

.   .   .   .   .

Take your ruler, and measure off 1/100,000 of an inch. Got it? That's how closely the diameter of the filament wire in an ordinary G. E. Mazda lamp has to be measured. It can't vary more than one one-hundred-thousandth of an inch.

(Used originally by the Graybar Electric Company, Inc.)

.   .   .   .   .

You can do it in the rain without an umbrella—in a hovel, a palace, or under a weeping willow. It is the supreme luxury, enjoyed by the poor and the rich. It starts revolutions, wars, tyrannies, banks, businesses, explorations—and *stops* them.

It is the beginning and end of civilization. They can abolish the movies, the stage, dinner parties, art galleries, musical instruments, and you'd still have it.

It is God's greatest gift to mankind...

(The next word gave away the secret. Are you curious?)

"He is not worth his salt."

Our word "salary" and its definitions—wages, pay, stipend, compensation—were derived from the Latin word, "salarium," which means "of salt." In the days of Caesar, the Roman soldiers received part of their pay in salt. Hence the saying— "He is not worth his salt."

(Interesting. And how would you like this payment plan?)

.   .   .   .   .

Sportsmen the world over will never forget Black Gold, winner of the Kentucky Derby way back in 1924. In size he was a peewee, but there never ran a thoroughbred with a bigger heart. And yet, it isn't his victory in the Derby that gave Black Gold immortality.

Many years have passed since he went to the post for his last race, but strong men who were at the track that day are not ashamed of tears when they tell you what happened.

Coming down the stretch...

(To lovers of the Sport of Kings, this is an especially interesting Star, but any reader would continue to find out what happened "coming down the stretch.")

.   .   .   .   .

The worst thing about a budget is that it will not stretch.

(Nothing unusual about this one, except that most people have budget troubles, and this beginning suggests the writer may have a solution for the difficulty.)

.   .   .   .   .

In the South Sea Islands, deep-chested natives dive time after time, bringing up great handfuls of oysters in the hope that some of them may contain pearls.

There is no way of telling which oysters *do* bear pearls, and the oysters themselves are strangely reticent. A diver may work for hours without acquiring more than the basis for a stew. But the law of averages dictates that every so often he *will* find a pearl...and the more oysters he brings up the more pearls he will find.

Your business, like ours, is based on that old law of averages.

(A Star used by Burgess-Beckwith, Inc. for a letter stressing the importance of continuous contacts with possible buyers.)

.   .   .   .   .

It's impossible—but it happened—near Anoka, Minnesota.

A tornado sucked an automobile off a highway and hurled it through the air for 100 yards. Sometimes it flew as high as the telephone wires. Then it was dashed to the earth and rolled over pasture land for a quarter of a mile. At intervals, bodies were hurled out to sprawl limply in the field. All five passengers were killed. The car was a twisted, shapeless mass of junk metal. (Another queer trait of human nature is the attraction held by horror stories. Many magazines take advantage of this fact— so do some letter-writers, especially when about to offer the preventive for such evils.)

Interesting facts to fit various letter-situations are valuable but hard to acquire on the spur of the moment. A fine plan is to keep a notebook in which facts for future possible use are recorded. Every business correspondent should have a scrapbook of such material. You never know when it will provide the inspiration for a good letter.

Interesting stories make good Stars. Most people are story-minded. You often see them huddled in the office, on the street, while a new one is being told. It is all right to take advantage of this human interest, *providing* your story is fresh, not "off-color," and that it is suited for the message of the rest of the letter. Unless the story does comply with these requirements, the reader's reaction will be negative, and more harm than good is done by the letter.

For example, consider the following letter inviting dealers to attend a meeting:

Gentlemen:

A farmer, after selling his produce in the city, planned to surprise his wife. He bought a new suit of clothes, a new hat, and a new pair of shoes, carefully placing the bundle under the buggy seat.

On the homeward journey, he pulled up beside the river, tied his horse, took off his old clothes, and threw them in. After a good swim, he enthusiastically reached for his new togs. THEY WERE GONE. Finally, he climbed into his buggy and said, "Well, we will *surprise* her anyhow."

There will be a WORTHWHILE SURPRISE in store for you at the Springfield Dealers' School on November 19th and 20th. With any number of new ideas and new sales plans to create profits for you, the program will be of real growth calibre.

Every phase of livestock and poultry feeding will be covered. Animal nutrition, advertising, and merchandising—each feed will be discussed individually. The vision of your possibilities will broaden and you will profit greatly by investing just a few days in a close study of new improved selling and business methods.

The return of the attached card WITH YOUR SIGNATURE will assure your firm representation at every session.

Sincerely,

Was the story used in this letter a good one? Did it tie in with what followed? Well, "no" to both questions. The story is very old, and nine out of ten people would have heard it. Moreover, the only connection between it and the Chain is the far fetched play on the word "surprise"; the farmer's wife would be surprised—so will the reader if he attends the meetings.

This one is better. It was used by the Equitable Paper Bag Company, Inc., as a follow-up to prospects who had ignored previous letters. The author was Colman O'Shaughnessy.

Gentlemen:

Val Briggens once stood in the heart of Times Square selling five dollar bills for $2.98. They were real honest-to-goodness five dollar bills—complete with Abe Lincoln's picture and the Treasury Secretary's signature. But there were no sales.

You can't fool New Yorkers.

And we haven't been able to fool you into inquiring about our low envelope prices.

Our prices on open-end catalog envelopes *are* unbelievably low. But we do make a lot of sales because a lot of people know we have our own paper mill, a large improved factory, and they know we have the lowest possible selling cost. In short, they know *why* our prices are the lowest they find anywhere.

In a letter like this, it's hard for me to back up my low price statement with specific figures—for I don't know what envelopes you use, or in what quantities you order.

But I would very much like to show you. If you'll just take samples of your present envelopes, mark them with the quantities you usually order, and put the whole business in the enclosed postage-paid envelope, I'll shoot you figures by return mail.

And when you see the high quality of our samples, you'll have the surprise of your envelope life.

Sincerely,

Assuming that you had not heard about Val Briggen's unsuccessful attempt to sell New Yorkers, the story must have been interesting. Furthermore, it illustrates a point made in the rest of the letter. The reader has been turning *his* back on a good thing, just as did the New Yorkers.

More introductions by O'Shaughnessy. The technique of starting business letters to capture reader attention—a device *deliberately* used by the

experts—is demonstrated in some more Stars taken from Colman O'Shaughnessy's contacts with prospects.

> The wife of the Consul to Timbuktu dressed for dinner in her
> silver-sequin gown...but it was all wasted on the desert air
> ...no one there to admire her beauty...no dances to grace
> ...just a thousand natives and one loving husband. She was
> all dressed up—and no place to go.
>
> But your products will go places, and be *seen,* and be *eaten.*
> Dressed in Equitable's glamorous Glassine bags, they will
> sparkle appetizingly—and stay that way.

.   .   .   .   .

> Remember the three sisters—Faith, Hope, and Charity?
>
> Faith and Hope went off to the big city to dig gold, and they
> came back wearing rings on their fingers and mink stoles on
> their shoulders. But when little Charity met them at the station,
> *she* had a sable coat, three strings of pearls, six diamond brace-
> lets, and money in the bank. For Charity began at home.
>
> That's a pretty good place to begin, if you want to make yourself
> a little present in savings. Right at home—on the things you
> buy and use every day.

.   .   .   .   .

> Just suppose...
>
> ...as you are sitting at your desk now I came in to ask you for
> a position. And suppose I needed a shave, and my suit wasn't
> pressed, and my shoes were muddy—what chance would I have?
> I might be a world-beater, but I surely wouldn't *look* it.
>
> First impressions are hard to change: They're often wrong but
> they last a long, long time.
>
> What sort of first impression does your catalog make?
>
> Today, Miss Susie Jones read one of your ads. And she liked it.
> She thought the pictures were swell. The copy moved her, and
> she honestly wanted to buy your product.
>
> But Susie couldn't buy. Susie is in the State Reform School.
>
> Of course, there aren't many Susies. But she, as an individual,
> represents waste advertising circulation—which brings me to my
> little sales talk. We have an advertising medium which has NO
> waste circulation.

.   .   .   .   .

> "Jim," I asked an old friend, just back from Europe, "what im-
> pressed you most during your months on the other side?"
>
> "Dirt!"

America is unbelievably clean in comparison. Cleanliness is the outstanding characteristic of Americans.

You know the truth of what Jim said. Entire industries have been built on this typically American trait. They thrive by catering to this insistent demand for cleanliness.

And that's why we're telling you about Equitable apron bags.

.   .   .   .   .

She walked out of the store...

...and continued shopping along the street. She stopped to look at the window displays. After going into several stores, she took a bus home.

Who was she? And what more about her? I don't know her name, but she bought several bottles of beverage at one of the stores. They were put in a handsomely printed bag—and she carried this bag as she continued on her shopping tour.

How many people saw that bag, and...

.   .   .   .   .

My grandfather had a wooden Indian in front of his store, and sold crackers from the barrel.

But the age of hitching posts, handle-bar mustaches, and loose, uncovered food is past. Today, things must be sanitary—and especially in your business. You must attractively package your food products today to keep up with competition.

Equitable has done some smart bag-thinking for you. We have created...

.   .   .   .   .

"The Little Toy Dog Is Covered with Dust."

Those are pretty sad words from a poem written long ago by Eugene Field. And they're mighty sad words when written today about a "little toy dog" or any other toy which has to stand the gaff of display—*unprotected*.

For shopworn toys do not sell.

But toys that are covered, not with dust, but with Equitable Glassine Bags have that added glamour which means SALES APPEAL.

All of the above Stars were used in letters to sell paper bags. Which conformed best to the requirements of being interesting, in good taste, and appropriate to the general purpose? Unless you take time to form opinions, and can justify them, the examples cited here and elsewhere are of no great value to you.

Other story beginnings. Because of their universal appeal, if they are interesting and to the point, Stars of the story-type seem to outnumber all the others, especially for sales letters. Here are a few more—good, bad, and indifferent—for your consideration. Some are too long, and rob the Chain of space, and some lack the dignity you expect in a business letter, but on the whole they are representative of the modern trend.

> An Oklahoma editor published two pictures. One showed a dilapidated house, the other an eroded field. He asked his readers to participate in a "You Write the Story" contest. The prize-winning letter came from an Indian, and it's a honey!
>
> "Both pictures show white man crazy. Make big tepee. Plow hill. Water wash; wind blow soil. Grass gone, land gone, door gone, window gone; whole place gone to devil. Buck gone. Squaw too. No chuckaway, no pig, no corn, no cow, no hay, no pony.
>
> "Indian no plow land. Keep grass. Buffalo eat. Indian eat buffalo. Hide make tepee, make moccasin. Indian no make terrace, no build dam, no give damn. All time eat. No hunt job, no hitch-hike, no ask relief. No shoot pig. Great Spirit make grass. Indian no waste anything. Indian no work. White man heap loco."
>
> •   •   •   •   •
>
> A certain gentleman, fishin' in a river down in Mississippi, pulled in his line and was surprised to find a minnow on the hook. Disappointed, he tugged a bottle of white mule from his pocket, took a pull, and then poured some on the tiny fish.
>
> Almost instantly, it flopped overboard, and his line went taut. After a fifteen minute battle, he got it back in the boat again, and would you believe it, that minnow had a five-pound bass by the throat.
>
> •   •   •   •   •
>
> Two frogs found themselves in a can of cream being shipped to the city. Both struggled to get out. One gave up, but the other kept on agitating in the hope he would find some means of escape. The end of the journey found one frog dead at the bottom of the can, the other sitting alive on a raft of butter.

Although there is little to be said for the "dignity of business," as contemplated by stiff-shirted old gentlemen who use Whiskers in their letters and who consider a smile in them very much out of place, yet discretion and good taste must still be used in the selection of a story. For example, you cannot commend the tone of a letter which began as follows: "As the little brown hen remarked to friend rooster, 'Seems like the worms aren't lying around any more, Old Cock, so we gotta scratch, that's all'—and forthwith, she began to throw dirt."

There is a wide gap between that which is really funny, and that which only attempts to be. Be sure that you know the difference. If you are not *sure* about the use of a story, remember—"When in doubt, *don't.*"

The big question—"Does it FIT?" As you have already noted, it is folly to drag a story into a letter, merely in the hope of getting attention when you know it has little or no connection with the subject matter. The big question is—*does it fit?* For example, when Vic Knight was promoting the use of classified advertising for a western newspaper, he sent the following letter to prospects. Not only is the opening story amusing, but it also seems to fit nicely with Mr. Knight's assertion that he does not intend to exaggerate what the ads will do.

> Dear Mr. Doe:
>
> They tell the story of an Alaskan sourdough miner who struck a mountain of pay dirt, and came to Seattle to go on a spree.
>
> He walked into a cafe and ordered $25 worth of bacon and eggs, and three cups of coffee.
>
> The waiter was something of a hand at "putting on the dog" himself, so he turned up his nose, and said, "You'll have to order more than that. We don't serve *half* portions."
>
> This just illustrates the point that no matter how strong a fellow goes, there's always someone who is ready to go him one better. So, if I said the Review-Chronicle classified ads were the best poultry medium on earth, somebody else would say they had a better way to advertise chicks, hatching eggs, or breeding stock.
>
> No, TALK doesn't prove anything. But the fact that the most successful poultrymen use Review-Chronicle classified ads year after year, and are coming in stronger this year than for several seasons, must mean they look for better business.
>
> How about you?
>
> If you are looking for more orders, the Review-Chronicle classified ads will help you find them, and they don't do any half-way job either. They bring home the bacon, and help you sell hatched eggs for $1.00 and up a dozen, instead of at the regular market prices.
>
> We don't serve *half* portions in results here. And if that seems like just talk, make us prove it. Try a few classified ads in the Review-Chronicle, and find out what they CAN and WILL do for you.
>
> Yours very truly,

When a story really "fits" in a letter-drama, it doesn't appear in the first act, and then never again. Instead, as the letter progresses, you will find the point of the story reappearing, as it does in the last paragraph of the Review-Chronicle mailing.

Okay! What about this letter, used to sell old cars? Is the Star a good one? Does it "fit" what follows?

> Dear Mr. Baxter:
>
> The used car problem you hear so much about reminds me of the man 35 years old who married a child 5 years old. He was then seven times as old as his wife. Five years later he was 40 and she was 10—he was four times as old. Twenty years more, and he was 60, and she was 30—he was then only twice as old.
>
> The question is, "How long would they have to live together to be the same age?"
>
> Used car sales have been coming closer to new car sales right along. Already, they amount to more in number of cars sold, and it's not impossible that this year they will be almost the same in dollars and cents.
>
> We've simply got to get rid of 100 used cars this month. If you'll help us solve our used car problem by buying any car in our stock, we'll give you a free auto license, and 50 gallons of gas.
>
> You can drive any car you select for five days before the deal is closed.
>
> Why not look them over today?
>
> Sincerely yours,

Did the story capture your attention? Probably, yes. Is it in keeping with good taste? You are not sure about that, are you? The reason is the absurdity of a middle-aged man marrying a girl of five. The thought is repugnant, if only imaginary. Does the story fit? Is there a logical connection between point of story and point of the attempted sale? No, very little.

All right! Now examine the letter on the next page. It also starts with a story of the humorous type. Is this story acceptable? Is there continuity between it and what follows? These are some of the questions you must ask yourself when judging the effectiveness of a letter-introduction. It's better to form your own opinions than always to be told. Put this letter through the wringer. How does it come out?

When the lead-horse does most of the work. There is always the danger in using a story for the Star that the writer will become so engrossed in the telling that insufficient time is devoted to the subject matter which should pull most of the load. Then the letter becomes dwarf-like, with a huge head and very short legs.

Dear Mr. Frailey:

You may have known the salesman who met a fellow canvasser and said that he had just called at a house where a nudist party was in session.

"I knocked at the door and out came the nudist butler."

"How did you know it was the butler?" asked his friend.

"Well," was the reply, "I knew it wasn't the maid."

That same sort of an attitude is often times an excellent way to judge a good Direct Mail Piece.

It isn't what you say but what you don't say that many times makes an impression in a sales letter. By that we don't mean the omission of any facts or truths.

Instead we mean assuming the "You" viewpoint of the customer. Good salesmanship, whether written or oral, simply means the creation of a desire on the part of your customer to want more the article you have to sell than the money it takes to buy that article.

The customer wants to know how your product can be advantageous to him. How will it benefit him? Not how capable you are to produce it or how long you have been in business.

He takes it for granted that you do business on an ethical basis and are set-up to meet his needs. Past history is not his concern ...what can you do for him today and in the future?

An especially created Direct Mail Campaign can tell your story simply and effectively. It will do so, at less cost, than any other personalized method.

If you have a sales problem, large or small, in which we can be of assistance why not call us? We'll be happy to offer suggestions. No obligation, of course. Just phone Pines 1212. Thank you.

Sincerely yours,

Here is a letter in which the Star pulls most of the load. It was submitted as a class assignment by a Northwestern University student and is probably imaginary. You might be smiling after reading this letter, but the big question is would it *sell* soap? That you may doubt.

Dear Mr. Doe:

If you like short, short stories—glance over this one which we clipped from one of our local newspapers some time ago (reading time 48 seconds).

Sweetheart, Ky.: Donald Bows, 12 years old, loafed around the school grounds, and the principal did not beckon him to come in. A neighbor saw him, and asked, "Sonny, don't you go to school?" "Yes, ma'am," he replied shyly. "Well, why aren't you in there now?" she demanded to know. "I skun me a polecat," he grinned.

Always on our toes, we wrote to the principal, and in a joking sort of way, suggested that perhaps a bit of "Wissell's Soap" might take care of some of these Huckleberry Finns. To our surprise, we received a wire to rush along a barrel of "polecat" soap. Swallowing our pride, we got the order off on the day received. Believe it or not, just last week we received a duplicate order by mail. Evidently, our soap deodorizes as well as cleans.

While we have never claimed to be deodorant experts, we do know soap. So if you have any small boys to scour, any floors and walls to clean, any automobiles to wash, maybe a canary to bathe, just write, wire, or phone—or better still,

Wissell for Soap.

Yours soapfully,

Yes, stories are good ammunition for the letter-writer. They *do* get attention. But when you use one, be sure it is *worth* the telling—that the point *does* fit the message you are trying to put across.

The power of famous names. It is no doubt true that most human beings are hero-worshippers. Thus the name of a great statesman, of a beloved author, or of any famous personage in history, may help to win reader-attention for a business letter. And here's how!

Mark Twain at one time was a newspaper editor. One day a subscriber wrote that he had found a spider in the folds of his paper. He wanted to know if this was good or bad luck. Twain replied:

"Finding a spider in your paper was neither good luck nor bad luck for you. The spider was merely looking over our paper to see which merchant is not advertising, so that he can go to that store, spin a web across the door, and live a life of undisturbed peace afterward."

So it is today in...

.   .   .   .   .

The late William *Rockefeller* used to tell a story that illustrates the financial genius of his brother, *John*.

"When John was a little fellow," he relates, "an Indian doctor visited our town with a cure-all. To get trade started, the doctor, took out a bright silver dollar, and said he would auction it off.

" 'How much am I bid,' he said, 'for this bright silver dollar?'

"But the crowd was cautious, silent, suspicious. No bids were made.

" 'How much am I bid,' shouted the Indian doctor, 'Come, come, gents! A nickel? A dime?'

" 'I bid a nickel,' piped up the youthful John D. at last.

" 'The dollar is yours, boy,' said the doctor. 'Hand up your nickel.'

" 'Take it out of the dollar,' chirped little John D., 'and gimme 95 cents change.' "

This story illustrates the situation today in...

.   .   .   .   .

Columbus never did know where he was going, and when he got back home, he didn't know where he had been. You'll remember, too, he made the trip on borrowed money.

Many men in business today don't seem to know...

.   .   .   .   .

"Allure" is the same today as it was when *Cleopatra,* the IT girl of Egypt, kept the Nile boys in a romantic dither. Daintiness is still the stock-in-trade of the eternal feminine.

And daintiness should be...

.   .   .   .   .

Horace Greeley, who always insisted that the word "News" was plural, exchanged the following messages with one of his reporters.

Dear L. A.: Are there any news? Horace Greeley.

Dear Mr. Greeley: Not a new. L. A.

Effective Personal Letters, by...

.   .   .   .

Robert Bruce, hiding in a cave, watched a spider spinning and climbing a web. Time after time the web broke, but always the spider began spinning and climbing again, until at last he reached his goal.

Watching this determined fellow, Bruce got renewed courage, emerged from his hiding place, and started his successful "comeback" to the throne of Scotland. Perhaps he or one of his followers coined the old maxim: "If at first you don't succeed—try, try again."

I don't want to pester you about...

There's a big difference between confidence and conceit. When *Babe Ruth,* in that World Series game, laughed at the crowd, and pointed to the exact place where he would hit the ball into the bleachers, maybe that was conceit in your book, but not in mine.

You see, Babe hit the ball just where he had said he would—for a home-run.

A lot of folks I know could stand...

Names have great power in proportion, of course, to how well they are known, and the particular individual's attention to them. It is hardly possible to think of *any* name that will win a favorable reception from *everybody*. Impossible as it may seem, there are probably some people who know nothing of Babe Ruth, and as time passes, there will be more of them. In the imagination of many men, Cleopatra still holds her own with the beauties of Hollywood, and long after some of the latter have been forgotten, she will still live on. But to one who has never heard of "Cleo," the name of Sophie Glutz would mean as much.

Use of an interesting quotation. Many a business letter gets off to a flying start with a quotation that makes the reader nod his head in agreement, or it may merely amuse him. Unlike stories, the statements of interesting people do not seem to suffer from repetition. The value of a story decreases rapidly with each telling, but this does not seem to be true of a proverb, a poem, or a striking utterance by some speaker or writer. If the quotation is one that the reader knows and *likes,* the use of it establishes a bond of mutual appreciation. Hence, in your scrapbook of possible material for business letters, reserve one section for quotations. You may be surprised how one of them will come to your rescue in a hurried moment.

Insurance agent Rupert L. Mills of Peoria, Illinois, used a Chinese proverb to good advantage in the following letter. Notice that toward the end he repeats the quotation for a better "fit."

Dear Mr. Nutter:

There's an old and bitingly truthful Chinese proverb that says:

"Man who sits with open mouth waits
long time for roast goose to fly in."

If we want the good things of life for ourselves or those who look to us for support, the only way to obtain those good things is to GET BUSY AND GO AFTER THEM.

Now, one of the eternally good things in life, but one that few enjoy, is peace of mind. There is no more comforting thought in the world than this: the complete certainty that when we grow too old to work, we can retire and enjoy a steady monthly income which is depression-proof, promoter-proof, and guaranteed to last as long as we do.

Just ponder that blessing a moment—the knowledge that when you want to quit work and spend your sunset years in leisurely independence, you will be able to do so—WITHOUT FAIL. If you could have that positive assurance *now,* wouldn't it remove those aggravating worries that flit through your mind every time you indulge in some financial "splurge" with today's hard-earned dollars? With the FUTURE safe, the PRESENT is far, far sweeter to enjoy.

But unless you DO SOMETHING about those years ahead, you will be very much like the chap who "sits with open mouth waiting for roast goose to fly in." Old-age prosperity must be planned in advance. We cannot put off indefinitely the business of getting started on our program of personal independence. The longer we delay our start, the harder the task will be.

For your own peace of mind, I'm hoping that after reading this letter, you'll decide TODAY to do something for your eventual comfort, while there's still time to do it properly and completely. This letterhead tells you how you can get in touch with me, so that I can show you the ideal, guaranteed way to financial security.

Sincerely yours,

This letter has a homespun tone that carries considerable conviction. It seems that one man has placed a friendly hand on the shoulder of another. "Don't wait for the roast goose to fly in," he says. "Come, let me help you while there is still time."

Let's see that scrapbook we were talking about. A real estate salesman wants to write a letter about the joys of home ownership. Is there a quotation in your book that might help him? Yes, there's one—"When you buy a *house* it becomes a *home*." And what about those others?

"HOME—a world of strife shut out, a world of love shut in."
"HOME—the father's kingdom, the mother's world, and the child's paradise."
"HOME—where Heaven touches earth."
"HOME—where we grumble the most and are treated the best."
"HOME—the only place on earth where the faults of humanity are hidden under the sweet mantle of charity."

Quite all right. Any one of those quotations, with the possible exception of the fourth, could be used as the Star in a letter to sell homes. The sentiment expressed in them is appropriate. It wouldn't do for selling locomotives, cement, or filing cabinets, but people are sentimental about owning their own homes. For this particular purpose, a serious quotation is much better than a humorous one. In fact, for *all* general letter-purposes that is likely to be true.

Use humorous quotations with caution. It is much easier to start a letter with something serious, of good attention value, and continue in the same tone, than to first make the reader laugh and then face the problem of bringing him back to the plane of sober contemplation. Besides, the situation becomes hopeless if the reader *doesn't* laugh.

There are all kinds of humor, and what strikes one man as funny may leave another person cold. For example, here's a letter which begins:

> You have heard what one big toe said to the other big toe—
> don't look now, but I think there's a couple of heels following
> me.

Is that funny? Well, I doubt if it would provoke much laughter in a meeting of college professors, but as it happened the letter went to salesmen whose bump of humor may not be so sensitive. Perhaps salesmen laugh more easily than professors.

The following are a little more subtle, and for that reason, not counting others, you would no doubt rate them higher.

> Mark Twain once said: "When a man goes to buy a collar, he comes back with the collar and maybe a necktie, but when he sends his wife, she comes back with a jar of face-cream, four yards of dress goods, some silk hosiery, and FORGETS the collar."
>
> .   .   .   .   .
>
> There's an old saying—"It all depends on whose kid has the measles." (Useful in letters where there is a clash in points of view.)
>
> .   .   .   .   .
>
> Says Jack Carr: "We know of no sadder case than that of the young man who joined the Navy to see the world, and then spent four years in a submarine."
>
> .   .   .   .   .
>
> You often hear it said: "Watch your P's and Q's." Well, I've got to watch them. That's my job. You see, I'm a proofreader.
>
> .   .   .   .   .
>
> "Always do right. This will gratify some people, and astonish the rest." (M. T.—that man again.)
>
> "They licked their platters clean."
>
> I am a cook—a very good cook. I know this for two reasons: First, my taste tells me. Second, like the people in the fairy story, my customers "lick their platters clean." (From a letter applying for a job in a company cafeteria. She *got* it.)

Touching the "soft spot." Earlier in this section, we saw how various appeals may be used to influence reader-response. Moreover, we agreed that no two individuals are likely to react in exactly the same way to the same appeal. Thus, the letter-writer considers each reader as a separate problem, and seeks a point of vulnerability—a soft spot—that might be entirely different if he were writing to someone else.

When the soft spot is known, the logical place to begin talking about it is in the Star, otherwise you may play your ace too late—after the reader has pushed the letter aside. To list all of the special interests to which various individuals may give attention is impossible, but you know the wide range they cover—sports, one of the sciences, collectors' items, any of the arts, dogs, horses, amateur theatricals, gardening, and all the many others. Sometimes the weakness, if it can be called that, may be the love of gin-rummy, or beautiful women, or even the desire to be the best-dressed man in the club, but whatever it may be, a reference to it can be the opening wedge for a successful letter. To be sure, this reference must be made in good taste, and not appear as a blatant attempt to curry favor, but when that requirement is met, there can be no wrong in talking to the reader about the one thing in which he is said to be the most interested. And thus many a strong Star is developed.

Don't tip your hand too soon. Remember that the purpose of the Star—the *one thing* it is supposed to do—is to capture favorable *attention.* This is a separate job, quite apart from what must be accomplished later. It is a good Star when the reader is sufficiently interested to continue, but it is not expected so soon in the letter that the reader is in the mood for immediate action. That comes later, when the reasons to *increase* interest have been offered in the Chain. By then, the reader should be ready for action, but seldom before.

With these facts in mind, you can realize the danger of exposing the real purpose of the letter before interest has been deepened, or desire created. This is especially true when the reader is asked to buy something he had not thought of buying, or to give of his time to a cause in which he has had no previous interest. By letting the cat out of the bag too quickly, the reader is put on guard and becomes much harder to persuade. He knows what you want, and the chances are he will either stop, or continue in a negative mood.

For example, a book house begins a letter in the following very dull and revealing way:

Announcing the Publication of ——'s
AN INTRODUCTION TO PUBLIC SPEAKING

Here is an eminently practical text which includes quantities of new information *not* contained in any other book.

In the very first sentence, the purpose of the letter is made known. If directed only to a list of people who buy everything published about public speaking, perhaps no harm has been done. But anyone else would know immediately that he is about to be asked to buy a book—and he knows that *before* anything has been said to make him *want* the book. The letter defies the principle of letter carpentry which says that the reader must be led *progressively* from ATTENTION to INTEREST to DESIRE to ACTION, and the steps must not be taken in any other order.

More cats out of the bag too soon. Many, many business letters are wasted because they suggest action before the reader is *prepared* for it— they go into the wastebasket for this one reason, although in other respects the proposition may be inviting and the arguments convincing. The letters from which the following Stars were taken are not at all bad when the whole of them is viewed, but the cat came out of the bag too early. In many a case, the reader must have stopped before he read all the fine reasons which might have appealed to him had he only been approached less abruptly.

> When you buy the policy I am going to tell you about, your worries about old age are "gone with the wind."
>
> (Oh, oh—trying to sell insurance! My good friend, Mr. Waste-Paper Basket, here's something for you.)

.   .   .   .   .

> May I suggest to you the convenience of a standing order for our country sausage and hickory-smoked bacon?
>
> (Thanks for the suggestion, but no sale. It costs too much to buy food by mail.)

.   .   .   .   .

> May we send you, at our risk and expense, a get-acquainted shipment of the most distinctive and most delicious food products that ever graced your table?
>
> ("At our risk and expense"—some catch in that. What's he talking about anyway—"food products" take in a lot of territory. No, my friend, you may *not* send me.)

Remember this point about the Star—*don't let the cat out of the bag too soon.* It is a costly mistake often made by letter-writers, but now you know better. Be sure to avoid this trap. Keep the reader guessing. Curiosity breeds interest. Get him *ready* for action before you ask for it.

How to start routine letters. Even though the job is simple, as when no reply is expected or no particular problem involved, it is still worth while to start a routine letter in a natural and interesting manner. This tends to be accomplished when the writer forgets any false ideas about the "dignity of business," and just sits down to *talk* to his reader as if they were both in the same room. However, there are a few little tricks of the trade, used by the best letter-carpenters, and you should know them.

First. Make the opening sentence short—just as your greeting would be if you met a friend on the street. If the previous correspondence has been pleasant, and you feel that you know the writer in a personal way, you can go so far as to say, "Hello, Mr. Gordon"..."Good morning, Mr. Gordon"...or any other natural thing you might use in speech. Even if the relationship is somewhat formal, or there have been no previous letters, you can still start "free and easy" with such sentences as,

> "You are right, Mrs. Jones."
> "Thank you for writing about the bill, Mr. Doe."
> "I am sorry, Mr. Black, that we let you down."
> "Yes, indeed, Mr. Barton, you can have the map."
> "Good news for you, Mr. Sickle!"
> "Don't worry, Mrs. Fisher, we'll exchange the lamp."

The trick is to just start talking, as if the letter you are answering had been spoken, and you are now taking your turn in the conversation. This does away with the foolish practice, so often encountered in business letters, of *rehashing* what the other party has said before getting down to the reply. Why say to Mrs. Fisher, "We have received your letter of the 15th, in which you inform us that the lamp recently shipped to you was damaged in transit"? What a lot of nonsense that would be. Mrs. Fisher *knows* that you received her letter or else you could not be answering it. She does not care on what date it was written. She *knows* the lamp was damaged in transit or someplace. What she wants you to tell her is that the lamp will be exchanged for a new one.

There is not the slightest reason for a preface in a routine business reply letter, as there is in playing a bit of music, when you might first strike a few chords. Don't waste any time telling *what* you are going to say, or referring to what the other fellow has already *said*. Just BEGIN.

> Dear Sir:
>
> Your letter of March 8th, relative to John Doe's application for employment, shall now claim my attention.
>
> From my personal knowledge of this young man, I am inclined to believe he will be fully competent if given a job within the limits of his capacity.

A pretty kettle of fish, isn't it? Why didn't the politician who wrote the letter omit the first paragraph, and simply say, "From what I know about John Doe, I think he will make good in your company"? But no, we forget that politicians are not, as a rule, so direct.

Second. Personalize opening sentence of the routine letter by including, when possible, the name of the reader. This is perfectly all right even for the first letter-contact. There is no discourtesy in the use of a person's name —in fact, it is more of a compliment. People rather like to hear their names pronounced, or to see them in print. It makes them feel important, and the use of the name in the opening sentence seems to put the letter on a conversational basis.

With this tip, there must go one caution: Do not *overdo* the practice. In a short letter of two or three paragraphs, one use of the reader's name is sufficient. In a longer letter, of one full page or more, the name might appear two or three times—but not any more. When overdone, the letter sounds flippant and too familiar.

There are times, of course, when the name cannot be used at all. A complaint from a woman who signs herself as Inez Goode, would be one of the exceptions. Is Inez married or single? Not knowing whether to call her "Miss" or "Mrs.," you would have to compromise by using neither.

Third. Use a positive and pleasant word or phrase to launch this first sentence. Go as far as you possibly can in *agreeing* with what the reader has said in his letter to you. This is especially important in adjustment letters. Keep the bad news out of the first paragraph. Begin with

> Right you are, Mr. Underwood,
> Your letter is appreciated, Miss Garner,
> Yes, Miss Jones, we understand perfectly,
> Thanks a lot, Mr. Wilcox,
> You are very patient, Mrs. Gardner,
> You can count on us, Mrs. Chapman,
> Everything is okay, Mr. Bates,

or any other appropriate statement that may start a reaction of goodwill in the reader's mind. To be sure, if a request is to be refused later on, the opening sentence can hardly be, "You are absolutely right, Doctor Long," but the sting could be lessened with, "You have been so frank and fair in giving us your point of view, Doctor Long, that we are encouraged to put our cards face-up on the table in the same friendly spirit."

Use these three simple devices to personalize the first paragraphs of your own routine letters. You will be surprised and happy to see how they help to smooth the rough spots in human relations, and give what you write a warmth which may have been lacking.

So much for the more common ways of getting attention at the start of a business letter—the "How" of the Star. Here they are in final review:

1. Reference to a previous contact
2. "Who, What, When, Where, Why"
3. A question
4. An interesting fact
5. A good story
6. Use of a famous name
7. An interesting quotation
8. Touching a "soft spot"
9. Personalization

There remains one other method—more spectacular—which deserves separate consideration. We will now see what it is.

4. Showmanship to Win Attention

The dramatized business letter. Somebody once said that all the world loves a parade. This is usually true, although there are some who sit unmoved in their offices as the bands march in the street below. However, they are likely to satisfy their thirst for something different by watching the grimaces, grunts and growls of a wrestling match every Wednesday night, by proudly wearing the colorful regalia of their lodge, or just by the selection of a particularly outspoken suit or overcoat.

This love for anything out of the groove may simply be the rebellion of the human race against the monotony of everyday existence, but the psychologists know best if that is true. At least, there can be no doubt that the average man likes a "show" and anything out of the ordinary quickly grabs his attention. This fact is well recognized by the "bigwigs" in sales and advertising, and there seems to be eternal competition among them to see who can turn the most somersaults. This is not said in a spirit of criticism, for if one makes his bread and butter by influencing human behavior, he must cater to the whims of his prospects and customers.

Certainly, we know that a dramatized business letter, if the idea is really clever and interesting, may often out-pull one of the more conventional kinds. This has been proved many times by actual test and comparison, so that no matter what our personal opinion may be, we cannot afford to overlook or scorn a device that has made many a letter an outstanding producer. Like every other idea or method used in business correspondence, the so-called "stunt" letter can be very sweet or very sour, depending on the quality of the idea and how deftly it is carried out. The letter-man who dares the unusual is always under fire. If the idea clicks—great applause! If it doesn't click—great derision! This, it would seem, should be a sobering thought for those who go in for showmanship, but there are still many who run amuck with ideas more stupid than clever, more likely to harm than to help.

But perhaps you are asking—"What *is* a dramatized letter?" Well, it is one in which an idea or thought is given *special prominence* by some illustrative or mechanical device that would not be used in the ordinary business letter typed in the usual way on the usual company letterhead.

No relation between cost and effectiveness. There is no end to the forms the special treatment may take in a dramatized letter. The idea may be quite simple and inexpensive, or it may be very elaborate and costly. Curiously enough, there seems to be no relationship between cost and effectiveness, as you might mail a dozen sales or collection letters, one each month for a year, and discover that the one which cost the least out-pulled all the others. The premium depends on the *originality* of the "stunt" used and on how aptly it fits the main purpose of the letter, *not* on what a big show it may make.

On the next two pages are dramatized letters used by The Rylander Company of Chicago. One is so simple that practically no extra expense was involved. The other gets away from the regular company letterhead, and of course the postage stamp in the man's hand was an added cost.

Both of these Rylander letters were two-color jobs, although this does not show in the reproduction. The second color was red—always strong in attracting attention. Only the line was red in the first letter; in the second, all parts were red except the typing. Neither could be called elaborate, but both were successful as business-builders.

Use of "gadget" to illustrate point. Many of the dramatized letters that you encounter are made more expensive by the addition of some object, usually in miniature, which is supposed to gain extra attention, and usually does. This attention-pull decreases, however, with repetition of the idea. The first time you received a Christmas letter with a miniature Santa Claus attached, it was an interesting experience. But if by now, as with most people, you have had a dozen or more Christmas letters with similar attachments, you are more repelled than thrilled.

Some of these gadgets are so clumsily conceived and so far removed from the point of the letter that they fail the first, and all other times, to make a favorable impression. We can give you a few examples. Although the

May 13, 19--

Dear Mr. Frailey:

There's no need of a long letter when our message is brief. So we'll just skip

down to here and say "The Rylander Company does good work, does it promptly, efficiently and cheerfully and does appreciate its customers"!

Sincerely,

Roy W Rylander

gadgets cannot be attached to the pages of this Handbook, a description may suffice.

The first is a letter with the caption, "You wouldn't drive a nail with a shovel." Then the first sentence reads, "It's the wrong tool for that kind of work—and efficiency demands the use of the right tool for each job."

130

There are two attachments stuck to the paper with Scotch tape. How the letter got through the Post Office is a mystery. One of the attachments, as you would guess, is a nail about two inches long. The other is a miniature shovel about four inches long. The general effect of the idea is preposterous, and after the first sentence there is no more mention of the shovel or nail.

THE *Rylander* **COMPANY** • DIRECT MAIL ADVERTISING

216 WEST JACKSON BOULEVARD • CHICAGO 6, ILLINOIS • RANDOLPH 6-4760

WE EVEN LICK THE STAMPS, Mr. Frailey

The other day a close friend of ours asked, "Say, just what does your organization do? You say your business is 'mail advertising service': Just what does that mean?"

"That", we answered, "is a rather difficult question. So many steps are involved in the handling of direct mail, and our service is so closely tailored to the needs of each individual customer that there is almost no limit to the things we do.

"When a firm like yours, for example, needs help in developing more business by mail - that's when we step into the picture.

"Often we supply names and addresses of likely prospects - suggest ideas for letters or mailing pieces, compose the copy - and draft layouts for presenting the sales story. We produced the finished material by any one of several processes...multigraph, mimeograph, planograph or letter press.

"We serve many customers on a strictly mechanical production basis. Mimeographing is a big department with us, and our modern equipment helps us do unusually fine work, at a minimum of time and cost. We produce form letters that look like typing. We do typing of all kinds and handle mailings, small and large, with economy and dispatch.

"We even lick the stamps!

"When you give us an order, you use the particular part of our highly skilled organization and modern machinery that your job requires. And you pay only for the time spent on your job. That makes for economy and efficiency and workmanship of high quality."

That is the information we gave our friend...and we're passing it on to you with the thought that you may not have known of the many services we render.

I hope you will find many ways in which we can serve you throughout the coming months. Call us. Our number is Franklin 5954.

Sincerely yours,

THE RYLANDER COMPANY

RGR:FT

PRODUCTION • LETTER PROCESSING • DUPLICATING • ADDRESSING (TYPEWRITER AND AUTOMATIC) • MAILING
CREATIVE • IDEAS • SALES LETTERS • CAMPAIGNS • ADVERTISING ART • MAILING LISTS
PRINTING • LETTERPRESS • OFFSET LITHOGRAPHY • PLANOGRAPH • MULTILITH

Difficult to mail, clumsy to look at, no punch, no pull—another letter-idea gone wrong!

"Cigars are on us—we've a new addition to our family," begins the second example. Stuck to the letter is a cigar, a match, and a piece of sandpaper. Everything so convenient!

But, oh, *what* a cigar! An anemic-looking, thin slab of tobacco, wrapped in cellophane.

Quite different from the *good* cigar, packed in a strong little box, which came with a similar letter.

.   .   .   .   .

A paragraph in the third letter reads: "People aren't buying buggies any more—nor bustles—nor petticoats—nor corsets."

The message in the letter is good. It urges the reader to forget old-time methods, and sell the modern way.

But my, my—what an attachment!

At the top of the page are two rows of punched holes, and woven criss-cross in them is a corset string. The two ends, dangling out, are at least five feet long—the whole string must be about five yards.

It seems to be a form letter, and no doubt a considerable number were mailed. To punch the holes and weave in the corset string must have been quite a job. And what would be the effect on the reader who pulled the letter and the long string from the envelope?

Good? That's very doubtful. Corset strings and business somehow don't seem to mix.

Questions to be answered. When you feel the impulse to dramatize a letter, and your idea includes an attachment to help catch the fancy of your reader, ask yourself these questions: (1) Will the reader be favorably impressed by what I am going to do, or will he make fun of it?...(2) Is the dramatization just an attention-winner, or does it also give emphasis to the main purpose of my letter?...(3) Is the idea original with me, or have I borrowed one with which the reader might already be familiar?...(4) Is the idea practical, so that it can be prepared easily at not too great a cost, or is my enthusiasm overshadowing my good judgment of results logically to be expected?...(5) Can it be mailed?

If your dramatized letter-idea can survive those questions, then no doubt it is a good one. Go ahead—use it. It pays to get off the old path now and then, and when you do, you may be pleasantly surprised to find how green the grass is.

The good letter-carpenter never places so much dependence on a dramatic idea that he neglects the importance of copy. In many of these stunt letters, the body text would stand alone if the showmanship were omitted. It is seldom intended that the dramatization should carry the whole load, or even the larger part of it. Instead, it is present to help win the reader's attention, to induce him to smile or nod his head, and thus make the body of the letter do a better job.

Importance of the dramatization varies. Since each letter problem is distinct from all others, it is impossible to set forth any fixed rules for dramatization, or to consider the importance of showmanship as anything but relative. If the letter answers the questions asked a moment ago, it will quite likely succeed, but the dramatization may vary from being only an attention-getter, consistent with the general purpose, to being the central idea around which all of the copy revolves. Its importance rates high in some letters, but in the following sales message, prepared by Advertising Manager D. M. Sweet for *Successful Farming,* the little bell only illustrates the story.

Dear Mr. Kimball:

Advertising, in one form or another, is a necessity for the life of business, not for just a month or a year—but always.

One day, a salesman seeking advertising for a local paper called on the village grocer. He was surprised when the gray-haired proprietor said, "Nothing doing. I've been established fifty years, and I've never advertised."

```
*********
* Small *    "What is that building on the hill?" asked the sales-
* bell  *    man.
* fixed *
* here  *    "The village church," said the grocer.
*  on   *    "Been there long?" asked the salesman.
* string *
*********    "About two hundred years."

             "Well, they still ring the bell!"
```

You must keep "ringing the bell" at customers' doors year in and year out. And by no means forget that FARMERS represent a vast, moneyed market that can bring you rich returns. ...But it takes a FARM publication to reach the farm market and it takes SUCCESSFUL FARMING to reach QUALITY farmers. SUCCESSFUL FARMING concentrates more of its circulation in the world's richest farming region—the "Heart"—than does any other farm magazine. That is where farmers are worth TWO for ONE!

Sincerely yours,

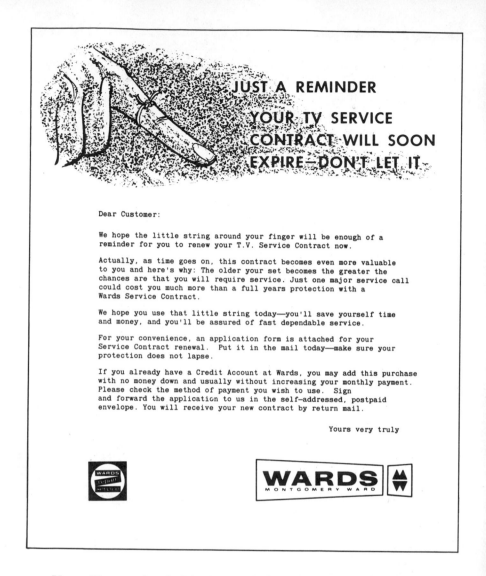

You will agree that in Mr. Sweet's letter the miniature bell had a small role to play. But when the curtain went up, the bell did help to get reader attention, and later it added a little reality to the story of the church-bell. Just how much—if at all—the miniature bell contributed to the *pull* of the letter, nobody could say. On Easter morning, Mrs. John Doe will wear a new hat—a very pretty hat. It will undoubtedly get plenty of attention, but how much will it increase Mrs. Doe's popularity? Who could say?

Nevertheless, it must be reasonable to assume that any illustrative idea in keeping with the theme of the letter, and helping to capture that important first-second attention, must be accorded some credit when the votes are counted.

You see in the letter with the bell, the gadget only illustrates something said in the copy. The text, without the bell, would be understood just as clearly by the readers. Similarly, in the letter prepared for the Montgomery Ward company, the picture and the message in large type serve only to supplement the copy.

Consider, also, the Hart Schaffner & Marx letter, used by dealer Baskin in Chicago, the story used for the Star would stand alone, but the horseshoe

Baskin OFFICES: STATE AT ADAMS · CHICAGO 3 · ANdover 3-1000

137 SOUTH STATE
EVANSTON
OLD ORCHARD
OAK PARK
OAKBROOK
CHAMPAIGN

Dear Sir:

"For want of a   shoe, the horse was
lost......"

"Remember that   old story? How because
one horse was minus one   shoe a whole army lost
a battle?

It illustrates the importance of seemingly small details.
And it's the painstaking attention Hart Schaffner & Marx pays to
such details that's made their Triple Test Worsted suit one of
the best suits in the country today!

For Triple Test is actually created to stand up under the
three tests most important in the minds of the majority of men
when they're ready to buy a suit of clothes. The suit must wear....
it must be a good value for the money...and it must be styled right.

Triple Test bats 1000% in all three of these leagues...
because Triple Test is subjected to scores of rigid tests before
it is ever allowed to carry the Triple Test label.

But we're not going to go into a long description about
the details that go into the making of this famous suit of ours!
They all add up to the sum total of one whale of a good value -
in authentic style (always smart, never extreme) in money-saving
upkeep (Triple Test has what it takes to hold its shape and press)
in topnotch service (here's a suit that really wears like iron).

We have a number of Triple Test Worsteds in the patterns
and colors we're sure you'll like. May we show them to you?

Their price? Only $58.00!

Cordially yours,

BASKIN

HART SCHAFFNER & MARX CLOTHES

(a miniature one attached to the page) commands instant attention, and thus helps the effectiveness of the copy.

In a similar way, there is no reason why the drawing of the members of a family in the Bankers Life Company letter could not have been omitted —except that the drawing does get special attention and makes the first impression all the more interesting.

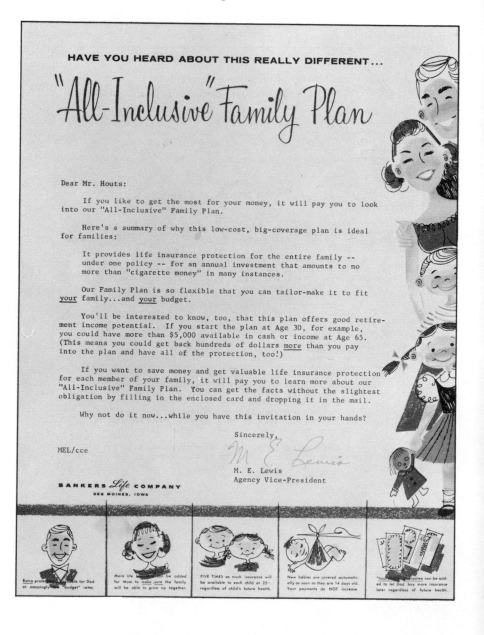

Letters where the "stunt" plays first fiddle. There are many ways to classify dramatized letters. One is to place them in two groups—letters similar to the above where the dramatization merely increases interest, and those in which it is woven into the copy, so that it could not possibly be ,omitted. For the second type, we may begin with a clever idea used by the circulation manager of *Life* magazine. The letter is dated March 4, and was typed on the back of the March 7th issue cover. The copy explains itself.

I'm sorry—

Sorry that I can't send you more than the cover of this week's LIFE (because your subscription has expired) . . .

Sorry that you are going to miss seeing all the exciting, important news stories pictured in this issue. . .

But let me send you *all* of LIFE next week.

I will gladly pay the Air Mail postage on the enclosed renewal card to save your missing another week of LIFE.

Sign the card and mail it today—and I will re-enter your subscription without a break.

Cordially,

You can imagine the reaction of the subscriber. Because the "joke's on him," he might smile and hasten to sign the card. To be sure, there is also the chance he might be the kind who only enjoys a joke on somebody else, so that the unusual approach would anger rather than please him. The important question is, would that dramatized letter, mailed to a large number of delinquent subscribers, bring more of them back than would a more conventional reminder? Yes, absolutely. It must have done so. However, good as the idea may be, it cannot continue to pull forever. Ideas lose power as they are copied, until eventually they are worthless.

Several years ago a most unusual eye-catcher went from Mandel Brothers to their lady customers. The things talked about are not for businessmen, but you can guess how many "Oh's" and "Ah's" must have been heard among the women.

The gadget used as the theme of the letter is a miniature pair of scissors attached to the page with a narrow strip of Scotch tape. The blades are slightly open, and are supposed to suggest two legs. The comparison is continued by the two round handles, which in a vague way complete the figure. Here's the letter:

Dear Mrs. Cahill:

Presenting
the newest

"SCISSORS"
SILHOUETTE

Inspired by
Schiaparelli,
and adapted
in Formfit
Foundations

You'll cut a pretty new figure this spring. Bustline high and separated...waist nipped to a shadow...skirts wide and flaring! You'll find your silhouette will look for all the world like a "scissors."

To help you achieve this "scissors" silhouette, Schiaparelli has conceived a new laced-in waist for Formfit foundations...that

holds your breasts high and separated...then laces down the front to take inches off your waist...and with utmost possible comfort.

This Formfit foundation is priced at just $10 and is but one of the many we are featuring during Formfit Week. New Formfit styles for every type figure are being modeled in our Corset Salon this week, February 20 to 25, and we want you to come and see them.

Enclosing a stamp to increase the chance of a reply is one of the oldest devices, still going strong, in the letter-world. That the pull is strengthened, no one can doubt. It doesn's seem honest to keep a stamp, so most people feel an obligation to do something with it. The following letter, used by TIME magazine, dramatizes the use of the stamp and makes it play the leading role.

Dear New Subscriber:

"Jones of Binghamton—he pays the freight."*

Thus, some fifty years ago, proclaimed Jones' Scale Works at Binghamton, New York, to its prospective customers.

We know you want to pay the enclosed bill promptly—that you like to keep small bills off your desk and out of your morning's mail.

So here is the freight—prepaid—in anticipation of your willingness to mail your remittance today.

With thanks for your promptness and for your interest in TIME.

                               Cordially,

    * This slogan did not originate with one of the great mail order houses as is popularly believed.

Even a couple of aspirin tablets can be made the heroes of a sales letter. The brand used is Bayer's—one of the widely advertised brands. The tablets are enclosed in a neatly imprinted, transparent envelope that seems to have been furnished by the Bayer Company. Because of their prestige and utility value they could not fail to arouse favorable and quick attention. The letter was sent to credit managers by The Credit Clearing House Adjustment Corporation.

> Dear Mr. Doe:
>
> 'Tis widely advertised that should you be smitten with a headache, aspirins will relieve it. Two are enclosed.
>
> But should that headache be the result of trouble with collections, then I unreservedly recommend our service—especially if you want to clear any old claims, hanging over from previous years.
>
> For best results on "headache accounts," I prescribe the following treatment: At the very first symptom of an account turning sour, GET IN TOUCH WITH US—our remedy consists of mail and male persuasion. It's potent!
>
> First, we send an ingenious PRESTIGE or FREE DEMAND LETTER— it commands respect—and usually collects a substantial number of claims right off. If your account is reluctant, we send a trained expert—an adjuster skilled in winning respect, adroit in selling the idea of honoring obligations, practiced in the art of holding goodwill.
>
> You'll find our Service penetrating the most inaccessible places, liquidating the most complex situations, freeing your frozen accounts.
>
> Yes, for "headaches," Bayer and Credit Clearing each is preeminent in its field. Acid test of Experience proves it. We've never lost a patient.
>
> Have your bookkeeper draw up a list of "Past Dues" for us. If we don't collect, you don't pay. If our PRESTIGE or FREE DEMAND LETTER collects, you don't pay. If we collect with Personal Service, the fee's moderate.
>
> You've everything to WIN—nothing to lose. Just *try* us.
>
> Clinically yours,

The copy in that letter is above average—it shows the hand of a skilled "carpenter." The aspirin tablets are cleverly used to gain attention and are woven throughout the fabric of thought. The letter should have done a good job.

Use of showmanship to sample the product. Among the very best of the dramatized letters used in business are those that manage to sample the company product, or some part of it. As all salesmen know, there is no better way to arouse interest in a prospect than to get the thing being sold *in his hands.* The *feel* of an object creates a sense of possession. This is just plain sales psychology, which can sometimes be applied in a written contact as effectively as in an oral one.

In a sales letter used by the Badger Paper Mills in Wisconsin, attention is called to a sizable little piece of spruce, enclosed in a glassine bag attached to the top of the page. "The paper on which this letter is written was once a chip like the one above. It is a piece of 100% American Northern Spruce, from which our Ta-Non-Ka Bond is made. The exclusive use of spruce fibre is one reason for Ta-Non-Ka's greater strength, higher white, and . . ."

Thus, the reader has for his inspection, not only a sample of the Bond being sold, but also a piece of the wood from which it is made. This is a simple but interesting demonstration, and certain to help the letter do its job.

Some companies are more favored than others in their ability to let a letter carry a sample of their craftsmanship. For example, a commercial photographer should have no problem in using a letter, containing a photograph, that will illustrate excellent quality photography. However, the subject of the photograph should not be so overpowering that the reader concentrates on the picture and forgets the letter.

A masterpiece of "sampling." If letters were rated like Hollywood actors, one of the "Oscars" would surely have been awarded to the oriental rug sales presentation prepared by Norman Focht for importer Joseph M. Eways of Reading, Pennsylvania. In fact, if *any* letter *could* be called perfect, this one would closely approach that distinction.

To this letter are clipped two pieces of yarn—one rust and one blue. As the letter tells you, the rust sample is machine-spun, but yarn like the blue is spun by hand "in far off Persia." From this simple explanation, the whole letter develops, and at the end the reader emerges with a most interesting conception of the value of oriental rugs. Can't you imagine the reader feeling the two samples, and seeing for himself how much stronger the one is than the other? This is *salesmanship* at its best, and yet the idea back of the dramatization is so simple and inexpensive that it puts to shame some of the other far more elaborate attempts that you see in this Handbook, and in the letters that cross your desk.

Certainly, of the dramatized letters used in this discussion, this one using two pieces of yarn wins the blue ribbon.

Joseph M. Eways

IMPORTER OF ORIENTAL RUGS AND CARPETS

213 North Fifth St. Reading, Pa.

Dear Mr. Jones:

Just two little pieces of yarn -- but what an important story they tell you.

Pull the ends of the rust yarn and notice how the strands separate and fray easily. Now pull the blue yarn and notice the difference -- it will not fray!

The rust yarn was spun by machine. The blue yarn was spun by hand in far off Persia.

Genuine oriental rugs are made only with the hand spun yarn. The wool for this yarn comes from the backs of sheep which graze most of the year in the warm, sunny pastures of the lands across the sea. It is the extra strength of this wool and the skill of the hand weaver which enables the genuine oriental rug to hold its beauty for centuries.

I would like you to see the exceptional oriental rug in my shop which was hand-woven so firmly that there are as many as 400 knots to the square inch, compared to 200 knots in the average oriental rug.

I would like to show you some of the genuine Orientals which have journeyed thousands of miles across oceans and continents to reach my shop from far-off lands. I can promise you one of the most pleasant half hours you have ever enjoyed, just "talking rugs" ... telling you some of the truly romantic legends behind these rugs and showing you the magnificent pieces which will add charm, distinction and character to your home.

Of course, you will not be under the slightest obligation. Either stop at the store the next time you are down town or telephone 2-3446 for an evening appointment if you wish.

Sincerely yours,

Joseph M. Eways
Joseph M. Eways

JME:LK

RUGS REPAIRED • CLEANED • STORED • PHONE 2-3446

Another good job of sampling is that used by Montgomery Ward in a letter sent out by store managers, presumably to customers who had previously purchased fishing equipment. Clipped to the page was a card that carried short pieces of two of the fishing lines sold by the company. Again, we see a very simple idea, although it must have been very interesting to those who got the letter. The copy is good, too.

Hello there, Sportsman:

You have heard fish stories a-plenty—but just absorb this little bit of news I'm CASTING your way, and ten to one you will find fishing a greater pleasure than ever.

Guess I've a REEL yearning for that "Brotherhood of rod and line—and sky and stream that's always fine." Maybe, it is simply that Ol' Spring is in the air.

But honestly, what's more thrilling than to land one of those glistening, nimble trout or scrappy bass? Well, fisherman, you know that high-grade tackle will help do this, and that's why I'm a little bit afraid of my own tackle. Noticed the other day my leaders were all stiff and dried out—a few of my lines beyond repair! Incidentally, how do you like these sample casting and fly lines?

Oh, yes, another thing—our sporting goods salesmen and I have just looked over a new shipment of fishing tackle that we have on display. No kidding, it really looks good to me. Why not drop in some day this week and look it over? And if you don't see what you want in our display, I'll personally see that you get it direct from the manufacturer, at Ward's usual low prices.

DON'T FORGET—the fishing season will be in full swing soon, and you'll be needing new tackle.

> MONTGOMERY WARD
> Store Manager

Other eye-openers in the Frailey collection. Of course, you realize the impossibility of hanging shark's teeth, corset strings, wedding rings, or four-leaf clovers on the pages of a Handbook. Many dramatized letter-ideas simply defy reproduction in book form. However, here are a few brief descriptions of "gadget" letters that may stir your imagination:

"THE POWER OF A SHARK"...in big red letters, that is the caption of a letter used by the Wizard Company in St. Louis. Above the title is fastened a *real* shark's tooth. The letter begins:

> The power of a shark is in its teeth. Nature keeps them sharp as you will find after examining the tooth attached. With teeth like this, a shark can sever a man's arm with one bite and a twist. The power of a shoe sale, too, is in the "teeth" that are put in it. The "teeth" are the "plus" that make the sale stick. Take Trimfoot—it's a natural "plus"...

.   .   .   .   .

"CONSIDER THE 'PEEP,' MR. JONES"...so starts a letter mailed by The Men's Shop in West Chester, Pennsylvania. Attached is a yellow cotton baby chick. The letter continues:

Along about this time each year, we see lots of pictures of this little fellow popping out of a cracked shell, and taking his first "peep" at a new world. He's a symbol of Easter, and he seems pretty happy about it.

Same way with a fellow in a smart looking Spring suit—he's a symbol of Easter too, and...

.   .   .   .   .

"HERE'S A SHAMROCK"...is the logical salutation which gets a Saint Patrick's Day message off on the right foot. It was used by Leonard H. Graves as a goodwill contact. The paper is green, and on it, over the typed letter, is the imprint of Mr. Graves' right hand. In one corner is a Shamrock, over which is tied a miniature clay pipe.

The letter isn't long. You may read the whole of it:

Here's a Shamrock, Mr. McNulty,
and my right hand goes with it.

"Good Luck to You on Saint Patrick's Day in the Morning!"

My son overheard a conversation at school in which the "Luck of the Irish" was mentioned, so when I got home that night he asked: "Daddy, what made the Irish lucky?"

"The luck of the Irish, son," I said, "is due to the fact that they work hard, talk little, and always wear a Shamrock on Saint Patrick's Day."

So today, I'll be wearing a Shamrock and doing everything that a good Irishman is supposed to do on Saint Patrick's Day.

And I hope that you will wear the Shamrock, too, for I have a sneaking feeling that the "Luck of the Irish" is hovering near, and that the wishes and plans which are uppermost in your mind will become a reality.

Yours for a real
Saint Patrick's Day,

P. S.   Believe it or not, one way to have "Irish Luck" on your mailing pieces and letters is to have our Irish crowd write and produce them.

.   .   .   .   .

"A FEATHER IN YOUR CAP, MRS. FOX"...that's the beginning for a letter used by Kaufman's, in Reading, Pennsylvania. Attached is a red feather about three inches long. The copy begins:

Perhaps you didn't realize it, but all you owe us on your account is a small balance.

That certainly is a "feather in your cap," as the saying goes. You can feel proud of the way in which you have handled this charge account, and your credit always will be A-1 at Kaufman's.

Because of the sincere effort to meet your payments regularly, I am very happy to extend a special courtesy to you. You can purchase any additional furniture and . . .

. . . . .

"RIVER FISHIN'S BEST" . . . printed in large type, this is the title of a letter used by the magazine, Down Beat. The letter-head reveals a plump old fellow, with pipe and rod. A red string (real) runs from the end of the rod to the lower right-hand corner of the page. On the lower end, is tied a metal fish. To keep the string in place, both ends are clipped to the sheet. Says the letter:

"According to Old Timer, 'You got more chance of ketchin' somethin' in a river, becus more fish see your bait.'

"Old Timer's philosophy isn't new to music advertising men, who also want to dangle their bait before the greatest number of prospects. They're river fishermen, too.

"Maybe that's why Down Beat carried more . . ."

. . . . .

"GETTING DOWN TO BRASS TACKS" . . . begins a letter used by Wurzburg Brothers, in Memphis, Tennessee. At the end of the first line of copy, two holes are punched about an inch apart. Into each is inserted a common brass paper fastener, head to the front. About as simple as any showmanship could be—but these old expressions are popular, and the dramatization of this one is quite effective.
Here is how the letter starts:

"GETTING DOWN TO BRASS TACKS" . . . it's your tag business we're after.

"Will you meet us halfway, and let us show you what we can offer on your tag requirements? It won't take . . ."

. . . . .

"HERE'S THE BRIGHT IDEA" . . . starts this letter used by the American Nickeloid Company, and to prove it's no joke, a disc of bright metal is attached—so bright you could almost trim your mustache looking at it.

"HERE'S THE BRIGHT IDEA"—try brilliant metal as it's used on this letter. Always distinctive, always . . .

Showmanship on the typewriter. Of course, you are familiar with the tricks so often played on the typewriter. Some are quite interesting and effective; others are so far-fetched or poorly executed that they repel rather than attract. Neither the good nor the bad ones are popular with the typists whose unfortunate chore it is to turn into reality the conceptions of their superiors. "Here is a Christmas message I worked out last night, Miss Gluts," says the boss. "Please see if you can't type it in the form of a Christmas tree." And he never knows how hard and long the girl has worked when she finally places the letter on his desk.

```
                                        By
                                     the time
                                    you receive
                                   this   letter,
                                  you will have on-
                                 ly about two or three
                                weeks remaining in which
               to           "tag your turkey". But in the meantime, we are
           sending          a dandy big picture of just what he looks like
         now that he        is grown up. Those of you who had the pleasure
         of winning         one of Colonel Morse's prize birds last year know
       that     there       never was a turkey that tasted so good.They're nice
       and      fat         and juicy. In the oven they take on that deep, rich,
       br-      own         color that makes your mouth water.   And of course that
              delicious taste of the bird itself when augmented by the fact that
              you won it in a nation-wide sales contest, makes it just that  much
              more wonderful to both you and your family.    I wish that I had some
              of the genius of Charles Dickens in his   "Christmas Carol"  in making
              words say what the heart feels,  so that  I could  bring out in the way
              that he does, the friendly spirit that prompts these Christmas Turkey
              Contests.   The interest that we here at headquarters have in watching
              your progress --.how much your attainment of your sales quota means
              to us -- and to you -- how the writer is glad when a chance to help
              you men in the field comes his way -- how the company appreciates
              your work and is genuinely interested in your success and wel-
              fare.   This is the spirit that prevails here not only during
              the Yuletide season but all through the year. And it's the
              spirit that you'll enjoy the more, when you receive your
              turkey with the Boss's compliments.  Don't forget, how-
              ever that a turkey is not the only thing you have an
              opportunity to win -- remember for each Branch House
              Sales Organization, there is a dandy fine F-M
              Radio as well which will be won by the high
              man.  Just a few weeks more now  -- and the
              winners will be announced.  So get go-
              ing.  Don't stop until you have
                 your turkey in the coop
                 and      sa      fely
                 ta       gg      ed.
```

Nevertheless, trick typing has developed some very good business letters. For example, salesmen often grumble over the number of bulletins they are expected to read, and any device that might lift one of them (bulletin not salesman) out of the groove is surely worth the effort. It may have taken considerable time to "carve" a turkey for salesmen of Fairbanks Morse & Co., but it should have gained more attention than the conventional bulletin would.

Trick typing need not always be so formidable. The following letter, used by the Central Manufacturers Mutual Insurance Company, Van Wert, Ohio, took very little extra time to type, but it rates high as an attention-getter. Moreover, the words typed in the unusual way gain extra emphasis for their meaning.

D the cost of your insurance protection considerably, because The Central, as you know, pays dividends to policyholders.

You're also able to gain other important advantages when you insure in The Central. For example, the wide range of available policies makes it possible to obtain combination coverages, eliminate duplicate protection and costs, receive more protection for less money.

Perhaps you have overlooked recent changes in the insurance picture, among them the fact that your home and possessions have become more valuable, would now be much more costly to replace.

That's why it will pay you to review all the facts about Central protection. For your convenience, this information has been condensed into an easily read booklet which shows you how to keep your property insurance more complete, more economical. Today you need such information more than ever before. So write for your free copy of "Facts about Mutual Fire Insurance" now. Just mail the attached postage-paid card. Your copy will be mailed promptly.

Yours very truly,

P. S.   If you have friends who would be interested in lowering the cost of their property insurance, do them a favor. Jot their names and addresses on the card when you send for your copy of "Facts." We will send them, without obligation, a copy of the same booklet.

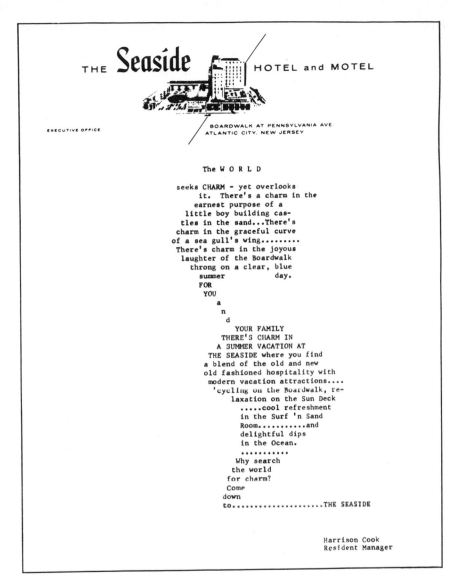

The Seaside Hotel and Motel letter is typical of the more complicated effects gained by typewriter manipulation. It is cleverly prepared to capture immediate attention. It does present one problem though, which the letter-carpenter must face when he elects a similar form of showmanship—a problem that tends to become more serious as the execution of the idea grows more complicated. The problem is the sacrifice that must be made in space for copy, with the dangerous possibility that the latter may be less interesting to the reader than is the dramatic idea. Furthermore, as the typed lines get further and further away from conventional length and position, they become more and more difficult to read. The man who plans

147

the "trick" letter to gain attention for the more serious purpose of his letter, *may* find himself in the lamentable dilemma of winning *all* attention and *no* action.

For the hotel letter, this may not have any significance, since it probably is not intended so much to impel immediate action, as to "prime" the readers for action when the proper time comes. In this sense, unusual typing is like billboard advertising which chiefly aims to make sure that certain products are *remembered* favorably, and to the exclusion of others. For such a purpose, the dramatically typed letter would seem to be perfect.

Remember that anything *different* seems to attract attention; a commonplace request can be given a bit of color simply by typing the letter in an unusual way. The following inquiry to put a mailing list in order should have had more than ordinary pull because of the type format. It was used by Prentice-Hall, Inc.

Dear Sir:

We're trying
To bring our records
Up-to-date.

So—
Will you do us a favor
And slide the card
Out of the pocket
At the top of this sheet
And correct
Any misspelling of your name—
Change of address—
Addition of your zone number—
Or anything else that makes
Our present method of addressing you
Inaccurate.

EVEN IF THE LISTING IS CORRECT,
We'd appreciate it if you'd
Check the "OK" box,
And maii the card.

Thanks
Ever so much.
Just drop the card
In your outgoing mail.
The postage will be paid
By us.

Very truly yours,

For those who think that copy is "everything," who always ridicule any form of showmanship as undignified and childish, your commentator has an example that still remains somewhat of a sales letter mystery. A young lady who was contemplating a career in advertising decided to seek a connection with a good agency. Accordingly, she sent a mimeographed letter asking for an interview to forty-eight advertising executives. As you can see, the copy was trimmed to the bone, and the emphasis placed on the rough sketch of the "copy cub" at large.

Dear Mr. Chittenden:

A "COPY CUB" WITH THE FOLLOWING QUALIFICATIONS IS AT LARGE.

Age: 26 years.

Education:
American Academy of Art.
Northwestern University.

Experience:
Copy, layout, sales letters,
art work, ideas, and
production. Three years.

Won't you use the enclosed reply-card to give this ambitious, hard-working, and capable young woman an interview?

(Signature)

It is doubtful that any of our letter experts would have predicted success for that sales attempt. And who could blame them? Except that the sketch may provoke a smile, what is left in the copy to make a big impression on high-powered advertising men? But here's the mystery: thirty-seven of these men took the trouble to reply, eighteen granted the interview, and three offered the girl a job. You couldn't ask for better success than that with an application letter—shooting in the dark at total strangers.

Why did it pull so well? It is *different* from the usual run of tiresome and stilted requests for employment that flow to the desks of business men throughout the year. You know the kind that start, "Having recently completed the secretarial course at King's Business College, the writer would appreciate an interview relative to a position with your company." Then, as a rule, there follows a blow-by-blow description of the applicant's education, age, weight, height, church affiliation, disposition, and whatnot—ending with reference to people who, of course, have been carefully chosen as sure to be kind-hearted and complimentary. But this "copy cub" knew better than to bore her readers with facts that could be saved for the interview. Maybe the results are not so mysterious after all. The letter did a fine job, and who are we to discount success?

Over-sized letters and telegrams. A very old idea for getting attention is the use of a letter or telegram many times the customary size. These blow-ups are simple to make, and not expensive. The master copy is typed the usual way on the letterhead or telegram blank, then sent to the printers for enlargement by a photographic process, somewhat similar to the enlarging of a camera print. Naturally, the reader is startled to encounter such a giant in the ordinary run of his mail, and tends to be favorably impressed. Here is the copy on a BIG letter used by Eastin 16 mm. Pictures Co., of Davenport, Iowa. The size of the mailing sheet was four times that of an 8½ by 11 letterhead.

> Dear Exhibitor:
>
> What's the BIG idea?
>
> We thought that 144 page catalog of ours was big enough to get your attention. But so far, neither the catalog nor our letters have brought any response from you.
>
> Therefore, I'm writing you a really BIG letter this time, and it's about a really BIG day for you—the day you start your summer roadshow circuit with those outstanding Eastin Films.
>
> Eastin is the only independent library with Hollywood connections and sufficient resources to bring you EXCLUSIVELY more late feature pictures for roadshow uses at roadshow prices, than all the other libraries in the country put together.
>
> Eastin Film alone has developed methods to maintain films in trouble-free running condition at all times. It is only here— week after week—that you get prints that are free from troublesome breaks while showing—that are cleaned, with all surface oil, grit and lint removed by our special process—that have good, long leaders for speed in threading.

Eastin gives you more for your money in every way...full insurance...topnotch subjects...good prints...prompt, dependable delivery. Audiences from coast to coast applaud the title, "Eastin Film," as identification of the finest in 16 mm. entertainment.

Your BIG opening day will be the beginning of your BIG profit

year with films from Eastin. Immediate booking means choice subjects. Don't delay. Shoot your order in today.

Most cordially,

You can see how the BIG letter idea can easily be adapted to a thousand and one uses in business.

"I am afraid that my previous letters about your unpaid bill have been too small to get attention, so now I am writing to you in the BIGGEST way I know how."...(Credit Manager)

"Men, this new product calls for BIG enthusiasm on the part of every salesman. It's your BIG opportunity for BIGGER income. Only a BIG letter like this could express how I feel about it."...(Sales Manager)

"This is a BIG way to tell you about the BIG campaign which begins next month in all the BIG magazines. It is the BIGGEST STORY ever told to your customers about radio, and it means BIG business for you."...(Advertising Manager)

"This is the BIG sale of the year—nothing held back. BIG values, BIG assortments to choose from, BIG savings for you! Everything BIG, except the prices."...(Retail Merchant)

"Best wishes to all of you for a BIG New Year. We have made BIG progress, in spite of BIG obstacles, and in that each of you has played a loyal part."...(President to employees)

"BIG news deserves a BIG announcement. The date is set for June 1, and a BIG night it is going to be. Nothing will be skimped or left out—BIG dinner, BIG entertainment, and your BIG chance to meet and hear our National President."...(Association Secretary)

Big telegrams, too, are useful in similar ways. Usually, they are not genuine enlargements, as that involves special arrangement with the telegraph company, but are made to resemble the real thing as much as possible. A good example is a message sent by Charles Kell when he was Western Life Director of Agencies; the layout on yellow paper was telegram-style, but titled differently.

Western Life
TREASURE-GRAM

St. Louis, Mo. February 20

Mr. Bill Bates,
2470 Estes Ave.,
Chicago, Ill.

HERE IS A BIG MESSAGE CONCERNING A BIG OPPORTUNITY. THE
MESSAGE IS OURS BUT THE OPPORTUNITY IS YOURS. SIX WEEKS
REMAIN IN WHICH YOU CAN WIN POINTS IN THE WESTERN LIFE
GREAT TREASURE HUNT SALES CAMPAIGN. YOU HAVE 234 PRIZES
FROM WHICH TO CHOOSE—MERCHANDISE EQUALED ONLY IN THE
BEST DEPARTMENT STORES. THESE AWARDS ARE YOURS. IN ADDI-
TION TO YOUR LIBERAL COMMISSIONS. SET YOUR GOAL FOR A BIG
BUSINESS...THEN MAKE EVERY DAY COUNT. THE ENTIRE HOME
OFFICE STAFF IS PULLING FOR YOU. GOOD LUCK.

CHARLES KELL
DIRECTOR OF AGENCIES

Telegrams of ordinary size get special attention because they are not received as frequently as letters. Obviously, a BIG telegram must have even greater power, especially when, with the cooperation of the company, it is delivered by a uniformed messenger.

It all sums up to being different. When you reflect on these sample dramatized mailings, plus others of your own observation, it is evident that they all handle problems common in business correspondence, and that what they *say* is the same as it would have been if done in the conventional way. Dramatic messages are all inspired by the fact that human beings tend to give special attention to anything out of the ordinary. Thus, they do the same job as does an ordinary letter, but they do it in a *different* way.

This is fine, provided the difference is *pleasing* to the reader. In the effort to get out of a rut, we sometimes see the writer wandering too far from the groove, and the reader's reaction is not as intended. For instance, you may have received letters with facsimile checks printed on the upper third of the page, and folded in such a way that through the window envelopes they appear to be genuine. The first reaction is wonderful. You say, "A check...swell...now the baby gets a pair of new shoes." But alas, the check turns out to be a swindle. It is *like* the check you *would get* if you were smart enough to own a certain policy and unlucky enough to break your leg before it expired. Perhaps you don't mind this form of deception, but it does lift the reader up and then throw him down. The effectiveness of the idea is doubtful.

Another experience that never seems to please is the reception of a letter on which there is postage due. The victim feels that he is expected not only to read the letter but to pay for the privilege. This tribulation was given a new twist by a clever letter-writer in Davenport, Iowa. He sent his mailing out knowing that one penny would be collected at the point of delivery. When the reader opened the letter, he found a card inside on which was mounted one penny—and the words, "Here is the penny you just spent to get this message."

Yes, this was a novel form of showmanship, and we must give its "daddy" credit for originality. No doubt, some of the readers accepted the stunt as a good joke on them, but others probably thought a childish device had been used to get their attention. The latter reaction may also have been strengthened by the fact that there was no connection between the idea and the rest of the letter. The writer knew he was taking a chance with the prank, but went ahead anyway.

Using the same approach of a shock followed by immediate recovery is the letter once mailed to prospects by one of the leading insurance companies. When the reader pulled the letter from its envelope, the first thing he saw was an itemized bill from the "Emergency Hospital." If he knew that such a hospital did not exist, the reaction was not too disturbing. Otherwise, he must have felt a chill running up and down his spine. However, the first lines of the letter ended the panic—"The thought of such a bill, if presented to you, gives an awful jolt, doesn't it? We will take the burden of responsibility. Pay all such bills promptly and completely! A modern shock-absorber at your service!"

But again, what was the reader-reaction? Were those who received the "phoney" bill so impressed with the seriousness of what *could* happen that they wanted to know more about the prevention, or did they resent the trick used to get their attention? The reaction was probably split both ways—only the insurance company could tell us.

"Just dip it in some water." Among the doubtful forms of showmanship that may backfire is a letter used by a Chicago printing company. Here is part of it:

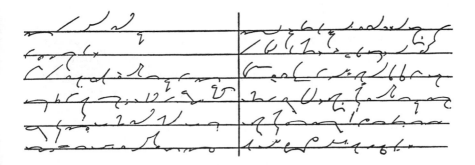

After several more paragraphs—the letter filled a page—there appears a postscript, typed in red: "You don't have to know shorthand nor even call your secretary to find out what this stenographic letter is all about—*just dip it in water.*" Now isn't that fine and dandy? A businessman should take time to walk over to the drinking fountain and wet this letter. Of course, by chemical process the real letter will then be revealed. Can you imagine the business man enjoying such a damp experience? There he stands, with the wet sheet in his hands, and after the letter has been launched, what does he do with it?

A letter in script. The passing from quill pen to typewriter was a great step forward in business correspondence, but it did eliminate a personal touch which only script possesses. To offset the coldness of a typewritten message, many letter-writers have the habit of adding a few words in longhand along with their signature. For example, on the bottom of the letter just signed, the credit manager may write "Please" or "Come on, friend Jones, let's get this thing settled." The salesmanager, on a letter to a dealer about some prosaic subject, may write, "Don't forget to bring your clubs on your next trip to the city," or "That is really a good buy, John."

The sight of the words in longhand is pleasing to the reader. They make him feel that he has received personal attention—that a cordial relationship has been recognized. It's a good idea to add a little warmth to the letter, but *not* when the addition in longhand is merely to take care of something forgotten in the dictation. A letter with scribbling all over the margins and at the top and bottom is most unsightly, and contributes nothing except the impression that the writer is both careless and lacking in pride.

Whole letters in script are also quite common. This may be done for a group mailing by using a mimeograph stencil, or better still, with a cut made from a master copy in India ink. The advantage of the latter is that the same person who made the master copy can then fill in the name of each reader and any other line or phrase left blank for that purpose. On the following page is a good example.

Sent along with this letter was a photograph of a young couple dancing; the young man is shown to be romantically interested in the young lady.

With this letter on hand in quantities, The Carlton Beach was able to send a copy to any prospect. Only one fill-in was necessary—the name of the prospect after "Dear." And if the name was carefully added to perfectly match the body of the letter, the effect of a personally written letter was attained. In fact, the "match" in the letter is so good that even now we cannot be sure how the job was done. It could have been written out, word

-2-

there last year and met a d
(single). She corresponds with
week and every two or three
corresponds with her too. Vir
she had a ~~fabulous~~ time a
Beach — even after the den
home! And a single girl
about a vacation than th
while Virginia is pretty
think she made the
opportunities. She kee,
how she practically
bed into the ocean, s
beach is right on t
Maybe if she had s
more te

-3-

Anyway, I've talked a girl friend of
mine, who is very nice, even if she
isn't exactly good-looking, into coming
along with me to The Carlton Beach
this year! We're considering your most
romantic, inexpensive room, as we're on
a budget.

Thank you,
Alma L. Walker.

P.S. This letter may be only an
advertisement for The Carlton Beach,
but doesn't it get you right here?

Dear Mr. Towle:
Would you please send me to The
Carlton Beach?
I'm 24 years old, single (although
I've been engaged twice — once to an
apprentice designer in Queens who had
certain designs on me that were not
exactly proper — see photograph — and
the ~~other~~ one time to a Chiropodist from
Sunbury, Pa., who thought I had cute
feet — did you ever?)
Anyway, as a single girl I'm looking
for the kind of place in Bermuda to
spend my two weeks' vacation having
a fabulous time.
My roommate, Virginia, told me all
about The Carlton Beach. She was

Letters in Longhand Always More Personal

for word, although the time involved would indicate otherwise. But what does it matter? The idea is splendidly executed, and it won quick and favorable attention.

However, The Carlton Beach was not content to confine its originality just to the letter. The matching envelope is completely personal; the address is handwritten; the return address is not that of the hotel, but of a young lady. This must have been done at the time the letter was mailed, and of course, had to be repeated for each contact with a prospect.

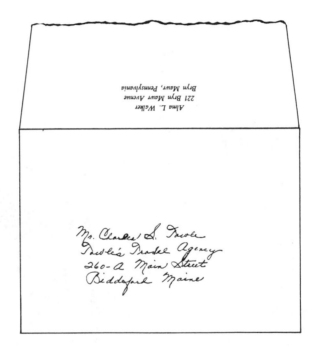

More examples for good measure. The forms that showmanship may take in business letters are so numerous and so different that a whole volume of examples would only scratch the surface. You have seen that they may be good or bad, depending upon the originality of the idea, how appropriate it is to the subject matter of the letter, whether or not it is simple enough to be practical from the expense angle—and, most important of all, the final effect it has on the reader.

For good measure, you may conclude your survey of this device used to win attention by examining a few more examples—all of them good enough that we may assume the letters did a fine job for those who used them.

TIME IS RUNNING OUT ON YOUR LAUNDRY EQUIPMENT WARRANTY...PROTECT YOURSELF WITH A WARDS SERVICE CONTRACT

Dear Customer:

Your one year free service and parts warranty on your automatic laundry equipment is about to expire. We think it highly important for you to extend this protection with a Wards Service Contract. This low cost, 12-month contract can really be a blessing. It covers all parts, labor charges and all service calls to your home necessary to maintain your equipment under normal use.

Why not safeguard your big investment and end all your service worries for the coming year. Even though your appliance is only one year old and was engineered to deliver dependable service...all automatic equipment is quite complex and its many parts are subject to the normal effects of usage.

So act today and make sure your protection does not lapse. Order your Service Contract now, before your warranty period ends and save the cost of an inspection call.

If you have a Credit Account at Wards, you may add this purchase without a down payment, and usually without increasing your monthly payment.

For your convenience, we have enclosed an application form for a Laundry Equipment Service Contract. Just check the plan that fits your needs and the method of payment you wish to use, sign and forward the application to us in the self-addressed, postage paid envelope. You will receive your contract by return mail.

Yours very truly

WARDS MONTGOMERY WARD

Continue ... Carefree Listening

Dear Customer:

Soon the warranty on your Hi-Fi will expire. Why not S-T-R-E-T-C-H your coverage--and your dollars--with a Wards Service Contract.

You can continue to enjoy beautiful music relaxed without a care in the world. With a Wards Service Contract the burden of repair expense and worry shifts from your shoulders to Wards. Your Hi-Fi is completely covered--all parts and all labor. Remember-- you get unlimited service in your home regardless of the number of calls you may require, and it can't cost you one additional penny.

It's the modern approach to the care and maintenance of electrical equipment. You plan ahead and budget your money, secure in the knowledge that there will be no unpleasant repair surprises for you. Doesn't it make sense to spend just a few pennies a day now, rather than be jolted by a major repair bill when you lease expect it?

There are many features that make our contracts unusually attractive--our nation-wide service--servicemen who specialize in your Airline unit--and a solid money-back guarantee on your Service Contract. You will be delighted to join the thousands of Wards customers who have responded enthusiastically to this new approach to repair service.

If you have a credit account at Wards, you may add this purchase without a down payment and usually without increasing your monthly payment.

Take care of this right now. Sign the enclosed application form for a Hi-Fi Service Contract. Check the plan that fits your needs and the method of payment you wish to use. Forward the application to us in the addressed, post-paid envelope. You will receive your contract by return mail.

29017

                              Yours very truly,

                              :***: **MONTGOMERY WARD**

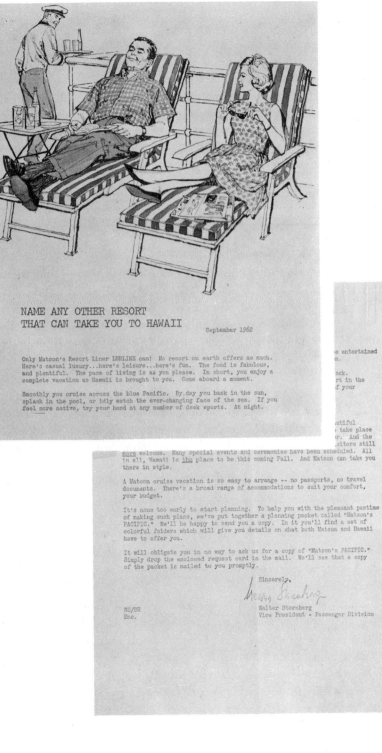

NAME ANY OTHER RESORT
THAT CAN TAKE YOU TO HAWAII

September 1962

Only Matson's Resort Liner LURLINE can! No resort on earth offers as much.
Here's casual luxury...here's leisure...here's fun. The food is fabulous,
and plentiful. The pace of living is as you please. In short, you enjoy a
complete vacation as Hawaii is brought to you. Come aboard a moment.

Smoothly you cruise across the blue Pacific. By day you bask in the sun,
splash in the pool, or idly watch the ever-changing face of the sea. If you
feel more active, try your hand at any number of deck sports. At night,

e entertained
n.

ock.
rt in the
f your

utiful
take place
r. And the
sitors still

more welcome. Many special events and ceremonies have been scheduled. All
in all, Hawaii is the place to be this coming Fall. And Matson can take you
there in style.

A Matson cruise vacation is so easy to arrange -- no passports, no travel
documents. There's a broad range of accommodations to suit your comfort,
your budget.

It's none too early to start planning. To help you with the pleasant pastime
of making such plans, we've put together a planning packet called "Matson's
PACIFIC." We'll be happy to send you a copy. In it you'll find a set of
colorful folders which will give you details on what both Matson and Hawaii
have to offer you.

It will obligate you in no way to ask us for a copy of "Matson's PACIFIC."
Simply drop the enclosed request card in the mail. We'll see that a copy
of the packet is mailed to you promptly.

Sincerely,

Walter Sternberg
Vice President - Passenger Division

WS/DB
Enc.

5. The Chain to Build Desire

Adding fuel to the fire. You will recall that the Chain of the business letter has the important job of taking the reader from a state of attention to one of increasing interest, so that finally he is *ready* to act as the writer will suggest in the Hook. Thus, after the spark that starts the fire, the Chain comes along to add fuel—not only to keep the fire burning, but to make it burn more brightly.

The Chain, of course, is the body of the letter, and of necessity is usually much longer than either the Star or the Hook. This is true because it takes time to parade before the reader the facts he must know if action is to be secured. The length cannot be avoided, as the reader will not jump directly from mere attention to favorable action, but it does present a serious problem for the letter-carpenter. This problem is the possibility that at some point, before all the facts can be marshaled and the whole story told, interest will be broken, and no more of the letter will be read. Hence, the facts in the Chain must be co-ordinated into a *swiftly flowing* message, with never a dull spot or let-up. Nothing is more important to the success of a business letter where action is to be requested than this "FLOW" from fact to fact— keeping the reader's mind on the subject and giving him no chance to think of something else.

HOW can this be done? Well, the answer to that question is a major purpose of this Handbook, and suggestions appear at almost any place that you might stop to read. For example, the letter-carpenter must construct his Chain with words, and so could not do the job unless he understood the language principles explained in Section 2. He must work with a plan (as emphasized in this Section) or surely the Chain will fall apart. He must also be familiar with letter-mechanics (Section 4), and if able to reflect a pleasing personality (Section 5), his chances of success will be increased. All through the other sections, matters important to the building of the Chain are set forth—some related more to one type of letter than another, but each having some connection with the major objective of making *every* letter do a good job.

Particularly in Section 7, How to Write the Sales Letter, you will find the Chain taken apart, and then put together again, and a survey of what can be done to make it strong, and of common mistakes that tend to make it weak. This information might, just as logically, be given in connection with the present analysis of the Star, the Chain, and the Hook, except that many of the points would need a second "airing" in connection with the sales letter, and there is no reason why you should be burdened with the repetition. So that the continuity of the formula will not be overlooked, there follow a few examples of that fast "flow" which is so essential if the purpose of the Chain is to be accomplished.

A fast-moving Chain. A short letter in which the reader is carried along rapidly once he has passed the introduction is one used by LaSalle Extension University. Notice that it has a title instead of the usual salutation.

"LEGAL KINKS AND TRICKS IN BUSINESS"

On my desk is a booklet that should be yours. May I send it to you?

Other readers have called it the most human collection of real-life narratives about what can "go legally haywire" with perfectly good business situations that was ever put into so little space. My guess is you'll agree after you have read it. And if you do, it will more than justify my entirely selfish motive in offering it —namely, to place one more goodwill builder for our Institution and its work where it will be most appreciated.

Here are a few instances of the bill of fare offered. Don't they suggest how rich the booklet is in food for serious business reflection?

> —the banker who should have written on his cuff, and didn't
> —the outlawed million francs that Baron Rothschild collected
> —the clubman who thought he had bought a $40,000 piece of real estate...only he hadn't
> —the bank whose birthday mistake cost $6,000
> —the coal company that had to pay $70 for a window it didn't break
> —the jeweler who left his name on another man's check and paid $2,000 for the privilege
> —the refinery that became an abandoned warehouse because a big executive "took something for granted"
> —the $5,000 that Benjamin Franklin's will turned into $1,631,000...and so on.

Every day your own duties present some aspect of the legal side of business to your attention; and if the subject of Law has ever appealed to you at all, I think you'll get an added "kick" out of this "Legal Kinks" booklet.

If you would like a copy, without obligation, simply have your secretary return the enclosed card.

Cordially yours,

The Chain in this letter carpentered by L. R. Alwood is superb. The facts are fired with machine-gun speed. "The banker who should"...bang! "The outlawed million francs"...bang! "The clubman who thought"... bang! "The bank whose birthday—the coal company that had to pay"... bang, bang! "The jeweler who left"—"the refinery that became"—"the $5,000 that Benjamin Franklin"...bang, bang, bang! When a letter *moves so fast,* there is no time for the reader to think of quitting. More than 16 per cent of those on the list replied, asking for the booklet, so beyond any question, the mailing was a big success.

However, there is no harm in wondering if that percentage might not have been higher, had two small changes been made—one in the Star and the other in the Hook. "On my desk is a booklet that should be yours." That is an interesting statement. The reader promptly asks himself, "What *kind* of a booklet?" But the question which follows seems to let the cat out of the bag—"*May* I send it to you?" So the reader could say, "There's a catch in this letter. He is asking my *permission* to send me the booklet." That *could* cause some people to stop reading, and who knows—perhaps it did.

The other possible error occurs in the Hook. As you will discover later in this section, "if" is a negative word when used in asking for action. "*IF* you would like a copy" means "perhaps you do, or perhaps you don't." The last sentence, then, would have been stronger had it read—"For *your* copy, simply have your secretary return the enclosed card"—thus implying no doubt that the booklet *would* be wanted.

But why criticize success? Has anything ever been written that might not have been made better?

A strong Chain forged by Jackson. Another letter which rates high in letter "flow" is one used by Merrill M. Jackson, of Kansas City, Missouri. It is especially noteworthy for the short sentences, the simple language, the interesting introduction, and the pile-driver speed with which the links in the Chain are put together. Before the latter starts to develop interest, two cards are played to win attention—the mention of the dog, "Snooks," and of the famous book which so many people have read. Also, a small picture of "Snooks" is attached.

> Good Morning Folks:
>
> My friend "Snooks" has never read Dale Carnegie's book—but she certainly knows how to make friends and influence people. She "ain't" got a thing but a bark, a cute little wiggle, and a heap of curiosity. She has never met a stranger in her life. She has the idea that if she's friendly she will get along. It's quite an idea —for it makes her life pleasant. It brings her plenty of attention, car rides and a good living.

Your ideas may do as well for you. For a good idea is the most potent thing on earth. An idea built Ford's business. Ideas built Katz and Luzier's. Ideas win wars. Here are a few brand new ideas that are building business today. Money making ideas! Ideas that are making jobs! Ted Ruhling of Independence, Missouri, has a new idea for fish stringers. He's selling loads of them.

George T. Cummings has a new portable vise, weighs less than four pounds. Can be carried in a tool kit, a car or a truck! It is stronger than any wrench. Every one who sees it wants it. The artist who retouched the photo bought four. My foreman bought one. My wife bought one for her brother-in-law, who has a home work-shop. Jobbers are buying them 500 at a clip.

Brunson has a "fishing gadget." Attach it to the end of the line! The instant the fish nibbles "Bingo" the hook is set. Fishermen are buying 'em as fast as Brunson can make them. Jobbers are flooding him with orders.

You may say, "Heck, those are all gadgets—nothing serious." O. K., my friend, Cheek has an improved wheel-barrow. The only real improvement for years! The load is perfectly balanced. A simple release automatically dumps the load. This makes all present wheelbarrows obsolete. So I still say that ideas make business, make jobs, make money.

Maybe a new idea will help sell your deal. A new approach: it could be a premium deal. A cooperative advertising campaign! A house organ! A mail order campaign! Your dealers, agents and distributors will need help. Perhaps your salesmen can't see them all. Direct-by-mail campaigns will help them.

There are many ways to use mail advertising. Why not find out just how it can help YOU? Our business is planning, writing and producing effective mail campaigns. If you're too busy, we'll do the mailing. In fact, we'll take care of all the details for you—get your mailing list if you wish.

So, my friend, it's a good idea to call HA6400 and ask for Jackson—or drop the card in the mail

Yours Merrill-y,
Merrill M. Jackson

P. S.   Printing by Jackson is a good idea, too. Have Jackson do yours. Fast automatic presses! Hurry-up service! Lowest prices!

"When you Advertise—Jacksonize"

Yes, there are faults in this letter. It's good that you are catching them. You are becoming a real letter-carpenter when you can. The twice used "my friend" might rub some readers the wrong way. But Mr. Jackson is **not** trying to curry favor. You would understand that if you knew him. He *feels* friendly. He writes as he talks. His personality is very much revealed in the letter, as you know by now it should be.

The postscript also is questionable. Postscripts usually are. This one tends to take the reader's mind from direct mail to run-of-the-mill printing. Thus it competes with the chief objective of the letter. This is not good sales psychology. Hammer on *one* thing—hammer it home. One big bullet shot from a rifle straight to the mark has much more power than a thousand pellets blown from a shot-gun. We'll concede that point. In this letter at least, the postscript does more harm than good.

But the Chain is a fast-stepper. It leads the reader swiftly from one money-making idea to another. Subconsciously, he begins to visualize what a good idea might do for *him*. Because that mental image is pleasing, he may do as requested—mail the card or telephone. Anyway, he is more in the mood for action at the end of the Chain than at the beginning. The Chain has quickened interest—and that's its job.

Another possible fault is that the introduction about the dog and the book are only remotely related to the message that follows. Thus, the Star gets attention, as it must, but there is no "carry-over" to the Chain; probably "Snooks" was forgotten long before the letter ended.

But these are minor errors in carpentry. The Chain is strong. No doubt the letter brought business back to Jackson.

In later sections, you will hear much about the Chain. At present, we will pause to examine the Hook.

6. The Hook for Action

The letter's climax. The Star gets attention. The Chain develops interest and desire. So at last, with those parts of the job completed, the letter-carpenter reaches the climax of his efforts. It is time for the Hook— that confident, forceful ending which makes the letter a success.

As you know, it would be folly to call any one of the three parts more important than the others. But we can agree on the utter *finality* of the Hook. It is then that the reader says "yes" or "no." No second-shots are allowed. When the letter is signed, and goes to Uncle Sam, the die is cast.

> The moving finger writes, and having writ
> Moves on: nor all thy piety nor wit
> Shall lure it back to cancel half a line,
> Nor all thy tears wash out a word of it.

Thus, thinking only of sequence, you could give the Hook the nod. It is the part of the letter that either carries the ball over for the touchdown, or leaves it short of the goal. You have seen football teams that seemed able to do everything but score. They could march up and down the field at will, but couldn't produce that one final punch. Well, many letters are like that. They start beautifully, sweep rapidly forward, and then stumble at the end. The trouble seems to be one of timidity—lack of confidence. The letter-carpenter works with precision until the time to ask for action—then he loses his nerve.

When doubt is catching. The end of the letter is, of course, the very worst place for any lack of confidence as to how the reader is going to react. He stands at the crossroads, still a little undecided on which path to take. Doubt is catching. If the writer implies lack of confidence in his own presentation, why should the reader take the step alone? Consider these closing paragraphs taken from actual business letters:

> We *hope* with the above facts in mind you will be favorably impressed with our proposition, and that we will soon receive your order.

> *If* you wish to give us a trial order, please be assured it will be appreciated.

> Now is the time when our customers are stocking for summer business. We *trust* you will join them by placing your requirements on the enclosed order blank.

> We appreciate your patience in reading this somewhat long letter, but it was necessary that you understand the many advantages of our service. *May* we now have the pleasure of sending our representative to see you?

In each of those flimsy Hooks, a negative word reveals that the writer is not at all sure of the reaction he is going to get. They are the "fatal four" that tend to defeat the purpose of any business letter.

> We HOPE you will be favorably impressed.

> IF you wish to give us a trial order.

> We TRUST you will join them.

> MAY we have the pleasure of sending our representative?

There they are, words that hold the reader back at the very moment when he needs a confident push forward—HOPE, IF, TRUST, and MAY. Never "hope" or "trust" for action. KNOW you are going to get it. Never say "if" or "may" because then you are confessing doubt in your own mind, and letting the reader decide what to do. Note the difference in these Hooks.

Weak....... "We trust that this price will meet with your favor. Hoping to have the pleasure of shipping you the range soon, we remain, respectfully yours,"

Strong...... "To save you time, a duplicate copy of this letter is enclosed. Just initial and return it to us, using the stamped envelope. You can then have the range to enjoy by the end of next week."

Weak....... "Considering the quality of our line, we feel our prices are reasonable. If you would like to have our salesman call with samples, please so advise."

Strong...... "When you buy our quality, you get more for your dollar than any other way. Jack Cook, a fellow you are going to like, will be around next Monday morning to show you samples, and service your order."

Weak....... "We feel you must realize this bill should be paid, as you have had the goods a long time and should appreciate our patience. If you agree this is only fair, we shall hope for a check soon."

Strong...... "There comes a time when patience is no longer a virtue, and the lawyers take over. Frankly, we now expect our money, and shall look for a check from you not later than Saturday."

Weak....... "If you will O.K. the card, we will gladly send you a copy of the bulletin. Trusting you will do this,"

Strong...... "Your copy of this interesting bulletin is waiting for you. Just O.K. and mail the card."

The difference in those Hooks is so apparent that it scarcely needs comment. The weak ones are very timid; they do not encourage *action*. The others are positive and confident; they *tell the reader* what he is expected to do.

Perhaps you think this is too commanding—that such a positive tone might be resented. That means you are overlooking the psychological background of the Star, the Chain, and the Hook. Remember, at first the reader is cold and casual. The hold on him is quite easily broken. So you "start easy and work up"—seeking only to increase interest until it becomes desire. In the early part of the letter, you wouldn't dare tell the reader what to do. That would be the quickest way to lose him. But as you go from point to point, as the fire blazes higher, a psychological change occurs in the reader's mind. He is now genuinely interested—he has confidence in what you are saying. He is more emotional—less rational. You can throw caution to the wind as you approach the Hook. It's time for "do" or "don't." The cat is out of the bag. The reader knows what you want. *Ask for it.* Not with "if" or "may" or "trust" or "hope," but with every indication that you KNOW the victory has been won.

You can soon convince yourself that the Hook demands a positive tone by examining the best sales letters that cross your desk. You will find without exception that courteously but firmly you are *told* what to do. Let's prove it. Here are the closing sentences of twenty-five successful letters chosen at random. Notice how they all ask for action, without limitation or equivocation—and not one "if" or "hope" or "trust" or "may" in the whole lot!

Send no money—simply mail the card.

We take all the risk—mail your order today.

Keep this letter as your guarantee, and mail the handy card—TODAY.

Be sure to get the enclosed order blank in the mail immediately.

Do not delay—do it today.

Simply check and return the card today.

Don't disappoint me—I shall expect your check by return mail.

Tear off the coupon and mail it with your order at once.

Put your check in the enclosed envelope, and mail it before you forget.

There is no red tape about it—simply mail the card.

Defy the summer slump by using the enclosed envelope.

So do the right thing by yourself   mail the card today.

Don't bother to write a letter. Just drop the card in today's mail.

Return the card now while you have it on your mind.

Just O. K. the card, and tell your secretary to be sure it is mailed promptly.

You will save yourself embarrassment by getting a check to us this week.

On the enclosed card let us know what you want.

Our supply is limited—use the blank today.

No satisfaction—no charge. Send no money. Simply mail the card.

There are no strings to this offer—just wire how many.

Your credit is good. Tell us what you need.

The card, mailed at once, will start the ball rolling.

It's your move. A telegram will get the order to you in ten days.

Come, come. Send a check immediately, so we can both stop worrying about this account.

The minute you tell us what you will need, the best assortment will be reserved for you. But tell us today.

Don't order your Spring stock until Bert Bemis gets to your store. He is worth waiting for, and will be in to take your order by the 15th.

No effort was made to sort these letters by purpose or style. If they are at all similar, it is because the writers were skilled in letter carpentry, and used the technique that they knew would get the best results.

Stilted endings break the charm. Remembering that the function of the Hook is to get quick action before the reader has a chance to cool off, you can understand why whiskers are taboo in the close of a business letter. Many a letter, otherwise good, is spoiled when the writer, by force of habit, thinks he must sign off with one of the old-time conventional phrases.

The following letter is quite bright and interesting, except for the rather tepid conclusion.

Dear Miss Ruhl:

It's Springtime...glorious Springtime here in the mountains...

...and that means handclasps, smiles, and greeting old acquaintances here at Sunrise Lodge. For at this marvelous season of the year many of our old friends visit us for a week-end, or a whole week of relaxation in the sublime beauty and restfulness of Spring in the famous Blue Ridge Mountains.

All nature seems to be saying "Welcome back to Sunrise Lodge" and with Easter coming so late this year you can spend a most enjoyable Easter week-end at Sunrise!

Our season will open on Friday, April 19th. Decide now to be among those present during the colorful Easter opening... renewing fond friendships here at Sunrise Lodge.

I have not missed a Springtime here in the mountains for thirty-five years, and I can't recall that the surrounding hills and valleys were ever more beautiful than they are this Spring. The vast panorama of nature's richest green and brown is a fairyland of enchanting colors. So you will surely enjoy your restful visit to Sunrise Lodge more than ever before.

The rates are very modest—$60.00 a week and up for single rooms and meals, or $10.00 daily.

Write to me immediately for your Easter reservations, or 'phone BU 7-1135, and I will have everything in readiness for you.

> [This is where the letter should have stopped.
> The urge for action has been made—and it is
> positive. But no, the writer was not content.

> So a new sentence drags in another sales point
> apart from Easter, and then a second sentence
> beginning with "May" spoils the positive urge
> for action.]

You *might* also let me make reservations now to assure your
favorite room for your summer vacation.

May I have the pleasure of hearing from you in the near future?

Cordially yours,

There is absolutely nothing that can be said in favor of stilted, moth-eaten language when used *any* place in a business letter. You have accepted that fact from the discussion in Section 2, and you will never be guilty of the practice in your own letters. But these old-time whiskers are particularly harmful at the time when action is being requested. The reader has been carefully nursed along through the early stages of attention and interest. As the Hook is reached, he is as close to saying "yes" as he ever will be, but he is still undecided, torn between desire and caution. And then, at this extremely delicate point in the psychological process, along comes a sentence so stiff and meaningless that the effect is like pouring a glass of ice-water down the reader's back. That is exactly what happened in the letter selling Sunrise Lodge. The climax was reached in "and I will have everything in readiness for you." That was a confident assertion. The writer *expected* favorable reaction. Period! So it would have seemed had he stopped there. But then came the glass of ice-water—"*May* I have the pleasure of hearing from you in the near future?"

So often you hear it said: "I never know what to say at the end of my letters," as if when the job is done there still must be a final flourish. This is nonsense, but it probably explains why so many business letters are handicapped by a totally unnecessary closing sentence, done in the best style of 1776, when men wore buckled shoes, knee breeches, and powdered wigs. The time to stop is when you've "had your say." Anything additional is superfluous, and only tends to chill the interest you have worked so hard to develop in the mind of the reader. If you, too, are one of those who "never know what to say" to finish off your letters, here is the answer to your problem. It's quite simple—say *nothing*. To prove that's good advice, consider this final example—the close of a letter soliciting club memberships.

> It costs nothing to be one of us. You simply pay $30.00 a year,
> and get twelve good meals for your money. There is nothing
> more to spend. So fill out the application blank, and return it
> with your check. Do this right away, so you can be with us
> next Wednesday.

Not a bad Hook, is it? The job is done. Put away your tools, Mr. Letter-Carpenter. You will probably get the check, and greet a new member next Wednesday. But wait a minute. What's this strange stuff you have added?

> Thanking you for your kind consideration of the advantages of membership in our organization, and trusting you will see your way clear to acceptance of this invitation, we remain, yours very truly,

Ho, hum, fiddle-de-dum! Another letter spoiled by that impulse to add just a little bit more. And what a contrast there is between the tone of the first paragraph, and the fish-market smell that pervades the second. Could it possibly be the same man that wrote both of those paragraphs? Why not? You see numerous examples of the same sort in every-day business correspondence.

Avoid the divided urge. It is a trait of human nature that if a man is told to do *one* thing, he may go ahead and do it, but if given the choice of *two* things, he is quite likely to do neither. An understanding of this fact will prevent a very common mistake in closing business letters—the divided urge for action. The following Hook taken from a collection letter illustrates the common fault of a divided appeal:

> Five dollars a week will clean up the balance in one year. If you cannot make payments that large, then send us three dollars every week—or, start with one dollar if that's the best you can do. At least, it is only fair that you should write us when you will start to reduce this debt.

All right, what has the credit man told his reader? Pay five dollars a week, or three dollars, or one dollar—or at least write and tell us when you will start paying. With such a divided plea before him, to which of the four suggestions is the debtor likely to respond? Probably none of them.

Examine these three closings:

> Let me tell you more about the convenience and comfort, the time and money-saving advantages of——service. Just return the enclosed card, marked for my personal attention—or call your local office, any hotel, travel bureau, or telegraph office for full information.

> Don't lose a minute. Write us a letter, telegraph, or send the enclosed card right now. If you are not ready to decide now, then please drop in to see us the next time you are in our city.

And now, during March only, you can save 5%. Simply give us your order now, for delivery as late as March 30, if you wish. See your painter right away if you want his advice, or I will be glad to call and tell you exactly what paint your home should have. Phone 7–3355. Or the enclosed card mailed will take care of everything.

In no one of these three Hooks is the suggested action specific or impelling. Instead, the many suggestions tend to confuse the readers, so that no *one best thing* is left for them to do. Thus, the situation facing the letter-carpenter as he decides what action to urge is somewhat the same as when he uses his garden hose. He may turn the nozzle to produce a strong stream of water that lands with force on a small spot, or he may turn it to produce a fine spray which gently covers a wide area with no immediate effect. It is the single, forceful stream that does the best job in the Hook. Of the many forms of action that might be requested in closing any letter, there should be one that stands out above the rest as probably the most acceptable to the reader. Concentrate your power of persuasion on that *specific* suggestion. Remember this point, because it is very important. Beware of the divided urge.

Use "dated" action. Here is a tip for letter-writers which is in no sense experimental or untried. It *works*. When used in your letters it *will* increase their pull. This simple device adds power to collection letters, sales letters, follow-up letters, or any other letters that ask for reader reaction. It has been thoroughly tried and tested. Use *dated action.*

What *is* dated action? Well, instead of telling your reader what to do in a general or vague fashion, as so often happens in business letters, *set a time limit.* Tell him *when* the reply is expected.

We will expect this check not later than *next* Saturday.

An *immediate reply by airmail* will enable us to ship your order day after tomorrow.

We must hear from you by *June 1.*

Doctor, in order to handle this claim promptly for your patient, it will be necessary to have your preliminary report by the *end of this week.*

Joe, be sure to give us this information along with the Daily Sales Record that you mail us *Thursday evening.*

This letter leaves for your city this evening. By using the enclosed stamped airmail envelope, you can get your reply back to us on *Friday.*

The lawyers will be ready to take over week after next. You still have ten days—until *December 31*—to spare yourself this trouble.

There is something about a *dated* request for action that makes it preferable to the one which goes at the job in a more general way.

Please let us have your reply at your *earliest convenience*.

Your *prompt* reaction to this proposition will be appreciated.

We shall expect to receive this report in the *near future*.

A check *without delay* is necessary to put your account in proper order.

Return the order blank *soon* so that no sales will be lost.

Such generalities sound all right, but apparently they do not prod a reader to quick action. In fact, do they *ask* for it? How early *is* "earliest convenience"? How near *is* the "near future"? How soon *is* "soon"? You see, generalities are hard to pin down. To one hundred people you can say, "not later than June 1," and they all know exactly how much time has been allowed. To the same group, "in the near future," might be interpreted in many ways, depending on the disposition and time-habits of each individual. Furthermore, when a *specific date* is suggested, the obligation of meeting that date tends to form in the reader's mind. It is something definite to remember. He has been told what to do and *when*. Quite often, he *does* it.

In this connection, the experience of an insurance company in Massachusetts is enlightening. One of the thorns in the flesh of this company was the time it took to get reports from examining physicians who were located all over the country. By test, over a three months' period, it was determined that after a certain blank was mailed, it was necessary, on the average, to follow each doctor 3.7 times by letter to get the blank back to the home office. In the department handling these follow-ups, eight full-time girls were employed. Only generalities were used to ask for action, such as, "We know you are busy, doctor, but won't you please get this blank back to us as *soon as possible?*"

Then it was decided to try *dated* action. All of the closing paragraphs in the follow-up letters were revised accordingly. The department head was willing to give the idea a trial, but he was quite sure it would make no difference. That opinion, however, he was very happy to change after another three-month test. With the action *dated,* the same follow-up letters were reduced to an average of 2.1 times per blank mailed. Not only were three girls transferred from the department, but clients with claims were given quicker service.

When preparing the Hook for your next letter—sales, collection, or otherwise—be sure to ask for *dated* action. Say WHEN it is expected.

Make the action as easy as possible. Probably it is true that human beings tend to follow the path of least resistance. Hence, in asking for action at the close of a business letter, common sense tells us to spare the reader as much time and bother as possible. How often are we tempted to say "yes" after reading a fast-moving, interesting letter, only to hesitate and then push it aside because at the end we are asked to fill out a long blank, answer a questionnaire, or just go to the bother of replying by letter? How often, on the other hand, do we say "yes" because there is only a card to sign, with the postage taken care of—nothing to do but put the thing in the mail?

The majority of the people you meet will tell you that they don't like to write letters, and perhaps this is understandable when you remember that eight steps must be taken to dictate and mail one. Do you doubt that? Well, count them:

1. Dictate, or write in longhand
2. Proofread for errors
3. Add the signature
4. Fold and enclose
5. Seal the envelope
6. Address it
7. Fix the stamp
8. Mail

Just a lot of little things to do, except the dictation or writing, but a ten to twenty minute job just the same, and big enough to cause many a letter never to be answered.

You are, of course, familiar with the devices used by letter carpenters to make action easy. The most common is an already-addressed card that needs only initials or a signature. When the postage is prepaid that's all the better. The enclosing of a stamped and addressed envelope is another action producer, especially if genuine United States postage stamps are used instead of the permit privilege. Receiving a stamp is, to most people, no different than receiving the equivalent in money. How, then, can an honest person keep the stamp and not reply? Of course, it can be argued that the reader didn't ask for the stamp, and is not bound to return it. That is true, but nevertheless there does seem to be a moral obligation to *use* the stamp.

Another very good plan for easing the reader's burden in making the expected reply is to tell him, "Just *initial* the carbon copy of this letter, put it in the stamped envelope, and it will come back to us in a jiffy." A busy man appreciates such an act of consideration. He initials the carbon copy, hands it with the envelope to his secretary, and his part of the job is done.

When order blanks are enclosed, they should be made as "short and sweet" as possible, with specifications already typed in, unless these are subject to the will of the reader.

Requesting that a telephone number be called, easy as the task may be, is not always a suggestion that wins favorable response. Some people shrink from a telephone call for fear that pressure may be put on them when the connection is made. We know of no test to prove it, but in our opinion a letter asking that a card be returned will usually outpull one asking for telephone calls.

In comparative analysis, the value of these plans to make action *easy* must depend on such variable factors as the nature of the problem at hand, the relationship between writer and reader, and those other conditions which are never fixed or static. The letter-carpenter builds to fit the particular time and need.

BUSINESS LETTER MECHANICS

BUSINESS LETTER MECHANICS

1. First Impressions

Fine feathers make fine birds. In the previous section when we had the Star under the microscope, we found that letters, like people, make a first impression which may or may not be helpful when the final effect is weighed. Since the factors which contribute to this first impression can be controlled, and may be as perfect as you are willing to make them, they can very properly be called the "mechanics" of letter-writing. There is no reason in the world why the correspondence of any company cannot enjoy the advantages of a good-looking letterhead, precision typing, and those other features that help to present a pleasing appearance. Anything short of this ideal can only be attributed to the indifference or ignorance of those responsible.

Furthermore, the attainment of distinction in appearance is not an item of great expense, because it may often cost just as much to prepare and mail sloppy, unattractive letters as those others which reflect pride and quality. True, the initial expense of a fine letterhead, designed and printed by craftsmen, may be higher than that of one which is cheap and commonplace, but the difference is many times offset by the better reception it is sure to get. The other factors, mostly in the hand of the typist, have no expense angle, and depend simply on the standard of performance which is considered acceptable. It costs no more to type fifty good-looking letters than to type fifty inferior ones. In fact, the girl who takes pride in her work is more likely to exceed the production of the one who is careless and not at all interested in making each letter reflect top quality.

We may therefore agree that the appearance of a company's letters depends largely on the attitude of those "higher-ups" who have the

177

authority to set the standards and to insist that they be met. If the president, the department head, and the dictator are not sufficiently interested to make sure that the letters reflect the same quality claimed for the company's products, then obviously the standards will be low and the performance inferior. But when you encounter an organization where the crusade for better letters has adequate leadership, plus the willingness to supply modern equipment, it is sure to follow that those of the rank and file are encouraged to do their best to keep in step.

It is hard to understand why any business executive would *not* want the letters of his company to make a pleasant first and *last* impression. When we remember, as was explained in Section 1, that letters are definitely a part of public relations, we realize that any indifference toward them is a form of business negligence. This, of course, is a condition not found in business as a whole, although there are still many lamentable examples of companies handicapping their own public relations with letters written on old-fashioned letterheads, typed in a slam-bang manner, and giving off an odor of indifference which smells to Heaven.

"Costly thy raiment as thy purse can buy...rich but not gaudy...for the apparel oft proclaims the man," said Polonius to his son. "Costly thy letters as thy purse can buy...rich but not gaudy...for the appearance oft proclaims the company," says Good Judgment to the business executive.

Impression begins with the envelope. This is not the place to discuss the various types of envelopes used in business, the value of color, or the different kinds of postage, but it is important that we recognize the relation of the envelope to the reader's first impression of a business letter. This reader may be a housewife who has just taken the letter from the box hanging outside the door, a farmer just in from the field he is plowing, or a businessman who prefers to open his own mail when he gets to his office. In any case the letter is unread, for the envelope must still be opened. For a few fleeting seconds, only that envelope speaks for the writer or the company he serves.

In some cases, this envelope may be a "dead giveaway." The recipient can tell at a glance that it is a form letter or circular. Designed to look like an ordinary sealed envelope, it has one end open, which seldom deceives anybody. Instead of the five-cent stamp, which would indicate a first-class letter, there is the insignia for the smaller amount bulk rate. The name and address are obviously stamped from a stencil. Everything on the envelope plainly says: "You are getting this letter because your name was on the list." Moreover, as is so often the case with these mass mailings, the paper and the printing are cheap and "circular" looking.

"Huh!" the recipient says to himself, "Somebody else wants to sell me something I don't want. Couldn't be important or it would have been mailed first-class. Why bother to read it?" And he *doesn't.*

In pleasing contrast is the letter which arrives in an envelope made of good quality paper, the name and address typed neatly and correctly, and a five-cent stamp giving it an air of importance. The "feel" of the paper is good, the typed address is flattering, and the stamp says "Personal." The letter inside may turn out to be a form mailing, but the man with the envelope in his hand cannot know it. There is always something rather exciting about getting a personal letter, especially if the name of the company is unknown to the recipient. "Who are they?" he asks. "Wonder what they want? Guess I'd better open it and see." And he *does.*

Naturally, you know that open-end envelopes that travel at a lower postage rate have a service to perform in the business world. You also know that stenciling machines and postage-meters are necessary for certain purposes. But there can be no argument about the comparative pull of a letter which travels first-class and one that takes advantage of these mass-production devices. For best results, when the cost is not prohibitive, use an envelope that speaks for quality, seal it, personalize the address, and up in the right-hand corner put one of Uncle Sam's genuine five-cent postage stamps. If you really want to attract the attention that transcends all others, make that an air-mail stamp.

Two letters of contrasting appearance. The impression made by the envelope is only the first hurdle that must be taken if the attention of the reader is to be retained. The second is the one made by the letter itself when it is unfolded. Here again, the cause may be lost if that first glance is displeasing. What the letter *says* might be interesting and convincing, but it is worthless unless the recipient decides to read it. This he is not likely to do, unless there is something in that first impression to gain favorable attention.

For example, on the following pages are two letters, one to sell neckties, and another extending an invitation to discuss insurance. Examine them as if you had just drawn them from the envelopes. Irrespective of copy, which you have not started to read, what impressions do they make? We can guess your reaction.

The letter about the neckties resembles an old-time handbill—every inch of space crowded with a conglomeration of pictures, type of various kinds and sizes, and the inevitable coupon. All in all, the layout is about as horrible as anything you could imagine. The printed part is an eighth of an inch off register, and crooked. In the original, three of the ties, the coupon, and the printer's type are in a bright red, making the whole effect even worse than the reproduction.

Would you be likely to read this letter? We doubt it. You would judge the quality of the ties by the cheapness of the presentation, and unless we are mistaken the wastebasket would receive, but quickly, another example of poor salesmanship.

Too Many Illustrations Spoil the Whole Effect

"A Few Minutes . . .
A Profitable Investment"

    Today's economic conditions make it extremely important that a man's life insurance and his other property be arranged to provide maximum benefits for himself and his family.

    It is our obligation to help every life insurance owner achieve that goal. Therefore, we offer you our "Key to Security" service. The few minutes it takes to see the scope and value of the service will, we are confident, represent one of the most profitable investments you have ever made.

    Within a few days our representative, whose card is enclosed, will call on you to show you how the "Key to Security" will help provide the maximum benefits for yourself and your family.

                Sincerely yours,

                Agency Vice President

As Nearly Perfect as a Letter Could Be

But what about the insurance company letter? If you like the reproduction you would be even more impressed by the original. The paper is at least fifty per cent rag content, and the color is a pleasing gray. The letterhead is printed in black and red, and the letter is typed in the same colors— a perfect match. In contrast to the other letter, which ran all over the page and almost fell over the edges, this one has wide margins and is beautifully balanced. The entire ensemble reflects the quality of this company and its service. We cannot imagine a letter so pleasing to the eye being tossed into the wastebasket.

181

The sad part about the necktie letter is that the copy isn't bad; the language is natural, and the argument rather persuasive. But how many men would read it?

Perhaps you are saying that the average company would not care to use letterheads as expensive as this one belonging to the insurance company. That is true, although "expense" is only a relative term, and cannot be fairly estimated apart from results. The extra cost is insignificant when reduced to the unit cost of a sheet and envelope.

However, even when plain stock is used and the printing is a simple black on white, a letter can still be made to catch favorable first attention if the design of the letterhead is in good taste, and the printer and typist do their part. A letterhead plus typed copy can put its best foot forward gracefully without costing any more than one that stubs its toe.

It didn't practice what it preached. A few years ago, the owner of a printing firm in a Northwestern city decided to mail a sales letter to several thousand companies in the same area. As you can see, the emphasis in the message was on quality of work and service.

Gentlemen:

A VERY INTIMATE PERSONAL WORD...

Our press is a capable organization engaged in assisting a few select clients with their direct mail advertising.
In short our policy is—to do addressing, folding and mailing...
perfectly, promptly, and in such a satisfying manner that you will not only employ our services, but gladly recommend them to your most intimate business friends.

Just last week a large store in this city requested us to take charge of a small mailing. They were so completely satisfied with our work, that today we have been informed that hereafter all their direct mail pieces will be sent from our offices. Confidence like this must be deserved. It is the inevitable result of our policy— "NOT HOW MUCH BUT HOW WELL."

We hold convincing evidence that large corporations do appreciate honest service; that they welcome being treated as we would want them to treat us. Our old friends are long familiar with this policy; our new friends will cordially endorse it.

Your telephone provides an easy way for you to immediately ask any questions which may have occurred to you while reading this letter. Just call Main 4–6663 and we can talk about it right now.

Sincerely yours,

While the above copy is not outstanding, it does preach from start to finish a sermon of painstaking, dependable performance. But unfortunately, the letter—a sample of what it talked about—did not practice what it preached. The chief offender was the typist whose touch was so erratic that it could be called no touch at all. Some of the letters are barely visible; others stand out like sore thumbs. Adding to the general messy appearance is an error corrected in ink. The talk about fine workmanship is belied by the company's very unsightly sample.

The man who sent the letter was surprised when it did not pull any telephone calls. He vowed he would never send out another sales letter—it was plain that new business could be obtained only by personal solicitation. What he didn't realize was that to talk about quality is one thing, but to demonstrate it is another. He had the chance to sample his wares in a pleasing way, but he fumbled. The letter could not possible gain a favorable first impression. It is doubtful if many who were on the list to receive it even bothered to see what it said.

A letter which worked under exactly the same conditions, but far more effectively, is the one on page 184. Here, the writer, who signs himself as "One of the Folks," is attempting to sell business stationery of high quality. In one place he says: "Nothing can call attention to your name and product more quickly than a distinctive letterhead." Thus, he puts himself squarely on the spot, for unless his own letter makes a fine impression, the claim of quality is sure to backfire. This challenge was well met. The letterhead *is* distinctive, although the reproduction in one color does not reveal its full charm. In the original, the small building and surrounding square are in red; the rest is a pleasing gray. The combination is delightful to the eye. The copy seems to be multigraphed, although the "fill-in" is so well matched that the effect is one of a perfectly typed letter. The paper is of fine quality, and of twenty-pound weight.

In this case the writer also set out to sample his wares, but he made a *good job* of it. It is easy to predict that this sales letter did produce a satisfactory number of replies, and also proved that new business can be gained by mail solicitation.

2. LETTERHEADS

The two objectives. To be called *completely* adequate, a business letterhead should accomplish two purposes. The first is that of winning favor and prestige for the company by fine appearance. The second is to provide for the reader such information as he may need if convenient contact with the company is to be continued. The two purposes are not unrelated, since the necessary information must be woven into the layout without the sacrifice of charm, and that is not always an easy compromise. Granted that the utility purposes of the letterhead come first, and that certain factual information is a "must," it is also true that charm and simplicity go together. It is a needless handicap to clutter the layout with items that might just as well be omitted.

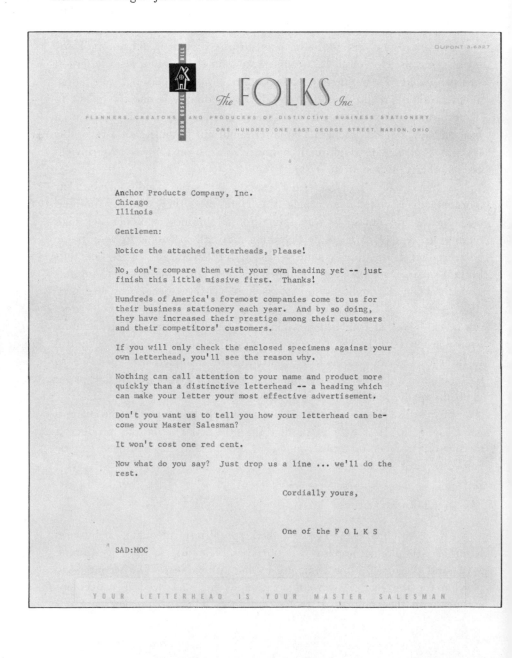

It is impossible to set forth any *one* combination of facts that all letter-heads should include. They vary according to the nature of the business, its location and prominence, and the judgment of the executives who must make the decision. In general, the following information may be considered necessary:

1. The full name of the firm or individual
2. Name of city and state
3. ZIP Code or zone number
4. Location or equivalent—such as street address, name of build-ing, or box number
5. Telephone number

In some cases, it is also advisable to identify the nature of the business —by a descriptive line, a commercial slogan, a trademark, or perhaps a picture of the product or building. It is scarcely ever necessary to use more than one of these identification devices, although you may have seen letterheads which run "hog-wild" with all of them. If not, be patient. We have some to show you.

The main idea back of the decision as to what information should be on the letterhead is that of *convenience* to the reader. Anything that at one time or another he may actually *need* should be provided for him. Anything else is likely to be an impediment to the other purpose, which is to make the letterhead as fine-looking as possible. Irrespective of what facts are finally selected to appear on the letterhead, the design and produc-tion should not be left to amateurs. There are experts who specialize in planning business letterheads, and money spent for their help is a wise investment. Once the design is chosen, it is likely to be used for several years, and it would be poor economy to save a few dollars at the sacrifice of interest-value and charm. Furthermore, the very best printer, lithographer, or engraver is none too good, no matter what the cost may be, when it comes to getting the perfect job you are after.

History of the business letterhead. An inspection of letterheads used only forty or fifty years ago will reveal the startling changes which have taken place in both form and content. In the Victorian days of coal-oil lamps, horse-drawn buggies, and stilted letter language, the average letter-head was a sight to behold. Not only was the printing and design extremely crude, but the items depicted included everything from "soup to nuts." Shaded letters, scrolls, flags, pictures of buildings and officials, all contributed to the confusion, and if a few clouds hovered over the whole that was the final touch of elegance. Plus all these pictorial effects, the names of company officials were often included, the date when the company was established, the date of incorporation, the amount of the capital and surplus, and whole paragraphs of information about terms, prices, and products. All in all, the result was a jumbled mess, but in those days it may have been considered quite distinctive.

English letterheads in the old style. As might be expected in a country where business relationships are maintained in a very formal and dignified way, many of the letterheads used in England resemble those of half a century ago in our own nation. This does not mean that our friends across the sea are lagging behind in business practice, but they do seem to cling more devoutly to certain traditions and customs. Possibly, to their way of thinking it would be almost sacrilege to tamper with a letterhead which has stood the test of a hundred years or more. The fact remains that English letterheads as a rule are more old-fashioned than our own, and hence, from our point of view, far less interesting. One sees the same characteristics that marked our own Gay Nineties—the shaded letters, trademarks, type of assorted faces, often set in curves, and a great abundance of factual information. An interesting side light about the language is that their letters usually end with "Yours faithfully," indicating a fondness for the expression in the country from which they came. This complimentary close was quite common in our pioneer days and until the turn of the century, but now rests in limbo, or wherever departing whiskers go.

Old-timers still common here. It would hardly be cricket to heckle our English friends about their letterheads, for we must admit that many of the old-fashioned conservative variety are still used in the United States.

The following letterheads are conspicuous for the limited space left for typing. This may be a subtle way of making sure that the dictators will not become too garrulous. Anyway, the allotment of space for copy seems too small for the business letter of average length. Of the 93 square inches on an 8½ by 11 inch sheet, the "Angostura" letterhead allows only 36 square inches for the address, salutation, body, complimentary close, and signature. But this might be called generous compared to another letterhead, not shown, where only 28 square inches, a little less than one-fourth of the total, are left blank. This may or may not be a world's record for cramping the length of a business letter. It would be interesting to know.

Of course, the reason for the overcrowding is obvious. The parties planning the letterhead had so many items they wanted to display, and each seemed so important, that they couldn't bring themselves to omit anything. There may even have been a debate in the office regarding the respective values of illustration and copy. Copy lost.

Letterheads are not catalogs or billboards. The illustration of a product or service on a business letterhead is not a bad idea if it can be done in good taste, and without violating the simplicity of the entire layout. You often see an attractive letterhead with a package or trademark a part of the general design—sometimes in color contrasting with that of the type. This is perfectly all right if the whole effect is pleasing, but the trouble is that too many letterheads are turned into catalogs or miniature billboards that offend the eye and destroy any chance of an attractive layout. After

187

all, the letter should do a bigger job than the letterhead. This is an impossibility if two thirds of the page is crowded with material competing for the reader's attention.

The mailing of the Graver-Dearborn Corporation is given a catalog appearance by the pictures of the prize items which run down the left side of the page. Take these pictures out, and the rest of the letterhead is both pleasing and distinctive. This was probably a special mailing, with the pictures added for the one purpose, but the result is quite displeasing to the eye. Also, because of limited space, the copy is printed with typewriter type of smaller size—and even then there is no margin on the right side. The entire page has an overstuffed appearance, and the first impression is not agreeable. In some cases the letter was probably tossed aside, because the reading of it looked like too much of an effort.

Why some executives hesitate to change. Certain businessmen cling to letterheads of ancient origin because they fear a change might result in loss to the company. They realize that the vehicle they are using is not attractive, and they would like to see it modernized. "But," they ask, "what would be the effect on sales?"

Then they go ahead with an old, old story—something like this. "The letterhead we are using has been known to our buying public for sixty years. In a pile of letters on the desk of a customer, it is recognized at first glance. It represents all of the goodwill we have been able to accumulate for the company during the many years we have been in business. This acceptance must be worth something to us. Why should we take the chance of starting all over again to develop this acceptance? After all, any long-established business has certain characteristics and trade practices which are traditional, and cannot be changed at the whim of the moment. Yes, we admit our letterhead is not modern as it would be if we were a new company. In the same sense, our company is old—very old—and we are proud of it."

This argument in favor of keeping the old letterhead would be quite convincing, except that the experience of other companies that *have* dared to make the change proves the weakness of the defense. There is nothing about a successful business that can be considered immune to the march of progress. If this were true, the argument for keeping an obsolete letterhead would apply with equal force to other "traditional" features of the company. Thus, deliveries would be made by horse-drawn trucks, packages would not be modernized and made more interesting for shelf display, windows and show-cases would be left as "they always have been," air-conditioning would be scorned, and new ideas ridiculed if they supplanted old ones. *And* soon spider-webs would be spun across the front doorways.

Any company that hopes to keep up with competition *must* change, and nothing warrants preservation unless it is still the *best* of its kind. To be sure, there probably are long-time customers who look fondly on a letterhead which has grown old with them. But to offset these few, are the many, many other people who may form the wrong impression of a company which clings to a peculiar old-fashioned letterhead. "This company can't be up-to-date," they think, "look at this funny, old-time stationery."

Fortunately, we do have the experience of those who have made the change to guide us, and we have never heard of any company that modernized its letterhead, used it for a while, and then went back to the old one. On the contrary, there is an abundance of evidence to prove that the modernization not only provoked favorable comment, but also led to increased sales.

A few years ago, a candy company in California had growing pains. A new letterhead was suggested, and finally adopted. But the president couldn't help wondering whether or not a mistake had been made. So a test was devised to find the truth. A list of old buyers who hadn't ordered for several months was split in two equal parts. To one half, a follow-up letter using the old stationery was mailed. To the other half, the same letter was mailed—on the new stationery. Nothing was said in the letter about the test. The readers did not know they were being used as guinea pigs. Thus, neither letterhead had any advantage over the other except for the difference in appearance, which might work either way.

What happened? At the end of thirty days, when the "votes" were counted, it was discovered that the old letterhead had pulled 15 per cent in replies, as against 40 per cent for the new one. Not all of the replies contained orders, but comparing those that did, the difference was even greater in favor of the new letterhead, the ratio being almost seven to one.

It pays to keep up-to-date. There can be no question about it. The company that sticks to an old-fashioned monstrosity is hindering rather than helping sales.

A guide for planning letterheads. Turning now from letterheads of the past, which are of interest only as something to be avoided, we can proceed with the more enjoyable task of surveying those which are modern, in order to find out what are the factors which contribute to their success.

A few years ago, John L. Scott, then editor of *The Printing Art Quarterly,* and a nationally known authority on letterhead design, offered ten questions to be used as a guide in determining the effectiveness of any business letterhead or in planning a new one. These questions are:

1. Is the letterhead appropriate to *your* particular type of business?
2. Is it distinctive—original—a letterhead that will be remembered?
3. Is it complete? Does it carry all the information—telephone, address, titles—the reader will need in replying?
4. Is it up-to-date? Modern? Does it suggest that your business is keyed to the tempo of the times?

5. Is it professionally designed by someone who knows what it takes to make a good job?

6. Is the paper suitable? Does it reflect good taste, quality, progress?

7. Is the letterhead adaptable to various kinds of letters—long and short—to bulletins, etc.?

8. Is it well printed? Are the colors vivid? Is the register perfect?

9. Is it designed to match the envelope?

10. Does it altogether speak for the spirit of your company, and the quality of your products?

You will agree that any letterhead would have to be good to meet the standards which Mr. Scott has established in these ten questions. Another step in the same direction is the Letterhead Rating Chart which was prepared for the benefit of friends and clients of the Whiting-Plover Paper Company of Stevens Point, Wisconsin. The plan of the chart is to grade the letterhead on each point, up to the maximum of 100. Then, by dividing the total of all the grades by 12 (the number of ratings) the final percentage is obtained. You will notice from the qualifying paragraph at the bottom of the chart, that the questions place the emphasis on the *utility* of the letterhead being rated, rather than on the more intangible factor of design. As the originator says, "The most beautiful letterhead, if deficient in the information it should convey, is not a good letterhead in the business world."

Choice of paper. Just as the beauty of a woman may be enhanced by the quality and style of the dress she wears, so may the appearance of a business letterhead be influenced by the choice of paper on which it is printed—its purity, its weight, and sometimes its color. Surely it is penny-wise and pound-foolish to skimp in the selection of paper for a company's stationery, since the best costs very little compared to the other items of expense in the preparation and mailing of a business letter. (See Section 1.) Moreover, although the difference in price between a cheap sulphite bond and a paper high in rag content amounts to a considerable sum when quoted by the pound, it is really nothing to worry about when reduced to single letter-sized sheets.

In this respect, another fact worth remembering is that from the point of view of reader reaction, and the good impression you want the letter to make, it may often be true that in the long run the best paper is the cheapest. Results are what count the most in business, and if the good paper does a better job, it can easily become the most economical.

Durability is also a factor that needs consideration. The cheaper papers, made entirely from wood, will not stand as much punishment in handling, or last nearly as long, as the better papers which are either all rag, or contain a high percentage of it.

The typist, too, deserves some consideration when the choice of paper is made. It is difficult to erase without leaving a smudge when the paper is thin and made from wood fiber, and many a letter is retyped that could have been saved had the paper been of better quality.

192

How quality of paper is determined. The three factors most important in measuring the quality of paper are: (1) content, (2) weight, and (3) the mill where it is made. The third point is often a matter of opinion, although it must be conceded that some mills do a better job than others. Thus, it is well to choose paper stock which comes from a mill of good reputation, rather than from one about which you know nothing.

The unit for measuring paper *weight* is a ream of folio size. This consists of 500 sheets, 17 by 22 inches. Each of these large sheets, when bisected both ways, produces four pieces of the conventional business letterhead size. Hence, when "20 pound paper" is mentioned, the meaning is that 2,000 sheets letterhead size weigh that much. In the same way, the weight of the ream, depending on the thickness of the sheets, may be 12 pounds, 16 pounds, 24 pounds, or a greater amount.

Twelve pound paper is very flimsy, and seldom used for business purposes. More business letterheads are printed on the 16 pound weight than on any other, although the 20 pound weight has a much better "feel" and deserves greater popularity. In many companies, letterheads on paper of different weight are provided for different uses. Thus, a 16 pound letterhead may be considered adequate for correspondence within the organization, a 20 pound letterhead used for letters to the general public, and a "superduper" 24 pound letterhead reserved for executives.

As has been intimated, the *content* of paper used for business purposes falls into one of three classifications: that made from wood fiber, that made from cotton fiber, or a combination of the two. The cheapest papers are "all wood"—of course, they are the least durable, and make the poorest impression. Newspapers, for example, are printed on paper made from wood pulp, and so are many of the inferior magazines. In contrast, the most durable and best-looking papers are made entirely from cotton fiber. Naturally, they cost the most. It is not necessary for letterhead uses, however, that the paper be "all rag." A mixture of about half and half produces a sheet that stands up well and is quite beautiful in appearance.

Compare a letterhead processed on "all wood" paper with one processed on a paper of at least fifty per cent rag content, and the difference in quality is easily discernible. The one with the high rag content is pure white and free from imperfections. The one made entirely from wood fiber looks gray and murky by the side of the other, and here and there are brown stains that could not be removed in the milling. The one is an aristocrat, the other a tramp, in the business world. One looks good, feels good, *is* good. The other is just another piece of paper, no different from many others that may now lie on your desk. It looks cheap, feels cheap, *is* cheap.

And yet, the difference in cost between sheets of the two kinds of paper may be no more, or even less, than a penny. Even the postage on a business letter is *five* cents. Doesn't it seem poor economy *not* to use paper for your letterhead which makes a fine impression, and speaks for the quality of your products and services?

Letterhead sizes. Having convinced ourselves that quality paper is a good investment, all things considered, our thoughts turn next to what size the letterheads should be. If general business practice is followed, the answer is 8½ by 11 inches. Four sheets that size can be cut without waste from a folio page, and that may be a minor argument for them. But there is no "law" or convention of business which prevents the use of another size if you happen to have a good reason, or even if you just like it better. Smaller sizes than the standard 8½ by 11 are not uncommon, although one is seldom seen any larger. For example, a size called "baronial" is often preferred by professional men, and sometimes used for the personal stationery of executives. Other variations are 8 by 11 inches, 7½ by 10½, 7 by 10 and "half sheets," eight of which are cut out of one folio page. But all of these departures from the 8½ by 11 size are merely ripples on the main body of water.

Frankly, we do not know how this "standard" size came to be the choice of Custom. But its use is now so universal that even filing devices and equipment conform to it. For this reason alone, there appears to be no good argument for a change. The size is practical, and most people seem to like it.

A good many of the letters that come from other English-speaking countries are typed on larger letterheads than our own. A sample is the one with the gun and the tiger, reproduced on page 196. The size of the original is 8⅞ by 12. The paper has an enamel finish, and the color is a light tan. This letterhead, by the way, leans toward the modern, although one flaw is the position of the gun, which seems to float in mid-air like a magician's suspended accomplice. The language, too, is far more "free and easy" than that of the average English letter, and even a cigarette is enclosed for the reader to smoke—a surprising bit of showmanship to come from "St. Mary's Row, Birmingham 4."

This larger letter, in its present condition, is an object lesson of what would happen if we started to use similar sizes in our country. Having been filed in a folder suitable for the 8½ by 11 letterheads, this English letter has had to take a lot of punishment. The edges are frayed, and in several places the page is torn.

As has been said, there seems to be no serious objection to the sizes smaller than our standard 8½ by 11. In fact, because they are *different,* they may have the advantage of claiming special reader-attention. However, even freedom of convention may travel too far from the beaten path, as seems to be the case with the letterhead used by a newspaper editor in Missouri. Here it is, one fourth the original size, to show the proportions.

The actual size of this letter is 6¼ by 11 inches. The stock is a pale blue, and the type is printed in red on a silver background. The general effect is startling, but not entirely pleasing. You might call it similar to seeing the "thin man" in the circus. Thin men may be more attractive than fat ones, but not, as with this letterhead, when they are only skin and bones.

Use of colored stock. Although white is preferred by a large majority of companies, this again is a matter of custom, and we often encounter an attractive business letterhead where tinted paper has been used. Some of these exceptions, especially those in the pastel shades, are very pleasing to the eye, and a delightful relief from the monotony of seeing everything in white. Others, from an unfortunate choice of color, would seem more appropriate for a carnival or circus than for a company that must operate with some dignity and restraint.

Certainly, there is plenty of evidence to prove that the average human being likes color, and is more pleased by the gay shades than by black or white. You see this fact reflected in the clothes we wear, the furnishings we select for our homes, and in many other ways. You may recall, for example, how one automobile manufacturer fought against colored bodies until the inroads made by competitors not so nearsighted forced him to change his mind. Look at the articles displayed by your grocer and you will see a mass of colors. Notice how the multi-colored advertisements in the magazines seem to get more attention than those in black and white. The love of color is deep-rooted in the human race, and businessmen may have been missing the boat in not using more of it in their letterheads and envelopes.

To be sure, color seems more appropriate for some types of business than for others. From a lawyer, a banker, a minister, an educator, or any company related to one of these professions, a letter on colored stationery would probably arouse unfavorable comment. A letter from a broker

Dear Sir,

      Will you do me a favour? It will not take you as long as it does to smoke a cigarette, and I am taking the liberty of sending this enclosed.

      I recently sent you my catalogue of sporting guns, and I am anxious to discover why I have not been favoured with your order.

      Do not bother to write a letter, jot your remarks on the margin of this one, then slip in attached envelope, no stamp necessary, I pay postage.

Have you yet reached a decision regarding your new gun?

If not, may I hope to be favoured with your order?

If not, will you kindly give a reason?

I am anxious to discover whether my prices are wrong, or if the models offered do not appeal to you - in what way they should be modified to suit you.

      I should be happy to do anything possible to meet your requirements by an adjustment of prices or terms, and your reply will help me a lot.

               Yours faithfully,
                 for W.W.GREENER LTD.

English Letterhead Interesting to Sportsmen

offering an investment in stocks or bonds would surely be handicaped if typed on colored stationery. Somehow, we expect certain professions and types of business to lean toward the conservative side, and any swing the other way is usually a dangerous experiment.

On the other hand, things bright and gay seem quite in keeping with other kinds of business activity—millinery stores, dealers in sports apparel, florists, candy manufacturers, gift shops, landscape gardeners, paint merchants, and the many, many others that you could add. Even when color seems appropriate, one shade may be better suited to a certain field of business than to another. For example, paper in a soft tint of blue might be ideal for the milliner, a canary yellow for the florist, and a light green for the landscape gardener. Even those selections, however, are strictly a matter of personal opinion.

As in almost every other phase of business correspondence, and its related problems, the question of when to use a color, and of what color is best, can only be decided by good taste and sound judgment. It is important that businessmen always keep their minds open toward color possibilities, and that they do not turn their backs on a use that might be highly productive. After all, if a company can get a higher percentage of replies—to sales letters especially—using tinted stationery, then why should it stubbornly stick to the white?

Showmanship from use of special materials. Now and then a business letter gains added attention because it is *not* written on one of the customary paper stocks. Instead, in the spirit of showmanship, some other material is substituted. When the reason for the substitution is not farfetched, this idea can be very effective. The best of the breed, of course, are those in which the material used is an actual sample of the thing talked about in the letter.

For example, a letter mailed to school superintendents by the Omaha School Supply Company arouses immediate curiosity and interest because the copy is processed—apparently by multigraphing—on an 8½ by 11 inch piece of window-shade cloth. The fill-in of the address and salutation is perfectly done, so that the whole effect is that of a personally typed letter. The best part of this idea, however, is that the piece of window-shade cloth is a *sample* of the product which the letter seeks to sell. Note the first paragraph:

> This letter, which is written on DuPont "Tontine" washable
> window-shade cloth, color 508 Afterglow, will introduce you to
> a window shade that admits light without glare.

In another paragraph, the use of the sample is given even better significance, when the writer suggests that it be put to a number of tests to prove its quality:

> "Tontine" is the last word in window-shade economy, cleanliness,
> and durability. It can be scrubbed clean as often as soiled and
> it will not crack, pinhole or fade. Scrub it—scuff it—boil it.
> Do the same for other types and see for yourself.

A second letter that does the same double job—winning attention by an unusual approach, and sampling the product—is one used by Hoff &

Company in Reading, Pennsylvania. It is one of the many clever letter ideas that have originated in the offices of advertising agents Beaumont, Heller, & Sperling. The piece of paper towel has rough edges, and is the size of a .section that might have been torn from a roll in actual use. Here again, the first paragraph justifies the showmanship:

> HERE'S NEWS, MR. ROGERS...It's an Announcement sure to interest you! It may be the first letter you've received on a paper towel, but then this letter is about the finest paper product on the market, and I'm sending my message right on that paper as PROOF.

Still more spectacular, but equally appropriate, is a letter once used by the Inland Steel Company, Chicago. You can imagine the surprise of anyone who got this message, when he pulled from a large envelope a letterhead-size sheet of metal on which the copy was quite plainly printed. Of course, no attempt was made to fill in the name and address of the recipient, but in the excitement of getting such an unusual letter, it is doubtful if that made any difference. Here is how it starts:

> A word
> concerning our
> new 44″ Mill
>
> Dear Sir:
>
> This sheet is one of the first rolled on our new 44″ Continuous Strip Mill, and cold reduced on our latest type cold finishing mill.
>
> Our new 44″ Continuous Strip Mill, which has just been completed and placed in operation, is the result of the growing demand for Inland uniform quality sheets. . . .

On another special "paper", perhaps a piece of percale, the sales manager of Appleford Paper Products Limited sent the letter below as a follow-up to prospects who had ignored previous sales attempts. Here again, the use of the fabric seems in keeping with good taste, and no doubt provoked many a smile. More important than that, it probably also brought back a good number of replies.

> Dear Mr. Doe:
>
> We do not like to think that you just read our recent letters, then tore them up and forgot all about our company, for we hold high hopes of getting your next order. We make good products, sell them at reasonable prices and ship promptly. You know that from previous orders you have sent us.

But we have not heard from you for months, so did you just tear up our letters after all?

You can tear this one up, but it will be just a little harder to r-i-p. So save your energy to write, not rip, stating you will be sending us an order soon. There's a stamped envelope enclosed.

                                        Very truly yours,

Obviously, letters typed on fabrics cannot be recommended as a regular diet. You can picture the trouble and confusion they would cause when it came to filing them. But surely now and then it can do no harm to get out of the rut with some novel or amusing idea which may add power and interest to the message.

Sometimes, you also see letterheads printed, and the letters typed, on paper with a wood surface finish. You might think, for example, that the letter which follows was on an actual piece of wood if you saw it on the desk of an associate. This letter was used by the Hartford Accident and Indemnity Company, and you may judge for yourself whether or not the idea was appropriate to the message.

FRIDAY THE THIRTEENTH
KNOCK ON WOOD

Probably you are not superstitious, but Friday the Thirteenth comes again in November.

SO—KNOCK ON WOOD!

Every day is Friday the Thirteenth on the calendar of accidents, and to knock on wood is no guarantee of immunity.

While you read this letter, eight persons in the United States will have met with some disabling injury.

Knock on wood, and then ask us about the form of policy which will protect your income and reimburse you for medical expenses on account of accidents.

                                        Sincerely yours,

Another letter, printed and typed on the same kind of imitation wood paper, does not rate approval as one in which the idea for getting attention has a logical connection with the thought of the copy. In fact, there is no connection at all. You will have to take our word for that, as the nature of the letter is too personal for reprinting. However, when the writer signed his name in brown ink, he added in longhand the following postscript... "Just to prove that we 'wood' be interested, here's your answer on wood." This could scarcely be called the best of humor, and so the adaptation of the idea leaves the reader unimpressed. As we have seen before, dramatic ideas to win special attention can be very sweet or very sour—depending on how clever they really are, and whether or not they blend logically with the thought of the copy.

3. Modern Letterhead Design

The trend toward simplicity. You have seen some of the letterheads of earlier days—conglomerations of information lines and illustrations which so cluttered the page that the effect was confusion and chaos. Although they accomplished—over-accomplished—the first purpose of a business letterhead, to give the reader the factual things he needs to know, they failed utterly to accomplish the second purpose—to impress the reader by their beauty and originality of design. Now, it is fitting that you examine some of our modern letterheads, and compare the new with the old to see what progress may have been made.

We are not so bold as to attempt a complete and scientific treatise on letterhead design. This is a job which only the highly skilled commercial artist might successfully undertake, and few businessmen have either the time or inclination to master the principles of such a technical and specialized art. Unfortunately, a great many businessmen fail to recognize their limitations in this respect, or to appreciate the need of expert help. They make the mistake of planning their own letterheads, or of turning to some local printer who does not have in his shop anyone capable of doing the job. This is one of the reasons why so many modern letterheads are still commonplace, even ugly, in design. No businessman of sane mind would buy a few yards of tweed and attempt to tailor himself an overcoat or suit of clothes. Why should he consider himself capable of "tailoring" his own stationery?

The one characteristic of the best modern letterheads which stands out above the rest is that of *simplicity*. This is attained by the omission of all factual information which the reader does not need, by good taste in the use of type faces and sizes, and by the discreet application of color, when it is used at all. The letterhead thus avoids that crowded appearance we saw in the "Gay Nineties" and other samples. There is plenty of space between the lines, and the one part of the whole ensemble considered most important is given the center of the stage. For example, the letterhead illustrated below is typically modern in its simplicity. It is engraved on heavy paper, and conveys the image of a progressive company:

You will no doubt agree that this letterhead has both dignity and eye-appeal. Moreover, all the facts the reader might want are presented—firm name, nature of the business, street address, names of city and state, and telephone number. An added touch is the trade mark, which properly gets a prominent position in the design—probably, the first thing you noticed.

Another letterhead conspicuous for simplicity is one used by Revlon. In reproduction, it loses some of the pleasing effect, because the original is in two colors, black and red.

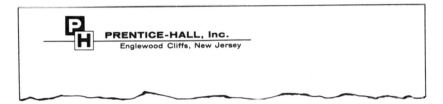

The publishers of this book have several letterheads for different types of uses, but they are all distinguished by as little copy as possible. One for general purposes gives prominence to the initials P and H.

Another of these Prentice-Hall letterheads is for executive correspondence, with a design that is both modern and pleasing.

Often a problem for the artist. Without meaning to disparage the skill of the artists who designed the three letterheads we have just inspected, it must be conceded that in attaining simplicity they were aided by the small number of items which had to be worked into the design. But this advantage is often lacking when a new letterhead is ordered. After all, the artist must use as much material in his design as the executives of the company or organization consider desirable, although his own artistic feelings may be severely jolted. Thus, the compromise between satisfying his client and still coming up with an attractive layout may be indeed a difficult problem.

For example, consider the letterhead reproduced on page 203. We have no right to question the necessity of what appears on it. No doubt the many names and titles of important doctors are intended to win reader acceptance of the good cause; perhaps, too, the doctors themselves are somewhat inspired to "get in and pitch." Nevertheless, here is the burden this letterhead is asked to carry.

> Name and location of the organization.
> Names of the officials and their titles.
> Names of 23 doctors who are members of the Executive Committee.
> Reproduction of the Christmas Seal, and slogan urging purchase.
> Line telling to whom checks should be mailed.
> Union label.

No one could deny that putting such a mass of items on one page made an attractive letterhead almost impossible; remember, too, that whoever did the job still had to leave some room for the typing of the letter. In view of these facts, we may be lenient in our criticism of the result. No matter how hard anyone might have tried, it is doubtful that he could have done any better.

As you would expect from professionals, the letterhead used by the Advertising Club of Minneapolis is a fine example. It shows how more than the usual number of factual and illustrative items can be assembled into a design. This design has both quality appeal and a distinction derived from originality in treatment. This letterhead is also printed in gray and red (a favorite combination) on 24-pound paper, high in rag content. The lines and the emblem are in red.

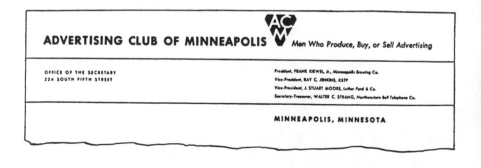

Letterhead with Handicap of Many Names

Using other parts of the sheet. There is no reason why a business letterhead must be designed to occupy only the top of the page. In fact, when there are many items to be included, a logical solution to the problem is the use of some other part of the sheet; keep in mind, however, that a major part of the entire space must be reserved for the typewritten message. If this is done, the best part of the sheet to use seems to be the left-hand side. This only narrows the space for the typed letter, and the design, using top and left, can be made quite effective.

203

Printing Industry of America Inc.

WOodley 6-1400 — 5728 CONNECTICUT AVE., N.W. • WASHINGTON 15, D.C.

LETTERPRESS · LITHOGRAPHY · GRAVURE [PA] AND ALLIED INDUSTRIES

November 14, 1961

*Officers
1961-62*

President
OLIVER R. SPERRY
R. R. DONNELLEY & SONS CO.
Chicago, Illinois

Vice President
MAX B. E. CLARKSON
GRAPHIC CONTROLS CORPORATION
Buffalo, New York

Secretary
MENDEL SEGAL
STEIN PRINTING COMPANY
Atlanta, Georgia

Treasurer
ARTHUR H. GRATZ
HERBICK & HELD PRINTING CO
Pittsburgh, Pennsylvania

Past President
FRANCIS N. EHRENBERG
BLANCHARD PRESS, INC
Garden City, L. I., N. Y

*President
Master Printers Section*
J. PAUL WHITEHEAD
HEMINWAY CORPORATION
115 South Leonard Street
Waterbury, Connecticut

*President
Union Employers Section*
ORAN I. BROWN
RAND McNALLY & COMPANY
Skokie, Illinois

*President
Magazine Printers Section*
GEORGE E. SHEER
McCALL CORPORATION
Dayton, Ohio

*President
Printers Rollers Section*
THOS. W. FORD, SR.
HARRIGAN ROLLER COMPANY, INC
Baltimore, Maryland

*President
Rotary Business Forms Section*
ARNOLD GREENFIELD
WATTS BUSINESS FORMS, DIV OF
ALFRED ALLEN WATTS CO, INC.
Clifton, New Jersey

*President
Ticket and Coupon Section*
JAMES S. ARCUS, JR.
THE ARCUS TICKET COMPANY
Chicago, Illinois

*President
Trade Binders Section*
ROBERT A. WUNSCH
BECKTOLD COMPANY
St. Louis, Missouri

*President
Web Offset Section*
PAUL LYLE
WESTERN PRINTING AND
LITHOGRAPHING CO
Racine, Wisconsin

General Manager
BERNARD J. TAYMANS
Washington, D. C.

Mr. L. E. "Cy" Frailey
21105 Bluebird Canyon Drive
Laguna Beach, California

Dear "Cy":

We understand you might have available a new long-playing record based on your successful booklets about effective letter writing.

If so, I'd be interested in receiving full details.

Very truly yours,

John Jay Daly

John Jay Daly
Public Relations Director

JJD:RL

I've used your slidefilm for so many years I'm not a bit abashed about addressing you by your first name.

[PA] logo

AN INDUSTRY JOINED TOGETHER FOR PROGRESS

On this letterhead, the problem of many names is handled very skill-fully. The letterhead and company symbols (blue to agree with color of names) are good complements for the listing. The small type·used for printing the names also helps the body of the letter to retain its prominence.

A very interesting example of this kind of layout is displayed on page 205. This letterhead seen in the original form is printed in two colors, and on tinted paper, so some of the eye-appeal is lost in the reproduction. You can see how cleverly the many items are worked into the design without the effect of overcrowding.

Before inspecting the letterhead of The Atlantic Department Store, you probably would have questioned the possibility of listing the names of seventy-two sales items, and floor numbers, with any chance of an attractive design. But there it is—quite pleasing to the eye, and useful, too.

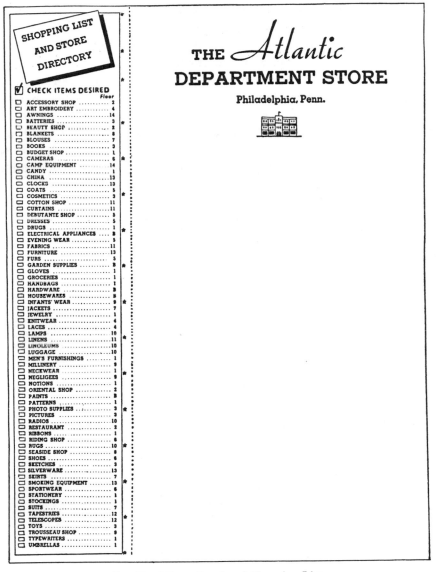

Combined Letterhead and Shopping List

All of these letterheads, where much material is depicted without confusion, emphasize the fact that the designing of a good letterhead is a job for the expert commercial artist. We shudder to think what any of these would have been had they been left in the hands of amateurs.

Four types of letterhead design. Although in a book that seeks to survey all of the many aspects of business correspondence, we cannot stretch too far this discussion of letterheads, but it is well that you have as wide a view as possible of the factors that contribute to their utility and charm. With that background, you may then be encouraged to continue your study of a subject which will prove both fascinating and of practical value.

In general, you may place almost any business letterhead in one of four groups, if you omit such variables as quality of paper, use of color, etc., and think only of their structural form. The first of these types, and the simplest, is the one that may be compared to the shape of a *triangle*. If you drew lines from above the center of the oval in the Coty letterhead, and connected them, the long line that runs from edge to edge would be a triangle. This triangular form has been used for many years; it is still a useful form and has been adopted by many modern companies.

Of course, the triangle could be in reverse to the one just illustrated, with the point at the bottom instead of the top. The Armco Steel Corporation letterhead is a very attractive example of the reverse triangle form.

The second of the four types is somewhat more flexible, although the items displayed are still centered with respect to each other and to position on the page. When you draw an imaginary line to follow the contour of the design, the resulting form is that of a *vase*. Many, many business letterheads are of the "vase" variety—like the one shown below.

The third type of letterhead departs considerably from the picture-on-the-wall effect of the *triangle* and the *vase*. The panel design runs across the page like the *frieze* on the wall of a room or building. This form has many interesting possibilities, which the modern designers have been quick to recognize. Some letterheads of the frieze classification are extremely simple, and yet very pleasing to the eye.

The fourth class of letterheads is by far the most interesting, and yet the most difficult to tag with a word. Perhaps, as defined in the dictionary, *"symmetry"* is as close as any other. According to Webster, "Symmetry is a due proportion of the several parts of a body to each other; harmonious relation of parts." Hence, a letterhead of this type does not attain balance by regularity of type, or by the centering of illustrative material on the page, but instead by "harmonious relation" in which blank space is as important as the printed parts.

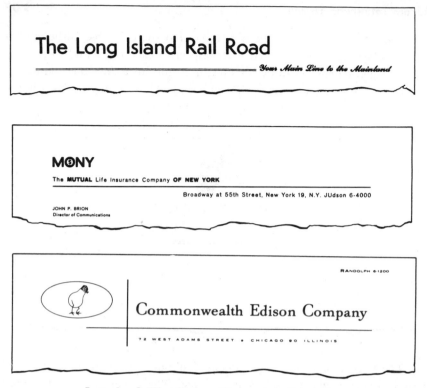

Letterheads That Express Harmonious Proportion

A great many of the letterheads displayed in this Handbook are interesting and suggestive examples of *symmetry* in design. On some of them, in their original form, color helps to achieve "harmonious relation of parts," by giving emphasis to a certain item in the layout which might otherwise seem to lack proportion. Even in these one-color reproductions, there is adequate proof that the parts of a letterhead may be put together without the old conception of regularity, and still be extremely pleasing to the eye.

However, we again need to remind ourselves that both skill and artistic sense are required to plan and execute a good design. This is a highly specialized, *creative* job, and not all are qualified for it. Some letterheads of the more modern type are obviously turned out by amateurs, and are painful to behold. If a business executive wanted an oil-painting of his wife, he would seek the services of a trained artist of established reputation. The same principle applies to the creation of letterheads in the third and fourth classes. It is far wiser to use one of the simpler forms—the *triangle* or the *vase*—except when a competent typographer is available, than to try for something more spectacular and make a botch of the job.

208

Letterheads symbolic of the business. Remember the influence of letter-contacts on sales; there is much to be said in favor of the letterhead which highlights the nature of the company, its products, or services. In a very attractive fashion, the letterhead following includes a map of the territory served by the Atchison, Topeka and Santa Fe Railway Company. Incidentally, the message on this fine letterhead shows how a small incident in the life of an organization can be used to express customer-appreciation, and thus promote friendly public relations.

Santa Fe all the way!

The Atchison, Topeka and Santa Fe Railway Company

ADVERTISING DEPARTMENT
Railway Exchange, 80 East Jackson Boulevard, Chicago 4, Illinois
A. A. DAILEY, General Advertising Manager
F. A. TIPPLE, Assistant General Advertising Manager

April 5, 1962
FILE: 75

Mr. C. L. Sullivan
Superintendent
Customers Department
Peoples Gas Light and Coke Company
122 South Michigan Avenue
Chicago, Illinois

Thank you very much for your letter of April 4th enclosing check for $8.72 covering dinner and refreshments served to Mr. and Mrs. Albert L. Tossell and Mrs. Mary Bruer on Santa Fe train #19 "The Chief" from Chicago, March 7th, 1962.

Expressions contained in your letter are sincerely appreciated and Mr. M. O. Strom of this office has been given an opportunity to read your letter.

All of us with the Santa Fe hope we may have the opportunity of serving your Company and your people frequently and continually.

General Agent, Passenger Dept.

WAF:emj

Four Letterhead Designs for Dude Ranches

The four "black and whites" above are designed for use by "Dude" Ranches, and distributed as a goodwill gesture by H. J. Justin & Sons, famous makers of cowboy boots and shoes. With or without imprint, each of these four letterheads reveals a phase of life on a ranch, and thus by the power of illustration alone, the reader's thirst for vacation on a "Dude" Ranch is sharpened. There is a very old saying attributed to the Chinese that, "One picture is worth more than ten thousand words." Certainly, pictures have great power in letterhead design.

Letterheads Displaying Nature of Service

Illustrating the building. There seems to be no reason for using the picture of a building on a business letterhead, unless there is something special or unusual about it to win favor. Banks, hotels, insurance companies, may be partially judged by the places in which they are serving the public, but if a building is only commonplace, a picture could do little more than please the vanity of tenant or owner.

Besides, it is difficult to blend a picture of any size into the design of a letterhead without letting it dominate the other items on the page. This was intended in designing the three letterheads reproduced on page 212. The pictures are so impressive that they deserved to rate higher than anything else that might have been included. You know that this thought was held by the creator of the letterheads, because the other items are reduced to a minimum. The pictures were allowed to carry the load, and they do it very well.

For example, the picture of the building used by the Provident Mutual Life Insurance Company of Philadelphia reflects a substantial strength which people expect of a life insurance company; and the huge plant of the John B. Stetson Company says plainly enough, "We must make fine hats, or why would the demand for them cause us to grow so big?"

Letterheads That Spotlight the Building

In connection with the use of a building on a letterhead, one kind of chiseling deserves severe condemnation. Sometimes a beautiful or massive structure is pictured, with the implication that it belongs to or is used by the company, when in reality only a small unit of the property is occupied by the company. This is downright cheating, because the users of the letterhead seek credit for prestige and magnitude which are not genuine.

The percentage of business letterheads carrying pictures of plants and office buildings is not large. In general, we think it could be reduced still lower without any great loss, as there are other possibilities much more interesting.

Use of trademarks. A very understandable feature in the design of many letterheads is the company trademark, slogan, or trade name. In some cases, it is a combination of two, or all of them. A company of long standing has every right to prize highly any means by which it is recognized and remembered by the buying public. Hence, if the identification device is clever and quite different from anything used by competitors, a determined effort is made to keep it alive and "kicking"—by using it on the package, on delivery trucks, in all kinds of advertising, and, of course, on the company stationery.

Trademarks, especially, are easily adaptable to letterhead design, the exceptions being those which are so ugly and uninteresting that they detract rather than add to the general appearance.

Trademarks and service marks are valuable because they help keep the product, service or company's name alive in the public consciousness. (A trademark is used for a product; a service mark is used for a service.)

Letterheads That Spotlight Trademarks or Service Marks

Executive letterheads. The most dignified, and sometimes the least interesting, of all letterheads used in the business world, are those prepared for the personal use of top executives. Often, they are engraved on paper of exceptional quality, and the size of the sheet is smaller than standard 8½ by 11 inches. Why high station demands so much formality is hard to explain, except that custom makes it so. Unfortunately, besides the coldness of the letterhead, there is now and then a similarity in language, so that the contact with the reader is not as warm and human as the writer probably wants it to be.

This charge is not filed against *all* business executives, because many prefer to use the regular company stationery with the addition of their name and title. In a later section of this Handbook, you will inspect representative executive letters, and many of them will please you by their naturalness and warmth.

Executive Letterheads

The letterheads shown above are typical of the executive type. Their chief characteristic is simplicity, attained by black or gray engraved copy on pure white paper of heavy substance and high rag content. Although they lack the attention value of many of the more colorful commercial letterheads, they do possess a dignity which must impress the reader.

Paper mills a source of information. Many of the best letterhead ideas have originated in the paper mills. They employ only outstanding designers, and now and then offer to their clients portfolios which include selected letterheads now in use, and suggested layouts for new ones. A contact with any of the major paper manufacturers should produce information and samples helpful in planning your own stationery. Consult business directories, or classified telephone books, for the name and address of the paper mill nearest to you.

4. Appearance of the Typed Letter

More variable than the letterhead. The best of letterheads on the finest paper cannot be held entirely responsible for first impressions. The reader sees everything on the page, and each part has something to say about whether or not the whole appearance is pleasing. Helping to contribute are such factors as the "touch" of the typist, the position of the letter on the page, the lack of erasures and smears, the form into which the various parts are molded, and even the condition of the ribbon and typewriter.

These factors are, of course, far more variable than that of the letter-head. Once the latter is designed and processed, it stays the same, but a typist may turn out one beautiful letter, and then an ugly one, depending on her mood of the moment and how faithfully she adheres to a standard of excellence. The attitude, too, of the person for whom the typist works helps to determine whether all of her letters will appear neat and in good propor-tion, for it is true that most people perform only as *expected*, and seldom any better.

Frankly, a survey of the mechanical features that contribute to the appearance of a business letter cannot possibly be as interesting as some of the other aspects of letter carpentry, but they are all important, and should be understood if a high level of quality is to be attained. A dictator must know what he wants his letters to look like, what will help and what will not, before he can properly instruct the secretary or transcriber. Moreover, he must be quality-conscious every day, for the moment his zeal falters, the level of performance is apt to sink.

Importance of the typist. As you know, among the several persons who contribute to the success of a business letter, the typist has the last word. Since almost all typists are women, this fact is not inappropriate, as they are accustomed to having it anyway. Be that as it may, the cycle is quite clear. The advertising manager usually goes to bat first. He plans the letter-head and selects the paper. Next, an artist makes the layout, the president approves the design, a printer does the processing, and finally the dictator spills his thoughts into a little microphone or directly across the table into the notebook of his stenographer. He never *sees* the letter he is dictating, until it comes back to him, ready for his signature. He must depend on someone else for attention to all those *little things* which will help to make the letter attractive, and in harmony with the letterhead. That *someone* is the typist.

Of course, you understand what is meant by "an even touch" in typing—the striking of each key with the same force, so that a whole line looks like a printed unit, no letter blacker nor dimmer than the others. Nothing is more attractive, from a letter point of view, than a page of copy typed with a firm and even touch; and nothing *less* attractive than one which resembles a furrowed lawn. Not only does an uneven touch hurt the charm of a letter, but it also makes it more difficult to read, for the eye rebels against the alternately bold and weak letters. Compare the two paragraphs that follow—both taken from actual business letters. It is foolish to ask which of the two typists had an even touch, because the contrast is too great. The one paragraph is a fine example of skilled workmanship; the other is just messy.

The
Fingers
of This
Typist
Hit with
Alternate
Puffs
and
Pokes

The writer has since having this report talked with Mr. Van ortwick of Kissick Company and in the absence of Mr. Kissick learned that he would suggest to Mr. Kissick that if he had not already written to you to do so, because he believed thoroughly in the Exposition, having previously obtained benefits from it. We are hoping that you have heard from Kissick Company and that you will now be inclined to consider exhibit space. We shall be pleased to have advice that you will wish to do so with an indication of the approximate amount of space that you could use so that we will be in good position to recommend the location to you.

But
This One
Hit the
Keys with
an Even
Touch

You know, we condemn liquor, and many happily await the day that for the second time it will pass out of the American picture, but an occasion like the one you and Carl and I enjoyed brings men closer together, and we find that we have many things in common which strengthen our friendship and our belief in each other. It was my real pleasure to enjoy that hour or so with you and Carl.

Above—Uneven Touch
Below—Even Touch

As it happens, the letterhead on which the first paragraph traveled is equally sloppy, so that there is nothing at all to create favorable attention before the reader begins to see what the letter has to say—*if* he ever does. But you can imagine how such a typed monstrosity would spoil the effect of *any* business message, even though the letterhead were an aristocrat of highest degree.

You might say, "If the typing touch of the girl who handles my letters is not even, what can I do about it?" This is an embarrassing question, for we have nothing against the fair sex, but obviously the only answer is, "See that she does better, or get a new one." There seems to be no excuse for an uneven touch in typing, because skill is acquired, as in every other human endeavor, by practice. Most of the business colleges are turning out good typists, but when one knows she has a poor touch the incentive of holding her job should be reason enough for improvement.

Certainly, in our opinion, no business executive can afford to put up with inferior workmanship, especially if the employee is indifferent to a fault, and makes no effort to correct it. The trouble has been, however, that many businessmen do not seem to be particular about the appearance of their letters, or interested enough to point out obvious faults. Any improvement in business correspondence is a matter of *teamwork* between those who dictate, and those who type.

Of course, the electric typewriter eliminates the "touch" problem, and any typist can do faster and better work on one. But not every office has or needs an electric machine.

A very simple and easily corrected fault in typing, one that makes the letters look "fuzzy," is the failure on the part of the operator to clean the keys of her machine regularly. Thus, certain letters like "W" and "O" become filled with dried ink, and the typing takes on a similar effect to that caused by an uneven touch. Good stenographers do not need to be reminded to do this cleaning job, and any evidence to the contrary is proof of indifference.

A sow's ear won't make a silk purse. In commenting on the relation between good work and the pride of the worker, it is well that we should remember the necessity of company co-operation in supplying adequate and up-to-date materials and equipment. The best typist in the world, eager to excel and proud of her craftsmanship, could hardly be expected to turn out fine looking letters if forced to labor under the handicaps of an obsolete typewriter, cheap ribbons that smudge at the slightest provocation, and paper so inferior in quality that it will not stand an erasure without leaving a smear. As the old saying goes, "one can't make a silk purse out of a sow's ear," and no typist can make a superlative letter unless supplied with the right tools.

A cheap typewriter ribbon not only tends to "fuzz" the typed lines, but the small saving over the cost of a good one is more than offset by frequent replacements. It is poor economy for any business executive to save a few pennies and let cheap-looking letters represent the company, when those reflecting pride and quality could earn dollars in goodwill and more sales. Thus, the typist who is expected to turn out work which is outstanding, and a credit to the company, should be provided with every facility for meeting that objective—a comfortable chair and desk, adequate light, a modern typewriter in perfect condition, the best quality ribbons, and stationery which will accentuate her own handiwork. On the other hand, if favored with those advantages, the same executive has the right to insist that the typist give in return the same degree of perfection.

Placing the letter on the page. From experience in typing many letters, it is easy to judge accurately how much space on the page a letter is going to take. With this forecast, the typist is able to "frame" any letter so that the margins are about the same width—narrow margins for long letters, and wide margins for short ones. The letter on page 219, typed by the secretary to Mr. Clyde W. Young, is about as near a work of art as any letter could be. An amateur typist might spend an hour trying to "frame" a letter so perfectly, but to this expert it must have been only a small incident in a busy day. This assumption is not farfetched, because other letters from Mr. Young's office are typed with the same feeling for beauty and balance on the page.

The same Monarch letter, retyped for comparison, has lost the impression of quality. With the narrow margins, and the high position on the page, it looks top-heavy, and like any other of the many letters that are dashed off with no regard for "harmonious proportion" on the page.

"But what difference does it make?" you can hear some businessmen asking. Yes, and they could just as well go on and say, "A letter is a letter like a pig is a pig." We heard that, too, as long ago as in the first section of this Handbook.

But it *does* make a difference—a whale of a difference—how a business letter *looks,* and what it speaks for, before a word of the message is read. An impression of quality carries over to the products or services offered by the company. To pull this Monarch letter from the envelope, to sense at first glance the care and pride in its preparation, is to make one feel that the insurance sold by the company *must* be of the same fine quality.

The format of the typed letter. When it comes to arranging the various parts of a business letter on the page, there is no one form that might be called "best." The decision depends on the personal taste of the man for whom the letters are typed, and the only limitation is that of consistency. For example, if indented paragraphs are preferred, then they *all* must be indented, and with the same number of spaces. It is not uncommon to see a very wide indentation in the opening paragraph, and a smaller one for the others, but this in our opinion is not pleasing to the eye, and there is no reason to justify it.

PARTICIPATING – NON PARTICIPATING LIFE · NON–CANCELLABLE HEALTH AND ACCIDENT INSURANCE

Monarch
LIFE INSURANCE COMPANY

SPRINGFIELD, MASSACHUSETTS

October 17, 1962

Mr. L. E. Frailey
1053 North Shore Avenue
Chicago, Illinois

My dear Cy:

Thanks a lot for your letter. If I have contributed
anything to the present-day thinking, I am happy.

In summarizing briefly this particular experience,
I think of the story that is told of Mark Twain's
first visit to the Atlantic Ocean. As he stood
looking out upon miles of water before him, his
host asked,

   "What do you think of our ocean, Mr. Clemens?"

To which Mr. Clemens replied,

   "It seems to be a huge success."

Tell Mary I am happy to have acquired another booster
and I hope that my friend, Joe Behan did not tire her
out. He is a remarkable man, has a host of friends
and an unlimited faculty for spreading good cheer.
It was nice to see you both, even if it was for only
a short time.

Hope this finds you well and may the enthusiasm,
originality and capacity for friendship of Frailey &
Associates continue to spread their beams of light.

      Sincerely yours,

CWY/HW
             President

A Letter Perfectly Framed on the Page

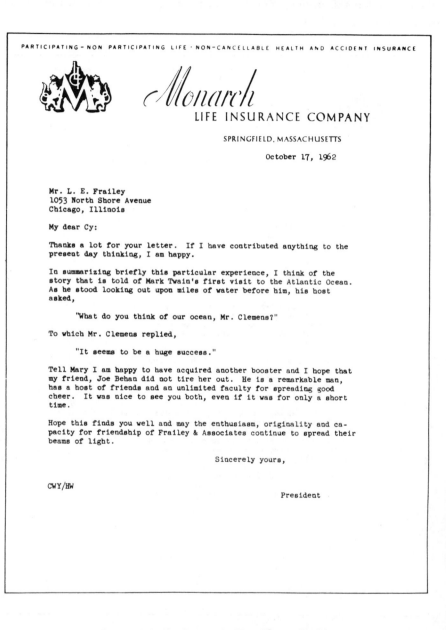

Copy of Same Letter in Top-Heavy Position

Surveying the letter to be typed on the page, the typist is conscious of one major part—the body—and several accessories. Not all accessories are used in every letter, but they may include:

The date	The complimentary close
Name of recipient	Name of writer
His title	His title
His address	Name of company
The salutation	Initials of writer and typist
Reference or identification line	Postscript

For the use of these various items, certain forms have been established by utility and custom, and we shall investigate what they are. It must be plain that they need to be assembled on the page in a format that is both practical and orderly. What that format is to be depends on the judgment and good taste of the individual responsible. It may be dictated by the man who writes the letters, or, in other cases, by company regulation. The latter is the best practice since it results in uniformity in style, and is the format considered "best" by the correspondence supervisor, or the officials of the firm. Certainly it is not a decision that should be left to the typist.

Suppose we see what some of the more common forms are like. There are others, of course, because some of the more adventuresome letter-carpenters are always experimenting with new ways of doing things. Here we will concern ourselves only with the forms generally accepted by business, which, of course, represent ninety-nine per cent of all the letters written.

So far as we know, no one has attempted to tabulate the use of these current formats in percentages, but it is our guess that the one most popular today is the *blocked* letter. This is the form in which all of the body lines start even with the left-hand margin, with only the date line, the complimentary close, and the identification of the writer, his title and company, remaining on the right half of the page. There are no indented lines to start each paragraph, or in the part which carries the recipient's title, company, and address. The effect, as illustrated on page 222, is both substantial and appealing. In our opinion, it is the best looking of all the forms now in use.

In some blocked letters, the practice is carried to an even greater extreme, with all items starting from the left-hand side. An example of the "all blocked" format is the letter on page 224.

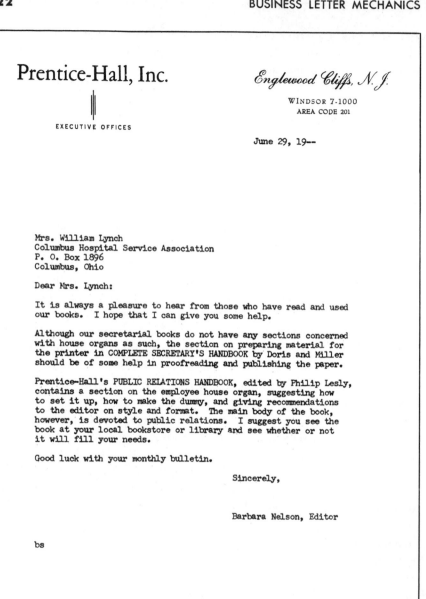

Prentice-Hall, Inc.

Englewood Cliffs, N. J.

WINDSOR 7-1000
AREA CODE 201

EXECUTIVE OFFICES

June 29, 19--

Mrs. William Lynch
Columbus Hospital Service Association
P. O. Box 1896
Columbus, Ohio

Dear Mrs. Lynch:

It is always a pleasure to hear from those who have read and used our books. I hope that I can give you some help.

Although our secretarial books do not have any sections concerned with house organs as such, the section on preparing material for the printer in COMPLETE SECRETARY'S HANDBOOK by Doris and Miller should be of some help in proofreading and publishing the paper.

Prentice-Hall's PUBLIC RELATIONS HANDBOOK, edited by Philip Lesly, contains a section on the employee house organ, suggesting how to set it up, how to make the dummy, and giving recommendations to the editor on style and format. The main body of the book, however, is devoted to public relations. I suggest you see the book at your local bookstore or library and see whether or not it will fill your needs.

Good luck with your monthly bulletin.

                                        Sincerely,

                                        Barbara Nelson, Editor

bs

A Blocked Letter

Prentice-Hall, Inc.

Englewood Cliffs, N. J.

WINDSOR 7-1000
AREA CODE 201

EXECUTIVE OFFICES

June 29, 19--

Mrs. William Lynch
    Columbus Hospital Service Association
        P.O. Box 1896
            Columbus, Ohio

Dear Mrs. Lynch:

It is always a pleasure to hear from those who have read and used our books. I hope that I can give you some help.

Although our secretarial books do not have any sections concerned with house organs as such, the section on preparing material for the printer in COMPLETE SECRETARY'S HANDBOOK by Doris and Miller should be of some help in proofreading and publishing the paper.

Prentice-Hall's PUBLIC RELATIONS HANDBOOK, edited by Philip Lesly, contains a section on the employee house organ, suggesting how to set it up, how to make the dummy, and giving recommendations to the editor on style and format. The main body of the book, however, is devoted to public relations. I suggest you see the book at your local bookstore or library and see whether or not it will fill your needs.

Good luck with your monthly bulletin.

Sincerely,

Barbara Nelson, Editor

bs

Same Letter Indented

A third style, and the oldest in business, is one with indented lines, as displayed on page 223. Probably it has retained its popularity because many people like the appearance of the indentations, but the reason for them—at least in the body of the letter—no longer exists. When, in the early days,

---

American
Institute
of
Business

GRAND AVENUE AT TENTH
DES MOINES 7, IOWA

KEITH FENTON, B. S., PRESIDENT

February 12, 1962

Miss Frances Bailey
F. W. Fitch Company
304 15th Street
Des Moines, Iowa

Dear Miss Bailey:

It is a real pleasure to have you in Mr. Frailey's letter writing class.

"Doc" Frailey is going to dispense a thousand dollars' worth of good, usable ideas on business letters during the next seven weeks.

He is a famous "doctor" for curing the pains, aches, and bruises caused by poor letters. For years Frailey has run a "clinic" for pale and puny letters, and his fame has grown by leaps and bounds until today he is "tops" in the letter writing field.

Here is an A.I.B. souvenir pencil. Make a note that you have a date at A.I.B. the next seven Wednesday nights.

The class is now going--and going places. Come early, if you can, and get acquainted.

I wish you increasing, continued success in your business, and pleasant personal progress.

Sincerely yours,

Keith Fenton

KEITH FENTON

KF:MLH

THE SCHOOL WHERE FUTURES ARE FORMED

"All-Blocked" Style

letters were written in longhand, and usually double-spaced, an indented line indicated the beginning of a new paragraph. But the coming of the typewriter has made that device unnecessary, since a new paragraph is indicated by simply double spacing.

There seems to be no established practice with respect to the number of spaces that should be struck on the typewriter before an indented line begins. Some use three spaces, some five, some ten, and others go almost to the center of the page before typing the start of the indented line. These variations are merely a matter of personal taste, and no one can say that one is better than the rest. After all, inasmuch as the indentations are used to improve the appearance of the typed letter, it is the job of those responsible to decide *what* number of spaces look best.

The worst of all the styles, as we view them, is the one displayed on this page. Every line in the body of the message is indented except the beginnings of paragraphs. To be sure, this format has the merit of gaining special attention, since it differs so widely from the others, but we doubt very much if the final reaction is favorable. To gain the reader's attention by trick typing is one thing; to please him with it is another.

May 15, 19——

Mr. John Doe,
111 East Main Street,
Kansas City, Missouri.

Dear John:

I was in Chicago the other day for the purpose of giving a talk to the executives of one of the banks, and while there I asked Miss Underwood to find out where you were. Her letter received today gave me the above address.

The principal reason I wanted your address was to send you mine in order that I might not miss seeing you if you happened through Denver any time soon. They are having a big real estate confab here this week, but insist that you are not on the program.

During these past years I have often thought of you. Our friendship has been worth a great deal to me, and I hope that someday we may have the opportunity of sitting down to "sorta" lick the chops of memory together.

I am still a bachelor and my brother and I have just taken over some bachelor quarters. That means you have a place to stay when you are here. Please remember me to the wife.

Sincerely yours,

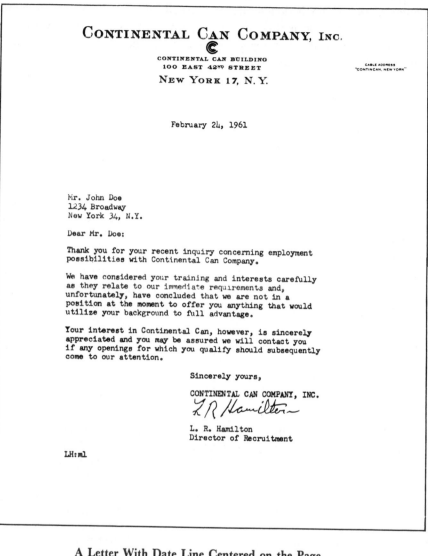

A Letter With Date Line Centered on the Page

The date line. The general custom is to place the date line of a business letter on the upper right-hand side of the page, so that it stands two or more spaces below the printed letterhead, and with the end of the line as even as possible with the margin made by the body. Since the latter is never exactly straight, as on the left-hand side, the alignment of the date line can only be made with approximate accuracy.

It cannot be set forth as an absolute rule that the date line *must* be in the above described position; in the "all-blocked" style, as we said, it

The Connecticut Mutual Life Insurance Company
HARTFORD

CHARLES J. ZIMMERMAN, C.L.U.
President

Mr. John O. Policyholder
140 Garden Street
Hartford, Connecticut

Dear Mr. Policyholder:

Welcome...as a new policyowner and member of Connecticut Mutual! We appreciate your decision to insure with our Company.

Since your policy is necessarily written in legal terms, we are enclosing a booklet that discusses it in non-technical language. After reading this booklet, perhaps you will want to attach it to your policy for future reference. Many do.

If you have questions about your life insurance, your Connecticut Mutual agent will be happy to help. Please feel free, also, to call on me or my associates in the Home Office.

We want you to feel that this is really your company.

Sincerely,

Charles J. Z
President

CJZ/W
(Enclosure)

Name and Address Blocked, Paragraphs Indented

starts on the *left*. Here again, we face a decision which depends more on personal judgment, and the willingness to go along with prevailing custom, than it does on any implacable authority which cannot be broken. In some cases, and particularly those where the design of the letterhead favors the variation, you run across date lines which are centered on the page immediately below the name of the city and state. For example, the position of the date line on the Continental Can Company letter seems to be a good one, and better from the appearance angle than if it had been typed in the customary spot, to the right.

Neither is it reasonable to establish, as some letter manuals do, any exact number of spaces that the date line should be typed below the letter-head. If the body of the letter is short and, to gain the best appearance, it is dropped down to the center of the page, the date line may well be dropped with it. There are also cases, although we do not like them, where the position of the date line is fixed by printing part of the numerals in the year on the page, so that the typist has no other choice than to fill in the missing number, and align the rest of the date line with it.

After the figure or figures designating the day of the month, the comma should follow immediately. It is unnecessary, and may be considered wrong, to use *nd, rd, st,* or *th.*

Wrong:	*Right:*
April 1st, 1964	April 1, 1964
March 3rd, 1964	March 3, 1964
July 20th, 1964	July 20, 1964
August 2nd, 1964	August 2, 1964

In the above examples, the periods were omitted at the end of the date lines, although they just as properly could have been used; the decision depends on whether the punctuation of the name and address lines is "open" or "closed."

It is not thought good form to abbreviate the name of the month, or to substitute a figure for it.

Wrong:	*Right:*
Feb. 1, 1964	February 1, 1964
Feb. 1, '64	
2-1-64	
2/1/64	

In earlier days, it was quite customary to use words instead of figures for the year and day of the month. This is still advocated by some authorities, for letters of extreme formality, but we can think of no business contact where such formality is necessary. However, this is a question that may be answered by the individual, rather than set up as a rule or "must" in business letter forms.

Wrong: July tenth, Nineteen hundred and sixty-four
Right: July 10, 1964

Variations in form of date line. The great majority of date lines are typed in the sequence of month, day, and year. This is purely a matter of custom, as it would appear more logical to start with the smallest unit (the day) and proceed to the largest (the year). The latter is the form officially used by the military services. Some letter-writers evidently agree with this logic, as you now and then encounter a date line typed in the following order.

25 September 1964 *instead of* September 25, 1964

When this newer form is used, and there is not the slightest objection to it, no punctuation is needed. The punctuation automatically becomes "open" for the inside address and signature lines.

That the form of the date line is not fixed, except by custom, is proved by the numerous attempts made to make it more interesting or ornamental. Often, the variation serves some special purpose for the company, as to call attention to an anniversary year. Other times it may simply represent the desire of the letter-man to get out of the groove and do something different. To ban such a device on the ground that it takes more time to type or read, seems rather like splitting hairs, as anything done to improve the appearance or effectiveness of a business letter can only be judged by whether or not the results are worth the time and effort.

The forms taken by these date line variations are too numerous for description. Some seem within the bounds of good taste; others, too "wild and woolly." The latter, of course, do not merit your approval, but there are always those who dislike *any* departure from the conventional standard even though it may be good.

These examples are typical of special date lines typed in forms that get away from the conventional. Since the first job of a business letter is to get attention, it may be that in their small way they support that purpose. At least, they are different, and not unpleasing to the eye. After all, there is no law that says this part of a letter must be typed on one line or in any certain position—nor is it a breach of business etiquette to use variety. The forms commonly seen have been developed by custom, and none are fixed or unchangeable.

August
26
1964

26
August
1964

August 26
1 9 6 4

26 August
Our 50th Year
1 9 6 4

Five More Days
26 August 1964
Clearance Sale

5. THE INSIDE ADDRESS

Useful for reference and filing. The lines that identify and locate the recipient are called the "inside address," and in content they should be exactly the same as those on the envelope which tell Uncle Sam to whom and where the delivery is to be made. The "rules" governing their use are given below, but again it is well to remember that in some respects they merely represent the preference of the majority of letter-writers, while those of the minority often take liberties with them.

The chief benefit of the inside address is to the company served by the writer of the letter, since it gives the information necessary for filing and future reference. Inasmuch as the recipient is thoroughly acquainted with his own address, it would seem foolish to type it under his name, were it not for the utility purpose of recording it on the carbon copy.

All right, here are the things to remember in connection with the inside address. Call them rules, if you wish, for they tend to create orderliness and uniformity when co-ordinated with similar conventions that govern the handling of the salutation, the complimentary close, and the other parts of the typed letter.

1. Position on the page. It is the first line of the inside address which determines what the margin shall be on the left side of the page. The whole appearance of the letter is influenced by how well the typist is able to select the position which will leave the right amount of space for the other parts, and thus achieve that "harmony of proportion" so necessary if the best possible impression is to be made.

The exact spot where the first letter of the first word is to be typed, as "M" in "Mr. John D. Doe," depends on the length of the copy that is to be balanced on the page. If the letter is a short one, the inside address may be started several spaces below the date line, but even if the letter is long, a minimum of two spaces is considered necessary to avoid the appearance of overcrowding. In the same way, the width of the margin may be varied, but should never be less than one inch. It is much better to run the letter to a second page than to disregard these two minimums in an effort to squeeze more on the one page than it should carry.

The lines of the inside address should always be single-spaced, but they may be blocked or indented according to the form selected for the rest of the letter. In either case, the first line of the inside address and the salutation start even and are aligned with all the lines in the body which are not indented.

In the second example, notice that all of the indentions are of the same number of spaces. In this case, the number is three, although some letter writers prefer five. In our opinion, the shorter number makes the best appearance. Some writers also like a longer indention for the start of paragraphs, but this practice is not recommended since it disturbs the uniformity which is most pleasing to the eye.

Mr. John W. Doe, President,
Universal Motor Corporation,
111 Washington Avenue,
Jefferson City, Missouri.

Dear Mr. Doe:

(Blocked)   I appreciated your letter asking how we like the car purchased from your good company six months ago. In these days, it is rather unusual to find a company interested in a customer so long after the sale has been made, and it speaks for the quality of your services.

Mr. John W. Doe, President,
  Universal Motor Corporation,
    111 Washington Avenue,
      Jefferson City, Missouri.

Dear Mr. Doe:

(Indented)   I appreciated your letter asking how we like the car purchased from your good company six months ago. In these days, it is rather unusual to find a company interested in a customer so long after the sale has been made, and it speaks for the quality of your services.

Although the logical place for the inside address seems to be below the date line and above the salutation, custom has decreed that in official or personal letters it may be typed at the bottom of the letter, two spaces below the signature. This is merely a matter of the writer's own inclination, or the procedure of the authority responsible for the correspondence. Here is an example:

...so please feel free to come to us any time you have a question to ask about our services.

Cordially yours,
Bernard B. Baker

Mr. George Browne,
888 Broad Street,
Columbus, Ohio.

When this position is used for the inside address, the letter starts with the salutation. Notice, too, that the lines of the inside address, although typed at the bottom of the page, are still even with the left-hand margin. In the above example the lines are blocked, but they should be indented if indentions are made of paragraph beginnings.

2. Punctuation. The oldest method of punctuating the inside address is to place a comma at the end of each line except the last, which ends with a period. This is called "closed" punctuation, in contrast with the "open" style in which no marks are used at the end of any of the lines—except when the name of a company ends with an abbreviated word.

The punctuation of the date line determines whether that of the inside address is to be "closed" or "open," since the form used in both of these parts must *agree*.

May 2, 1964.

Mr. George Browne,
888 Broad Street,
(*Closed*)   Columbus, Ohio.
Dear Mr. Browne:

May 2, 1964

Mr. George Browne
888 Broad Street
(*Open*)   Columbus, Ohio
Dear Mr. Browne:

May 9, 1964.

Mr. John Jones, Secretary,
Jones Costume Co.,
234 East Gay Street,
(*Closed*)   Decatur, Illinois.
Dear Mr. Jones:

May 9, 1964

Mr. John Jones, Secretary
Jones Costume Co.
234 East Gay Street
(*Open*)   Decatur, Illinois
Dear Mr. Jones:

Two facts need to be remembered in connection with the punctuation of the inside address. The first is that no matter which form is used, open or closed, the salutation is commonly followed with a colon. The second is that "open" does not mean any of the punctuation marks can be omitted *except* at the end of the lines. Thus, in the first and second examples above, a comma properly appears after the word "Columbus."

Also notice that in the second line of the third example the word "company" could not be spelled out to agree with Secretary, Street, and Illinois, because the abbreviated form is a part of the official firm name.

Later, in the fourth example, which was open, the abbreviation, "Co." had to be punctuated with the period, although the comma was omitted to agree with the other line endings. This illustrates a law which in all cases must be followed—it is not permissible to alter in any way the established form of a firm or association name. If a word is abbreviated, or if & is used for *and,* the typing must conform.

3. Content. The simple rule for the make-up of the inside address is that it should contain everything necessary for the easy delivery of the letter, a duplicate of the address on the envelope, and that it should give proper recognition of title when the recipient holds a position of importance in the company. In typing the sequence of lines, the practice is to start with the smallest item and work down to the largest—name, title, company, street address or box number, city, and state. Also, if the letter is going outside the United States, the name of the country would come last.

To be sure, not all of these items appear in every inside address. If the letter is dictated to an individual, and the contents are personal, the name of the company or association is not used unless it is necessary as a guide to delivery.

The shortest form of all is that of two lines—name, city, and state—as when the letter is going to some very small village where the street address is not needed, or to a public official whose address is well known to post office authorities. A none-too-popular example of the latter is, "Collector of Internal Revenue, Detroit, Michigan."

Here are examples, in the order of their complexity.

Mr. Hiram Cornplanter,
Minonk, Illinois.

Mr. John Q. Public,
Rural Route 2,
LaGrange, Indiana.

Mr. Jonathan Doe,
505 Oregon Street,
Urbana, Illinois.

The Purina Mills,
Seventh and Gratiot Streets,
St. Louis, Missouri.

Mr. William B. Black, Treasurer,
The Continental Corporation,
10 Rut Road,
Newark, Ohio.

Mr. Frank Hesselroth, Manager,
Advertising & Sales Executives Club,
913 Baltimore Avenue,
Kansas City, Missouri.

Mr. James Doe,
Superintendent of Maintenance,
The Buckeye Building,
42 East Gay Street,
Columbus, Ohio.

Mr. Oscar Merriwell, President,
Springfield Advertising Club,
Petterson and Hogart,
987 Washington Avenue,
Springfield, Illinois.

Mr. Morgan Hanford Goodfellow,
Assistant to the Vice-President,
Johnstown Construction Company,
4454 Riverside Road,
Cleveland, Ohio.

Mr. Burton Maxwell McPherson,
Chairman, Entertainment Committee,
Sales & Advertising Club,
McPherson, Mack, and Monihan,
333 Grandville Avenue,
Grand Rapids, Michigan.

To avoid the formidable appearance of the six-line address, it is desirable to place the name and title of the individual on the first line, but this is not always possible—see last address above. Had the first and second lines been combined, the one line would have stretched across the page to a point below the date line; moreover, it would have appeared off balance with the rest of the inside address.

Just how far across the page the first line of the inside address may properly reach is a debatable question of no great importance. As in all matters which influence the appearance of a typed letter, the aim is to make the best possible impression, but what determines "best" is often a matter of opinion. Some letter authorities say that the first line of the inside address should not reach beyond the center of the page. Roughly, this is probably as good a guide as any, although no harm is done if the line happens to exceed that point by a few spaces.

To keep the first line within the limitation of half the page, one of the leading experts, William H. Butterfield, approves the "carryover" of part of the line to the space below. According to Mr. Butterfield, "if this is done, the continuation should be indented five spaces when the paragraphs of the letter body are not indented, and the same amount as the paragraphs when the latter are indented." He gives the following examples:

Dr. Edward J. Bell, Director
Department of Aeronautical
        Engineering
The University of Oklahoma
Norman, Oklahoma

Dear Sir:

We have given much thought to your suggestion...

Professor H. Carl Brighton
Massachusetts Institute of
        Technology
Cambridge Station
Boston, Massachusetts

Dear Professor Brighton:

It was a pleasure to hear from you regarding...

Although none of the above examples have included postal zones or ZIP Codes, they should appear when known to the writer. These notations, suggested by our Government, speed letter deliveries and deserve our cooperation. The postal zone goes after the city—Chicago 38, Illinois. The ZIP Code, which includes the postal zone number, goes after the state—Chicago, Illinois 38205.

4. **Numbers.** The use of a sign or word before a street number is taboo in the inside address. The number can stand on its own legs.

Wrong: Mrs. Jacob Goldman,
           #3561 Lindell Boulevard,
           Louisville, Kentucky.
Wrong: Mrs. Jacob Goldman,
           No. 3561 Lindell Boulevard,
           Louisville, Kentucky.
Right: Mrs. Jacob Goldman,
           3561 Lindell Boulevard,
           Louisville, Kentucky.

When the numeric names of streets and avenues are composed of single numbers, they should be spelled; when composed of compound numbers, use the figures.

Wrong·   Seventy-third Street
Right: 73rd Street or 73 Street
Wrong: 4th Avenue
Right: Fourth Avenue

A possible exception to the above rule is created in those cities where numbers and words are used to identify streets and avenues of the same names, as "4th Street," and "Fourth Avenue"—the one thoroughfare usually running east and west, and the other north and south. In such cases, the typist uses the forms established by the city, as otherwise there might be confusion in delivery.

5. Abbreviations. To an extent, the use of abbreviations in the inside address of a business letter is dictated by custom, or by the personal inclination of the writer or company. You should never abbreviate the name of a city. Even when "to do or not to do" is a matter of choice, the fact still remains that most typed words look better when *not* abbreviated, and nothing is gained by the shortened forms except a little saving of space and time. Certainly, good taste decrees *consistency* in the one direction or the other.

Wrong: Mr. John T. Williamson,
             1876 Parkview *Avenue,*
             Atlanta, *Ga.*

Right: Mr. John T. Williamson,
             1876 Parkview *Avenue,*
             Atlanta, *Georgia.*

Right: Mr. John T. Williamson,
             1876 Parkview *Ave.,*
             Atlanta, *Ga.*

In general, the abbreviations used may be grouped in three classes: obligatory, customary, and permissible. Those in the last group are left to the choice of the writer, but it is not wise to disregard those in the second group dictated by custom. Those in the first group may not under any circumstances be spelled out.

(a) Abbreviations that *must* be used in both the outside and the inside address are those already fixed in the official name of the company or association as indicated on their letterhead. Even though the abbreviated word may not appeal to the writer of the letter, and he would much prefer to see it spelled out, there still remains no choice. This also is true of the substitution of the sign *&* for *and.* While not technically an abbreviation, it may logically be included with the others, such as *Co.* for *Company,* and *Corp.* for *Corporation.*

(b) There are many of the abbreviations so firmly established by custom that they should not be tampered with. For example, the use of *Mister* instead of the abbreviated form would be rather sure to attract unfavorable attention, and thus in its small way detract from the success of the letter. These abbreviations established by custom are listed below:

> Mr., Mrs., Messers., Mmes., Esq., Jr., Sr.
>
> Those of professional or official significance—such as C.P.A. for Certified Public Accountant, Ph.D. for Doctor of Philosophy, and M.D.S. for Master of Dental Surgery.
>
> Those that stand for trade associations, such as A.A.A. for American Automobile Association.
>
> Names of honorary significance, such as D.A.R. for Daughters of the American Revolution, D.S.O. for Distinguished Service Order, and F.A.M. for Free and Accepted Masons.
>
> The other very common forms, such as P.O.B. for Post Office Box, or M.P. for Member of Parliament.

(c) The abbreviations left to choice are many. For example:

> Titles, such as Prof. for Professor, Rev. for Reverend, and Hon. for Honorable
>
> The names of the states, with certain exceptions.
>
> Business designations, such as Pres. for President, Sec. for Secretary, and Treas. for Treasurer.
>
> Words standing for street direction, such as S. for South, W. for West.
>
> Names of thoroughfares, such as St. for Street, Blvd. for Boulevard, or Ave. for Avenue.

As previously stated, these abbreviations in the flexible group are best when used only for a good reason, such as to shorten a long line in the inside address. They do not improve the typed letter's appearance.

A few additional facts should be understood with respect to abbreviations in the inside address.

(a) When the person addressed holds more than one degree, indicate only the highest, unless there are two or more in different fields of endeavor.

> *Wrong:* Professor Albert S. Jones, A.B., A.M., Ph.D.
> *Right:*   Albert S. Jones, Ph.D.
> *Right:*   Asa B. Underwood, A.M., LL.D.

(b) When only the last name is known, it is considered discourteous to abbreviate the title.

Wrong: Prof. Bagby...Dr. Schreiner
Right: Professor Bagby...Doctor Schreiner

(c) If the last name only is used, the word *Reverend* should be followed by *Mr.*—or *Dr.* if the clergyman is a D.D. It is customary to abbreviate this word, unless preceded by *The.*

Wrong: Rev. Boardman
           Reverend Boardman
Right: Rev. Mr. Boardman
           Rev. Dr. Boardman
           Rev. James Boardman
           The Reverend Mr. Boardman
           The Reverend Doctor Boardman
           The Reverend James Boardman

(d) The use of the word *Honorable* and its abbreviation is the same as that of *Reverend.*

Wrong: Hon. Bricker
           Honorable Bricker
Right: Hon. Mr. Bricker
           Hon. John W. Bricker
           The Honorable John W. Bricker
           The Honorable Mr. Bricker

(e) The word *Esquire* or its abbreviation is sometimes used after the names of prominent attorneys or other high ranking professional men who do not have other titles. The custom dates back to early days and is fast fading in popularity. When a title precedes the name, the use of the word or its abbreviation is not permitted.

Wrong: Mr. L. E. Mackie, Esq.
Right: L. E. Mackie, Esq.
Wrong: Dr. Claude Minton, Esq.

(f) The use of *Messrs.* is not permissible in addressing companies or association with impersonal names. It is okay for a company where the names in the title represent men, or men and women.

Wrong: Messrs. General Electric Company
           Messrs. Illinois Central System
Right: General Electric Company
           Illinois Central System

Right: Messrs. Brown, Brown, and Brown
            Messrs. Marrison Parks and Bros.
            Messrs. Wollett and Kirby

(g) When the company or organization is headed by women, married or single, either *Mesdames* or *Mmes.* may be used.

Right: Mesdames Darby and Moore
            Mmes. Darby and Moore

(h) A widow should be addressed as *Mrs.*—and socially she continues to be known by her husband's name. In legal and financial affairs, however, her given name is substituted.

Socially: Mrs. Abner Carter
Legally: Mrs. Julia Carter

(i) A divorced woman may continue to use her husband's full name, or a combination of his and her surnames. She does not use her given name, as that is supposed to indicate her guilt in the incidents leading to the divorce. However, if she has legally resumed her maiden name, she may be addressed as *Miss.*

Right: Mrs. Andrew H. Bronson
Wrong: Mrs. Bernice Bronson
Right: Mrs. Baker Bronson
Right: Miss Bernice Baker (if legal)

6. Capitalization. Prevailing customs for capitalization within the inside address are as follows. Some are a matter of correct English practice, others are rules developed by common usage.

Capitalize—

(a) Initials, given names, and surnames.

(b) All words and abbreviations in the names of companies, trade associations, and other organizations, *except* conjunctions, prepositions, and articles. However, an *exception* to the exception is that an article must be capitalized if it starts a line.

Right: Empire Service Corporation
            The Brokers' Institute
            Peoria Advertising and Selling Club
            Baker, Brown, and Buggins, Inc.
            The City of Columbus

(c) Names of thoroughfares, and words that describe direction.

Right: 22 East Gay Street
            431 West Fifth Avenue
            33 Park Terrace
            5676 Oleotangy Boulevard
            6654 Riverside Drive
            377 Linden Place
            111 Lee Circle
            4443 Magnolia Plaza
            7982 Rock Terrace Highway
            4433 Cemetery Road

(d) Words to indicate post office delivery, and rural mail routes.

Right: Post Office Box 99
            P. O. Box 333, Station B
            Care of General Delivery
            Rural Route 3

(e) Names of buildings, and units in them.

Right: The Buckeye Building
            Room 777, Federal Insurance Building
            Apartment D, the Park Plaza
            Suite BB, Jefferson Hotel

(f) Names of cities, counties, territories, provinces, states, nations and their abbreviations.

Right: Columbus, Franklin County, Ohio
            Washington, D. C.

(g) Abbreviations for degrees and other official designations.

(h) Titles and designations of rank or position, such as Miss, Mrs., Mr., Professor, Dr., the Reverend, Messrs., Mmes., Secretary, Vice-President, Chairman of the Board, Manager, Editor, Personnel Director, and the others. When the title consists of more than one word, all are capitalized except articles, conjunctions, and prepositions.

(i) Names of divisions or departments within an organization or company, except for articles, conjunctions, and prepositions.

Right: Department of Finance
            Maintenance and Repair Division
            Committee for City Planning

7. The attention line. Considerable difference of thought exists in the business letter world with respect to the necessity of the attention line and where it should be placed. It is discussed here, in connection with the inside address, because it is the opinion of your commentator that nine out of ten of the attention lines encountered in business correspondence could just as well, or better, have been omitted. We see no reason, at least generally, why a letter should be addressed to a company, and then bounced back into the lap of an individual through an attention line. Why not address the letter to the individual, followed by the name of the company? This is a controversial question, and after you have examined the evidence on both sides, you may make your own decision as to which plan you prefer.

John Doe, for example, is about to write a letter, with a check enclosed, to the Canary Cracker Company. He would have sent the money sooner, but an argument has been going on as to whether or not he is entitled to a special discount he thought he would get. Several letters have passed back and forth between John Doe and Robert Black, Credit Manager for the cracker company.

Okay, that is the simple background, and here is the problem faced by John Doe. Obviously, he owes the money to Canary Cracker Company, but all of his correspondence has been with Mr. Black. How shall his letter be directed? That is the point where the opinion of business men and letter experts seems to split. One group says that John Doe should write to the company, and ask that his letter be called to the attention of Robert Black. The other side says that is nonsense. Mr. Black's delegated responsibility in the company is understood. He is the Credit Manager. He *represents* the company, and has authority to make decisions. Why go around and around the mulberry bush? Write to Black direct.

Well, if you want to get into the fight, take off your coat. You are welcome. Here are the two ways that John Doe might address his letter.

With *Attention* *Line*	Canary Cracker Company Main Street at Drexel Hijinks, Colorado Attention Robert Black Gentlemen:
The *Direct* *Approach*	Mr. Robert Black, Credit Manager Canary Cracker Company Main Street at Drexel Hijinks, Colorado. Dear Mr. Black:

If one looks with impartiality at both sides of the question, it is apparent that the attention line can at times serve a useful purpose. The chief objection is that it adds a formal touch to the appearance of the letter, and thus works against the major aim of making every letter a personal contact between writer and reader. Furthermore, it seems that some businessmen fall into the habit of using the attention line a lot more often than is necessary. But if there are circumstances which make its use advisable, as when some legal question is involved, or when the name of the head of a department is unknown, the attention line merits approval. However, it is safe to say that the attention line is declining in popularity.

Sometimes the need is also felt for a reference line, such as the order number, the file number, or the subject of the letter being answered. In a consideration of the appearance of the letter, and the necessity for keeping it as simple as possible, it is much better when the letter does not need to be cluttered with any of these special items; when absolutely necessary, the following position is recommended:

Iowa Mail Order Company
343 Chapel Avenue
Davenport, Iowa
Attention John B. Duffy
Gentlemen: *Order No. 7889*
The lawn mower which you billed on the above order number is being returned today because...

Sometimes, to facilitate the handling of mail, large organizations *ask* that an identifying number or initials be mentioned when the reply to a letter is dictated. This leaves the writer no choice but to follow instructions, as otherwise his letter may not get to the right party, or receive prompt attention. There are also companies that ask, on their letterheads, that all mail be directed to the company, rather than to any individual in it. Here again, the writer should accept the fact that there must be a reason for the request, and comply with it.

There are two positions for the attention line that are favored by many executives today: one is opposite the salutation; the other is below the name of city and state.

There is one style for the reference line which is out of date and especially displeasing in its suggestion of formality. This is the use of *Re:* with respect to the letter being answered, an order number, or the subject.

Even if the caption must be used, as it seldom has to be, the *Re:* is totally unnecessary, as the mere giving of prominence to the item tells the reader it is going to be the subject of the letter. Notice how some of the formality is lost by the omission of this little "throwback" to early letter-writing days.

Re: Your letter of March 10	*Your letter of March 10*
Re: August Sales Contest	*August Sales Contest*
Re: Order No. 8873	*Order Number 8873*

8. Names. Accuracy in the use of names is a most important requisite for the inside address, as well as any other place in the letter or on the envelope. The average individual holds high respect for his name, and wants nobody to take liberties with it. Furthermore, he has selected for his own use the form which he likes best, and any variation by others is likely to irritate him. He expects you to spell the words correctly, to use the right initials, and he doesn't like any combination to which he is not accustomed. Offhand, you might think that any error which does not interfere with the delivery of the letter must be a small thing to worry about, but that is not true. It is discourteous to write any part of an individual's name incorrectly, and doing so is quite likely to hinder the success of the letter. For example:

John D. Jones does not appreciate being addressed as John B. Jones.

Conrad C. Nutter wants his first name spelled out, or he wouldn't sign it that way. He doesn't want you to write to him as C. C. Nutter.

J. Alphonse Goodfellow has some reason sufficient to himself for not spelling out the first name. Even though you knew it to be James, it would be unwise to address him as James Alphonse.

Wm. H. Warren likes the abbreviation for William. Then why take the chance of displeasing him by spelling out the name?

L. E. "Cy" Frailey may look like a funny way for a fellow to sign his name, and probably it is. But go along with him. He likes it, so humor the codger.

If Mr. Boone uses the signature Marshall V. Boone, III, then that's your cue. Address him the same way.

There may be no real reason for John Jacob Heinbaugh to place "Jr." after his name, because you know his father is dead and there could be no confusion in delivery of his mail. But follow his lead. His signature carries the "Jr."—respect his preference.

When replying to another man's letter, his signature is your guide—*if* you can read it. Of course, if the name seems to have been written in a wild frenzy by a contortionist, you may not be able to decipher it. However, if he is a courteous fellow and considerate of your feelings, he no doubt has his secretary solve your problem by typing the correct name underneath the spot where he intends to have his fling. Or his name may be printed on the letterhead. Otherwise,, you are in for it, and can only do your best.

Other times, the letter may be going to an individual as the first contact, and only the last name is known. For such a predicament, the solution may be found in the telephone book, the city directory, *Who's Who,* or some other national compilation of names and titles. Or, it may be that someone else in the company has had previous correspondence with the same individual. It is surprising how much information the files of an organization may produce for those who will turn to them.

Accuracy in writing company names is also important, as any error indicates lack of familiarity with the company, and it may detract, in the mind of the reader, from the good impression which the writer wants to make. There is seldom any excuse for a mistake of this kind, as usually there is a letterhead available which carries the correct form.

With a letterhead before you, there is no problem. When in Rome, do as the Romans do. What you might like, if the firm were yours, is of no consequence. Your typist must type the name exactly as it is used by the company.

The variations in name forms are numerous, and that requires alertness in copying the style of each particular company. Some begin with *The,* and others do not. Some prefer abbreviations such as *Inc., Corp.,* and *Co.,* and others like these words spelled out. In a sequence of surnames, some firms use a comma preceding *and,* and others omit it.

> The Pierce Brokerage Company
> Union Clothing Company
> Bates and Gerry, Incorporated
> John C. Featherweight, Inc.
> The Dartnell Corporation
> The American Mutual Benefit Corp.
> James W. Underwood Company
> The Universal Motor Co.
> Baker, Jones, Brown, and Bean
> Walker, Bechtel, Doe and Flesh

When the exact form of the company or organization name is not known and there seems to be no way to check it, you may use the forms considered best. This would mean, with respect to the variations illustrated above, that you would use *The* when the rest of the name permits; spell out Incorporated, Corporation, and Company; and not use the comma between the last two names of the sequence. But these choices would endure only until the official forms became known. After that, you would properly frame the inside address to conform with company usage.

Street names should be spelled exactly as they exist, although sometimes this rule is disregarded. For example, *St. Louis* is the official form for that city, and not Saint Louis. To be sure, a few firms in that city may use the longer form in an effort to lend glamour to the name, but the practice is not to be commended.

In connection with street names, there are the words which designate direction, and when space permits, they should not be abbreviated. Usually, the qualifying word appears after the number and before the generic name, but when placed last in the line it should be preceded by a comma.

> 999 *North* High Street
> 3232 *East* Broad Street
> 121 *South* Parkview Drive
> 4996 S. E. Connecticut Avenue
>   (Abbreviated to conserve space)
> 3333 Grand Avenue, North
> 237 Lindell Street, East
> 6543 Tchoupitoulas Street, S. W.
>   (Abbreviated to conserve space)

When a street number immediately follows a house number, confusion must be avoided by one of two devices. Either the space between the numbers should be doubled, or a comma should be placed between them. Of course, there is no problem when a word standing for direction appears between the two numbers.

> 656 32 Street
> 656, 32 Street
> 924 East 15 Avenue

For corner addresses, it is often customary in business to use the names of the intersecting thoroughfares, omitting numbers. If both are of the same type—streets, avenues, roads—the designating word may be used only once in the plural form. If they differ in type, both of the designating words must be used.

> *Right:*   Grant and McKinley Streets

Wrong: Grant Street and McKinley Street
Right: Lee Avenue at Clay Street
Wrong: Lee and Clay

Earlier in this section, pages 231 to 241, other facts related to the street address were covered. It would help to review them in connection with the material just presented.

9. Titles. No one has to go through life without a title, even though the three most common lack the distinction of rarity. They are, of course, *Mr., Mrs.,* and *Miss,* the first two being abbreviations of *Mister* and *Mistress.* Only the abbreviations are ever used in business correspondence, but their acceptance is so wide that to omit them, when no other higher title is sanctioned, is not considered good taste.

Any man may be addressed as *Mr.,* and any woman as *Mrs.* if she is married, a widow, or a divorcee who has not gone back to the title of *Miss.* As explained previously, a married woman uses her title in connection with the full name of her husband, but a widow also has the choice of substituting her given name for that of her departed husband. If the choice is known to the letter writer, he properly complies with her wishes.

Married: Mrs. Albert K. Kissell
Widow: Mrs. Albert K. Kissell, or
           Mrs. Mary Anne Kissell
Divorcee: Mrs. Mackey Kissell (husband's surname)
           Mrs. Mary Anne Mackey (maiden name)
           Miss Mary Anne Mackey (as before wedding)

The title of *Miss* is used to address a girl or older unmarried woman. It is not an abbreviation, and so requires no period. One of the problems which often confronts the business letter writer is how to address a lady when he does not know if she is single or married. He may have a letter before him, signed by "Elisabeth Long," with the designation, "Credit Department," but he has no way of telling whether her proper title is *Mrs.* or *Miss.* He decides that even if he is not correct, a single woman objects more to being addressed as *Mrs.* than does a married woman to being addressed as *Miss.* So he takes a chance on *Miss.* This reasoning is approved by the letter authorities. When you don't know and can't find out, use *Miss.*

However, a little better co-operation on the part of the feminine workers in business would go a long way toward removing the problem. Thus, it might be insisted by a business executive that any lady writing letters for his company should use *Miss* or *Mrs.* in connection with her signature. Instead, the situation is sometimes encountered where a woman in business is allowed to sign only her initials and surname. Thus, a customer might write letters over a long period of time to B. L. Garner, and never realize that this company representative wore skirts, and that the initials stood for Betty Louise. This is hardly fair to either party, as the customer might say things in his letters not appropriate for the feminine sex.

Questionable:	B. L. Garner (a woman)
Better:	Betty L. Garner (but confusing)
Best:	(Mrs.) B. L. Garner
	(Miss) Betty L. Garner

Titles belonging to a man do not carry over to the use of his wife, and are not to be combined with *Mrs.* in the outside or inside address of a business letter.

Wrong:	Mrs. Professor J. B. Maynard
	Mrs. Dr. Wayne Brooks
	Mrs. Reverend George Rook
Right:	Mrs. J. B. Maynard
	Mrs. Wayne Brooks
	Mrs. George Rook

Women should be addressed by titles other than *Mrs.* or *Miss* only when they themselves hold right to them. For example, a woman may be addressed properly as *Dr.* if she has been awarded a doctor's degree by a university in such branches of knowledge as law (LL.D), Divinity (D.D.), medicine (M.D.), or philosophy (Ph.D.).

In the same way, women may hold many other titles, along with men— all to be recognized in addressing business letters, or those for other purposes. Thus, when the right exists, a woman may be addressed as *Professor, Dean, Honorable, Reverend,* or by any of the business designations, such as *President, Treasurer, Director, Manager,* or *Superintendent.* While women are not found in all of the positions of rank held by men, for example, President of the United States, nor in equal numbers, the same forms of address and salutation are used, with two exceptions. One is the substitution of the word *Madam* for *Sir* and *Mr.,* and the second, the avoidance of masculine terms such as *Congressman* and *Assemblyman.* Of course, most of these changes are necessary in the greetings rather than the addresses.

Inside Address	*Salutation*
The Honorable John L. Doe,	Sir:
The House of Representatives,	Dear Sir:
Washington, D. C.	My dear Congressman:

The Honorable Clara B. Jones,   Madam:
The House of Representatives,   Dear Madam:
Washington, D. C.   Dear Representative Jones:

It will greatly simplify your understanding of titles and their uses if you will think of them with respect to the major groups into which they may be classified. The rules for each group are limited by tradition and custom, so that modern letter writers are forced to obey conventions and formalities which are a hindrance to the general objective of making every letter a natural, man-to-man contact. If some of these old threads could be cut, without in any way ignoring the demands of courtesy or lessening respect for authority, it would be a step forward in business correspondence. Probably the trend is already moving in that direction, but it may be many years before convention will permit any person to be addressed in the first line as "Mr. John Doe," followed in the second by a simple statement of his position or rank. Should this ever come to pass, it will not decrease the prestige of any person of importance, as public respect is surely created more by performance than by the mere bleating of titles or the insistence on forms handed down from the past.

Until that much-to-be-desired day, there are forms which need to be followed for the inside address and salutation, and persons who violate them are open to the accusation of ignorance or disrespect. In general, persons of rank fall into one of several groups including: the Military; the Governmental—National, State, and Municipal; the Judicial; the Educational; the Clergy; the Diplomatic Service, local and abroad; the Nobility; and those of Business. Each of these groups has its own set of conventions, and some are characterized by key words, such as "Doctor," "Reverend," "Honorable," and "Esquire"—as previously noted in the discussion of abbreviations. In each case, an agreement in style exists between the inside address and the salutation, so that the letter writer needs to survey both of them in his effort to inform himself as to what are the correct forms for each situation.

6. Salutation and Complimentary Close

The salutation. When you walk into a man's office, come down to the breakfast table, or meet an acquaintance on the street, your natural impulse is to extend some form of greeting. You say, "Good morning," or "Hello," or "How do you do?" and the other person would consider you rude if you didn't.

This is exactly what happens in the business letter when you write the salutation. You are greeting the other party before starting the message to be presented in the body of the letter. The ice is broken, and your reader sits back to see what you have to say.

Unfortunately, the greetings used in business letters are not nearly as natural or friendly as those used in personal contacts. Instead, they have been so standardized by custom, in stiff and stilted forms, that little warmth is left in them. This is especially true of the salutations considered proper for persons of rank. They are cut and dried, and serve no good purpose except to satisfy the demands of established custom. To omit them would be called an act of discourtesy and might offend the "bigwigs" to whom the letters are addressed, yet few writers feel that they add in any way to what they are trying to accomplish.

For this reason, no doubt, a revolution against the salutation has been under way for several years in certain business organizations, including some of our largest companies. They have gone so far as to omit entirely the salutation in their letters, and most of the pioneers who have led this crusade will tell you that there has been no loss of goodwill or effectiveness as a result of the bold departure. Whether or not the idea of this omission appeals to you is beside the question. At least, it is at work in business circles, and you should know about it. The number of companies that omit the salutation seems definitely to be increasing, too.

For example, the salutation is not used in letters mailed from one of the nation's largest utilities. Instead, the reader's name is used in the first sentence of each letter, with a tone of cordiality which more than takes the place of the missing salutation. Thus, these letters begin: "Yes, indeed, Mrs. Leary, we will be glad to turn on the gas for you at your new home next Saturday," or "Thanks, Mrs. Bailey, for your letter about the April bill," or "As you requested, Mr. Gordon, we are enclosing an itemized list of your gas bills for last year." These sentences, we think, do a better job in getting the letters started pleasantly, than would the conventional salutations of "Dear Sir," or "Dear Madam," or "Dear Mrs. Bailey." After all, the letters of this company have been remarkably successful in building customer goodwill, although no one can say how much the omission of the salutation has contributed to that accomplishment.

How does a business letter look without a salutation? Well, like this:

July 6, 1964

Mrs. James C. Wood,
4961 South Wabash Avenue,
Chicago, Illinois

Yes, you are right. Your check for $15.86 paid in full your bills for July and August. You owe us nothing, Mrs. Wood.

We want you to know that we have appreciated having you as
a customer, and we hope you will enjoy your new home in Joliet.

Should you later return to Chicago, we will be happy to have
the privilege of serving you again. Your credit will remain very
good with us, for you have been very prompt in meeting every
obligation.

Sincerely yours,

Would the omission of the salutation in such a friendly letter make
any difference in its reception by the customer? Frankly, the answer to
that question is a matter of opinion. You may draw your own conclusion.

In the meantime, consider the various aspects of the salutation, as it is
still commonly used in American business letters:

1. Position. The salutation should be typed two or more spaces below
the last line of the inside address; it helps to establish the left-hand margin
of the letter. The preferred number of spaces is two, since otherwise the
inside address seems to dangle apart from the rest of the letter. However,
when window envelopes are used, it is sometimes expedient to increase the
number of spaces, and the same device is used by some letter writers for
very short letters. The great majority, however, favor the two-space separa-
tion, and it probably results in the best appearance. For those letters where
the inside address is placed below the body, the salutation is typed several
spaces below the date line, but of course on the left side of the page. The
actual number of spaces depends on the length of the letter and the judgment of the typist or her superior.

2. Content. The salutation may be singular or plural, depending on
the nature of the first line of the inside address. It should be singular if the
letter is sent to one individual, and plural if to a company, organization,
a box number, any group such as a board of directors or a committee, or
to more than one individual.

The most common plural forms are *Gentlemen* and *Mesdames* or
Ladies. The first word, of course, is used in letters going to companies, or
associated persons, as a committee or partnership, where the heads are
either all men, or a combination of men and women. The other two words
are used when the company or group consists entirely of women. When
there is any doubt as to an all-female cast, the masculine word should
be used.

In military and official correspondence, but preferably in no other
kind, *Sir* or *Sirs* is a correct salutation. It is a very formal and uninviting
greeting and has nothing at all to recommend it for business letters, not
even when combined with *Dear* or *My Dear.*

Obviously, a letter to a company or group is more formal in nature than one to an individual, and for the latter considerably more freedom is allowed in choosing the appropriate salutation; the selection will depend on previous relationships between writer and reader and the contents of the message, which may be "strictly business," or semi-personal. In today's business correspondence, salutations run a wide gamut from formal to personal, and the only problem is that of using the one which best fits the particular situation.

This range in choice for salutations to an individual runs from "cold to warm," and covers a lot of ground, but the following are typical:

Sir:	My dear Blake:
My dear Sir:	Dear Blake:
Dear Sir:	My dear Carl:
My dear Mr. Blake:	Dear Carl:
Dear Mr. Blake:	

Another form not often seen, but which seems to have an added warmth, is that in which both given and surname are used—"My dear Carl Blake." Then there are the other more personal forms allowable only when the relationship is very friendly, and of long standing. Among them are:

Dear friend:	Hello, Carl:
Dear friend Carl:	Thanks, Carl:
Good morning, Carl:	Right you are, Carl:

Because of the extreme informality, the salutations just mentioned are only a sample of the many variations which these non-traditional greetings may take. On the whole, their use is dangerous, and for that reason not recommended for everyday business correspondence. On the other hand, they do come closer to the greetings exchanged in speech, and when appropriate they help to make the letter a personal contact.

Salutations to ladies follow the same pattern as those for men. In the order of decreasing formality, they include:

Madam:	{ Dear Mrs. Blake:
My dear Madam:	{ Dear Miss Blake:
Dear Madam:	My dear Phyllis:
{ My dear Mrs. Blake:	Dear Phyllis:
{ My dear Miss Blake:	

For some reason hard to explain, the form "My dear," followed by the name, is more commonly used in letters to women than in letters to men. For the latter, the "Dear" without the "My" seems to be more popular.

When the title *Dr.* is used in the salutation, it takes the place of *Mr.* The same is true of *Professor* or its abbreviation. Otherwise, letters to doctors or professors run the same gamut of decreasing formality, except that the more personal forms of greeting seem to be used less frequently—perhaps because some writers are awed in approaching men of such importance:

<table>
<tr><td>My dear Sir:</td><td>My dear Sir:</td></tr>
<tr><td>Dear Sir:</td><td>Dear Sir:</td></tr>
<tr><td>My dear Dr. Battin:</td><td>My dear Professor Roe:</td></tr>
<tr><td>Dear Dr. Battin:</td><td>Dear Professor Roe:</td></tr>
<tr><td>My dear Fred:</td><td>My dear Emanuel:</td></tr>
<tr><td>Dear Fred:</td><td>Dear Emanuel:</td></tr>
</table>

The words, *Honorable, Reverend,* and *Esquire,* are not used in the salutation, even though they appear in the inside address. If he holds a doctor's degree, a clergyman with the title of *Reverend* should be addressed as *Dr.* in the salutation. If he does not hold a degree, the proper word is *Mr.* The use of a clergyman's surname with *Dear* or *My dear* is not considered good taste. Do not say in the salutation, *Dear Worthsbey* or *My dear Worthsbey.* When the relationship is extremely personal, however, you may correctly address the clergyman by his first name—*Dear Harold* or *My dear Harold.*

<table>
<tr><td>My dear Sir:</td><td>{Dear Dr. Worthsbey:</td></tr>
<tr><td>Dear Sir:</td><td>{Dear Mr. Worthsbey:</td></tr>
<tr><td>{My dear Dr. Worthsbey:</td><td>My dear Harold:</td></tr>
<tr><td>{My dear Mr. Worthsbey:</td><td>Dear Harold:</td></tr>
</table>

For *Esquire,* substitute *Mr.* in the salutation. Thus, the proper form is *Dear Mr. Mills,* and not *Dear Esq. Mills* or *Dear Esquire.* In connection with the last mentioned error, it should be noted that no title should be used in a salutation without the surname. It is just as wrong to say, *Dear Doctor, Dear Reverend,* or *My dear Professor.* Use, instead,

Dear Doctor Merkle:
Dear Reverend Harms:
My dear Professor Pate:

Occasionally, business letter writers omit *Dear* or *My dear* in the salutation, and simply use the reader's name and title—*Mr. John Baker* or *Dr. Arthur Jones;* even the first name is sometimes omitted—*Mr. Baker* or *Dr. Jones.* Since the authorities disapprove the practice, you cannot afford to copy it, but it is easy to understand the motive. One of the great inconsistencies in all forms of correspondence, and especially in that for business purposes, is the use of the word *Dear* in any of the common forms. It is, for example, hard to justify a word of affection in a greeting from one business man to another. John Bates and Oscar Prine may never have met, and yet Mr. Bates says to his secretary. "Take a letter to Oscar Prine ...*Dear* Mr. Prine." Credit Manager Albert Smith writes to a customer that his patience is exhausted, and that unless a check is soon forthcoming legal action will be taken. But he still says, *"Dear* Sir." The clerk in a mail-order house writes to a woman in North Dakota, and though he knows her not, he says, *"Dear* Mrs. Malstrom."

You can see that custom has sanctioned a word which logically has no place in impersonal contacts. Perhaps this fact will be recognized eventually, and those who now defy the authorities by refusing to use the word will be hailed as worthy pioneers. Perhaps! We hardly think it ever will be so; therefore, you may continue to use the term until the experts frown upon it.

In the salutation of a business letter it is not permissible to substitute a designation of rank or position for a name, title, or for both. A similar designation after the name of the individual is also taboo.

Wrong:	Dear Comptroller:
	My dear Mr. Comptroller:
	Dear Comptroller Williams:
Right:	Dear Mr. Williams:
Wrong:	Dear Mr. Williams, Comptroller:
	My dear Mr. Lait, President:
	Dear Mrs. Brown, D.A.R.:
Right:	Dear Mr. Williams:
	My dear Mrs. Brown:

Some authorities object to the salutation, *Dear Friend,* but under certain circumstances, your author sees no objection to it. If the man to whom you are writing *is* a friend, why not address him as such? Certainly, the use of the word cannot be as illogical as that of *Dear.* Moreover, it does not stretch the imagination too greatly to think of even a customer as a friend, and for some form letters to customers of long standing, the term does not seem too farfetched or unreasonable.

3. Abbreviations. The only titles that may properly be abbreviated in the salutation are *Mr., Mrs.,* and *Dr.* Particularly offensive are such contractions as *Gents.* for *Gentlemen,* or in lesser degree, *D'r* for *Doctor.* We can think of no better way for a letter-writer to label himself as an ignoramus, than to address a company or group as "Dear Gents," although now and then this monstrosity is met in business correspondence. The title *Messrs.* or the feminine version *Mmes.* should not be used as a salutation, or as any part of one.

> *Wrong:* Messrs.:
>   Mmes.:
>   Messrs. Bailey and Bailey:
>   Mmes. Helen Rupert, Inc.:
> *Right:* Gentlemen:
>   Ladies:

4. Capitalization. There are four things to remember in connection with capitalization in the salutation of a business letter. Always use capitals for: *Sir* and *Madam,* given names and surnames, titles, and the first word.

A *don't* for good measure is that the word "dear" is never capitalized unless it starts the line.

> *Wrong:* My Dear Miss Jones:
> *Right:* Dear Miss Jones:

ADDRESS AND SALUTATION FORMS
FOR INDIVIDUALS OF RANK

(When two or more forms are suggested for the same title, they are listed in the order of decreasing formality. To complete address, the street and number, and the names of city and state, need to be added.)

Abbot

The Right Reverend Abbot Denn, O.S.B. (or other initials of the Order)

Right Reverend and dear Abbot:

Dear Father Abbot:

Admiral, Full, Fleet

The Admiral of the Navy of the United States

Admiral Jonathan Doe
Chief of Naval Operations

Dear Sir:

Dear Admiral Doe:

Alderman

Alderman James B. Noon

Dear Sir:

Dear Alderman Noon:

Ambassador (American)

His Excellency	Sir:
The American Ambassador	
to Great Britain	Your Excellency:
The American Embassy	
London, England	Dear Mr. Ambassador:

The Honorable Carl Reid
The American Ambassador
    to Great Britain

Ambassador (Foreign)

His Excellency	Sir:
The Ambassador of the French	
Republic	Excellency:
French Embassy	
Washington, D. C.	Your Excellency:

His Excellency
M. René Lenoir
Ambassador of the French
    Republic

Archbishop

Most Reverend Albert B. Dean	Your Excellency:
	Your Grace:

Archdeacon

The Venerable the Archdeacon of	Venerable Sir:
Philadelphia	

The Venerable Woodson Ware,
    Archdeacon of Philadelphia

Assemblyman

The Honorable Walter B. Goon	Dear Sir:
Member of Assembly	
	My dear Mr. Goon:
Assemblyman Walter B. Goon	
	Dear Mr. Goon:

Assistant Secretary (Cabinet)

The Assistant Secretary of the
War Department

Sir:

(My) Dear Sir:

The Honorable Russell C. Doe
Assistant Secretary of the War
Department

My dear Mr. Doe:

Dear Mr. Doe:

(*Never* Mr. Secretary:)

*Associate Justice of the Supreme
Court*

The Honorable William H. Black
Associate Justice of the Supreme
Court

Sir:

Mr. Justice:

The Honorable William H. Black
Justice, Supreme Court of the
United States

Your Honor:

My dear Mr. Justice:

Mr. William H. Black
United States Supreme Court

My dear Justice Black:

Dear Justice Black:

Attorney General
(See Cabinet Officer)

Baron

The Lord Scarborough

Sir:

Dear Lord Scarborough:

Baroness

The Lady Scarborough

Madam:

Dear Lady Scarborough:

Baronet:

Sir James Kinsman, Bart.

Sir:

Bishop (Methodist)

The Reverend Bishop Carl Crew
Bishop of the Eastern Area

Dear Sir:

My dear Bishop Crew:

Dear Bishop Crew:

Bishop (Protestant Episcopal)
The Right Reverend Samuel   Right Reverend and dear Sir:
Seabury
Bishop of Cleveland   My dear Bishop Seabury:

Bishop (Roman Catholic)
The Most Reverend James   Your Excellency:
Bartley
Bishop of Baltimore
                                   My dear Bishop:
The Most Reverend Bishop
Bartley

Bishop (Anglican)
The Right Reverend the Lord   My Lord Bishop:
Bishop of (name of bishopric)
                                   My Lord:
The Lord Bishop of (name of
bishopric)

Bishop (Scottish)
The Right Reverend Bishop   Right Reverend Sir:
James B. McPherson

Brigadier General
Brigadier General   Dear Sir:
Arthur C. Clandleman
                                   Dear General Clandleman:

Cabinet Officer
The Honorable the Secretary of   Sir:
Agriculture (or War, State,
Commerce, etc.)   Dear Sir:

The Honorable the Postmaster   Dear (My dear) Mr. Secretary:
General (or Attorney General)   (Postmaster General, Attorney
                                   General)

Cadet
Cadet Harrison Slagle   Dear Sir:

                                   Dear Cadet Slagle:

                                   Dear Mr. Slagle:

Canon

The Very Reverend Canon Walter Woodsberl

The Very Reverend Walter Canon Woodsberl

Very Reverend Canon:

My dear (or Dear) Canon Woodsberl:

Captain

Captain William Fahnestock United States Army (or Navy or Marine Corps)

Dear Sir:

Dear Captain Fahnestock:

Cardinal

His Eminence, Frank, Cardinal Cantell

His Eminence Cardinal Cantell

Your Eminence:

My Lord Cardinal: (to those of foreign countries)

Cardinal (if also Archbishop)

His Eminence the Cardinal, Archbishop of Baltimore

His Eminence Cardinal Smythe, Archbishop of Baltimore

Your Eminence:

Chargé d'Affaires

The Chargé d'Affaires of Mexico

Mr. Salico Gonzoles Chargé d'Affaires

John Shrewsbury, Esquire Chargé d'Affaires

Sir:

Dear Sir:

My dear Mr. Gonzoles: (or use title if there is one—hereditary, military, or naval)

Chief Justice of the United States

The Honorable John W. Bates Chief Justice of the Supreme Court of the United States

Chief Justice Bates United States Supreme Court

The Chief Justice of the United States

Sir:

Mr. Chief Justice:

My dear Mr. Justice:

Dear Justice Bates:

Chief of Police
 Frank Minton   Dear Sir:
 Chief of Police

            Dear Chief Minton:

Clergyman
 The Reverend Donald Beard Reverend Sir:

 Reverend Dr. Donald Beard My dear Sir:
  (If Doctor of Divinity)

            My dear Mr. Beard:

            Dear Mr. Beard:

            Dear Dr. Beard:

Clerk of the House (or *Senate*)
 The Honorable James Pierce Dear Sir:
 Clerk of the House (or Senate)

            My dear Mr. Pierce:

            Dear Mr. Pierce:

Colonel
 Colonel Gerard B. Goodman Dear Sir:
 United States Army (or Marine
  Corps)   Dear Colonel Goodman:

Commander
 Commander B. C. Winters Dear Sir:
 United States Navy

            Dear Commander Winters:

Commissioner of a Bureau
 The Honorable William Dorset Sir:
 Commissioner of the Bureau of
  Education   Dear Sir:
 Department of Interior

            My dear Mr. Dorset:

Comptroller of the Currency
 The Honorable Robert C. Roberts Sir:
 Comptroller of the Currency

            Dear Sir:

            My dear Mr. Roberts:

Congressman

The Honorable Howard Reamer   Sir:
House of Representatives
                                                Dear Sir:
The Honorable Howard Reamer
Representative in Congress   My dear Congressman Reamer:
    (When away from Washington)
                                                Dear Representative Reamer:
Representative Howard Reamer
House of Representatives   Dear Mr. Reamer:

Congresswoman

The Honorable Clara O. Booth   Dear Madam:
House of Representatives
                                                Dear Representative Booth:
The Honorable Clara O. Booth
Representative in Congress   My dear Miss Booth:
    (When away from Washington)

Representative Clara O. Booth
House of Representatives

Consul

Mr. Richard D. Mann   Dear Sir:
Consul of the United States of
    America   Dear Mr. Consul:

                                                My dear Mr. Mann:

Corporal

Corporal Charles Hayes   Dear Sir:
United States Army or
United States Marine Corps   Dear Mr. Hayes:

Countess

The Countess of Sheffield   Madam:

                                                Dear Lady Sheffield:

Dean (Ecclesiastical)

The Very Reverend the Dean of   Sir:
    St. Joseph's
                                                Very Reverend Sir:
The Very Reverend Dean
    George Conant   Very Reverend Father:
                                                    (Roman Catholic)

Dean (Graduate School or College)
    Dean Casper Millwright   Dear Sir:
    School of Commerce

                              Dear Dean Millwright:

Diplomat
    (See Ambassador, Chargé d'Affaires, Minister. For diplomats of lower rank, use the common forms of address, unless they have military, naval, or hereditary titles.)

Duchess
    The Duchess of Ashleigh   Madam:

                              Dear Duchess of Ashleigh:

Duke
    The Duke of Ashleigh   Sir:

                              Dear Duke of Ashleigh:

Earl
    The Earl of Scofield   Sir:

                              Dear Lord Scofield:

Ensign
    Ensign E. W. Brown   Dear Sir:
    United States Navy

                              Dear Mr. Brown:

Envoy
    (See Minister, Diplomatic)

General
    General Henry S. Hatch   Sir:
    United States Army

                              Dear Sir:

                              Dear General Hatch:

Governor
    His Excellency   Your Excellency:
    The Governor of Ohio
                              Sir:

    The Honorable the Governor of
      Ohio   Dear Sir:

    The Honorable John W. Bricker   My dear Governor Bricker:
    Governor of Ohio

Judge

The Honorable Harold Lemming   Dear Sir:
United States District Judge
                                 Dear Judge Lemming:
The Honorable Amy O'Neil
Judge of the Circuit Court   Dear Madam:

                                 Dear Judge O'Neil:

Knight

Sir James Parkersdam   Sir:

                                 Dear Sir James:

Lawyer

Mr. Carl Benbow   Dear Sir:
Attorney at Law
                                 My dear Mr. Benbow:

                                 Dear Mr. Benbow:

Lieutenant

Lieutenant Ralph Maloney   Dear Sir:
United States Army
                                 Dear Mr. Maloney:

Lieutenant Colonel

Lieutenant Colonel John Beam   Dear Sir:
United States Army
                                 Dear Colonel Beam:
   (Omit the *Lieutenant* in the Salutation.)

Lieutenant Commander

Lieutenant Commander   Dear Sir:
   C. O. Blue
United States Navy   Dear Mr. Blue:
   (The salutation to a naval officer of or below the rank of Lieuten-
   ant Commander should not refer to his title. Use *Mr.*)

Lieutenant General

Lieutenant General Casey Shea   Dear Sir:

                                 Dear General Shea:
   (Omit the *Lieutenant* in the Salutation.)

Lieutenant Governor

  The Honorable Hiram B. Snooks   Sir:
  Lieutenant Governor of Arizona
                                    Dear Sir:

                                    My dear Mr. Snooks:

Major

  Major Robert C. Wolling   Dear Sir:
  United States Army
                                    Dear Major Wolling:

Major General

  Major General T. T. Thaad   Dear Sir:
  United States Army
                                    Dear General Thaad:

     (Omit the *Major* in the Salutation.)

Marchioness

  Marchioness of Huntleigh   Madam:

                                    Dear Lady Huntleigh:

Marquis

  The Marquis of Huntleigh   Sir:

                                    Dear Lord Huntleigh:

Master in Chancery

  Honorable Hugo B. Bauman   Dear Sir:
  Master in Chancery of the Circuit
      Court   Dear Judge Bauman:

Mayor

  The Mayor of the City of Chicago Sir:

  The Honorable Anton J. Kelly   Dear Sir:
  Mayor of the City of Chicago
                                    My dear Mr. Mayor:

                                    Dear Mayor Kelly:

Midshipman

  Midshipman E. C. Obear   Dear Sir:
  United States Navy
                                    Dear Mr. Obear:

Minister (Diplomatic)

The Spanish Minister	Your Excellency:
The Spanish Legation	
Washington, D. C.	Sir:

His Excellency A. B. Coe	My dear Mr. Minister:
Minister of the United States of America	
Madrid, Spain	

Minister (Religious)
(See Clergyman; Priest; Rabbi)

Monk
(See Priest)

Monsignor

The Right Reverend Monsignor Malcomb McComb	The Right Reverend and dear Monsignor:
	The Right Reverend Monsignor Malcomb McComb:
	My dear Monsignor McComb:

Mother Superior

The Reverend Mother Superior Convent of the Sacred Heart	Reverend Mother:
	Dear Madam:
Mother Mary Louise, Superior Convent of the Sacred Heart	My dear Reverend Mother:
Reverend Mother Mary Louise (Plus initials of the order)	Dear Mother Mary Louise:

Nun

Sister Mary Angelica	Reverend Sister:
	Dear Sister Mary Angelica:

Pope

His Holiness Pope Paul VI	Most Holy Father:
	Your Holiness:

Postmaster General
   (See Cabinet Officer)

President (College or *University)*
   President Robert Lee Jones   Dear Sir:
   Ohio University
                                       My dear President Jones:

   Robert Lee Jones LL.D.
   President, Ohio University
      (Use initials of only the highest
      degree, unless in different fields)

   Very Reverend Robert Lee Jones   Very Reverend and dear Father:
   Loyola University
      (If a Catholic College)

President (State Senate)
   The Honorable John Doe,   Sir:
      President
   The Senate of Oklahoma

President (United States Senate)
   The Honorable the President of   Sir:
      the Senate of the United States

   The Honorable James J. James
   President of the Senate
   Washington, D. C.

President of the United States
   The President of the United States   Sir:

   The President   My dear Mr. President:
   The White House
                                       Dear Mr. President:

Priest (Roman Catholic)
   The Reverend Father Harold   Reverend Father:
      Harms
      (Plus initials of the Order)   Dear Father Harms:
      (Above are regular forms; note exceptions below.)

6

Benedictine, Cistercian, or *Canon Regular*
The Very Reverend Dom Harold Harms
(Plus initials of the Order)

Reverend Father:

Dear Father Harms:

Carthusian
The Venerable Father Harold Harms, O. Cart.

Venerable Father:

Dear Father Harms:

Secular
The Reverend Harold Harms
(Plus initials of the Order)

Reverend Sir:

Dear Sir:

Dear Father Harms:

Priest (Episcopal)
Reverend Hector M. Heath

Dear Father Heath:

Professor
Mr. Robert C. Wilcox

Dear Sir:

Professor Robert C. Wilcox

Dear Professor Wilcox:

Dr. Robert C. Wilcox
(If he holds the degree)

Dear Dr. Wilcox:

The Reverend Professor Harold D. Esper

My dear Sir:

Dear Professor Esper:

The Reverend Harold D. Esper D.D.
(If he holds the degree)

Rabbi
Rabbi Jacob Solomon

Reverend Sir:

The Reverend Jacob Solomon

Dear Sir:

Dr. Jacob Solomon

My dear Rabbi Solomon:

Dear Doctor Solomon:

Representative
(See Congressman)

Secretary of Agriculture, Commerce,
  War, etc.
(See Cabinet Officer)

Secretary to the President

The Honorable John Doe	Sir:
Secretary to the President	
The White House	Dear Sir:
	Dear Mr. Doe:

Senator (United States or State)

Senator Alvin E. Tobin	Sir:
The Honorable Alvin E. Tobin	Dear Sir:
United States Senate	
	My dear Senator Tobin:
The Honorable Luther Mack	Dear Senator Mack:
Senate of North Carolina	

Sergeant

Sergeant Terry McGuire	Dear Sir:
U. S. Army or	
U. S. Marine Corps or	Dear Mr. McGuire:
U. S. Air Force	

Sister of Religious Order

The Reverend Sister Mary Louise	My dear Sister:
Sister Mary Louise	
(Plus initials of Order)	Dear Sister Mary Louise:

Speaker of the House

The Honorable the Speaker	Dear Sir:
House of Representatives	
	My dear Mr. Speaker:
The Honorable William Petts	
Speaker of the House of Repre-	Dear Mr. Speaker:
sentatives	

Undersecretary of State

The Undersecretary of State	Sir:

The Honorable Ralph Richey Undersecretary of State	Dear Sir: My dear Mr. Richey:

Vice Admiral and *Rear Admiral*

Vice Admiral Carl Garner Rear Admiral John Case United States Navy	Dear Sir: Dear Admiral Garner: Dear Admiral Case:

Vice-Consul
    (Same forms as Consul)

Vice President of the United States

The Vice President Washington, D. C.	Sir: My dear Mr. Vice President:
The Honorable John Doe Vice President of the United States	Dear Mr. Vice President: Dear Mr. Doe:

Viscount

The Viscount Huntleigh	Sir: Dear Lord Huntleigh:

Viscountess

The Viscountess Huntleigh	Madam: Dear Lady Huntleigh:

Note: The above list includes positions of rank most likely to confront the business letter-writer, but it is not intended to be complete. When two or more forms of address are suggested for the same person of title, any one of them may be accepted as correct. The suggested salutations are only those most commonly used. Any of them are correct, but the more informal ones are recommended.

The Complimentary Close. It is not difficult to understand why below the body of practically all business letters there is added the phrase rather aptly called the "Complimentary Close." That's exactly what it is—a parting gesture from the writer of the letter to his reader. Just as you feel the impulse to end a conversation with "Good-by now" or "Thanks a lot," so does a letter seem to require some similar courtesy to avoid too abrupt an ending—"Yours very truly," "Sincerely yours," or one of the other commonly used expressions.

With the motive for the custom there can be no serious objection, since anything that might tend to humanize a letter-contact must be accepted as quite worthwhile and desirable. But when you remember that the same set of stock phrases are used over and over millions of times every year, you must concede that the complimentary close adds very little warmth to a business letter. It is simply another of the conventions which has come down from the past, and is quite likely to persist for no better reason than "this is the way we've always done it."

To prove that the complimentary close is merely a convention to be taken as a matter of course, like the tipping of your hat to a lady, try to remember which of the customary phrases was used in the very last business letter that came to your attention. Was it "Yours very truly," "Cordially yours," or just *what* was it? Probably you haven't the slightest idea what the words were, and that is no reflection on your memory. It was there, as you would expect it to be, but you paid no attention to it. We think that is what happens ninety-nine times out of a hundred when business letters are read. The complimentary close is taken for granted, and adds nothing to the message in the body of the letter.

Does this mean that the practice might just as well be discontinued? Well, it has been by some companies, and those responsible tell us there has been no criticism from those receiving the letters. The reason is possibly that business-contacts are less likely to be formal and traditional than in other fields of human relations. The businessman, writing to customers and prospects, is less bound by custom than he would be if writing to a high government official or to some other important individual of title.

However, the complimentary close is commonly accepted as a necessary part of the business letter, and so long as the majority of our companies continue to use it, you must understand the rules which govern its form and content as approved by the authorities for different letter situations. Certainly, we do recommend that when choice is offered between the formal and informal forms, that you use the latter.

This leaning toward informality in the complimentary close is strictly in keeping with the modern trend with respect to other aspects of the business letter—the turning away from the old-fashioned stilted phrases, the growing preference for the more intimate forms of salutation, and the general effort to write as we *talk*. Already, the most extreme formal forms of the complimentary close, as seen in the letters of our forefathers, have passed into the letter limbo. We no longer encounter letters ending with

"Your obedient servant," "Yours faithfully, Sir" or those other equally cold and exaggerated forms so common in the past.

1. Position on page. Usually, the complimentary close is typed two spaces below the last line of the body of the letter, but there is no hard-fast rule that it must be in exactly that position. On the contrary, when the letter is very short, a better appearance may be gained by dropping the complimentary close a greater number of spaces. When this is done, however, more space should be allowed for separating the other parts of the letter, as otherwise the complimentary close would seem to dangle alone and remote from the rest of the structure.

The line ordinarily starts a few spaces to the left of the vertical center of the page, and in that position it tends to balance best with the inside address at the top. Here again, the choice of the starting point depends more on the judgment of the typist or dictator, than on any rule that says where it must be marked. You have noted, perhaps, the practice followed by some letter-men of starting the complimentary close in line with the left-hand margin. This radical departure from the more conventional position on the right-hand side is not favored by authority, but it cannot be called an act of business discourtesy or lack of good taste. We have seen some letters typed this way that made a fine appearance, and who would be so hide-bound as to say that any new style is taboo simply because it differs from the old? The American Institute of Business letter illustrates this point. While the position of the complimentary close may be disturbingly different because you are not accustomed to it, one must admit that the general appearance of the letter is both interesting and pleasing.

No matter what the starting place of the complimentary close, it should never extend beyond the line made by the right-hand margin.

2. The common forms. Although there are no rules to tell you exactly what form the complimentary close should take for a particular letter, common sense suggests that in the degree of formality it should conform with the salutation which has been selected as most appropriate for the individual who is to receive the letter. For example, in a letter to a well known business acquaintance or friend it would be absurd to greet him with "Dear Mr. Carter," or "Dear John," and then sign off with "Very respectfully yours." In like manner, it would be just as inconsistent to begin with a blunt "Sir," and then conclude with "Cordially yours." At least the latter fault is not condoned by modern practice, even though you might ask why any gentleman of high rank would object to an expression of cordiality?

As you may have guessed, your author has none too much sympathy with the inherited conventions that tend to stiffen and make unnatural the tone of a business letter. However, we must recognize that these conventions exist, and that they are followed by the great majority of letter-writers, including even those who strive to make the body of their letters human and conversational. Hence, it is well that you should be familiar with the forms of the complimentary close that are commonly used, particularly with their respective degree of formality.

American Institute of Business

KEITH FENTON, B. S., PRESIDENT

GRAND AVENUE AT TENTH
DES MOINES 7, IOWA

May 7, 1962

Mr. L. E. Frailey
1053 North Shore Avenue
Chicago, Illinois

Dear Cy:

When I received your file on your letter writing clinics, I was rather disappointed in the puny efforts of some of those advertising geniuses.

Now I have labored and brought forth a mouse. Let me know what you think of my efforts. Of course, I don't care what you think--if it doesn't get results it won't be worth a dime.

The point is that you are to speak to the group on Wednesday morning, June 15, at nine o'clock. I hope you will rouse the Rock Island engineer and see that he gets you here on time. If there is any slip-up on this, it will be my most embarrassing situation in all the twenty-nine years of my life.

Get yourself a glass cage and stay in it until June 15.

If this clinic "clicks," it will be an annual affair.

May I have your reaction to all this activity?

Very sincerely yours,

Keith Fenton

KEITH FENTON

KF:CW

Complimentary Close and Signature Blocked at Left

The most formal of them all are those that were used by our ancestors. Fortunately, these monstrosities have just about disappeared from business correspondence, although it is surprising to note one book of high authority recommending that a letter to the President of the United States should close with, "I have the honor to remain, Sir, Your most obedient servant," the last four words being the complimentary close. Frankly, we do not think that even our President expects such servility from one of his citizens. For that reason, we do not propose to include such obsolete forms in the list below which contains, in the order of their formality, the phrases now in common use.

Very respectfully yours,	Very sincerely yours,
Yours very respectfully,	Yours very sincerely,
Respectfully yours,	Sincerely yours,
Yours respectfully,	Yours sincerely,
Respectfully,	Sincerely,
Very truly yours,	Very cordially yours,
Yours very truly,	Yours very cordially,
Truly yours,	Cordially yours,
Yours truly,	Yours cordially,
	Cordially,

The above list includes all of the forms recommended by the authorities, but they shut their eyes to many variations which are seen every day in business correspondence. Some are the more intimate forms used by business friends, and others are suggested by special occasions. For example, here are a few typical ones taken from incoming mail:

> Yours with appreciation,
> Best regards,
> Gratefully yours,
> Always a Buckeye,
> Bottoms up, Cy,
> Your Texas friend,

While we realize that these forms may be too personal for general use, there can surely be no harm in them when a friendly relationship exists between writer and recipient. In fact, they have a human touch which would be entirely lacking in any of the old cut-and-dried forms. If one man has done a favor for another, why shouldn't the latter end his thank-you letter with "Yours with appreciation"? "The complimentary close," writes one of the best authorities, "is to a business letter what the expression 'Good-by' is to a conversation." All right, agreed! Then why not make it *conversation?* Not in all letters! Unfortunately, no. If the letter goes to a stranger, to a mere acquaintance, to someone of higher rank, then drag out the proper formality. But there are many occasions in business, when we can be as natural in saying "Good-by" as we would be in speech.

3. Rules to remember. Following are facts about the complimentary close that the business letter-writer needs to know.

(a) Capitalize the first word only.

Wrong: Yours Very Respectfully,
Right: Yours very respectfully,

(b) The last word should be followed with a comma. Even if open punctuation is used for other units of the letter, the comma should be used.

(c) Do not abbreviate in the complimentary close.

Wrong: Yrs. very truly,
          Respy, yrs.,
          S'c'ly yrs.,
Right: Yours very truly,
          Respectfully yours,
          Sincerely yours

(d) "And oblige" is a throwback to early times. Avoid its use.

Mail the check this week,
          And oblige,

(e) Do not confuse the word *respectfully* with *respectively.* This is so often done that it deserves the red flag signal.

Wrong: Yours respectively,
Right: Yours respectfully,

Since there is some latitude in choosing the form to be used for the complimentary close, it would be interesting to know which form or forms, if any, are the most frequently used. Perhaps a survey of fifty to a hundred thousand letters would produce an authoritative answer to this question, but so far as we know nothing of the kind has been attempted. However, for what it may be worth, here are the forms that appear on twenty-five business letters recently received, with the writers identified as to rank or position.

Complimentary Close	Times Used	Type of Executive
Very sincerely yours,	1	President (1)
Very sincerely,	1	President (2)
Sincerely yours,	4	President (3) Sales Manager (1)
Sincerely,	4	Secretary (2) Vice-President (1) President (1)
Cordially yours,	5	President (2) Hotel Manager (1) Circulation Manager (1) Publisher (1)
Cordially,	5	Sales Manager (2) Circulation Manager (1) Advertising Manager (1) Editor (1)
Yours very truly,	3	Sales Manager (2) Secretary (1)
Very truly yours,	1	Advertising Director (1)
Faithfully yours,	1	President (England) (1)
Thanks a lot,	1	Manager of Research (1)

Although twenty-five letters are far too few to use as a basis in forming dependable deductions, the information revealed in the above list may at least point the way to more exhaustive research. Remember, too, that this batch of letters was taken at random from those of "recent date" received by one businessman. It might be a fairly representative sample of what would be exposed if a far greater number of letters were examined.

Several facts seem significant. First, the twenty-five letters were all written by businessmen of high position. If it were true that rank and formality go hand in hand, you would expect the complimentary close in these letters to lean the formal way, but twenty of them use "Sincerely" and "Cordially" in one combination or another. Only four take the more formal road, ending with "Yours very truly," or "Very truly yours." One of the men is a radical—he dares to end his letter with "Thanks a lot"— and of all things, he is the Manager of Research, one whom you might expect to be the most conservative.

By now, perhaps you have discovered what appears to be an inaccuracy in the figures. There are twenty-six letters listed instead of twenty-five. Right you are, but one doesn't count. It came from London, England, and is not representative of American letters. You seldom see "Faithfully yours," at the bottom of our letters.

Formality still rules in England. A good illustration to prove this statement is the experience of an American executive. He had written to an executive in London, addressing him as, "Dear Mr. Doe." In his reply, the Englishman said, "We are confident no discourtesy was intended, but perhaps inadvertently your letter to the writer was incorrectly addressed to him by name rather than the more proper form, Dear Sir." Yes, this is a true story, and it shows that even in letter-writing, one must respect custom or take the chance of being called a boor.

7. Signatures and Other Notations

The signature. The signature on a business letter is far more important than it might seem at first thought. It not only serves to place responsibility for what has been said in the letter, but also may add or detract from the general appearance of the whole ensemble. It may also be assumed that the reader has the right to know, easily and without the slightest inconvenience, to whom the signature belongs, and how it is spelled. Thus, we have the simple "must" that either the written name and initials should be legible without question of doubt, or they should be duplicated by the typist. In the latter case, the writer can have as much fun as he wants in signing his name; otherwise, the slightest inconvenience to the reader in trying to decipher a signature is inexcusable. Any thought that this comment is superfluous may be canceled by an inspection of the "cockeyed" signatures on page 276. They were taken from business letters where no other means was supplied to identify the writers—nothing on the letterheads, and no duplications in type. In each case, the writer signed his name in a way to indicate that he had just swallowed a hornet, and the reader was left to decipher the spelling as best he could.

The rules that govern the position and content of the signature are far from ironclad. They are based on prevailing custom, the will of the individual, and the practice of the company as may be ordered in the correspondence manual. Some serve a utility purpose, and others are merely a reflection of what seems to be common sense and good judgment. You are not forced to follow these rules as they are set forth below, but you cannot "go wrong" in doing so. They represent the opinion of the leading authorities, and for that reason may be accepted with confidence:

1. Position. Usually, the signature on a business letter consists of three or more lines—the name of the company, the name of the writer in longhand, and the typed copy of the writer's name, with designation of department or title. These lines are arranged in an orderly fashion, somewhat similar to those in the inside address and salutation. The best appearance is gained when no one of these lines extends far beyond the others. One line may be sufficient for name and title if both are short, or two lines may be necessary to keep the entire signature in harmonious proportion.

Very Truly yours,

A MASSIVE sprawly signature
Peps up a letter, I'm quite sure:
Huge flourishes, though superficial,
Make it look much more official;
Crisp swirling strokes, placed here and there,
Denote the writer's savoir-faire;
Dots and doodads, smartly placed,
Proclaim his dignity and taste;
Combined, they add much snap and class
To correspondence, but alas!
They sometimes drive the reader plumb
Daffy, figuring who it's from!
    By G. B. Walton,
    Saturday Evening Post

Cordially

Very truly yours,

Assistant Advertising Manager

Division Manager

Sincerely yours,

Sincerely yours,

President

Sincerely yours,

President

If the first line is typed, it may be dropped two spaces below the complimentary close, to agree with the space allowed between paragraphs and between the other letter units. However, if greater space has been allotted between these other units, the same should be true of the space between complimentary close and first line of the signature. Particular care should be taken to allow sufficient space for the longhand signature of the writer.*

---

* All longhand signatures are shown here in italics.

It may be from three to six spaces, depending on the size of the name as it is customarily penned. Some men write with generous flourishes; others with minute precision. The typist soon learns how much space is required.

When two lines are typed consecutively, they should be single spaced for two reasons. First, to save space, and second, because they look better that way.

Not	Cordially yours,
Good	
This	The Doe Supply Company
Way	*Albert S. Grace*
	Albert S. Grace
	Advertising Manager

Okay	Cordially yours,
with	
Last	The Doe Supply Company
Two	*Albert S. Grace*
Lines	
Single	Albert S. Grace
Spaced	Advertising Manager

In the opinion of most letter experts, the signature lines make the best appearance when *blocked,* starting at the same distance from the left edge of the page as does the complimentary close. In every case, this should be done when the other parts of the letter are arranged in the blocked form.

> Very cordially yours,
> Caldwell Processing Co.
> *Leslie J. Caldwell*
> Leslie J. Caldwell
> Director of Personnel

This blocking of the signature is recommended, even when the other parts of the letter are indented, with the exception that the lines no longer start even with the first word in the complimentary close. The one indention assures consistency with the general form of the letter.

> Very cordially yours,
> Caldwell Processing Co.
> *Leslie J. Caldwell*
> Leslie J. Caldwell
> Director of Personnel

One rule for the position of the signature which should never be disregarded is that none of the lines should reach beyond the right-hand margin of the page. This creates a problem for the letter-writer and his typist when one of the lines is extremely long and cannot be broken. In such a case, the long line cannot be blocked with the rest of the signature, and still kept from stepping over the right-hand margin. Hence, some other form must be followed.

> Very truly yours,
> Blue Bonnet Oil Co.
> *Martin T. Williams*
> Martin T. Williams
> Assistant Superintendent of Production

> Most sincerely yours,
> Larson Lithograph and Printing Company
> *James C. Donovan*
> James C. Donovan
> Credit Manager

While neither of the above solutions to the problem of the unusually long line present the neat, orderly appearance of a pure block, they are probably as good as the circumstances will permit. As has been said, the signature rules are not ironclad, and when two of them oppose each other the best compromise must be left to the judgment of the sender.

Of course, another possible solution to the problem is the one illustrated on page 271. The unorthodox alignment of the signature with the left-hand margin, allows considerably more space for any overstuffed line.

2. Variations in content. The simplest of all forms for the signature is the one in which only the pen-written name of the writer appears. It looks best and is best, unless additional information is necessary or desired by the company. This form is also especially appropriate in correspondence between business friends; the titles, being understood, do not require repetition which would only be an indication of vanity. In such cases, the writer assumes full responsibility for the message in the letter as there is no company name coupled with his own.

> Yours cordially,
> *John E. Doe*

Another form almost as simple is the one where the name is typed as well as pen-written. This also looks good, and is a courteous procedure when the writer knows his signature is not easily deciphered. The typed copy of the name is unnecessary if it also appears on the letterhead. The only exception to this rule is when the letterhead also contains in printed form the names of several other officials. This forces the reader to study the list of names to see which one compares most closely with the written signature—an inconvenience to which he should not be subjected. Again, since the company name does not appear in this form, the assumption is that the writer assumes responsibility in a personal way for what he has said.

> Yours cordially,
> *Howard H. Wainwright*
> Howard H. Wainwright

Sometimes a two-line signature consists of the pen-written name plus a typed line giving the title or department. This form is often desirable in business, as it helps the reader to understand the source of the information he has received, or the authority of the writer in supplying it. Thus, if Mrs. O'Brien has written to a mail-order house about the poor performance of her new stove, she may have more confidence in the suggestions offered in the reply if it is identified as coming from the "Chief Engineer," rather than just from a name which might belong to a mere clerk whose job it was to handle any complaint. In similar fashion, a collection letter with only a name at the bottom might not carry as much weight as if that name were designated as belonging to the Treasurer. Or, a letter identified as coming from the Vice President in Charge of Sales might make a customer feel more important than one coming from an unknown member of the Sales Department, whose position or authority is not stated. You can think of many other situations where the mention of title or department strengthens the effect of a business letter.

> Yours very truly,   Very truly yours,
> *Oscar Bauman*   *Charles Gast*
> Chief Engineer   Charles Gast, Treasurer

> Sincerely yours,
> *Carrie C. Goode*
> Service Department

In one of the preceding examples, it was possible to place both title and typed copy of the pen-written name on the same line. But when this results in too much length, so that the signature is thrown off balance, a three-line form becomes necessary.

Yours very truly,
Fred C. Wood
Fred C. Wood
Advertising Manager

Cordially yours,
Malcomb Hennapenny Bates
Malcomb Hennapenny Bates
Superintendent

So far, we have inspected only the signature forms that do not include the name of the company or organization. When the latter is included, the procedure becomes more complicated. Not only are more lines usually required, but several problems present themselves with respect to the position of the company line, and just how it is to be typed. For example, note the different treatments of the following four-line signature.

(a) *Company name first*	Very truly yours, The Cameron Rug Company *Russell T. Geho* Russell T. Geho Sales Manager
(b) *Same, all capitals*	Very truly yours, THE CAMERON RUG COMPANY *Russell T. Geho* Russell T. Geho Sales Manager
(c) *Writer's name first*	Very truly yours, *Russell T. Geho* Russell T. Geho Sales Manager Cameron Rug Company
(d) *Same position but company name all capitals*	Very truly yours, *Russell T. Geho* Russell T. Geho Sales Manager CAMERON RUG COMPANY

These four forms for the same signature illustrate two problems. The first is where the name shall be typed, and it is inconsequential. The person in authority may decide whether or not he wants the company name to have the added display gained by all capitals. Once the decision is made, however, it should be adhered to in all departments and by all individuals. A company should develop a style for its correspondence, and not let every dictator "roll his own," which results in lack of uniformity and no style at all. Particularly is the last point true with respect to the second problem—in what position the company line shall be placed. If there seems to be a good reason for having it precede the name of the individual (examples *a* and *b*), then the form should be followed in all of the company letters.

The point of difference between the two positions is largely one of determining the responsibility for the content of the letter. If the company name is typed first, then the implication to the reader is that the company has stated the facts, and the individual who signs the letter has acted in the capacity of interpreter or transmitter. Thus, the concept of complete company responsibility gains greater emphasis than when the individual's name comes first, and he seems to speak for himself.

The question of whether or not the company name shall be used at all in the signature may be influenced by the inclination of the executive in charge of such matters, or sometimes by the more urgent factor of necessity. If the letter is typed on a blank sheet of paper, which could hardly happen in an organization of any prestige or importance, then obviously the company name must appear in the signature, unless the subject matter is purely personal, and the writer is acting strictly for himself. In the vast majority of letter situations there is a letterhead to tell the reader plainly the source of the message. When this is true, the company name in the signature is only a repetition, and may be considered as unnecessary. The person receiving a letter on the stationery of *Blank & Blank, Inc.,* and signed by *John Doe, President,* hasn't the slightest doubt as to the identity of the organization of which Mr. Doe is the head. Neither would he question the authority to act for the company of a man who signed as Credit Manager or Sales Manager.

A signature of more than four lines does not enhance the appearance of the entire letter—in fact, it tends to have the opposite effect—but sometimes the long form is necessary. For example, this is true when both title and department need to be mentioned.

(a) *Better balanced with company name placed first*	Sincerely yours, PARAMONT MOTOR COMPANY *Horace P. Oliver* Horace P. Oliver Assistant Superintendent Used Car Department

	Cordially yours,
	Alvin S. Fritsche
(b) *The four consecutive*	Alvin S. Fritsche
lines look awkward	Manager Experimental Farm
	Research Department
	BRUNSON FEED MILLS

So far as is reasonable and possible, the best procedure in determining signature forms is to keep them simple and short by eliminating all unnecessary information.

3. Punctuation. As with the date line and inside address, the punctuation of the signature may be either *open* or *closed,* but the form used must agree with the other units. Hence, the punctuation of the date line sets the style for the rest of the letter. Remember, however, that the complimentary close is *not* a part of the signature, although it teams closely with it. The complimentary close ends with a comma, no matter which of the two punctuation forms is used for the other parts. In contrast, the pen-written name of the writer has no punctuation mark following it in either form, unless an abbreviation concludes the name:

(a) *Open punctuation*	Sincerely yours,
	MCNULTY & MINTON, INC.
	John Selby Graham
	John Selby Graham
	Sales Manager
	Textile Division
(b) *Closed punctuation*	Sincerely yours,
	MCNULTY & MINTON, INC.,
	John Selby Graham
	John Selby Graham,
	Sales Manager,
	Textile Division.
(c) *Open punctuation*	Yours very truly,
	John Gore
	John Gore, Secretary
	The Battin Company
(d) *Closed punctuation*	Yours very truly,
	John Gore
	John Gore, Secretary,
	The Battin Company.

4. Abbreviations. In the preceding example (*a*), the word *incorporated* was abbreviated in the signature because in that form it was a part of the official company name. There can be no deviation from this rule—as the name stands on the letterhead, so it must appear in the signature. On the contrary, personal names, with certain exceptions, should not be abbreviated. The authorities do not approve such contractions as *Geo.* for *George* or *Jno.* for *John,* but there are occasions when an exception must be conceded. For example, we know of one great business leader whose first given name is *William,* but for more than fifty years he has used the contraction, *Wm.* To suggest to this individual that he should start signing his letters with the full name, *William,* would surely be the height of absurdity.

The abbreviations, *Jr.* and *Sr.* have become so standardized by common use that they also are exceptions to the rule. It is very seldom that the longer forms are ever seen in personal signatures. Approved, too, by the censors are initials, although the preference is for at least one of the given names to be spelled out. Thus, *James C. Hardy* undoubtedly has a more balanced appearance when written or typed in the signature of a business letter, than does *J. C. Hardy.* However, if an individual prefers to use both initials, it may be considered his personal business, and no one has the right to criticize the practice.

Designations of position and departments should not be abbreviated. For example, *Advertising Manager* should never be typed *Adv. Mgr.*— *Circulation Department* should never be typed *Circ. Dept.*

5. Capitalization. The following rules apply to capitalization in the various signature forms.

Capitalize—

(a) All initials, given names, and surnames.

(b) All words designating title or position, except prepositions, conjunctions, and articles. The latter, however, should be capitalized if they begin the title or position.

Wrong: Sales manager
Director Of Personnel
Assistant to the treasurer
the Grand Marshal

Right: Sales Manager
Director of Personnel
Assistant to the Treasurer
The Grant Marshal

(c) Abbreviations *Jr., Sr.,* and *Mrs.,* and the designation *Miss.*

(d) All words and abbreviations in the name of a company or association, except prepositions, conjunctions, and articles. The latter, however, should be capitalized when they begin the name.

(e) All words in the names of departments, except prepositions, conjunctions, and articles. The latter, however, are capitalized if they ·begin the name.

Wrong: National association of real estate boards
Department of traffic control
Credit And Collection Division

Right: National Association of Real Estate Boards
Department of Traffic Control
Credit and Collection Division

6. Signatures for women. So that the recipient of a letter may address his reply properly, he should not be left in doubt as to the sex or marital status of the correspondent. The latter refers only to women, as the title of *Mr.* is used for both single and married men. Consider the following rules:

(a) It is an unwarranted, if innocuous, form of deception to allow a woman employee to sign only the initials of her given names.

Wrong: H. I. Williams

Right: Hazel I. Williams
(With Miss   Hazel Williams
or Mrs.)   Hazel Imogene Williams

(b) If the signer is single, the word *Miss* in parentheses starts the typed copy of the name. However, *Miss* should not appear in the pen-written signature.

Right: Cordially yours,
Hazel Williams
(Miss) Hazel Williams

(c) A married lady preferably uses her given name in the pen-written signature, but the typed name is that of her husband preceded by *Mrs.*

Right: Very truly yours,
Mary Jane Beach
Mary Jane Beach
(Mrs. Carl W. Beach)

(d) A widow may sign her name as she did before the death of her husband, or she may just use her given name, or names. In either case, she still uses the word *Mrs.*

Right: Yours very truly,
            Blanche B. Browne
            Blanche B. Browne
            (Mrs. James D. Browne)

Right: Yours very truly,
            Blanche B. Browne
            (Mrs.) Blanche B. Browne

(e) A divorcee, unless she has legally resumed the title of *Miss,* should continue to use *Mrs.* in the typed signature. She may either use her own surname, or that of her husband, depending on the form chosen after the divorce, but she may not use her husband's given name or initials.

Right: Yours very truly,
            Katherine Coe
            (Mrs.) Katherine Coe

Right: Yours very truly,
            Katherine Coe Smith
            (Mrs.) Katherine Smith

Wrong: Yours very truly,
            Katherine Smith
            (Mrs.) John E. Smith

7. Other suggestions. Although the discussion so far covers the major points with regard to the signature in the business letter, there are other important facts that should be recognized. Here they are:

(a) If it helps to harmonize with the general appearance of the letter, there is no objection to a color other than black for the pen-written name. For example, if a brown ribbon is used to type the letter, the pen-written name in the same shade may be effective.

(b) In earlier days, the use of a rubber stamp to affix the individual's name was quite common. This practice is no longer considered good form, and it also weakens the message of the letter by making it seem too casual.

(c) Another old custom, probably a carry-over from legal documents, was the typing of the word *Signed* at the start of the line where the pen-written name is to appear. This is a bit of formality which does no good, and it should be avoided.

(d) Similarly, the prefixing of *per* or *by* on the name line is an unnecessary formality.

(e) Titles should never appear on the same line with the pen-written signature, either before or after the individual's name. They are bad form if typed this way, but especially uncouth if written in ink along with the name.

(f) The person signing a letter should remember the appearance value of his signature. He should not write over the other lines, or at an angle. He should also stay within the limits of the space provided, and not allow the name to stick out beyond the right-hand margin.

A very bad habit, but one often followed in business letters, is the attempt to avoid responsibility for what has been said in the body of the letter (or for the errors that a reading might detect) by the addition of a qualifying statement such as, "Dictated but not read," or "Signed but not corrected." The reader has the right to resent such a sloppy and careless device, and his opinion of both writer and letter may justifiably be negative. When it is impossible to check or sign a dictated letter, the initials of the pinch-hitter should appear below the pen-written name, and in some cases a postscript by the secretary or typist may explain why the situation required special handling.

With initials of the pinch-hitter	Very truly yours, *John B. Whittier B.E.F.* John B. Whittier Advertising Manager
With postscript signed by the *secretary*	Very truly yours, *Harry S. Wheatley* Harry S. Wheatley

P.S.   Mr. Wheatley left for Toronto before this letter could be typed. To avoid any inconvenience to you, he asked me to sign and mail it for him.

> *Julia Groves*
> Secretary to Mr. Wheatley

Identification devices. It is a business custom to place certain coded information below the signature lines and aligned with the left-hand margin. In some cases this serves a useful purpose, but in others it might just as well be omitted. This statement clashes with some of the authorities who insist that these identification marks are always necessary. There are others who believe to the contrary, however. The author cannot recall one single instance in his years of business experience when he made any practical use of the identification symbols, although during that stretch of time he has handled many thousands of letters. Yet it is desirable that we keep our minds open toward any practice pertaining to business correspondence. When there is a sound *reason* for an identification line, as there may well be for certain companies, then there can be no objection to it. When the reason does not exist, as frequently it doesn't, then it becomes only another thing to clutter the page, serving no good purpose for the company which mails the letter, and certainly none for the person who receives it.

What *are* these identification symbols, and why do they rate such a controversial paragraph? Usually they consist of the initials of the person who dictated the letter, of the person who typed it, and sometimes, also of a third person for whom the letter was dictated, and who usurps the privilege of signing it. You know, initials like these: LEF/CM   FHR: 36 GHH-WH-fj.

Deciphered, they mean that a man named Luther Elijah Flesh dictated the letter, and a girl named Crystal Mooch typed it. That's the first set decoded. Jumping over to the third one, the meaning is that Walter Hoop signed a letter which George Henry Hapwood dictated and Freda Jacombs typed. Freda, of course, is only small fry in the company, and so her initials are not capitalized. But that is more recognition than the typist got in the second example, for she is only number 36.

All right! You know that symbols like those just cited are generally encountered in the lower left-hand corner of business letters. But why? What's the *reason* for putting them there? "The identification line," says one of the nation's best letter-men, "provides an easy, accurate, and inconspicuous means of recording the identity of the dictator and transcriber. Its use enables a business organization to ascertain the identity of either individual by merely consulting the correspondence file."

With half of that definition at least, there must be complete agreement. Probably the typist or transcriber could not, in many cases, be identified any other way. Her initials, coming last of course, are a sort of trade-mark, and perhaps she takes pride in seeing them on the letters that she types. Also, because of those initials, she can be quickly brought on the carpet if she has made an error in typing embarrassing to the company.

Okay, so far, so good! But what about the initials of the dictator? If under his pen-written signature, his name is typed, then what purpose is gained by repeating his initials in the identification line? Our good authority says that they enable his identity to be known by merely consulting the correspondence file. In other words, a glance at the initials on the carbon copy quickly puts a finger on the writer. Yes, that is true. But why isn't it just as easy to look at the name typed under the pen-written signature?

Of course, if the name of the writer is *not* typed under the space left for his penned signature, then we have a very *good* reason for identifying him in some other way. In this contingency, however, a rather recent development seems to have much in its favor. This is the typing of the *whole* name in the identification line, instead of just the initials. It may or may not be punctuated, according to the wish of the dictator or of his company correspondence supervisor.

> Abner L. Rich: AC
> A. L. Rich/AC
> ALRich-AC
> ALRich
> AC

Any of the above forms are acceptable—the best would be the one least conspicuous. A great advantage of the idea is that it takes one of the lines away from the signature which, as we have seen, is too cumbersome in many of its forms.

Sticking to our premise of accepting the initials or name of the dictator in the identification line when there is a good *reason* for it, we must admit the necessity when a third party enters the picture, as the one who signs the letter even though he did not write it. For example, in some companies the lamentable practice still prevails of having all letters dictated within a department signed by the highest in authority. Thus, all collection letters are signed by the Credit Manager, all sales letters by the Sales Manager, and similarly throughout all the company units. This means that if the company is large, a number of subordinates may dictate the letters signed by one man. The idea is to give each letter greater importance in the mind of the reader, since it apparently comes from the "head man," but except for this questionable advantage (which in the strict sense may not be ethical) the practice has nothing to recommend it. It must be demoralizing for a person to dictate letters all day long, and to receive no visible credit for his work. Under such a condition, there is less incentive for superior dictation, and the company surely loses more than it gains.

From what has been said about the identification line, the following policy is presented as being, in our opinion, the most consistent and logical:

1. Let the initials of the typist always be displayed—for reference purposes, and for whatever beneficial effect it may have on her morale.

2. If the same person dictates and signs the letter, use only one identification form—either his name typed under the place where he is to sign, or his name in full typed in the line with the transcriber's initials. But don't do both.

3. If the dictator does not sign the letter, then let his initials or name appear in the identification line. (Better still, abolish the procedure with which one man takes credit for another man's labor.)

Although some authorities may not agree with this policy, which is surely their privilege, we believe it will hold water with the majority of individuals who have had considerable business experience.

Other notations. It is sometimes considered desirable, outside of the body of the letter, to call the reader's attention to some special feature of the mailing, such as the presence of an enclosure, the sending of an extra copy to some other individual, or some particular form of handling. These notations are customarily placed in line with the left-hand margin and below the identification marks; the number of spaces depends on the length of the letter and the judgment of the typist or dictator.

It is not always necessary to refer in this special way to an enclosure, but usually the plan has merit. For example, in a large company where all letters are folded and prepared for mailing in a centralized department, the word *Enclosure* tells the clerk that something besides the letter-page is intended to go into the envelope. Thus, the simple device helps to reduce the possibility of error.

Another benefit is to the recipient of the letter. The word calls his attention to the fact that something extra accompanies the letter. You probably have had the experience of removing a letter from the envelope and overlooking an enclosure. If it was a check, you no doubt were put to considerable inconvenience in getting a duplicate. Had the word *Enclosure* been plainly typed on the page, or better still, the words, *Check Enclosed,* the catastrophe would have been prevented.

The preferred position of an enclosure notation is immediately below the identification line. It may be abbreviated, but commands more attention if spelled out. If there are two or more enclosures, that fact is also indicated either by word or numeral. Here are some of the forms commonly used.

RCHunter: WV
Enclosure
GAF/fc
2 Encls.

MH: ACE; MJ
Enclosures 2
Carl F. Lunt: ad
Check Enclosed

J. J. Cartwell: 6
Enclosure:
Mortgage

In the same manner, the notation may call attention to a special form of mailing.

MLFahnestock: lef
Registered mail

KIUtterbach: OR
Special delivery

JSC/GRT
AIR MAIL

When the writer wishes his reader to know that a copy of the letter is being mailed to another individual, a notation to that effect is placed in line with the left-hand margin. To give it special emphasis, the notation is usually the last item typed on the page, and if possible, a few spaces removed from any other items. The full name and title of the individual is typed, but the symbol C.C. (Carbon Copy) may be used if desired instead of the word, *Copy*.

Very truly yours,
The Maxwell Company
J. H. Cambleton
Sales Manager

JHCambleton: AC
C. C.—Mr. John Doe

·   ·   ·   ·   ·

Cordially yours,
Luther G. Long
Luther G. Long
Credit Manager

MLF
Copy to Miss Alice Dill

·   ·   ·   ·

Sincerely,
R. C. Bellwether
Advertising Director

RCBellwether: MJK
Copies to:
Mr. James Duncan
Dr. R. L. Defoe

Sometimes, for good reason, the writer of the letter does not wish the recipient to know that other individuals are getting copies. Then the notation is placed only on the carbon copy. To make it more conspicuous, the position generally preferred is at the top of the page several spaces above the inside address.

The postscript. Opinion as to the value of the postscript in the business letter is divided—some think it serves a useful purpose, and others believe it should never be used. The latter hold that anything that needs mention can be adequately covered in the body of the letter, and that the postscript is merely evidence of careless preparation and thinking. We believe this is true in the great majority of cases, as it is very easy to overlook a point until the main part of the letter has been dictated, and then say, "Oh, yes, put this in a postscript." This, of course, is inexcusable. Possibly if all postscripts were outlawed, better letters would be the result.

When *purposely* used, the postscript gets a spotlight position which gives an emphasis to its content that might otherwise be rather difficult to attain. It is a device often used with powerful effect in the sales letter, and we hardly think it should be ruled out completely. It does not particularly injure the appearance of a letter, certainly to no greater degree than some of the other notations we have been surveying. However, postscripts should never be longer than a few words, or the one argument of gaining special attention is eliminated.

When a postscript is used, the common practice is to place the initials, P. S., in line with the left-hand margin, and two or more spaces below the last line of the signature. This puts it ahead of the identification initials, but occasionally you see the positions reversed. The message of the postscript should follow on the same line as the P. S., and should be punctuated like any sentence. As justified by those who cling to it, the postscript highlights some special fact. It may be a repetition of something told in the body of the letter, or something in the nature of a digression from the general message.

P. S.   Remember—June 2—don't fail us.

P. S.   Confidentially, you will save money by ordering before August 1. You can guess the reason.

P. S.   I saw Joe Warner yesterday. He spoke highly of your hospitality.

P. S.   It hurt me to have to write this letter, Jim. Please try to understand my position.

We see no harm in postscripts of the above variety, but you may decide for yourself whether or not to use them. Be sure you do it *purposely,* and not as an afterthought.

Devices to gain emphasis. To capture special attention for a word or phrase, several devices are commonly used. One is to underscore, another is to use all capitals, and a third is to type the word or phrase in a different color of ink. The latter, of course, necessitates a two-color ribbon, and adds somewhat to the expense. There are other methods, such as circling the desired part of the letter, drawing a hand or arrow that points to it, or placing a cross in the margin with a red pencil, but in general these are messy in appearance and cannot be recommended. Your opinion, however, of any of these devices must be tempered by the results which they attain.

The two devices used the most, and sometimes in combination, are underscoring and capitalization. Consider the following examples.

Underscored: This is the first time we have made such a liberal offer, and we do not expect ever to repeat it. You actually save two dollars, and you cannot afford to delay, as only the first thousand who reply will be accepted.

With Capitals: This is the first time we have made such a liberal offer, and we do not expect ever to repeat it. You actually SAVE TWO DOLLARS, and you cannot afford to delay, as only the FIRST THOUSAND who reply will be accepted.

Combination: This is the first time we have made such a liberal offer, and we do not expect ever to repeat it. You actually SAVE TWO DOLLARS, and you cannot afford to delay, as only the FIRST THOUSAND who reply will be accepted.

A comparison of the above three paragraphs will prove that the underscored words stand out more boldly than do those capitalized. In the same way, the combination of both gains still greater force as an eye-catcher. A further step would be typing the words in red ink. However, there is one caution to be remembered about the use of these devices. When you *overdo* them, they tend to irritate more than please. Furthermore, if too many words and phrases are underscored or capitalized, the purpose of the device is defeated, since all of the parts emphasized compete for attention against each other. This is illustrated when we increase the underscoring and capitalization in the third of the above examples.

Overdone: This is THE FIRST TIME we have made such a LIBERAL OFFER, and we do not expect ever to repeat it. You actually SAVE TWO DOLLARS, and you CANNOT AFFORD TO DELAY, as only the FIRST THOUSAND who reply will be ACCEPTED.

Only confusion is created with so many words emphasized. In fact, it is questionable which parts stand out the most—those highlighted, or those left untouched. The letter reproduced on page 293 is an example of emphasis sought with considerable restraint. Only three words are capitalized, but as paragraph starters they hold special prominence. Incidentally, the writer, Mr. Robert Stone, is a highly successful sales-letter writer, and you will notice that he uses a postscript for a thought connected with the body of his message but somewhat remote from it.

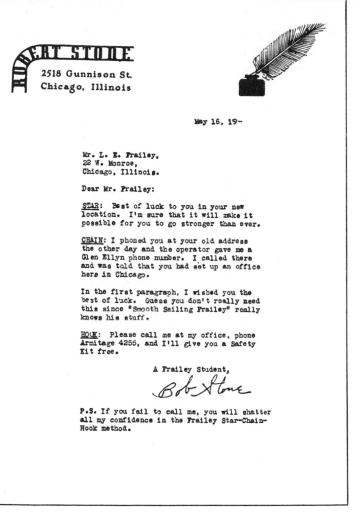

ROBERT STONE

2518 Gunnison St.
Chicago, Illinois

May 16, 19-

Mr. L. E. Frailey,
22 W. Monroe,
Chicago, Illinois.

Dear Mr. Frailey:

STAR: Best of luck to you in your new
location. I'm sure that it will make it
possible for you to go stronger than ever.

CHAIN: I phoned you at your old address
the other day and the operator gave me a
Glen Ellyn phone number. I called there
and was told that you had set up an office
here in Chicago.

In the first paragraph, I wished you the
best of luck. Guess you don't really need
this since "Smooth Sailing Frailey" really
knows his stuff.

HOOK: Please call me at my office, phone
Armitage 4255, and I'll give you a Safety
Kit free.

A Frailey Student,

Bob Stone

P.S. If you fail to call me, you will shatter
all my confidence in the Frailey Star-Chain-
Hook method.

Original Letterhead Has a Red Feather Attached

Second sheets. When two or more pages are necessary for a business letter, the second page should be typed on exactly the same paper as that used in the official company stationery. It is a poor form of economy to have a special paper of inferior quality and weight for the extra pages, even though the practice is not uncommon. The saving is inconsequential, and certainly the effect on the average reader is negative.

Custom varies as to what the notation on the second sheet shall be. Usually it consists simply of the numeral 2, in parentheses, typed about four spaces below the top of the page. If on the left side of the page, the designation also sets the margin line, which should be of the same width as on the first page.

293

There are those who like dashes with the number, and we won't split hairs about that. If-2-looks better to them than (2), or if they prefer *Page Two* to the numeral, that's okay, too. There does seem to be good reason for adding two other items—the name of the recipient, and the date. In the event the second sheet was detached from the first (perhaps in the mailing department where incoming letters are received), this additional information becomes valuable. Just how the three items are to be placed on the page is a matter of personal preference, but the following form is both attractive and consistent with the position of the name and date on the first page.

(2)

Mr. James A. Cook　　　　　　　　　　　　　　　　November 1, 1964

In transcribing a letter, the typist sometimes finds that the body has taken all of the first page and only complimentary close and signature remain. This results in an odd-looking second page; even if the letter has to be done over, it should in every case be avoided. After making a few of these major corrections, the typist soon learns to plan her margins so that at least two lines of the body will be carried over, and to understand that nothing less will be accepted.

The typist, of course, is an important member of the team which gets out the daily run of business letters. She may travel with the imposing title of *Secretary,* or she may be just one of the girls in the *Transcription Department,* but in either case she is the one who actually puts the letter on the page.

Some of the hints given under the following heading may prove useful to secretaries facing the task of presenting a business letter in its best possible format.

8. Devices to Make Reading Easier

Paragraphing. We have noted that short words and short sentences tend to improve the effectiveness of a business letter because they impose less strain on the reader's mind than do long words and long sentences. In like manner, the thought is easier to absorb if the paragraphs are not too formidable, and so constructed that each one covers a separate and complete unit of the message. The reader knows at the beginning of each paragraph that the previous division of thought has been completed, and that he is about to be presented with a new one. Of course, this is true only when the paragraphing has been done by a competent and logical thinker. A paragraph composed of unrelated material causes confusion, and hinders the assimilation of the central thought.

The chief responsibility for the arrangement of paragraphs in logical and compact form belongs to the dictator. If he has planned his letter properly, he knows what points he intends to present, and in what order. When one point has been thoroughly covered, he is ready to say "new paragraph," and proceed to the next, which will present a new point, completely and without digression. However, if the point is complex and requires lengthy discussion, the dictator faces the choice of using a long paragraph, or of breaking the thought into several paragraphs to cover separate sub-points. The choice of several shorter paragraphs is preferable, since a lengthy one is tiresome to the eye and tends to repel the reader before he has started to read the letter.

Placing the burden of responsibility on the dictator does not mean, however, that the competent secretary has no part in proper paragraphing. When she notices that her superior has forgotten to signal a new paragraph, she may, without exceeding her authority, go ahead on her own initiative, and make the division in the copy which she is typing. Moreover, some dictators make no pretense of indicating paragraph beginnings. In this case, even though it cannot be approved as the best practice, the secretary must do the best she can to make the paragraphs presentable and logically cut to the pattern of what seems to have been the dictator's intention.

We have seen paragraphs that filled an entire page of typing, and many more that ran a half page or longer. This indicates both careless and loose thinking on the part of the dictator, and a low grade of efficiency on the part of the typist or secretary. The influence of these long paragraphs cannot possibly be favorable. They tell the reader that the letter is going to be difficult to read, and they set up a negative mental attitude which puts the writer behind the eight ball at the very start. This fact is well recognized by the majority of business letter-writers, and the modern trend is toward paragraphs that will not impose on the eye or mind of the reader. Sometimes the tendency is overdone, with each paragraph consisting of a single sentence or a couple of short ones. This succession of small bits of copy is just as objectionable as the other extreme. Hence, you will gain the best results by sticking to the middle of the road, and making your paragraphs neither *too long* nor *too short*.

One factor influencing length of paragraphs is the nature of the message in the letter. Certain phases of business, for example, are more technical and complicated than others. The paragraphs in a sales or adjustment letter might be expected to run somewhat longer than in a letter which merely thanks a customer for his order or asks when a bill is to be paid.

Another variable factor is the mental background of both writer and reader. Probably the head of the Department of English in a large university is more accustomed to reading material arranged in long paragraphs than is his landlord, who happens to be a man of no great education or native intelligence. In the same sense, one writer may be able to use longer paragraphs, and make them easier to read, than can another. As in all other aspects of business letter-writing, paragraphing should take into consideration the probable reading habits and intellectual status of the individual to whom the letter is addressed. Generally, you may be sure that it is better to write short paragraphs than long ones—no matter who the potential reader may happen to be.

Highlighting special material. In many business letters there are certain facts or figures that the writer particularly wants the reader to remember. In such cases, the special material may be highlighted by contrasting forms of indentation, by tabulation, or by some other similar method. Facts buried in the middle of a paragraph are much more likely to be overlooked by the reader than when they are given a more prominent display. For example, consider the different typings of the following letter to a salesman.

> Dear Jimmy:
>
> First, let me tell you that I am much pleased with the way you have taken hold in your new territory. If you keep on at the same pace, there is a big bonus assured for you at the end of the year. Your success gives me personal satisfaction, because as you know there was some opposition to your appointment on account of your youth.
>
> During the coming week, I want you to spend a day in Cairo. Talk to John Doe, president of the Doe Implement Company, and see if you can revive his business. He was a steady buyer until last December, when he suddenly left us cold. Probably something happened to displease him, although I cannot think what it could be. Also, while in Cairo, see old man Roe again. You said last month that he would make a substantial payment on his account, but nothing has happened. Be courteous, but make it plain that we are about ready to call on the lawyers to get our money. In Centralia, be sure to get the contract signed with Black and Black. You seem confident this business will jell, but from my own field experience I can tell you that no order is any good until the buyer puts his John Hancock on the dotted line.
>
> Here in the office, we are going ahead with plans for the national convention. This will be your first, and I know you will get a tremendous kick out of it. By the way, if you want a room reservation, don't neglect returning the card to Hotel Jefferson— the one sent to you three weeks ago. If you overlook doing this, it will be your hard luck as there won't be a chance to get a room after you arrive.

Again, Jimmy, I compliment you on your efforts. You may not
be satisfied to see your name twenty-ninth on the list, but that
is a fine rating for a beginner, and I have no double before the
year is over, you will be crowding the leaders.

Report to me on the matters I have mentioned.

> Sincerely yours,

Probably, Jimmy was pleased with the letter from his boss. But in
addition to the compliments, it contains certain instructions which are
more or less covered up in the body of the message. Without any major
changes in wording, these instructions could have been highlighted by the
following form of typing:

Dear Jimmy:

First, let me tell you that I am much pleased with the way you
have taken hold in your new territory. If you keep on at the
same pace, there is a big bonus assured for you at the end of
the year. Your success gives me personal satisfaction, because
as you know there was some opposition to your appointment on
account of your youth.

Jimmy, along with your other calls, here are three things I want
you to do this coming week:

1. Talk to John Doe, president of the Doe Implement Company, in Cairo, and find out why he stopped buying from
us last December. An order from him will be another
feather in your cap.

2. While in Cairo, also see old man Roe again. He has not
made the substantial payment, as promised to you last
month. Be courteous, but make it plain we are ready to call
on the lawyers to get our money.

3. In Centralia, be sure to get the contract signed with
Black and Black. An order is never an order until the
buyer's John Hancock goes on the dotted line.

Be sure to report to me on these three special assignments by the
end of the week.

Here in the office, we are going ahead with plans for the national
convention. This will be your first, and I know you will get a
tremendous kick out of it. By the way, if you want a room
reservation,

> don't neglect returning the card
> to Hotel Jefferson—the one sent
> to you three weeks ago.

If you overlook doing this, it will be your hard luck, as there
won't be a chance to get a room after you arrive.

Again, Jimmy, I compliment you on your efforts. You may not be satisfied to see your name twenty-ninth on the list, but that is a fine rating for a beginner, and I have no doubt before the year is over you will be crowding the leaders.

Sincerely yours,

Your eye tells you that numbering and indenting the three points gives them a special emphasis they did not have in the first version of the letter. In the same way, the indentation highlights the reference to the room reservation. With these assignments so prominently displayed, Jimmy is not likely to forget or neglect them.

Explanatory material presented in tabulated form is usually easier to read and understand than when worked into the body of paragraphs. For example, compare the two typed forms that follow:

Thank you, Mrs. Doe, for writing, and for the payment of $5.00 to apply against your unpaid bills. We appreciate the effort you are making to bring your account up to date, and your offer to send us another payment of $5.00 in two weeks is quite satisfactory.

The total amount which you still owe is $16.35, and not $14.00 as mentioned in your letter. The difference of $2.35 is the amount of the March bill, which you thought was paid. The confusion, no doubt, is caused by the fact that both the February and March bills were for the same amount. The receipt you enclosed covered the February bill, but left the one for March still unpaid.

Since the first of January, you have made four payments: $3.42 against the January bill; $2.35 against the February bill; $3.29 against the April bill; and your latest payment of $5.00. This is a total of $14.06.

During the same period, the following bills have been issued: January, $3.42; February, $2.35; March, $2.35; April, $3.29; May, $4.01; June, $3.17; July, $3.99; August, $4.10; and September, $3.73—a total of $30.41.

Thus when you deduct the total paid from the total billed, there is a balance of $16.35 still due.

We hope these figures are clear to you, Mrs. Doe, but if you have any question to ask about them, we will be very glad to answer it. It was nice to know that your husband has now recovered after his long illness, and that he has found such a good job.

Cordially yours,

The above letter is about as clear as any exposition could be, but the many figures make the deciphering a slow process. When these figures are tabulated, the job is much simpler.

> Thank you, Mrs. Doe, for writing, and for the payment of $5.00 to apply against your unpaid bills. We appreciate the effort you are making to bring your account up to date, and your offer to send us another payment of $5.00 in two weeks is quite satisfactory.
>
> The total amount which you still owe is $16.35, and not $14.00 as mentioned in your letter. The difference of $2.35 is the amount of the March bill, which you thought was paid. The confusion, not doubt, is caused by the fact that both the February and March bills were for the same amount. The receipt you enclosed covered the February bill, but left the one for March still unpaid.

	Bills		*Payments*
January	$3.42	$3.42	Paid February 2
February	$2.35	$2.35	" March 22
March	$2.35	$3.29	" May 6
April	$3.29	$5.00	" November 6
May	$4.01		
June	$3.17	$14.06	Total
July	$3.99		
August	$4.10		
September	$3.73		
Total	$30.41		
Less	$14.06		
$16.35	The amount you still owe.		

> We hope these figures are clear to you, Mrs. Doe, but if you have any question to ask about them, we will be very glad to answer it. It is nice to know that your husband has now recovered after his long illness, and that he has found such a good job.
>
> Cordially yours,

Obviously, this second version of the letter is easier and quicker to read. It could hardly be misunderstood. Business letter-writers should use these and similar forms of typing to clarify the letter's message, and to put emphasis on items that deserve it.

Another method of highlighting material is the use of *exclamation marks*. These may be used to close a word, a group of words, or a full sentence when the thought is more emotional or dramatic than the ordinary sentence carries. When not overdone, its use adds spice and color to business writing, especially in advertising copy and sales letters. With the exclamation mark, the writer can vary the monotony of conventional sentence forms, and thus create extra interest in the minds of his readers. Unfortunately, the majority of businessmen make small use of this punctuation mark probably because they have not learned what it can do for them.

Listen a few minutes to conversation on the street, in the office, or any place where people meet, and you will agree that everyday speech is not made up of a steady sweep of full-rounded sentences. Far from it! Instead, in between the sentences are numerous exclamations, couched in single words or short phrases, adding life and interest to what might otherwise be rather dull language. Well, if we are still sticking to our major premise—that we should write as we *talk*—*why* shouldn't our letters have some of the same atmosphere? What's wrong with a word or phrase interjected in the flow of thought that makes the letter sound like a man *talking?* What's wrong, for that matter, with a dash of emotion? Is there anything so phlegmatic or academic about business that one connected with it cannot be his natural, interesting, often excitable, self? If you think business is immune to emotion, watch the sales manager as he nears the end of a quarter, with a fighting chance of making quota; watch the advertising director as he contemplates the million dollars he has risked on the new campaign, wondering if his judgment was sound. The "dignity of business" is only a pose—a thin shell which hides situations, experiences, frustrations, and ambitions, as dramatic as any you will encounter in other walks of life.

Yes, we cast our vote for the exclamation mark, and the kind of business language which makes it necessary.

> All right, Joe! You say you are discouraged, and you will be solving a problem for me by quitting. Nonsense! You never have been a problem to me in all these ten years we have worked together. Nobody here in the office wants you to quit, Joe. Nobody has been discouraged about *you.*
>
> But there *is* a problem, Joe. Yours! It's in your own mind, and either it will lick you, or you will lick it.
>
> We have no room for men who get discouraged, and start to pity themselves. You are right about that. If you really have lost your grip, if your blood has changed to water—okay! But I never expected to see the day when Joe Doe's guts ran out— when he couldn't take the rough spots with the smooth.
>
> Sure! You can quit, or you can be your old self again, and tell me to tear up this damnfool resignation. But I'm not telling you *what* to do. The problem is in your lap, Joe—with a swell wife and three kids sitting on the sidelines to see how you solve it.

Listen! You go fishing next week at our expense. We owe you that for all the ten years you have fought the good fight and never weakened. So, go ahead, and see if you are too discouraged to catch a few big ones.

No argument about this, Joe! When you get back, write me your final decision. I still want you around. You know it! But you'll have to get those bugs out of your bonnet.

It's you in the driver's seat, Joe. Good luck!

From the above letter written by a sales manager—he got a telegram to tear up the resignation—you can see how handy exclamation marks can be. *All right, Joe! Nonsense! Yours! Okay! Sure! Listen! No argument about this, Joe! You know it! Good luck!* None of those words or phrases *had to be* in the sales manager's letter, but don't they add naturalness and power to it?

Of course, you may be saying that the situation of the salesman wanting to resign is naturally emotional, and not a fair sample of the more prosaic things generally handled in business letters. Yes, that is a very good comment. It is true that salesman Joe Doe left himself wide open to the personal, man-to-man language used by his sales manager. Most letter-situations in business are far less dramatic, but even if dry-as-dust, can't they be handled in a human, conversational manner?

Please! Won't you sit down right *now* and write us a check? We know the amount of your bill is small, but with several thousand other customers also holding out on us, the size of the total might surprise you.

Your letter about the mistake in your assortment of canned goods leaves me with no explanation that would hold water. How we could have sent pears instead of peaches, I don't know. *Queer!*

We did appreciate this first order, and wanted so much to please you. *Is my face red!*

Right you are! Your June bill is paid. The check and our letter must have crossed in the mail. *Sorry!* Please excuse us for the trouble we have caused you.

Good news for you! Effective July 1, you will be entitled to an extra discount of five per cent.

Yes, indeed! You can have two of our trucks all day Sunday, and we will supply the drivers. You folks at the Red Cross deserve our hearty cooperation. *Congratulations!* Feel free to come to us any time we can help.

Listen! We cannot sell your products unless you keep us supplied. Where is the shipment you said we could count on last week? We aren't angry. *Not much!* But it's bad business to change our customers over to your feed, and then run short. *Please!* Get on your horse, and give him the whip.

There you are! Even the run-of-the-mill letters can be made to sound as one man talking to another. There's a lot of power in an exclamatory word or phrase.

Other methods of highlighting material will be found in Sections 3, 7, 9 and 14. These techniques include the use of large capital letters for emphasis, color-writing, illustrative devices, and various other forms of showmanship.

PERSONALITY IN BUSINESS LETTERS

PERSONALITY IN BUSINESS LETTERS

1. WHAT MAKES A LETTER INTERESTING?

Reflecting writer's personality. You do not need to be told that some writers manage to make themselves more interesting than others. Among those from whom you get letters, no doubt two or three are especially favored, and when one of them is represented in a newly arrived batch of mail, you push everything else aside until the message is read. But why? What are these writers able to do that others cannot? Is there some one quality in their letters that makes them outstanding? Is it a quality that anyone might attain if he only knew how?

Well, yes. There is no reason why most business letters should be so dry, so dull, so colorless. There is no mystery about an interesting letter. It simply reflects more of the *friendly personality* of the writer than do messages which are lifeless, cold, and stiff. In the interesting letter you hear a man *talking*, and you feel his smile between the lines. He isn't trying to be clever, nor is he doing anything purposely to attract attention to himself, but you sense that he is there with you, and the warmth of his presence is a pleasant experience that you miss in the letters which seem to be only a collection of words.

Of course, in some letters the subject material is in itself more interesting than in others. That gives the writer a running start. Generally speaking, sales letters talk about more exciting things than do collection letters; letters about advertising have more interesting content than letters about traffic. But these advantages in nature of material, or the lack of them, make little difference to the writer who has the gift of *putting himself* in his message. Personality is a quality that has few limitations. Certainly, you must admit the truth of that statement, for you have read letters about

305

simple routine matters that made you smile, and you felt attracted to the writers; and in contrary fashion, you have read letters that had every chance to be interesting, but left you cold and yawning.

Meaning of the word. Before we go any further in talking about *personality* in the business letter, we should define its meaning. In the broadest sense, every individual has a personality, although it may not be pleasing. This fact is brought out in Webster's definition.

> *Personality* 1. Quality or state of being personal, or of being a person; personal existence or identity. 2. That which constitutes distinction of person; individuality; as, a *striking personality*. 3. A personal being; a person. 4. Quality of relating to a particular person, esp. disparagingly or hostilely; as, *vulgar personality*. 5. A personal remark, esp. one disparaging or offensive;—usually in pl.; as, to indulge in *personalities*.

It is the second of the five definitions which comes closest to what we mean when we offer *personality* as a quality to be desired in the business letter. We want "distinction of person" to be evident in the dictated words; and more than that, distinction of a likable, *friendly* person.

If you still lean to making business letters as short as possible, countless examples could be cited to prove that brevity and interest are not incompatible. Remember?

> Dear Governor: They are fixing to hang me on Thursday, and here it is Tuesday.
>
> .   .   .   .   .
>
> Will you please send me the name of a good lawyer in your town? I may have to sue you.
>
> .   .   .   .   .
>
> Yes, John Doe did work for us several weeks. When he left, we were satisfied.

And added to those short ones, might well be Elbert Hubbard's collection letter: "Come Brother, dig! You'll never know the difference and, God knows, we need the money."

None of the examples just cited are letters in the conventional style. Instead, the writers dared to get out of the groove and to express themselves as they would in ordinary speech. People like things which are *different*— shoes cut in a new way, a breakfast food unlike any they have eaten before, a play with a fresh plot. They also are receptive to a new approach in letters. At least, this must have been Miles Kimball's thought when he dared the following unusual collection letter. He had a lot of small accounts to collect, and several of the customary conventional appeals had failed. There was nothing much to lose in trying something entirely different, even though he hesitated at the last moment to mail a message so remote from the "dignity" of business. But out it went.

> Dear Mr. Doe:
>
> The worst has happened! Elmer, our treasurer, has found out about your account, and is threatening to write you a letter.
>
> As a friend of yours, I implore you to pay now before it is too late! People who get Elmer's collection letters never recover. We hide the Accounts Receivable Ledger from him, but sometimes he finds it and gets out of control. If you realized the horror of it, you would mail your check at once. If you had seen the pitiful results as we know them! Young men prematurely aged, and strong men broken—babbling in a corner through palsied fingers. It is hideous!
>
> Usually, Elmer's letters result in 40 percent collections and 60 percent suicides. He may have other words in his vocabulary besides "sue," "legal action," and the unrepeatables, but no one has heard him use any since the spring of 1928.
>
> Elmer's old mother (who has been in a sanitarium since he was seven) tells us that he was a happy, normal boy until he was five. Then a neighbor child persuaded him to trade two old pennies for one shiny new one. When Elmer found out he'd been hornswoggled, the change came over night. He earned his first dime drowning kittens, worked in a slaughter house when he was fourteen, and is now treasurer of our company. He is president of the League for Restoration of the Death Penalty, and has filed a standing application for the job of public Hangman.
>
> You see the situation. I like people, and I just can't stand the thought of having Elmer destroy your will to live. So please, for your own sake and the sake of my conscience, mail your check today for the $17.65 owing to us—or you may get a letter from Elmer—God forbid!
>
> > Urgently yours,

Miles Kimball, president of Direct Mail Associates, Inc., Oshkosh, Wisconsin, had used many collection letters in his business career. But never one so shockingly different. Before you join the businessmen who could not tolerate anything so unconventional, consider also the fact that this letter outpulled by a wide margin all of the others that had been mailed by the company over a period of many years. Why? Perhaps because people like to be amused. Perhaps *humor* in some intangible way is connected with *personality* in a business letter.

Another example, of similar vein, is the celebrated letter written by a prominent business executive to the manager of one of the large Chicago hotels. In condensed form, here is the correspondence between the two men:

Dear Mr. Doe:

Upon making the customary room inspection after a guest's departure, our housekeeper advises that two brown woolen blankets, replacement value $15 each, were missing from the room you occupied. . . . Guests frequently, we find, in their haste inadvertently place such items in their effects and, of course, return same when discovered.

The accusation, politely made in the guise of "inadvertently," would have angered the average human being. But the executive to whom it was mailed was more of a philosopher. He realized, no doubt, that hotels do suffer considerable loss because of the "haste" of certain guests. Anyway, his reply is a classic in funpoking; it bubbles over with the calm personality of a man who chooses to see the humorous side of the experience rather than to write back in righteous indignation.

Dear Mr. Manager:

I am desolate to learn that you have guests who are so absent-minded. I suppose that passengers on railroad trains are apt to carry off a locomotive or a few hundred feet of rails. Or a visitor to a zoo may take an elephant or a rhinoceros, concealing same in a sack of peanuts after removing the nuts (replacement value of $.25).

It happened that I needed all the drawer space you so thoughtfully provide. The blankets in question occupied the bottom drawer of the dresser, and I wanted to put some white shirts (replacement value of $6.50 each) there, so I lifted said blankets (replacement value of $15 each) and placed them on a chair. Later, I handed the same blankets to the maid, telling her in gentlemanly language to get them the hell out of there.

If you'll take the trouble to count all the blankets in your esteemed establishment, you'll find them all present.

Very truly yours,

P. S.   By the way, have you counted your elevators lately?

Thus confronted with a guest who refused to take his first letter too seriously, the manager of the hotel removed his stiff shirt, and did his best to write a second letter in the same spirit. You need not be bothered with the whole of it, but from the following paragraph you can see how different is the language—how much more human is the writer.

> Dear Mr. Doe:
>
> Yes, we do a lot of counting around here. I've counted the elevators. What I want to count now is more important to me. I want to keep on counting you as a friend of the ——— hotel. ...As the song says, "Let's Call the Whole Thing Off."

Perhaps by now you are beginning to catch the meaning of "personality" as it may be expressed in business letters. It is not something that can be weighed, or counted, or painted; nor is it ever manifested twice in exactly the same manner. The latter is impossible because no two persons are exactly alike, and *personality* as nearly as your author can describe it, is the reflection of a *man*—of his disposition, his mental attitude, his feeling toward the world in which he lives, and the other human beings in it. All of this sounds intangible, but it isn't really. A letter gives out personality when you forget it *is* a letter—when you feel the *presence* of the writer, and hear him *talking* to you.

2. How to Express Your Own Personality

Loosen your belt. In an earlier chapter of this Handbook you were urged never to think about writing letters. Instead, you were to say, "Today I must *talk* to these people." And if from these many pages only one idea were to be culled, the one of *talking* and not writing is probably most valuable. The chief reason why so many letters—the great majority of letters —are dull and uninteresting, is because those who write them cannot shake off the concept that they are preparing something to be *read,* rather than *talking* to other human beings. The difference in these two approaches is so wide and radical that the one produces letters dry as dust; the other, letters which sparkle with human personality.

Hence, if you wish *your* letters to be interesting—to reflect *your* friendly personality—the first requisite is that you adjust your own mental attitude toward the job. Take off your necktie, loosen your belt. Forget the silly formalities. Sit down, and be comfortable. Remember the slogan: "Relax—be natural—just TALK." If your letters are drab and colorless, it isn't because *you* lack personality. It is because you keep it bottled, so that not a drop can escape to lighten your words, or to make you sound like the friendly, interesting person that you really are. No modern businessman can express his real personality when using the stilted language of 1776; no one can make his letters vital and human while sitting behind his desk with the same austere dignity that he may affect in a box at grand opera.

Good manners are as necessary in writing letters as in any other human relationship. We do not mean that you should wisecrack, try to "show off," or that you should write a letter in the same spirit that you might shoot a game of pool. On the other hand, neither do we think that business relationships need to be any more formal than those of everyday, decent, pleasant living. The person who is to read your next letter is probably just another human being—like your neighbor, your friend, or your boss. He doesn't want you to slap his back on first acquaintance; neither does he want you to talk as if he were an old fuddy-duddy, allergic to a smile. Maybe you are saying, "But his letter to me was cold and formal. . . . I must go back at him in the same way." *Why* must you? Perhaps he learned to write letters in the old school. He doesn't know any better. Must you keep your personality undercover because someone else does? No. Keep your letters on a high plane of courtesy. Write with respect to those of higher station, and to those older in years. But *be yourself.* Relax. . .be natural. . .just TALK. There is no logical reason for assuming a personality that is false—no reason why you should be cold and formal in a letter, if in reality you are not that kind of a person.

Homely language helps. In the writer's scrapbook is an old clipping titled "Every letter ought to make a friend." The author's name has been lost along the way, but his comments are pertinent to the subject of our quest—how to put personality in a business letter. Read what he says about Bill Galloway:

> When Bill Galloway was president of a farm implement company in Waterloo, Iowa, he made a fortune for himself and others because he knew how to write a good letter. I think Bill's chief qualifications for letter writing were that he KNEW people, and LIKED people.
>
> Galloway never wrote a form letter. He could always find time to *talk* to a farmer. Every letter, even though the same copy would go to a hundred thousand farmers, was a personal letter to him. Bill was a great believer in friendliness. Even in form letters he could manage to put in some personal touch.
>
> One time he had some letterheads printed with a picture of his office building in the upper right-hand corner. One of his favorite stunts was to draw a crude cross in ink over one window. Under this cross he would write, "Here is where I sit."
>
> That simple cross-mark and phrase added a friendly note to a letter which made a deep impression on farmers. They were

accustomed to doing business in a personal way. The idea made Bill into a human being who reached out from the envelope and shook hands with every reader.

There are homely words in our everyday language, and combinations of words, which seem to fit the pattern of the average, commonplace, likable human being. When used in business letters, they contribute a man-to-man touch which helps to bring reader and writer on the same plane. You know these expressions, because you use them every day—that's water over the dam...he would give you his last shirt...let's take the bull by the horns...don't swap horses in mid-stream...you can't burn a candle at both ends...and the thousands of others which make our language interesting even though they may not be favored in college classrooms. The power of these homespun expressions is generated by the fact that they are mutually understood. The average American is suspicious of "fancy" language; he likes best the common words that are a part of his own vocabulary. *Folks,* for example, is a word with great popular appeal. When you *talk* to *folks*—or about *folks*—you are really writing a persuasive letter.

Adding the personal touch. An old and effective device used by letter-writers to season the meat of their message, is the addition of a sentence or two of a personal nature. Usually, these "extras" are type near the end of the letter, but sometimes they are written in ink at the time the writer signs his letter. For example, here are three of these personal touches taken from letters dictated for the Jefferson Standard Life Insurance Company, of Greensboro, North Carolina. The subject matter in the three letters was not interesting, as it included references to policies, rates, premiums, and the like; but the sentences thrown in for good measure help to give the message life and personality.

> *In a letter to an agent in California:* What about letting me know how you like the Sunshine State. Have you crashed the movies yet?
>
> *To an agent in Augusta, Georgia:* I enjoyed visiting in your office Friday morning, and I hope it will not be my last visit to your beautiful city.
>
> *To a policyholder:* We enjoyed having you with us yesterday. Come to see us again.

None of these letters actually *needed* these personal touches. In a business way, they would have done their job had the digressions been omitted, and a little time could have been saved by sticking strictly to the subject. But who would say that the time taken to personalize the letters was wasted?

Some remarks on this subject appeared in a Better Letters Bulletin, issued by the Dartnell Corporation, and edited by Cameron McPherson. The bulletin was entitled *The Finishing Touch,* and some of Mr. McPherson's comments are most illuminating:

> Just as the genius of an old master is reflected in the finishing touch which he gave to his paintings, so the skill of a correspondent shows in the finishing touch which he gives to his letters.
>
> In a recent bulletin I showed several closing paragraphs which had outlived their usefulness. They lacked individuality. They were cold and insipid.
>
> In this bulletin I am suggesting a type of close which appeals to the friendly instincts that most men have beneath their masks of formality.
>
> Of course, these closes will not do in every case. There are times when reserve and formality are necessary. But nine letters out of ten can be improved by a human touch at the close.

We agree heartily with Cameron McPherson. Except when used for a very formal occasion, there seems to be no sensible reason why the human touch will not improve any business letter.

Use of reader's name. The value of working the reader's name into the body of a letter has already been mentioned. It is also one of the ways that personality is gained. In speech, we use over and over again the name of the person to whom we are talking. While this must be done with more restraint in letters, it is still one of the simplest methods of making the reader feel that his identity as an individual is recognized. In his fine book, *Goodwill Letters That Build Business,** William H. Butterfield says: "Every normal person likes to be noticed, not as a name in the company ledger, but as a flesh-and-blood human being. Mr. John Q. Public is proud of his individual identity; so he is complimented and flattered when a personal letter makes him feel that someone has noticed his existence and appreciates his patronage. . . . Any evidence of office routine is a death blow to letter tone, and it kills the reader's enthusiasm instantly. He realizes that he is not being written to as John Smith or William Jones, but merely as one of the firm's customers."

Then Mr. Butterfield tells how destructive to the personal tone is the robot-like reference to company records. And to that comment, amen! No human being wants to feel that he is merely a matter of record—a name in the file of customers. Nevertheless, thousands of business letters are

---

* Prentice-Hall, Inc., Englewood Cliffs, N.J.

written every day with the deadly, impersonal beginning, "According to our records." What does this indicate to the reader? Why, simply that someone in the company has been going through the files, and happened to see his name as one who hadn't been buying recently; or as one to whom, for some other reason, a letter might be written.

Think of your readers as *people,* not *names.* Address them directly, and without any explanation or apology. To be sure, every company has records, and from them may come the impulse to write to a particular person. But don't *tell him* that the kick-off was prompted by seeing his name in the file. "Accoding to our records," writes the promotion manager, "you have not used your charge account during the past six months. We have missed you in our store, Mr. Doe, and would like to know why you have been giving us the cold shoulder." What a ridiculous thing to say to a former customer! He knows you have not missed him as an individual. He knows, too, that none of the clerks have remarked about his not being in the store. How did you know he had stopped buying? You *told* him in the first four words. The *records* said he had not used his charge account. How differently the letter would have sounded had the start been, "Mr. Doe, you haven't used your charge account in the last six months, and we are getting concerned about you. Will you do us a favor? Write and tell us what happened; or better still, come in and let us serve you again."

This last letter begins with the customer's *name.* That makes him feel important. Then it gives the fact that he has not used his charge account. That warms his ego—he has been missed. Finally, a favor is asked. That is especially pleasing. He, John Doe, can do a big company a favor. All of this is a matter of psychology, but what are business relationships if not psychological? The more you recognize that fact, the better your letters will be.

Don't overplay your hand. As has been explained previously, the personal tone *can* be exaggerated in a business letter, and in proportion to how deeply the writer falls into that trap, the less sincere he seems. Simply telling you that a letter is improved by the direct use of the reader's name in the body does not mean that you should use it with sickening frequency:

> Thanks for your check, *Mr. Doe.* We were glad to hear how pleased you are with the shipment, and that makes us wonder, *Mr. Doe,* when we may expect another order. Please remember, we are here to serve you, *Mr. Doe.* And believe us, *Mr. Doe,* we do appreciate your business.

The use of John Doe's name four times in one paragraph would be absurd, and no doubt more offensive to him than to use it not at all. Nobody likes to be bombarded with his own name. Doing so makes the letter sound flippant and insincere. Stick to the middle of the road. Let your reader know that he is recognized by name. Use it once or twice in the letter, but not so often as to sound like a ward politician out for votes.

The use of nicknames without benefit of authority can be particularly obnoxious. No one has the right to address another individual with such familiarity unless a friendly relationship has been established, and in sufficient degree to warrant doing so. Any step beyond this limitation is bad manners, and quite likely to be resented. Consider, for example, the absurdity of the letter which was addressed, "Dear Si," and closed with the postscript, "Did I spell your nickname correctly?" Certainly, if the spelling were not known to the writer, he could not claim a friendship that would sanction the nickname's use.

3. How to Spotlight the Reader

More YOU and less WE. Some business letters make us wonder if the writers were not thinking more about themselves than about their readers. They are full to the brim with *I* and *We,* but contain hardly a drop of *You.* This is fundamentally so wrong an approach that it would seem

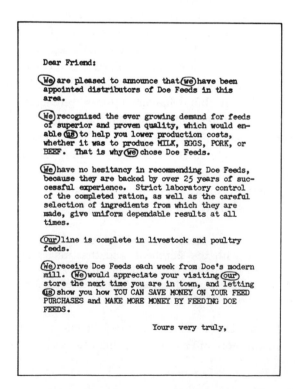

apparent to anybody. But you know from your own observation how often in business writing the reader is forced to play second-fiddle. For example, note in the following letter how the emphasis is placed on the company. Four paragraphs beginning with *We,* and the fifth, with *Our.* The purpose of the letter is to bring buyers to the dealer's store, and we cannot believe the writer meant to take the play away from his prospects. That is exactly what he does, though.

The personality expressed in the above letter is selfish and egotistical. The writer is "blowing his own horn" and quite happy to be doing it. He isn't really thinking about the money the readers of his letter can make by using Doe Feeds; instead, he is contemplating the money *he* is going to make with the new account. In the first four paragraphs, the reader gets the call only once. In contrast to the one *you* in the middle of the second paragraph, there are five *we's.* At the very end of the letter, *you* and *your* get a better break, but long before he reads that far, the recipient's sense of importance has been rudely shattered. We doubt very much if this letter pulled many prospects to the store. It never had a chance, because the spotlight was turned on the wrong fellow.

Another letter with the emphasis just as badly placed is the four-liner below. The man who got it wrote in the margin: "Give this letter to Frailey as a letter that should never have been written. Look at the first word of each line. This is truly a horrible example."

Gentlemen:

We	are returning herewith Connecticut policy #1887, which
we	have signed, consenting to the assignment of interest.
We	regret that it was necessary for you to return it to
us	for this signature.

Yours very truly,

Of course, the fault of this letter could have been made less conspicuous had the typist shortened the length of the lines, but after all, the average girl who transcribes dictated copy is not a sales psychologist. The blame properly falls on the man who wrote, and then signed, the letter. He *could* have noted how the four lines started and had the letter retyped, even if he did not bother to reword it.

Letters that star the reader. Turning to the more pleasant side of the We-You problem, notice in the following letter how the reader is given the center of the stage—the place where the reader always belongs. It was written by advertising manager Martin F. Maher, of the Florsheim Shoe Company, in an effort to win co-operation of dealers in a direct mail campaign:

Gentlemen:

We know that this time of year finds *you* very busy, and that's why we are reluctant to bother *you* again about a detail that may seem small to *you,* but one that can have a marked influence on *your* Spring Florsheim business.

We are holding 1180 Florsheim "Styles of the Times" booklets, all addressed to *your* mailing list, and properly imprinted with *your* store name; and we think it important that *you* give us mailing instructions as soon as possible.

It is now the first of May and *you* are getting into *your* spring selling season, and Florsheim Style Booklets should prove a helpful aid.

For *your* convenience, a business reply envelope is enclosed. All *you* have to do is to indicate at the foot of this letter the date on which *you* want these booklets mailed from Chicago.

                                        Yours very truly,

Throughout this Florsheim letter, the reader is allowed to play the leading role. He is made to feel that the request made of him is for his own benefit. Mr. Maher knew that mailing the booklets would help Florsheim, but he appears more eager to help the dealer.

Robert Ray Aurner, Wisconsin University maestro of letters, says in his interesting text, *Effective Business Correspondence:* *

There is one person in whom your reader will forever be most interested. That is *himself.* From this fact is drawn one of the important principles of business writing: Take the "You" attitude. You have heard the saying, "Put yourself in his shoes." That applies here. Talk about the reader, and you are discussing the most interesting thing in the world—to him. Make his interests, his wishes, his preferences, his hopes as nearly as possible yours. See, if you can, what he sees, through his eyes. Assume his viewpoint. Interpret your business through his sight channel, and you reinforce your appeal with the motive power of his self-centered attention. In your imagination take up your position beside him, look back at yourself, and ask, "What would I like to have myself say if I were over here with my reader instead of in my own office?"

> To sell John Smith
> What John Smith buys,
> You must *see* John Smith
> With John Smith's eyes.

Thus runs a convenient little verse that contains both rhyme and reason. It applies to every business relationship.

---

* Reprinted by permission from the publishers, South-Western Publishing Co., Inc.

To see through the reader's eyes, to talk his language, to present your message in the light of *his* thinking—this is the field from which you must take off, if your letter is to possess that intangible something we call *interesting personality.*

A matter of mental attitude. Keeping out of the rut called *We* is not difficult, once the business letter writer grasps the fundamental fact that to gain favorable acceptance for what he says he must *please his reader.* On the other hand, it is only natural that we should take for granted that others react as we do. This fallacy, coupled with the sense of our own importance, leads us with lamentable ease away from the *You* approach. It is a temptation against which we must ever be on guard if we wish our letters to attain maximum results—and of course we do.

The determining factor with respect to whether or not you are able to meet your reader on his own ground, is your own mental attitude. "The psychological fallacy," said William James, "is the almost universal tendency of people to think that others see a problem as they do themselves. On the contrary, they see the problem from one angle, you from another. Your duty is to see clearly, and understand both points of view."

Although some authorities do not approve the practice, we see no harm in the writer of a letter revealing himself as an *individual,* speaking for himself or for the company he represents. This means there is no objection to the use of the pronoun *I,* but it must never be allowed to "steal the show" so that the reader, cast in the leading role, is forced to yield his favored position. However, this can hardly happen as long as the writer holds steadfastly to his reader's point of view, and does not prattle about things as he, himself, happens to see them.

The use of *We* instead of *I,* which in many companies is a law that must be obeyed, is another queer custom we seem to have inherited from earlier writers. When a business writer speaks wholly for the company, as in telling a customer, "We will ship your order tomorrow," obviously he should not speak for himself. On the other hand, if he means to see personally that the order is shipped, why shouldn't he say, "I will personally look after this order, and you can be sure we will ship it tomorrow"? Thus, in the same sentence, both *I* and *We* properly appear, and logically there is no reason why they shouldn't. The idea that a business writer must always speak in the sense of "We, the King," seems utter nonsense. Certainly, the insistence on *We* to the exclusion of *I* in all cases is a barrier to the goal of "writing as you talk"; no writer can be his natural self if he must forever conceal his presence as an individual person.

In the following insurance letter, the writer often uses the pronoun *I.* Although the purpose is to get the policy reinstated for the company, it is nevertheless plain that the writer is responsible. Surely the letter would lose much of its human, friendly personality if it started, *"We* feel a little like Bill Stebbins," and continued in the same impersonal manner.

> Dear Mr. Doe:
>
> I feel a little like Bill Stebbins. At plain and fancy cussing, Bill could give cards and spades to anybody in Blair County. On even the most ordinary occasions, Bill's conversation smelled of brimstone, and under provocation—well, it simply burned your ears off.
>
> One day, after the express had gone through, when everybody and his brother were coming down the steep hill from the station, Bill was driving his team with a load of the White Star Orchard's finest Elberta peaches.
>
> Halfway up, the binder rope broke and every darned peach in the load fell out and rolled downhill. Somebody yelled at Bill— and the women and kids, fingers in their ears, ran for shelter.
>
> Bill hopped off the seat, walked back, and looked things over. Then he let fly a mouthful of tobacco juice—took a reef in his overalls—and turning to the assembled citizens, said quietly: "Ladies and Gentlemen, I know what you're expecting. But, honest, I'm not equal to the occasion."
>
> To date, I've written you several letters about your lapsed Reliance Life policy, something you need and should take care of. I hate to see you lose it, because I know you'll always regret doing it. But I've never had a word from you. I guess I'm like Bill—"not equal to the occasion."
>
> Won't you either send in the completed health certificate, or at least write on the back of this letter: "It's all right, old timer; you've done your part," and shoot it on to me, so I can get this matter off my conscience? I'll certainly appreciate it.
>
> >   Sincerely yours,

All right, what do you think? Would that letter have been as natural and interesting if the writer had hidden his personality by using *we's* instead of *I's?*

4. Sauce to Season the Letter

The world loves a cheerful writer. You remember, of course, the old adage, "Laugh and the world laughs with you; weep and you weep alone." There's truth in it. The most interesting letter writers seem to have the knack of seasoning the meat of their message with a little sauce of humor. Thus, the reader not only sees the face between the lines, but on that face is a friendly smile, sometimes even a chuckle.

And why should it not be so? When you step into a room, crowded with strangers, are you not immediately drawn to those of cheerful manner; repelled by those who appear glum and distant? Isn't it only common sense that the same people might make the same impressions in their letters? In your own business experience, have you not responded more freely to the salesman of pleasing personality than to the one who is blunt, argumentative, or gloomy? Isn't it only reasonable to think that the letter writer who can make his reader smile a little bit will get better results than the one who curtly states his case, and ends with an abrupt "Yours very truly"? It doesn't matter what the purpose of the letter may be—to sell, to collect, to correct an error, to build goodwill—it may still reflect a smiling personality, and is more likely to succeed when it does. The following examples, serving various needs of business, are proof of the pudding.

Humor in adjustment letters. Handling the complaint of a customer is always a ticklish problem. The writer loses face by being too apologetic; he offends by taking the matter too lightly. The best place to stand is near the middle of the road: sorry, but not begging for mercy; eager to make a fair adjustment, but not wasting any time in useless explanation; disturbed, but not without poise. Something like this:

> Dear Mr. Jones:
>
> Your letter of December 6 blasted me right out of my chair and into the circulation records—a distance of twenty feet and probably the longest non-stop circulation hop on record.
>
> En route I grabbed the plaid two-peak Sherlock Holmes cap, polished off the magnifying glass, and yelled lustily for Watson. However, the case didn't prove to be as baffling as the "Study in Scarlet," because we quickly located the source of the crime. That's too bad, too, because I was all ready to say in a loud voice, "Why doesn't somebody tell me these things?"
>
> Here is the post mortem. I tried to locate you by sending copies of the October and November issues to your old address, hoping somebody would put your new address on them and forward them to you. This neighborly act did not take place, so then I tried to locate you through the National Sportsman, and they were sportsmen enough to send the letter on; but by the time your reply arrived it was November 1, and the December issue had been made up and sent out. But the change was made on our galleys so we could send you future copies and promotional material.
>
> After twenty years of seeing accidents like this happen, I just refuse to tear the hair out any more. As a matter of fact, there is very little of it left; but in accordance with good circulation custom, I will either send you the copies missed or extend your

subscription for that number of copies, and leave it up to you to advise the number of them. October, November, and December issues came back.

However, if you feel that personal persecution has been perpetuated with malice aforethought, and alienated your original interest, I will cancel and refund. You're the customer in this case, and whatever you say goes.

Kindest regards and greetings from one c.m. to another!

Cordially yours,

In that letter, John H. Reerdon, then circulation director for *Popular Photography,* was neither too abject nor too blunt. To soothe the feelings of his angry customer, he chose the man-to-man approach summarized by the closing sentence, "Greetings from one c.m. to another." In other words, he said in a friendly, half-humorous way, "You should understand how these mistakes can happen, because we are both circulation managers." The approach was successful, as it brought back a friendly letter from the customer.

The next exhibit is a reply made to an outraged customer who had received a nasty collection letter, although his account was fully paid. This situation, which occurs too frequently in business, has put gray hairs in the heads of many credit managers.

Dear Mr. Doe:

Twenty years ago D—— T—— and I both had .22 rifles. We used to sit on the fence at the city piggery and shoot rats. Big guys they were. African game hunting had nothing on that for sport.

That's what I would like to do now to the *competitor* who wrote that putrid collection letter. It must have been a competitor. It couldn't possibly be genuine because certainly this business was not built by calling customers names.

The most oafish person on our payroll in all of our 63 years wouldn't have written that letter. Certainly, nobody would write it when the bill had been paid four months, because we've got the swellest bookkeeping system since Noah checked the passenger list for the Ark. It just couldn't have happened here.

The only explanation is that some competitor of ours wants your business, and plans to heckle you by writing letters and signing our name. Please let me know who the first competitor is that calls and asks for your business. Hold the rat until I get there. I'll shoot the bastard.

Sincerely yours,

Yes, that was a dangerous letter to write, for it could have backfired if the customer had taken it seriously. Evidently the writer was sure of his man and could predict his reaction. The result was a reply in the same spirit, and a satisfied customer. In fact, Mr. Doe liked the letter so much that he commented. "This fellow's sense of humor kept my business for his company." And that must have been its purpose!

Now we will climb over the fence, and read a letter of complaint, quite unlike the usual sort that rant and rave. It was written to the superintendent of the Doe Freight Lines by a lady who had a large bump of humor, and could laugh at her own troubles—a more effective way to get them removed than to loose a tirade of abuse.

> Dear George:
>
> Short of strapping my belongings to my frail back and striding up Highway 101 to San Francisco, I'm beginning to believe there's no tougher way to get hold of them than through your lines.
>
> Things are loused up good now. I'm leaving here on Monday, December 14th, and will not return until Tuesday, December 22nd. Unless the things can be delivered before next Monday, it looks like we'll have a dizzy Christmas.
>
> If you try to pry open the doors and deposit them while I'm away, there won't be anyone here to pay you. Not that I feel like it.
>
> Your Frisco office seems to be staffed by persons of bad temper and subnormal intelligence.
>
> First, they refused to take the order; second, after the fifth vain call I am still unable to persuade them to jot down my phone number. Now really, I can remember the not-too-distant day when men FOUGHT over my phone number, and blood flowed freely.
>
> Today's call to the Frisco office was typical.
>
> I phone. A female answers and cuts me off. I wait ten minutes. I hang up. I phone back. She says, "Did you want something?" (Do I want something? Oh, dear Lord!) I say, yes, and explain my business. She gives me Mr. Smith. Mr. Smith listens ten minutes before explaining he is the wrong guy, and I really want Mr. Jones. I say I don't want Mr. Jones—I only want some sense to the whole thing.
>
> Mr. Jones, after a decent interval of twelve minutes, deigns to answer the phone. He will not, however, deign to (a) take down any instructions, (b) jot down my phone number, or (c) do anything. I explain that you suggested it, and he implies that the

Frisco office is far, far above the Los Angeles office. So you, George, will have to attach the phone number and instructions firmly to my trunk, and hope for the best.

My mother and father live at 654 Hunters Drive. Their home, a large brown house in need of paint, is located at the corner of Hunter and West, if that is any help.

Before removing the things from the garage, please ask one of my parents to instruct your men. The whole darned family stores things in mother's garage, and I don't want any of Aunt Maggie's old junk. The items I do want are:

1 filled, locked trunk
1 couch
1 coffee table
1 heavy chest of drawers

There are four pieces in all, unless you have me confused too. We live in a firetrap located at 0000 Sacramento Street, San Francisco. Do not ring the bell. It is dead and nothing happens. I've begged my husband to fix the darned thing, but he only hides behind his paper and says "wump."

Enter the CENTER door (painted red). Take the long flight of steps to the extreme right. On the top floor, turn to the left and continue to third floor back. That's us—Apartment 33. I'll admit it's a bother to climb all those steps, and my husband nearly broke his neck when he came in the other morning from a Legion meeting, but the rent is cheap.

Now, George, I'm awfully easy to please, but I do have my little whims, so will you indulge me just this once. You see, people have an unhappy way of delivering things out in the street to me. This is where I do NOT want them, so I demand that the Frisco office send me a second brawny back to help the driver lug my chattels up these 56 steps.

Now, are we straightened out? I understand the charge is $3.98 per 100 pounds, and I will have to pay extra for apartment delivery. Try to keep it cheap, huh? You've cost me so much already in phone calls and postage that I'm considering sending YOU a bill.

I'm not really angry, George, because this is the way things always happen to me. I was even born in a taxi.

Thanks for your cheery note, and best wishes for a Merry Christmas.

Frustratedly yours,

Admitted that the above letter is longer than it needs to be, and that the intimate tone would not be appropriate in the average business letter, there is no doubt but that the lady reveals a personality which is both delightful and strongly tinged with a sense of humor. The comment made by the party who contributed the letter was, "Incidentally, the gal got prompt apartment delivery!" It did the job, which is the best that can be said of any business communication.

Routine letters can be interesting. No matter what the business letter talks about, or how routine in nature it may be, there is no reason why it cannot contain a dash of personality. The following are run-of-the-mill illustrations: a letter about a check gone astray and a request for glossy prints. Even though the subjects are not life-or-death, the writers manage to season them with a smile.

(1)

Gentlemen:

The invoice which we received had not the slightest intimation of where we should send it. We scanned it on both sides with much precision, and even applied a match to it to see if, by some chance, you had used invisible ink.

After much deliberation, we took a shot at Evansville, but a miss is as good as a mile and the check, which we crave to spend, was returned to us as is evidenced by the envelope.

Now you may be a large concern and think that everyone down in these hills, even I, should know where to address your mail; but it seems that even Uncle Sam was somewhat befuddled, and this alleviates my inferiority complex in no infinitesimal manner.

We have gone to great pains to make this remittance to you; and if, by the time it does reach you, we have disintegrated to dust, please don't blame us.

Very truly yours,

(2)

Dear Cy:

I was greatly intrigued by your latest letter and particularly by your mention of the fact of how much easier you are able to sleep in a Pullman because of the motion.

Needless to say, this is a subject which I would like to take up with you in greater detail at our next convention aboard His Majesty's Ship Yacht Club at the Edgewater Beach Hotel.

The purpose of this letter is to ask if you could forward me several 8 x 10 glossy prints of your handsome fizzog.

I feel that displaying your "Rogues' Gallery" photograph will do more to kill the sale of the film than anything else, but after all, we must give you a little break on the publicity.

Sincerely yours,

Nothing remarkable about those two letters, was there? Nobody expects every routine business letter, done in a jiffy and without special thought, to be a precious gem. Nevertheless, in each of those letters a man seems to be *talking*—a friendly fellow with a sense of humor.

5. PERSONALITY IN SALES LETTERS

Easier to express. The sales letter-writer has at least two advantages over those who handle other types of correspondence, when it comes to making them express personality: the subject matter is naturally more interesting, and he is expected to spend more time on them. In the section two steps ahead, How to Write the Sales Letter, you will find many samples of the masters' skill which are interesting to the "last drop." It is not difficult for a writer of imagination to *relax, be natural, just talk,* when explaining the merit of products or services which themselves have plenty of "oomph." He has a big edge over his associates who must write about traffic regulations, unearned discounts, shipping specifications, and other matters no more exciting. You would think that every sales letter would sparkle with the personal touch, but as you will also find out in Section 7, this is not always true.

In no other kind of business letter writing is it so important that the personality of the writer be expressed. The urge to buy is usually more emotional than rational. You are swayed by the enthusiasm of the clerk in the store where you are trying on a new hat more than you are by the reasons why the hat may be worth the price. If that enthusiasm is lacking, you probably walk out without the hat. The problem of the sales letter-writer is much the same as that of the man behind the counter. He must make his prospect feel that he is proud of the thing he is talking about; that he himself would like to own it, or does.

Three letters to sell clothing. Two of the letters that follow were mailed for clothing merchants, the third by a tailor in London. The latter (see page 328) is reproduced in its original form. It was sent to two hundred prospects, and made one hundred and fifty sales—a remarkable pull of 75 per cent. Of course, the fact that it was written in script increased the . feeling of a personal contact. Letters in longhand are not practical as a rule, but in this case it seems to have been a happy choice.

The other two letters are extremely novel in their approach. One is pure slapstick comedy, but it probably made many readers laugh. You may decide for yourself whether or not you like these out-of-the-rut sales attempts, but at least you will concede they are not deficient in personality.

My dear and faithful companion:

This letter deals with a very ticklish subject. It concerns the Christmas gift you are going to select for me.

Last year you gave me a box of cigars, some screaming green and yellow seat-covers for my car, and a red leather volume of Love Lyrics.

The cigars broke Henry, our office porter, of his smoking habit; the seat-covers have been a source of real enjoyment to Uncle Nathan, who is color blind; and the Love Lyrics went over in a big way with little Patricia.

This letter I'll admit is a trifle cruel, but I am determined to help you avoid past mistakes.

Old age has made my golf bag unfit for further service; my riding trousers are fast giving up the ghost; I long for a set of matched irons. I wear size 38 sweater, and 10½ hose. Dark blues, maroons, and golden browns are my favorite colors.

These are a few of the things I noticed the other day on the Fourth Floor Sports Gift Section at BOYD'S.

BOYD'S, by the way, is my favorite store. Need I say more?

Lovingly,

Your Lord and Master.

Boyd's, St. Louis store of high standing, had considerable success with this Christmas-time sales letter. It was mailed, of course, to wives of customers. The one below was mailed by Ed Day, "The Genial Clothes Bandit," of Akron, Oho.

 Just as a reminder to the gentleman whose picture appears on the left, my records show that he made his last purchase on—

July 4, 1776

Might I, with great humility, suggest to this gentleman, that if he will present himself at 325 E. Market St., with his Social Security number, his driver's license, and his Unfit-for-Work Certificate, and insist on buying a new suit, topcoat, or overcoat, and if, after strict examination, I find that he really is in need of one or more garments, it is possible that I might be bribed, or persuaded, if caught in a weak moment, to allow him to select one or more garments that would prove to be a credit to both of us.

Under a recent ruling of the Supreme Court, I am not allowed to mention the very low prices of these garments, which start at

$27.50—the woolens represent some of the finest domestic and imported creations it is possible to get. This low price of $27.50 is made possible through our tremendous "No-Volume" business, and the extreme need of ready cash. These garments are made to your individual measure in the model that will make you look your best.

I have just received 40 beautiful stolen suit patterns, that would sell anywhere, even in ready-made, for at least $55.00 or more, but which, on account of the purchase price, I am tearfully and reluctantly offering for $39.50 for the suit. Sales are limited to no more than six suits to each customer—don't crowd, boys.

You don't have to worry about parking here. There's plenty of parking space and it's FREE. During the month of October we will discontinue stripping accessories from customer's cars. This service will be continued, however, after the November elections, with several added features.

Style note—trousers with patches on the seat, and holes in the toes of sox, will again be popular this Fall with the style-conscious men of both political parties

says

"The Genial Clothes Bandit."

The pictures used in this mailing were genuine. Snapshots of customers were on file; they had been taken at time of the first sale.

Importance of tone. One danger the novice faces in trying to put his personality in a sales letter is that he may exaggerate, so that the general tone becomes irritating to the reader. It is for this reason that beginners are reminded to be *natural* and *not to press* for effects that under the pressure may seem artificial. There is hardly anything more irritating than a writer *trying* to be clever.

Furthermore, what may be a proper tone for a sales letter to one type of reader could be a very wrong tone for a sales letter to some other class. Thus, people of very little education or culture might enjoy greatly a letter that would be considered too flippant by a group of bankers, lawyers, or college professors. This fact takes us back to the necessary steps in planning an important letter. You will remember that two of the steps were (1) to visualize the reader, and (2) choose the approach most likely to please him.

Following are four sales letters quite different in tone. Obviously, they were not intended for similar types of readers. For example, the tone of the English letter would be considered stiff and uninteresting by the average American reader, although it is very courteous and the picture of the writer gives it a pleasing personality. On the other hand, at least two of the other letters would be considered far too flippant by our cousins across the water. Never can we afford to forget that underneath all business writing certain psychological principles are always at work. Since no two individuals are exactly alike, then no two letters should be written in the same way if you hope to achieve the best results. This, to be sure, is only an ideal to be talked about and never entirely attained, because no business letter writer has the time to tackle everything he dictates as a psychological problem.

Nevertheless, the nearer the match between letter tone and reader individuality, the greater will be the sales pull.

Letter to sell advertising. The next of the four letters of different tone is shown on page 330. It attempts to sell printing and advertising services to business executives. Notice the not too farfetched play on the writer's name in the complimentary close—"Merrill-y yours." Notice, too the unconventional salutation, "Good Morning Friend:" But the body of the letter contains no horse play. The writer is friendly, but not intimate. You can guess that the people on his list were of a different type than those on the list to get the clothing letter. Vary the tone to fit the intended readers. That's only sound sales psychology. If you think your reader likes brass instruments, get out your trumpet; if you think he likes stringed instruments, get out your violin.

Letter to sell letters. A man of many years' experience in writing letters is Jack Carr, creator of *Cordial Contacts*—monthly mailings for companies to use in holding the goodwill of customers. On page 331, you see a Jack Carr letter to his own clients. The tone is lively and very informal. It would please a lot of people, but not *all* people. Of course, Carr, the expert writer, knows the limitations of the tone he uses in all of his Cordial Contacts. But like printerman Jackson, he has specific types of readers in mind, and seeks to match their moods.

Mr. Carr's letter would probably fall flat if mailed to the customers of Mr. Vernon S. Porter, whose letter is reproduced on page 332. But to make it tit-for-tat, so would Mr. Porter's letter fall flat if mailed to those on Mr. Carr's list. Hence, we have another demonstration of our salient point— no letter writer can hope to shoot at the moon and blast the whole of it. He must be content to aim for a certain slice, and use the ammunition most likely to hit the particular target.

All four of the sales letters cited have personality—but no two are of the same variety.

Dear Sir,

I admit that it is unusual to write a personal letter of this kind — but then what I have to say is unusual!

I want to make you a Suit. The suit I want to make would cost you 12 guineas anywhere in the West End from any first-class Tailor. I will charge you only 8 guineas for it and give you 90 days credit as well, if you want it.

All my friends say I'm crazy to do it. I don't think so. I know if you have one suit you'll buy another — and another — and that I'll be making your suits ten years from now. Isn't that sound sense?

So I am writing you this personal letter because it really is a personal matter

This Letter, Mailed to 200 Prospects, Gained 150 Orders for a London Tailor

The "how" of it. Perhaps by now, through summary and review, we can devise a formula for injecting the writer's personality into a business letter; remember that anything so abstract and intangible cannot be reduced to an exact science. However, the following road-marks may point in the right direction:

1. Try to begin with the concept of *talking*, not writing. Hold fast to this feeling of a man-to-man contact to the very end.

2. Use the language that is yours in everyday speech. Do not "press" or try to be clever. Relax. Be yourself.

3. Avoid the stilted expressions that make business writing stiff and colorless. Use, when you can, the homespun words like *folks, home,* and the others that have pleasant meaning to the common man.

4. Reflect good manners, rather than the "dignity" of business.

and rather than spend £4 in advertising,
I'd prefer to give the value in your suit.
Don't you agree?

If you're busy just give me a ring
at MAYfair 3688 and I'll be glad to
come down with patterns and measure
you. Alternatively, I'd prefer you to come
up here and see for yourself that what
I say is true.

In either event will you let me know,
please? I can only cater for 100 clients
and still give the service which has
(with all due modesty) put my name
amongst the 10 best Tailors in the
West End!

Now let me prove it!

Very truly yours

L. J. Titchmarsh

Managing Director.

Telegrams
SVERTRATA. LONDON.

Telephone:
MAYFAIR No. 3688

Brander & Co. Ltd.
CIVIL & MILITARY TAILORS.
ESTABLISHED 1871
10 Hanover Street Hanover Square London W. 2
L. J. Titchmarsh
Managing Director

There is no more dignity in business than in any other ordinary form of human activity.

5. Let the reader know he is being approached as a fellow human being. Call him by name a time or two. Add an "unnecessary" line about him, his city, a previous contact, or anything that may be of mutual interest.

6. Put the emphasis on *him*. Start sentences with *you*—avoid *we*. Interpret everything you talk about in terms of benefit to your reader—keep yourself and your company in the background as much as possible.

7. Keep in mind above all else that you must *please your reader*. See through his eyes, not your own.

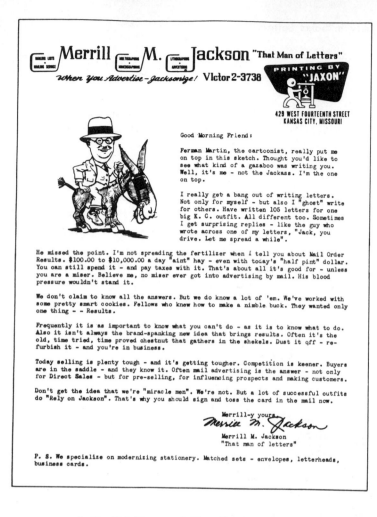

A Cordial Contact Selling Cordial Contacts

8. Cultivate a sense of humor, but do not *force* for it. If you have to stop and think about something funny to say, by all means don't say it. But don't be afraid to unbend. A smile is a million times more inviting than a frown.

9. Try hard to make the tone of your letter fit the personality of your reader.

10. Never dictate when you are cross or irritable. To be friendly, you must *feel* friendly.

Sober contemplation of these 10 points brings one fact to mind which cannot be disregarded. Not every person in business is qualified to write letters. You cannot write in a friendly way unless you *are* friendly; you

330

cannot make the reader feel you are interested in him unless you *feel* that interest; expressing a pleasing personality is impossible unless you *have* one. It may be that your letters have been cold although your heart is warm. If that is true, then your problem is simple. Open the gate, and let the warmth flow out. But if at heart you are contentious, sarcastic, suspicious, unfriendly, keep the gate closed. You can't make a silk purse out of a sow's ear; you can't express a pleasing personality when there is none to express.

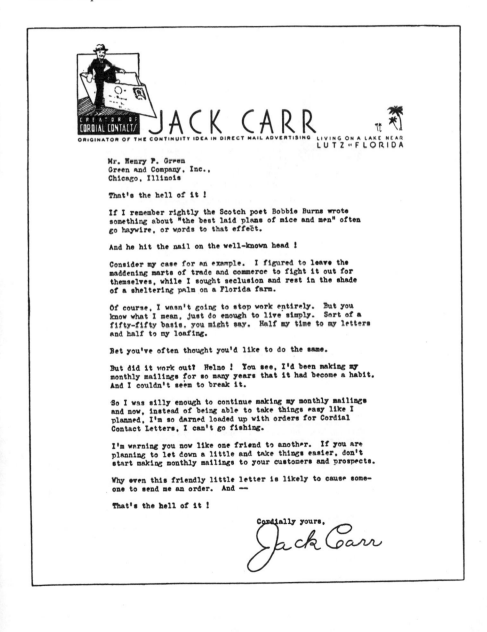

CREATOR OF CORDIAL CONTACTS

JACK CARR

ORIGINATOR OF THE CONTINUITY IDEA IN DIRECT MAIL ADVERTISING   LIVING ON A LAKE NEAR
LUTZ " FLORIDA

Mr. Henry P. Green
Green and Company, Inc.,
Chicago, Illinois

That's the hell of it !

If I remember rightly the Scotch poet Bobbie Burns wrote
something about "the best laid plans of mice and men" often
go haywire, or words to that effect.

And he hit the nail on the well-known head !

Consider my case for an example. I figured to leave the
maddening marts of trade and commerce to fight it out for
themselves, while I sought seclusion and rest in the shade
of a sheltering palm on a Florida farm.

Of course, I wasn't going to stop work entirely. But you
know what I mean, just do enough to live simply. Sort of a
fifty-fifty basis, you might say. Half my time to my letters
and half to my loafing.

Bet you've often thought you'd like to do the same.

But did it work out? Helno ! You see, I'd been making my
monthly mailings for so many years that it had become a habit.
And I couldn't seem to break it.

So I was silly enough to continue making my monthly mailings
and now, instead of being able to take things easy like I
planned, I'm so darned loaded up with orders for Cordial
Contact Letters, I can't go fishing.

I'm warning you now like one friend to another. If you are
planning to let down a little and take things easier, don't
start making monthly mailings to your customers and prospects.

Why even this friendly little letter is likely to cause someone to send me an order. And —

That's the hell of it !

Cordially yours,

Jack Carr

S. MAW, SON & SONS, LTD

(G.P.O. Box No. 54)

7 to 12 ALDERSGATE STREET, LONDON, E.C. 1.

TELEPHONE:
NATIONAL 2488
(PRIVATE BRANCH EXCHANGE)
TELEGRAMS:
" ELEVEN, CENT,
LONDON "
CABLEGRAMS:
" ELEVEN, LONDON "

DIRECTORS:
MOWBRAY T MAW
ARTHUR T MAW
ALBERT F PORTER
VERNON S. PORTER
NORMAN M. PORTER

Manufacturers of

TOILET BRUSHWARE, TOILET PREPARATIONS, SURGICAL DRESSINGS
CLINICAL THERMOMETERS, DRUGGISTS' SUNDRIES, ETC. • SHOPFITTERS

FACTORIES: NEW BARNET, HACKNEY, HAGGERSTON

SEASONAL EXHIBITION OF CHRISTMAS MERCHANDISE,
GRAND HOTEL, BOURNEMOUTH. COMMENCING 8.10.

Dear Sir,

We are pleased to advise you
that our special range of
Christmas Merchandise has had
a most encouraging reception
at the hands of the trade in
all parts of the country.

Special exhibitions have
already been held in such
centres as Birmingham, Glasgow,
Edinburgh, etc. at which
attendances and sales have broken all our
established records for many years.

In fact, we have had such a high degree of
interest, that it has been difficult to
attend to all customers on certain days,
despite the use of trained auxiliary staff.

We are writing to tell you that so far as
Mr. John Swan's exhibition at the Grand Hotel
is concerned, we have arranged for Mr. Phillips
of our Showroom Staff, to be in attendance with
him for the rest of the week, to ensure proper
service.

We are looking forward to a personal visit from
you, and if you can possibly telephone and make
an appointment, it would be of assistance to us,
but in any case you can be sure of the most
cordial welcome.

This is going to be a vintage year for Maw
Christmas Merchandise, and it promises to be the
finest season for our customers that they have
ever known.

We do hope that you will come along to our Stock-
room, so that you may judge for yourselves just
what we are doing to help you.

Wishing you the most successful Christmas you
have ever known, and thanking you for your
support,

                         Yours very truly,
                         S. MAW, SON & SONS LTD.

                         (VERNON S. PORTER)
REF: VSP/P   MANAGING DIRECTOR.

The Picture Helps to Personalize This English Letter

6. Spirit of the Company

Another form of personality. Business organizations, like the people in them, have personalities to express. Some are forbiddingly cold; some are warm and attractive. Others, clinging to the fetish of "business is business," have the best of intentions toward their customers, but hide them behind a barrier of formality. The writer who serves an organization which is either cold, or appears to be, works under a severe handicap. If he writes friendly, man-to-man letters, sometimes flavored with a touch of humor, he is quite likely to be called on the carpet and told his letters must stick strictly to the business at hand. This is lamentable, of course, as the very spirit which would help to get results is prohibited.

In the largest sense, the business correspondent writes for his company more than for himself. This though is expressed in the book, *Smooth Sailing Letters*,* in the chapter called "A Pint of Molasses or a Barrel of Vinegar." The title, of course, refers to Abe Lincoln's familiar saying that a pint of molasses catches more flies than a barrel of vinegar. The application to business letters is quite obvious.

> It's the company that writes the letters—not you or me. And the company is bigger than any man or woman on the payroll. The company has just one purpose—to render an honest service and thereby reap an honest profit. Everything that helps the company to achieve that purpose is good—anything that works against that purpose is bad. There is no middle ground.
>
> What good could an angry, impudent, or sarcastic letter do the company? You could sock a fellow in the eye for calling you a liar. You wouldn't be much of a man if you didn't. But the company can never take a punch at a customer. Customers are the root of the business. Without customers, there would be no business. Without customers, there would be no job for you.

If the above sounds reasonable, then it must be conceded that the letter-writer has a double purpose to attain; first, to express his own personality in a pleasing way; second, to express the *spirit of goodwill* that exists in his company. To be sure, the second purpose is missing if the company spirit is not friendly. But we are not talking about exceptions. We believe the great majority of organizations that comprise American business are genuinely eager to render an honest service. Some of them may not *express* goodwill as well as they could, but the spirit is there just the same.

---

* *Smooth Sailing Letters,* by L. E. Frailey; Prentice-Hall, Inc., Englewood Cliffs, N.J.

A provocative letter. If you take time to study the letters that come your way, you no doubt are amazed at the two extremes which they often represent in helping or hurting public relations. It is difficult to understand how any business executive could have dictated the following letter, and then signed his name to it as general manager. The letter was written several years ago, and from the spirit reflected in it, we may assume the company is no longer in business.

> Gentlemen:
>
> You had a few shipments of our harmless active ———— ————.
> You have not purchased for a long time.
>
> From our viewpoint there can be but one conclusion. You have no business, or, you do not know what ———— ———— is, or what it should be.
>
> Manufacturing firms having brains leading them, use this ————, as we can prove by transportation records, so that we and our dealers are supplying more ———— consumers than those supplied by all other ———— producers combined.
>
> The reordering goes on while you slumber.
>
> However, we shall be glad to supply you when in the market.
>
> Very kindly,

If it were not such a horrible illustration of tactless writing, you could smile at that letter. After insulting the former customer by insinuating he is asleep and has no brains, the writer ends with "Very kindly." If you can find anything kind in the letter, you are a wizard. The spirit expressed is utterly selfish. The general manager is irritated because the customer stopped buying. He plainly says what he thinks of such stupidity.

When the customer is very angry. Under no circumstances can a business correspondent be justified in slapping back at a customer. The former may have received a provoking letter; he may have good reason to resent it. But his job is not to add more fuel to the argument. He must, if possible, smooth the ruffled feathers; the old saying that a soft answer often turneth away wrath is true. Consider the very fine example that follows:

> Dear Jerry:
>
> Whatever you may say about us, you will not deny that we have developed an almost fiendish accuracy in treading on your toes. I won't insult your intelligence by giving you a lot of baloney about why these mistakes happened, or why they won't happen again. I can't even promise that.

But I will do my best to set things right, and I am sorry that you feel I am personally responsible for these blunders.

No doubt if I were in your shoes, I would echo your "Nuts to you" with vehemence. But I'm not—I am on the other side of the fence, and honestly you haven't left me a leg to stand on. Sorry, Jerry! But I hope you don't feel too angry to accept my sincere apologies, and best personal wishes.

Sincerely,

Your could hardly ask for a finer illustration of good letter writing than the above. It reveals a man of pleasing personality expressing the goodwill of his company—a spirit which carries on in spite of trying circumstances.

Section 6

COMPANY BETTER LETTER PROGRAM

6. OTHER DEVICES TO IMPROVE LETTERS

COMPANY BETTER LETTER PROGRAM

1. CONDITIONS NECESSARY TO SUCCESS

Must start at the top. Many companies in recent years have undertaken programs to improve letters. Some attained temporary results that were eventually nullified by lack of sustained effort. Others, equally successful at the start, have managed to keep the fire burning. But many fizzled, either from inadequate supervision or lack of executive backing. It is useless to consider a letter program in your company, in spite of the good one might accomplish, unless the top executives are thoroughly sold on the need, and will let it be known that cooperation is expected from all employees who have anything to do with company correspondence. This, of course, includes themselves, since cooperation does not permit exceptions.

An interesting example is the contrasting experiences of two companies that launched letter programs at about the same time, and under the same leader, a man who had been able to improve correspondence for many other organizations. There were many other similarities that make the comparison even more convincing. In both companies, the number of people handling letter writing totaled about eighty, and the preponderance of the letters went to customers. No attention had been paid before to letter improvement, and those being written were stilted, curt, and often unfriendly.

Since the program and conditions in both cases were identical, it would seem that the results should have been no more gratifying for the one company than the other. This was far from what happened, however. Company A came through the program with flying colors. The improvement in the letters was so marked that even many customers remarked in a complimentary way about them. Sales letters produced more orders; collection letters brought back the money with less friction; complaints were

339

handled more tactfully; the company felt an unmistakable improvement in public relations.

But the results in Company B were quite different. Some of the letter writers improved, others did not. The program was carried out as agreed, but with lukewarm cooperation. At the end, nothing was done to keep it going. Here and there some individuals were doing a better job, but the majority slipped back quickly to their indifferent, and often rude, manner of writing. In a few months, no one would have known that a better letter program had ever been launched in that company. The results could hardly be called worth the effort.

Why did Company A succeed, and Company B fail, with the same letter program? Well, because of one very important reason. In Company A, the president and all of the other officials were highly interested. They set an example for every employee to imitate. They encouraged every letter writer, irrespective of rank, to attend the meetings. The president announced the course in advance, and asked for complete cooperation. He said that his letters would be treated like any others, and that he and the other officials would attend the meetings. And they did, without exception.

In Company B, the attitude of top, executives was the reverse. The program was placed in the charge of a junior department head, who probably was the one who had sold the need for better letters. Unfortunately, he was one of the poorest writers, and not popular among the other men. No announcement or call for teamwork came from the president's office; none of the officials appeared at any of the meetings. Of course, their letters were not put through the wringer. From the beginning, it was obvious that the program was intended to be only a school for down-the-line employees—and they resented the idea. They were expected to improve their letters, but the big men in the company were immune to the treatment. Some department heads came to the meetings as observers, but a sure way to kill even this casual interest was to find a fault in their letters. Naturally, the program failed to gain a fraction of the results gained in Company A. The cause was lack of executive backing!

Inception of program. The better letter program can originate in any department, but, as previously mentioned, it must have the interest of company officials to give it the impetus needed for success. For example, the idea for a better letter program in the New York Life Insurance Company was born in its public relations department. However, that is not an important fact. What was crucial to the success of this program was the backing it got from company executives. This company has been in the forefront in the development of a better letter program, and the author wishes to thank its personnel for constructive guidance in the writing of this chaper.

If you are the one who wants to initiate the program, do some research first and you will be in a good position to make recommendations to your superior. The following memorandum was adapted from an actual one. See how well the initiator has done his work; he presents a well-thought-out program for his superior's consideration.

PROPOSED PROGRAM FOR IMPROVING COMPANY CORRESPONDENCE

There are two broad approaches to the problem of improving correspondence: By employing an outside agency to do a complete survey and wholesale revision of letters, as in the case of the ABC Company; or by developing a program from within the Company, as in the case of DEF Company. Among the objections to the first approach are the antagonisms and resistance which an outside organization is likely to encounter when dealing with department heads, the danger of reverting to old habits when the outside organization has completed its task, the fact that an outside organization would require considerable assistance and direction on the part of people within the Company, and expense.

It is recommended that the second approach be adopted, with this office taking on the task of developing a plan which would have the full-time attention of an expert writer.

The plan, in brief, would cover a broad, overall program for stimulating interest in better writing, and secondly, assistance and guidance for particular departments and individuals. The general principles and procedure, as outlined below, were developed after studying the experiences of other life insurance companies with this problem:

1. A course, consisting of six or seven one-hour lectures, to cover the general principles of how to write a better letter. The course would be given to groups of fifteen or twenty, generally from the same department at weekly intervals. This procedure has proved very successful at DEF company.

   a. Organize material and prepare lectures, which might be illustrated with slide film.

   b. Enroll members and deliver lectures.

   c. Provide summaries of each lecture.

   d. Prepare and provide study material.

2. Prepare, and send periodically, reminder follow-up bulletins to those who have taken the course, to keep them from backsliding into old habits. Experience of other companies has indicated the advisability of this.

3. Enlist the cooperation of department heads. We feel that this may best be accomplished by having a particular department head recognize the need for better letters and come to us to assist him. In this way we could cooperate with the department head to find a satisfactory solution to his problem, and avoid the natural resistance which usually arises in these situations. It is not expected that they would hesitate asking for help when it becomes known that the top officers of the Company are interested in improving the quality and character of correspondence, and that there is a set-up to help department heads in this regard. As a good job is done in one department, we believe that word would get around and that there would be heavy demand for the service we would be ready to provide.

4. The procedure by departments might be as follows:
   a. Review an extensive file of letters and classify the various types of letters written in the department.
   b. Prepare model letters and guide paragraphs for the most common types of letters.
   c. Provide each letter writer in the department with a correspondence manual on how to write good letters for his department.
   d. Review printed forms going to customers and agents, and suggest ways to improve them in appearance and phraseology.
   e. Work in close collaboration with the department head, lawyers and actuaries in making all revisions.
   f. Counsel with individual letter writers and show how particular letters can be improved.
   g. After completing the job in a particular department, inaugurate a system of periodic review to make certain high standards are maintained.

5. Review with the Committee on Procedures the relative advantages and disadvantages, from the viewpoints of economy, efficiency and public relations, of individually typed letters, automatically typed letters, multigraphed letters with typewritten fill-in, printed letters with typewritten fill-in, and printed forms.

This program may seem rather ambitious and comprehensive, and obviously all of it cannot be accomplished immediately. DEF spent a full year developing a program before introducing it; and ABC employed a considerable staff of outside consultants who spent several years before completing a program of departmental correspondence manuals. It is certainly enough to occupy the full time of one man. As the program is new, it would probably be advisable for us to feel our way, especially in the beginning, to make certain we are on the right track, although the fundamental procedures and principles are based on the experience of other companies.

A plan so well thought out had to be approved, and it was. There are so many sound ideas presented in this memorandum that companies of all types and sizes can find some that are useful for their purposes.

Announcing the program. Since the logical next step in a better letter program is the announcement, it is important that a high-ranking executive sign this call to arms so that it is given the proper weight. The announcement should stress the purpose and importance of the program. Following is a letter that can be a guide for you.

> As you know, letters written by the company to customers, agents and the general public play an important part in determining the nature of public feeling toward the company and toward the business as a whole. Except for the agents, the only contact in many cases between a company and its customers is through written communications.
>
> In view of the importance of the letters we write, the Public Relations Committee for some time has been trying to work out some way in which it could be helpful to those who have the responsibility of writing letters in the Home Office. As a result of this study, an "Effective Letters" program has been developed. It will include a series of round table conferences for those who write letters, review and analysis of individual letters, and consultation with the head of the department on correspondence problems.
>
> The general plan will be administered by the Public Relations Department under Assistant Vice President Doe, and conducted by Mr. John Smith of the Department. Before joining the Company, Mr. Smith was a successful writer for leading national magazines, and he has had considerable experience in the field of business letter writing.
>
> The program will be started in one department at a time, and eventually it will cover all departments of the Company. Department heads wishing to take advantage of the Effective Letters service should get in touch with Mr. Doe. He and Mr. Smith will be glad to explain the program in detail and work out plans to fit particular needs.
>
> John Jones
> Executive Vice President

Adequate leadership. If maximum results are to be secured, a necessary condition is the selection of a qualified person to plan and supervise the program. As in any other similar undertaking, the net gain is sure to be in proportion to the knowledge and experience of the instructor, plus his ability to present his material in an interesting and practical manner. Some companies are blessed with such an individual within the organization, and that person can do the job as a part-time activity, which he is often glad to do if paid a bonus for the extra effort. Many of the bigger organizations, however, maintain full-time correspondence supervisors. This is the ideal setup, and it pays high dividends to the company that can afford the cost.

Outside help. When the company considers the cost of a full-time correspondence supervisor prohibitive, and there is no person in the organization ready to take over, the only alternative is to look outside for help. Fortunately, this alternative is not a restricted one. Many companies are located in cities where universities, colleges, and business schools offer good courses in letter composition.

In addition to the helpers that may be drawn from the college field, there are also a limited number of professional business letter consultants. Some of them conduct letter clinics in the larger cities. These are valuable in laying the groundwork in principles, and in motivating correspondents who lack the understanding of the relation between their letters and pleasant public relations.

The company library. A business organization need not be large to maintain a library of books for the training of employees in various aspects of business. However, the number of companies offering this service is surprisingly small. There are several exceptionally good books on business letter writing, and any person who handles correspondence should be encouraged to read them. Sometimes, a small group may be organized to study the same book, with weekly get-togethers for discussion, and systematic application of the subject matter to the company's letter problems. Many a company school has started in this informal way. The average employee is receptive to the idea of self-improvement when those higher up provide the opportunity.

It is foolish for any executive to say that he would like to see his letter writers do a better job but that no means of training them are available. He may have to scratch here and there, but he can always come up with some kind of a letter program. It may not be the best in the world, but it will be better than nothing. If sincerely offered, with genuine executive encouragement, the results are bound to outweigh the cost in time or money.

Need of sustained effort. A lot of better-letter programs go up like a rocket, and fall like a dud. Someone in the company gets the idea that correspondence needs a shot in the arm, and he sells a bill of goods to his chief executive. The stimulant may have been a letter that caused the company much embarrassment, or the person inspired may have heard about the results gained by some other organization. Anyway, the program is launched with the best talent available, and the company spares no cost in turning old methods upside-down. In some cases, the intentions are better than the procedure; results are negligible. In others, the immediate progress is even better than had been expected. The letter writers are all doing a much better job. The executives agree the program is a swell idea—and then they promptly let go of it. Better letters are an accomplished fact in the company. They can now think of other things.

But that is not true. The minute the program is put on the shelf, it begins to lose its effectiveness. One by one the letter writers return to their old bad habits. With nothing to keep them on the new trail, they soon return to the old and easier one. They, too, stop thinking about better letters. In the course of time, most of the progress is erased. And all for the lack of *sustained* effort.

This fall from grace and return to the old inferior way of doing things is common in business. Factory workers slip in quality and quantity of production unless the incentives to do good work are kept fresh and alive. Advertising copy tends to become impotent unless somebody continues to prod those who write it. Errors increase in the shipping department unless the work there is kept under continuous observation. It is just human nature to take the easy road when there is no one to lead the way on the hard road. No letter program will continue at maximum speed unless a competent driver stays at the wheel.

If this fact sounds discouraging, let it not be so. The bulk of the job is done when the letter writers, and the others helping them, have mastered the principles of letter construction and have caught the idea that their output is directly connected with sales and public relations. With that much accomplished, they *know how* to write effective letters. When they slip back to former bad writing habits, it is not because they don't know better, but because nobody continues to check their work, nor seems to care any longer whether it is good or poor. Thus, the incentive to fine performance is gone.

The companies that manage to keep the quality of their letters high throughout the years are those that maintain an adequate form of supervision. At regular intervals, and sometimes unexpectedly, carbon copies are checked. Bulletins, too, are sent forth regularly to keep the principles alive and to present new ideas. Praise of good work is freely given, and now and then a prize is awarded to the writer of an especially good letter. Never are the writers allowed to forget either the principles or the need for their application to company correspondence. Thus, the program never dies— because somebody is around to keep it fresh and vital.

Periodic announcements. As part of its program, a company should send announcements to department heads before the beginning of each course. Department heads are thereby reminded of the program and invited to submit names of employees who are interested in taking the course. The announcements, in memorandum form, should be clearly written and fully explain the program. The following memorandum is an example:

> Next month, we will begin another course in writing improvement as part of our continuing Effective Letter Program. To help us do this, will you please send the names of those under your supervision you would like to be considered for training. Please submit the names by Monday, March 5, as follows:
>
> > Type separately on 3×5 cards the name of the employee who will participate in the program:
> >
> > > John Doe   (Group Classification)*
> > > Insurance Department
> > > Room   , Tube
> >
> > > * Group Classification will be either 2A or 2B: "A" for those who will attend the 2 morning workshop meetings and "B" for those who will attend the afternoon sessions.
>
> HOW DOES THE COURSE WORK?
>
> The course will be given in the same manner as the most recent one, which was successfully concluded in February. Two lectures, based on the principles of effective business writing, will be followed by 26 weeks of carbon analysis. That is, each week, trainees will submit carbons of their letters, which will be analyzed and returned to them with comments. The "Effective Letters" manual will be distributed. At the end of the program, we will send a progress report of each trainee's writing to his department head or division head.
>
> WHO IS ELIGIBLE?
>
> While the program concentrates on our special type of correspondence and is intended mainly to build good will through our letters, it is not restricted to those who write letters only. It is open to anyone who writes or is expected to write *in any media* as part of his job responsibility. Those who have had previous training are eligible. Only letters will be criticized, however, not memorandums or reports—but the principles and skills learned

will be useful in all kinds of writing. *If the writer has no letters of his own to submit* for evaluation, he will be asked to complete exercises that will be furnished him each week.

Enrollment is voluntary, of course, but it is expected that trainees—once enrolled—will do all assignments until the end of the course.

A report on the just-concluded program is in preparation and will be distributed soon.

Please send the names of your prospective trainees, on the 3×5 cards, by Monday, March 5, to Effective Letters Program, Room 3311. If the first evaluation of a participant's writing shows that he has no need for training, we will notify you immediately to that effect.

Announcement to participants. After the names of employees who are going to take the course are submitted, the supervisor of the program should send a memorandum to each participant welcoming him to the course and restating the importance of better letters to the company. Included in this memorandum can be general information about the course. The following is an example:

Effective business letters are a vital part of our Company's public relations, and we are delighted to learn that you will participate in our Effective Letters Program. We know that you will find your assignments to be both interesting and useful.

The program consists of 2 major elements: Lecture-workshop meetings, and comments on your letters from expert writers and teachers.

LECTURE-WORKSHOP MEETINGS

There will be 2 of these meetings, conducted by a professor of Business Writing at New York University. He is the author of several books and articles and is a past president of the American Business Writing Association. Meetings will be held on the following days in the 13th Floor Conference Room.

	Group 2-A	Group 2-B
Friday, March 23	9:15 a. m.	2:00 p.m.
Friday, March 30	9:15 a.m.	2:00 p.m.

You will find your group classification underneath your room and tube number on the white slip at the top of this page. Please use this slip when submitting your first set of carbons.

COMMENTS ON YOUR LETTERS

From now on, beginning the week of March 21, we would

like you to make extra carbons of all your letters, and to select *every week* the 5 that you think are the best, for comments. Your editor will comment upon how they conform to our principles of effective writing, and return them to you. Your editors will be Robert Cain and Lionel Dael, experienced editors in this field.

You will receive 6 months of such training—in 2 periods of 3 months each. This will involve 26 different sets of carbons. The first period will begin the week of March 21 and end during the week of June 20.

NOTE: At the conclusion of the program, a progress report will be sent to your department head. To help us with this, we will need a sampling of your letters before the Program begins. Therefore, the carbons you submit on March 21 will not be returned to you. However, the carbons you submit on March 28 and thereafter will be returned to you with comments.

The program coordinator in your department has already let you know, or will soon let you know, the schedule he wishes to follow when he collects your carbons. They will always be collected on the *same* day every week. Also, because comments are only a week apart, no late carbons can be accepted; and no more than 5 carbons can be submitted in any one week.

The carbons, with comments, will be folded and stapled and returned directly to you through the tubes. In this way, the comments made will remain confidential between the instructor and yourself.

YOUR NAME SLIPS

At the first meeting, you will receive 15 slips containing your name and other information. Please clip (**NOT STAPLE**) one of these slips to your carbons every week when your coordinator collects them. The same slip will be used to return the carbons to you. (If you should lose these slips, please prepare new ones.)

We will have further information and materials about the program for you at the meetings. This material will be packaged, labeled with your name, and placed on tables at the side of the Conference Room. The material will be arranged in alphabetical order. As you enter the Conference Room, please pick up your material *before* taking your seat.

Meanwhile, if you have any questions, will you please get in touch with your program coordinator immediately.

We are looking forward to seeing you at our first meeting on Friday, March 23.

2. First, the Letter Audit

To know where you stand. The logical beginning of any better-letter program is to take inventory of the letters currently mailed. In the New York Life Insurance Company's program this job is done by more than one person. Other companies leave this to the program leader. By making this audit, the man in charge gains useful information to guide his steps. He finds out the major faults of the company's correspondence as a whole, and puts his finger on the letter writers who need the most correction. This is a necessary "first" because in no two companies will the same conditions prevail, and the program should be custom-built to fit the letters at hand.

This information is very simple to get. Several weeks before the program is to begin, a period is named during which extra copies of all letters are made for the program leader. These carbon copies should be placed in folders: there should be a set for each correspondent, sufficient in number to give a fair sample of his work. The leader then proceeds to read and mark the carbon copies, in preparation for a personal conference with each letter writer. These conferences should be kept strictly between the leader and the letter writer, as it encourages cooperation if the latter knows his faults are not to be called to the attention of his executive. Inasmuch as some men and women are keenly sensitive about their faults, the program leader needs to search for good points in the carbon copies as well as bad, even if he has to stretch his imagination a little bit to find something worthy of commendation.

Carbon copies are audited throughout the entire course.

Future inventories. At the end of the formal meetings and personal conferences, if the leader really knows his subject, considerable improvement should already be noted in the work of the various writers. A second audit is then necessary to know exactly how much ground has been gained. Based on this second analysis, a report to the executive responsible for the program is in order. This report can show by comparison the improvement made, and it may also call attention to certain individuals whose ability has been overlooked. The executive thus has a guide for the future selection of employees to handle important letter jobs. The report may also point to certain individuals who have not benefited by the program, and who are not likely ever to produce effective business letters. By transferring these persons to other jobs that do not involve letter writing, a benefit is created both for them and the company.

If an outsider has been employed to head the program, the second audit of carbon copies and the final report on results is the signal for his departure. But while he has built the foundation for better letters in the company, and the principles are understood by all who write them, this is by no means the end of the job. If the gains are to be held, the letter audits must be continued indefinitely, preferably twice a year. The carbon copies may be reviewed by someone in the company who has developed the inclination and ability for the job, or they may be sent to the outsider who directed the initial stage of the program. These semiannual check-ups, coupled with the regular distribution of better-letter bulletins, should keep the program alive.

Training of beginners. Because of the recurring turnover in personnel in the larger companies, one troublesome question pertaining to the letter-program is what to do about correspondents who are new on the job, and have not had the benefit of previous instruction. Of course, when their number is large enough to warrant the cost, the initial steps of the program can be repeated in a beginners' class, conducted either by the man in the company who has taken over the supervision of correspondence, or by the same outsider who launched the program. It is also a good idea to save complete sets of bulletins for these beginners.

3. How to Conduct the Meetings

The physical set-up. It is important that meetings for letter improvement be held in a place where interruptions or distractions can be avoided. If the company has a large conference or director's room, the problem is solved. Whatever the place selected, it should be apart from the rest of the business and free from noise, so that the program leader will have undivided attention. For example, one professional letter-consultant will never forget the conditions under which he was forced to operate in a certain company. Arriving for his first lecture, he was taken to an upper floor in the factory part of the building where a space had been cleared for the first and subsequent gatherings. On the other side of a temporary partition certain machines were pounding and thumping. The noise was so great that he had to shout to make himself heard. When he asked if the machines could not be stopped until after the session, one of the executives replied, "Certainly not, we are away behind in filling orders, and those machines must run night and day." You can imagine how successful the meetings were under those circumstances!

It is also important that those attending the meetings should be made as comfortable as possible. They should be provided with armchairs, or seated near tables so that notes can be taken. The instructor should have a rostrum on which to lay his papers, a large blackboard, and plenty of chalk. These may appear to be minor details, but unless someone looks after them the program will be hindered.

Attendance. The need for complete co-operation, so that every letter writer attends every meeting, has been mentioned. Not only should they be expected to be there, but punctuality also needs to be stressed. It is distracting to the group members and to the instructor when persons arrive late, or leave in the middle of a meeting to take telephone calls or for some other purpose. If a letter program is to be launched at all, it should be considered important enough to set aside everything else for it.

Material to be covered. The material that will be covered at each meeting should be clearly outlined before the beginning of the course. How much should be covered will be dictated to a great extent by the needs of the company and by the program leader's preferences. The first two meetings in one company's program were devoted to the tone of a letter and to saying what you mean. You might decide to cover more or less, or to discuss something entirely different at your first meetings.

4. Devices to Rate Letters

Too intangible for exact rating. A business letter cannot be rated as a piece of meat is weighed on the butcher's scale. There are too many factors that must be working in the right combination, too many psychological forces that may play on one reader with different effect than on another. Even the experts are often fooled in advance about a letter, calling *poor* the one that later gets fine results, and rating *good* the one that later turns out to be a flop. Nevertheless, there are evaluating devices that may be used with a reasonable percentage of accuracy. Even though they may at times miss their mark, they do have the great merit of forcing the writer to judge his letter with a more critical eye. He may discover a weakness that would have been lost in a more casual examination of the letter.

The trouble is that most people hastily read a letter they have written, consider the general effect, and then jump to the conclusion that it is good or bad. They do not stop to take the letter apart, or to view it from several angles, as the Rating Scale on page 353 requires them to do.

To rate your own letters. This scale places before you—one at a time —six major factors in the success of a letter. First, you are asked to consider only the *appearance* of the letter, and nothing else. If there is a fault in the letterhead, the position of the letter on the page, or the way it is typed, it should be noticed because you are concentrating only on appearance, and its importance is not overshadowed in your mind by your enthusiasm for something else.

Then, in sequence, but always only one factor at a time, you are led by the Rating Scale to a consideration of Language, Argument, Carpentry, Personality, and Spirit. When weighing the language of the letter, you have pushed aside the question of its appearance. And when you come to argument, language in turn takes a back seat. Hence, if there *is* a deficiency in any óne of these six respects, you are more likely to spot it than if you had taken a once-over view of the whole.

The system of grading is simple. You are not asked to pare your judgment to a hair's breadth, as must be the case when a teacher says that one composition is worth a grade of 86 and another a grade of 87. Instead, when considering *appearance* you come up with one of four valuations, worth in points as follows:

If extremely good	15 points
If better than average	10 points
If questionable	5 points
If obviously poor	0 points

Any person willing to look at his own letter with an impartial eye can tell very quickly which of the above four ratings it deserves on appearance. If "5" is the answer, then he knows that from one angle the letter has a serious weakness. Probably, he decides immediately that it must be retyped, or that he will call his printer and have a new letterhead designed.

With the appearance graded, *language* takes its turn. Perhaps the words are short and expressive, the sentences neatly turned, with not a whisker to mar the naturalness of the message. Okay! No doubt the proper rating on language alone is 15 points. Or, if not that good, at least it rates above average—10 points.

When the last of the six points is reached, the points can be totaled, perhaps like this:

Appearance, better than average	10
Language, extremely good	15
Argument, questionable	5
Carpentry, better than average	10
Personality, extremely good	15
Spirit, better than average	10
Total points	65

Finally, when the rating is completed, and not before, there is one question to be answered, and it is the only time that the letter is considered as a whole. *Does this letter do the job?* If the writer sincerely thinks it *does,* then he gives his letter an additional 10 points. But if he has any doubt in answering the question—if he is not *sure* it does the job—no additional

CY FRAILEY'S RATING SCALE FOR BUSINESS LETTERS*		
! = 15　　　+ = 10　　　? = 5　　　− = 0		Points
Appearance	How well is the letter groomed?　Is the letterhead attractive without being wild?　Does the letter sit nicely on the page?　Is the typing good and free from erasures?　Does the letter appeal to the eye as one easy to read?	
Language	Are the words short and natural?　Would the average person know their meaning?　Is the letter free from whiskers?　Does it carry the distinction of simplicity?　Is the language the same that the writer would use if he were talking to the reader?	
Argument	Has the story in the letter been well told?　Do the facts seem complete?　Is all the information presented that the reader needs?　Does the letter "ring true"?　Does the writer seem to know what he is talking about?　Does the purpose of the letter stand out sharply?	
Carpentry	What kind of craftsman does the writer prove to be?　Between the lines can you see the skeleton that all good letters must have?　What about the Star the Chain, and the Hook—are they all there?　Do the paragraphs cling together?　Does the story move along?	
Personality	Does the writer succeed in getting himself into the letter?　Does he take the reader on an interesting journey?　Does he get out of the rut of the commonplace?　Does the letter sparkle with originality?　Is the interest sustained from beginning to end?	
Spirit	Will the letter win goodwill for the company?　Is it free from sarcasm, ridicule, anger, and bluster?　Does the reader get the impression that he is being well served?　Is it a letter the writer would be proud to show to the head of his company?	
Result	And now, beyond all of those six points, what general impression does the letter give?　Does the writer seem to have accomplished his purpose?　Does the letter do the job?	
	Final Rating	

points are given. For example, it would not be consistent to say a letter does the job, if the argument in it has been rated questionable—as in the hypothetical rating, which totaled 65.

As can readily be seen, only what appears to be a perfect letter with not a flaw in any of the six qualities could receive a final rating of 100. Since perfection is rare in business correspondence, the writer who rated his own effort 100 would do well to question his judgment, and repeat the procedure. On this Rating Scale, a total grade of 80 indicates a very good letter, although it might rate so low on just one point that a serious weak-

* This scale is from L. E. Frailey's *Smooth Sailing Letters*. Englewood Cliffs. N. J.: Prentice-Hall, Inc.

353

ness would obviously demand correction. Little is to be gained by leniency in the evaluation of our own handiwork. Why should we fool ourselves?

Check carbon copies of letters. Carbon copies of letters that are actually sent to customers can be submitted to an editor for appraisal and criticism. This practice is the backbone of the New York Life Insurance Company better letter program. The following is an example of the type of comments that a letter writer who is taking this course can expect:

EFFECTIVE LETTERS PROGRAM

NEW YORK LIFE INSURANCE COMPANY

Mary Doe:

Welcome to the course.

I didn't think we were handling inter-office letters and memos, but since you sent them on I'll be glad to read them. First, I would like you to work on tightening up your prose--be concise, say what you must say in simple language. You'll find that writing becomes more effective when you get the message across in few words. And, it's obvious that a clear, concise letter reveals a writer who knows what she's talking about.

If you're interested in learning a bit more about the subtitles of syntax, you might read <u>Plain Words, Their A B C</u>, by Sir Ernest Gowers. It's interesting and has always helped me.

A Note From Your Editor: I have tried in my comments to reflect your Company's policy toward letter-writing. Always, I will put myself in your reader's place; if your letter seems ineffective to me, probably it will not satisfy your reader either. But sometimes, when I don't have the technical information relevant to a particular reply, my remarks may be inappropriate. If this should happen, I hope you will let me know.

Mary Doe:

Who is the "she" mentioned in the Tripp letter? Is Dr. Howard a woman? Then why didn't you give the reader a clearer idea of this. When you use a personal pronoun the antecedent must be clear. Where is the antecedent to "she"?

I think you could be clearer in your letters. You tend to get caught up in medical jargon. Re-read your letters, and rewrite them if they're not clear.

The Barrett letter is a little better. But, even here, you use starchy expressions: "in reference to" (about); "shall advise you further".

Sir Ernest Gowers gives one good rule you might follow: "Use words with precise meanings rather than vague ones."

Mary Doe:

Your letters are improving. The tone is getting friendlier, and you are writing with more clarity.

"Forward" is one of the words classified under the heading "Non-conversational", which we try to avoid in writing letters.

"The above" is jargon. Just say, "this policy", or "the item."

Be careful in using commas. They can be important in making an idea clear, or in getting the wrong idea to the reader. There is no set body of rules in punctuation. Writing changes, and the rules change. If you can, read Strunk and White, The Essentials of Style, on this subject.

Jane Doe:

You can be more concise--and effective--in your letters, if you try to avoid superfluous language. In the Bradley letter, you mention "measured height" and "scaled weight." Isn't "height" always "measured?" "Scaled" is also a superfluous word. Re-read the section in the manual on how to "eschew surplusage."

"Furnished" (sent), "contact" (write), and "indicate" (state) are non-conversational words--try to use more specific, friendlier words.

Jane Doe:

Try to be more concise in writing. In the Avill letter, for instance, notice the changes I made in the last paragraph: "Please let me know if you want this coverage..." is friendly and effective. "Is desired..." is stiff. And "outlined above..." is unnecessary--and sounds like commercialese.

"Prefer the familiar word to the far-fetched. Prefer the concrete word to the abstract. Prefer the single word to the circumlocution." These are a few of Fowler's rules. Think about them.

Isn't that jargon in par. 1 of the Vanel letter?

Jane Doe:

I would like to give you one method of judging conversational and non-conversational words. You can "furnish" a home; but you can not "furnish" a statement, you can only "read", "receive" or "send" one. "Furnish a statement" is commercial, not popular, usage.

"It may be necessary for us to," is a round-about way of saying "we may have to...." Why not use the latter.

The second sentence in the Kucharski letter might be written in a more direct manner: "You said we were getting a statement from Dr. M. Bernstein."

It is a good idea to re-read the finished letter. Then you might not make typographical errors such as the two in the Bennett letter.

Progress report. Illustrated here is a progress report that can be sent by an instructor in the company program. It helps gauge the participant's progress, or lack of it, and describes in detail strong areas, weak areas, and areas where improvement has been made.

TYPICAL INSTRUCTOR'S EVALUATION

INSTRUCTOR'S EVALUATION OF TRAINEE

Please complete in duplicate, and return no later than
Tuesday, February 20th.

1. How many weekly comments did you return to this trainee during the 13-week period just completed? *13*

2. How do this writer's letters compare with his letters written at the beginning of this 13-week period?

Now		*Then*	
Excellent		Excellent	
Better than Average	X	Better than Average	
Fair		Fair	X
Poor		Poor	

3. How would you describe the improvement, if any, in this writer's work since you began to work with him?

   He was addicted to the use of stiff, formal language and wasted no time being friendly toward the reader. Lately, his style has begun to loosen up and his tone has been warmer, more personal. His improvement in tone has been particularly striking and he has maintained it consistently for the last 4 or 5 weeks. I feel that he has really grasped the concept of creating good will for the company with his letters.

4. What problems still appear to bother this writer?

   He could loosen his style a little more. His phrases are still somewhat stiff and when in doubt, he often heads for some cliches.

At the end of the course, a questionnaire can be sent to the participant to get his views on the effectiveness of the program.

OFFICE MEMORANDUM   DATE February 8, 1964

To   PROGRAM PARTICIPANTS   SUBJECT: Effective Letters Program

FROM _____   Evaluation

Please return by Friday, February 16.

May I congratulate you on completing your work in the Effective Letters Program? At this point we would like you to complete another questionnaire. Your cooperation will help us not only to evaluate this program, but also will help us improve all future programs. You need not sign your name.

EFFECTIVE LETTERS QUESTIONNAIRE

1. Do you think that your writing has improved as a result of this program?

    Yes, very much _____
    Yes, a little _____
    Very little _____
    Not at all _____

2. Did you feel at the beginning of the program that your writing was relatively satisfactory? *Yes* _____ *No* _____ .

3. Now that you have completed your carbon analysis, do you still feel that your writing was satisfactory at the beginning of the program? *Yes* _____ *No* _____ .

4. If your writing has improved to any extent, in which of these areas did you find your training to be especially helpful?

    Writing more concisely _____
    Writing more conversationally _____
    Using passive voice less _____
    Avoiding cliches _____
    More aware of readers' interests _____

5. What do you consider to be the greatest strength of this program?

6. What was the greatest weakness of the program, if any?

7. Would you like more time to be devoted to any other aspects of writing? If so, which ones?

8. You had a different instructor for the last 13 weeks of the program. How would you compare the second instructor with the first one?

9. Do you think you could be helped by further training? *Yes* ____ *No* ____ .

10. Any other comments?

11. Are you in Group A _____ or B _____ ? (check one)

    Please Return to:
    Director of Home Office Training

Many companies have found a questionnaire to be helpful in keeping its better letter program geared to the needs of the employees. For example, the following are actual replies to two questions on the questionnaire:

WHAT DO YOU CONSIDER TO BE THE GREATEST STRENGTH OF THIS PROGRAM?

In each case where the instructor made corrections or offered advice, I felt the suggestions were excellent. I wouldn't hesitate to follow his advice, and I feel he pointed out weaknesses.

The effective letters manual and the professor's criticisms every week I think proved beneficial both to the company and particularly to the individual.

Without question, the personal carbon analysis in 2 periods of 3 months' duration.

Making the writer conscious of what he is writing and the kind of impression made on the recipient.

The program has helped me to be more conversational in my writing. It has helped me to feel that the person to whom I am writing is actually present in the room. Lastly, I have learned to avoid cliches and other bad habits which I picked up in the past.

It is helpful to know how your letters sound to someone else.

Self-criticism can be very difficult and I think that the comments of an objective reader are valuable. I'm always interested to hear the impressions of a reader and to discover whether I have succeeded in conveying what I wanted to say, the way I want to say it.

Other effective letter courses lacked the follow-up that the carbon review gave us during this course.

Learning to write more concisely and conversationally. Pointing up these two factors seems to be the greatest help to me.

Two meetings at beginning together with carbon analysis so that we could tie in our own work with what was talked about at the meetings.

The constructive criticism indicated on the carbons of the letters used daily.

Its help in alerting the writer to think of the reader when preparing a letter. Pointing out phrases and business terms which are of no interest to the person receiving the letter.

WOULD YOU LIKE MORE TIME TO BE DEVOTED TO ANY OTHER ASPECTS OF WRITING? IF SO, WHICH ONES?

More original writing. Professors could give us a theme and ask us to write a 2-3-4 paragraph letter on it. For example: How would you tell an insured he had been declined for insurance?

No, I think criticism of the actual everyday letters that we write is most helpful.

Yes, offer more substitutes for opening and closing sentences of the letters.

Have discussions during the term of the course. These would create a better understanding between correspondents and instructors.

No, the people who write to me in this jet age of ours have a greater interest in getting the word in a word, than they have in beauty of expression or purity of language. What I need most is writing ideas, those little touches which give life or color or force to a dull story. My instructors can teach me correct literary deportment. But they can't teach me how to "invent" ideas which will result in my writing letters with sentences that sing or sentences that succeed.

Once a month lectures throughout course would keep course up to date by criticizing letters submitted during course and give students opportunity to ask questions that arose *after* course started.

The company does a lot of writing to their general offices. We write letters to the public, but write memos to offices. Can we have lessons on this subject? (Inter-office memos.)

5. BETTER LETTER BULLETINS

To keep the fire burning. Bulletins distributed with reasonable regularity help to keep a letter program alive; their value depends on how attractive the contents are made to those who receive them. As is true of messages to salesmen, the first requisite of a bulletin to letter writers is that it be *interesting*. If it contains nothing but a rehash of things the reader already knows, it is rather sure to suffer a quick burial in the wastebasket. Too often, the preparation of letter bulletins is left to someone with only a casual interest in the assignment; consequently, they are dashed off just before the deadline with little thought or care.

On the other hand, many companies have found letter bulletins a fine means of keeping their correspondents and secretaries on their toes, and the quality of the material in them is just as high as you will find in the best books on business correspondence. The bulletins for the New York Life Insurance Company are typical examples.

Letter bulletins may be used for various purposes:

1. To illustrate faults in letter writing, and to explain principles.
2. To call attention to outstanding letters that have been written by certain employees, and thus to encourage similar work by others.
3. To quote interesting and helpful passages from books and magazine articles.

4. To promote interest in better letter contests—a very effective device in the general program.

5. To present new ideas, or old ones used by other companies.

While the above are major purposes for letter bulletins, there are others that may arise to meet the need of a particular company.

Above all other reasons for their use is the fact that they are an inexpensive method of keeping everybody letter-conscious. Thus, they serve in a way similar to the kind of advertising that is designed more to keep products before the public than to lead to their immediate sale.

Two of the New York Life Insurance bulletins. It is regrettable that space will not permit the reproduction of the entire series of New York Life Insurance Company bulletins, for they constitute a neat course in business letter writing presented with a practical viewpoint. Beginning on page 362 are two samples.

Checklist of reminders. New York Life Insurance Company letter writers are asked not to mail their letters before checking seven important points. These points are put in question form on a card that is distributed at the end of the program. The card is reproduced here and can serve as a guide for other companies, both large and small, to help them formulate a similar checklist. (See the opposite page.)

6. Other Devices to Improve Letters

Contests based on company letters. Probably more than any other nation, the people of America love competitive sports. This will to beat the other fellow can be made a powerful asset in a better-letter program by staging contests to see which letter writer can excel the rest in solving a correspondence problem. The best results are obtained when actual situations, taken from the company's experience, are used to test the writers' skill. It may be a letter of complaint received from a customer, an attempt on the part of another to deduct an unearned discount, or any other real letter-problem that somebody in the company had to handle.

The procedure is simple. A carbon copy of the letter that had to be answered—the more recent the better—is given to every letter writer—or printed in the company bulletin. All who write letters may be requested to dictate their idea of a reply, or volunteers may be called. The weakness of the voluntary alternative is that only the better letter writers are likely to try their hands at the problem, and thus those who need the practice most are self-eliminated.

Of course, a time limit is set for the replies to be returned to a certain party—the correspondence supervisor if there is one, or to anyone else

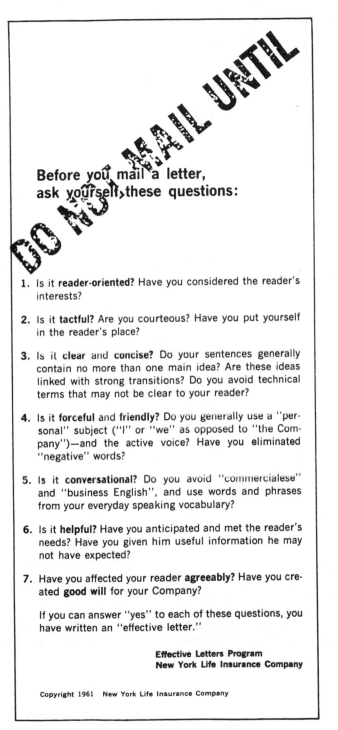

DO NOT MAIL UNTIL

Before you mail a letter, ask yourself these questions:

1. Is it **reader-oriented?** Have you considered the reader's interests?

2. Is it **tactful?** Are you courteous? Have you put yourself in the reader's place?

3. Is it **clear** and **concise?** Do your sentences generally contain no more than one main idea? Are these ideas linked with strong transitions? Do you avoid technical terms that may not be clear to your reader?

4. Is it **forceful** and **friendly?** Do you generally use a "personal" subject ("I" or "we" as opposed to "the Company")—and the active voice? Have you eliminated "negative" words?

5. Is it **conversational?** Do you avoid "commercialese" and "business English", and use words and phrases from your everyday speaking vocabulary?

6. Is it **helpful?** Have you anticipated and met the reader's needs? Have you given him useful information he may not have expected?

7. Have you affected your reader **agreeably?** Have you created **good will** for your Company?

If you can answer "yes" to each of these questions, you have written an "effective letter."

Effective Letters Program
New York Life Insurance Company

Copyright 1961   New York Life Insurance Company

Afterthoughts and notes of interest to business correspondents,
published bi-monthly as part of
New York Life's continuing Effective Letters Program.

Effective Letters

BULLETIN
MARCH
APRIL

THE GENTLE ART OF SAYING "I'M SORRY"

It seems easier for most people to face death and taxes than to admit they've made a mistake. At least that's the impression we've gotten from a number of business letters that have come our way recently. For instance, the following letter which a friend of ours received from his insurance company:

> *Dear Mr. Green:*
>
> *Upon checking our records we noticed that we had charged you the wrong amount for the proportionate premium for December, 1959. The correct amount is $105.70. Since we only collected $103.67 our file and your records are incomplete. Would you please send us the difference in the two amounts which amounts to $2.03.*
>
> *In addition to this will you please sign the attached form so that our records will be corrected?*
>
> *Your attention to this matter will be greatly appreciated.*
>
> *Sincerely yours,*

Reduced to its simplest terms, the letter seems to be saying "We made a mistake. You straighten it out."

Then there's the relentless emphasis in this letter on "our records." It seems to us a safe bet that a reader doesn't care a whit about company housekeeping. Harping on "our records" or "our files" is not likely to impress him and is almost sure to irritate him. In this case, the reader knew the company wanted $2.03 because it was due, and not because "our files and your records are incomplete."

And what about the phrase "proportionate premium?" Most policy owners have little or no knowledge of insurance terms. Involved technical expressions are apt to baffle, or worse, annoy them.

Then there's the word *only*, first paragraph, third line. The phrase should read "collected only . . ." not "only collected . . ." Faulty grammar is not a cardinal sin perhaps, but it is surely a breach of etiquette, indicating disrespect for your reader as well as for your subject.

The final discourtesy was, according to our friend, "the perfect parting shot." The writer enclosed a self-addressed envelope — not stamped. Not only did he have to sign a form and send another check, he had to pay four cents to rectify a mistake he hadn't made in the first place.

Now, we're not saying this was an easy letter to write. It wasn't. But surely there are other ways to do it. Here's one way:

Dear Mr. Green:

We always appreciate the opportunity to be of service to our policy owners, but I'm sorry to tell you that last month we did you — and ourselves — a disservice. The correct amount of your December, 1959, premium was $105.70, and we billed you for only $103.67 a difference of $2.03.

May we ask you to sign the attached form and send it to us with your check for $2.03?

I'm certainly sorry to bother you with this, Mr. Green, but you can be sure we'll do our best to see that it doesn't happeh again.

Sincerely,

This, plus a stamped envelope, might not send the reader into transports of joy, but surely it wouldn't set him smoldering, as the first one would — and did.

Being courteous takes more time, maybe, but it's time well spent, since discourteousness can lose for you and for your company the confidence of your reader. That's no small loss.

"Our representative will be in Chicago from March 14-18. Please look him up when you arrive at the convention; he will be manning our booth."

This is part of a letter which was dictated to a secretary. When she finished transcribing and typing it, she brought it to her boss for his signature. The last sentence read: "Please look him up when you arrive at the convention; he will be Manning R. Booth."

WHAT DOES THIS MEAN?

It has come to our attention that herbage, when observed in that section of enclosed ground being the property of an individual other than oneself, is ever of a more verdant hue.

AND THIS?

Inasmuch as dividends under your above-mentioned policy are payable under date of December 6, it is impossible for us to issue and forward our check in payment of such dividend until the due date, making it, therefore, impossible for you to pay your August, 1959, premium with the dividend to be payable on December 6, 1959.

THIS MEANS

The grass is always greener in the other fellow's yard.

AND THIS

I am sorry to tell you that we cannot apply your December, 1959 dividend toward your August, 1959 premium.

IT'S THE STYLE

As a general rule, italicize (or underline):

TITLES OF PUBLICATIONS:
 The New York Times, Saturday Review, The Diary of Anne Frank
Occasionally you will see titles of publications set off by quotation marks instead
of italics. But the best practice is to reserve quotation marks for articles from
publications, chapter headings from books, short stories, poems, quotes, and the
like.

FOREIGN WORDS AND PHRASES:
 e pluribus unum, vis à vis, Zeitgeist
There are a number of words — *chauffeur, ballet, beau, cliché, opus, data, via,
hoi polloi* — which, though certainly foreign, have been so incorporated into our
language that they're no longer considered so. However, foreign words and phrases
less well-known should always be italicized or underlined.

WORDS USED AS SUCH:
 "You have used *may* when you should have used *can*."
You'll notice that in the example under foreign words and phrases we italicized
those words which we said need no longer be italicized. That's because they were
used not to represent concepts or ideas, but to represent words as such.

LETTERS USED AS SUCH:
 "The *p* in *ptarmigan* is not pronounced."

TITLES OF MUSICAL COMPOSITIONS, WORKS OF ART, NAMES OF SHIPS AND AIRCRAFT:
 Bach's *Jesu, Joy of Man's Desiring*
 Rodin's *The Thinker*
 U.S.S. Missouri
 Columbine II

FOR THE SAKE OF EMPHASIS:
 "Not only *can* we go, we *must* go."
On this point — a word of caution; too-frequent use of italics for the sake of
emphasis defeats its own purpose. As Fowler, the distinguished compiler of
Modern English Usage puts it, "To italicize whole sentences or large parts of
them as a guarantee that some portion of what one has written is really worth
attending to is a miserable confession that the rest is negligible."

Afterthoughts and notes of interest to business correspondents, published bi-monthly as part of New York Life's continuing Effective Letters Program.

Effective Letters

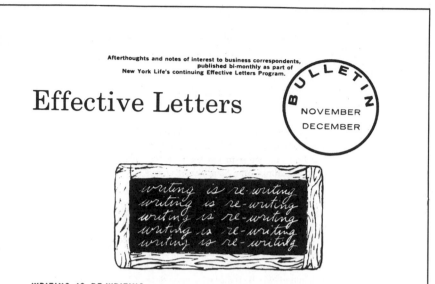

WRITING IS RE-WRITING

Mining a diamond does not produce an engagement ring any more than a random collection of facts produces a good letter. It is rewriting, the writer's refining process, that turns the raw material into the finished product. Let's look at an example of raw material:

Dear Mr. Jones:

We have received your inquiry of November 6. Regarding this inquiry, we would like to state that we are in no position to comply with your request, changing the method of premium payment on your above-numbered policy to the monthly basis, because the monthly premium must amount to at least the sum of $10 per month, inasmuch as the Company has found it impractical to issue policies with a monthly premium of less than this amount.

We might, however, make mention of the fact that your policy contains an Automatic Premium Loan clause and under this clause, unpaid premiums can be taken care of by loan provided there is sufficient cash value in your above policy to warrant doing so, and provided small repayments are made on your loan from time to time.

If it should be your desire to do this, kindly contact us and we shall be pleased to comply with your request.

Sincerely yours,

The raw material is there, but certain refinements seem to be in order. First of all, because the sentences are overloaded, the letter demands a second or even a third reading — hardly fair to the reader. So on the first rewrite, let's take out the linking words — *and, because, since, inasmuch as* — and make separate sentences out of what follows:

> *Dear Mr. Jones:*
>
> *We have received your inquiry of November 6. Regarding this inquiry, we would like to state that we are in no position to comply with your request, changing the method of premium payment on your above-numbered policy to the monthly basis. This is because the monthly premium must amount to at least the sum of $10 per month. You see, the Company has found it impractical to issue policies with a monthly premium of less than this amount.*
>
> *We might, however, make mention of the fact that your policy contains an Automatic Premium Loan clause. Under this clause, unpaid premiums can be taken care of by loan. This can be done provided there is sufficient cash value in your above policy to warrant doing so, and provided small repayments are made on your loan from time to time.*
>
> *If it should be your desire to do this, kindly contact us. We will be pleased to comply with your request.*
>
> *Sincerely yours,*

This seems to be a lot clearer. At least it can be better understood on first reading. But what about all the gingerbread — "We are in no position to," "We would like to state that," "If it should be your desire,"? A second rewrite could take care of those:

> *Dear Mr. Jones:*
>
> [handwritten: I am sorry to tell you that we cannot change]
>
> *~~We have received your inquiry of November 6. Regarding this inquiry, we would like to state that we are in no position to comply with your request, changing~~ (the method of premium payment on your ~~above-numbered~~ policy to the monthly basis. This is because the monthly premium must amount to at least $10 ~~per~~ [handwritten: a] month. You see, the Company has found it impractical to issue policies with a monthly premium of less than this amount.*
>
> *~~We might,~~ however, ~~make mention of the fact that~~ your policy contains an Automatic Premium Loan clause. Under this clause, unpaid premiums can be taken care of by loan. This can be done provided there is sufficient cash value in your above policy ~~to warrant doing so~~, and provided small repayments are made on your loan from time to time.*
>
> [handwritten: Let us know if you want us to do this, won't you?]
> *~~If it should be your desire to do this, kindly contact us.~~*
> *~~We shall be pleased to comply with your request~~*
> [handwritten: It will be a pleasure to take care of it for you.]
>
> *Sincerely yours,*

The language sounds more courteous and clear, but what about the order of the letter? Is the reader seeing first what's most important to him? What if it read like this:

Dear Mr. Jones:

Since your policy contains an Automatic Premium Loan clause, we can arrange to have your premiums paid by loan provided there is enough cash value in your policy. Then you can simply make repayments toward your loan and all will be in order.

I'm sorry that we cannot arrange to have you pay premiums on the monthly basis, as you asked, but monthly premiums must amount to at least $10. However, this Automatic Premium Loan arrangement will; in effect, accomplish the same thing.

Let us know if you want us to do this, won't you? It will be a pleasure to take care of it for you.

Sincerely yours,

Admittedly, such revisions take time, but with practice, rewriting becomes habitual and takes less and less time. It's part of the correspondent's job to be an editor, too.

Begin by relying, as we did here, on only 3 simple rules of editing:

1. Look for overloaded sentences. When you find words like *and, because, since, inasmuch as, which, for the reason that,* you can usually begin a new sentence at that point.

2. Look for words and phrases of traditional "Business English." Delete them and substitute the language of conversation.

3. Look at your reader. Arrange your material so that he will see first what is apt to interest him most.

WHAT DOES THIS MEAN?

It has been observed that an enclosing barrier, for the purpose of discouraging and preventing intrusion upon that which it encloses, tends to enhance the amicability of those whose property abuts on said barrier.

AND THIS

The current dividend notice from you has been received on which was indicated your election of option to have the existing and latest dividend under your above policy applied to reduce future premiums under this policy and we are pleased to advise that this, and further future dividends, in accordance with your election will be duly applied to reduce future premiums.

THIS MEANS

Good fences make good neighbors.

AND THIS

We'll be happy to apply your current and future dividends to reduce premiums on your policy, as you asked.

IT'S THE STYLE

Division of words should be avoided whenever possible, but when it's unavoidable, the following guides should help:

1. Divide according to pronunciation — in other words, make sure that the part of the word left at the end of the line will suggest the meaning and the sound of the whole word:

    pro-gress (noun), *prog-ress* (verb), *epi-taph, epit-ome*

2. Never divide words of one syllable:

    asked, named, strolled, height
        not
    ask-ed, nam-ed, strol-led, hei-ght

3. Never divide words with only 4 letters:

    only, also, into, open
        not
    on-ly, al-so, in-to, op-en

4. Never divide a syllable of only one letter:

    about, away, again, enough, mighty
        not
    a-bout, a-way, a-gain, e-nough, might-y

5. Usually divide compound words between the members:

    laundry-man, under-secretary, astro-naut

6. In verbs ending in *ing*, usually divide before *ing*:

    offer-ing, say-ing, danc-ing, ask-ing

    But there are exceptions; for example, words in which the consonant has been doubled before the ending:

    admit-ting, prefer-ring, stop-ping

7. When 2 different consonant letters appear together, or when a consonant letter is doubled, usually divide between rather than after them:

    sym-bol, fal-ter, abun-dance, advan-tage, exces-sive, dif-fer

    However, if this rule conflicts with Rule 1, Rule 1 takes precedence:

    demo-cratic, camp-ing, stick-ing

8. Never, ever, hyphenate at the end of the page.

who is directing the better letter program. The ideal plan is to code the replies in some way so that the identity of the contestants is not revealed until after the prize-winner has been selected. The person heading the program may do the judging, or he may ask some outsider, who is an expert in business letter writing, to serve in that capacity. First, second, and third selections are usually made.

The reward for winning need not be anything of great value—perhaps a new hat, a pen, or a good 'new book on letter writing. Cash prizes are not considered advisable, since the competition may become too bitter and losers may not accept their defeat gracefully. The highest reward for human achivement is not material. People will try just as hard for the honor of being first as for some gadget that may go with it. The important thing to remember, however, is that each winner in a contest should be publicly praised. It may be announced in another bulletin, at a meeting of the letter-class, or at some company function.

If the company has some' kind of a school, with one or more classes in letter writing, a sequence of problems may be used, a new one assigned at each weekly meeting, and the winner of the previous contest announced.

Better letter contests, as briefly outlined above, serve at least three beneficial purposes: (1) since the letters to be answered are taken from all parts of the business, they give each contestant a better idea of what goes on outside his own department; (2) by co-ordinating training with the deep-seated thirst for competition, contests tend to make the training more interesting; and (3) they encourage the best kind of practice in letter writing, since each assignment represents an actual company experience.

Perhaps a fourth benefit that should have been mentioned is that often in the contests some hitherto unrecognized writer of ability comes to the foreground. The executives thus discover an asset in their personnel that later may be required to solve a manpower need.

Correspondence manuals. Another helpful instrument in maintaining a high standard of correspondence, and for use as a reference guide, is the manual of information prepared by some companies for their letter writers and typists. Since these manuals are assembled independently and slanted at the needs of the particular company, no two of them are ever found to be alike. Every executive in charge of correspondence has his own preferences with respect to letter mechanics, and the manual he puts together is sure to differ from the one in use in the company across the street. Generally, the contents include sample letters to show the typist the forms she is expected to follow, and information with respect to titles, punctuation, capitalization, abbreviation, and such other matters as the compiler may consider important. Perhaps the biggest value of the manual is that it assures consistency, so that all letters mailed from the company are similar in appearance and form.

The manual is usually prepared only in the larger companies where many letters are written, and where some one person devotes his full time to keeping of correspondence on a high level. Unfortunately, however, some of the manuals now in use do not reflect modern letter principles, and many of the rules they set forth are those of the hidebound past. In some cases this may be because they have been in existence a long time and never revised; in others, it simply means that they have been prepared by individuals not familiar with modern letter practice.

Correspondence manuals are also valuable in getting the newly hired typist or correspondent quickly acclimated to company letter-practices. In this sense, they are time-savers and mistake-eliminators. They cannot, however, take the place of personal training; nor do they provide the challenge to better work which the novice gets from a well-directed letter program.

Form letters and paragraphs. A form letter is essentially no different from any other letter, except that it is mailed to more than one person, with the name and address of each recipient filled in at the top. When the fill-in is a perfect match with the part already prepared, the average reader does not realize that the same letter has been sent to other people. Unfortunately, however, the "perfect match" is more of an exception than the general rule, and this is the great weakness of the device. When the reader knows that he is only one of many to get the letter, much of its power is lost, since the effect is no greater than getting a circular or some piece of advertising.

Another weakness in the use of form letters is the failure to rewrite them at regular intervals. Result: They are no longer up-to-date, or they are mailed to the same individuals more than once. This, of course, creates a poor impression in the reader's mind, unless the purpose of the letter is purely routine, and the recipient does not care whether it is a form letter or not. For example, a form letter might be used to notify dealers that orders had been shipped. In this case, the only purpose of the message is to give information.

In spite of the fact that form letters are black sheep in the opinion of certain writers, and that some companies rarely use them, they do serve a useful purpose in business. If properly handled, there can be no logical objection to them; in fact, some form letters rate higher than those individually typed. The reason is that they are carefully tailored to fit certain situations, and often represent the best skill and thought available in the company. This is not likely to be true of the other letters, often written on the spur of the moment by various individuals of different abilities.

Another advantage of interest to the average business executive is the immense saving in time and money. In an hour or two, numerous copies of the form letter can be processed by mimeograph, multigraph, or automatic typewriters, and the time spent in placing the names and addresses on them is only a fraction of what it would have been to type them individually. Furthermore, an even greater saving is the time it would have taken to write the letters personally. This time saving not only leaves the typists and letter writers free to do other work, but it represents a considerable reduction in cost—a fact no company can very well afford to disregard. What this reduction represents in actual money is difficult to estimate, since the possibilities in one organization for the use of form letters, and the nature of their content, may differ widely from those in another. However, it is safe to say that the average form letter costs, to prepare and mail, no more than one fourth of what the same letter would cost if individually written and typed.

Except in a general way, it is difficult to state the uses of the form letter. It is quite satisfactory for repetitive and routine situations where no attempt is being made to slant the message at a particular reader. On the other hand, when the purpose is more important, or involves special circumstances, the use of a form letter cannot be approved. For sales letters, the form letter gets the green light only when it is necessary to contact a great many prospects quickly but little is known of their individual characteristics or buying habits.

Personalizing the form letter. Since we know the importance of making the individual feel he is getting a special letter prepared for him and nobody else, it is plain that the form letter should be made to appear as if it were a personal message. Whether or not this object is ethical you may decide for yourself, but it may be justified on the ground that the reader would get the same message if it were individually written.

As we have pointed out, many of the form letters mailed in business would not fool a moron. The type of the name and address does not match the type of the body. The ink of the two parts is of different shades. The spacing and alignment are dead giveaways. Another fact to cause suspicion is the use of a salutation made to fit all those who are going to get the letter; the condition can easily be avoided by *not* including the salutation in the form part of the letter. Naturally, the letter is more likely to pass as personal if it starts "Dear Mr. Doe," than if it starts "Dear Friend," or in some other general way.

To personalize the form letter, several simple steps may be taken. Why they are ignored is hard to say, because there is no logical reason for handicapping a mailing any more than is necessary. You should, therefore, observe these steps:

1. Use a letterhead of good appearance, printed on paper of at least average quality—not a cheap substitute, poorly processed on thin paper, that any reader would know could not be the company's regular letterhead.

2. Use an envelope to match the paper. It will look better with the firm name neatly printed on it than it will blank.

3. Let the salutation be filled in by the typist, along with the name and address.

4. Insist that the fill-in be a perfect match with the rest of the letter. This means that the proper equipment must be provided, and that the work must be supervised.

5. See that the signature is personal, and affixed with ink. Processed signatures are easy to recognize. Never use a rubber stamp.

6. Mail the letter, first-class. Seal it. Use regular postage stamps. This is not the cheapest method, but it is the best. Before you decide the cost is prohibitive, consider comparative results.

It will pay the company using many form letters to consider the purchase of automatic typewriters. One girl can easily manage a battery of four. After she types the names and addresses, and the salutations, the same machines will automatically complete the letters. A perfect match is then absolutely assured.

The use of automatic typewriters also makes further personalization possible. For example, the reader's name may be typed in the body of the letter. This takes more of the typist's time and adds to the expense, but the added touch of personalization may sometimes be more than worth the cost.

Do not turn a cold shoulder on form letters. Use them in their proper place, but use them *properly*. Make every one as much like an individually typed letter as is possible. Form letters serve a useful purpose, but keep them up-to-date. Change the copy at *regular* intervals, not just when you happen to think about doing it.

A part of the letter program. Since form letters are just as important as any others, assuring that they are doing the best possible job is a logical part of a company's better-letter program. In those cases where an outsider has been called in to start the program off, one of his chief duties is to examine the form letters currently in use, to suggest others that might be used, and to assist in such revisions as may be necessary.

The work does not stop with the departure of the expert, however, nor after the first house-cleaning is finished. At least four times a year the entire ensemble of form letters should be reviewed; most of them should be rewritten that often.

The fact that form letters are devised to take the place of those that are personally written does not mean that, like a piece of machinery, they can be left alone until they wear out. A great many companies make the mistake of thinking of form letters as a necessary evil—paying little attention to them, even though they may be giving a lot of attention to the improvement of general correspondence. Form letters are not black sheep unless the company treats them as such. They deserve better consideration than they usually get.

THE SALES LETTER

THE SALES LETTER

1. How to Construct a Sales Letter

Supreme test of writer's skill. No letter written for business purposes can be called unimportant, but the relation of sales to profit makes the sales letter stand out above the rest. Furthermore, in the writing of the sales letter, the skill of the business correspondent is put to the greatest test.

Unfortunately, in many kinds of business writing it is not easy to *measure* results. For example, letters mailed to gain goodwill may do the job, but except in specific cases where evidence is developed, the exact accomplishment is still intangible. This is not true of the sales letter. It either sells or it does not, and the extent of the pull is known by the number of orders received. Thus, the sales-letter writer is always under fire. Unless the results of his efforts are considered satisfactory, he is quite likely to lose his job or be transferred to some other type of less difficult letter writing.

On the other hand, the reward for the successful sales-letter writer is usually high. He is the man who is bringing orders to his company, and orders are precious. The greater the pull of his letters, the greater is his prestige. Besides, there is much personal satisfaction to be derived from the writing of a letter that does a good sales job. Out it goes to a list of prospects—or to just one important prospect—and then comes that period of waiting to see what the result will be. And then, the orders begin to come in—perhaps, lots of orders. What a thrill it is to be able to say, "This sales letter of mine had a pull of ten per cent." Ten per cent is considered good in the average instance, but what if it is twenty, thirty, or even higher? Then, indeed, the writer's cup of joy runneth over.

The letter carpenter at work. To get the most value out of this discussion of how to write the sales letter, a review of Section 3 is suggested. There, the principles of letter carpentry were explained as they apply to any kind of business correspondence in which an effort is made to influence

377

human behavior—letters to collect money, letters to adjust complaints, letters to motivate salesmen, and all the others where the object is to get the reader to *do something* desired by the company. These principles of letter carpentry are broad enough to cover all business correspondence, with the possible exception of those that are merely routine and commonplace. Now we are going to narrow the arc of the spotlight, and see how they apply to the one type of business correspondence for which they hold the greatest importance—the sales letter.

No doubt you remember the necessary steps in planning a letter. They are especially important in the construction of the message that goes out looking for orders. First, determine clearly the *purpose* you want to accomplish. Second, know all the *facts*. Third, *visualize* your reader. Fourth, select the *appeals* to which he will most likely be vulnerable; or, if there are to be many readers, the best appeals for the group. Fifth, *arrange* the arguments you plan to use in the order to gain maximum continuity and conviction.

In Section 3, you considered how the reader must be led carefully from *attention* to *interest* to *desire* to *action:* how fatal it is if that sequence of psychological reactions is changed or interrupted. For example, you found that action cannot successfully be induced until desire has been created; that increasing interest eventually creates desire; that getting attention is the first step toward arousing interest. You saw what happens when the writer lets the cat out of the bag too soon; when he begins so dully that no more of the letter is likely to be read; when his conclusion is not positive and impelling.

For accomplishment of these four psychological reactions in their proper order, you were given a formula to follow—the *Star,* the *Chain,* and the *Hook.* The purpose of the Star was to stop the reader, so that he might go a little farther with you in the letter. The purpose of the Chain was to make him more and more interested, until finally he *wanted* to do as you desired. The purpose of the Hook was to produce immediate favorable reaction—before desire began to chill.

You found that the construction of the Star was a separate problem from the construction of the Chain or the Hook. For each of the three parts in the job there were different factors to consider, different principles to apply. You saw letters that illustrated strong and weak Stars, strong and weak Chains, strong and weak Hooks. You found there were definite *ways* to get attention, to build interest and desire, to impel action. Thus, by now you understand the use of the Star, the Chain, and the Hook for all *letters*. But here we are to apply the formula strictly to sales letters—the kind of business writing in which it is most needed, and where it exerts the greatest power.

Psychology of a sale. As the well-written sales letter travels its course, certain psychological changes take place in the mind of the prospect. To be sure, he has to *be* a prospect. The best sales letter ever written would not cause a reader to buy a country estate if he already had owned one or detested country life. A man might be moved mightily by a letter presenting the merits of a Cadillac automobile, but if he had no money to buy one and couldn't get it, the presentation would be sheer waste. Wastage of this sort is to be expected in the use of any list of possible buyers. Some of them are not prospects because of their total inability or disinclination to buy.

But when the reader *is* a potential buyer, it may be assumed that a change in mental reaction is usually taking place as he reads from paragraph to paragraph. At first, he is politely indifferent—controlled by *reason,* and well versed in all the objections that may exist. Moreover, he is strictly on the defensive against any effort to high-pressure him into action. Thus, if the positive urge appears too soon—as so often happens in sales letters— he is quite likely to be frightened or irritated, and into the wastebasket goes the letter.

On the other hand, if the reader is gently led from point to point, the things talked about may begin to appear in a new and pleasant light. This simply means that interest has quickened, and desire has begun to form. The reader by this time is not nearly as suspicious or as indifferent as in the beginning. His reactions are colored with *emotion.* Objections are fading out.

You know how the application of the Star, the Chain, and the Hook, has brought about the above described change in mental attitude. The chart on page 380 shows the thought sequence.

A study of this simple chart quickly reveals why so many sales letters flop. They do not *take time* to do a complete job. They expect and ask for action while the reader is still only cold or lukewarm toward the item or service for sale. They disregard the necessity of changing rational reactions to emotional reactions. They either do not use the Star, the Chain, and the Hook, or they do it so awkwardly that the letter falls apart. Some fail for *lack* of a Star; others, for *lack* of a Hook. Some turn the formula upside down, revealing the purpose of the letter before the reader has had a chance to visualize benefits. Truly, this is not a formula to be tampered with, or one in which any of the three parts can be left out. You must take all of the four steps, and always in the same order.

S T A R	Indifferent Cold Mildly attentive	Reactions
		are
	Casual interest	
	Lukewarm	RATIONAL
C H A I N	Deeper interest	
	Visualization of benefit	
	Begins to want	
	Desire increases	Reactions
	Objections pushed aside	
		are
H O O K	Ready for action	EMOTIONAL
	Hot	
	Needs only a push	

First—get ATTENTION. Think about nothing else. In what logical, appropriate way can you win a little favor at the start— enough so that the reader is willing to read on? That is the job of the Star. Nothing more. Just that.

Second—arouse INTEREST. A deeper and more sustained interest than you had at the start. This is the first job of the Chain. In this stage, you are not trying to make the sale— simply paving the way.

Third—build DESIRE. Desire comes as the natural result of increased interest. Make the reader see himself enjoying the benefits of your product or service. And that's the second job of the *Chain*. Now the sale is coming up. Your reader *wants* what you have to sell.

Fourth—impel ACTION. That means *ask* for it. Make it easy. That is a problem different from the rest. Think only of that. It's time for the Hook.

Remember, you have four jobs to do in your sales letter, and no two of them are alike in purpose or technique. Take one at a time and concentrate on it alone. It's something like scoring a run in baseball. You go from first, to second, to third—each base reached means a problem solved.

When you stand on first base, you have the reader's attention. But many a player gets no farther. Neither may you. If you get to second, you have aroused interest; if you get to third, you have built desire; if you cross home plate, you have stimulated action. The sale is made.

If you want to carry the analogy a point further, consider the pitcher as your reader. When you go to the plate to bat against him, he knows nothing of your proposition; he has no thought of buying what you have to sell. His main object is to strike you out so that he can give attention to something else. But step by step you wear him down. Each base that you advance stands only for temporary success. You may not arouse his interest—you are caught trying to go to second. You may get as far as third, but never score. You didn't completely overcome his resistance. You were close to success, but lacked the final drive that would have sent you home. A lot of sales letters die at third. Some have Hooks which are too weak; some have no Hooks at all.

Examples of sales letter carpentry. Now that we have discussed the theory of constructing sales letters, let us consider some actual examples taken from the business world. The first is a letter that seeks to sell a merchandising plan to dealers in footwear. It was written by M. H. Cable for Roberts, Johnson & Rand, a branch of the International Shoe Co. of St. Louis. The very logical appeal is to the desire of the dealers to make more money. The Star opens with this appeal in a rather spectacular way which could hardly fail to get attention.

> Dear Mr. Doe:
>
> You would be surprised, wouldn't you...
>
> ...if you walked into your store tomorrow morning, glanced at your shoe stock, and saw two fresh green dollar bills hanging out from every box lid?
>
> Money, as you know, has no value unless it is working. If you invest money in something that does not earn anything, it costs more money to leave it there. This is why a large group of our customers willingly go to a little extra time and effort to harness their shoe stocks with our Concentration Plan. This plan helps them drive those slow moving shoes off the shelves. It spotlights every pair that should not be there.
>
> In every carton of shoes on your shelves there is merchandise representing at least two dollars per carton. It is your money that is invested. But, do you know definitely how many of those pairs have no right to remain on your shelves?
>
> Our Stock Control System is a part of the Concentration Plan.

Properly used, it will dig out all of those buried dollars that you can use to buy new shoes.

For what little time and effort you put into it, the Concentration Plan can earn mighty big dividends for you next year. Install it in January, and it will be operating smoothly when you commence selling spring shoes. It costs nothing except your willingness to start it and keep it going.

Please read the attached Concentration Plan agreement. Fill in the information on the second sheet and we will forward the necessary supplies and information. Thaw out those frozen dollars in your shoe stock. We will help you put them to work next year.

Yours very truly,

This sales letter to dealers did not waste any time in explaining the details of the plan; the agreement contained that information. Instead, the emphasis throughout the entire Chain was on what the plan would *do* for the dealer. The appeal would be of interest to any retail merchant—how to keep stock turning over and thus increase profits. Even the end of the Hook repeats that theme—"Thaw out those frozen dollars."

The letters reproduced on pages 383–385 are additional examples of effective use of the Star, the Chain, and the Hook in sales letter construction. In both cases the Hooks are positive and courteous. "Either order card will start your subscription," says Mr. Westerfield. "Order now...," says Mr. Marshall. As you discovered in Section 3, the tone of these two conclusions is correct, although it might offend if used earlier in the letters. The end of your sales message is no time to pussyfoot or play church-mouse with "If" or "May" or "Hope." These are negative words that betray the writer's lack of confidence in his own sales message. Messrs. Westerfield and Marshall tell their readers what to do, and leave no hint that they fear an unfavorable answer.

Letter from Moline Business College,
Signed by A. L. Due, Manager.

Dear Mr. Doe:

Would you like to receive a nice salary check every week, soon after finishing high school; and to know that the future held for you opportunities for outstanding success?

If you are like most high school seniors, you have this picture in the back of your mind, but you are wondering WHEN and HOW you will be able to fulfil it.

TIME THE WEEKLY NEWSMAGAZINE
540 NORTH MICHIGAN AVENUE, CHICAGO 11, ILLINOIS

April 26, 1963

Dear Sir:

   TIME, of course, is a magazine you know. It's a favorite of
business and professional people; a prime source of news, a powerful medium for advertising, a magazine that has earned the respect
(and readership) of the country's leadership community.

   If you see only an occasional issue -- or receive it regularly
but don't always have a chance to read it thoroughly -- it's our
feeling that you're missing TIME's true value as <u>a continuing
service</u>.

   <u>Our suggestion</u>: accept a trial subscription, delivered either
to your home or office -- sample TIME for less than 10¢ an
issue. Put <u>one of the two</u> order cards in the outgoing mail
now; if TIME disappoints you, cancel your subscription and
we'll return the pro-rated balance of your payment.

   If you'd like to know more about the news and the people who
shape it than you are ever likely to get out of just the daily
papers and the broadcast reports --

   -- if you consider it worth your while to keep up with all
the <u>extra</u> fields that TIME covers (art as well as politics; business as well as foreign affairs; religion as well as sport) --

   -- and if you're willing to take your news, not just in a
bare recital of facts, but in a story told as thoughtful reporters
and editors see it

   ... then accept our invitation to subscribe on a trial basis.

   Formalities (like a bill) can wait until after you begin to
receive copies. Either order card will start your subscription.

                              Cordially,

                              Putney Westerfield
                              Putney Westerfield
                              Circulation Manager

PW:LM

Enclosed:
(1) home delivery order card (21 weeks/$1.87)
(2) office subscription (52 weeks/$5.00)

Esquire

SUBSCRIPTION OFFICES/BOULDER/COLORADO

Dear Sir:

No purveyors of pigs in pokes, we.

Before we invite you to join the ranks of ESQUIRE readers (and, indeed, before you accept our invitation) you ought to know something about today's ESQUIRE. Not what we say about it, of course (we're biased), but what it's contributors have said in it.

How?

Well, one way would be to have Norman Mailer, Terry Southern, Gay Talese, Kenneth Tynan, Gore Vidal, Dwight Macdonald, Elsa Martinelli, Thomas Morgan, Federico Fellini, David Schoenbrun, Graham Greene, Jack Paar and a few hundred others drop in on you some rainy evening to talk ESQUIRE.

But the impracticality of it all!

You'd soon run out of food and drink. Your quarters would get as crowded as Grand Central Station on a football weekend. You'd have to give up the idea of inviting all your friends and you'd likely lose some of them forever once they discovered what they'd missed out on. Fares alone would cost you a fortune since at any one time ESQUIRE's scores of contributors are scattered over at least 28 countries and anywhere from 3 to 6 continents.

And finally, just as the President of the United States and his Vice President must by law travel via different routes and in separate vehicles to avoid the loss of both in the same catastrophe, so it would be imprudent in the extreme to gather so much of the world's wit, wisdom, and authority in the very same living room.

So, short of having you hold an ESQUIRE Symposium in your apartment, we've done the next best thing.

> See the enclosed GUIDE TO BEING A GENTLEMAN which
> is yours free. No strings attached. It's a delightfully
> representative sampling of today's ESQUIRE, though it's
> limited to the one subject - Gentlemanliness. Other equally
> delightful GUIDES (TO BEING A BOULEVARDIER, WORLD
> TRAVELER, SPORTSMAN, LITERATEUR, WIT, MAN-IN-
> THE-KNOW, etc.) might as easily have been compiled from
> the varied pages of today's ESQUIRE.

But remember, please: one GUIDE doesn't make for the full tour;
a mere sampling doesn't really give you the full scope and range
of today's ESQUIRE. (Try describing your jazzed up, fully equipped
and accessorized, Ultra-Super-Deluxe _____mobile by showing off
a set of its hubcaps.)

If you like the GUIDE, good. Enjoy it. Use it. Share it with a
friend. Quote from it at the next party. And if you'd like more
of the same -- lots more and not really the same -- here's what
to do:

> Turn your attention to the enclosed order form and
> the postage-paid, self-addressed envelope that
> accompanies it. The form entitles you to ESQUIRE
> at half-price for the next 8 months. (ESQUIRE's
> regular per copy price is 60¢; regular subscription
> price, $6 a year). The envelope speeds your order
> back to us so we can enter your subscription with the
> very next issue. Promise: it's a dilly!

So much for the arithmetic and the mechanics. One request: act soon,
please. While the GUIDE is long-lasting and near to indestructible,
this half-price offer is limited to a matter of days.

Cordially,

J. L. Marshall

J. L. Marshall
Subscription Manager

JLM:sss
3948

Bonus: Order now and your subscription will include at no extra cost
ESQUIRE's splendid $1-a-copy Christmas issue, celebrated
by all who appreciate magazine quality -- including our
fellow publishers -- as the big publishing event of the year!

There IS a way by which you can protect yourself against the uncertainties and idleness which face most young people; and assure yourself of pleasant and profitable employment...

And—best of all—it is a way which does NOT require from four to seven years of study, or a college investment of several thousand dollars. It builds towards life's greatest goal—financial independence—without demanding that you postpone your earning period for a long interval. You can enjoy a good income, make your parents proud of you, have money to spend in your younger years, and advance to substantial success while you are still young—while other high school graduates are still going to college, waiting for "something to turn up," or are sidetracked in "blind alley" jobs.

There is nothing theoretical about this plan. It has worked for other high school graduates year after year—even during the darkest days of recession.

Today it provides one of the safest and surest methods by which high school graduates can win early success that it is possible to conceive.

Would you like to know more about it?

The enclosed card will bring you complete information, entirely without obligation. It requires no postage. It is ready to mail as soon as you fill in your name and address.

Very truly yours,

In this sales letter, the Star is a question which no doubt would be successful in getting the attention of the average boy just out of high school, unless he were already registered for a university course. But any letter mailed to a graduating class would be wasted on a certain percentage of the members.

The Chain continues the theme sounded in the first paragraph. The reader is told he doesn't have to worry about being idle—that in a short time he can enjoy a good income and be on the way to success while other lads are still in college, or side-tracked in blind-alley jobs. The plan, he is told, has always worked for other high-school graduates—why not for him?

Then in the Hook, which begins with "Would you like to know more about it?" he is impelled to sign and return the enclosed card. The object of the letter is attained if the card comes back—a personal call will complete the enrollment.

Teamwork between Star and Hook. Although it is true that the functions of Star and Hook are quite different, and each is an independent problem for the sales-letter writer, they can be teamed to help gain the major objective. In this way, they perform like two players on a football team: the Star stops the reader with a momentary block; the Hook makes the tackle. Consider the Star and the Hook in the following letter:

Dear Sir:

On the high seas, there are none who enjoy a more enviable position than do the captain and officers of a great ocean liner. They represent the last word in navigation—on the high seas.
When the liner nears port, a weather-beaten man whose oil-skins contrast sharply with the golden splendor of the ship's officers comes aboard.

He's the port pilot, whose job it is to bring the ship through the maze of harbor channels, buoys, lights and congestion, to a safe berth.

The Chicago Elevated Advertising Company is comparable to the port pilot. We live in Chicago and are in intimate contact with local conditions and market information. We understand the current of preferences and prejudices. We are familiar with channels of distribution.

Our knowledge and experience regarding this one market is of inestimable value to those seeking safe anchorage for a worthwhile product, in Chicago.

So when it's "all aboard" for Chicago—just remember a satisfactory landing is made with greater assurance with a "port pilot" aboard.

Cordially,

Obviously, this letter was not intended to make an immediate sale. Its purpose was to drive home the one point that a local advertising firm is in the best position to understand its own market. Looking to future business, this one point might win the order, and it is very well illustrated in the story about the port pilot. But having used this story to get attention, the writer does not entirely discard it. Instead, the importance of "knowing the channels" is emphasized in the body of the letter, and the "port pilot" himself reappears in the conclusion. Thus, the story is the skeleton that holds together the flesh of the whole letter.

Need of balance. Since each of the three parts of the sales letter has an important job to do, it is generally poor procedure to let one part steal the show to the detriment of the other two. The following election letter used by a printing company illustrates the point. The writer has a very interesting introduction, based on the coming Derby in which donkey and elephant are to run. He also manages to echo the idea in the conclusion, but there is no balance of emphasis on the three parts, because the sales argument consists of exactly one sentence. Thus, the message consists of a fine Star, a fairly satisfactory Hook, and practically no Chain.

Dear Friend:

Here it is again, the grand old Election Derby, with the donkey and the elephant staging a whirlwind race before 186,000,000 enthusiastic citizens. Fireworks all along the way, with perhaps a bit of mud from a flying hoof now and then. What a race!

The man on the donkey lays on the leather, lashing the long-ear down the stretch. The elephant fights for the pole, running under the goad as a deputy jockey gets in some fancy hard-riding at the rear. Battle! Dynamite! Storm! But onlookers, hotter than a campaign speech, will cool down the minute the race is ended.

We have fourteen salesmen, covering the entire state, at your service. Call on us and we will show more speed than you can get out of either the donkey or the elephant.

(No complimentary close)

The italicized sentence is the Chain. The company has 14 salesmen to serve the reader. That's fine. But what about the service? Is it especially beneficial and outstanding?

In contrast, here is a sales letter with a Chain and a Hook that could hardly be beaten, but with a Star so weak that it might bring about the demise of the message without any more reading. That would be a tragedy, for if the reader pushes past the dull generalities at the beginning, he goes the rest of the way on a very interesting and persuasive journey. The lack of balance is in the Star. You wonder if the same man could possibly have written the other two parts:

Dear Mr. Doe:

APPETIZING, HEALTHFUL, and SATISFYING — [here reader yawns].

This is the SKITLE—born in the shadows of Hollywood hills and nurtured by famous movie stars.

Friend of the waist-line, easy to digest and nemesis of hunger, SKITLE is a sandwich three times bigger than the low-born hamburger and five times as good.

Ground veal from itsy-bitsy baby calves snatched from clean, green pastures, garnished with mild dry-eyed onions, topped with blushing tomatoes and a crunchy, spicy relish, all tucked in a big, over-sized bun that's been toasted to a golden brown and—ah! You have a creation of the gods—the SKITLE.

It's truly a meal in itself and all for a paltry fifty cents! You will want to try one, and as a get-acquainted offer we will furnish one for half the regular price. Here's how you do it:

Just bring this letter and a friend some time before the first of March. You order the first one, and the second will be on the house.

We're located at 4937 Main, on the east side of the street. There's lots of room to park your car and we stay open until 2:00 A.M.

Come up and see us some time. Bring your friend and the letter.

Cordially yours,

P. S.   We have dandy chili, too.

It is the Hook in the sales letter that is most likely to get insufficient attention; at least, you will find a lot more letters slumping at the close than in the middle or beginning. This, of course, is unfortunate because the function of the Hook is to *complete* the job.

The following letter was written by a master in the use of words. In a novel and interesting way he sells the prestige of his company and the quality of its services. But where is the Hook?

Dear Mr. Doe:

In Chicago it's 15¢, no matter whether we ride the streamliner on Madison Street or the oldest model bus in town—the price is established.

But *not so* when we think of operations; of clothing; of furniture —yes, and of landscape work!

"I'll remove your appendix for $125.00," says one physician. "Five hundred dollars is my charge," says another. "Milady's dress will cost her $35.00," declares the sign in the window, while across the street we see a similar appearing creation for $85.00. The dining room set for $750.00 is laughed at by the table and chairs which claim to be "just as good" for $200.00.

So we shop around, pitting price against reliability, until at last we find the place where, in our judgment, they meet.

It will be the same with the work on your grounds: Sometime soon, after calm consideration, you'll select a company where price and reliability go hand in hand.

Before the first horse-drawn car left the barns; before modern medical science had come into being; and while milady in crinolines rode her carriage on the cobblestones of the Avenue, and furniture was still being made from the forests surrounding the swamp city of Chicago. . .

As far back as that, this company founded their business on the proposition that in all their work, price and reliability must travel together—and through the years they've proven trustworthy companions.

Sincerely,

You can see the lack of an urge to action in the above cleverly written letter. The prospect may have been impressed by the message, favorably disposed toward the company—but what is he expected to *do about it?* Perhaps it was never intended to be a sales letter, but only a bit of promotion to pave the way for a salesman's personal call. In that sense, it would not be necessary to worry so much about the missing Hook.

In the same way, the next letter is interesting and convincing, but it does not ask for action. In that respect, it is inadequate as a sales letter; on the other hand, it does a good job if intended only to keep the reader conscious of the company's services, as does a piece of effective institutional advertising. The Star takes two thirds of the space; the Chain, one third. There is no Hook.

Dear Mr. Doe:

Maybe you've heard this story—but it's good enough to repeat any day.

Recently, a firm installed a large piece of machinery. When everything was set, ready to let 'er rip, the thing simply wouldn't start "nohow."

Engineers were called in right and left, and each in turn fiddled around, but no luck. She just wouldn't go, and that was that! Finally, as a last resort, the foreman called in a two-bit mechanic. (So they thought)

In he strolled with his small sledge hammer, and walked over to the machine. He glanced here and there for a moment, and then set his eyes on one spot. He struck three blows with the hammer; and lo and behold, much to the surprise of the on-lookers, off she went!

"Just how much do we owe you?" yelled the foreman.

"One thousand and three dollars," replied the mechanic.

"What's the thousand and three bucks for?" asked the foreman.

"Three bucks for three blows, and a thousand bucks for knowing where to hit," the mechanic retorted.

So, in the long run, if a fellow knows his business, it's a cinch; and if not, it's too bad for him and the other fellow he's doing it for.

We've got a grand bunch of mechanics working here, and believe me, they know "where to hit" when it comes to numbering machines—making them, and repairing them.

You are taking no chances when you let them serve you. As a matter of fact, it's the best assurance you have of turning out ACCURATE NUMBERING, and at the same time, SAVING yourself TIME, WORRY, and EXPENSE.

Numerically yours,

Even though the above letter, minus the Hook, asks for no immediate business, it deserves praise as a reminder of the services of the company. It was used by the Wetter Numbering Machine Company, and won Gold Medal recognition from the Dartnell Corporation in one of their annual selections of representative letters in American business. Interesting also is the fact that a feminine letter writer, Kathleen Simpson, did the job.

A neatly balanced letter, with each of the three parts doing its share of the job, is one used by the Naylor Corporation, Chicago, as a follow-up to a mailing of samples. The Star is especially appropriate, and would serve equally well for any follow-up letter.

Gentlemen:

Did you ever drop a stone over the edge of a cliff and wait for the echoing sound to come back to you?

If you heard nothing at all, then your curiosity really was aroused and you wanted to find out what was at the bottom of the cliff, and how deep it was.

We are in the same position today, but the stones we dropped were the samples of our Tap-A-Way set and Cash Register. They were dropped in your direction last July, and since then we have heard—nothing.

Frankly, the samples were sent to you to arouse interest in our line. If they have accomplished that purpose, we are human enough to want you to tell us so; and at the same time, to tell us what the chances are of your buying some of these items.

The enclosed literature tells the story of Naylor toys, and we invite you to read it, keeping in mind that these toys offer you a real merchandising opportunity. Hundreds of other department stores are arranging for Tap-A-Way demonstrations, and for promotion on the Earl Toy Register sales.

Now that a second stone has been dropped your way, we will listen intently for the echo. When can we count on getting your order?

                                                                Yours truly,

Strive for balance in your own sales letters: let each part do its fair share of the work, with no one part overcrowding the others.

The undisguised form letter. Many attempts to sell by letter are directed to groups of prospects, rather than to separate individuals. This means that the sales message must be broad enough to cover all members of the group, even though by matching the fill-in and by other devices, an effort is made to make the letter seem to be a personal contact. Disguising the form letter is thus considered an innocent and justifiable deception by most sales-letter writers, although they realize the negative effect when the disguise is obvious.

Some writers, however, make no bones of using the form letter openly without trying in any way to hide it. In their opinion, if the letter is interesting and convincing, the average reader doesn't care whether or not he is the only one to get it. Of course, in taking this position, the users of the undisguised form letter save themselves considerable trouble. The need of a perfect fill-in is eliminated, and for the names of the readers an attention-pulling caption can be substituted. A good example is the letter reproduced here.

Plainly a Form Letter, But Convincing Nevertheless

Dear Friend,

Try it. Sip it, savor it, taste it, puff it, sample it. Test drive
it. Use it on a trial basis in the comfort of your own home. Ciga-
rettes, appliances, cars, foods, gadgets -- everyone's doing it, we
noticed, so why not Esquire?

>   Why not, we thought, give a man a
>   chance to sample our wares -- have
>   him sip, savor, puff, test drive
>   our magazine and provide for his
>   continued enjoyment if he likes what
>   he samples?

And so we devised our Quarter Plan, your risk-free, satisfaction
guaranteed introduction to Esquire.

>   Send us 25¢ and we'll rush you a
>   copy of next month's Esquire. (It will be
>   selling at the newsstand
>   for 60¢.)

This will be our signal to send you the next 8 issues at 25¢
apiece for which we'll bill you later. If after inspecting the copy
for which you sent your quarter, you decide you want no more, write
"Cancel" across your bill. We'll stop service immediately and
you'll be under no obligation whatever. Fair enough?

                              . . . .

I think that on receipt of your first copy you'll agree that never
did 25¢ go out and bring back so much.

                              . . . .

Take fiction. Esquire carries the best available for two good
reasons. First, Esquire's editors have a fondness for solid, lean,
imaginative writing and they spare no effort in unearthing it.
And secondly, Esquire has a tradition to uphold. The Snows of
Kilimanjaro, Ernest Hemingway's unforgettable masterpiece, was first
published in Esquire, as were the works of thirteen other Nobel
Prize winners. Esquire feels bound then by virtue of tradition and
reputation to continue presenting the work of the finest new and
established authors writing today.

Which authors? John Updike, for instance. Philip Roth, Alan Paton,
Budd Schulberg, John Cheever, J. Edgar Grove, Wallace Stegner, Isaac
Bashevis Singer.

                              . . . .

<u>Take fashion</u>. Whatever your interests -- what to wear, what to eat, what to drink, what to see, hear, read -- Esquire will serve you as a knowledgeable guide, for Esquire stands for Authority in a Man's World. Yes, Esquire covers the full range of leisuretime interests of today's modern man who knows that leisure means more than Beer, Bowling, and To Bed.

But let Esquire speak for itself ...

. . . .

"You can sell it tonight and turn
around and sell the same pugnuckling
again tomorrow. You ain't lost
nothing. Likely if they tried to
put that blue law onto pugnuckling, the
police would come in and stop them."

Give up? It's a bit of William Faulkner -- an excerpt from his last novel <u>The Reivers</u>. And it was previewed, in advance of publication, in the pages of Esquire.

"A contest for the heavyweight
championship is more than a fight,
it is a celebration, a ceremony,
a profound rite, as truly a blood
ritual as the sacrifice of the
fighting bulls."

That was Budd Schulberg, an avowed romantic, who looks at leather and canvas and finds in them beauty, poetry, and truth.

. . . .

Mailed today, your quarter, like in days long gone, will bring you back something really worth having ... hours and hours each month of the most unusual and exciting in magazine entertainment.

Cordially,

J. L. Marshall

J. L. Marshall
Subscription Manager

JLM:sss
3900

2. MAJOR APPEALS IN SALES LETTERS

Man and his inner self. From the time that he begins to be aware of the world about him, and perhaps even before, man is driven by inner forces which influence and direct the molding of his own personality, and his reactions to the things, people, ideas, opportunities, and beliefs he meets daily in his own world. Call these forces what you will—instincts, emotions, inherited tendencies, or those acquired—the fact remains that they are ever present, and must be understood by any person who seeks to influence human behavior, as, for instance, in a sales letter.

We have neither the inclination nor the ability to approach these inner motivating forces from the scientific viewpoint of the savant who may hold the highest degrees in psychology, philosophy, and sociology, and who knows how to take man's emotional being apart and sometimes put it together again. That can never be the approach of the practical businessman, although it might be helpful could he use it. On the other hand, it may be best that he cannot, since too much emphasis on theory is not always constructive.

Even the layman knows, however, the major inner forces by which his own life is directed, and his judgment and common sense tell him how one or more of the drives may be used to build a successful sales letter. The ability to select the right appeal for a given situation grows with time and experience. Psychology, in the language of the layman, is the study of human nature, and many a salesman who lacks a formal education, who might not even know how to spell the word, is a psychologist in practice if not in name.

You know—we all know—that *fear* is one of the forces which governs the actions of all human beings; never in the same degree, perhaps, but always present. To *protect* himself and his family, his business, or some group to which he belongs, against the things he *fears,* John Doe will buy insurance, vitamin pills, a football helmet for his boy, or new tires for his automobile. Thus, if the product or service to be presented in the sales letter guarantees protection against any of the evils that the reader fears, then that may be the major appeal which the writer should use. Never, however, will this appeal have the same effect on different individuals, or under different conditions. Knowing *when* a certain appeal may have the greatest effect, and when it may be disregarded as not the best for the particular occasion, is one of the skills of the expert letter writer.

Why do people buy? The appeals that may be used in sales letters are numerous and varied. Often, too, the reason that leads to a sale is so small that only the buyer knows why it was important to *him*. A home is sold because the wife of the buyer likes the color of the kitchen walls. A hat is sold because of a feather stuck in the band. A book is sold because the title sounds interesting. None of these reasons *appear* important, but they were to the buyers. The smart salesman looks for these *little* things that may count *big* in the mind of a prospect. He doesn't care *why* the prospect feels that way—he is glad to find *"a peg to hang the sale on."*

But aside from these unexplainable reasons why some people buy, the clever sales-letter writer is well acquainted with the smaller number of major reasons that are common to *all* people, and he is alert to the possibility of using any one of them for a specific sales situation. He analyzes his product or service to decide what benefits are supplied; he analyzes his prospect to decide what needs or desires exist, knowing that if a benefit and a need can be matched, the sale is likely to follow.

What *are* the major forces that influence the thoughts and actions of the average human being? Well, *fear* has been mentioned. If protection against something feared is the major benefit, then protection is the thing to talk about in the letter. Another primary force which seems at work in every human being is *pride;* who among us all is entirely without it? Another is *love:* love for children; love for parents; love for animals; sometimes, love for self. *Loyalty, greed, hate, ambition*—you know the others. Even *sex* may be the "peg to hang the sale on," and often is in a sales letter. The point is that among these many possible appeals, there is always at least one most likely to have the greatest effect for a particular letter situation. The problem is to make the right selection.

Letters that appeal to fear. Much of the "scare copy" that you see commonly in advertising, and in some sales letters, is an insult to the intelligence of the reader. To be urged to buy some remedy which "might" cure a disease that "might" develop, is a form of high pressure which any reader has good right to resent. However, if the condition that the letter seeks to correct is common to mankind, and men have *reason to fear it,* then the writer is a benefactor and not a quack; the appeal is logical and its use is ethical.

There are many kinds of businesses whose services or products may properly be offered as protection to offset fear. The insurance companies, for example, have good reason to talk about the various forms of protection provided by their policies—and each form is the answer to something dreaded by the average individual. Hence, the sales letter that quickens one of these fears to the point of action has used an appeal as beneficial to the individual as to the company. In this sense, the letter on page 397 reminds the reader that men die and leave their families homeless, but that no one need fear for their family's welfare if protected by the right kind of insurance policy.

Overcoming price objections. Companies that sell products or services of the highest quality are forever faced with price objections. "Too high," says the prospect, and unless he can be convinced that he is getting just as much or more for his dollar, he is quite likely to buy elsewhere. The

---

EQUITABLE

Life Insurance Company of Iowa

FOUNDED IN 1867 IN DES MOINES   D E S   M O I N E S ,   I O W A

*a Mortgage
Is A Wonderful Thing . . .*

     Do you have a mortgage? Most families couldn't enjoy living in their homes if there were no mortgages.

     But mortgages are obligations that have to be paid. Right now you're paying on yours, and you fully expect to continue to meet your payments. But what would happen to your home - to your family - if you should suddenly be taken away?

     We have the answer. It's a simple plan of life insurance that promises, in event of your death, to pay off the mortgage. It means that your family will have their home as you planned it. It means a home if they want to live in it, an asset if they want to sell it, an income if they want to rent it. It means all these things, for only about 1% of your mortgage annually.

     Surprising? Yes, but it's true. Our representative, whose card is enclosed, will call on you within a few days to give you facts and figures.

            Sincerely yours,

               Agency Vice President

individual who does pay the extra amount for the extra quality is influenced by at least two of the inner forces we have been discussing—*pride,* and the *fear* that something cheaper may turn out to be unsatisfactory. Both of these appeals are often used by sales-letter writers, and the two letters that follow are excellent examples. One was written by direct-mail executive Henry Field, of Shenandoah, Iowa, and the other by Ken Raetz for the Badger Printing Company, Appleton, Wisconsin.

Both of these letters are conspicuous for their man-to-man style, and both are extremely adroit in selling the wisdom of buying quality—the folly of buying "cheap." Consider first, the letter by Mr. Field:

Friend Jones:

I admit it is a temptation for you to go ahead and buy cheaper alfalfa seed than I have offered you. I used to be tempted to pay less and be able to sell for less myself.

But when I look over the wholesale offerings of cheap seed, my temptation is all gone. I would never have the nerve to sell it to my friends and customers. Mostly, it is a sorry lot of seed. Generally dull and small and wrinkled. None too clean. And nobody knows for sure how many weeds are in the lot.

Our alfalfa seed is big, plump seed. It has a bright, healthy color that you will recognize as fresh and full of vitality. It is cleaned, mighty carefully cleaned. All the chaffy stuff and all the light, small seeds are removed. They wouldn't grow, anyway. And it is absolutely free of noxious weeds.

In order to get the good heavy stand of alfalfa you want, you will have to sow from 15 per cent to 25 per cent more cheap seed than quality seed like ours. And you will have to take the weeds as they come whether you like them or not.

Now, just figure it out for yourself. My price is higher. It ought to be. But when you figure it out you will need enough less of my quality seed to make up the difference and then some. Goodness knows, I like to see every man save money, but I never heard of one who saved any by planting seed because it was cheap.

That is pretty straight talk, but I believe you will appreciate it. Get good, honest seed, whether you send your order to me or to someone else.

If you like my kind of quality seed at a fair price, send your order along in the enclosed envelope. You will never regret it, and I will be glad to get your order and see another farmer on the right road.

Very truly yours,

You will look far and wide to find a sales letter that talks the reader's language any better than this one selling quality seed. In pile-driver fashion, one phrase after another hits the prospect between the eyes. No doubt you noticed them.

"never have the nerve to sell it"
"a sorry lot of seed"
"nobody knows how many weeds"
"they wouldn't grow anyway"
"take the weeds as they come"
"figure it out for yourself"
"price is higher—ought to be"
"whether you like them or not"
"make up the difference and then some"
"Goodness knows, I like to see"
"who saved because it was cheap"
"get good, honest seed"
"you will never regret it"
"another farmer on the right road"

You don't encounter any fancy words in that sales letter. But the language used is common sense talk, and so are the ideas. The man talking is a *friend*—he wants to put *another farmer on the right road.*

Mr. Raetz in his letter to Charlie is just as direct and persuasive, but he talks to a business executive, not a farmer. The language isn't quite so homespun, but it's still man-to-man.

Dear Charlie:

Let's sit down, figuratively speaking, and talk this thing over. I'll admit you've got reason enough to stand, but I think we'll get places quicker if we're comfortable.

It's a ticklish business, Charlie—this price business, and yet it's the most important item in your and my existence. It has been our contention all along that *price is but part of printing.* A printer can break down his cost only to a certain point. He can allow so much for composition, ink, type, paper and printing, but the one thing that no guy's been smart enough to figure is an arbitrary cost on *craftsmanship.*

I think all the heat's been raised on account of our refusing to do a job that we know in advance won't come up to our standards because of a too-low estimate. And, Charlie, there *is* a difference in good and bad printing even in the simplest jobs. Ed

Boetcher will be glad to call and explain further our point of view on this matter.

But probably more important to you is again this angle of price and profit. You're in a good business. You've got clearly defined grades of meat and prices adjusted accordingly. For example, when a customer complains (maybe one of our employees for all we know) about a piece of beef liver being tough you can always say that *calves* liver is a better kind of meat. While your beef liver is the best obtainable, it still doesn't compare with your calves liver. You carry both of them because some people like beef liver.

We only stock one kind of quality, Charlie, because it's our native cussedness to insist that people should only like the best. You and I have grown to be the biggest concerns in our respective fields around here. The quality of our efforts always has been high, and neither one of us intends to lower the standards that have earned us the reputation we now enjoy.

We do quite a bit of business with you, and damn-it-all, we'd like to do this job for you. It'll be a bang-up one too, I assure you.

Expectantly yours,

Again, you have a letter full of simple but expressive phrases—the kind heard everywhere in everyday speech.

"and talk this thing over"
"a ticklish business, Charlie"
"price is but part of printing"
"no guy's been smart enough to figure"
"all the heat's been raised"
"And, Charlie, there *is* a difference"
"you're in a good business"
"is a better kind of meat"
"because some people like beef liver"
"it's our native cussedness"
"and damn-it-all"
"to do a job for you"

You notice, too, that in this letter selling quality above price, the reader's own business is tactfully brought into the picture. Also, his name is used several times but not too often, although the men seem well acquainted and the length of the letter permits the repetition.

With sample to prove quality. The following letter was used by the Gates Rubber Company to sell garden hose to dealers. The appeal throughout is based on the quality of the product, with a sample sent along to prove it. Four hundred and fifty hardware dealers got the letter; orders were pulled for 14,700 feet of hose.

(No salutation)

"Spring is just around the corner"—

Businessmen with vision are NOW giving serious thought to their Garden hose requirements for the coming season. The Gates factory in Denver is prepared to solve this problem, and to help make this YOUR most profitable year.

Here is YOUR opportunity to deal direct and take advantage of factory prices, just as many other thoughtful buyers are doing. Complete stocks carried in our Denver and Chicago warehouses enable us to give prompt attention to your orders for Gates "factory fresh" Garden hose—the kind that gives your customers extra service *without* extra cost—the kind of service you want them to have.

The sample in the attached bag is our 2-braid Greenlawn DeLuxe Garden hose. Test it anyway you want to. Twist it, try to tear it, try to chip the tough, thick inner tube with your fingernail. Press the sides together and notice how quickly the hose springs back to its original shape. The attractive dark green cover with its deep corrugations insures long life and prevents cracking.

Each type of Gates Garden hose is THE outstanding value in its particular class, built to give maximum service; and you will be surprised at the moderate cost. Gates Garden hose is available in all sizes, in grades ranging from All Rubber to the Greenlawn DeLuxe—in black, red, and green.

Each brand is distinctively paper-wrapped to make it stand out and attract your customers' attention—actually selling itself. Each length of standard braided hose carries its own guarantee tag, enabling your customers to see and feel the QUALITY.

The attached card requires no postage. Fill it in, and drop it in the mail-box. Without obligation to you, samples and quotations on our complete line of superior Garden hose will be sent to you immediately.

You will profit by dealing direct with us, so be sure to mail the card TODAY.

Cordially yours,

Garden hose is not a glamorous thing to talk about, since it serves only a utility purpose. Hence, the Gates letter-man, R. J. Gentles, wisely chose to pack his sales attempt with solid facts.

1. This is the season when garden hose will sell.
2. You can buy our quality hose at factory prices.
3. The sample *proves* our claim of quality. Treat it rough. See how it fights back.
4. Surprisingly low price for each grade.
5. Wrapped to invite customer attention.
6. Each length tagged to guarantee quality.

All of these facts are up the hardware dealer's alley. Supported by the sample, they could hardly fail to impel interest among those who had not already purchased seasonal requirements.

Unseen quality hardest to sell. The job of the sales-letter writer is not nearly so difficult in talking about quality which is obvious as in talking about quality which is hidden. A sample of shirting, attached to a letter, can be seen and felt; it can be compared to other pieces of similar cloth. Mr. Gentles invited various tests of his sample of garden hose; he knew quality could be demonstrated on the spot. Mr. Field's problem was not so simple. How can anyone looking at a handful of alfalfa seed *know* whether or not the seeds of weeds are included? Perhaps an expert could tell, but not the average farmer.

The quality of many products is revealed only in *use*: by their length of service; by performance; by comparison with results attained with other inferior makes. Two homes may stand side by side on the same street—both newly built, equally attractive in appearance and interior arrangement. They *look* alike, but they are not. The builder of one knew how to cut corners; how to cheapen construction in ways that would be hidden. The builder of the other used quality construction throughout. The one home will last thirty or forty years longer than the other, but the real estate man who sells it cannot wait that long to prove the fact. He must tell his prospect *how* the home was built: about the extra precautions to insure durability; about the quality of materials that went into the house, even though they are now concealed.

Unseen quality must be sold more consistently than that which is apparent. Buyers must be kept conscious of the values they are getting. Not always by letters that ask for orders, but at regular intervals new fuel must be added; otherwise, the customer may be lured into buying that which *seems* "just as good."

Quality appeal to personal pride. Most people like to put their best foot forward; they are receptive to anything of quality which may enhance their appearance or prestige. Of course, many merchants and manufacturers base their sales programs on this appeal to pride. Millions and millions of dollars are spent annually on advertising in an attempt to create an image of quality for certain brands, products and services; and once these concepts of quality are established, the buying public gratifies its pride by paying a premium for better-known products. But these are the methods of the big corporations that have millions to spend for magazine ads, billboards, direct mail, and other forms of promotion. The smaller companies, the retailers, and certain types of service organizations may logically turn to sales and goodwill letters as the most inexpensive means of enhancing the quality of what they have to offer.

Any local merchant, if he is willing to take the trouble, may build a list of prospects and customers; without much ado, he can keep it up-to-date. Letters can be sent to these people at regular intervals—announcements of new merchandise just received; the news of special sales; talks about goods to fit seasonal needs; or messages serving no other purpose than to keep the merchant's name and the quality of his products or services in the public consciousness.

Pride in personal courage. You see, there is no end to the tangents pride may follow or to the appeals that it makes possible. Perhaps one of the most potent is pride in personal courage. Even if an individual wears the white feather, he likes to imagine himself a combination of Tarzan, the Three Musketeers, and Joe Palooka. Any insinuation that he is a quitter will either challenge him to prove he isn't, or send him snarling to lick the wound. Because one never knows what the reaction will be, the appeal is a dangerous weapon in the hands of the sales-letter writer. It may work, and it may not, depending on the ability of the reader to "take it."

The following letter used by International Correspondence Schools, and signed by Paul V. Barrett, used this appeal:

THIS...IS...FIGHTING...TALK

If you are a quitter you won't read this letter. But—

If you are not—if you have the courage to face facts—you want to know who is responsible for your not getting ahead faster.

Do you accept the challenge? All right—

It's YOU!

The man who *won't* be licked *can't* be licked.

The world is filled with men who *wish* something would happen. But it takes men of determination and purpose to *make* things happen.

Maybe you are making things happen for yourself and for your family. A lot of men like you, then, are making them happen faster by acquiring more practical training through International Correspondence Schools Courses.

If things are not happening, and if you are a fighter, you will do something about it!

You'll get the special training that fits you for advancement, and you'll go on to a bigger job and better pay.

In your spare time, right at home, you can get the training you need. Through I.C.S. Courses thousands of other men have lifted themselves out of the rut into well-paid, responsible positions.

They're no better men than you. They had ambition and they seized opportunity.

Here's opportunity for you. Mark and mail the enclosed card. It will bring you news that can change the course of your whole life. Do it today.

> Sincerely yours,

So much for the various forms which the appeal to *pride* may take. There are many others of which you are conscious because they influence your own life. But there is another and more worthy inner force at work in human beings which we can contemplate with considerable pleasure.

Sales letters with appeal to love. Fortunately, man is not entirely selfish. In many of his activities and associations, *love* for others has a strong influence on what he thinks and does. This force is manifested in numerous ways—love for parents, love for children, love for friends, love for animals, and for others—and because of this love, he is often moved to protect them against misfortune. Thus, the sales-letter writer, in surveying his product or service, may often find therein a protection against the evils that man wishes to keep away from those he loves. It may be that the writer has a policy to provide monthly income for the prospect's wife in the event of his death, or a food product that helps to keep his children strong and free from colds, or even so small a thing as a powder that chases insects from a pet. In every case, if the offer is accepted, the motivating force is love of others, not love of self.

The chief danger in using the appeal to love is that the writer may become so engrossed with his subject and its sentimental aspects that he overpaints the picture. People as a rule do not like to wear their hearts on their sleeves; they are moved by sincere sentiment, but turn away from abject sentimentality. Hence, the writer using this appeal should be careful not to "gush" or let his message become too "sticky." When this happens, a tone of exaggeration and insincerity creeps into the letter and its purpose is defeated.

The following letter, used by St. Louis Union Trust Company, is written with restraint and tact. The incidents mentioned in the introduction are sufficient to arouse the protective instinct in those who received the message. No doubt, some of them were impelled to see this trust company about their wills.

Dear Mr. Doe:

I know of a case where through a mistake a man's entire estate went to his wealthy brother-in-law, leaving his dependent parents in want.

In another case, a man worth $500,000 provided bequests of $75,000 in his will and left the residue to his children. When he died, he was worth barely enough to pay these bequests and his children received nothing. In a third case, a childless man worth $50,000 neglected to make a will, and consequently, his wife received but half his estate, the other half going to his brother.

These are but a few of many cases which have come to my attention in which an ample estate, for some reason, has failed to provide for those who should have benefited, or has been subject to heavy unnecessary loss. Some unfortunate provision in a will, the failure to make a will, or the mistake of an inexperienced executor, is the usual cause of such—often tragic—miscarriages of purpose.

If you haven't made a will, I urge you to do so without delay. If you have made a will, I suggest the advisability of reviewing it carefully.

In either case, you will find our booklet "Your Will" interesting and helpful. It is written in simple non-technical language and crammed full of information pertaining to estate matters of vital importance to people of means.

A return card is enclosed for your convenience in sending for a copy of this helpful booklet.

Very truly yours,

No doubt you noted the strong Star in the above letter. The three concrete examples are powerful attention-getters. The reader naturally wonders if his own will might contain similar flaws, or, if he has not made one, the urge is strong to do so.

Letter with double love appeal. Lovers of dogs can never understand why anyone else doesn't love them. To the great majority of people, especially men, any reference to these devoted tail-waggers is liable to receive immediate attention. The letter which follows, however, serves a double purpose: it appeals to the lady, particularly if she is a dog lover, and if she isn't it still touches her desire to make her children happy. The message was used by Realtor G. K. Masterson of Philadelphia.

> Dear Mrs. Doe:
>
> Do your children love dogs?
>
> Do you like dogs?
>
> Does your husband like dogs?
>
> The affectionate fellow that looks up wistfully at you and wags a doubtful tail—how could you help but love him?
>
> But the boys can't keep a dog in the city. That is, *really* keep him.
>
> It isn't safe to let him run, and he *must* run to be a happy, natural dog.
>
> What if you had a real home in the suburbs where a dog can really live?
>
> There's some satisfaction in being a dog in the suburbs. And there's some satisfaction in being a boy or girl.
>
> Why not have a real home, where children can be children and dogs can be dogs, and you can all be free and happy together?
>
> The cost? Nonsense! We have plans that will carry you safely and easily over the cost, whatever your income is.
>
> Why not let us tell you about them? At least, you ought to *know*. Telephone City 4800, or return the enclosed card, and our representative will call on you.
>
> Cordially yours,

To save time or money. Numerous products and services have as buying bait a saving in time or money, or a combination of both. The sales-letter writer who is able to offer something of equal value at a lower cost is rather sure of success *if* he is able to *prove* the equality. In similar fashion, his chances are good if he has some convenience, such as a saving in time or labor, to talk about. This is simply because one of the inner forces in man is the craving to possess as much as he can with the least possible effort. This may be an unworthy trait of the human race, but you know it is present to some degree in practically all individuals.

Most of the inventions with which modern man is blessed are the result of this craving. If conservation of time and money had held no special meaning, we probably would still be using primitive machines and working from the rising to the setting of the sun. The first wheel was no doubt conceived by some savage whose back was tired from dragging heavy objects over the ground. He thought how much nicer it would be to push a lot less and move a lot faster. Be that as it may, a great many sales letters are based on a possible saving in one form or another. The following message written for Williams Oil-O-Matic Heating Corporation by J. M. Cullinan offers added comfort and convenience without any great drain on the prospect's purse—an appeal to which he may be very receptive. The letter starts with an interesting comparison—always an effective device for the Star.

Dear Mr. Doe:

TWO MEN WENT DOWN
TO THE BASEMENT

One went down to fire the furnace. He wasn't in the mood. He would far rather have plumped into his easy chair with his favorite pipe and the evening paper. But this was out of the question. The house was cool—uncomfortably cool. So down to the basement he went.

What happened then?

First, a battle to coax warmth from a stubborn heating plant. Perhaps the shovel hit the furnace door a few times, jarring the man's disposition and spilling coal dirt on the floor. This mess had to be swept up after numerous other furnace tending tasks had been performed. Next, grimy hands were washed. Then upstairs to a round of draft regulating and a brief interlude of comfort. This day-after-day routine can leave no doubt in our minds. *The heating plant is boss.*

Consider the second man. He also went down to the basement. But what a difference! His basement was clean and bright. In one corner was an easy chair, reading lamp, and smoking stand. An ideal spot for a quiet smoke and a look at the news. There was no voice from upstairs reminding this man of coal to be shoveled, or of grates to be shaken. Every thought of these distasteful tasks vanished after a grateful glance at the Williams Oil-O-Matic.

Don't let the heating plant dominate your home life.

Find out now—before another day has passed—how little it really costs to enjoy Oil-O-Matic heat without work or worry. Telephone today for a FREE Heating Survey. This will provide an accurate estimate of how much Oil-O-Matic heating will cost in your home—installed in your present heating plant in but a few hours time.

Act now while present prices are in effect.

Very truly yours,

While in many parts of the country this experience is no longer common, there is no exaggeration in this letter, as any man will agree who has ever fired a coal furnace with a grimy shovel. The work and worry Mr. Cullinan talks about is real to the reader he is trying to reach—hence, the appeal of sparing himself in the future is tempting.

Another variation of this type of sales letter is the one that offers to spare the reader the expense and annoyance of some kind of unsatisfactory service. You know how often you have taken your car to a garage, and then taken it away later, wondering if the fault has been permanently corrected and if the bill you paid was fair and reasonable. You had no way of knowing the truth until the car was tested on the highways—because you couldn't stand around to see the work being done, and you had no way of checking it.

The writer of the following letter very adroitly seized this common state of mental uncertainty and used it as a powerful appeal in his message. The reader is told that visitors are always welcome in his shop; that the mechanics are proud of their work and like to have it inspected. Note, too, how the name of a famous and beloved person is used in the Star to win attention.

> Dear Mr. Doe:
>
> Mark Twain once remarked: "Always do right. This will gratify some people, and astonish the rest."
>
> Perhaps that is one of the reasons our Service Department is so popular. Our aim is always to do right by our customers and their cars.
>
> But there isn't any trick to that because our shop is well equipped to keep cars in perfect running condition. More so, we believe, than any other non-specialized headquarters in the city.
>
> The boys here are born mechanics. Visitors and customers are always welcome to thoroughly inspect their work. They don't attempt to hide it, because they are proud of it. Besides giving efficient service, they are mighty interested in seeing that you get friendly treatment. You'll feel at home here...and like it.
>
> From the first analysis of your car's trouble by Ed, the foreman, every mechanic wants to give you his best. And *does*.
>
> So this, our first letter contact with you, is just a real friendly invitation for you to visit us. When your car is ill, let our doctors examine it. The diagnosis costs you nothing—obligates you to nothing.
>
> In all friendliness,

The foregoing letter doubled business over the preceding month for the garage. It was written by a master sales-letter composer, C.D. Craddock.

The appeal of something free. Watch the people leaving any kind of a business show, carrying paper bags full of give-aways, and you have tangible evidence of another deep-seated human desire. Perhaps it is fair to call it *greed,* but not in its baser forms. Many of the gadgets and samples in the paper bags are later tossed into the junk pile, but just the same it seems to be a commonly shared thrill to get something free.

This weakness in man, if you want to call it that, is frequently used by sales-letter writers, and even by credit men, as an approach to the sale. Although the reader might know that the cost of the bait is included in the sales price of the article or service, he still likes to fool himself with the idea he is not paying for it. This comment, however, is not intended as a criticism of the method, provided the buyer still gets his money's worth.

A good illustration of the appeal at work is the following letter used by Circulation Manager R. R. Rountree in an effort to get subscriptions to the magazine, *Advertising & Selling.* The book offered as an inducement, *My Life in Advertising* by Claude Hopkins, is extremely interesting and instructive. Those who took advantage of the offer were in no way deceived.

Dear Mr. Doe:

I see that your name is not on the list of executives to whom we have mailed a copy of "My Life in Advertising"—free.

I am sure you will not want to miss the outstanding advertising book of the last decade, so I urge you to mail the enclosed card promptly.

Claude Hopkins' autobiography relates his sensational career in advertising. He was personally responsible for many of advertising's greatest successes—Palmolive, Pepsodent, Edna Wallace Hopper, Puffed Wheat, etc. He wrote a single advertisement that brought in 1,460,000 coupons for Van Camp's Evaporated Milk. He tells you the inside story in his amazing book, "My Life in Advertising."

He describes intimately his experience with Swifts, Liquozone, Studebaker, Schlitz beer, etc.

Mr. Hopkins earned as much as $185,000 in one year by writing advertisements. He was President of Lord & Thomas for seven years, and when he left he was receiving $120,000 per year for half of his time. He describes in detail why campaigns worked—why others failed. He tells the schemes he used—his methods of testing copy—why the public buys. His book is filled with facts and usable ideas that will be of tremendous value if you want *your* advertising to pay its way.

The question is—how can you get your copy of "My Life in Advertising" free?

The answer is—a copy will be sent to you without charge if you will authorize your subscription to Advertising & Selling on the enclosed card.

The combination of Hopkins' book and Advertising & Selling is an unbeatable bargain—one that will pay you dividends. The book will present ideas that you can use in your business right away. Advertising & Selling will bring you every other week adaptable ideas on all phases of advertising and sales: copy, media, markets, research, etc.

The supply of books is limited and this offer is limited to January 30. Make sure of your copy by using the enclosed card now.

Cordially,

Because the above sales letter is fundamentally sound in construction, a review of its strong points should be helpful to any other sales correspondent. Notice:

1. That the appeal of getting something *free* is started in the first sentence, thus inviting the reader to continue.

2. That mention of the enclosed card early in the letter is an exception to the rule which says we should hold the Hook for the conclusion. In this case, the reader is only being urged to take something free, not to buy. That comes later.

3. That more than half of the letter is used to sell the free book. If the reader can be made to want the book first, he will be ready later to take the subscription also.

4. That a flock of big names are used to impress the reader with the author's importance. This as you know by now is a powerful sales device.

5. That the impression of author's importance is strengthened further by mention of the huge sums of money he has earned.

6. That the author's ability is *proved* by the mention of the 1,460,000 coupons one of his ads brought back to Van Camp's Evaporated Milk.

7. That the reader is told how the ideas in the book are usable in his own business.

8. That before swinging to the discussion of the magazine, a second mention is made of the appeal—"your copy *free*."

9. That the impetus developed by the sale of the book's value is not retarded by a too-long sale of the magazine. The writer chose to gamble on the pulling power of the book, and was too smart to let the reader's mind wander too far from it.

10. That quick action is impelled by mention of the limited number of books on hand.

Offer to solve financial problems. Another twist of the money appeal is that used by the personal loan companies. In a different sense, the soft spot touched is man's natural desire to free himself from worry. You know, of course, the argument on which practically all of these letters are based— "it is better to owe us a lump sum of $500 than to owe ten different people or companies sums of $50 each." Financially it may not seem that the man who takes the large debt is any better off, especially if interest charges increase. However, he is spared the annoyance of being pursued by many bill collectors. A second advantage of the one debt is that it may be stretched over a longer payment period.

The Cure for Financial Worries

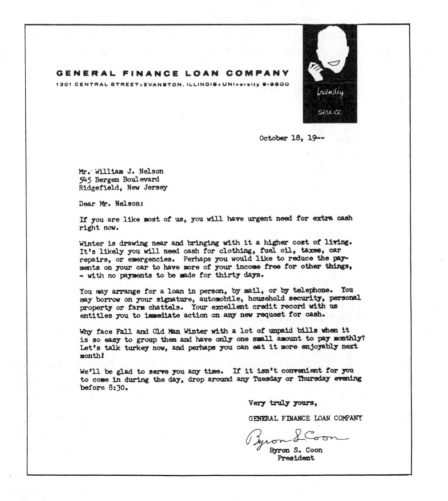

GENERAL FINANCE LOAN COMPANY
1301 CENTRAL STREET·EVANSTON, ILLINOIS·UNIversity 9-9500

friendly service

October 18, 19--

Mr. William J. Nelson
545 Bergen Boulevard
Ridgefield, New Jersey

Dear Mr. Nelson:

If you are like most of us, you will have urgent need for extra cash right now.

Winter is drawing near and bringing with it a higher cost of living. It's likely you will need cash for clothing, fuel oil, taxes, car repairs, or emergencies. Perhaps you would like to reduce the payments on your car to have more of your income free for other things, - with no payments to be made for thirty days.

You may arrange for a loan in person, by mail, or by telephone. You may borrow on your signature, automobile, household security, personal property or farm chattels. Your excellent credit record with us entitles you to immediate action on any new request for cash.

Why face Fall and Old Man Winter with a lot of unpaid bills when it is so easy to group them and have only one small amount to pay monthly? Let's talk turkey now, and perhaps you can eat it more enjoyably next month!

We'll be glad to serve you any time. If it isn't convenient for you to come in during the day, drop around any Tuesday or Thursday evening before 8:30.

Very truly yours,

GENERAL FINANCE LOAN COMPANY

Byron S. Coon
President

From the letters you have received from loan companies, it may not appear that they are overcrowded with expert correspondents. At least, some of their collection letters could stand considerable improvement. This, of course, is merely a personal opinion, and you may not agree. The sales letter reproduced on page 411 has much that you may commend. It starts briskly with an observation which in many cases is likely to provoke the mental reaction, *yes*. It then mentions some of the common needs for money and concludes with a friendly offer of service. The language is talkative—mostly made up of short words. An interesting sentence is the one that says, "Let's talk turkey to eat turkey enjoyably." The message contains no exaggeration or insincerity. The writer does not pose as the big-hearted brother, as is too often the case in this type of a sales letter.

The appeal for fair play. Asking the reader to apply the Golden Rule is an appeal more often found in collection letters than in sales letters. However, the justice of reciprocity can be made an effective sales argument—"I've been scratching your back, now you scratch mine." If offered tactfully, as in the following message, the idea will sometimes produce the desired result; on the other hand, if the appeal smacks of high-pressure it may do more harm than good.

This, we think, is the right way to use it:

Gentlemen:

This income tax business gives me a pain in the neck. I have been through my canceled checks half a dozen times, trying to find some deductions.

I didn't have much luck with the deductions, but I did run across a lot of checks payable to you fellows. We've been trading with your stores for years, because we like good merchandise and you give good service.

We, also, have a service which is that of things pertaining to real estate. Our service here in Tulsa is selling, buying, renting, and leasing property.

When you or any of your organization need the help of a Realtor, it would be nice to have you call on us.

Sincerely yours,

Written in such a polite manner, without insinuations or threats of withdrawing as a customer if business were not forthcoming, the above letter at least keeps the writer's name before the reader. It might lead to an immediate service; if not, it at least might develop goodwill looking to the future.

Getting away from business, you often encounter the Golden Rule as the major appeal in sales letters that reach out for charity of civic donations. The soft spot touched is the reader's better self; a spot which fortunately runs to larger size in some individuals than in others. Following is an excellent letter of this type—with an extremely interesting story for the Star.

> My dear Mr. Doe:
>
> Have you ever heard the old fable about the villagers who each agreed to contribute a sack of grain for those of their neighborhood who were ill or poor?
>
> A large vat was put in the village square where the sacks were to be emptied. The day appointed for the opening arrived; the villagers assembled; the vat cover was lifted.
>
> It was empty. Each villager, thinking, "My grain will not be missed," had forgotten.
>
> In a drawer in one of Glenwood's files stand 1121 cards, the records of 1121 people who know and believe in the worthwhileness of giving homeless, friendless boys a chance to become the right sort of men. But those 1121 men and women, for one reason or another, have forgotten to send their checks; there is not only a blank space on each card, but a corresponding lack in Glenwood's treasury.
>
> Your card is among the 1121.
>
> Please don't think that your contribution hasn't been missed— even though it may be a one-figure amount. No donation is too small to be helpful; none too small to be missed. All together, these donations accomplish a wonderful work.
>
> Won't you please, remembering the story of the empty vat, send your check? We *need* it more than ever this year.
>
> > Sincerely yours,

It is impossible to say how the 1121 people responded to this letter, but one man who got a copy sent a check for double the amount of his pledge. When asked *why,* he replied, "Well, I had forgotten to send my check, even though I knew the good work that school does for boys—then that letter got under my skin. I made up my mind right on the spot to put at least two sacks of grain in that empty vat." In that case, then, it was the story that stirred the reader's imagination and goaded him to action—as good stories often do in sales letters.

Indirect appeal to customers. The letters we have been viewing, to see how they probed for soft spots, were slanted largely at prospects, rather than customers; they were after new business. Getting orders from customers is an entirely different job. It is not necessary to talk to them about the nature of the service or product, or to sell them on the reliability of the company. In a way, they are already members of the family; they will continue to buy as long as they feel satisfied, or until some other company lures them from the family .circle.

Smart businessmen, however, do not take customers for granted. They appreciate the necessity of keeping their goodwill, and many letters are written for no other purpose. And, of course, some of these goodwill letters properly reach for orders. Letters of this class are especially effective when signed by the company's president; they make the customer feel important. An example is the letter below, one of many similar customer contacts made throughout the years by the Kalamazoo Vegetable Parchment Company:

Dear Mr. Doe:

What the Business World
Needs Isn't a Better Five-Cent Cigar
But a Good Hearty Laugh

When we were youngsters on the farm, we devoted considerable time to feeding chickens and hunting eggs.

One year, one of our chickens got the pip and it spread to the entire flock. We did not know at the time and we do not know now what caused the disease; but we do know that it spread until all of our egg producers were non-producers, and they wobbled around the barnyard, glassy-eyed, and with their tail feathers dragging in the dust.

An old farmer told us to mix cayenne pepper with their feed and it worked wonders. In a short time they had pep instead of pip.

So, as the entire business world has been suffering with the pip for the past twelve months or more, we suggest that the pippers, instead of taking the cayenne pepper, indulge in a few hearty laughs occasionally. Having tried this remedy ourselves, we can testify to the fact that we have saved ourselves from a perfectly good nervous breakdown by substituting a good laugh for a glum look and a groan.

Sincerely yours,
Kalamazoo Vegetable Parchment Company
J. Kindleberger

P.S. Since dictating the above, our mill manager informs me that the biggest need of the mill just now is another order.

3. SALES ARGUMENTS OF SPECIAL POWER

The point of difference. Blessed is the sales correspondent who has a "point of difference" to talk about in his letters. It may not be so important compared to other features of the product, but it still has special power to charm his readers. People are instinctively interested in anything new or different, and the desire to own the item is always potent.

What are these *points of difference?* Well, you were asked to smoke *Luckies* because they were *toasted.* Whether or not this difference of being toasted made Luckies any better we must let the cigarette smokers tell us, but the fact appealed to people's imagination, and was a sales argument no other cigarette maker possessed. A few years ago, one of the television set manufacturers featured a new type of cabinet, and for a while there was a point of difference—*no squint, no squat, no stoop.* No doubt that point of difference sold many sets until the other manufacturers caught up with it. Compared to picture, sound selectivity, power, and other selling qualities, the tilting of the screen couldn't be so tremendously important, but it was *something new to talk about*—interesting bait to attract buyers.

A good sales letter that talks about a point of difference is the one below—written by C. A. Winser for the Gates Rubber Company:

Gentlemen:

Away back in the beginning of history, some primitive ancestor got tired of dragging his worldly belongings around on a sledge. Perhaps by accident, perhaps by intent, he conceived the idea of wheels. It was such a ridiculously simple invention—yet how tremendously important it was!

Thousands of years later another man thought of the *Cone Belt Drive* as a means of changing speeds on a machine. That was another simple invention—but *you* know how much it means in the textile industry.

And now we've come along with an improvement for the Cone Belt used on those drives. It's just a slight change too—but *what* a difference it makes.

The secret? Gates Cone Belts are built with a CURVED INNER FACE.

Study the attached illustrations. See how curving the inner face of this belt—the face that runs next to the cone—overcomes the tendency for the belt to climb and fight the shifter fork. It is that "fighting," that jerk and change of speeds, that makes an uneven yarn. Then remember that the curved face that eliminates this is a patented Gates feature.

No other Cone Belt has it.

Naturally, a belt that runs smoothly produces an even, smooth yarn—you see that immediately. But the improvement doesn't stop there. For there is less strain on the belt, easier service, and so you'll find the Gates Cone Belt outwearing every other Cone

Belt you ever have used—and giving you a better yarn every minute it is in service.

Take advantage of this saving now by writing Small and Parkes, Limited, Hendham Vale Works, Manchester 9, England. They carry a complete stock and will be eager to work with you on any drive problem.

Cordially yours,
Export Division

Commenting on this letter, Mr. Winser says: "It was sent to a list of textile mills in Holland, and very shortly afterwards our English representatives, who handle Holland also, wrote in that they were surprised at the volume of orders they were receiving." You see, Mr. Winser had a point of difference to talk about in his sales letter—the curved inner face.

Even if the company has no entirely exclusive feature in its product or service, patented or copyrighted, it may be possible to *develop* a point of difference worthy of the spotlight in a sales letter. It may be something that another, but not every, company would also have the right to claim. There are a number of magazines that feature brief, terse copy, but any one of them can use that point of difference in comparing their style with magazines of contrasting editorial policy. Illustrating the point of difference is the letter on page 417.

Writers of sales letters should look long and hard for a *point of difference* to talk about. There are few products or services on the market that are not duplicated in many respects by others. Consider the various automobiles in the low-price range: they are so similar in price, quality, power, etc., that not one of those factors makes a strong sales argument. However, just one of these cars might have a new patented feature which would be a point of difference—something worth talking about. Or, it could be that the *appearance* of one make of car is far superior to the others.

Waste few words on arguments that your competitors can also use. Pound hard on something which is *yours,* and yours *alone.* Then you develop sales power—and nobody can stop you.

Proof by testimony. It sounds big and means little to say in a sales letter, "Thousands of famous men, whose names you would quickly recognize, have worn our shirts for years." That is a generality, pure and simple. Who *are* the famous men? Mention just two or three of them, and the statement immediately has power. The average human being is a natural-born hero worshiper. He is easily influenced by reference to people he has learned to admire. Quotations, of course, are even more powerful; but just the names will often give your letter the "teeth" that it needs.

TIME
THE WEEKLY NEWSMAGAZINE

TIME & LIFE BUILDING
ROCKEFELLER CENTER
NEW YORK 20

Dear Reader:

If you will mail the enclosed card, I shall be happy to see that twenty-one stimulating issues of TIME, The Weekly Newsmagazine are delivered to your home.

The cost of this trial subscription is one dollar and eighty-seven cents -- a reduced price available to you and other discerning readers, on an introductory basis only. And here are a few of the things that can make TIME your most trusted weekly companion ...

TIME's approach to the news is an unusually fresh and engaging one. You'll be pleasantly surprised by the way in which it appeals to the intelligence and keen enthusiasms of subscribers such as you:

> From each issue's initial article on national events
> to its final trenchant book review, you'll find only
> the highest standards of writing and reporting in
> TIME. There is no tempering of tone, no sacrifice in
> style, to mar your enjoyment of its precise and uniquely
> rewarding news coverage.

With more than twenty special departments, TIME regularly delves into topics you might not otherwise have an opportunity to explore: Art, Music, Science, Education, Show Business. Not to mention all that's important to you in the fields of Politics, Business, Sport ... and so on.

Give TIME a chance, and I think you'll find it will soon become an essential part of your regular reading. It's the easiest, most stimulating way to keep up to date and still maintain your usual busy schedule.

The price you pay -- $1.87 for 21 weeks of TIME -- is just 9¢ a copy. Therefore, your savings on this introductory subscription are quite substantial.

See for yourself why so many active, successful people enjoy TIME -- and know they can depend on it, week after week. Mail your card today, and we'll bill you after your subscription begins.

Cordially,

Putney Westerfield
Circulation Manager

PW:LF

Sales Letter Stressing a "Point Of Difference"

The following letter, for example, would be far less convincing without the mention of certain highly respected customers. The use of these names makes the sales message a hundred times more convincing than if the writer had said "Many well-known companies use Stanley labels."

> Gentlemen:
>
> Do you remember the story of King Midas? You know, he was said to have the golden touch. Everything he touched turned to gold.
>
> Now, honestly, we are no Midases. But hundreds of firms— Palmolive, Wahl Pen, Colgate, Hudnut, C. C. Conn, Ltd., just to mention a few—will tell you that Stanley metal seals and labels on their packages are making *two* sales grow for them where only one grew before.
>
> A shabby, unkempt man may be just as worthy as the chap who is spic and span. But he is under a big handicap. So are many mighty good products bearing commonplace labels. Clerks are often merely order-takers. They *won't* push your goods for you.
>
> Stanley metal seals and labels do their own talking. Beautiful, artistic, distinctive, they draw the eye to *your* package, and not to your competitor's.
>
> That's why so many of the country's leading concerns are putting Stanley seals and labels on their packages. In the rich, colorful Stanley labels of deeply embossed metal, they have found the best little silent salesmen in the world.
>
> It's nothing to hear of instances where Stanley labels and seals have increased sales for manufacturers on packaged goods anywhere from 15% to 150%.
>
> And they are so modestly priced—so easy to put on. You will be delighted.
>
> Turn the page. Examine specimens of Stanley seals and labels. Then mail the enclosed card for your copy of the Stanley catalogue. Mail it today.
>
> Why not do it NOW?
>
> Sincerely yours,

On page 419 is another sales letter taken from the same field of business. It, too, has labels to offer; it, too, mentions the names of prominent customers.

The letter to poultrymen (page 420) which heralds the benefits of classified advertising features three testimonials in a most interesting fashion. Each is tagged "RESULTS" with a golden egg to tie in with the introduction.

THE TABLET & TICKET CO.
BUILDING DIRECTORIES   LABELS, EMBOSSED TAGS
CHANGEABLE LETTER SIGNS   ADVERTISING SPECIALTIES
1021 WEST ADAMS STREET, CHICAGO 7, ILLINOIS

WILLSON SPIELMANN
President

John Brown Distilleries
Rockford
Illinois

Gentlemen:

We don't claim to know the first thing about liquor and we
can't guarantee you repeat business. But - if it's new business you want, if you're looking for new customers to develop
into steady ones, here's a real tip for you.

Hiram Walker, the Schenley folks, Gooderman & Worts, Arrow,
Philip Blum, Paramount and others you know, are no longer experimenting on their labels. They know from experience that a
cleverly designed foil label creates sales and pays for itself
over and over again.

If you are not satisfied with your label and are open to suggestions, we will send you a collection of beautiful foil
label samples. Furthermore, if you wish, our Art Department
will reproduce any one of your labels on foil, through a
sketch. Then you can see exactly how your favorite brand
will appear dressed in a bright, attention-getting label produced through the Perfect-O-Cut embossed foil method.

Here is more good news, too. Modern equipment, plus quantity
production, has lowered costs, so that the finest foil label
costs surprisingly less than you would suppose.

Let us send you samples, or better yet, send us a sample of
your label, so we can submit a sketch.

No obligation to you, of course.

                              Very cordially yours,

                              Geo. L. Candler
                              THE TABLET & TICKET CO.

                                                    AREA CODE
                                                        312
Executive Offices: Chicago, Illinois.   HAymarket
NEW YORK, SAN FRANCISCO, LOS ANGELES, SEATTLE, PORTLAND, DALLAS, KANSAS CITY, ST. LOUIS, ST. PAUL, MILWAUKEE, DETROIT, BOSTON 1-3883

You've heard of the hen that laid the GOLDEN EGG

M. E. Atkinson
Hollywood Poultry Farm
Woodinville, Washington

Dear Mr. Atkinson:

   The hen that laid the golden egg is an old story. So is
it an old story that Review-Chronicle Poultry Want Ads get results
for advertisers.

RESULTS H. Kincaid, Freshlaid Farm, Colfax, Washington
writes, "Your papers have played a very important part in selling the 4,000,000 chicks we
have hatched since we have been in the business."

RESULTS Elmer Tucker, Tucker's White Leghorn Farm,
Coeur d'Alene, Idaho, writes, "The combination
of morning Review and evening Chronicle gives
an ideal advertising medium that brings results."

RESULTS I. D. Casey, Walla Walla, Washington, Pacific
Northwest pioneer poultryman, writes, "Year after
year the Casey Hatchery has used the Spokesman-
Review and Chronicle Want Ads to sell poultry
with excellent results."

   Of course, results are more interesting when you are the
person who is getting them and making the profit from the orders
Review-Chronicle Want Ads bring.

   By starting a Review-Chronicle Want Ad now you can have a
RESULT story of your own to tell before long. The poultry business
is so much better than it was two or three years ago that there is
no comparison. People are ordering chicks and breeding stock. One
large hatchery is already booked to capacity for the entire season.

   Review-Chronicle Want Ads will help you get your share of
the business.

        Yours very truly,

    THE SPOKESMAN-REVIEW and SPOKANE DAILY CHRONICLE

      J. J. Tierney
    Manager Classified Advertising Division

More About The Golden Egg

Inasmuch as those receiving the sales letter probably knew the spokesmen
personally, the effect of what they say is bound to be considerable. A possible
weakness in what is otherwise a strong message is the lack of any request
for action. In other words, the letter has no Hook. Of course, the answer to
that criticism may be that this letter is one of a series—the purpose being
to build acceptance for the power of advertising in the two papers.

  Sometimes, the testimonial may be offered in the form of an interesting
story, as is done in a sales letter to fire chiefs, composed by Advertising

Manager W. E. Cox, of the Quaker City Rubber Company, Philadelphia. The value of the story is increased because it describes the experience of another chief whose name is also mentioned.

This letter must be conceded a success, for it brought back orders totaling almost seven thousand dollars. Thus, we are again reminded that under the right circumstances letters may be as effective as salesmen; don't forget, too, that they are paid no salary.

> Dear Chief:
>
> Yeadon is a nice suburban town near Philadelphia. They are building there a new $800,000 municipal building. In the tower there's a fine new siren. It went off the other day. It's so loud and uses so much air it nearly blew the workmen off the tower. It was necessary for Wayne Ross, chief of the fire company, to go back to the smaller siren until the workmen finish the new building.
>
> Give Chief Ross credit for installing a siren that will be heard in all sections of his town. His judgment was also good when it came to the selection of fire hose, for his town uses Quaker Fire Hose. He is in good company, for many intelligent fire chiefs all over the United States, from New York to small cities, use Quaker. They are free from the worry of bursting hose when the pressure gets high and action is at fever heat.
>
> For over fifty years we have been building fire hose. The inside pages give you a graphic description of the largest single order for fire hose ever placed...and it was for Quaker.
>
> Quaker Fire Hose is built by master craftsmen who realize their responsibility to humanity. I wish you could see the care exercised in the selection of the materials, the precision in compounding the rubber, the smoothness of the tube and the uncanny accuracy of the machines in weaving the jacket, and finally, the rigid test and inspection to which every length is subjected. If you could take a trip through our plant, you'd say, "No wonder the larger cities buy Quaker Fire Hose."
>
> We have a nifty little souvenir you'll be glad to possess. Something for nothing you say? Then beware! You have to work to earn this article. Easiest kind of a job though! Just fill out the enclosed card and mail it. No postage required. We'll be looking for the card. Hope you won't disappoint us.
>
> Very truly yours,

The use of local testimony in selling is a powerful procedure, when and if the information is available to the writer. It takes time to assemble testimony of this kind, but the time is well spent. A prospect is far more

The PAUL E. STARK Company • One West Main Street • Madison 3, Wisconsin • ALpine 6-9011

Dear Sir:

   How is one to really advertise an expensive home -- one that cost a lot of money fourteen years ago when it was built, but which is now, for a number of reasons, offered at a price which places it within the reach of many of Madison's discriminating families?

   We have concluded that the best way is to address this letter to quite a number of such "discriminating families" with the hope that they might be interested for themselves or might be glad of the opportunity of passing along the information to a friend.

   We are reliably informed that the owner of this house once refused an offer of $51,000. The present owner has authorized us to accept $25,000 just a portion of the former incumbrance. That does place it within the reach of many Madison families. Does it not?

   Now about the house--its location on the highest spot in University Heights is unique. This can but be appreciated by standing in the solarium and viewing the city park system and the lakes as far as eight miles to the southeast. Because of this elevation the slightest breeze from the south and east is effective.

   The architecture is definitely Italian--tile roof, arch windows, balustrade and all. Its white cement walls are set off with green shutters and wrought iron trimmings. The front entrance is impressively done in light Italian marble with seven marble steps to the main hall.

   The first floor rooms are unusually large, the living room being 14 x 35; dining room 18 x 17 and the music room 10 x 18. Then, too, there is a solarium 12 x 32. The black Belgium marble fireplaces in the living room and dining room are a striking contrast to the light walls.

   The second floor has five bedrooms, two baths, and two sleeping porches. The English basement contains additional bedrooms, kitchen, and bath for servant accommodations.

   The two-car garage is heated and accessible from the basement.

   One immediately assumes that the cost of heating such a house would be large but we are informed that the annual fuel cost does not exceed $300.

   Perhaps you have a friend who is looking for a home. He would appreciate your passing along this information. Photographs and additional information will be mailed to you or to him at your request.

   We trust you will forgive this intrusion. We confess we go a long way to serve our clients. Perhaps we can do something in a real estate way for you sometime. If so, we should be most happy to have you call.

                                        Most cordially yours,

The Facts Make This Home Seem Worth Buying

impressed by the favorable experience of someone he knows locally, than by some generality like "Many prominent executives in your city are using our protection," or, "Many housewives in your city are delighted with the cooking qualities of this stove." In contrast would be:

> "Here are the names of banks in your city using our blanket bond insurance." (Followed by list)

> "Mrs. Doe, why not talk to Mrs. Oscar Judd, who lives in your block, about the cooking qualities of this stove? Six months ago, she purchased the same model, and by now she knows from experience all its fine points."

Use testimony when you can. It will surely increase the pull of your sales letters.

Facts and figures. You will remember from Section 3 the necessary steps in planning a sales letter. The second was to know the *facts*. The more facts you can parade in a sales letter the greater the conviction it will carry; keep in mind, of course, that facts should be interesting, pertinent to the subject, and directly or indirectly of benefit to the reader. As facts are piled one upon another, the presentation of the product or service seems to gain speed; an accumulation of power drives hard into the mind of the reader; until at the end, unable to resist such a combination of persuasive force, he is swept to the place where favorable action takes place.

The above is what happens—a mental process—when the facts are wisely chosen, interesting enough to induce reading, and move at a swift pace through the letter. Unfortunately, the result can be just the opposite, too. If the facts presented are *not* pertinent, are *not* interesting, and are *not* connected with the benefit being offered to the reader if these things are true, the letter is sure to be dull, hard to read, and slow moving. Many a sales message is doomed to failure by factual content either too remotely related to the subject, or because of the deadly dry way it is handled.

Survey with an extremely critical eye all the facts you mean to use. Be sure they *help* your cause, and not *hurt* it. Put yourself in the shoes of the man who will read what you are going to dictate. Would *you* be impressed, interested, moved to action by these same facts? Can you present them from *his* point of view, instead of glorifying the product, or satisfying company pride?

Figures put power in the following sales letter mailed to prospects by Merrill E. Jackson—starting with the question, "You would hardly think that a man could make a million dollars selling onion plants by mail, would you?"

Good Morning:

You would hardly think that a man could make a million dollars selling onion plants by mail, would you?

Yet that is essentially what Clyde H. Melton of Texas has done in the past few years. He tried growing Bermuda onion plants and selling them to his neighbors. His finances permitted him to plant only a few acres, and at first his sales were made in person.

Then he tried mail advertising. It is said he has an investment of $3,500,000.00 in the Bermuda onion plants and the means of producing them. He frequently has four to five thousand acres of irrigated land planted exclusively in Bermuda onions. He has shipped as many as one hundred million plants a day. Seeds for one crop were imported from an island off the coast of North Africa, and cost $375,000.00.

He started with a few dollars. He built a business that has gone into millions. It is another example of what can be done by mail advertising; by the right kind of copy, the right plan, and the right product—sent to the right people.

If onions can be sold successfully by mail, don't you think that your product can be successfully sold by mail too?

What it took to sell onions by mail was a well-formed plan with the right ideas and printing behind it. The same plans have sold hearses, caskets, cosmetics, raincoats, baby buggies, septic tanks—or what have you? Jackson's will be glad to submit a plan to sell your products, with money making ideas behind it—ideas that have brought from ten thousand to one hundred thousand dollars in sales per month to others.

There is no obligation to you. Just drop the enclosed card in the mail, and find out what we can suggest for your business. Then judge for yourself as to whether or not it will be as successful as the plan that sold onions.

Yours Merrill-y,

Most people do not realize how much money they pay in rent over a period of years, but in the realtor's letter on page 425, the figures tell the story to "Mary and John." Twenty-four thousand dollars wasted. "One house paid for—most people pay for *three!*"

You have seen in an earlier section how some companies manage to use their products in the construction of letterheads. Thus, while reading the letter the prospect *sees* the thing talked about. The use of samples in any form in a factual sales letter carries great conviction. The reader knows that the company has confidence in its own wares, and is not afraid to place

DOUGLAS VAN RIPER *INC.*
REALTOR & INSUROR

Douglas Van Riper
Chairman of the Board
Douglas M. Van Riper
President

154 PLANDOME ROAD
MANHASSET
LONG ISLAND

TEL. MA. 7-2800

BROOKVILLE OFFICE
Northern Blvd. & Cedar Swamp Road
MAyfair 6-1800

Dear Mary and John:

During the past ten years to my knowledge you have never paid less than $200 per month rent, and most of the time a higher amount than this. This means you have paid out approximately $24,000 for shelter during this period.

It's time to own your front door key!

As you know a tenant takes no credit on his income tax for rent, whereas if you are an owner, your mortgage interest and taxes are deductible, which would reflect a great saving on both federal and state income taxes. Furthermore, each month as you make a mortgage payment you add to the equity in your home and in a specified number of years you will own it outright. Pride of ownership not only for you but for your children will really pay dividends in satisfaction, security, prestige, and in many other ways. It pays to have your roots down.

Renters rarely retire. How true this is. Don't you think it's time you became a home owner and enjoy the manifold blessings and benefits of home ownership?

I am sure if you analyze the situation you will find that you have paid for at least one house so far. Most people pay for three. Why not own one now? May we show you how easily this can be accomplished?

Cordially yours,

Douglas Van Riper

Douglas Van Riper:f

MEMBER OF LONG ISLAND AND MANHASSET REAL ESTATE BOARDS

Figures Used to Sell Home Ownership

evidence of quality in his hands for inspection. Naturally, the confidence of the company and its representative carries over to the reader. This tends to increase the pull of the letter in a manner hardly possible otherwise. The quality talked about is a *fact* actually demonstrated, and not merely a word description.

Of course, the use of samples in letters is limited by the nature of the product. You cannot attach a can of peas or stewed tomatoes to a sales letter—or an outboard motor, a vacuum cleaner, or a furnace. But the use of many other products is not so restrictive. For example, in the following letter the Ohio Rubber Company attempts to sell a safety flooring. The writer couldn't attach a large enough piece to prove how easy and safe the material is to walk on, but he could and does send along a sample two inches square. It is glued on the upper right-hand corner of the letter-head—a visible proof of quality.

> Gentlemen:
>
> That small square you see above is a sample of Orco Safety Flooring.
>
> Try rubbing your thumb over it. Do, you notice the resistance it gives? Well, imagine walking on an area covered with this material—you'd feel safe and it would be comfortable, too.
>
> Your rubber heels have taught you that rubber is resilient—comfortable. You also know that you feel safe with them as well. We combine those natural qualities of rubber with wear-resisting abrasive Norton Alundum for extra safety, add an attractive color, and we get Orco Safety Flooring.
>
> It is the best insurance against accidents due to falls that we know of.
>
> And speaking of falls, I hope this request for payment of your past-due account for August, amounting to $15.00, does not fall into the discard. We imagine our first request for payment slipped your attention. This bit of Orco Safety Flooring is to prevent that, and to establish your interest in our new material. May we expect your check soon, and an inquiry regarding our new product?
>
> Very truly yours,

Combination collection and sales letters are infrequently used in business. Perhaps there should be more of them!

Printing companies have a natural advantage in the use of samples in their sales letters. In the first place, the letterhead itself speaks for the quality of the business, although sometimes it does not speak as convincingly as it should. Also, it is easy for the printer or lithographer to enclose some evidence of his originality and skill. Blotters, for example, are doubly good; they serve a useful purpose as well as sample the company's work. Mailed once a month throughout the year, they keep the sender's name constantly before the prospect, as a blotter is something seldom discarded. The following letter includes such a reminder.

> Gentlemen:
>
> Here's your March blotter.
>
> It has been said, "Whichever way the wind doth blow, someone is glad to have it so." Well, we won't argue because we've been told that you can't sell and argue in the same breath, and we're supposed to make this letter SELL SOMETHING.
>
> SELLING SOMETHING in our case naturally means printing, and the services pertaining thereto so back to the blotter.
>
> The last two blotters we've sent to you portray a different technique in art work; also, a little different type of printing. The art is what we call a free poster style. The printing is done from rubber plates, and is particularly adapted to the style of art work for comparatively short runs.
>
> Do you like it?
>
> Perhaps you have something in mind that could be handled this way—a counter card, calendar, poster, label, blotter, placard, or any other item where masses of color and a small amount of detail work is desired. This economical process fits any of those needs.
>
> To have more details as to cost and application to your job, USE THE CARD; or maybe you are considering another type of printing. We're still interested. Again, just use the card.
>
> > Sincerely yours,

The reference to the blowing of the wind in the Star of the above letter was a tie-in with the illustration on the blotter—a man trying to hold his umbrella against a high wind. Another handy part of the blotter is a calendar for March. This mailing, one of a monthly series by the McCormick-Armstrong Company, of Wichita, Kansas, was made with excellent results.

4. SALES LETTERS SLANTED AT SPECIAL GROUPS

The third step in planning. As you will recall, the third step in planning a business letter (Section 3) is to visualize the reader. Then, in the later steps, the arguments are selected that seem most likely to win that particular individual's favor. This procedure is of special importance in sales letters. The ability of the sales-letter writer to match approach and content with the mental reader-picture determines whether or not the letter is to succeed or fail.

Even when the sales letter is directed to *one* prospect, the problem of making the "match" is not simple, unless the writer knows the addressee's characteristics and buying habits. When the letter goes to a *number* of possible buyers, and must be slanted at them all collectively, then the problem is extremely difficult. Nevertheless, for certain groups in which the members are closely related in ways of living, type of work, degree of wealth, education, or other similar respects, it is usually possible to form a *composite* mental picture that may be used as a guide in preparing the letter.

Obviously, a sales message aimed at business executives should not use the same approach or arguments as might be appropriate in a letter about the same product or service to a group of clerical or factory workers. In the same way, the approach and content would differ in a letter to college professors and students; professional men and laymen; politicians of the "left-wing" variety and those known to be conservative; members of a University Club and manual laborers; chorus girls and choir singers; society women and wives of factory workers; literary men and baseball players; and on through a thousand other comparisons. To be sure, we are citing average cases rather than exceptional ones. In any group mailing, there must be assumed to exist a certain percentage of waste—variations from the typical composite picture. All the sales-letter writer can do is touch as many of the group as possible by the appeal to common interests; to keep the percentage of "misses" as low as could humanly be expected.

The types of groups to which sales letters may be addressed are as numerous as the leaves on a tree, but they tend to become standardized for a specific company; at least, as to the number that must be approached. A company offering expensive overcoats for men is not bothered about how to sell them to women or to men of low income. A company publishing a so-called "high-brow" magazine is not likely to mail a sales letter to a list of factory workers. The manager of the local dance hall is not concerned with selling a course of dancing lessons to elderly people. For each kind of product or service there are likely to be well-defined groups of potential buyers. What kind of people they are, and how they commonly react, tends to become known as the sales-letter writer continues on the job.

Probably, there is no greater degree of difference in buying habits, and the appeals that match them, than between men and women. The two letters that follow illustrate how this difference influenced the sales approach for exactly the same type of service.

1. *The Letter to Women*

Dear Mrs. Doe:

Of course, her name is confidential, but she is one of the social leaders in our city—probably, quite well known to you. She came last week to have her eyes examined, and seldom in my thirty years' experience have I encountered such a pitiful example of visual neglect. You see, for a long time this lady had suspected the need of glasses, but she couldn't stand the thought of wearing them. She was afraid they would detract from her beauty.

So year after year, she had suffered with headaches, and nerves on edge. Once, fine embroidery had been her hobby, but she gave it up because she couldn't see the stitches. Even reading had been abandoned—the type would dance and blur after a page or two in any book. She finally gave up the struggle and came almost tearfully to ask my advice.

But the sad part of this story is that when I helped her select the glasses for her type of features, she was amazed to find they made her even more beautiful than before. All those years she could have been protecting her eyes without the slightest detraction from her physical charm.

I think a lot of women are like this society leader—they suffer in silence because they do not know how cleverly nowadays glasses are custom-built for every style of beauty. Now, I don't mean that *you* are having the same experience, but I do know you will be glad that never will you have to worry about glasses spoiling your beauty. And if you will pardon me for saying so, there is no one who knows better than I do what glasses to recommend for each style of feminine personality.

In fact, stop in at my office on State Street any day next week, and I'll be glad to show you dozens of styles in glasses—how each one is designed to add charm to a different type of beauty. It's a demonstration in which you will be tremendously interested—so please do come next week.

Yours very sincerely,

That letter to women attempts to do only two things: first, remind the readers what dreadful things can happen if eyes are neglected; second, to answer the fear that glasses may detract from beauty. The second appeal, of course, plays the major role.

But what about men? Are they worried so much about glasses detracting from their appearance? Well, a few might have that objection, but certainly not the great majority. How *can* they, then, be induced to have their eyes examined?

2. *The Letter to Men*

Dear Mr. Doe:

A businessman doesn't want to be bothered with a long letter... so I'll make this a short one.

Nowadays there is such a fine line between profit and loss, that all of us are constantly seeking ways to increase efficiency without increasing cost.

Has it ever occurred to you that your eyes have more to do with your efficiency on the job than any other factor over which you have control?

Strained or tired eyes sap vitality, foster sleepiness, and weaken the power to concentrate. And the strange part of it all is that you, yourself, can seldom tell when your eyes are causing these troubles.

But your efficiency is diminished surely.

The only way of assuring that your eyes are up to par is to have them examined about once a year. And we would like to perform that service.

If an examination shows that you need glasses, our reputation for dependability will guarantee the best. If you don't need glasses, we will be frank in telling you so.

But not knowing is not good business. Come in some day this week, and let us give you a quick but thorough examination. You couldn't make a better investment of the half hour it will take.

Sincerely yours,

Women, glasses will not spoil your beauty. Men, protect your efficiency on the job. How widely apart are those two reasons for eye examinations; and yet, could they be more intelligently chosen to hit their respective marks.

Other sales letters to women. It is not our intention to imply that the *only* thing of interest to women is their personal appearance. As a group, they are receptive to many other approaches—the one most effective depending on the nature of the product or service being offered, their special interests, and their place in the social pattern. A woman may be attracted to a new food product because one of her chief delights is setting a good table; because it may contribute to her children's health; because it is something different to serve at parties; because she thinks her husband may like it; because it is reputed to be a good conditioner against old age;

because it is cheaper than some similar product she has been using; because—oh, because of many other reasons. For a particular sales letter, the problem is to decide which of the many approaches has the greatest chance of touching the largest number of the group.

The following sales letter used by Marshall Field & Company is based on the fact that just before Easter so many women are thinking what to wear on that Sunday—it solves the problem with the lure of New York styles to be had at very attractive prices. The women were asked to be in the store on a Thursday morning—it may be assumed that this particular department of Field's was crowded at that time.

The Letter from Field's

My dear Madam:

I have such good news for you that I'm sending this letter from New York to ask you to save time on Thursday, April 25, for a visit to Fields to let me tell you more about it.

The days just before Easter are the most favorable time of the whole year to buy in the wholesale clothes market. Spring coats, suits and dresses, finished too late for delivery to the retail stores before Easter, may be bought at extraordinarily low prices. The good news is that Fields again has turned this situation into an enormous advantage to its customers.

We (the buyers for the departments on the Sixth Floor and in the Evanston and Oak Park stores) hurried to New York last Thursday, found some of the most charming Spring clothes we've seen all season, and bought them for prices that make it possible to sell them for $29.95 each. Of course, there are just a few of each style, and not complete colors and sizes, but there are hundreds of styles from which to select.

We are bringing many of them home on the train with us. We aren't taking time for a newspaper advertisement—instead, we're rushing these letters off, and tucking into them some hasty sketches to give you an idea of the clothes.
Aren't they grand? Do come in as early as you can on Thursday morning. I want to show you the things before any of them are gone.

Yours most sincerely,

On pages 432 and 433 are two additional letters aimed specifically at women readers. The first sells the services of a Beauty Shoppe to newcomers in the city—a form letter for new residents. The second asks wives to help their husbands sell tickets to the Lion's Bingo Party, the funds to be used for a charitable purpose.

Beauty For Sale At Lowest Possible Cost

Dear Mrs. Snyder:

These are BUSY days for you. Moving to a new city always means a lot of running around, trying to become familiar with the shopping district, and how to get here and there.

When you say to yourself "I wonder where I can find a good Beauty Shop" you need not bother looking around for one moment, because our shop is the EASIEST to find...and the most popular in the entire city.

We are located in the very heart of the business district, on historic old "Penn Square"...at the southwest corner of Fifth and Penn Streets.

Here you will find 18 *experienced,* licensed beauty operators ready to give you personal, careful attention. We employ the largest personnel in the city, in order to serve our many satisfied customers speedily and efficiently. Because of the large volume of our business we are in a position to offer you the fairest possible prices for high class workmanship!

Won't you give us the pleasure of serving you real soon? Our phone number is XY2-1500...I suggest that you phone for an appointment to avoid unnecessary "waiting".

Cordially yours,

R. J. Rickert, Manager

An Appeal To Reader's Sympathy

Just for one minute, Mrs. Jones...

...picture yourself in THIS position with Christmas coming on—Suppose you were twenty-one, a young wife and mother prematurely grown old with the worries and strife of life. Suppose you had a husband who tried his best, but was the victim of unfortunate circumstances and sometimes could not bring home enough food for the table. CHRISTMAS would be sad enough for you two, but you both would be old enough to understand and bravely "make the best of it."

But suppose you had a little girl, a good youngster, and as deserving of Santa's blessings as any other child. And as Christmas day draws near, you are both sorry for her because you do not want her to know how selfish and cruel the world can be.

If only this day of days would not have to be a meaningless, drab day for her, who has never had much cause to smile as other children smile.

Like other mothers in this sad position, you would find it hard to put your child to bed and know that there would be no Christmas for her.

Imagine then your utter happiness if, to your complete surprise, someone would notify you that your child was invited to attend the Lions' Club Christmas Party for deserving, underprivileged children—that she would enjoy a good warm dinner with all the trimmings—could sit on Santa's lap and get a few little toys and things to wear and fruit and candy that would bring her joy for many, many days to come.

Wouldn't you and your husband be thrilled, for her sake? Wouldn't you be thankful that the Welfare Committee of the Lions Club had been so thoughtful? Of course you would, and you will want to help us make our Annual Christmas Party a grand success this year, by attending the special Lions' Bingo Party described on the attached sheet.

Your husband has been assigned ten tickets. *Please* help him sell them, and more, if possible. One of our members has already sold over fifty tickets to friends in bridge clubs, etc. The success of our Christmas Party this year depends largely upon the success of this Bingo Party which is being sponsored to raise additional funds. So please do your best, for the sake of the sixty-five unfortunate boys and girls we're going to entertain on December 23rd!

Appreciatively yours,

WELFARE COMMITTEE

The two letters illustrating different approaches to women were used in Reading, Pennsylvania, and were prepared for the respective clients by Beaumont, Heller & Sperling, a firm which has helped many merchants with ideas and copy for sales letters.

Letters slanted at men. As we saw in the letters to women and to men about eye examinations, what may be a good approach to the one sex is not likely to be good for the other. It is true that men and women may be equally interested in the purchase of many things—a home, an automobile, tickets to take them on a vacation trip, membership in a book club, an insurance policy, and thousands of others. But the *reasons* that impel the purchase may be far apart. A sales letter to women about a vacation hotel might properly talk about the luxurious appointments, the social activities, the famous people who are frequent guests, and the facilities for reducing baths; whereas to men, the things talked about might be the nearby trout-filled stream, the thick steaks served in the dining room, the poker room, the facilities for keeping in touch with the grain and stock markets, and the polo field where famous teams compete.

Furthermore, sales letters to men must differ in content and approach according to the nature of the respective group—their financial level, their social position, their occupation, and the many other factors that might influence their reactions. For example, the following letter, used by Alexander Hamilton Institute, is directed at young men in business who have yet to reach high position. To *them,* the letter should have considerable appeal; to *executives* near the top, it would probably fall on barren soil.

My dear Sir:

I once figured that I throw into my wastebasket every year at least $50.00 worth of literature which people send me in the mistaken notion that I have nothing to do but read.

You are probably in the same position.

I mention this frankly because we have just published and are sending without cost to interested men a booklet entitled "Forging Ahead in Business." It's rather unusual. Just as an insurance company, from its study of millions of men, can make a pretty shrewd guess as to how long you will live; so, from our twenty-five years of watching men promote themselves through business study, we have a good measure of just what a normal man can accomplish in six months, twelve months, eighteen months, and two years of definitely guided effort.

We have put the results of that experience into this booklet and I want to get a copy into the hands of every man who has a real reason to be interested in it. But I don't want to feed anybody's waste basket.

Will you tell me frankly whether it's worthwhile to send this book to you?

Of course the book has a good deal to say about the work of this Institute but it also deals with problems you are facing every day. We do not claim that the Institute meets every man's needs, but if you are on the lookout for broader business knowledge, then what we have to offer is invaluable to you.

The Institute has reached a point of national acceptance in the business world; its problem is not one of RECRUITING but of SELECTING the men who can get the most from its service in the shortest time. In this process of selecting we try to appeal only to mature men who are actively engaged in business. We have nothing to offer boys and can be of no service to men who are not keenly interested in business.

We want you to decide for yourself whether or not the booklet is intended for you. If you are not interested in business training, don't send for it. If you are seeking new ways to add to your knowledge of business, we want ·you to have a copy with our compliments. Simply fill in and mail the enclosed card and the booklet will reach you by return mail.

Cordially yours,

The level on which the above sales letter travels is quite plain. It is trying to reach men in business who represent neither of the two extremes in attainment; neither the top executives nor the novices, but those in between who are mature enough to know what business is about, young enough to be reaching for greater success. The idea of letting the reader qualify himself to get the booklet is also worth noting. In this letter it is very cleverly handled, but it might be difficult in the hands of a beginner.

A moment ago you read Field's letter to women. Here is how Saks Fifth Avenue approaches men. The tone of the letter is light and pleasing, but still in good taste for business executives. The offer presented solves a problem which bothers many men near Christmas time. It must have brought orders to Saks.

My dear Mr. Doe:

We spent about three hundred days getting thousands of rare gifts under one roof. We know that men appreciate them because they are rare and hard to find. Our only problem now is to bring together all the busy men who want them. But *this* is where our Gift Counsellors come in.

The Gift Counsellor, a fast-moving, quick-witted young person, is our "middle-man" between a store full of rare gifts, and the busy executive. You will find her, and her associates, in the Main Floor Foyer near the elevators. She will select the entire list of gifts for you, getting your official scrutiny on them all, have them wrapped and sent, and not budge the budget if you say so.

Call her—up to 6 P.M.—for an appointment, and you will find your Christmas shopping the most painless you ever did.

Cordially,

Another sales letter that seeks to solve the same shopping problem is one mailed to business firms and executives by Berea College Student Industries. In the letter from Saks, the emphasis was on saving time for the busy executive; in this one, there is the added possibility of helping mountain boys and girls get an education. As has been pointed out, a lot can be learned about business letter writing by *comparing* the efforts of those working toward similar objectives. Which of these two sales letters developed the most business?

Gentlemen:

Once a year we have a chance to write this kind of letter, and we get a big kick out of it. So here goes.

You know Berea's story—how we make it possible for seventeen hundred boys and girls from the mountains to get an education by means of our Student Industries. No fancy frills here, just downright earnestness and hard work. You and your organization have had a part in this enterprise.

We can show our appreciation by extending to you our wholesale prices. And you can show your approval of Berea's work at this Christmas season to your own benefit and satisfaction.

How? Give to your preferred customers, to your own staff, or to your personal friends, a remembrance which comes from Berea. If you are racking your brain now for something different, give our suggestion an ear.

All we ask is that you allow your secretary or some volunteer to act as a clearing house. Orders can be pooled then, and we can make shipment economically.

And does this sound familiar? Please give us your orders as *early* as you can, specifying a later shipping date if you wish, so we can serve you as well as you have served us.

Very cordially yours,

In writing a sales letter to executives, it is well to remember characteristics which they generally possess. Disregard of any one of these characteristics is likely to destroy the letter's chance for success.

1. He is interested in anything that will improve the operation of his business: the conservation of time or money; the speeding of production; new ideas or methods to better the quality of his products; anything that will smooth employee relations.

2. He has many responsibilities, and has no time of his own to waste in reading long-winded letters. This does not mean that he will react unfavorably to a long letter, provided it is direct, factual, and *worth* his attention.

3. He is serious-minded, and expects to be met in the same spirit. Letters of too light a tone, such as might be sent to younger men, tend to irritate him and handicap the effectiveness of the letter.

4. He reads quickly, and likes his information in condensed form without unnecessary explanation. This means he appreciates simple language, and any other devices that help him to grasp the "meat" of the message—tabulations, sum-

maries of facts, captions that lead him surely from one point to another.

The characteristics mentioned above seem to have been carefully respected in the two letters that follow. They were used by the TelAutograph Corporation; the first pulled a 25 per cent response, and the second 15 per cent. The two mailings were separated by a three-week interval. Although a form-letter job, the first letter achieved some personalization by the fill-in of the reader's name at the beginning of the fourth paragraph.

1. *The Opening Shot*

We have just completed a job for you. We are now ready to submit, in folder form, the results of our experience in working with basic systems and procedures of a sizable cross section of manufacturing companies. We invite you to accept copies without charge and without feeling obligated in any way.

These folders will prove valuable to you as a check on your own operations. They offer you a means of comparing your own systems with those of other plants. You'll find much helpful information in them that may enable you to cut corners in time and cost.

Our facts are based on actual in-the-plant surveys made by specially trained engineers—aided in many companies by executives like yourself. They represent our experience in a cross section of plants, both small and large, differing widely in physical layouts, nature of products, and in volume of business.

Mr. Doe, other manufacturers of equipment such as your own have basically similar procedures. Of course, they vary in terminology and in scope for different types of business and for different plant sizes—simple in small plants and complex in large ones.

We present six basic systems: SALES ORDER...PRODUCTION PLANNING AND SCHEDULING...INSPECTION AND QUALITY CONTROL...WAREHOUSING AND SHIPPING...JOB COST ANALYSIS.....OFFICE RECORDS, CREDITS, AND CASHIERING. Each of these systems is discussed fully in an easy-to-read, graphically illustrated four-page folder. Three such folders are now ready to be placed in your hands.

SALES ORDER—Answers such questions as: What is the crucial test of an efficient sales order procedure? What are other companies doing to keep their hard-won customers from slipping through their fingers?—by insuring fast, errorless service on orders...avoiding slip-ups on delivery promises...handling unexpected delays and order changes easily and quickly.

PRODUCTION PLANNING AND SCHEDULING—Gives you a quick picture of a typical planning and scheduling system. Tells how companies have developed systems that enable them to plan production on quick-turnover basis...how they get quick action on schedule changes...stop production on not-so-urgent stock items...make way for rush orders...and keep inventories at a minimum. Discusses management's problem of correlating the responsibilities of the production and sales departments.

INSPECTION AND QUALITY CONTROL—Show what other companies are doing to reduce their scrap losses, lower salvaging costs, hold down "off-standard" products, or "seconds," and eliminate production delays due to late reports from laboratories. Cites specific examples in six different types of industries.

Experiences summarized in folder form, analyzing the last three of the six procedures, are now "in work." These will be available to you in a short time. All have this single purpose—to help executives like yourself compare their present mode of operation with systems now in use in other companies.

Since we are sending these folders without charge or obligation, it occurs to us that you may want copies sent to several of your department heads or systems men—in addition to your own copies. Please feel free to requisition as many as you need.

To avoid unnecessary delays in getting them to you, we are enclosing a convenient requisition form. Please check which of the folders you desire for yourself, and which ones we should send to other men in your company. Slip this form into the stamped envelope attached and drop it into your out-going mail.

Cordially yours,

2. *The Follow-Up*

A short time ago I wrote you in regard to several new folders we've prepared for free distribution to the management of a cross section of manufacturing companies. As mentioned in my previous letter, these folders summarize our company's experience during many years past in working with basic manufacturing systems and procedures.

I firmly believe that you'll find these folders, as described in the leaflet enclosed, of great value. Each one represents a system common to your plant, to ours, and to the majority of all plants. These folders not only offer you a means of comparing your own operating procedures with those in other plants, but included is a considerable amount of helpful information designed to aid you in cutting time and cost in your operations.

Since I wrote you, we've received requests from hundreds of executives like yourself, manifesting great interest in our presentation of systems. We've supplied these men with copies, as well as their various department heads and systems men.

May I repeat my invitation to you to obtain copies of these folders. They will be sent to you without charge or obligation. We want you to feel perfectly free to request as many copies as you need—for yourself and for other men in your company responsible for basic operations.

A requisition form and stamped addressed envelope are enclosed for your convenience in requesting copies. Please check which of the folders you desire, and which ones we should send to other men in your company. It will be a pleasure to see that they are sent without delay.

Very truly yours,

In this letter and the follow-up, signed by "W. F. Vieh, President," we have the practical demonstration of one executive talking to another. Obviously, Mr. Vieh should have known, and did, the language of his group. Both letters put the emphasis on things dearest to the heart of the average executive—methods, costs, how to cut corners. To younger men of less experience in business, these two messages would have been tiresome; to the executives *for whom intended,* they are just the opposite.

An interesting digression of no great consequence is—why did Mr. Vieh use "Cordially yours" as the complimentary close in his letter, and "Very truly yours," in his follow-up?

The offer to solve a problem. Shot-in-the-dark sales letters which assume the reader has a problem that the writer proposes to overcome can be extremely irritating. You have probably received letters which start, "Here is the answer to your fuel problem," or with some other equally brash statement. It may be that you are living in a hotel, or are blessed with the finest type of heating equipment—the writer puts the problem in your lap whether it belongs there or not. Unless the assumption happens to hit the mark, letters of this type promptly tell the reader that he is only a name on a list, and that the writer *hopes* he will be interested.

On the other hand, the approach may be quite all right if the problem is known to exist. The reader then feels that you have come to him with a helping hand, and he willingly continues to see just how valuable your assistance may turn out to be. For example, the program chairman of any business group is likely to welcome an offer to solve the problem of finding speakers or talent for entertainment. The following letter is of his type, and it does a very good job.

Dear Mr. Doe:

When you plan the entertainment for your coming convention, you naturally want the very best that your budget will afford.

You are eager to give your members something they will long remember and talk about.

But probably you are saying, "Where can I turn for talent? Who can be trusted not to let me down?"

Well, Mr. Doe, that question is my cue. I've been helping other program chairmen with their shows for fifteen years, and I can just as surely help YOU. It doesn't matter what kind of entertainment you want—musicians, dancers, singers, actors, magicians, novelty acts—I am able to give you the best. You can have your pick of local talent, or I can bring you artists from other cities who are tops in their specialty. And the cost in either case will be a lot lower than you may expect.

This isn't just an idle statement on my part. Many businessmen in Columbus will tell you that Dorothy Doe knows *how* to plan and stage an entertainment which really goes over in a big way. You tell me what you want—how much you can spend—and I do the rest. You won't need to worry about the success of your show, or the danger of getting a lemon when you thought you had a plum.

A reply to this letter will bring me to your office any time you wish. I have pictures and press notices to show you that are very helpful in deciding what acts to use.

Please do give me the opportunity to give you the benefit of my experience. You will be under no obligation to follow my suggestions, but I *do* have ideas which will make your entertainment the best you have ever had.

When *can* I see you, Mr. Doe?

Sincerely yours,

In the letter-situation just reviewed, the assumption of a problem was logical and not just a guess. The offer to solve it is pleasingly made, and sounds convincing.

Letters to occupational classes. To approach effectively the members of a class engaged in the same kind of work or activity, the sales-letter writer must have a reasonable knowledge of what they are doing, their special needs, and how the benefits of the product or service offered may touch their daily activities. The more he knows about these things, the better he is able to select the best appeal for the particular problem. In a letter to army officers, H. N. Fisch, sales manager for H. J. Justin & Sons, uses pride in immaculate appearance as the appeal because he knew that military men are especially receptive to it. Also, to gain their interest, he starts his letter with the story of Napoleon's reprimand after the battle of Jena.

Dear Major Doe:

History tells us that Napoleon, recognized as the greatest military genius of his day, was a "stickler" in matters pertaining to the neatness of his officers and enlisted men, although he himself dressed rather slovenly.

Reviewing his troops after the battle of Jena, October 14, 1806, he severely reprimanded one of his higher officers because of the appearance of his uniform and his mud bespattered boots. This officer, being next in command, first excused his appearance with the statement that the previous day had been a strenuous one, and he had not found time to clean up; then commented on the fact that the uniform of the great Napoleon was also rather disreputable.

The great General's reply is interesting: "Only Napoleon can afford to dress and do as Napoleon does." But I venture to suggest there is one thing that even Napoleon overlooked—the importance of setting a good example for those of lower rank.

On regular duty, as you so well realize, you dress properly to retain the respect of the men under your command. On the Parade Ground, in the Hotel Lobby, on the Ball Room Floor, and among your fellow officers, you maintain the appearance of one who is interested in reflecting the dignity of the rank designated to you.

There isn't anything that improves the personal appearance of an officer as does a pair of neat, snappy, well-built Army boots. They are a mark of distinction, an insignia that pictures your pride of service to your country—and their selection means much to you.

The enclosed folder illustrates and describes some of Justin's finest boots; built to exacting specifications and bearing a trade mark of 54 years of satisfactory dealings as your guarantee. Boots that are unsurpassed by any American or foreign makers.

Perhaps, you have been saying to yourself, "I really need a new pair of boots." With the attractive prices now in effect, this is decidedly the time to buy.

Yours very truly,

Perhaps you are thinking that the foregoing sales letter is interesting enough, but that it lacks evidence to prove the quality and attractiveness of the boots. That would be true were it not for the folder mentioned in the next to the last paragraph. In it, six steps in the making of Justin Boots are described, with pictures of different workmen illustrating each step. The copy with the "steps" is done in very human language, and helps to make the sale. Here are the six steps:

1. When your order comes in, either John or Earl Justin carefully compares the measurements you have given. They have hundreds of wooden feet to select from, but they must get the correct one, for the fit of the boot depends upon the last— and Custom Built Justin Boots are guaranteed to fit. We also keep a record of your foot so you may reorder at any time.

2. The second step is to take the last selected for you, and build an exact duplicate of your actual foot—little pieces of leather must be added to take care of corns, bunions, broken bones or any irregularities that may be necessary. Our Superintendent, S. E. Brady, has been duplicating feet in wood for over 35 years—Justin Boot wearers know that he knows his stuff.

3. From these built-up wooden feet, patterns must be made to cut the leather by. Hides are not the same all over so knowledge and skill must be used in cutting to secure the best part of the leather. Our pattern maker has a gift of cutting leather so that the separate pieces have an even quality and color. This skill in making, selecting and cutting the hides assures you of perfectly matched and fitted boots.

4. The tops of Boots are individual—they reflect taste—they show hobbies—they are the real "front" of a boot. To have beautifully stitched tops it requires an artist, and Vane Justin is just that—for he has designed and stitched cowboy boots for over eighteen years. He can create the most fascinating designs with his varied-color silk threads—he uses silk thread because it wears longer and gives a boot class.

5. The vamps are soaked and crimped on boards where they stretch and dry for twenty-four hours. This step is the one that controls the future shape of your boot—for all the stretch must be taken out of the leather. It is interesting to watch this expert work. He knows just how long to soak each grade of leather—for he has stretched thousands of pairs of vamps during the years he has worked in the Justin plant.

6. Now your boot takes shape—comes to life. It is hand lasted— which means the tops are joined to the bottoms, the insole, the counter and practically everything except the outersole— even a strip of 10-ounce pre-shrunk duck reinforcing is added. The boots stay on the last eight to twelve days and are then finished with the outersole and heel. Pat Rix has been doing hand lasting for over ten years—and Justin Boots reflect his skill.

A strong feature of this copy describing boots in the making is the use of the workmen's names, and the telling of their many years of experience in the plant. And the personal touch is strengthened by the pictures of the men talked about!

In many cases, the sales-letter writer has a strong argument in the story of how his product is manufactured, but the difficulty in using it is that the body of the letter becomes too long. Mr. Fisch got around this barrier by using the three page, 8½ x 11 inch folder—a device open to anyone with the same problem. The letter on the first page serves the purpose of getting the reader interested enough to look inside; the story there goes ahead to complete the sale. Actually, the Star and the Hook are in the letter; the bulk of the Chain appears on the inside pages.

Another sales message of the same type is one that was sent to school teachers by the Fidelity Investment Association, Wheeling, West Virginia. The letter on the first page aims for attention and interest by telling the story of a teacher who is enjoying life in Florida because she followed the company's Income Reserve Plan. Then on the inside pages desire is awakened by additional copy and pictures. The whole would be too much for the ordinary letter form. The key-note of the inside sales copy is the caption: "When the zest for your job is lacking...when working days are over...GO *where* you please—when you please...there's nothing to prevent!" The choice of this appeal is evidence that the writer understood one of the biggest worries of the average school teacher—how to accumulate money for old age, and to have enough to do some of the things that were impossible during the many classroom years.

Good as the letter is, it would not do the job if left to stand alone, for the Hook is merely a question and suggests no action. However, as was true of the letter to Army officers, the inside pages complete the job; also, this mailing is one of a series of three mailed by the company to teachers, and did not have to carry the entire load.

Dear Miss Doe:

Last winter—when a blizzard hit Chicago, Anne Andrus, Chicago school teacher, went to Florida.

You will be interested in the following paragraph from the letter she wrote to us from St. Petersburg.

> "The reason I am able to bask in the sunshine all day with pleasant companions, surrounded by blossoming plants, growing fruits and tropical birds, while your Northern newspapers are carrying headlines about zero weather, is because I adopted the Fidelity Plan some years ago...I do not attribute my good fortune to

either wisdom or luck. It was because I felt that here was something that would compel me to save systematically. And while there were times when it pinched a bit, especially during the long summer vacations, I managed—and now I am thankful that I did."

What Anne Andrus did—you, too, can do! Only you will find it infinitely easier with the new and improved Income Reserve Plan, which calls for no deposits during the teachers' vacation season.

The Income Reserve Plan, sponsored by this twenty-five year old, $27,000,000 company, is safe—simple—convenient. Accumulating money is made easy, almost automatic. And each month finds you nearer your financial goal.

If you've found it difficult to save in the past—if you are not satisfied with the money you have accumulated to date, isn't it time you gave the Income Reserve Plan your most earnest consideration?

Sincerely yours,

Examples of sales letters to different types of occupational groups are far too numerous for complete coverage in any business book, but the most important principle in preparing any of these messages is always the same— acquaint yourself with the problems of the particular group, and try to connect your sales message with one or more of them. You have seen how this was done in Mr. Fisch's letter to military men, and in the letter to school teachers. Here are a few sales letters that went prospecting in other fields. In each case, the appeal is to some special interest or activity of a particular reader.

Sales Letter to Doctors

Dear Doctor:

"QUIET ZONE," say the street signs in front of your hospitals. And even the most careless of us give heed.

"Absolute rest and quiet," you prescribe for your patients. And gradually, as we learn the value of silence elsewhere than in the sick room, we eliminate noise from our offices and our homes.

The kitchen can be in a "Quiet Zone," too. Clatter and noise need no longer go hand in hand with automatic refrigeration. Servel, the Gas Refrigerator, has changed all that.

Servel freezes with heat—without machinery—no noise, no loud starting and stopping. The chilling action is continuous—and silent. Servel produces constant, healthful cold, and ice cubes aplenty, with never a whisper of sound—and saves its price in food and ice.

Knowing as you do, doctor, all about the cost of operations, I believe you will be much interested in the cost of operation by Servel. I should like the opportunity of giving you (briefly, of course) this and some other facts about this remarkable refrigerator.

Will you mail the card, please, permitting me to call?

Yours very truly,

The above letter seeks to use the language of the medical man, and the comparisons are taken from his professional life. Below, the same company approaches lawyers in a different way—*their* way.

Sales Letter to Lawyers

Dear Sir:

Haven't you often heard of cases where the true facts were so inconceivable that the strongest sort of testimony was necessary to obtain a favorable verdict?

It is hard to believe that ice cubes can be made by heat, that a constant temperature of 50° and less can be maintained in a refrigerator without machinery of any kind. Yet Servel, the Gas Refrigerator, does just this. "Incredible," you'll say until you know the true facts in the case.

I want to tell you in very few words, as a good witness should, the story of Servel. I know you will find it amazingly interesting.

Will you return the enclosed card summoning me for questioning?

Yours very truly,

Unless they were teaching those subjects, the comparisons used in the letters to the experts in medicine and law would have little interest or significance in a sales message to college professors. But the latter are receptive to any classroom help—and that's where the emphasis is placed in the next letter.

Sales Letter to College Professors

Dear Professor:

I am writing to extend a cordial invitation for you to join us as a Life subscriber at Life's special Educator's Rate—which saves you $1.00 under the regular subscription price.

But it would be presumptuous of me to claim that you should see Life each week because it is a "textbook" in the accredited sense. It is not.

Life is a running visual record of the world in which we live. . .
and that is exactly why I believe you as a college faculty member
will find Life not only absorbing to see and read yourself, but a
classroom tool of very real value.

> For Life has undertaken to record, with all the dis-
> crimination and intelligence its readers expect of it, one
> of the world's most critical eras. . .to record it with all
> the fact-gathering facilities available to man. . .to
> record it as a living history.

And because from the very beginning Life's editors have held
that the news is not all in the headlines, Life has developed a
new form of pictorial journalism, a form uniquely qualified to
present news of the normal pursuits of life, news of the forefronts
of knowledge, news of this era's cultures—and make the significance of that news immediately apparent.

So I believe Life will prove useful in your classroom, interesting
in your home. And I hope you will take advantage of the Educator's Rate of only $3.50 *for a full year* of Life (instead of the
regular $4.50 price) —

—by filling out the enclosed nontransferable card and returning it to me today.

Cordially,

Sales Letter to Laundries
[A Dartnell presentation]

AN OPEN LETTER TO
ALL LAUNDRIES:

Every so often, you buy tags of one style or another to mark
bundles for delivery. Perhaps you've often considered changing
your present tags, so you could get more value for the money
you spend.

After making all sorts of laundry tags for many years, we naturally have a lot of ideas about them. We know that many
laundries are constantly looking for new ideas—ideas that will
mean economy in buying, and ideas that will make it possible
to use the tag as a means of identifying inactive accounts and
collecting for deliveries.

So—here's what we have done. . .

. . .we've prepared several sample folders that show the almost
numberless types of tags we make for other laundries. These
folders include samples of inexpensive route tags, and they
include samples of complicated system tags that are used in
conjunction with machine tabulating of accounts.

One of these folders is yours for the asking. Just mail the enclosed card—TODAY—so we'll know whom it should be marked for. It's bound to prove interesting since it will show you the sort of tags used by other laundries in all parts of the country.

We've also included some samples of practical items for advertising in each folder. These include bridge score cards, contract calculators—and similar novelties.

Mail the card—TODAY—for your copy. It's FREE.

Yours very truly,

Without knowing a great deal about the laundry business, the writer, B. J. Quinlan, could not have prepared the foregoing sales letter. The average letter-man, expert though he might be, would not be informed about the tags that laundries use, or why they use them. The mailing was made by Dennison Manufacturing Company. To those who did not reply, a copy of the same letter was mailed a month later. In red ink at the top of the page was this notation.

Two hundred and eight laundries asked for a copy of the folder mentioned in my February letter. With the thought that the original of my letter went astray, I am sending you this copy. Just mail the card enclosed, to get one of these folders.

Sales Letter to Clothing Merchants

Gentlemen:

You know how it is in business; there are a lot of people that you'd like to sell goods to who don't trade with you. Quite likely you can name a dozen, right in Indianapolis, just your kind of fellows, who don't come to you. You wish they would; you believe honestly that it would pay them to do so; and you'd like to know why they don't.

That's the way we feel about the good clothing men who don't buy our goods. We don't expect to sell everybody in the business; it wouldn't be a good thing if we did.

But your concern, somehow, seems to be our kind; we feel that, with a town like yours, and a trade like yours, and a business sense like yours, we ought to be working together to build up a fine trade for both of us.

Now, you know us; you know our goods. There's probably some reason why you're not buying them, and you know what it is. We wish you'd tell us what it is, very candidly. If we're "in wrong" we ought to be told, and if there's something here that's a good thing for you, then you ought to know about it.

Let's write a few letters to each other and see if we haven't some common ground of advantage.

Yours truly,

If you are at all familiar with the famous letters of the past, you have recognized the above sales letter as one used many years ago by Hart, Schaffner & Marx. It was only the opening shot, and two more rounds were fired to conclude the series. They were written by the late Henry P. Williams, and produced so many new accounts that the company continued to use them for a long time. Just in case you have not read them before, here are letters two and three.

Second letter:

Gentlemen:

You had a letter from us the other day; it wasn't a circular letter either; it was "personal"; so is this one.

In that letter, which used up quite a good many words, we really asked just one simple question—Why don't you handle our goods? We put it much more delicately than that, but that's really what it amounts to.

Now we can't decently insist on your answering that question; but we'd like very much to have you answer it. You may have so good a reason for not selling Hart, Schaffner & Marx Novelties that when we know what it is we'll say, "You are right," and that will be the end of it.

But we're not going to be quite satisfied until you tell us. For fear you haven't our stamped envelope handy, we enclose another. Tell us very plainly.

Very truly yours,

The third letter:

Gentlemen:

The fact is, we really want to know, and you haven't told us yet—Why don't you handle Hart, Schaffner & Marx goods? Is there a good reason? Maybe you don't like the goods; maybe you don't like us.

You needn't feel that you are committing yourselves to anything by answering our question; but we don't feel that we are being fair to ourselves unless we know why so good a concern as yours, and so good a concern as ours, are not on closer terms.

We don't want to bother you with calls; letters are really more convenient for both of us. But letters don't get anywhere unless the other fellow answers them. Drop us a line and tell us.

Yours truly,

We doubt if a series of three sales letters ever was written that hammered on one thought so steadily as these for Hart, Schaffner & Marx. Mr. Williams evidently decided that his ace was the thought that two good concerns should be together. The quality of the goods made by this company needed no explanation or proof; his readers *knew* that. But, Mr. Williams must have thought, he could appeal to pride—the idea of two "champs" playing doubles together.

Letters to those with mutual interests. There are, of course, many bonds that tie people together beside those of trade, profession, or some other work connection. In fact, many of the activities man considers important are those in which he amuses himself; sometimes they are even more important than those connected with earning his daily bread. All of these outside activities tend to bring people of a type together, although within the groups there may be some exceptions. You know what these groups are: golf players, particularly members of a specific club; bridge players, baseball players, football players, all kinds of groups interested in a certain sport; those of the same religious belief, and especially, of the same church; members of a business association, a fraternity or sorority; a little theatre, or a musical organization; even so thin a bond as owning the same kind of automobile, or smoking the same brand of cigar, may tend to develop mutuality of interest, and make those brought together open to a common sales appeal.

5. Special Inducements to Increase Pull

A part of the Hook. You have studied the blueprint from which the letter-carpenter constructs his sales message: starting with a Star to get attention; followed by a Chain to arouse interest and awaken desire; and ending with a Hook to impel action. You have seen many examples of successful letters built from this blueprint. It has been demonstrated that no one of the three steps in letter-construction can be called more important than the others, since each must do a job necessary to the success of the whole.

However, the Hook is the final blow, and unless it induces the desired result, the whole structure might just as well not have been erected. It is the climax of the sales presentation—the reader either does what he has been asked to do, or he does not. If his decision is unfavorable, the writer has no chance to continue the argument in an effort to change the reader's mind. Once the letter is mailed, nothing more can be done. There are no second shots in letter-writing. The attempt succeeds or fails according to whether the reader says "yes" or "no," and you are not with him when the decision is made.

You have seen, too, in Section 3, how the Hook must be constructed to attain the nearest possible chance of success: how the request for action must be offered in a confident and positive way; how such negative words as *if, may, hope,* and *trust* weaken the request; how the action suggested must be made as easy as possible for the reader; how *dating* the action will tend to increase the pull. All of these "how's" must be understood and applied if the letter is to have the maximum pull.

Assuming, however, that the writer has followed the principles, so that his Hook is fundamentally proper and sound, there are still other inducements that can be used to make the urge to action even more forceful. These special inducements in no way lessen the necessity of a correctly constructed Hook; they simply help it do its job.

What are these special inducements? In sales letters, particularly, there are numerous ways to increase the power of the Hook by offering special inducements. Not all of them, however, and sometimes not any of them, are suitable on every occasion; their use depends on the nature of the product or service, the type of people to whom the sales message is going, and the policy of the company. For example, one letter offered a free trial of the company's cigars; the reader could even smoke ten and then return the rest if he did not like them. But no fruit grower would be likely to ship a crate of oranges on the same basis—eat ten and return the rest if you don't like them. Spoilage would make such an offer too costly. Some products cannot even be guaranteed beyond date of delivery, or for a limited number of days, because control over their use or abuse is impossible once they reach the customer.

The following list is consequently offered only in a general way. The inducements mentioned may or may not be possible for a specific sales situation. When advisable, they can and do tend to increase the chances of a favorable reply. This must be true or they would not be used so frequently in the sales letters of so many companies.

(a) *Just sign and mail the card; we will bill you later.* This merely postpones the day of settlement, but the average human being worries less about the future than the present. Also, the offer gives him a chance to wiggle out if not satisfied.

(b) *You have nothing to lose; within ten days send us your payment, or return the goods.* This gives the buyer complete control of the situation. The inducement is not justified, however, if the percentage of returns is high. Of course, the allowed number of days may vary.

(c) *Enjoy it as you pay; take advantage of our easy terms.* The terms vary according to the will of the respective company, but the offer is tempting. Many people buy things on the installment plan that they could not buy for cash.

(d) *You take no risk; with the goods you will receive our unqualified Guarantee Certificate.* Of course, the guarantee may have strings tied to it, but the buyer still feels safer.

(e) *You get both for the price of one.* Everybody likes a bargain, and combination offers often impel action.

(f) *To show our appreciation for your order, we will include without charge a handsome sterling silver tie-clasp.* Premiums have helped to develop millions of dollars worth of sales, both by mail and in other forms of selling. Often, the premium is offered only with full payment.

(g) *Be sure to send your order TODAY, as this offer will be withdrawn soon.* There is no great urge to action in this statement. *How* soon *is* soon?

(h) *Please hurry, as no orders can be accepted on these terms after July 31.* Here the time limit is definitely established, and the reader is more likely to believe the statement.

(i) *We have only 59 more to offer at this unusual price; do not delay in sending the card.* A limit in number seems more impressive than one in time. Always a strong urge to action.

(j) *Frankly, we want you as a customer, and to prove it, we will allow you a special discount of 10% on any order placed within two weeks.* Offers such as this have pulling power, but the special price—if genuine—sets a precedent that may cause trouble later.

(k) *Please rush the card back immediately, as the price positively goes up $10 on the first of next month.* Statements like this have caused many sales; also, much ill-will if the advance does not take place.

(l) *To prove we have not over-sold this new open-air theatre, we enclose two complimentary tickets good any night next week.* Assuming the recipient would not otherwise visit the theatre, this inducement really costs nothing; the value is in the repeat visits that may follow.

(m) *All we ask is ten minutes of your time; our representative will also bring you a very useful reminder of his visit; it's yours whether you buy or not.* Not telling what the gift is makes the inducement more attractive; the reader agrees to find out.

(n) *We cannot tell you why, but confidentially, there is one*

special reason why you should not delay. A good inducer
if true; otherwise, not ethical.

The above list by no means covers all of the special inducements that
you yourself may be offered in a month's batch of incoming letters; but
there is no need to stretch it out any longer. Anybody who understands
human nature will know *why* these inducements do help to get action. In
some ways, man is a funny animal: he thinks it will be easier to pay later
for what he can't pay now; he buys and hoards things that are scarce, even
though he may not need them; he thinks he is getting a premium for nothing
when common sense should tell him the cost is included in the price of the
product. Thus, the appeals of *deferred payment, limited number, free gift,*
and all the others are often used to put added power into sales letters.

Examples. The following letters show how some of these special inducements have been used by various companies. Before we put them under the
microscope, here is one important caution—*never let the buyer down* with
any special reason for action. If a gift is offered, don't oversell it, causing
the recipient to be disappointed when it gets in his hands; if the offer is
limited in time or number, be sure to do exactly what you said would be
done; if a free trial is the inducement, and the goods are returned, make no
effort to high-pressure the buyer into keeping them. The only sound basis
for any special inducement is absolute *sincerity*—they are *not* clever tricks
to lure the buyer into some action he may later regret.

The first of the examples is a sales letter used by the Neil Barron Fuel
Company in Kansas City, Missouri. As a token of appreciation for orders
received during the summer months, the readers are offered a beautiful
colored etching, and to give some idea of its appearance, a miniature copy
was clipped to the letter. The letter sounds sincere—the gift appears worth
while. Thus, the inducement is of the better sort, and deserves our approval.

> Dear Mr. Doe:
>
> I am writing you this personal letter because I have a gift for you.
> You have admired beautiful etchings; particularly, those colorful
> types depicting rural life in the old country...the scene of a
> quiet English country-side, or one of a picturesque mill on the
> banks of a Dutch canal.
>
> I have one of these etchings for you; tastefully created by the
> artist, Wettel, who is famous for his artistry in the field of etch-
> ing. The size of the picture is 24×28 inches and I can truthfully
> say that it will grace the loveliest of living rooms, when properly
> framed. The retail price of this picture is from $4.00 to $5.00.

I want to ask a favor of you, and in asking this favor I can save you money. Most everyone knows that in the coal business the months of July and August are rather slow periods as far as sales are concerned, and our firm is no exception. We want to make it worthwhile for you to order during these months.

If you will place an order for coal for delivery during the months of July or August, you will receive our usual discounted summer price, which saves you from fifty cents to one dollar per ton; and, in addition, I will present you with one of the beautiful etchings described in the first part of this letter.

My supply of these etchings is limited; consequently, I am writing to only a small number of my preferred customers.

I have arranged with my salesmen to carry several of these pictures with them, and if you would like to see one before placing your order, I will be glad to have one left at your home for inspection. I know you will be more than pleased.

Call me today at Chestnut 0–0000.

Very truly yours,

This letter, a winner of the Dartnell Gold Medal Award, contains three of the special inducements to action which have just been listed. First, it offers a nice gift with the order, and to make it seem truly worthwhile, the retail cost is mentioned—$4.00 to $5.00. Furthermore, the miniature copy is visible proof of value. Second, it tells the reader that the supply of etchings is limited. Third, it mentions the discounted summer price—a saving of fifty cents to one dollar per ton.

A considerably less valuable gift—but interesting to many people—is the drink offered by the Chicago eating place, Martini's. This was some time ago—the prices will have changed, but the letter doesn't need changing:

Dear Mr. Doe:

Every day several people walk into our place, lay one of these letters down and say, "Now let's see if your food is as good as you say it is."

We'd like to have you put us on the spot that way. We know you'd soon be a regular customer like the rest of them and get real enjoyment out of our Italian home cooking.

There's boneless chicken, spaghetti, ravioli, green noodles, steaks, chops, roasts, served with sauces that you'll smack your lips over.

But no orchestras or fancy fixtures—just good food and good drinks—and to show you how easy the prices are—we serve a Chef's special dinner for $1.25—a regular dinner for $2.00—and at luncheon on week days we serve cocktails for 55¢.

On Sundays we're closed so that we all have a little breathing spell and are ready to serve you better during the week.

That offer of mine still goes for you—I'm ready to buy the first introductory drink myself—I hope it will be soon.

> Yours very truly,

To personalize this sales message still further, the signature is simply "Johnnie." Two special inducements help to power the sale—low prices, and the free drink. The idea brought many new customers to Martini's.

Unusual letter offering special discount. A few years ago, in the letter problem contest conducted by *Printed Salesmanship*, the following combination sales and Christmas message was submitted by Dorothy Marie Johnson, one of our better writers of business material and fiction. The special inducement to make the Hook more impelling is a discount of 5% during the month of December. Of course, not all business men can handle the King's English as gracefully as does Miss Johnson.

Dear ——:

Your first sled—you thought there might be one, but you didn't see it by the tree, so you pretended for Dad's and Mother's sake that you didn't care at all. And then you found it in the dining room!

What do children remember longest—the things they had, or the things they wanted and never got?

Godwin's will help you play Santa Claus this year—not just with a red Santa Claus, though he's here too, but by making Christmas giving easier for you. Further on in this letter you'll learn of our gift to you.

Christmas is the time when you make up to your loved ones for the things they didn't have on other Christmas days, when grown-up boys and girls get things to take the place of the tricycles and talking-dolls Santa Claus forgot in other years. Christmas is the time when you make dreams come true.

Your own dream comes true at Godwin's, too, for every gift you give can come from here. The small, the large, the quaint, the beautiful—all these are here for you to choose. We've gathered from across the world the fruits of its people's labor. You'll want to spend a day or two in Godwin's. Your packages can be mailed direct from Godwin's post office; stamps and ribbons and tissue and wrappings are ready here.

But all these aisles and floors of useful and lovely things are lacking in this, that only you can furnish—the spirit of Christmas giving. Your gifts are waiting at Godwin's, but in your own heart alone is the priceless ingredient that you must wrap into each package. The gift without the giver is bare; yours must be wrapped with the invisible finery of human affection.

To make Christmas giving more pleasant, and because we want to show you our appreciation of a friendly relationship, we are presenting you with this card as our gift. It entitles you to a special Friendship Discount of 5% at any time during the month of December. It is good throughout the whole vast Santa Claus workshop of Godwin's store.

More than nineteen hundred years have passed since three wise men rode down to Bethlehem, but the spirit of giving has grown, not lessened, through them all. When Christmas morning dawns, may you, too, have. . .

A Very Merry Christmas

Yes, you are right. The letter was planned primarily for home mailing— to women with charge accounts at the store. Women are made in finer molds than men—they will read and like longer letters as a rule.

How to use gifts as inducements. The sales letter used by the Kansas City fuel dealer, offering a $5.00 etching to those who would buy their fuel in the summer, was good because the reader could clearly understand the motive behind the gift. The dealer wanted orders, and said so. He did not start with an extravagant promise, which he later failed to keep. But not all sales letters offering gifts approach the reader so frankly. They lead him to believe he will get something absolutely free, letting him trip later on the strings attached to the offer.

Particularly obnoxious are those sales letters which begin: "Within five days, you will receive absolutely without charge or obligation a handsome, durable, efficient pen and pencil set which you will be very proud to own and show to your friends." Or, some similar form of deceptive palaver! Later, it turns out the set is free provided something else is purchased; meaning, if the reader is smart enough to figure it out, that what he pays for the one article includes the cost of the "free" one, plus a nice profit for the seller on the whole combination. This use of so-called free gifts was mentioned in our discussion of the Star (Section 3) ; it is equally taboo when used to impel action.

Quite different in color, and without the odor, are those sales letters in which the reader is offered the gift free-and-above-board and with the reason understood by both parties. The gift may be a prize in return for a purchase, or the payment of a bill; it may be a token of welcome to a new resident, presented with the hope of gaining his goodwill; it may be in the

The Connecticut Mutual
Life Insurance Company

Hartford, Connecticut

Date

Mr. John Q. Prospect
Hartford, Connecticut

Dear Mr. Prospect:

     Will you accept with our compliments an attractive and
useful Dur-O-Lite pencil, rich in appearance, and precision built
for years of dependable service? It is yours for the asking.
Just return the reply card.

     We make this offer because we want you to see our new
"Insurance Indicator." The indicator has helped many of our
clients settle for themselves two questions which seem uppermost
in the minds of people when they consider their own life insurance.

                    How much should I own?
                             and
                    What kind?

     There isn't anything magical or complicated about the
"Indicator." But it will enable you to find out for yourself how
much and what kind of life insurance you should own.

          Just fill out the enclosed card and mail it to me today.

                         Sincerely,

                         Senior Vice President

RWS:hkop
(Enclosures)

SAVE $5 ON A
LAUNDRY EQUIPMENT
SERVICE CONTRACT

Dear Customer:

We would like to thank you for calling us recently to repair your
appliance—we trust it is now in fine working order.

If you liked our fast, dependable service, you can purchase a full
years protection for just a small investment...and if you do it now,
you can save $5. Why not do away with "service worry" with a Wards
Service Contract...all parts, labor and service calls are included
in one low price. You will receive unlimited service repair throughout the year without any additional cost.

TAKE ADVANTAGE OF THIS 10-DAY OFFER TO SAVE $5

Enclosed is a $5 coupon which you may use as cash toward the
purchase of your Service Contract.

Also enclosed is a Laundry Equipment Service Contract Application.
Just check the plan that best suits your needs and the method of
payment you wish to use. Deduct the $5 from the price shown on the
plan you have checked. Sign and forward the application to us in
the self-addressed, postpaid envelope, along with the $5 coupon.
You will receive your new contract by return mail.

For your convenience, if you have a Credit Account at Wards, you
may add this purchase without a down payment, and usually without
an increase to your monthly installment.

                                        Yours very truly

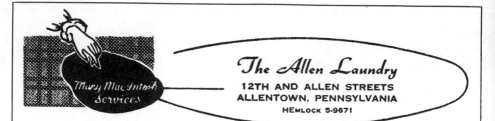

Dear Parents:—

CONGRATULATIONS!

We, at Allen, were very happy to hear that you have been blessed with a child. In this complex age of atoms, missiles, and ever more astounding scientific discoveries, the miracle of birth still dwarfs all man's knowledge and inventions.

As tangible proof of our good wishes, we enclose a free coupon which we sincerely hope you will feel free to use at no further obligation. Simply dial HEmlock 5-9671 and ask our Operator to have the routeman stop. Give him this coupon, together with the soiled articles, and they will be returned to you in 3 days looking like new.

This is our effort to lighten your burdens at this important time in your life.

Sincerely

Mary MacIntosh

This coupon entitles you to **your choice** of the following:
EITHER
ONE COAT, SUIT, OR DRESS expertly cleaned and pressed without charge
OR
An average family's laundry for **ONE WEEK FREE** (up to 15 lbs.) processed in the famous Mary MacIntosh coin-op service. All shirts and linens ironed, everything else fluff dried and neatly folded.
FREE PICK-UP AND DELIVERY
This coupon must be attached to soiled work

Not Good After June 4, 19__
ALLEN LAUNDRY AND DRY CLEANING

nature of a sample of the product sold, or the service. Of course, nothing can be given away in business without being an item of expense, and thus a drain on profit—unless enough additional volume is created by the device so that the cost is more than offset by the extra business. In many types of selling, the premiums, discounts, large samples, souvenirs, and the like, more than pay their freight; in others, they do not. The decision as to their use is an executive responsibility. In any case, the sales-letter writer has no legitimate right to offer a gift under false colors. In one way or another, it is a device for getting business—and that's the way most readers understand it.

Consider, for example, the letters on pages 456, 457, and 458. The first one offers an attractive pencil. The second offers a five-dollar saving upon purchase of a year's service contract. The third offers the parents of a new arrival free washing for one week; but could the baby's parents have any doubt as to the motive?

6. Sales Letters That Stir Imagination

Highest form of salesmanship. You will find no better sales letters any place than those which you are about to read, although some that you have surveyed in this Handbook rate just as highly. They are truly the work of the masters, and from them you may gain ideas that will be extremely helpful. Nevertheless, it is very difficult to say *why* they are so outstanding, or *how* the writers went about the job. Perhaps the common characteristic is that they succeed better than ordinary letters in arousing mental images in the reader's mind—they stir his imagination, and make him *see* or *feel* the things talked about.

If you take time to examine carefully the language of these letters, you will see that it is colorful but not fancy. The pictures painted with words are very vivid. The reader sees *himself*—enjoying a benefit or suffering from the lack of it. Each of the letters *takes time* to build these mental images. Concrete examples are supplied to back up any generality. In many cases, they take a product or service and show the *romance* in it. Thus, they charm and interest the reader as might a good bit of fiction. He has no thought of stopping, because what he reads is too exciting.

He is caught and held by the description of Gloucester fisherman; he is intrigued by the brief recounting of the history of paper; he is chilled by the thought of his own boy, lost like eight-year-old Billy in Union Station; he pictures himself on Island lake, pulling in the big, fighting bass. Always, the experience is *personal*. The reader *himself* is the leading character in the letter, enjoying or fearing what happens there. All of this is an imaginative process, started and kept going by the ability of the writer to paint word pictures that seem *real*.

But no one can stir the imagination of another human being unless he, too, sees and feels the thing he is describing. It takes imagination to create imagination. A lot of people say they lack the imagination to write the kind of letters that follow. What they mean is that they are afraid to let themselves go—to sit and dream of romance in their business—to put that romance on paper. Of course, it is always wise to keep our imagination within the boundaries of our own experience. Mr. Smith, for instance, was qualified to write of seafaring because of his close affiliation with it.

In the same way, Harold McQueen, long a resident of Chicago and a student of that city's early history, had the necessary background to write about John B. Sherman's mansion. And Mr. Voorhees' knowledge of Travelers Aid Society gave him the credentials to describe actual cases handled by the organization.

The lesson that we learn from these, and the other letters that follow is—*let your imagination run, but keep it on the highways you have traveled.* Otherwise you may come up with a "Midsummer Night's Dream," rather than a sales letter.

Romance of fishing. Perhaps the use of imagination in business correspondence seems a difficult skill to master. You might even feel that most merchandise is lacking in qualities that might strike an imaginative chord. Well, are you sure about that? At first glance, *fish* might seem to be unappealing to the sense of romance and adventure. We all know that fish are cold, dead and slimy in the market. But wait! What about the fish in the sea? Could there by any romance in a business that catches them for commercial purposes?

Yes, plenty of it. Putting the story in words has built a big consumer acceptance for the Frank E. Davis Fish Company of Gloucester, Massachusetts. Over the years, the letters written for that company by John A. Smith have sold millions of pounds of fish, and the emphasis in these letters has always been on the romance of the business. Mr. Smith has put "oomph" in the fish business. It was there all the time, but this sales-letter writer had to *see* it. Check the historical background, the methods of manufacture, the sources of materials, and you will usually find in any product enough glamour to talk about in an interesting and exciting manner. Here, for example, is one of the fish letters:

Dear Friend:

Way back in 1623, a small group of Pilgrims gathered in their small huts to name this fishing port Gloucester. They were a hardy lot of folks, living mostly on game and salt water fish. They built small boats and braved the treacherous waters off Gloucester to get fish for their families. In those times women folks helped too—for every hand meant more food for the cold winter months to come.

I remember, as a small boy, my grand father telling me about being lashed to the mainmast in a stiff blow, when his schooner was half buried in the plunging sea. It was a hard life. But still, Gloucester boys follow it year after year. It's in our blood. It's our way of living. Nature has located us close to the richest waters there are.

Have you wondered why Gloucester is one of the greatest fishing ports in the world? You see, we have many varieties of delicious fish landed here daily. More good fish come right in here to Gloucester than any other port in the world. That's why you can never say you've tasted fish at its perfect prime unless you get it direct from Gloucester.

So you won't mind, will you, if I ship some of my fish direct to your home? It won't cost you anything, unless you feel like keeping it. All I ask is that you try the fish at my expense, and judge for yourself whether it isn't exactly what you have always wanted.

On the enclosed cards you will find a full description of the THREE SPECIAL OFFERS I am making. If you are like most of my regular customers, you will choose my Special Get-Acquainted Assortment. I've made up this package to let people know how good all my fish are.

You see, I can tell people that I give them the first pick of the finest, primest catches. But the best way to let them know that my fish are exactly what I say, is to send a generous meal-size package of 14 different kinds of seafoods—to taste! That's just what you get in my Get-Acquainted Assortment; fourteen different varieties of delicious seafoods, that will tell you as no fine writing ever can, what a real treat it is to eat fish shipped direct to your home from the fishing smacks.

Then, there's my special deep-sea Lobster Offer! Each package comes to you with no shell, no waste, just the tasty, flavorous meat of a two pound lobster And when you come to compare prices, you will find that my lobster—even though more tender than the ordinary kind—COSTS LESS THAN HALF for what you actually eat! And on the third card, you'll find dainty Sardines in Olive Oil—a new pack, delicious, and each package ready for instant use.

For 52 years we have been selecting the primest grades of ocean fish to be sent direct from the fishing boats to our customers.

And it is real pride on our part to know that thousands of families have found our fish so much better than any they could get locally, that season in and season out they send us their orders.

Today, I invite *you* to join them. I want you to know the satisfying taste of fresh-caught, prime-grade seafoods. If you have never tasted anything but the kind you get in stores, there's a real treat awaiting you. Read the cards enclosed now, and see how you can get one, or all of my Introductory Offers without sending a penny in advance. All you do is check the offer you want, fill in the card, and your seafoods will be on the way to you the very day I hear from you. You pay nothing, unless you are perfectly satisfied that my fish are really the best.

It is just this way that we secured our thousands of customers. So you know beforehand that you can send your order with full confidence. You know in advance that you will get the choicest, tenderest, fullest-flavored seafood that you have ever tasted. Check and sign the enclosed postcards and mail them to me— TODAY. They require no stamps.

                                        Sincerely yours,

There is much to appeal to the reader's imagination in the sales letters of the Frank E. Davis Fish Company. The one you have just read is personalized from "Dear Friend" down to the title under the signature of Mr. Davis—"The Gloucester Fishman." Notice, too, that the pronoun *I* is freely used. The letter just *talks* to the reader—about early days in Gloucester—about folks and fish.

Use of historical background. People are naturally interested in the origin of things: in the battles, love affairs, ways of living of the human beings whose bodies long ago returned to dust; in any historical fact with which they do not happen to be familiar. This thirst for news of the past is often the basis of imaginative sales letters. For example, Norman Alper starts a letter for the Equitable Paper Bag Co. Inc., Brooklyn, with the early history of paper-making:

Gentlemen:

More than eighteen hundred years ago Tsai Lun, a Chinese, first manufactured paper in the modern, beaten-pulp manner.

But almost six thousand years ago—as far back as 3500 B.C.— the Egyptians were making a type of paper called *Papyrus*. The Egyptians peeled the thin, inner layers off the stem of the Papyrus plant. These strips were laid side by side on a hard, smooth surface. Then more strips were laid across—at right angles.

The strips—now a mat—were soaked in Nile water, with some starch added. As a final step, pressure was applied to the Papyrus for hours, followed by polishing with hard stone or glass.

That was the beginning—in Egypt. The art of Papyrus-making spread. The Romans made more than 20 kinds of Papyrus. Some grades were used for wrapping goods. But for 4,000 years the process was done entirely by hand.

These old Egyptian Papyrus makers would surely marvel at the enclosed large Reply Envelope. For it was made of wood pulp. Huge machines changed the pulp into tough yet attractive paper —22 Substance, Ivory Kraft. And then...we at Equitable formed the paper into envelopes at an unbelievable speed. Printed at the same time, too, on a rotary press attachment of the envelope machine!

Check Equitable's low prices on the envelopes you use—28 and 32 Substance, Fawn Kraft, and 32 Substance Ivory Jute Finish (carried in stock) for PROOFS—a wide variety of papers made-to-order in minimum quantities of 25 thousand for your PROMOTIONAL MAILINGS and JOB PRINTING.

Just write the quantity you usually buy on samples of your envelopes. Mail them to me in the enclosed Reply Envelope. An attractive Equitable quotation, samples, and money making suggestions, will be sent to you promptly.

Very truly yours,

Here is another example of the ability to make words stir the imagination. Notice how cleverly Harold Pitcairn McQueen, a business-letter writer of Chicago, used the historical background of an old home in placing before his readers the services of landscape gardeners Swain Nelson & Sons Co. The lack of a strong Hook is explained by the fact that the purpose of the letter was to break ice for a personal call later.

Dear Mr. and Mrs. Matot:

One evening, sixteen years after a pioneer family had cleared a piece of forest land on Lake Michigan and built their farm house, they stood in their yard and watched the reflection of one of the greatest fires in history.

These folks lived a good day's journey from that swamp city of Chicago, which covered but 18 square miles of—mostly mud. When Mr. Heinzen built his home in 1855, Chicago had but 159 miles of wood sidewalks and 27 miles of plank streets. Cobble stones had been tried—only to disappear in the mud. The Illinois Central had just laid its tracks along the shore, and the Democratic Press, one of Chicago's first newspapers, was telling the world to "Come West." George M. Pullman came—in time to raise our only skyscraper (the four-story Tremont House) on some 5000 jackscrews; followed by Carter H. Harrison of Kentucky—whose son was to serve Chicago five times as mayor.

And so, from that time till this, the old farm on the lake has seen the rise of Chicago—from village to mighty city.

Now I hear this landmark is to be your home—and I'm interested because in 1856 this Nelson company came into being, growing with and serving the men who built Chicago, many of whose sons now live along the North Shore.

I wonder whether you feel we could help you to make your grounds an appropriate setting for your most interesting home.

                                              Cordially yours,

Another sales letter—seeking to arouse interest in the British West Indies—is the one written by James Hawkins for agents Defoe & Stevenson, Port Royal, B.W.I. Here is a business communication that fiction could not excel: full of the names of pirates and buccaneers that excited our imagination when we were children; crowded with historical facts that make the reader's heart beat faster. Emotionless, indeed, would be the person who could read this letter and not feel an urge to visit the West Indies. It is truly magnificent writing—as good as you will ever encounter in a sales letter.

Historical Sales Letter

Defoe & Stevenson - agents - Port Royal, B.W.I.

CODES: BENTLEY'S & A. B. C.

Howard Smith Paper Mills Limited,
407 McGill Street,
Montreal, Canada.

Dear Sirs:

PUNCH

        If you took three puncheons of rum and two hogsheads of sugar;
dumped them in a well; then drew up the mixture in buckets: you would have
what might truthfully be called a magnificent punch.
        It's exactly the kind British soldiers had when they landed on
Trinidad during the Napoleonic Wars and broke into a sugar-house and a
distillery.
        I always liked that story. There is a grandeur and a magnifi-
cence about the business which seems so in keeping with the native grandeur
of our islands. The sea is so brilliantly blue; the flaming tropical
foliage so glorious. Hills blaze with the orange-red Bois Immortel; there
are giant trees and tree ferns, scarlet poinsettias, purple bougainvilleas,
golden poui, many-hued hibiscus ....

BUCCANEERS

        When Defoe wanted a satisfactory island for his Robinson, it was our Tobago he chose; when Jim and Long John Silver set out for Treasure Island, it was here they came. Drake still lies beneath the Caribbean waters, "waiting for the drum"; Raleigh came to Guiana in search of El Dorado; Morgan, admiral of the buccaneers, ruled at Port Royal and Blackbeard in the Bahamas; the little island called "Dead Man's Chest" is here, and the old pirate harbour of Tortuga.

FOUNDER

All through the islands there are so many reminders of our turbulent past, there are so many interesting historical events to recall, that some of the most important are easily forgotten. For example: one of our showplaces is our "Gibraltar", the fortifications on St. Kitts' Brimstone Hill; while three miles from them is a practically unknown memorial of much deeper historical significance -- the grave of a forgotten Maker of Empire, Sir Thomas Warner. The first English settlement in the West Indies was his establishment on St. Kitts, from which he sent settlers to colonize Nevis, Antigua, Montserrat and St. Lucia. Briefly, this son of a Suffolk yeoman was the founder of the Empire's oldest group of colonies.

ACCIDENT

The first English foothold in the central Caribbean was obtained in more accidental a manner. Some, I suppose, would say "more English" a manner, more typical of the haphazard and absent-minded fashion in which an Empire has been built. Penn's "disorderly rabble", having been soundly beaten off from Santo Domingo, desperately grasped at the idea of getting something to show for their pains, so they landed on Jamaica. From that time on, English buccaneers had a headquarters in the very middle of Spain's dominions.

That's all ancient history now. The buccaneers have joined Columbus and the Conquistadores and the battle fleets of England and of France in our West Indian story. Modern Port Royal could hardly be called "the wickedest town in the world", and nowadays we don't see many "stately Spanish galleons" dipping past our shores richly laden from the Main.

TREASURE

A treasure remains, however: eternal sunshine and rest, beauty of land and sea, and the health-giving breezes of the Trades. No wonder West Indian cruises are popular, and that every year we welcome more visitors from Canada.

For you in Canada there is another, and a more practical, interest in our islands -- one more closely connected with pieces of eight and double castellanos. I refer, of course, to the question of Canada-West Indian trade.

TRADE

The complementary character of our climates and our products makes the development of such a trade seem natural, and much has been done to stimulate it. Did you know that your first Trade Agents, appointed under the auspices of your Department of Finance, were sent to the West Indies? Trade treaties have been negotiated assuring preferential treatment for each of us in the other's markets. Regular steamship service has been supplied. The Canadian-West Indian League has done magnificent work in strengthening business ties and fostering goodwill between you in Canada and us in the Bermudas and the British Colonies of the Caribbean. Indeed, this letterhead is one specific example of our trade, for, like many of our office forms and business communications in the West Indies, it is printed on your Progress Bond.

Much has been done for the expansion of trade and travel between us. I think even still more can be accomplished, and even greater advantage taken of the opportunities offered us to work together for our mutual prosperity.

You can easily obtain full information as to specific trade possibilities from governmental sources, or from the League, or from your various financial institutions interested in the West Indies; and you can count on their helpful co-operation in any matters promoting trade and travel between your great Dominion and these islands -- the Crown Colonies which lie closest to you.

Yours sincerely,

James Hawkins

P.S. I certainly like your Progress Bond, White, 40(m).

Characters the reader can visualize. As has been mentioned, generalities don't get very far in a sales letter. Any broad statement about the merits of a product or service must be proved with concrete cases. This ideology is the keynote of a sales letter used by H.B. Voorhees to raise money for the Travelers Aid Society. He was not content merely to state that the organization does "good work" and let it go at that. Instead, he documents this work with a random sampling of true stories. Accordingly, the reader's imagination is exercised; the people he reads about are there with him; he visualizes himself or some person dear to him in the same predicaments.

Dear Mr. Doe:

Clipped to one of the checks we received last December was a card bearing this message:

"For someone stranded on Christmas Day!"

I thought, as I held that card, of eight-year-old Billy, who had come to us that morning in the Union Station. The terminal was filled with a happy holiday throng—arriving travelers being met by smiling friends and relatives and packed off into cars and taxis—all except one lonely little boy.

Billy was not met. The Travelers Aid worker found him standing alone beside his shabby little suitcase, and trying awfully hard to be brave. Someone, he said, was supposed to meet him, but he guessed they "just forgot."

I thought, too, of young Joe Barnes, whose tragic story is told on the next page, stranded here in Chicago with his three small children, and the body of his wife. And of twenty-year-old Jennie, incurably ill and going home on a stretcher—to die. And of barefoot Peter and John, stranded three hundred miles from home because of careless planning on the part of some careless grown-up.

And then I thought of the thousands of others who come to us throughout the year; some of them needing merely a sympathetic listener; others, in desperate need of the help that Travelers Aid alone gives to the traveler in trouble away from home.

Some of their stories are briefly told on the inside pages of this letter. We ask you to read them, and if you will, to make yours a happier Christmas by sharing it with these other less fortunate folk. Tear off the coupon and please mail it with your check to Travelers Aid today. Mark it, if you wish,

"For someone stranded on Christmas Day!"

Sincerely yours,

Perhaps you have received other letters from Travelers Aid. They are almost always fine examples of sales letter carpentry, supported by stories to set the reader's imagination on fire. The one you have just surveyed was reinforced on the inside pages with specific cases to turn the heart inside-out. Like this:

> With a thin three-weeks-old baby in his arms, and two tear-stained children clinging to his coat, Joe Barnes timidly approached the Travelers Aid desk at the railroad station. He was taking his wife's body to her parents, who had promised a home for the children.
>
> Grief-stricken over the loss of his wife, Joe was on the verge of collapse, and the baby's sudden illness terrified him. He had very little money and had not eaten in 24 hours, but "It don't matter about me," he remarked, "it's the kids I'm worried about."
>
> *   *   *   *   *   *   *   *
>
> "You see, my son's wife doesn't like me—and I can't stay where I'm not wanted"—Mr. Lane's voice trembled and his mild blue eyes filled with tears as he told the Travelers Aid worker why he was "running away" from home at age 87.

What have appeals for charity to do with *business* letters, you wonder? Well, in one sense, nothing; in another, plenty. The technique used in the Travelers Aid letter is one of the best for selling the product or service to which it may be applied. Support your claims with actual cases; let your reader *see* living people in what you say, rather than mere words about them. Personalities—not platitudes—stir the imagination.

Consider the following illustration—a sales letter used by the Robertson Paper Box Company, Montville, Connecticut. The writer (it is signed by the president) doesn't just say his company can supply an idea to meet any box problem; he talks about the man from whom the ideas come, and thus makes his message far more interesting.

> Good Morning, Mr. Jones...
>
> ...and do you know Walter Tiskey?
>
> Well, he's a young fellow here at Robertson's who stands behind a drawing table with a rule, pencil, cutting knife, and a head full of ideas.
>
> Everybody around here marvels at the way he snaps them out. Ideas, we mean. Ideas which our die-cutters take, pass on to our technical men and printers, who pass along to customers some of the most unusual Folding Display Boxes that this era of smart merchandising has known.

Robertson salesmen come to Walter with a handful of knives
...a water bottle...shotgun shells...a new toilet preparation
...a batch of noodles, biscuits, candy, or bakery products...
sheets, pillow cases, blankets or lingerie...in fact, ANYTHING
that needs a container—and Walter "sparks" a sample box
(made by his own hands) which the customer falls for, head
over heels.

In this day, when new IDEAS are so important to the winning
of the customer's dollar—when EYE-APPEAL is just about the
most important essential to store selling, it's good to have a fellow
like Walter Tiskey around.

The reply card enclosed is for your use—so that you may profit
from Tiskey's help.

Cordially yours,

Another letter that presents characters for reader visualization is the
one sent by The Plaza Hotel. The interplay between Mary O'Sullivan and
Paul Sonnabend is entertaining, but it never overshadows the sales message.

The lure of vacation spots. Letters that seek to arouse interest in
vacation spots have a great opportunity to stimulate the reader's imagination. The things described are those that the prospect has dreamed about
during the long work months when he has had his nose to the grindstone.
He is ready for any mental spree the letter may encourage, and if the place
offered sounds at all interesting, the more facts presented the better. This is
one sales-letter problem where the writer has no need to worry about length;
the greater the array of advantages, the more likely he is to touch points of
vulnerability in the reader.

Where would you like to spend your next vacation? Well, perhaps the
letters coming up may lead you in the right direction. The first one lures you
to Blake Lake, Wisconsin. See how C. D. Craddock tells of all the fun you
could have at Sugar Bush Lodge; he wrote the letter for Roy and Mae
Shattuck, the owners. This *purposely* long letter (sent to those who asked
for it) turned the trick; the lodge was filled all during the season.

Dear Vacationist:

Have you *time* to really live?

In this day of speed many people, long before their time, find
themselves flat, discarded tires on the brutal highway of life.
The stress and strain of seeking "success" is terrific. The price
we pay for prosperity is high.

When the summer sun is scorching hot, like red rivets, and city
streets are ready to blaze, it takes just such a place as the famous

FIFTH AVENUE AT FIFTY-NINTH STREET, NEW YORK 19. N. Y. · PLAZA 9-3000

OFFICE OF THE
VICE PRESIDENT-MANAGING DIRECTOR

October 25, 1962

Dear Mr. Mersel:

I have a problem.

It's like this. Recently, one of our chambermaids, Mary O'Sullivan,
wrote a sales letter which you may have received. (A privilege that
I usually reserve for myself, as I am rather good at it.) But, after
all, it made her happy, and I'm a big one for employee morale... we
have company picnics, bowling leagues, elevator races and all that
kind of stuff. Well, the point is, Mary O'Sullivan got 387 replies
to her letter including over 100 orders. (We have a quaint custom
of calling them reservations instead of orders.)

But her letter talked only of our bedrooms! She didn't say a thing
about the function rooms. (As perfect for Boards of Directors meetings
as wedding receptions.) And the fact that we spent $175,000 to restore
the unsurpassed beauty of our Ballroom escaped mention altogether. She
probably thought you never planned a lunch, speech or special event in
your life! It's not that I have anything against boudoirs, but Mary
O'Sullivan simply ignored everything else.

Now tell me...as one businessman to another...what should I do?

              Fire Mary O'Sullivan?
              Sentence her to 6 months in the laundry?
              Bar her from the Persian Room?

I would appreciate your valued advice. By the way, if you have any
thorny problems bedeviling you, let me know. I'll be glad to return
the favor and do whatever I can...particularly if your problems involve
one of the many services of the Plaza.

                    Very sincerely yours,

                    Paul Sonnabend
                    Vice President and Managing Director

P. S. I hope Mary O'Sullivan cleans better than she writes, I think
I'd better check on that...

HOTEL CORPORATION OF AMERICA

Sugar Bush Lodge to keep you cool, cheerful and comfortable It's a safe bet that the chap who wrote "The Melancholy Days Have Come" never spent any time at Sugar Bush, because we don't have any melancholy days here. Let me tell you why!

Sugar Bush Lodge, an ideal summer resort, is a perfect setting tucked away on the forest-studded shores of Blake Lake, with a picturesque background of deep-hued, enchanted hills. Fifteen miles north of Amery, Wisconsin, in Georgetown, Polk County. Its name is derived from its grove of Maple Syrup and Sugar-producing trees. It offers anyone a respite from world cares, strife and struggles.

Mother Nature must have planned this place for her personal playground—she put so *many* things there. With a gesture of generosity she gave Sugar Bush everything that the vacationist wants in such an atmosphere—a delightful realization of every expectation. A paradise to live in—play in—loaf in. Once you come you'll want to stay for good—your *own* good.

Here the days are uniformly warm; the summer sun tempered by cool northern breezes—nights delightfully cool and refreshing. Sparkling lakes, crystal-clear creeks; a climate conducive to health, happiness and comfort—a place of hospitality, contentment and well being. Beautiful beaches of sand in contrast with the blue and green of restless, glimmering lakes. Wondrous scenic beauties, lost ravines, shady woods, colorful hills, green prairies, smooth highways, perfume-scented trails. And solitude! Then there's boating, bathing (a safe place for the youngsters, no drop-offs), hiking, picnicking, hunting, fishing. Dancing and golfing near by! Outdoor sports and games!

The lakes and streams abound in Bass, Northern Pike, Crappies, Sunfish, and the fightin'est Trout that ever knocked the fire out of a rod and reel. If you can bait a hook, we won't dare name your catch!

Good roads radiate in various directions, leading to the beaches, points of natural and historic sights, thrilling reminders of adventurous days of our forefathers. There's the fascination of traveling roads and lanes lined with richly-colored foliage, and shady trees swaying in the northern breeze, remindful of the rhythmical rhumba. Within short distances there are 25 (count 'em) gorgeous lakes and streams. All these attractions in a place where you live as you please, combine to create recreational supremacy.

The enclosed map points the way to your magic destination. The snapshots give only a bird's-eye view of the attractions.

The cottages are spotlessly clean. All dishes, cooking utensils, tables, cooking stove, refrigerator, fuel—are **FREE**. Groceries, including fresh milk, are procurable at a nearby store, at reasonable prices. Fresh vegetables from our own farm!

And here's the good news! It doesn't cost a fortune (but worth it) to spend your never-to-be-forgotten vacation at Sugar Bush. If you want to "housekeep" and cook your own meals, cottages are available in three classes. One group with 4 beds or more to each cottage is only (hold your breath) $50 a week. Cottages with 3 beds only $40 a week! Others with 2 beds only $35 a week! Special free services are included—free boat, fishing poles, blankets. Many people bring their own linen, but we can furnish it at only 50¢ extra per week per bed.

You can board at Sugar Bush and enjoy Mrs. Shattuck's wholesome, tempting meals. And just wait until you tickle your palate with her old-fashioned, delicious home cooking! For those who board, room is included in the rate of $4.50 per day per person. A family can board, occupy a cottage, and pay only half price for each child under 12.

If you want to eliminate cooking during your vacation, then why not board? Imagine getting up some brisk, lake-tanged morning with the appetite of a bear...and wading right into a stack of delicious wheat cakes, flanked by oodles of pure maple syrup (made right on the farm), a pitcher of pure Guernsey milk—Nature's beauty tonic, the kind that puts the blossoms in your cheek and a sparkle in your eye! Then, a platter of real fresh eggs, slices of Canadian pork loin roll, or farm breakfast sausage! All you can eat!

Although we've only given you a part of the story about Sugar Bush Lodge, and why it is the ideal summer resort, this is our personal invitation to you to come and share the pleasures of a memorable vacation...in Nature's own playground. Make your reservation in advance, sending a $5 deposit, and tell us how many will be in your party. Write or telephone for additional information.

We'll be seein' you—right soon.

Sincerely yours,

Okay, but before you start for Sugar Bush Lodge, let's see what Ken Raetz has to offer us at Normandy Court. The folder that described the location has been lost, but as we recall, Normandy Court is located in Michigan—not too many miles from Chicago.

Dear Mr. Frailey:

Right now Mr. LeRoy is up at Normandy Court, the lucky stiff, and as a result, a part of my job is to try to whip up prospects into a frenzy of dissatisfaction with their present surroundings and give them positive assurance that Normandy Court is one place where "All's well with the world."

I speak from experience, too. Last Memorial Day week-end we crammed more fun into three altogether too short days than I had ever thought was possible. You'll recall that that week-end was a scorcher in Chicago, but up at Normandy cool breezes ruffling the pine trees were either a pleasant lullaby or an exhilarating cocktail...as you preferred.

I am not a fisherman, but one of the guides showed me a place where a No. 7 spoon enticed three beautiful Wall Eyes into my boat. You play hard or you luxuriate in your own laziness, but it's ten to one when nightfall comes that you sleep like a baby on your Simmons Beauty Rest. And food, Mr. Frailey! People actually come from miles around, and even from other lodges, mind you, to revel in the chef's gustatory miracles.

If Joe was literary minded, we would call him Merlin, for it's my feeling that "Joe" is entirely too prosaic a name for a man accomplished as he.

Quite a few ad men and others associated with the graphic arts have made the Court their stamping grounds. You will have a good time and I am quite sure that Ed LeRoy would enjoy meeting the man whose "Bulletins for Dictators" have been such a source of constant inspiration in our regular advertising work.

                                                              Cordially yours,

In the foregoing letter, you saw at work a master in the use of the English language. Many of the words are little barbs that prick the imagination. The tone is intimate and personal, but not "sticky." From one advertising man to another, the approach is perfect. The message is short, but long enough to make the reader feel that the writer is thoroughly sold on Normandy Court. Some of the phrases are extremely vivid: a pleasant lullaby or an exhilarating cocktail...enticed three beautiful Wall Eyes... luxuriate in your own laziness...to revel in the chef's gustatory miracles. Yes, this letter gives the imagination an exciting prod. Result—a strong urge to be off to Normandy Court.

But wait a minute—this workout of your imagination is not over. Perhaps you will prefer the cabin Hassenpfeffer, up in the North Woods. Rose Kreuser tells you about it—for the owner.

Dear Mr. Doe:

Do you still feel yourself in the clutches of "Ole Man Winter"? Are you weary and tired of cold, sleet, ice—one sunless day after another? Has battling the elements for nothing less than five months just about worn you out? Do you have that listless feeling—just a casual interest in the things that used to seem so vital?

Man—what you need is a rippling lake full of fighting bass— trout—pike; a rowboat with a lazyback chair—a can of worms— a box of spinners and flies—a reel. You need a sun-kissed white sand beach—cool, restful evening—and nights bathed in silvery, shimmering moonlight—moonlight peeking through tall, imposing pines—short, bristling cedars—green furry spruce.

Man—you need to rub the soles of your feet on a carpet of spongy pine needles—you need to hear the chatter of the chipmunk—the screech of the loon—the hoot of the owl—the "whippoorwill" of that odd night bird. You need the distant wail of the coyote—the sight of a frightened deer.

Man—you need the North Woods—the Land of Hiawatha.

North on M-94, just eleven miles from Manistique, Michigan, on the upper peninsula, here in the heart of Hiawathaland, on the edge of Island and Dodge Lakes—the "cure" awaits you. The doors of a big brown log cabin—the cabin Hassenpfeffer— are swung open to you. Here in the thickest woods on the lapping water's edge, you'll welcome the sight of dozens of cottontails romping about the place—hiding under ferns—cottontails that gave Hassenpfeffer its name.

Hassenpfeffer is no ordinary cottage, such as you would expect to find in a near-city resort. It is a two-story cabin, constructed of hewn logs—logs felled on the very spot where Hassenpfeffer was built. It has a stone foundation, and the inside is finished in natural white birch, taken from wooded acres around the cabin.

A large, bright kitchen, equipped with oil stove, inside pump, and ice box, a dining room with natural stone fireplace, and a rambling screened sun porch covering the whole front of the cabin, occupy the main floor. Up the stairs off the kitchen, the second floor is an airy, comfortable bedroom which will accommodate at least six people. This second floor can easily be curtained or partitioned—as you wish.

Unlike other cabins that must be closed at the end of the summer, Hassenpfeffer is so securely built—so snug and warm in winter, it is an excellent hunting lodge. In fact, it's only two years old. During open season, you can hunt raccoon, pheasant, duck, wild geese, bear, deer, coyote, fox, wolf.

Hassenpfeffer stands on a little hill, about 130 feet from the white sand beach of Island Lake. The cabin itself is literally hidden by pines, cedars, and spruce—all of which throw soft, welcome shade over it on hot summer days. For decades, pine needles have been dropping to the ground, until now they have formed a spongy carpet over the whole territory. It is a delightful sensation just to step on Nature's own inimitable carpet—a sensation you will never forget.

Nor will you forget the air, permeated with pine and cedar. You can't help noticing the difference the moment you breathe in. The whole upper peninsula is a refuge for hay fever sufferers. And—there are no snakes or reptiles anywhere on the upper peninsula.

Island Lake joins Dodge Lake about halfway across. Both lakes are full of big, fighting bass, trout, and pike—to say nothing of the thousands of game little perch, sunfish, bluegills. Here you fish at dawn—by day—at twilight—by moonlight. Some beauties are just waiting to be caught—there's never a dull moment.

Nor is there any danger that either Island or Dodge Lake will be some day fished out. Every year, at the end of the summer, the Michigan State Fish Hatchery replenishes the supply with hundreds of tiny fish that will one day grab your hook.

Island Lake has a yellow sand bottom; the water is so clear you can see right down. It's perfect for diving and swimming.

If you wish to play golf, the Hiawatha daily fee course is just two miles from cabin Hassenpfeffer; the private club, five miles out. Both courses are in excellent condition.

When you start on your vacation, wouldn't you like to *know* that you are going to a heavenly spot in a movieland setting? A spot where you can have every vacation advantage? Where you will be really secluded—away from the noise and heat of the city? Where thrills and excitement await you? Where you will enjoy cool, restful nights?

Hiawathaland has all this. It can be yours not only this year, but every year, because we're selling cabin Hassenpfeffer and five acres of woodland for $10,000. As you wish, you may make a downpayment of $1,000, and we will arrange convenient terms— or you can purchase it outright.

Mr. Doe, we promise you a vacation such as you never have had before. Come up for a few weeks—live in Hassenpfeffer cabin— see for yourself why you should own it.

The attached reply card supplies the details. Mail it right away, so that we will know when to expect you.

Sincerely yours,

Well, there you have them—three sales letters out to do a similar job. Did they stir your imagination with their many interesting facts? Where would you choose to go—to Sugar Bush Lodge, to Normandy Court, or to Hassenpfeffer cabin?

Excitement of home ownership. There are few families in the world that do not crave to own their own home; and many of those that have a home are dreaming of the day when they can own a better one. A home is not just a mass of bricks, lumber, or stone. It is a place where the owners may do as they please, where no landlord can tell them they must move, where the children and their pets can play unmolested, where loving care can shape the grounds with trees and flowers and shrubs—so that everything more and more reflects the personalities of those who live there. There is

Sales Letter to Flower Lovers

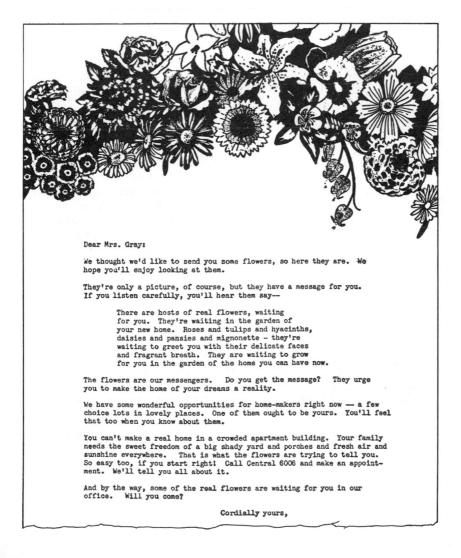

Dear Mrs. Gray:

We thought we'd like to send you some flowers, so here they are. We hope you'll enjoy looking at them.

They're only a picture, of course, but they have a message for you. If you listen carefully, you'll hear them say—

> There are hosts of real flowers, waiting
> for you. They're waiting in the garden of
> your new home. Roses and tulips and hyacinths,
> daisies and pansies and mignonette – they're
> waiting to greet you with their delicate faces
> and fragrant breath. They are waiting to grow
> for you in the garden of the home you can have now.

The flowers are our messengers. Do you get the message? They urge you to make the home of your dreams a reality.

We have some wonderful opportunities for home-makers right now — a few choice lots in lovely places. One of them ought to be yours. You'll feel that too when you know about them.

You can't make a real home in a crowded apartment building. Your family needs the sweet freedom of a big shady yard and porches and fresh air and sunshine everywhere. That is what the flowers are trying to tell you. So easy too, if you start right! Call Central 6006 and make an appointment. We'll tell you all about it.

And by the way, some of the real flowers are waiting for you in our office. Will you come?

Cordially yours,

so much about the thought of owning a home that stirs the imagination of a family that doesn't have one. Is it any wonder that many of the most colorful letters are those selling homes? Or selling something to make them more precious?

In its original form, the sales letter on page 475 was far more spectacular than the reproduction in black and white, because the flowers at the top were in their natural colors. And love of flowers is the soft spot which the letter seeks to touch! Most people are flower lovers, particularly, the women—and it is the women who usually make the decision when homes are bought. Although the writer is offering lots instead of completed dwellings, the imaginative appeals are just the same.

Another letter (by Harold McQueen) seeks to picture what a few trees, set in the right places, might do in beautifying the exterior of a home—hoping that the picture will grow in the reader's mind until action is impelled. It reads:

Dear Mr. Doe:

Christmas—New Year's—and now the ever-welcome breathing spell. Dare I ask you to day-dream for a moment—about next summer?

It's July!

Once more the sun is bearing down in much too generous proportions for comfort. Around the rustics seat, we again wish those spreading Sugar Maples were making that spot more attractive. The bare corner of the house should be set off by the decorative Honey Locust we've spoken about so often. And our porch! For two years now our next door neighbors have used theirs every hot afternoon, protected by the cool shade of the Elms they planted.

Desires that come too late! "If only we had thought about them sooner, we would be enjoying them right now," you say to yourselves.

Now let's skip back again—to today—and suggest:

Whatever your desires for next summer may be, they can be fulfilled if you plant your trees NOW.

Moved best (and at less cost) when they are dormant—their life-giving sap will start to flow weeks BEFORE the first signs of Spring.

A word from you on the enclosed card will start the ball rolling. Yes, come to think of it—a ball of earth—holding the tree you want in use next July.

Sincerely,

REALTORS, DESIGNERS, BUILDERS, MANAGEMENT, INVESTMENTS
2550 CRAWFORD AVENUE · EVANSTON, ILLINOIS · UNIVERSITY 9-1000 · BROADWAY 3-4080

Dear Mr. and Mrs. Frailey:

I have just finished a lovely home in the Williamsburg tradition at 1211 Chestnut Street, East Wilmette, which has been awarded the Good Housekeeping shield for excellence in design and construction. Needless to say, I am mighty proud of the award and certainly would like to have you see this new home.

It was a massive double-door entry with shutters on either side flanked by potted cedars; a circular staircase; a huge bowed picture window in the living room; a natural wood-burning fireplace with a marble-faced mantel; and a shuttered door screen between the living room and dining room. One entire wall of the dining room is a glass window.

The kitchen, if I say so myself, is a masterpiece of efficiency, beauty, and design, with its snack table, Dutch door, and serving pantry. The family room is paneled in pickled pine and opens out to an outdoor screened porch. One side of this porch is in the new modern glass brick. A separate staircase leads directly to the servant's quarters.

There are three master bedrooms with two master baths, beautifully tiled (one bath has a glass-enclosed, tiled shower stall) -- in addition to a downstairs powder room.

The decorations throughout the house were selected by Mrs. Blietz, and I think she has done a beautiful job. Why not drive out this way some Sunday soon and see for yourself? I'll be at the house every Sunday from two until six, and would really enjoy showing it to you.

Incidentally, I wonder if you saw the publicity that the Chicago metropolitan papers carried regarding the Connecticut Village of thirty-nine homes that I am starting just one block south of the Kenilworth Station of the Northwestern and North Shore Railroads in East Wilmette (walking distance to the lake).

In this Village I will have winding streets, James River lamp posts, evergreen landscaping, and outstanding character such as made the Indian Boundary Park development so famous. The homes will all be in the better Colonial tradition and will range in size and price from 6 rooms, 1 1/2 baths at $19,500 to 9 rooms, 3 1/2 baths at $37,500. I mention this village thinking that you or some of your friends might be interested.

If you know of anyone who is thinking of buying or building a home, I will be happy to send them complete details about this development, if you will furnish me with their names and addresses on the enclosed card.

Looking forward to a visit from you, and with my best wishes for the New Year.

Sincerely yours,

Irvin A. Blietz

DESIGNERS AND BUILDERS OF: KINGS COVE ON THE EAST FORK, CARRIAGE HILL ON THE WEST FORK CONNECTICUT,
NEW ENGLAND, PARKWOOD, PINE TREE, PANORAMA WILLIAMSBURG, SPRUCEWOOD, ELM TREE, HILLSIDE, LINDEN
VILLAGES, PEBBLEWOOD LANE, INDIAN HILL NORTH AND OTHER FINE NORTH SHORE HOMES AND APARTMENTS

Letter to Create Mental Image of the Home

In the above letter there is no concealment of purpose. The writer says, "Dare I ask you to day-dream for a moment?"—he wants the reader to *imagine* the trees he talks about—to see them as they might stand next summer, if only he will start the ball rolling. And if successful in creating those mental images, the writer stands a good chance of transforming imagination to reality.

In another letter, Irvin A. Blietz, Wilmette home builder, is offering one of his own houses, and he takes time to describe every point of utility and beauty. This is a very wise procedure for a letter of this type. A woman wants to know all the details that Mr. Blietz supplies. They may stretch the letter longer than might seem necessary, but time is not a worry of the average woman home-buyer. She wants all the facts.

7. Mistakes to Avoid in Sales Letters

Things the masters never do. Many of the costly mistakes made in sales-letter writing can easily be avoided. They are the result of ignorance rather than intent, as no writer *wants* to lessen the chances of success for what he is trying to do. Consequently, it is well that we listen to the voice of experience and view with an open mind the tips the masters give us. Probably you know by name at least some of those who pioneered the way in selling by mail—Homer Buckley, Charles Wiers, John Howie Wright, Louis Victor Eytinge, Jack Carr, Henry Hoke, and the others—some still on the job. To this group can be added the younger men who have followed up the trail—many represented by letters you have seen or will see in this Handbook; all making their personal contribution to the principles of sales-letter construction as we now know them; all helping to develop an art that still has many secrets untouched.

Although the work of these masters varies according to their respective personalities and beliefs, there are nevertheless certain cardinal points on which they all agree: things *to do* that will increase the pull of a sales letter; things *not to do,* that will decrease that pull—so much that it may not pull at all. Throughout the pages of this Handbook, you have seen what these principles are, and there are still others yet to be revealed. We have surveyed chiefly the positive side of the picture: devices and procedures developed because they are known to be helpful. Here, however, you are to let them tell you about the negative side: traps to avoid; *don'ts* in sales-letter writing. They are all simple enough, and yet the frequency with which they are disregarded in business correspondence indicates they are not generally understood. Consider these errors carefully, for any one of them might easily cause a letter of your own to fail.

DON'T belittle your reader. Often a sales-letter writer, in his eagerness to make the sale, comes up with an assertion which tends to belittle, humiliate, or ridicule either the reader or something about his business. The statement may be merely an insinuation, but it is likely to cause offense. Here are statements taken from actual business letters. Probably none of the writers realized the negative reaction set up in the reader's mind. Ignorance may be bliss, but it still doesn't pay off in sales letters.

From a letter offering detective services:

"We are of the opinion that there is something wrong, or that you suspect there is something wrong in your place of business."

Even if true, this is an irritating remark. The reader may close his mind to anything else that is said in the letter. What right, he thinks, has any stranger to make such a bald accusation.

From a letter offering mailing lists:

"Your own mailings and those taken care of by so-called mailers, often reach the wrong prospects. That's the reason for your failure."

Fighting talk, with two barbs to prick the reader! First, the writer takes a crack at his competitors, the "so-called mailers"; second, he uses the nasty words, "your failure."

From a letter offering wallpaper:

"Why do you depend on luck to increase your business?"

This question is insulting. The reader is told that he is inefficient. He depends on luck.

From a letter selling boiler equipment:

"Don't close your eyes to changing times. Don't feel that you can continue to operate with inefficient and wasteful equipment."

First, the writer insinuates that his prospect is not up-to-date. Then he makes the plain accusation that the present equipment is inefficient and wasteful. The word "continue" does the dirty work.

From a letter selling glassware:

"These dealers are letting someone else go after the pennies— they go after the quality merchandise trade at a real profit. Why gamble with your future?"

The other dealers are smart but this one is dumb, insinuates the writer. Worse than that, this prospect doesn't use his head—he "gambles" with his future.

From a letter offering typewriters:

"Do you fumble the sales inquiries that come to the Doe Corporation?"

Pleasing question, isn't it? The writer doesn't exactly call his prospect a "fumbler," but he wants to know if it could be true.

This was the opening sentence. The man who got the letter—the president—doesn't know what was said later. He didn't read it.

From a letter offering accounting systems:

"There's mighty little fun in being robbed day by day, dollar by dollar, by antiquated accounting and collection equipment in your own office."

Since the writer is selling the "cure," it must be taken that he means his prospect's equipment is the antiquated kind. No doubt this is true, but some things are better not mentioned.

If you agree that the quotations just exposed were humiliating to the men to whom the letters were sent, then you are in the proper mood to inspect an even more horrible example of tactlessness. The writer is a business consultant offering his services.

	Gentlemen:
Insinuates the prospect has not been efficient	In view of the economic situation, it has become imperative that you...operate more efficiently if you intend to show a proper return on your investment and effort.
Insulting questions	Do you know the facts about your business? Do you face them squarely? Because of our broad experience...we believe we can help you do that and more.
Ends with tactless question	The writer is frequently in the vicinity of your office. Are you sufficiently interested to extend him the courtesy of an interview?
	Yours very truly,
Conceited implication; smart men value my importance	P. S. Years ago, a similar letter went to a junior executive of a company, who referred it to the general manager. I served that company many years, more recently the second generation. This junior executive is now head of the institution.

The tragedy of the examples just reviewed is that the thought behind the belittling statements was well intended; at least, the writers had no idea they were handicapping their own efforts. The same thoughts could just as easily have been expressed in a tactful way. For example:

Negative	"Your own mailings and those taken care of by so-called mailers, often reach the wrong prospect. That's the reason for your failure."

Positive   "You know how it is with mailings. Unless they reach the right prospects, they are doomed to failure."

The negative sentence places the blame on the reader; states the failure as a fact. The positive sentence presents the problem impersonally—assumes the reader will agree how important it is that the right prospects are reached.

This is a very important point in sales-letter writing; *don't* put your reader on the defensive. *Don't* insinuate. *Don't* humiliate. *Don't* belittle.

DON'T exaggerate. The bridge-player who consistently over-bids his cards soon loses the confidence of his partner; the sales-letter writer who over-bids his product soon loses the confidence of his reader. And that means, loses the sale! Truly, exaggeration is a poor weapon. Guard against it. You know the importance of sincerity in any contact with a fellow human being; you know that it is impossible to stretch facts beyond reality and at the same time be sincere. If a letter-writer isn't fooling himself, how can he expect to fool his reader? Of course, you may make a sale with facts you know are not true, but in the long run you are sure to lose a customer; never forget that in business there are ethics that must be respected.

However, much of the exaggeration seen in letters and advertising is not necessarily meant to deceive; the people responsible for it simply seem to proceed on the basis that those who read are very small children or morons. For example, a while back we were told in the national magazines that the easiest way to make a hit with the men is to make party sandwiches with a certain food preparation. That may be a good tip, but we doubt if many young ladies would endorse it. Another magazine advertisement showed a gay young couple driving down the highway, with this foolish dialogue beneath the picture.

He: Is that trooper following us with arresting intent?
She: He wouldn't give *you* a ticket, darling. You look too impressive in your new ——— hat.

You encounter a lot of that kind of piffle in modern advertising; you encounter far too much of it in sales letters. "Do you want your sales letters to produce the maximum number of orders?" asks one sales manager. "If your answer is *yes,*" he continues, "be sure to use our envelopes." Nonsense, isn't it? The envelopes *could* help, but there are numerous other factors that team to produce the maximum number of orders. The statement is pure exaggeration, and the reader is chilled rather than warmed by it. Note the exaggerated statements that follow—the words in italics that are overdrawn.

Your last letter gave me the thrill *of my life.*

John, I *won't be able to sleep* until I know you got this order.

You know I hold your opinion *above all others.*

Nothing could please me more than to grant this concession, if company policy would permit.

We are *worried sick* about this mistake, and will *never* be so embarrassed.

It *hurts us more* than it *could possibly* hurt you.

You might *search the world over,* and *never find* an opportunity like this.

Joe, there are a *thousand reasons* why you should not quit under fire.

We appreciate your business *more than we can say.*

This is the *biggest chance you have ever had* to double your sales.

It's the opportunity *of a lifetime.*

I am *amazed* that one in whom we placed *implicit* confidence should refuse to pay this bill.

You are one of a *carefully selected few* to whom we are making this offer.

Remember as a sales-letter writer that facts need no stretching; exaggeration *weakens* your arguments, lessens your chances of success. Put your best foot forward—write with enthusiasm—but be sure it *is* your foot, just as you describe it. Exaggerated copy is only an insult to the reader's intelligence—it never pays. This is one of the things that all good letter-writers know.

DON'T try to trick the reader. Experienced and ethical writers do not hold feed bags in front of their readers, as may be done with a horse or mule to get him to move forward. Neither do they make statements not strictly true, in the effort to flatter or please them. As was said a moment ago, sincerity is the only foundation for a sales letter which will stand firm to the end. Notice how the following letter begins:

Will you accept a beautiful fountain pen and pencil—WITH MY COMPLIMENTS?

With your permission, I am going to send you a big new fountain pen and pencil, oversized, self-filling, with 14 karat gold point —FREE.

And if you care to pay the small cost of engraving (only 25¢), I'll have your full name die-stamped on it in solid gold leaf.

The circular enclosed shows you this beautiful new pen and pencil in its exact size. It looks as good, and works as well, as the pens which sell in stores at $3 to $5, and the makers guarantee it to give as satisfactory service. More than that, your name on it in letters of gold gives it a distinctiveness often lacking in high priced pens.

Are there any strings tied to that offer? Not a one. Of course, the words "with your permission" tell any intelligent person that there is something fishy which has yet to show up. An extremely gullible reader might think he is about to get the pen and pencil free, as the letter plainly states, but the next paragraph in the letter destroys that dream.

I am going to send this fountain pen and pencil to you, just to get you to TRY our new letterheads and envelopes with your name and address on them in raised letters.

So the truth comes out. In reality this beautiful pen and pencil, the kind that sells in stores at $3 to $5, is not free. Here is what the reader has to do to get it:

The regular price of the 100 letterheads and envelopes, with monogram and address on them in raised letters, is $2.98. If you mail the enclosed Reservation at once, you get them for the $2.98—AND IN ADDITION you get the beautiful fountain pen and pencil FREE OF CHARGE.

What does common sense tell you about such an offer? If the pen and pencil is worth $3 to $5 how can the company afford to sell the stationery and envelopes for $2.98? Either the reader will pay far more for the latter than they are worth, or the pen and pencil don't have the value described. Obviously, the company has to come out with a profit on both items—the reader is being deceived one way or the other.

The above is not intended to criticize the use of premiums, when offered as such and without any attempt to hoodwink the reader. But it does criticize the *way* the pen and pencil set was offered, and with the obvious impossibility that a $3 item could be given free in a sale amounting to $2.98. The value is simply too big compared to the price of the stationery.

Another form of deception, although it may be mild, is when a condition is described as an excuse for writing the letter—a condition that will hardly hold water in the light of human intelligence. It is something more than mere exaggeration, because the writer must have his tongue in his cheek as he states the condition. Here are some examples:

Hundreds of letters have been received asking if our kits would be available as Christmas gifts. This national approval leads

> us to suggest to you the attractiveness of the Christmas wrapped. . . ."
>
> "Although our Fifth Birthday occurred in October, we have been amazed at the requests we are getting for an extension of our remarkable combination subscription offer. . .so by popular demand, we are going to reopen this special offer to a selected list of old friends only. . . "
>
> "Many of my customers have written me, asking if I could quote a quantity price on my pipes and tobacco, to be given to friends, relatives, employees, and business associates at Christmas."

In all of the above letter introductions, the writers seek to convey the impression that they have been swamped by requests for the action later explained. "Hundreds of letters" cannot properly be interpreted as "national approval"—the number is too small. In the second quotation, it seems the writer was rather easily "amazed" and the idea of a "selected list" is extremely stale. It is also a fortunate coincidence that in the letters to the pipe merchant, all groups of possible prospects were mentioned—"friends, relatives, employees, and business associates." These, of course, are the same groups the writer would have mentioned had the letter been written on his own initiative, instead of by popular request.

Neither can we swallow without a wink the introduction used by another circulation manager.

> This letter, coming to you in advance of any public announcement, is intended for your eyes alone. It contains information we ask you to regard as confidential. You will see why in a moment.
>
> We are sending this letter at this time to only a few of our old customers, because we feel that they are entitled to first chance at this remarkable offer.

Here the reader is given a little secret. For some reason not explained, only a few of the old customers are to have a shot at the remarkable offer—he is one of the chosen few. If true, it is easy to see why the matter must be a secret. What would the other old customers think if they knew they were not cut in? We could be wrong, but it seems more logical to think that *all* of the old customers who were in good standing with the company got the letter. If not, those left out certainly had cause to feel slighted.

Perhaps you have respected the memory of the famous violin makers of the past; certainly, you know how their violins are prized by the great players, and the prices they bring when sold. Well, maybe we have been deceived about violin-making. Maybe you or anyone else with a workbench can turn out a fine violin. That at least is the impression developed by a sales letter from a company which has all the "makings." Here are the bits that can be quoted:

> Dear Friends:
>
> What a thrill to hear the rich golden tone of a violin made with your own hands in your own home! How you can amaze your friends! And this at a cost of only a few pennies a day.
>
> ...Of all the hobbies today, violin making is easily beginning to take the lead with men and women who are eager to make things with their own hands that are really worthwhile. Things that were formerly considered impossible!... It is a most unique hobby—intensely interesting, yet actually simple enough for you or any home craftsman to master at once.... No wonder hundreds of people are now adopting this hobby, and other hundreds have already satisfactorily completed one or more technically perfect instruments.
>
> ...All of the materials in our Kits are of the very finest to be obtained, assuring you of a fine instrument—one that you'll be proud to play and to show to your friends.
>
> ...Don't deprive yourself of this supreme enjoyment another day. BEGIN THIS FASCINATING HOBBY NOW!
>
> Sincerely yours,

Yes, we think it would be fun to build a violin, but is the job as easy as the writer of this sales letter leads us to believe? How does he say it—"Actually *simple enough* for you or any other home craftsman *to master at once.*" Be still, old masters in the art! Don't turn over in your graves! This writer has just eaten too much spinach.

And what do you think of the conflicting statements in the following opening and closing paragraphs of another sales letter? The first one says, "Don't worry—I won't shoot." The second fires the shot.

> Naturally you will think this another letter asking you to renew your subscription. It isn't. Your subscription has been canceled and I am writing now simply to ask some assistance from you....
>
> If you have changed your mind and do want the subscription then I'll know my work wasn't so badly done. In that case, just put your initials alongside this paragraph, return to me, and I

will see that a NEW subscription is entered to begin with the current issue.

Of course, the writer does leave himself one loophole, but one too small for squeezing through. He declares the OLD subscription has been canceled—all he wants is a NEW one.

DON'T be too flippant. The margin between cleverness and flippancy is sometimes rather thin. One man has the ability to write in a gay and nonchalant manner without irritating his readers; another tries the same tactics, and arouses only antagonism. The difference is intangible, but real. Certainly, beginners who are not sure of themselves should not attempt to spread their wings too far.

In the attempt to lighten the tone of their letters, you often see writers using slang words or expressions. The attempt usually fails. Especially irritating are such words as "Gosh," or "Golly," or "Heck." They make the letter sound too juvenile; the writer, too immature. Also in the same objectionable class are such combinations as "Wotinhel," or "Damitall," or any similar form of disguised profanity. The use of slang and profanity was discussed in an earlier section of this Handbook—the suggestions given are especially important with respect to sales letters.

DON'T abuse your competitor or his product. A commendable trait in the average person is his love of fair-play. He does not admire the man in business who runs down his competitor, or another product or service. If the man thus attacked were present to tell his side of the story, it might be different. But sales-letter writers who disparage competition orally or in writing are seldom received with favor. Read the following contrasting letters—written to customers by partners who had severed their relationship. Which of these letters do you think the customers liked best?

(1)

Gentlemen:

This is to advise you that I have bought the interest of my former partner, John Doe, in X-Y, Incorporated, and that he is no longer connected with the company.

I want to thank you for your many courtesies in the past, and for your loyalty to the company, which I hope will continue.

Our name, our products, our package and our catalog are known throughout the Industry, and the business will continue to be operated as usual, and under the same high standards.

It is our aim to contribute everything possible to your continued growth, and we will be constantly seeking new ways in which to serve your business.

In grateful appreciation of your goodwill,

Sincerely yours,

(2)

I hate to hang out
the dirty wash BUT

...my partner and I have split up...we're quite washed up...through...we've kissed each other goodbye...and now HE'S sole owner of X-Y, Incorporated (there I go giving him free advertising already).

So what? Well, I thought you might be interested to know that although my former partner bought ME out, I'm by no means quitting the automotive parts business. Not by a long shot. After all, I've been eating...sleeping...dreaming...buying... selling...cataloging automotive parts for a good many years... and people who should know have told me that I've done a pretty good job. Now, without any ENCUMBRANCES, handicaps, etc., etc., I believe I can do a better job.

And that's exactly what I'm doing right now...building the finest automotive replacement parts business to be found anywhere.

Judging from the congratulations and good wishes I'm receiving from old customers, manufacturers, sources of supply and many good friends, this new ——————————— CORPORATION will really and truly be worthy of your business.

I'm all set...in our own building   0000 S. Michigan Avenue. So won't you please try to save a little piece of an order for a guy who has always appreciated your business?

All kidding aside! I've got my sleeves rolled up an I'm earnestly going into the replacement parts business in a big way, and soon one of our representatives will be in to see you. When you happen to be in Chicago, I hope you'll drop in for a handshake and a hello.

Cordially yours,

It is impossible to decide from these two letters what caused the split in partnership and which of the two men, if either, had the greater reason to be provoked. But clearly the writer of the first letter puts himself in a far better position with the old customers. He says nothing at all to the detriment of his former associate.

To be sure, there is much temptation for a sales-letter writer to compare the strength of his own product with the weakness of another; to expose some deficiency in the other company's service; to play tit-for-tat with other organizations that have not been ethical. But an eye for an eye, a tooth for a tooth, is never a winning slogan in letters, or any other part of business. In the long run, the writer who concentrates on the advantages and quality of his own product is the one who comes up with the most goodwill from customers and prospects. Yes, of course, if he has a "point of difference," he can and should put the spotlight on it, because if the prospect cannot find this advantage elsewhere, he will surely come to his company for it.

DON'T ballyhoo. Some sales letters call to mind the spieler outside the circus side-show—big noise and fervor, nothing specific to back his claims. Plenty of ballyhoo, but no ballast! Merely to make a number of empty assertions about a product is the lowest degree of salesmanship. You have witnessed the value of *proof* in getting favorable action; you know that a generality is only a shell without the oyster. And yet how often you read in sales letters:

> "The astonishing performance of this razor will"...
> "You will appreciate the many modern refinements in this utterly different automobile"...
> "Right from the can, as good as mother could make, and yours without"...
> "With gay lines in the modern trend"...

Just a lot of ballyhoo! How shall the reader interpret it? *How* will he be astonished when he puts the razor to his face? What *are* modern refinements? How different is *utterly*? *Nothing* from a can could equal mother's cooking—at least, *prove* it. Just what *are* gay lines in the modern trend? Do any of these high-sounding phrases paint sharp pictures in the reader's mind? Absolutely not—no pictures at all.

Here's a sales letter from a laundry. The writer wants Mrs. Doe to try the "finest laundry service" in Cleveland. But any laundry could talk in terms of "finest." *Why* is it the finest? Where's the proof?

A hotel in New York wants Mr. Doe to stop there on his next trip. The writer says his hotel is "truly different." Yes, a lot of hotels are "different"—unpleasantly so. Anyway, if he means there are advantages in staying there not found in other hotels, just what *are* they? Where's the proof?

"You should attend this annual banquet. The entertainment will be *unusual* and the speeches will be *outstanding.*" Wonderful! But you said after the banquet last year, that you would never be hooked for another—

ten dollars for a tough steak, a boiled potato, and the inevitable apple pie; a couple of tap-dancers and a funny ·man who wasn't funny; a soap-box speaker who prattled about world affairs. Should you try again? Why? Unusual entertainment! Unusual in *what way?* Outstanding speeches! What does the writer *mean* by outstanding? Could this banquet be worth ten dollars, and a whole evening of your time? Where's the proof?

Generalities need to be *explained*. They won't stand alone. "Save for the future—practice thrift while you are young, and you will be protected when you are old," says a sales-letter writer. The sentence sounds all right, but what is there in it to be remembered a half hour later? *Thrift* is an abstract word. So is *protected*. They are like drops of water—soon evaporated. Why didn't the writer *interpret* "thrift" and "protected": money in the bank when too old to work; travel, contentment, independence; not left destitute and unwanted when the sun of life begins to set.

Don't be a circus spieler in your sales letters. Come down from the clouds—put your feet on solid earth. If you have something *worth* buying, tell the reader *why*. Be specific. Give him proof.

So there you have them—things the master letter writers don't do.

Don't belittle your reader. The man humiliated is never your friend.

Don't exaggerate. A truth needs no stretching. The reader knows you are taking him for a ride. You fool only yourself.

Don't try to trick your reader. Don't put false bait under his nose. All of the cards belong on top of the table.

Don't be flippant. Buying is a serious matter to the reader, if not to you.

Don't disparage your competitor or his product. Show the reader what *you* can do for him. It doesn't matter what the other fellow *can't* do.

Don't ballyhoo. Thunder is only a big noise; a bolt of lightning gets attention.

Simple enough—these "Don'ts"; disregard them, and your letters will not sell.

8. Dramatized Sales Letters

To win special attention. In Section 3 (pages 128 to 159), you have seen how the business-letter writer may use some form of showmanship to make his message different. The idea is that it may capture preferred attention in competition with letters of the more conventional type. You have seen, too, the qualifications of a good dramatized letter, and the faults that may cause one to be ineffective. You know that the idea must not be farfetched or remote from the central thought of the letter, and unless it is really clever, it may do more harm than good.

When used with discretion and good taste, a dramatized idea may be especially effective in a sales letter. It tends to break down the reader's initial resistance, and to put him in the mood to continue the message. Psychologically, however, showmanship in selling faces the danger of being received as an attempt to "show off," so that the prospect feels he is being maneuvered into buying by a clever person and must guard against him. The idea should never be so spectacular that it over-shadows the rest of the letter. In other words, it should *aid* the general sales thought, rather than *compete* with it.

The very best of all dramatized sales letters are those that manage to sample the product. A fine example was the letter (page 141) with the pieces of yarn attached—illustrating the difference between hand-made and machine-made yarns used in rugs. The purpose of the idea was to *instruct* more than to *impress* the reader, although the final result was as convincing as any sales message could possibly be. Perhaps in some similar way your own product can be dramatized for presentation to prospects. If so, go ahead and prepare the letter. It will probably outpull any of the conventional letters you have used.

The following dramatized letters will complete the collection started in the earlier section; you should be able to pick out from the collection a number of ideas adaptable to your particular type of business.

Showmanship by The Cincinnati Inquirer. Here's a letter used by *The Cincinnati Inquirer* to sell accident protection—probably as an inducement to subscribe to the paper. The letter does not attempt to complete the deal, but paves the way for a personal call.

With a large question mark, a note in script on the back of the bill, which is enclosed with the letter, hastens to cushion the shock—"Suppose this bill were YOURS —could your pocketbook stand this unexpected expense?" Then the letter explains:

Dear Madam:

I'm writing to you about your husband.

If he were to come home with a broken arm who would pay the doctor and hospital bills? Suppose he were hit by an automobile or fell down the stairs or was otherwise disabled by accident, would your income stop?

As long as nothing unexpected happens, your husband's income just about covers your living expenses with possibly a few dollars left over for savings.

BUT—accidents, like lightning, strike without warning. Every minute 17 persons are accidentally injured or killed! Suppose your husband were to have an accident today. The unexpected expense for doctors, hospital, druggist, etc. would seriously interfere with your income and might wreck your savings account too.

There's only ONE way to protect yourself and your family from the heavy expense of accidental injuries.

It will be a real pleasure for me to tell you how you can get this protection easily and inexpensively. I will call within a day or two to discuss this vital problem with you.

It will take only a few minutes and you will not be obligated or disappointed.

Yours very truly,

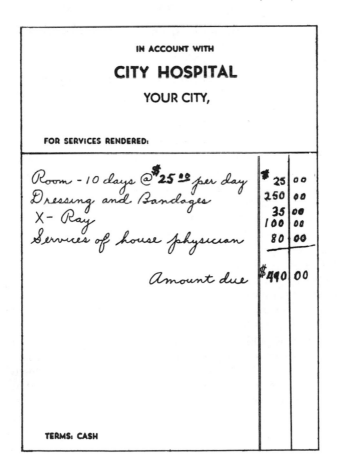

IN ACCOUNT WITH

CITY HOSPITAL

YOUR CITY,

FOR SERVICES RENDERED:

	$	
Room - 10 days @ $25 00 per day	25	00
Dressing and Bandages	250	00
X-Ray	35	00
	100	00
Services of house physician	80	00
Amount due	$440	00

TERMS: CASH

Of course, you noticed that this letter is addressed to the lady of the family, rather than to the husband. The dramatized idea should have even more appeal to women, than to men. Housewives probably get fewer letters, and seldom one so spectacular. Because of the implication of moderate income, it is also plain that the letter is slanted at wage earners. Persons of greater wealth might resent the implication.

Reader's name in large script. If it is true that an individual is most interested in himself, then the sales letters that dramatize his name should have special attention value. Instead of the conventional address and salutation, the following letter, written for *Tide* by Harry H. Costello, carries the names "Sutton & Peterson" at the top in red script. The letters are about an inch high and stretch across as much of the page as does the body of the message. In addition to this attention device, you will admit that the letter is written with refreshing humor and frankness.

THIS LETTER IS GOING TO BE DIFFERENT.

I'm not going to start out by saying that just because 7100 busy executives read TIDE—that is any reason why you should read it.

And, I'm not going to tell you how TIDE keeps your mind refreshed and brings you the really significant news of advertising and marketing dished out in short pithy paragraphs, piquantly flavored with anecdotes and personalities.

All I'm going to say to you is this:

> "Friend—TIDE is a good magazine for you to read.
> It's entertaining and full of interesting news that might
> suggest a new business opportunity or a new slant on
> some problem in your work. It certainly is worth 6¢ a
> week. You ought to have it."

TIDE is so good I read it myself. So, I know what I'm talking about. And, you'll like it too—once you read a copy. You see, TIDE has an editorial style all its own—the newsiness and accuracy of TIME, the compactness of READER'S DIGEST and the whimsical flavor of THE NEW YORKER—all put together in a way that makes business reading entertaining and interesting as well as useful and informative.

> TIDE is published twice a month—costs only $3 for a
> full year's subscription. You can start your subscrip-
> tion now by simply filling out and mailing the enclosed
> postage paid card. The modest fee can follow, later,
> when we send a bill.

I'm sorry I can't offer you a set of books or ten easy lessons on playing the Hawaiian guitar along with your subscription. It seems as though the boss got the crazy idea that people would buy TIDE—because they wanted to read it—and so far more than 7100 readers have backed him up. But, see for yourself what TIDE is like—fill out and mail the card TODAY.

Cordially yours,

Another way of dramatizing a sales letter is to get a prospect's license plate number and display it, along with his name, prominently in a letter. For example, if you were "Mr. Roberts," you would no doubt be pleasantly surprised to see a picture of a gasoline station attendant holding your license plate in his hand. This was done in a letter prepared by Harry Latz, which reads as follows:

THE LICENSE ON YOUR CAR, MR. ROBERTS!

Just for fun check up and see if we're not right...then drive to your nearest Gulf station and see for yourself that we have your number...especially at this time of the year!

Have you thought about the coming winter...ice, snow, hard starting, harder gear shifting...probably not...so we would like to recommend that you stop at the Gulf station right away for a Gulf winter lubrication.

You'll find a smiling attendant ready to serve you...ready to refill your crankcase with winter-grade Gulfpride Oil...the world's finest motor oil...100% pure Pennsylvania...Alchlor Processed and free-flowing in any weather. He's ready, too, to drain the worn heavy summer lubricant from your transmission and differential and refill with Gulf Transgear Lubricant winter grade...no more hard starting...grinding gears...worn parts.

Let him give your car a real Winter Lubrication...with lubricants that are made specially for winter temperature...rain-proof, slush-proof, mud-proof. Then you'll be all set for the coming season...mild or severe. Be sure to use That Good Gulf Gasoline...it's kept in step with the calendar...refined to suit the weather...it'll be your guarantee of quick starting.

There's a Gulf station near you...drive in today and have your car prepared for winter...your local Gulf man appreciates your business. Visit your Gulf dealer and get acquainted.

GET HIS NUMBER

Cordially yours,

[A Dartnell presentation]

Pictures to illustrate copy. A mild kind of showmanship in sales letters, and one that nobody can call out of place, is that where the copy is reinforced with suitable pictures. There is a heart-tug in Valentino Sarra's picture of a child's shoes.

The letter was used by B. A. Roloff as Extension Secretary for the Travelers Aid Society in Chicago. You will concede that it puts appeal in the message.

A child is missing from his home tonight—and parents wait with anxious hearts for some word of reassurance.

It makes no difference that they are poor people and the child has probably not been kidnapped—he is their child, and he is gone, and his mother lies awake tonight wondering where he is.

Thousands of children leave their homes each year without parental permission and in Chicago alone last year 777 such youngsters came to the Travelers Aid. These are the cases of which you seldom hear, because in so many of them the nation-wide chain of Travelers Aid Societies quickly intercepts the young runaways, learns their stories, and returns them safely to their homes.

This is truly a remarkable service and one of which the public knows comparatively little because it functions speedily, smoothly and without publicity. Obviously, the value can not be measured in dollars and cents. Just try to set a price on a mother's gratitude!

Wouldn't you like to help us continue this important work? Five dollars will mean a great deal to us and even one dollar will be mighty welcome. Your check in the enclosed envelope will bring happiness to grieving mothers through the return of their missing children.

Gratefully,

Illustrations of this type are just as appealing in sales letters as in any other form of selling. The reader *sees* what he is urged to buy, and if the sight is pleasing, the urge is strengthened.

Drawings made on the typewriter. You saw in Section 3 how some sales letters are dramatized by drawings made on the typewriter—usually in forms.to represent the thing talked about. Many of these attempts are too fantastic, too difficult to read, but the one reproduced for you on this page seems quite appropriate for the occasion. This message used by the Senator Hotel in Atlantic City invites the reader to arrive in time for the various Christmas functions planned by the hotel manager. Hence, the stocking

Dramatic Sales Idea for Christmas Season

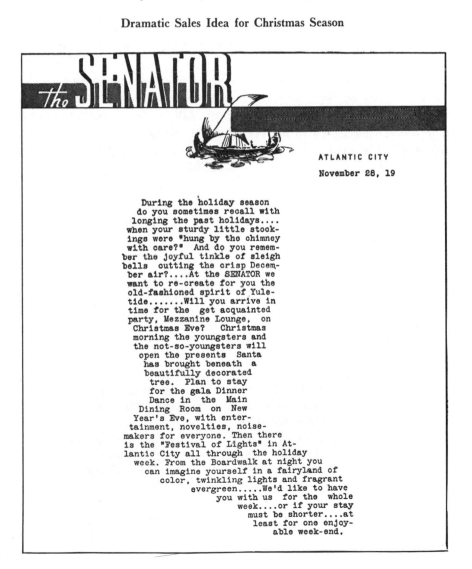

ATLANTIC CITY
November 28, 19

During the holiday season
do you sometimes recall with
longing the past holidays....
when your sturdy little stockings were "hung by the chimney
with care?" And do you remember the joyful tinkle of sleigh
bells cutting the crisp December air?....At the SENATOR we
want to re-create for you the
old-fashioned spirit of Yule-
tide.......Will you arrive in
time for the get acquainted
party, Mezzanine Lounge, on
Christmas Eve? Christmas
morning the youngsters and
the not-so-youngsters will
open the presents Santa
has brought beneath a
beautifully decorated
tree. Plan to stay
for the gala Dinner
Dance in the Main
Dining Room on New
Year's Eve, with enter-
tainment, novelties, noise-
makers for everyone. Then there
is the "Festival of Lights" in Atlantic City all through the holiday
week. From the Boardwalk at night you
can imagine yourself in a fairyland of
color, twinkling lights and fragrant
evergreen.....We'd like to have
you with us for the whole
week....or if your stay
must be shorter....at
least for one enjoy-
able week-end.

made on the typewriter seems quite effective and in tune with the holiday season. Because the length of the lines does not vary too much, the copy is not difficult to read. The letter is the cover of a four-page folder; on the inside, effective pictures of the hotel add more power to the mailing.

Simple ideas as good as any. Showmanship in sales letters sometimes takes such an elaborate form that one wonders if the game is worth the candle; the expense appears so great that only a very high pull in orders would enable the idea to pay its own freight. For those who like now and then to get out of the rut and do something different, a simple idea of very little cost may be just as effective as one that is complex and expensive. The letter with the two pieces of yarn, which rates as high as any, involved nothing more than the cost of the yarn and the time it took to staple the two pieces on each page. Anyway, it isn't the expense that counts; the result has little relation to it.

Another illustration of this fact is the effective, simple Christmas sales letter prepared by Norman Focht for The Men's Shop in West Chester, Pennsylvania. To this letter is clipped a small tag on a red string—the dime-a-dozen kind used to identify gifts. On the tag, where the name of the recipient is usually written, are two words in longhand—"To myself." And here's how the tag ties in with the 'message.

> It's this way, Mr. Doe...
>
> ...I don't believe in anyone being selfish and thinking of himself first. But I do feel as though it's all right for a fellow to give some thought to himself when he remembers others at Christmas time.
>
> And here's why...there's no one more deserving of a gift than yourself. You plug along, like most fellows, for 365 days in the year, putting in a lot of hours of hard work. So, when it's time for Santa to slide down the old chimney, you are entitled to a treat as much as Aunt Emma, Cousin Ted, the cop on the beat, and all the others.
>
> So for goodness sakes, don't skimp on yourself...give yourself something worthwhile. Tie a tag on a new suit, topcoat or overcoat from Kauffman's...a gift that will bring you a lot of happiness and satisfaction.
>
> Stop in and look over our new winter selection. It's a grand array of clothes that says "Merry Christmas" to you in no uncertain tones. And remember, we have a Budget Charge Account Plan which makes paying easy—if you desire to take advantage of it.
>
> Merry Christmas!

Whether or not the psychology back of this appeal is sound, the manner of offering the suggestion is unique. Besides, the profit on one order probably would offset the cost of the tags and labor.

How to dramatize unseen quality. Somewhat similar to the sales letter idea comparing the two pieces of yarn, but doing a more difficult job, is the one comparing the two kernels of corn. Could you think of a better way to demonstrate how a product may have hidden qualities which make it worth more than other products that *appear* just as good?

Selling hidden quality was also the purpose of the yarn letter, but the comparison was more obvious. The reader could *feel* the red and blue

In the Bag Appeared Two Real Kernels of Corn

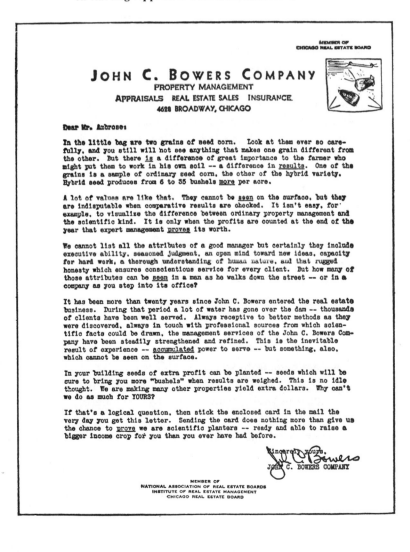

JOHN C. BOWERS COMPANY
PROPERTY MANAGEMENT
APPRAISALS   REAL ESTATE SALES   INSURANCE
4628 BROADWAY, CHICAGO

MEMBER OF
CHICAGO REAL ESTATE BOARD

Dear Mr. Ambrose:

In the little bag are two grains of seed corn. Look at them ever so carefully, and you still will not see anything that makes one grain different from the other. But there is a difference of great importance to the farmer who might put them to work in his own soil -- a difference in results. One of the grains is a sample of ordinary seed corn, the other of the hybrid variety. Hybrid seed produces from 6 to 35 bushels more per acre.

A lot of values are like that. They cannot be seen on the surface, but they are indisputable when comparative results are checked. It isn't easy, for example, to visualize the difference between ordinary property management and the scientific kind. It is only when the profits are counted at the end of the year that expert management proves its worth.

We cannot list all the attributes of a good manager but certainly they include executive ability, seasoned judgment, an open mind toward new ideas, capacity for hard work, a thorough understanding of human nature, and that rugged honesty which ensures conscientious service for every client. But how many of those attributes can be seen in a man as he walks down the street -- or in a company as you step into its office?

It has been more than twenty years since John C. Bowers entered the real estate business. During that period a lot of water has gone over the dam -- thousands of clients have been well served. Always receptive to better methods as they were discovered, always in touch with professional sources from which scientific facts could be drawn, the management services of the John C. Bowers Company have been steadily strengthened and refined. This is the inevitable result of experience -- accumulated power to serve -- but something, also, which cannot be seen on the surface.

In your building seeds of extra profit can be planted -- seeds which will be sure to bring you more "bushels" when results are weighed. This is no idle thought. We are making many other properties yield extra dollars. Why can't we do as much for YOURS?

If that's a logical question, then stick the enclosed card in the mail the very day you get this letter. Sending the card does nothing more than give us the chance to prove we are scientific planters -- ready and able to raise a bigger income crop for you than you ever have had before.

Sincerely yours,
JOHN C. BOWERS COMPANY

MEMBER OF
NATIONAL ASSOCIATION OF REAL ESTATE BOARDS
INSTITUTE OF REAL ESTATE MANAGEMENT
CHICAGO REAL ESTATE BOARD

strands—test their texture—and quickly tell the difference. But the two grains of corn are not so easily identified. One kernel is far more productive than the other, and worth a lot more to the planter, but the extra value must be proved in use.

Any company having difficulty in getting across to prospects the point of unseen quality can use advantageously this very graphic comparison of the two grains of corn. The idea carries a fact to the prospect that many pages of sales copy might not explain so effectively. It is just as good a demonstration for a service as for a product. In this particular case, the John C. Bowers Company seeks to make plain that not all property managers work with the same effectiveness; some are able to produce more income from given properties than others. There is no way of selecting the most skillful manager, however, until his services are tested in the various duties of management. Neither is there any way of knowing—at least by the layman—which of the two kinds of seed corn will produce the most bushels. But the difference in value is *there*, whether it can be seen or not.

The sales letter with the corn was one of a series used by this Chicago Realtor—the majority of the mailings being of the dramatized variety. Last of the series was one of the "big" letters described in Section 3. It was enlarged to twice the size of the ordinary business letterhead. The copy is in keeping with the "big" idea, and reads as follows:

So we decided
to make it
BIG

Several times recently you have had letters from us in which we craved the privilege of talking to you about our ability to serve you in a very special and pleasing manner.

Thus far, that privilege has not been granted, and we think it must be our fault. Either we have been too bashful in explaining what we can do for you—or we failed to make our letters stand out in your mail.

So now we are coming to you in a BIG way.

Maybe we should always use BIG paper because BIG benefits should be called to your attention with BIG emphasis.

Anyway, we are making this message short, as we don't want the BIG point to be cluttered in your mind with a lot of puny words.

It all sums up to this. We are burning with a BIG desire to serve you with BIG satisfaction to yourself.

We want to hear you say, "Come on over with your BIG ideas about managing real estate—but they had better be BIG or you'll get a BIG invitation to leave."

To make it easy for you to reply, we are attaching a letter all ready for you to mail back to us.

The letter contains one BIG word—and when it gets back to us our thanks will be BIG too.

Yours for BIG profits,

The letter the reader is asked to return continues to emphasize the "BIG" idea. The one BIG word "Yes" does the job. This return letter is reproduced for you below. Together—the letter to the prospect and the one he is supposed to return—they are an example of showmanship in sales-letter writing at its best.

Dramatizing the Important Word

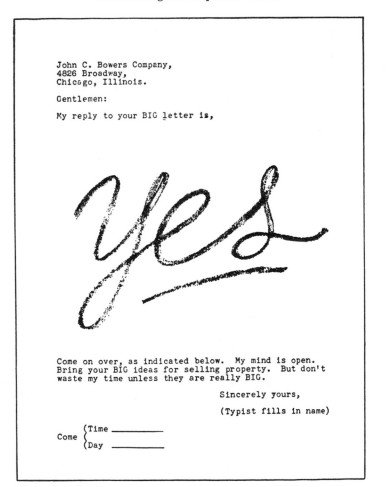

```
    John C. Bowers Company,
    4826 Broadway,
    Chicago, Illinois.

    Gentlemen:

    My reply to your BIG letter is,
```

Yes

```
    Come on over, as indicated below.  My mind is open.
    Bring your BIG ideas for selling property.  But don't
    waste my time unless they are really BIG.

                            Sincerely yours,

                            (Typist fills in name)

            (Time _____
    Come  {
            (Day  _____
```

SUPPLEMENTARY
SALES LETTERS

SUPPLEMENTARY
SALES LETTERS

1. How They Help to Increase Sales

To have and to hold. In business, the strength and depth of the roots are proportionate to the goodwill content of the soil. If the amount is sparse, the company must continuously struggle to get new customers to replace the old ones that are lost; if the amount is plentiful, sales increase and the company prospers. Very few organizations neglect making the effort to get orders. The methods of one company may be better than those of another, but they all work hard and consistently to make sales. But that is only *half* the job; it is just as important to *hold* an old customer as it is to *gain* a new one.

Unfortunately, many companies concentrate most of their efforts on getting business. They blandly assume that customers once in the fold will continue to remain there. They leave the customers alone, except for the necessary routine contacts, the calls of the salesmen, and fervent appeals for *more* orders. They forget the little courtesies, the evidences of appreciation, that might build goodwill and make the customer less vulnerable to competition. In their sales program there are no planned letters to keep the customer conscious of a friendly business relationship; none to show appreciation; none to make the salesman's job easier. Occasional efforts along this line are spasmodic and ineffective—crumbs thrown to the customer in a hit or miss manner.

This emphasis on getting orders, with the lack of emphasis on holding goodwill, is in the long run a costly procedure. Often the sales expense on the initial order exceeds the profit; the company looks to repeat orders to place the account on the right basis. Repeat business is almost always more profitable than new business, and this fact would seem sufficient to encourage every possible effort to keep customers satisfied and loyal to the company.

503

It doesn't take long to dictate a letter thanking a customer for his order; a letter telling him later that the order has been shipped; and a letter after delivery, asking "How do you like it?" All of these letter contacts, or any one of them, tell the customer that the company is interested in *him* as well as in his order; that the desire exists to follow through until it is known he is thoroughly satisfied.

Why more of these *supplementary* sales letters are not written is difficult to understand, for anything that helps to *increase* sales must deserve a place in the company program. "You are right in theory, but not in practice," says many a sales manager. "We are too busy to waste any time on unnecessary correspondence." Common sense tells us, however, that such an excuse doesn't hold water. The sales department finds time for other activities—why must this one be neglected? Why call letters that *help* the sales program *unnecessary?* The sales executive who sees the need of one kind of selling, to the exclusion of another, is like a horse that wears blinders. He can only see straight ahead. He doesn't know, or will not admit, that to either side there may be opportunities just as fertile as those in the direct sales program. What he should be after is a *whole* and *complete* program of sales activities, with *nothing* skimped or slighted that might contribute to the success. If there is no one in the sales department who has time for these supplementary sales letters, then someone can be hired for that purpose. He will always more than pay his cost in the business that he *saves* for the company. To have is fine; to hold is wonderful.

Letters used by Kansas City Coal Dealer. Supplementary sales letters need not be long. The subject matter is not nearly so important as the fact that the reader has been reminded in a friendly way that he has not been forgotten. No man wants to be just a name in the records of the company with which he deals. He wants to be recognized as a human being. The letter that he gets accomplishes that purpose—makes him *feel important.*

How letters may do this job is illustrated by the following cordial contacts made, as the occasions present themselves, by the Wiedenmann-Simpson Coal Company, Inc., of Kansas City, Missouri. None of these letters, prepared by the Norman Glore Corporation, can be considered time-wasters, for they are only a few paragraphs long. Neither are they any more remarkable than many of the other supplementary sales letters you will see later in this section. No, they are just a valuable addition to this coal company's sales program—sensible, simple, and sincere letter contacts which, over a period of years, are certain to increase sales.

In one sense, they are form letters, but in a short time a typist can turn out a day's quota of originals so that the effect on the reader is exactly the same as if the message had been dictated solely to him.

(1)

Welcome to New Resident

Welcome to Kansas City!

We know you are going to enjoy your residence in Kansas City. Its many parks and boulevards are known throughout the world. It is a beautiful city with its magnificent Nelson Gallery of Art, its stupendous Municipal Auditorium and its many other attractions, almost too numerous to mention.

You will be greatly impressed by Kansas City's outstanding residential district. Beautiful homes for mile after mile! Kansas city is warm in friendship, warm in cordiality, and we know that you will consider yourself a part of it in but a short time.

We cannot help but feel that we, in our business, have had some part in the warmth of Kansas City, at least as far as winter heating comfort is concerned, because we have been rendering a service since 1914 in that direction.

When you are ready, we should like to serve you, too.

Yours very truly,

(2)

Letter to New Customer

It is indeed a pleasure to welcome you as a new customer of the Wiedenmann-Simpson Coal Company. We hope to please you always.

We attempt to show our appreciation for the business given us by rendering a service which is just a bit more than is expected. We are constantly on the alert to handle only the finest of quality coals, so that no matter what price coal you buy from us, it is unquestionably the best in its class.

We sincerely hope that you are pleased in every respect in doing business with us. It shall be our endeavor at all times to see that you are entirely satisfied.

Very truly yours,

(3)

Thanks for Past Orders

When Spring rolls around, a coal dealer either has something for which to be thankful or just the opposite. He either has had a satisfactory winter season, or things haven't gone quite so well.

We are privileged to be in the former group—we have reason to feel quite happy over the season that has just passed. We wish, however, to place our appreciation where it is most appropriate, and that is with you—our customer. We thank you for having given us the opportunity to be of service to you during this past season.

We want to extend to you our best wishes for an enjoyable Summer, and a most pleasant vacation.

Very truly yours,

(4)

Thanks for Sending a Friend

Thank you very much, Mrs. Jones, for recommending our company to a friend.

It is indeed a real pleasure to know that we have pleased you to the extent that you have felt inclined to tell someone else about our service.

Many, many thanks for your thoughtfulness.

Very truly yours,

(5)

To Lost Customer

When we lose a customer at Wiedenmann-Simpson, it is a serious matter.

We don't immediately fly off the handle and loudly exclaim, "What's the matter with those folks anyway?" We sit down and very seriously summon all of our thinking energy to determine what we have done here at Wiedenmann-Simpson that was wrong. Why have *we* failed to please the Jones family?

We are of the opinion that we must have made a misstep somewhere along the line, and we want to ask the personal favor of you to write on the back of this letter, just what happened to cause you to end your business relationship with us. A stamped envelope is enclosed for your convenience in replying.

Will you do this, please?

Very truly yours,

(6)

Follow-Up of Letter Five

Some time ago, we wrote to you expressing regret that you had not done business with us recently. We asked you very frankly to tell us why. So far we have received no reply.

We realize that there are many reasons for discontinuance of business with a firm; however, if in any way it was our fault, we want to know it. If we are doing something wrong, we want to correct it.

Won't you reply by letter, or call me personally by phone and tell me just what happened? I will be ever so thankful to you for this favor.

Very truly yours,

The above six letters might all be called "unnecessary" by businessmen who do not sense the importance to sales of cordial contacts with prospects and customers. But this opinion does not hold up in the light of the results obtained by companies who *do* use letters to foster friendly public relations. Nobody can say how many tons of coal the above six letters have sold, but enough, surely, to make a long train load.

Has anybody seen Jones? You will recall that one of the basic methods of the letter-writer is to visualize as nearly as is possible the person to whom he is writing. The mental image helps to bring out that man-to-man tone that makes the written words a conversation rather than a letter. The better the image, the closer the writer can come to using the right appeals for a particular reader or group. Names in a card file or on sheets of paper are cold and impersonal. When they stand for *real people,* they take on life and personality. This was the thought, of course, that motivated the following rather remarkable letter. It is the brain-child of H. A. Lufkin, of the Newton Manufacturing Company, Newton, Iowa.

Dear Mr. Jones:
????????

Who is this man *Jones?* Is he fair, fat and forty, or thin, dark and seventy? Does he live in one room, boil coffee on an electric grill, or does he have a fine family, a bull-dog, and old-fashioned friendly neighbors? Does he smoke big black cigars and carry a cane, or is his weakness red neckties and chop-suey?

Does he sing in the choir, play the pipe organ, hunt ducks, or shoot pool? Is he an expert with a dry fly, a 30-30, a camper's skillet, and a cribbage board? Has he a wooden leg, a big black mustache, and cauliflower ears?

These are some of the questions which run through our minds from time to time when we sit down and start a letter to a man we have never seen.

Writing to a name is one thing, but writing to a real live human sort of a fellow is quite another. Of course, we know we can't see every man personally, but if you have no objection, Mr. Jones, we'd like to know something about yourself, your family, your likes and dislikes, so we can write to you a little more personally than has been possible in the past.

Here's a stamped envelope; we'll pay the freight. What do you say?

Yours truly,

In explaining how he happened to dictate such an unusual message, Mr. Lufkin said: "It's only once in a blue moon we get to know these men personally. Naturally, it is a tremendous help when we can know more about them. Finally, I hit on this semi-humorous tangent, and the replies came back nearer to 100 per cent than on anything else I ever hope to write."

Yes, it seems reasonable that a letter so unique should develop a large number of replies, and after Jones became a *person* instead of a mere *name,* it must have been easier to correspond with him. But the supplementary sales letter, in any of the forms it may take, does not need to be so spectacular. If it's just a pleasant contact with the prospect or customer, it may help to keep the human relationship alive. In doing that, it is a real asset to the sales program.

But what *are* these supplementary sales letters? What particular purposes do they serve?

2. Letters to Those Who Have Not Replied

Three choices. When one or more sales letters have been sent to an individual or company without provoking a reply, and the chances seem slim, three courses of action still remain. The first is to lose your temper, and give the other fellow a piece of your mind. You can be very self-righteous and ask, "Don't you think we are entitled to the *courtesy* of a reply?" This is a neat way to blow off steam, but it also completely alienates the reader. Your chance of selling him is consumed in the heat of your reproach. Number one course is good for those who cannot control their patience, but very bad for business.

The second course is to file the correspondence, and look for other game. This is better than the first, because no matter what you may think about an impolite fellow who will not yield to your persuasion, he knows nothing about it. Eventually, he may come through anyway, but it's not a good bet.

The third solution is to *try again.* If you really concentrate, a new approach may occur to you—something different, which may bring the rascal out of his shell. Of course, it usually isn't fair to call him a rascal, for he may not have been under any obligation to answer. After all, who is at fault if a sales letter, or a series of sales letters, fails to get a response? It *could* be the writer.

A sure way to close the file. A good example of the type of follow-up that scolds the reader for his failure to reply is the one below. The company from which the letter was mailed doesn't matter, but it is interesting to know that it is signed by the president. You can tell he is no longer thinking much about getting the order, but he does mean to put the other fellow in his place.

> Dear Sir:
>
> On December 13 we received a request from you for some prices on signs.
>
> In your letter you informed us that the sign you had in mind would be used in a container made by the Doe Company.
>
> We replied to your letter on December 15th, and when we did not hear from you, we wrote again to you on December 29th.
>
> At the same time we wrote the Doe Company, and got the necessary information from them.
>
> After getting the required information, we again wrote you on January 19th, asking that you be good enough to acknowledge receipt of this information, and let us know if you were interested.
>
> To date we have not had the courtesy of hearing from you.
>
> Don't you think that when you ask for certain information, and a company goes to the trouble of getting it for you, then at least you should show some interest and repay them with a reply— even though it is to say that you are not interested?
>
> Very truly yours,

To be sure, it is no fun to be stymied, and after so many vain attempts to get a reply, it is easy to understand why this president lost his temper. On the other hand, he sent his protest to the purchasing agent of a much larger company than his own, and presumably a company that he hoped to sell. But the one blast of temper killed that dream. The purchasing agent sent the letter to your commentator with this remark, written with a red pencil: "Here's a dandy way to destroy goodwill—he'll get no orders from us."

The stinger in this follow-up is the insinuation of discourtesy on the part of the man who didn't reply. The latter might have swallowed the last paragraph, even though the implication is not complimentary, but that one sentence did the dirty work. A man cannot accuse another of discourtesy and still retain his goodwill.

The temptation to scold a prospect who has not come through in the way desired is strong, but better judgment tells us that his goodwill is worth more than any satisfaction to be derived from hauling him over red-hot coals. Resisting the temptation is even more difficult when an expected order is lost, as had happened to the photographer who wrote the following goodwill buster.

Dear Mrs. Doe:

Your letter was a shock, I assure you. Business, in a chaotic condition anyway, would be in a much worse state if everyone were as unethical in their dealings as some photographers are.

"A competitive sitting!" That is just too much. This work is creative—it isn't like a piece of merchandise one can hold up and compare with something sold by another merchant. If we failed to please you in our attempt, in all fairness you should have given us another chance. You saw the type of work we do and should feel reasonably certain that if the first sitting did not please, another one would.

We went to you in good faith, traveled 160 miles, used our time and materials, and did not even ask for a deposit on our work. That is the confidence we had in you. Now, I am not really scolding. I am just telling you this because you are an intelligent girl, and should know that these practices are unethical and should not be shared in by anyone of ordinary social instincts.

Naturally, you were interested in getting the best possible picture of your child, but the point is *we could have* given it to you. If another photographer had come along after Z & Z and you had let him try again—then Z & Z would have had their work for nothing and you can see it is an endless chain of entirely *wrong thinking* and harmful practice. If you had ever had any business experience I would not need to tell you all this.

Now our minimum sitting charge is $18.00. On receipt of this we will mail you the usual three photographs, for we are unwilling that your money represent nothing. We will select the pose that we consider the best—and finish it for you. I am really sorry about all this—however, I do thank you for your very nice letter.

Very truly,

In the foregoing letter, the writer fell into one of the traps described in Section 7—DON'T abuse your competitor or his product. It seems he had some cause to complain, but the tirade should have been mailed to the Secretary of his Trade Association, if mailed at all. It was of no particular interest to the wayward customer. Besides, she had to share his wrath, along with the unethical competitor. The insinuations in some of the things he said to her could not be pleasantly received—"In all fairness" (she isn't fair) . . . "You should know" (she is dumb) . . . "By one of ordinary social instincts" (She doesn't have them) . . . "If you had ever had any business experience" (dumb again). So, it isn't surprising that the girl's reply was brief but sharply pointed.

Dear Sir:

I enclose my check for $18.00, which I finally gathered from your letter is the amount owed you.

You can buy some dandy books on how to write business letters for a mere fraction of that.

Yours very truly,

There is a great lesson for business letter writers in this exchange of correspondence. Perhaps it should have been another "DON'T." Never scold a customer, even though he may be wrong. Never let your anger toward a competitor fall on a customer's head.

The right kind of follow-ups. The tone of the letters which follow is good; the writers try in a friendly way to get the elusive replies. They don't insinuate, and they don't scold. They simply imply, "Come on, now. Be a good fellow and write that letter—just as I would do for you if our positions were reversed."

The first one goes all-out in making the reply easy for the reader. Copies of the previous letters are attached—an old idea involving some trouble for the writer's secretary, but not too much trouble if the reply is secured.

Gentlemen:

Enclosed are copies of two letters written you. It will only take a moment to run over them again.

Won't you just make a notation on the bottom of this letter as to when you will be in the market, and for what?

No need to write a letter, just place your answer on the bottom of this sheet.

Thank you.

Yours very truly,

The next follow-up was dictated by Vice President Earl Hollingsworth of Fine Products Corporation. The location of the company is cleverly revealed in the message which appeals to a special interest of the reader. It would be hard to resist such a friendly contact.

Dear Mr. Doe:

It was way back on a bleak day in February...on the 10th to be exact, when I wrote you and sent you a package by Parcel Post. Now Spring is here. The sap's rising, the trees are budding and the flowers are blooming...still no word from you.

I have never seen the Dogwood more beautiful around Bobby Jones' Golf Course. Come on down to Augusta to see the Masters' Golf Tournament, which takes place the last of this month. It's a great show and I know you would enjoy Augusta at this season...and please bring an answer to my letter of the 10th with you.

Cordially yours,

The little questionnaire at the bottom of the following letter may help to draw the reply. All the reader has to do is scribble *yes* or *no* three times, and shoot the page back in the enclosed stamped envelope.

Dear Mr. Doe:

Did you ever write a man about a matter you felt sure would interest him—and then wait and wonder why he didn't reply? That's what I'm doing now.

When I wrote you my last letter I tried to make it easy for you to answer. This time, I'm not only going to make it easy, but I'm going to make it PROFITABLE, as well.

Just look below—take your pencil and write "yes" or "no" opposite the questions that apply in your particular case. Then return this letter in the enclosed stamped envelope.

Do this now—IT WILL PAY YOU.

Yours sincerely,
ALLEGHENY TUBE & STEEL CO.
Sales Manager

Are our prices in line?_____

Are our couplings suitable?_____

Are you in the market?_____

A follow-up used by Cunard White Star Limited also encloses a copy of the previous letter. Unlike the previous examples, this one takes time to advance a strong sales argument for immediate action—do it now, or you may be disappointed.

Dear Mr. Doe:

Do you remember the letter we recently wrote you on March 10th? For your convenience, I am enclosing a copy.

You will surely want to go to Europe this year, and inasmuch as advanced bookings are so unusually heavy, I am calling your attention to the advisability of reserving accommodations as early as possible.

If, by any chance, your plans or the plans of your friends include a trip abroad between June 15th and July 10, by all means make reservations now. There is a very strong likelihood that no space of any sort will be available during this period.

The volume of travel this year is so great that it far exceeds available accommodations, and we do indeed want to see that you and your friends are provided with desirable space.

Won't you let us know on the enclosed card if you or your friends are planning a trip abroad this year, so that we can be of assistance to you in securing just the type of accommodations you desire?

Cordially yours,

P. S.   Even at this early date, there are a number of sailings for which it is already difficult to secure accommodations.

The repetition in the above letter seems to have been intentional. The writer had just one point to drive home—accommodations going fast —and he made sure that "Mr. Doe" would not overlook it.

A follow-up by *Forbes* magazine is appealing because of the novel implication that the magazine will keep on working for the reader for a salary of only $5 a year instead of the usual $7.50.   This idea carried throughout the letter makes the subscription cost seem very low.   The question in script—"Are you firing me?"—helps to capture reader attention, too.

3. How to Answer Inquiries

Begins with the Chain. When the sales-letter writer answers an inquiry about a product or service, he is not faced with the problem of getting attention. It may be assumed that the reader is already at least mildly interested, or he would not have requested information. Hence, that part of the sales formula which we call the Star has already been accomplished —only the Chain and the Hook remain.

The purpose of the Chain, you remember, was to increase interest until it becomes desire; the purpose of the Hook, to impel action. The first—to increase interest—is the one immediately before the sales-letter writer as he sits at his desk with the prospect's inquiry about to be handled. What can he say to transform the casual interest to something more deep-seated and real?

His position at the moment is similar to that of a retail store clerk, whose turn it is to meet and serve the man who has just entered. The latter is enough interested to have stepped inside, but he is far from being sold. The clerk's problem is to show the merchandise, explain its good qualities, and make the prospect *want* to buy. The fact that many clerks

Are you firing me?

I've tried to do a good job for you.

I've kept you in touch with what's going on in business. I've given you new ideas, accurate forecasts of what to expect. I've shown you many ways to make or save money. I've told you of good investments and warned you of bad ones.

Are you going to take me off your payroll now. . . when my salary is so nominal. . .when you have so many problems I can help you solve?

I want to prove my worth. Won't you keep me on for the next three years at only $15? It saves you $7.50 on my annual salary. . .means I'll work a whole year for you FREE. . .insures my services with no raises for the next three years.

I'll punch in on the 1st and 15th of every month and keep you posted on latest corporate developments. . .interpret them in terms of your career, your business, your investments . . .make certain you're "IN" on the inside story of business and finance.

All you've got to do is use my services fully and I guarantee that I'll become not only a valuable employee, but a living, producing, inseparable partner.

How about it? I'll pull my weight! Simply check and return the enclosed "time card" now and I'll be back on the job bright and early.

Hopefully,

Forbes Magazine

5R

70 FIFTH AVENUE, NEW YORK 11, N. Y.

fall far short of this responsibility, and are merely order-takers and not salesmen, does not in any way change the picture. Merely to lead the way to a showcase, and pull out a few trays for the prospect to paw over, is not *selling*. And neither is it selling when a correspondent simply sends a booklet or some other form of advertising to the person who has inquired about a certain product or service. It may be a very good booklet, but it still lacks the personal touch that a letter can add.

Suppose you had written to a firm of nationally known manufacturing chemists for information about one of their products—what would have been your reaction to the following reply?

> Dear Sir:
> Your request for a sample of Z—— is being given immediate attention.
> We gladly send you this sample and hope the results will convince you of its worth. You can replenish this supply from your druggist. Thanking you for your interest in Z——, we are,
> Very truly yours,

A magnificent sales letter, isn't it? Yes, if the moon is made of green cheese. The man who wanted the sample is the head of the biggest business of its kind in the world. An order created by the sample and the letter would have been substantial. But on the letter, the interested executive wrote—"Why should I buy it from this firm?" Well, he shouldn't—and he *didn't*. A sales correspondent without any concept of salesmanship had destroyed a fine opportunity for his company. If he had any reasons *why* this executive should buy, he kept them to himself. He only "hoped" the sample would convince the reader of its worth. He couldn't be sure, or tell why—but he did *hope*.

Unfortunately, too many inquiries are handled this way in American business. A booklet is tossed in the mail, a sample forwarded, a blunt letter with a generality or two about the product is dictated—and that's all. The tragedy, of course, is twofold. First, it costs money to develop inquiries, and it seems a pity not to make the most of them. Second, when the prospect's interest is cooled, it may never become warm again.

A time when facts are important. In general, the reply to an inquiry can be longer than the usual sales letter which goes unsolicited to a cold prospect. Unless the reply is very dry indeed, details about the product or service will not disconcert or tire the reader. He *wants* the facts. He has asked for them. He is interested enough *at the start* to take all of the information that may help him in deciding whether or not to make the purchase.

Thus, the best replies to inquiries are crowded with *facts* the writer thinks his reader may want to know. He omits nothing that might help to gain the order, because he knows this is the one best chance he probably will ever have to sell this particular prospect.

Compare, for example, the weak effort of the writer who handled the inquiry to the chemical company, with the thorough, convincing reply by the Deltox Rug Company to a furniture dealer in Louisiana. Two fine features of this letter are the way the spotlight is focused on the reader's home state, and the attached list of other dealers who are already in "the Deltox family". There is an interesting story connected with the use of these lists in various states—but first read the letter:

> You certainly wrote to the right manufacturer, Mr. Doe, when you asked for our Catalog and Prices, for Deltox is the leading line of fibre and wool-texture rugs in Louisiana.
>
> Look over the attached list of Louisiana stores selling Deltox Rugs. As a group, these stores sell more fibre rugs than all of the others combined. But why did they select Deltox Rugs in preference to others?
>
> There is but one answer. Deltox is styled for the Louisiana and other Southern trade. Hence, Deltox rugs sell easily down your way. And because of this, you can be assured of a profitable season with our line.
>
> A Catalog and Price List are being mailed you separately. The Price List is properly marked with your trade discount.
>
> Mailed also are samples of our best selling summer fabrics— Delfibre and Delweave. The color plates of patterns on these lines will be found in the catalog. And it makes no difference what patterns you select. They are all good. But the colorings of Brown, Rust, and Green sell best in Louisiana.
>
> James C. Barr, our District Manager, will visit with you on his next Louisiana trip, but you will need rugs before he calls. We suggest, therefore, that you select the quantities of sizes in the patterns and colorings you want, and send us your order on the enclosed handy form.
>
> *(No complimentary close)*

It is a long way from Oshkosh, Wisconsin, to Louisiana, but the writer of the Deltox letter succeeded very nicely in taking his rugs "close to home." Five times, the dealer's state is worked into the message. "For Deltox is the leading line...in Louisiana"——"Look over the attached list of Louisiana stores"——"Deltox is styled for the Louisiana...trade"——"Brown, Rust, and Green sell best in Louisiana"——"On his next Lousiana trip."

All right—now the story as told by George Hughes, then Sales Manager for the Deltox Company. Originally, lists of sold dealers in the various states were not attached to letters answering inquiries about Deltox rugs. You can understand why, as it takes considerable time and labor to compile such lists and keep them up-to-date. However, when the idea was finally given a workout, it was found to be worth many times the cost; the percentage of orders received was several times higher when the lists were used! There is no mystery in this fact. The reader could always find on the list names of other dealers he knew and respected. Thus, he had local testimony for Deltox rugs—a lot more powerful as a sales argument than a generality such as, "Over half the furniture dealers in Louisiana are handling Deltox rugs."

Backing up the booklet. Many companies use booklets to help sell their products; the idea is that they can be produced in more attractive form, and do a more complete job, than letters which might carry the same information. This may be true, but on the other hand, booklets lack the man-to-man, personal touch which is so important in making a sale. It is a mistake, therefore, to answer an inquiry with a booklet and nothing else— no matter how interesting the copy may be. The ideal procedure is to include a letter that will serve a double purpose: first, to arouse reader interest in the booklet; second, to put in a sales lick or two. This double job is done very well by Mortimer B. Fuller, Jr., in a letter for the International Salt Company:

> Dear Sir:
>
> Your request for a copy of "The Farmers' Salt Book" is appreciated. We welcome the opportunity to become acquainted.
>
> Years of hard work of many experts gathering together the best practical experience on this subject have gone into the creation of this booklet. If it is as useful to you as we have tried to make it, we will be more than happy.
>
> As in all businesses, farming in recent years has been tough. That's one reason we became so interested in helping farmers to know more about the correct use of salt.
>
> It takes so little money in salt to return a lot of money in results. You're as welcome as you can be to all this information but we would like to be still more useful to you. We have a fine research bureau that knows or can find out anything you want to know about the use of salt on your farm.
>
> So, if there is anything in this book that isn't clear to you now or at any time, you will please us if you will write us about it. If you are unable to purchase our Smoke Salt or Sausage Seasoning from your dealer we will forward them to you C.O.D., or

upon receipt of money order. The prices are—10. lb. can Smoke Salt $2.00 postpaid, and 10 oz. can Sausage Seasoning, 50¢ plus postage.

                                        Sincerely,

P.S.   After you have looked over "The Farmers' Salt Book," if you would like us to send one to any farmer friend of yours, just send us his name and address.

An inquiry for a booklet, or any other material distributed by a company, is also a tip-off that the time is ripe for the nearest salesman to call. These two shots, first the booklet and then the salesmen, often land the order. Pfaelzer Brothers of Chicago, meat packers, use this two-edged sword whenever possible. To make sure that the salesman is recognized when he gets to the prospect, his picture (about one inch square) is attached to the letter:

> (*No salutation*)
>
> Thank you so much, Mr. Doe, for your interest. The booklet, "Personalized Service," has been mailed to you separately, and it is a real pleasure to send it.
>
> You will enjoy reading this book because its contents conduct you on an interesting picture tour of our plant—at the same time, clearly pointing out the advantages of our service that reaches 50 states.
>
> To the many restaurants it serves, Mr. Doe, "Personalized Service" has a truly great value. You, too, will find it a source of greater satisfaction and increased profits.
>
> I also have taken the liberty of sending you a copy of our latest price list. You will find it complete and interesting because in it are displayed various cuts, qualities, and weights, so that you can easily find the best items for your needs.
>
> We have suggested to our representative, Mr. Jones, that he call on you the next time he is in your vicinity. He should have an opportunity to do so in about a week or ten days. Meanwhile, the back page of our price list explains just how to order—the booklet tells how your order will be filled.
>
> A postage-free mailing card is enclosed for your convenience. Mail it today, and "Personalized Service" will begin working in your interests.
>
> Kindest regards!
>
> (*No complimentary close*)

As indicated, this very friendly Pfaelzer reply to an inquiry does not carry the conventional salutation and complimentary close. Neither did the equally friendly Deltox letter you read on page 516. In the section devoted to letter mechanics, it was pointed out that a considerable number of business organizations have discarded these rather unnecessary forms. While such firms are still in the minority, the trend seems definitely in that direction, because the omission does not detract from the personal tone that modern writers cultivate.

Co-ordination with dealer. When the company does not sell direct, and this is usually the case, best results are not obtained from an inquiry *unless* the dealer or agent know about it. A carbon copy of the reply, or some other notification, should be mailed to the distributor. This impresses the dealer with the power of the company's advertising program, and gives him the chance to follow through locally. While some dealers may be remiss in taking advantage of these inquiries, the alert ones find them helpful.

Teamwork of this kind is illustrated by the next two letters: one the reply to the inquiry, and the other the notification to the local merchant. The letters are signed by Advertising Manager, Harold O. Leiser—pitching for the Walter Booth Shoe Company of Milwaukee.

Reply to the Inquiry

Dear Mr. Doe:

As you requested, we are immediately sending you the booklet, "Shoes from Authentic Fashion Sources."

In this little booklet you will find the type of men's shoes that gentlemen prefer. You will find shoes for all wearing occasions—for campus wear—for business wear—for sport wear—and for dress wear, all authentic reproductions of the kind of shoes that usually are much higher priced.

As the name of this booklet implies, the shoes illustrated are inspired from different fashion sources. The shoes themselves are not fantastic creations like one does find in certain lines, but they are the type of shoes that you will be proud to wear, as you will know that they are correct fashions.

The various models shown in this booklet retail at a price range between $10.00 and $16.00, so you can find in CROSBY SQUARE the grade of shoes you want, and we assure you that dollar for dollar you will receive a full measure of fine appearance, good fit, and honest material.

Below we are listing the authorized dealer in your vicinity who features CROSBY SQUARE Authentic Fashions. Won't you drop in at his store at your earliest convenience?

Yours very truly,

Notice to Dealer

John B. Doe,
3333 Main Street,
Your City,

wrote in for our booklet, "Shoes from Authentic Fashion Sources," advertised in TIME, ESQUIRE and THE SATUR-DAY EVENING POST. This we immediately sent him and wrote him a letter, advising him that he could purchase a pair of CROSBY SQUARE shoes at your store.

Don't you believe it would be a good idea for you to get in touch with him by phone, or by dropping him a short letter, inviting him to your store?

Turn his interest into a sale for you.

Yours very truly,

The above complete job is worthy of imitation by all companies that advertise to create sales opportunities for their agents. It seems like half a job to reply to an interested prospect, and not let the man most interested in on the secret.

A customer who couldn't shop. The companies that sell direct by mail receive many out-of-the-ordinary inquiries; the majority are developed by the catalogs which are the backbone of their sales program. Because they come from all kinds of people, from all kinds of homes, some of these inquiries are obviously not so promising as others; but to the credit of the companies concerned, it must be admitted that each letter from prospect or customer is handled as carefully as if it were the only sales opportunity of the day. In this respect, Sears, Roebuck, Montgomery Ward, and most of the other big mail order houses are doing a letter job comparable to any in American business. Every inquiry is answered completely, clearly, and cordially. The will to serve is conspicuous in every reply.

A good example of the care taken to give each inquiry the very best attention is this Montgomery Ward letter. The circumstances provoking the letter were unusual—perhaps, pathetic. To this good company came one day an inquiry from an inmate of the New Mexico state prison. He couldn't very well go shopping for what he wanted, so he wrote:

Gentlemen:

Have you some person in your organization who can advise me as to the proper things to purchase for an elderly lady of 75 years, for Spring and Summer wear?

I wish to buy a Spring coat, hat, shoes, etc., and of the things you have listed in your catalog, I am at a loss to know what to choose. The lady in question is 5′1″ tall, and weighs around 120; has dark eyes, with black hair turning grey.

I know the sizes of everything but would like you to advise me what is the correct thing.

Yours very truly,

P.S. I have one of your general catalogs for the current season.

Here was a sales opportunity that some business correspondents might have handled indifferently, since it was rather obvious that the prospect was not in a position to question the advice given to him, and that he probably did not have a lot of money to spend. Yes, in some cases, it might have been pushed aside as not worthy of reply. But not by the Montgomery Ward sales correspondent; to her, the occasion was a challenge, and she did her best as the convict's shopper. A picture of a model, dressed in the described outfit, was included:

Dear Mr. Doe:

Behold the charming little lady with the dark smiling eyes and black hair so generously sprinkled with silver! She's on parade for your inspection after a tour through the smartest shops in Chicago. From the top of her head to the tip of her toes, she is correctly attired wherever she goes.

The dress, as you'll see, Mr. Doe, is of lovely acetate rayon crepe in soft beige color (light tan). The dainty lace trim and soft shirring at the neck gives it such a dressy look. Somehow, they always seem to be a necessary part of the elderly woman's costume. See how her medium brown, hand-woven straw hat, smartly trimmed with soft velvet ribbon and brightly colored flowers, blend with the dress, and the neat fitting one-strap brown pumps. There is comfort as well as style in her Foot-Health shoes.

The most important part of her costume is the becoming polo coat of all wool, in the new treebark weave. The well-dressed woman, old or young, likes the new polo coat, as it is so becoming to every figure and can be worn for every occasion. Of course, no costume is complete without a purse and gloves to match the shoes and hat. The shaded brown steer-hide purse so easily carried on her arm, and the smartly tailored brown cape-skin gloves add the finishing touch to her very practical and becoming, yet inexpensive, outfit.

Seventy or seventeen—the woman of today wears what is most becoming to her—the colors and the styles that bring out her individuality, making her different from anyone else. That's just what this lovely costume I have chosen for your lovely lady will do. One thing nice about it too, it can be worn the year around, with the possible exception of the coat and the hat.

The order blank is all filled in, ready for you to return to us with your check or money order. All you have to do is to fill in the sizes. New clothes and a new thrill, and a new interest in life for old or young. You, alone, know the happiness this will bring to your lovely lady. Can't you just see her in this costume now?

Yours very truly,

Perhaps, you are saying that the language of this letter was "over the head" of inmate Number 0000. But how can you judge except by results? The order blank came back to correspondent Miss Lucy Young with everything specified exactly as she had suggested. Furthermore, the buyer wrote to her: "Please send me some idea of what to buy the lady in question for summer dresses." You see, there is no limitation in place or condition for a good sales letter—not when the writer is willing to do a complete and sympathetic job.

An ace for the last trick. When several attempts to secure a reaction from the prospect have failed, it is good to have an especially strong point in reserve for the final approach. This procedure is illustrated in the following letter used by Pacific Manifolding Book Co. Ltd., and signed by Philip T. Farnsworth. The true story of the garage man who almost lost $284.00 for lack of an adequate recording system would be likely to make any businessman take serious inventory of his own methods.

Dear Sir:

I've written to you before about the new Wiz Register. In looking over the copies I'm afraid they were pretty ordinary letters. They couldn't have been very good, because they didn't get a reply.

I want to tell you about something that happened to me some time ago. I was showing the machine to a garage man. The garage man didn't want to buy—thought his old sales books would do all right. He had used them for twelve years and didn't know of any mistakes. While I was talking a man dropped into the store and just stood there listening while I talked. Pretty soon he spoke up.

"That's what I thought too, Ed," he told the garage man, "but about a year ago I bought one of those machines and it saved me plenty." He went on to tell how one of his men had made a sale the day before leaving town for a vacation. In his excitement he forgot to file the billing copy. A month later, the man found the error when he looked over the audit slips in the locked refold compartment of his Wiz Register. The refold slip saved him $284.00, enough to buy two dozen Wiz machines.

That's a true story. I'll vouch for it. Naturally, things like that don't happen every day, but if you'll put a sample of your present sales slip in the yellow envelope, I will see if I can work out a Wiz System that will protect the records of your business.

Sincerely yours,

It paid to get tough. The experienced salesman knows that not all prospects can be handled in the same way. Although in general it is better to serve milk and honey to the individual or company that has asked for information or prices, now and then a case develops where a firm and independent reply may get quicker action. This is true in the situation where the sales manager has reason to think that the inquiry has not been made seriously, and that the prospect has no real intention of buying.

The following reply deals with a company which year after year had applied for quotations—and year after year had ignored them. Finally, the sales manager decided the time had arrived for plain talking. The letter was written quite a while ago, but just the same it might have been sent only yesterday.

Gentlemen:

In yesterday's mail we received a letter from you advising that on September 27th you asked for quotations. Our filing clerks have made a very thorough search for this letter and it seems that we did not receive it. We make a special effort to reply promptly to all correspondence.

We regret very much that our reply is not going to be just what you expect. For several years past, it has been customary for your company to ask us for quotations. We have always given you our very best. Our letter quoting you prices on our SUPE-RIOR QUALITY MILK BOTTLES has always been the last bit of correspondence between our companies for another year. At the end of each year we go through the same procedure. Our quotation letters have never been acknowledged and we have not succeeded in securing your business, all of which is evidence of the fact that your company believes in buying on price instead of quality.

We have repeatedly tried by correspondence and through the calls of our representative to assure you we could save you money because our ware would give you "more trips per bottle" and hence be cheaper in the long run. We have absolutely failed in putting this idea over with your company in spite of the fact that similar companies all over the country are using our bottles exclusively.

Last year we quoted you on a twenty-five car basis and we note from your letter that you are interested in a fifteen-car contract.

For that reason our prices would not be as attractive as they were last year, and since we were unsuccessful in securing your specifications then, we certainly would be this time. As a matter of fact, our prices have not changed since we quoted you last year.

We have been extremely anxious to secure your business, as we feel that we are particularly well-equipped to take care of companies like your own, that are big not only from the standpoint of size, but also with regard to quality of the goods demanded.

Our bottles are sold strictly on their merit and not on a price basis. We believe that every manufacturer knows the real worth of his product and when other manufacturers cut under our prices to secure the business, we think it is significant and proves that the business could not be had on an equal price basis.

Yours very truly,

Obviously, the writer of the foregoing letter staked all on his unusual reply, but he had nothing much to lose. After the experience of several years —price quoting and no sale—there was little to be gained by repeating the process. So he used an old appeal which often moves people to buy—the attitude of indifference. In other words, some folks are more impressed when no effort is made to sell them. It is not the best approach under most circumstances, but in this case it *worked*. A week after the letter was mailed, an order for twenty carloads of the bottles was received. As the writer of the letter commented, "It pays sometimes to shoot straight from the shoulder with customers and prospects who shop around."

4. Letters to Show Appreciation of Orders

Thanking the new customer. When we think of all the time and expense involved in getting a new customer, it seems only logical that every effort should be made to consolidate the victory. The position of the new buyer is not as fixed or sure as that of one whose name has been on the books for a long period. The new buyer still has his fingers crossed. He hopes he has made a wise purchase, but he cannot be certain until later. His mental attitude is that of doubt, and the company is strictly on trial both as to the goods sold, and the nature of its services.

During this preliminary time when the new customer and the company are getting acquainted, any action is worthwhile that will please the former, and help him to form a favorable first impression. A little extra courtesy at the start may go a long way toward winning goodwill and the confidence that leads to repeat orders. Granted that this is just straight thinking, it is hard to understand how any company could fail to thank a customer for his first order. Furthermore, the letter of appreciation can do the additional job of *reselling* the buyer at the very moment when he is wondering whether or not he should have made the purchase.

A "thank-you" letter supplements the work of the salesman, and helps him on his next call; it puts the company in the class of those who *appreciate* business; it does a whale of a job compared to the small effort required in its preparation. In many circumstances, it can even be a form letter, although it should always be individually typed and personalized.

Examples from everyday business. To reveal how various types of companies do the "thank-you" job, the following letters are presented as typical. Most of them are fairly short, as thoughts of appreciation should be. Gratitude is not an emotion that can be stretched without creating an impression of insincerity. Letters thanking new customers are similar in this respect to Christmas messages—they are best when done simply.

(1)

Dear Mr. Doe:

First of all, "Thank You" for your order calling for electrical supplies.

Then we want you to know that the quality, delivery and prices which merited this order are also to be found in all of the other electrical supplies we carry; such as electrical devices manufactured by the Westinghouse Manufacturing Company, and other substantial organizations.

And as our acquaintance ripens, and you become more familiar with our stock, the feeling will grow that for anything and everything electrical, you can depend on Hyland as a sure and constant source.

Please be assured of our appreciation for this initial order. We shall strive to do all possible to cause it to be the first of many.

Yours very truly,

(2)

Gentlemen:

Old friends are essential in any business, but one must get acquainted with new folks to grow and increase the number of old friends. Right?

This is a greeting from Weatherbest and a personal thank you for the recent order that we believe is the first you have given us.

We appreciate your thinking of us and frankly it is our hope that you will find the quality of the product and the service so satisfactory that you will feel it to your best interests to call upon us real often.

Cordially yours,

(3)

Dear Mr. Jones:

Personally, I want to thank you heartily for your order. It has been shipped and we think you will be well pleased with the goods.

It has been called to my attention that this is the first order you have given us.

It is not as easy to become acquainted with a man through the mail as it is when you look him in the face, shake hands and hear his voice.

Yet many friendships have been formed by mail.

So, although I can only write to you, I feel I have made a friend. I want you to think of us as a friendly institution, always ready to render whatever service it can. Our catalog is enclosed for your convenience in ordering.

Several thousand years ago Socrates remarked: "There is no pleasure like having a new friend." I think he was right.

We of the Aloe Company hope to have the pleasure of meeting you personally some day—perhaps at a convention—perhaps you will come to St. Louis.

In the meantime, let us hear from you again.

Very truly yours,

(4)

Dear Mr. Doe:

We are indeed glad to say "welcome" and thanks for your order of the 6th, which arrived this morning. The shipping department is working on this order, and will send it to you within the next two days.

It gives us great pleasure to be able to write this letter welcoming you to Reliance, and we sincerely hope that this order will be just the first of many during the year.

Cordially yours,

(5)

Dear Mr. Doe:

It is a pleasure to greet you as a customer of the Home laundry, and to thank you sincerely for this opportunity to serve you.

I hope you will avail yourself of the many benefits to be derived from our laundry services, as outlined on the enclosed pamphlet, and enjoy them, too. For your convenience, we also offer various "special" services, such as the laundering of pillows, curtains, and blankets; and, for your finer garments and wraps, our FAULTLESS DRY CLEANING SERVICE.

As I take a very real and personal interest in your satisfaction, I should greatly appreciate your letting me know, by mail or phone, how you liked our handling of your first laundry and dry cleaning.

Further, I want you to know that my interest does not stop with your first bundle. If at any time our workmanship or service should fail to merit your entire approval, I should consider it a favor if you would call me, or Miss White, at once.

We will be ready and willing to serve you in any and every way possible.

Cordially yours,

(6)

Dear Sir:

This letter is our personal representative to shake your hand and welcome you among us. For over 120 years we have been welcoming new customers and making new friends, and we look forward with pleasure to counting you among them, and to serving you with our best efforts.

Since 1841 we have been specializing in coffee; and during that time have learned many things about roasting, blending, packing, and selling. That experience is yours for the asking.

We are waiting to help you in all your coffee problems. Whether it is about bulk coffee, package coffee, or making coffee in a small restaurant or large one, please feel free to call us and see how much we can help you.

There are also many other items in our stock which you will find profitable. Let us be of service. We will do everything possible to please you, so that we may have many years of pleasant business relations together.

Sincerely yours,

The close of this last letter might well be the key thought of any thank-you message—"We will do everything possible to please you, so that we may have many pleasant business relations together." Care should be taken, however, not to let too much emphasis rest on getting *more* orders, to the detriment of the main purpose, which is to show appreciation of the order just received. The goodwill letter that carries a greedy palm outstretched may do more harm than good.

The perfect "thanks-for-your-first-order" letter may accomplish the following purposes, although not all of them may be necessary in every case:

1. Shows appreciation of the order
2. Welcomes the buyer as a new customer
3. Tells when the order will be shipped
4. Assures the customer he has bought wisely
5. Mentions facts to build confidence in the company
6. Expresses the desire to *merit* further orders

Use of salesman's name. When a new customer is being thanked for an order taken by a salesman or agent, it is good business procedure to work his name into the letter. In such cases, it is the salesman who will continue to contact the buyer, and he needs every possible help from the company. The mention of his name not only makes him share the appreciation, but it also helps to keep his identity fresh in the mind of the customer. The following letter, used by International Salt Company of Scranton, Pennsylvania, features the salesman in the very first sentence:

Dear Sir:

Our Mr. Walter has thanked you in person for your order of January 3rd, but I also want to thank you on behalf of the company. This is your initial order. and I know of no greater kick a sales manager can get than the beginning of business with a new customer.

The signing of an order is an expression of confidence, and I want you to know that we recognize the responsibility we have for maintaining that confidence.

The most important thing to the buyer of any product is the character of the supplying organization; its resources; its facilities; its reputation; and its standards of service.

You have at your beck and call every facility of our company. We would like to be useful to you beyond the mere necessities of business transaction.

The experience and services of the International Salt Research Laboratory are freely available to you in any salt problem you ever may have. We would like to have you use them.

In any emergency when Mr. Walter may not be available, do not hesitate to write, wire or phone us here at headquarters.

We appreciate your business. We want to continue to deserve it.

Sincerely,

Standard Oil Company
INCORPORATED IN *New Jersey*

30 ROCKEFELLER PLAZA, NEW YORK 20, NEW YORK

M. J. RATHBONE
CHAIRMAN OF THE BOARD

June 25, 1963

Dear Mr. Smith:

    I would like to extend a warm welcome to you as a new shareholder. The other Directors and I are pleased that you have chosen to make an investment in this Company.

    To provide you with current information about the Company and its affairs, we are sending in a separate envelope a copy of the annual report which contains financial data and a review of last year's operations. During the year you will also receive a magazine, "The Lamp", and an interim report, the Jersey Shareholders' Quarterly, which is enclosed with the dividend checks in March, June, September, and December.

    As do many of our shareholders, you might enjoy the convenience of having the credit card of our domestic marketing affiliate. If so, please sign and return the enclosed post card. In purchasing the products of our affiliate you will be supporting your investment.

    I hope your association with Jersey will be long and satisfying, and that if you have any questions or comments about the Company or its management you will write to us at any time.

              Sincerely,

              M. J. Rathbone

In a similar way, a letter used by the Lion Oil Refining Company, El Dorado, Arkansas, mentions in the last paragraph the names of the two men who secured the new dealer and who no doubt will continue to work with him.

Dear Mr. Doe:

We're mighty proud of our new friendship and want to say, "thanks" for your contract to sell Lion products. We really appreciate it. And we hope we'll always merit your friendship. That's exactly our ambition.

Lion products are exceptionally good. We are proud of them. And we believe you, as one of our dealers, will be equally proud to serve them. You will find that Lion customers are loyal customers, and that they are real boosters for Lion products.

Just as soon as we possibly can, we will have one of our merchandising men call on you. He will be glad to assist you in every way toward increasing the profits of your business.

We are proud of the fact that each dealer who has gone with Lion has been successful in increasing his gallonage. This, we think, is due to the superiority of our products; our company policies; the help they give to our dealers; and to the natural preference of Southern people for products made in the South.

Because this is your first association with us, Mr. Doe, we want to thank you for the confidence you have placed in Mr. Hinds, Mr. Clark, and our company. We sincerely believe this is but the beginning of a long and mutually pleasant association between you and our organization.

Sincerely yours,

Standard Oil of New Jersey welcomes new stockholder. We doubt if a company can ever grow so big that it can afford to eliminate goodwill contacts with customers or the public. At least, that is the opinion of Standard Oil of New Jersey, which even stops to welcome a new stockholder, irrespective of whether he buys ten shares or a thousand.

The average individual who had bought a few shares of stock for the first time would naturally be pleased and impressed by getting such a welcome as the one on page 529 from the Chairman of the Board.

How a Master said "Thank you." The business world lost one of its best letter writers at the death, a few years ago, of H.J. Cocking, then sales promotion manager of Quaker City Rubber Company. No matter what the problem, he always came up with a well-nigh perfect letter solution. And here is how he welcomed a new buyer of Quaker City Belting:

Dear Mr. Doe:

It was just fine of you to send us that nice order for Belting. Thanks a lot.

For the confidence you have placed in Quaker and its products, we are very grateful. In return, we shall leave no stone unturned to justify a continuance of that confidence.

You'll always find the Quaker organization happy and ready to give you the fullest measure of assistance, so make your Mechanical Rubber problems ours. Don't feel you'll be putting us to any trouble, because besides selling quality rubber goods, it is our job to create satisfied customers.

Quaker will not forget you after this, your first, order. No Sir! It could not have carried on for fifty-two years—successfully weathering every business upheaval—were that its policy. This order will be the beginning of a long and pleasant business relationship. Anyway, that's what we shall try to make it.

So kindly think of us the next time you need Mechanical Rubber Goods, and if we can help you in any way, please call on us. Don't hesitate, will you?

Our one desire is to serve you faithfully. More is humanly impossible. Less, we will not tolerate.

Cordially, indeed,

The language of Mr. Cocking's letter is simple, man-to-man talking; the spirit is sincerely friendly. No doubt you noticed, too, that he defied tradition with an unusual complimentary close.

Four-letter plan of Bowers Company. On the four pages starting with page 532 are reproduced the *four* letters—not one—which go from the Bowers Battery and Spark Plug Company to welcome a new dealer. By the time the latter has emerged from such a bombardment of goodwill, he must indeed feel welcome, and about to be favored with unusual service.

The first letter is signed by C. P. Bowers, President—in ink, not rubber-stamped. Mr. Bowers tells how he personally made the first batteries by hand, and then personally took the trouble to talk to the buyers about them. He assures the new dealer that he is just as eager now to keep in touch with him.

The second letter is signed by Roy W. Shreiner, Sales Manager—in ink, not rubber-stamped. He talks mostly about service, and how he is ready to help the new dealer make more money.

The third letter is signed by John R. Dreibelbis, Production Manager—in ink, not rubber-stamped. He tells about the men working in the plant, carefully making and testing the thousands of batteries and plugs shipped out every few hours. Then he

BOWERS
Battery and Spark Plug Co.

(A Division of GENERAL BATTERY and CERAMIC CORP.)

READING, PENNA.

February 28, 19--

I learned this morning that you recently sent us your first order.

It is a pleasure for me to welcome you as a new customer friend of ours!

When I started out in the battery business I made only four batteries the first month. Made them alone, and by hand, and then discussed their construction features with the first four men who ever used Bowers Batteries in their care.

I was determined to <u>satisfy</u> them in every way. I made up my mind from the very start that every new customer of mine would always be given not only the best battery which it is humanly possible to build, but also personal attention and 100% cooperation.

So today, even though the busy company bearing my name has grown to be one of the largest manufacturers of batteries and spark plugs in America, I still like to take the time to personally welcome each and every new customer.

Please let me know if I can help you at any time and feel free to write to me with any suggestions, criticisms or comments about our batteries, spark plugs, or our service. I am eager to work with you in a close, friendly manner!

Sincerely,

BOWERS BATTERY & SPARK PLUG CO.

C. P. Bowers

President

FACTORIES
READING, PA
NEW PHILADELPHIA, OHIO
GREER, S C
FRENCHTOWN, N J

BRANCHES
BALTIMORE, MD
BUFFALO, N Y
CHARLOTTE, N C
COLUMBUS, OHIO
MACON, GA
NEW HAVEN, CONN
PHILADELPHIA, PA
PITTSBURGH, PA

EXPORT DIVISION
READING, PA

Letter From the President

BOWERS
Battery and Spark Plug Co.
(A Division of GENERAL BATTERY and CERAMIC CORP.)

READING, PENNA.

October 9, 19--

Thank you for your initial order.

We appreciate this opportunity you have given us to serve you.

You will find, as hundreds of other satisfied dealers have found, that Bowers products will "click" with your customers and the Bowers setup with "click" with you.

Your customers will like the dependable quality built into every Bowers product.

You will like our prompt, personal, factory-to-dealer service -- our friendly cooperation -- and, best of all, you'll like the customers you will win and hold as a result of selling them good quality, dependable products.

Again I thank you for your initial order and hope that this is the beginning of a long and pleasant association. Let me know if there is anything further I can do to make your battery or spark plug business more profitable, enjoyable and successful as time goes on!

Very truly yours,

BOWERS BATTERY & SPARK PLUG CO.

Roy W. Shreiner
Sales Manager

FACTORIES
READING, PA
NEW PHILADELPHIA, OHIO
GREER, S C
FRENCHTOWN, N J

BRANCHES
BALTIMORE, MD
BUFFALO, N Y
CHARLOTTE, N C
COLUMBUS, OHIO
MACON, GA
NEW HAVEN, CONN
PHILADELPHIA, PA
PITTSBURGH, PA

EXPORT DIVISION
READING, PA

Letter from the Sales Manager

BOWERS
Battery and Spark Plug Co.

(A Division of GENERAL BATTERY and CERAMIC CORP.)
READING, PENNA.

December 30, 19--

I wish you could be with me this morning, to spend a couple of hours "out in the shop," of our various plants!

I'd like to show you how Bowers Batteries and Ceramite-Sealed Spark Plugs are really BUILT TO "TAKE IT."

As Production Manager, I make-the-rounds every day, and I know that you would be greatly impressed with our modern, up-to-the-minute production facilities.

You would enjoy meeting the hundreds of men who have spent most of their working years right here with Mr. C. P. Bowers. You would like the way they work; the care and skill with which they use their hands and tools. You'd find our testing laboratories of real interest as well as our rigid inspection. You'd see the most modern equipment known to the industry, and thousands of batteries and spark plugs being shipped out every few hours.

Perhaps sometime you'll be in or near Reading. If so, stop out at our plant and let me show you around. Meet Mr. Bowers and his key men in both the battery plant and the spark plug plant. You'll enjoy your visit with us and you'll go home feeling confident that we fellows here at Bowers are "looking after YOUR orders with care and interest."

Sincerely,

BOWERS BATTERY & SPARK PLUG CO.

J. R. Dreibelbis

John R. Dreibelbis
Production Manager

FACTORIES
READING, PA
NEW PHILADELPHIA, OHIO
GREER, S C
FRENCHTOWN, N J

BRANCHES
BALTIMORE, MD
BUFFALO, N Y
CHARLOTTE, N C
COLUMBUS, OHIO
MACON, GA
NEW HAVEN, CONN
PHILADELPHIA, PA
PITTSBURGH, PA

EXPORT DIVISION
READING, PA

Letter From the Production Manager

BOWERS
Battery and Spark Plug Co.
(A Division of GENERAL BATTERY and CERAMIC CORP.)

READING, PENNA

December 30, 19--

When I arrived at the office this morning, there was an inter-office memo on my desk from Mr. C. P. Bowers.

He said that he wrote to you recently, and suggested that I also drop you a get-acquainted note.

That's the one thing which makes this company different from most manufacturing concerns. There's a "spirit of service" from top to bottom. The men who make our batteries and spark plugs -- the office staffs -- all of the executives -- everyone does his and her part to make your selling of Bowers products more profitable.

As Advertising Manager, I am keenly interested in helping you to establish new sales records by giving you all the advertising assistance possible.

You will be receiving material from us from time to time, and I am anxious to know how you like it. If you think it can be improved in any way, let me know. If you want to recommend the use of other promotional ideas, your suggestions will receive careful consideration.

My job is to HELP YOU. And if you can help me to do a better job, you'll really be helping yourself. Let me hear from you!

Sincerely,

BOWERS BATTERY & SPARK PLUG CO.

C. G. High

C. G. High
Advertising Manager

FACTORIES
READING, PA.
NEW PHILADELPHIA, OHIO
GREER, S. C.
FRENCHTOWN, N. J.

BRANCHES
BALTIMORE, MD.
BUFFALO, N. Y.
CHARLOTTE, N. C.
COLUMBUS, OHIO
MACON, GA.
NEW HAVEN, CONN.
PHILADELPHIA, PA.
PITTSBURGH, PA.

EXPORT DIVISION
READING, PA.

Letter From the Advertising Manager

invites the new dealer to visit the plant—see how things are done there.

The fourth letter is signed by C. G. High, Advertising Manager— in ink, not rubber-stamped. He talks the top-to-bottom spirit of service in plant and office; how he wants to help the new dealer by developing prospects. And he asks for suggestions—help me help YOU.

With so much goodwill flowing toward him from important men in the company, the new customer can hardly help feeling that he has indeed become a part of an alert and friendly organization. Does this feeling impel him to push Bowers batteries and plugs? Well, why not? And especially, if some of the other companies happened to give his orders no special attention!

Appreciation letters to old customers. If many companies fail to give proper recognition to orders received from new customers, the number is still insignificant compared to those that pay little or no attention—with never a word of thanks or appreciation—to the "old faithfuls" who continue to buy month after month, year after year. This is shockingly poor business procedure, for the customer neglected today may turn out to be the customer gone over to a competitor tomorrow.

It is human nature to take things for granted, and never to lock the stable until after the horse is stolen. Why worry about satisfactory old accounts which seem so safe and sure, when there is so much new business to fight for? But the sales manager who clings to that kind of thinking is frequently rudely awakened. The customary orders *don't* come in, the salesman can't explain why he no longer seems welcome, and then the truth comes out—the buyer has simply been persuaded to give his orders to another firm. Of course, this will happen in spite of hell or high water in a certain percentage of cases, for some turnover among customers in our highly competitive business markets is unavoidable. But if that turnover can be *held down* by some evidence of goodwill and appreciation on the part of the company, surely the effort is worthwhile.

The sad part, too, about the loss of business from lack of customer appreciation is that no company is really indifferent to the value of a good account. Far from it! The steady and consistent buyer who pays his bills promptly and never causes any trouble rates very high in the mind of the sales executive—but the latter just doesn't get around to expressing his appreciation in visible form until the fire is out.

How some companies are doing the job. There is no set routine for showing order appreciation that could be advocated to fit all, or even the majority, of cases. It is very desirable and proper to send a thank-you letter for each order to the occasional buyer, but it would be a foolish waste of time to write a hundred or more times a year to the buyer whose orders are received every day or so. For the latter, a special note of appreciation, sent three or four times a year and signed by major executives, is much more effective. The only general rule to follow is that every customer must be contacted often enough to let him know that his orders are sincerely appreciated, and that the system be airtight enough to make sure no single customer is denied his share of company recognition.

The following letters thanking old customers for orders are typical of the better sort seen in business correspondence:

(1)

Used by Salisbury & Satterlee Co., Minneapolis

Dear Mr. Doe:

Habit, custom, even the language of a people, may undergo great changes in the course of a lifetime. Yet one habit, one custom, one old phrase, continues unchanged into the fourth generation of our business.

Even today as we repeat it again to you, it has lost none of the sincerity and depth of responsibility that it carried when Tom Salisbury stepped out on the loading platform to say "Thank You" to that pioneer Minneapolis merchant, first caller at the new factory overlooking Saint Anthony Falls.

Your orders number among the newer and brighter links in that long chain of confidence begun back there in 1877—links which are the driving force of an organization whose responsibility it is to serve you to your complete satisfaction.

The shipment made to you today combines the up-to-date improvements in the bedding industry with the best workmanship our long experience can provide. May it be our privilege to continue to serve you.

Thank you.

Very truly yours,

(2)

Used by Nicholson File Company, Providence

Dear Mr. Krueger:

Probably at various times you have checked the orders that come into your plant—perhaps you do it every day. I find it interesting to go over the orders we receive—for a dozen files here, a hundred dozen there—every one representing faith in our products and our company.

Ever so often, in looking over our order records, I have the desire to write to those names on our books—to tell customers like you, Mr. Krueger, that every order for a dozen or a hundred dozen files is important to us, and that we are doing our best to deserve your business.

I hope that if you have any special problem or requirement in your use of files, you will let me know, so that we can give you all the help we can.

Cordially yours,

(3)

Used by Sun-Maid Raisin Growers Association, Fresno

Gentlemen:

They tell me that in China a fellow never sees the girl he marries until after the wedding. Even during the ceremony she keeps her head in a sack. Now, that doesn't appeal to my idea of business any more than of matrimony. I want to know the people I'm dealing with, and in thanking you for your last order, wish that we could talk over Sun-Maids face to face.

Our organization is more than a machine—it is people— thousands of California vineyardists banded together in a co-operative effort to make raisins profitable to themselves and to the trade. For twenty years they have advertised Sun-Maids. By their marketing foresight, carton raisins were popularized and the bag pack introduced. They turned raisins from a luxury into a regular seller and even put them in our daily bread. Through their research such improved products as Nectars and Puffed have been developed.

But what does the personality of this organization mean to you? Simply that when you deal with us you are trading with the leader, the one packer who has consistently tried to build your business as well as get it.

But I'm not going to ask for your support on sentimental grounds. When you bought our raisins you didn't get a "bride in a sack." We shipped you something you and your customers know—the quickest selling, because it is the finest quality and proportionately lowest-priced raisin line on the market. You can't afford to buy anything else and, naturally, I'm glad you didn't.

Sun-Maid hopes to serve you in the future as it has in the past. We are human beings out here, interested in you and your problems. Please think of us in that light.

Very truly yours,

(4)

Used by Lee Clay Products Company, Inc.

Good Morning, Gentlemen:

We take our pen in hand...

It's an old-fashioned way of starting a message...but that's the kind of a message we want to write. That is, it may *seem* old-fashioned according to certain modern schools of thought.

A high-salaried, high-powered, button-down-collared sales executive...the kind that eats in a private dining room at the Ritz, recently said: "Don't thank a man for giving you an order. The moment you thank him, you weaken your position with him. You must feel that you are doing him a favor in accepting his order."

Well, sir, if that's the modern way, then we must admit we are old-fashioned. When we look over the accounts on our books we are convinced that frank gratitude mixes well with honest values.

We may be taking an awful chance by showing our hand this way and thanking you for the order being shipped in the car to Whitehurst-Wilbur Company. But here goes—we *mean* it!

Cordially yours,

(5)

Used by Maurice Weiner, Reading

Dear Mr. Doe:

Even though I did say it the other day here in the store when you made your purchase, I want to say it again...

"Thank-You!"

I want you to know that I sincerely appreciate your patronage. And remember...now that the sale has been made, Maurice Weiner just BEGINS to serve you.

I won't feel that the sale is "closed" until you receive full wearing service and lasting satisfaction from your purchase...until you honestly feel that you have received full value for every dollar spent!

It is my earnest hope that behind this personal service our business relations may long continue.

Very sincerely yours,

(6)

Used by S. Maw, Son & Sons, Ltd., London

Dear Sir:

Thank you very much for the order which you have just placed in our new Showroom. We appreciate your continued support, and we are pleased to again have the opportunity of cooperating with you. We believe these goods will be of assistance to you in increasing your sales in a satisfactory manner.

We are constantly producing unique ranges of modern merchandise, and a considerable proportion of the goods, and all the packages, are designed or styled by us.

It is only when ranges of these goods are bought and sold by our progressive customers that we feel our efforts are successful. We have written our representative, telling him of the order you have placed with us, and you will be pleased to know that he receives full credit for it.

We both hope that we shall deserve the pleasure of another visit from you in the not too distant future.

Yours very truly,

P.S. The Spring Programme will break all records. It's a promise!

Letter number 6 is worthy of special comment. There is a common feeling that our business friends in England and other foreign countries are still overly stiff and stilted in their business letters. This may be true, at least from the American viewpoint. However, not *all* English writers are sticking to the inherited traditions, as can be seen from this particular letter. It was written by Managing Director Vernon S. Porter, whose letters invariably are modern in language, pleasing in tone, and as friendly as those done on this side of the ocean.

Notice of delivery date. When possible, it is desirable to tell the buyer exactly when his order will be shipped or delivered. In some cases, this information can be given in the thank-you letter, in others a simple card or notice can be mailed separately. The procedure tells the buyer his order is receiving special attention; also, it helps to complete the sale when the order has been taken subject to payment on delivery.

Follow-up of sale or service. A business courtesy not extended often enough is a contact with the buyer some time after his purchase to find out if he is thoroughly satisfied. Letters of this sort not only show that the company is interested *after* the sale, but they also may result in additional business. Sometimes, too, they unearth faults in the goods or service which need to be corrected. It is not good for business to have a dissatisfied customer keep his troubles to himself, since he is rather sure not to return to the place where he feels he was not well served. Moreover, if the complaint is legitimate, the reputable company *wants* the opportunity of making things right, and of eliminating the chance of similar difficulties in the future.

From your own experience, however, you know how seldom these after-the-sale contacts are ever made. Perhaps you purchased a new TV a few months ago, maybe a new automobile, or re-roofed your home. Last summer you may have purchased oil from a new dealer for your home or factory, had your basement waterproofed, or your yard landscaped. You can think of hundreds of things and services for which you paid out good money during the past year. But how many of the companies that benefited by your patronage took the trouble later to inquire how well you were pleased, or if there could be any additional service they could render? Very few, we'll wager. But if you *did* receive one or more follow-ups of that nature, you were pleased and no doubt said, "Now there's a *good* company."

Wouldn't that have been your reaction, had the letter arrived after the purchase of your last new automobile? Wouldn't you remember this special courtesy the next time you were buying?

That letter went to an individual buyer. Here are two more, mailed to companies. Both accomplish two purposes: first, they check customer satisfaction; second, they politely reach out for future business.

Letter from Coal Dealer

Dear Mr. Doe:

What did you think of your first shipment of Famous Reading Anthracite? I am in hopes that it received a favorable vote on its arrival at your yard.

In past years great importance was often attached to appearance of the coal alone. Today, the emphasis is placed on quality—the absence of impurities. And rightly so.

That's where Reading excels. Impurities such as rock, bone and slate are removed by the most modern methods.

It means a great deal to you to distribute fuels in which you can place unlimited confidence. Reading is one of them, and we shall look forward to another opportunity of serving you well.

Yours very truly,

Letter from Standard Register Company

Dear Mr. Smith:

We are constantly striving to improve our products and service to our customers. This effort is justified because our business must be operated profitably if it is to exist and continue to give gainful employment to hundreds of sales representatives, factory men and women.

I am writing, therefore, to a few customers like you who have installed a new Form Flow Register. We want you to know we deeply appreciate the confidence you already have shown in our company and our products. We have great hopes in our Form

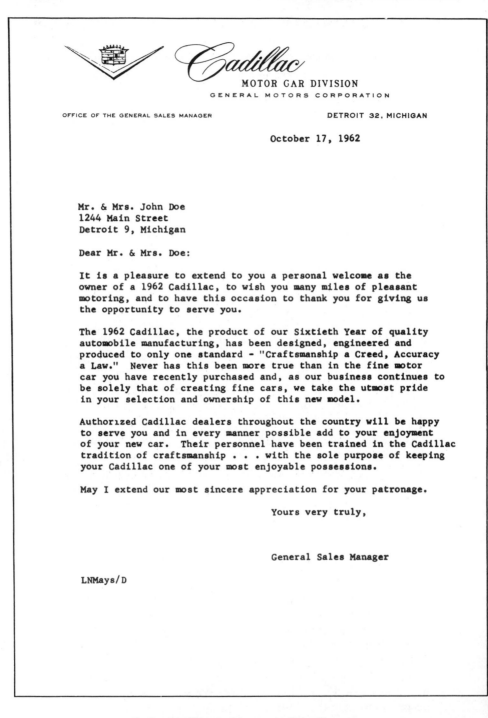

MOTOR CAR DIVISION

GENERAL MOTORS CORPORATION

OFFICE OF THE GENERAL SALES MANAGER   DETROIT 32, MICHIGAN

October 17, 1962

Mr. & Mrs. John Doe
1244 Main Street
Detroit 9, Michigan

Dear Mr. & Mrs. Doe:

It is a pleasure to extend to you a personal welcome as the
owner of a 1962 Cadillac, to wish you many miles of pleasant
motoring, and to have this occasion to thank you for giving us
the opportunity to serve you.

The 1962 Cadillac, the product of our Sixtieth Year of quality
automobile manufacturing, has been designed, engineered and
produced to only one standard - "Craftsmanship a Creed, Accuracy
a Law." Never has this been more true than in the fine motor
car you have recently purchased and, as our business continues to
be solely that of creating fine cars, we take the utmost pride
in your selection and ownership of this new model.

Authorized Cadillac dealers throughout the country will be happy
to serve you and in every manner possible add to your enjoyment
of your new car. Their personnel have been trained in the Cadillac
tradition of craftsmanship . . . with the sole purpose of keeping
your Cadillac one of your most enjoyable possessions.

May I extend our most sincere appreciation for your patronage.

                              Yours very truly,

                              General Sales Manager

LNMays/D

Reflecting Sincere Interest in New Customer

Flow Register because we honestly believe that it will give improved service to the user. However, irrespective of how we may view it, we know that its quality can only be determined by the user.

Consequently, while I realize the request may be a little unusual, I am wondering if you would write me personally and frankly, expressing your viewpoint toward this new product. Tell me if it is serving you well, giving you satisfaction, and in general, exactly what you think about it.

Quite often our salesmen relate to us experiences of our users that we can pass along as helpful to other businesses. Possibly you have experienced some unique advantage in the system you are using. It's possible, too, that there may be further applications for registers in your business, or you may know where an application could be installed profitably in some other business— or possibly you would like our representative to make a complete survey of your record system.

At all events, Mr. Smith, I want you to know that I would deeply appreciate a letter from you commenting as has been suggested. May I thank you in advance for your co-operation?

> Yours very truly,

Hotel contacts with guests. Many of the first class hotels in the country send thank-you letters to guests after their departure. This is especially good practice for any type of service which is so highly competitive that people are led to shop around and make their own comparisons. In the following letter used by the *Bismarck* in Chicago, the customer is not only urged to return, but he also gets a courtesy card to pass to a friend.

Dear Mr. Doe:

I am writing to tell you how much we appreciated the opportunity of serving you recently at the Bismarck Hotel.

It is my hope that you found our accommodations and services entirely satisfactory and that we may have the pleasure of counting you one of our regular guests.

It occurs to me that you might like to give the enclosed card of introduction to one of your friends. This will enable us to give him special attention.

Looking forward with pleasure to your next visit to the Bismarck, and with kindest regards,

> Cordially yours,

A similar letter, used by the *Fifth Avenue Hotel*, New York, goes a step farther by asking for criticisms or suggestions.

Dear Mr. Doe:

It was most pleasant to have had the opportunity of entertaining you recently, and we are looking forward to having you with us soon again.

We would very much appreciate hearing from you as to whether or not the service, cuisine and accommodations were satisfactory in every way, and if you have any criticisms or suggestions, they will be most welcome.

For your convenience we are enclosing a Courtesy Card. With sincere good wishes,

Very cordially yours,

The *Congress* in Chicago uses the opportunity to thank the guest graciously, and also acquaint him with other hotels under the same management. Since the letter is written in February, a special gesture is made toward the resort hotel in New Hampshire.

Dear Mr. Doe:

Mr George V. Riley, Manager of the Hotel New Yorker, wrote me urging that I get in touch with you and determine whether or not you enjoyed your recent visit there to the fullest extent. He earnestly hopes you did.

While writing you, I thought it a good opportunity to advise that I am prepared to make advance reservations for you if you are planning to return at any time in the future.

Some of the other fine hotels operated by the National Hotel Management Company, Inc. for which I will be glad to extend this complimentary service, are the Book-Cadillac, Detroit; the Van Cleve, Dayton; the Adolphus, Dallas; the Netherland Plaza, Cincinnati; the Nicollet, Minneapolis; and the Eastern Slope Inn, a fine winter and summer resort in the New Hampshire White Mountains.

I sincerely hope you will give me an opportunity to cooperate with you in this respect.

Cordially yours,

P.S. Plan now for ski-larks in the White Mountains this winter. Details regarding the Eastern Slope on request.

The *Homestead,* Hot Springs, Virginia, in its letter to the appreciated guest includes a copy of magazine—"for those of our guests who like to be reminded of us now and then."

Dear Mr. and Mrs. Doe:

Every day it's proven to us that The Homestead is hard to forget.

Anyone who has once sampled the way of life which makes The Homestead what it is, who has once been here, can almost certainly be depended upon to want to come back.

And, sooner or later, practically all of them do come back.

You're one of them, you know.

And though your taste of the way of life here may have been brief, we wonder if you didn't catch at least something of its flavor; and if you may not feel, sometimes, that the memory of it is pleasant.

So we'd like to remind you of it; and we're sending you a copy of the little magazine we issue from time to time—in the hope that you'll recapture a bit of the "feel" of The Homestead. "The Spectator" is published for those of our guests who like to be reminded of us now and then—who have, they tell us, pleasure in having their memories of The Homestead renewed.

And in case you're of the same notion, we'll be happy to count you among them. Just send back the postage-collect card, and you'll get "The Spectator" from time to time—as frequently as we issue it.

With Homestead-y greetings,

In Section 4 an occasional urge on the part of a few writers to humanize the complimentary close was mentioned. We can see no objection to the example in the foregoing letter—"With Homestead-y greetings." It seems to fit the style of the message.

The *Mayfair* letter, page 546, is an almost perfect example of customer follow-up: distinguished letterhead, interesting copy, expert typing; a combination hard to resist. On the Rating Scale which you saw in Section 6, it gets 90 out of a possible 100 points. Few business letters rate that high.

> Appearance 15
> Language 15
> Carpentry 15
> Argument 10
> Personality 10
> Spirit 15
> Yes, it does the job 10
>   —
> Rating 90

5. OTHER TYPES OF SUPPLEMENTARY SALES LETTERS

Inviting use of other products and services. It is a strange trait of human nature that a man may buy his hats in one clothing store, and his shoes in another; may have a checking account in one bank, and a savings

Mayfair-Lennox
Hotels, Inc.
825 WASHINGTON AVENUE
ST. LOUIS 1, MISSOURI

C. GORDON HEISS
PRESIDENT AND MANAGING DIRECTOR

CENTRAL 1-7200
AREA CODE 314

Mr. L. E. Frailey
1053 North Shore Avenue
Chicago, Illinois

Dear Mr. Frailey:

As a Mayfair guest, you probably know some of the more important
things that distinguish Mayfair-Lennox service. These are the
traditionally personal hospitality, impeccable housekeeping, and
innovations such as our courtesy airport limousine.

Together with fine food and service at realistic rates, these
are features that seem to appeal to experienced travelers like
yourself.

We are taking the liberty of enclosing a new brochure pointing
out those benefits of Mayfair-Lennox hospitality which are so
important to today's traveler. We'll be grateful if you will
pass it along to someone else you know, who may appreciate the
extra comfort and service we try to provide for visitors to
St. Louis.

It has been a real pleasure to have you with us at the Mayfair.
Our aim for the future is to make each of your visits more enjoyable than the last, be it at the Mayfair, the Lennox, or the new
Mayfair-Lennox Inn at the airport. When there is any special
service we may render you or your friends, I hope you will call
on us.

                                   Cordially yours,

                                   C. Gordon Heiss

CGH:eo

An Ideal Customer Follow-Up

account in the one across the street; may buy his letterheads from one printer, advertising booklets from a second, and office supplies from a third. This may be good for business in general, since it tends to scatter the plums, but any company offering a complete supply of products or services naturally wants to get all of the customer's orders.

The reasons why an individual or company passes favors around are numerous, but often the simple fact is that the buyer is not *invited* to increase the scope of his purchases, nor is he made conscious of opportunities to buy which he has not happened to think about. The following supplementary sales letter, used by the Wilkinson-Grey Company, New York, has a blotter enclosure that lists commodities in which the customer might be interested. Irrespective of whether or not the latter already knew the items were sold by this company, the very fact that they were put before him on the blotter might be an urge to buy them.

GOOD MORNING, MR. DOE!

As another year rolls around—it is just three years ago today since you made your first purchase—the following questions come to mind.

How can we do more for you? How can we render a better service or a more unusual one? What is there that we can do to make it easier or more pleasant for you to do business with us?

We appreciate your cooperation during these years a great deal and more so than words can adequately express. May we take this occasion to thank you most sincerely and assure you of our continued effort to do our utmost in serving you to your entire satisfaction?

There are still a few items which we either have not sold you at all or have not sold you recently, and we are taking the liberty of indicating them on the Commodity Blotter, enclosed for your use.

If there is anything further that we can do, Mr. Doe, to justify your placing this additional business with us, kindly do not hesitate to make your suggestions.

"Wrappingly Speaking,"

A similar letter that goes fishing for a bigger catch is one used by the Kimball Laundry Co., Omaha.

Dear Mr. Doe:

You remember poor Oliver Twist, Dickens' little boy who dared to "ask for more," and was held up to the other inmates of the workhouse as a shining example of ingratitude.

In writing you this letter, I am emulating that unfortunate

youngster, but hoping you will not visit his punishment upon my head.

To end more briefly than I began, I am grateful for the laundry business you've been sending us, but very, very eager that you should try some of our other services—dry cleaning, for example.

You know that our laundry work is distinguished by a more-than-ordinary amount of care and attention. Please believe that you will be equally delighted with our unusual dry-cleaning service.

Will you try it?

Sincerely yours,

The above sales letter reveals the hand of a good carpenter. Even though short, it plainly follows the formula of the Star, the Chain, and the Hook. The reference to Oliver Twist gets *attention,* which quickly becomes *interest* as the story is applied to the writer's desire for "something more." Then to arouse a little desire, the reader is reminded of the quality service he is already getting—followed by the confident, action-impelling question, "Will you try it?" Just as expertly constructed is another try by the same company for more business.

Dear Mr. Doe:

Robert Bruce, hiding in a cave, watched a spider spinning and climbing a web. Time after time the web broke but always the spider began spinning and climbing again, until finally he reached his goal.

Watching this determined fellow, Bruce got renewed courage, emerged from his hiding place, and started his successful "comeback" to the throne of Scotland. Perhaps he or one of his followers coined the old copybook maxim:

"If at first you don't succeed—try, try again!"

Realizing you have a good reason for not giving us your laundry business right now, I don't wish to pester you about it.

But your circumstances may alter—you may need a first-class laundry service—and when you do, I want you to think of Kimball's.

That's why I keep reminding you with these letters—in the spirit of "If at first you don't succeed" I'll keep on trying until your need and one of my letters happen at the same time.

Meanwhile—thanks for the business you are giving us. It is much appreciated.

Sincerely yours,

These two Kimball letters, and others of the same caliber, were prepared for the company's use by Allen & Reynolds, Inc., also of Omaha.

Letters used by Mobile bank. A company may increase sales by getting more customers, or by getting larger purchases from those already in the fold. The letters you have just been reading were seeking the second objective—trying to get individuals interested in items they had not been buying. The Merchants National Bank in Mobile, Alabama, had the same idea in the use of the three sales letters which follow. Each is directed to people already among the bank's customers, but each seeks to interest them in services of which they are not taking advantage. Notice how the first of the series stresses a "point of difference"—the posting of transactions by machines in clear, indelible type.

(1)

Dear Mr. Doe:

I was very glad to notice that you opened an account in our Checking Department recently, but we in the Savings Department are wondering if you will permit us to have the pleasure of serving you also. It might be that you could very conveniently use our Savings facilities.

While in the bank transacting other business, it would take only a few more minutes to step around to the Savings Department and make your deposits. These deposits need not be large, but if regularly made they will soon amount to a sizable sum.

A feature of our savings service which should particularly appeal to you is the method used in the handling of transactions. The Merchants National is one of only six hundred banks throughout the nation that has machines through which all savings transactions are posted in clear, indelible type. It was the first commercial bank in Alabama to make this installation.

These machines are a guarantee against error as there is never any question as to the accuracy of the figures—and there are never any blots or splotches to mar the appearance of the books. This system is so much neater than the old-fashioned way of posting with pen and ink that it is naturally appreciated by savings depositors. You will enjoy watching your account grow, as the record of your financial progress will stand out in clear, sharp figures.

The personnel of my department are constantly working to make and hold friends, and I can assure you that we will do everything we can to make saving with Merchants National a pleasure.

Cordially yours,

(2)

Dear Mr. Jones:

You opened a savings account with us about three months ago. By now, we hope you are well acquainted around the bank, and familiar with the services we provide for customers.

Just to give you a little of the history of the bank with which you are doing business, we were organized in 1901, employing five men. Now, there are ninety-five people employed, of which twenty-one are woman. The incentive of these men and women is pride in performance and in doing a good job.

You know, of course, that every man and woman with Merchants National—your bank—is at your service any time and will be glad to discuss business and financial problems with you. Don't think for a moment that you intrude on the time of our officers or employees when you ask for information or advice. They are here for the very purpose of working with you. Ask questions, get all the facts, make use of the facilities that are here at your beck and call, and we predict a better understanding between you and your bank.

Add systematically to the savings account you opened just ninety days ago, thereby building a surplus fund that will increase the joy of living, and make it possible for you to enjoy more fully the good things of life.

We want to see you in the bank often.

Cordially yours,

(3)

Dear Mr. Smith:

Everyone has his individual problems, and today, on account of changing conditions, each of us is seemingly confronted with more financial problems than ever before.

You are a friend and customer of the Merchants National and, therefore, are privileged to consult us about your banking or any financial business in which you are interested. If you have failed to capitalize on this service, we now invite you to take advantage of every source of information which has been provided for your benefit.

No one man at the Merchants National endeavors to specialize in all lines of banking and finance. But for virtually every problem in these fields we have at least one man who is qualified by experience to take care of your requirements.

The savings account that you already have is the avenue to the solution of many difficulties that may arise. By adding to it systematically, and with frequent consultations with us about your financial affairs, a cash reserve fund can be established that will justify every effort on your part.

We are taking an interest in your progress and will assist in any manner possible.

Cordially yours,

Letters to imply partnership of interest. Making the customer feel that he is part of the company goes a long way toward *keeping* his friendship and support. One way to do this is to ask him now and then for criticisms and suggestions—not necessarily as they apply to his own relationships, but also to the company's operations in general. The latter, you will remember, was the approach used by Mr. Rathbone in his fine letter to stockholders. He conveyed the idea that the reader was a partner in Standard Oil of New Jersey, and that his interest was considered important.

When you mail a letter asking for suggestions and criticisms, you are accomplishing at least three things: *first,* you give the customer the definite impression that you want to improve your products and services; *second,* you appeal to his pride by the implication that his opinions are considered valuable; and *third,* from the replies you will occasionally get something of real value—the knowledge of a weakness you did not suspect, or a practical idea that is worth adopting. But even if the third accomplishment never happened, the first two more than justify the customer contact as a goodwill builder.

A supplementary sales letter of this type is one used by Guthrie-Morris-Campbell, dry goods merchants of Charleston, West Virginia.

Gentlemen:

In looking over Mr. Wood's accounts, we are very glad to note the nice business you have given him, and want to assure you of our appreciation.

However, in view of the somewhat larger volume received from you last year, we are just wondering if any difficulty has arisen which is within our power to remedy.

If you have not received full satisfaction from us in every way, either in merchandise or service, we would deeply appreciate your letting us know about it; not only because of our earnest desire to serve you well individually, but to help us avoid disappointing other customers, if you have discovered a weakness in our operations.

Please understand that we appreciate your continued business even though it is of less volume, but we want to be sure that we are rendering the kind of service you deserve, and will appreciate a word from you as to whether or not anything may have gone wrong.

With fine regards,

Sincerely yours,

Although the above letter did not develop a worthwhile criticism, it did result in a vote of confidence for the salesman and the company; there's also the good impression made on the dealer, as is evidenced by his prompt reply.

Dear Mr. Morris:

There is no particular reason for our not buying as much as last year, except we have found that a few of the items we were handling are not profitable for the furniture store.

The service that you render and the quality of goods sold does not enter into the picture at all.

We have as high a regard for Mr. Wood as any salesman that calls on us, and if all the merchandise that he sells were sold more extensively by us, we would surely give him a great deal of business.

Very truly yours,

A serious problem for many companies is how to control personal contacts made by employees who are working outside the office or plant. It is difficult to know whether or not the contacts are as cordial as the executives in charge want them to be. A very able effort to throw some light on this problem, is a letter used by C. L. Sullivan, head of the Customers' Department of the Peoples Gas Company, Chicago. The writer is successful in avoiding any suggestion of a behind-the-back check-up of the meter reader; the latter is included in the request for criticisms after a fine tribute to his work.

(This company does not use salutations)

Once a month you are visited by a faithful representative of your gas company. He doesn't stay long because he has many places to go, and he must keep up with a stiff schedule. Day after day, in all kinds of weather, he goes about his job. Just as the actor clings to an old tradition that "the show must go on," so is this man taught that his service to you must be rendered.

He can't wear fine office clothes, but in his heart he has the same spirit of cooperation that you'll find in all of our employees. He tries to meet you with a smile, to answer your question cheerfully. Not only must he be accurate in what he does for you— but we expect him also to be helpful and courteous.

Of course, you know this man—the reader of your gas meter. Maybe, you've never given him much thought, but he really is a fine fellow. Some of the most important positions in the Peoples Gas Company are held by men who began by reading meters. And one of their best assets now is that they got to know our customers long before they became executives.

But, of course, with more than 800,000 meters to read every month, there are many things to try the patience of our meter readers. Sometimes, they may be blamed for mistakes over which they have no control—sometimes, they are just physically tired from a hard day's work in rain, snow, and sleet. So being human, it is not surprising if one of these men now and then gets "grumpy"—forgets for the moment that a customer's good-will can only be earned by cheerful service.

Once in a while, we like to ask our customer-friends how they enjoy their contacts with these meter readers. Often, by doing that we get valuable ideas for improving this branch of the service—ideas which the meter reader appreciates just as much as does the company. Or, there may be small wrinkles that need to be ironed out—but we can't do anything about them unless we know what they are.

So—please, as a favor—will you return the enclosed card and tell us about *your* meter reader? Give him a pat on the back if he deserves it—give him any help in the way of a criticism where you think it is needed.

(No complimentary close)

Needless to say, the foregoing letter does not go in one mailing to more than eight hundred thousand customers. The idea is to "sample" this particular feature of Peoples Gas Company service by contacting a fair cross section of gas users—sometimes as many as five to ten per cent of the whole number. Meter reading is not the only operation checked, as similar letters are mailed at regular intervals to develop suggestions and criticisms of other types of service. The idea has helped to build the unusually fine reputation held by this company among its customers—it should do the same for any other public-minded organization.

The request for customer opinions does not have to be in the form of a letter, although it may be the most personal. President C. J. Leonard of the M. B. Cook Company, Chicago, once did the job with a two-color

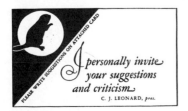

double postcard to give the mailing a little added interest. One half of the card was used to invite suggestions and criticisms; the other half was for the customer to mail back to the company. The latter carried the company's permit number, and required no postage except that paid by the company if returned. Here is the part of the double card which the recipient saw first.

On the other side of this attention-winner appears the following message.

> You have made it possible for us to produce and merchandise the finest quality carbon papers and inked ribbons throughout our business history of nearly fifty years. This year has been the biggest ever.
>
> Your comments on our service and our merchandise will be treated in *strictest confidence*—and will at the same time help us greatly in improving our relations with you. After all, you are the judge who can best point out how we can further improve our service, our products, and the courtesy of our employees.
>
> *We'll be ever so much obliged.*
>
> The M. B. Cook Company

Quite properly, for a check-up of this nature, the customer's part of the job was made just as easy as possible; no lengthy questions to answer —just a few lines for him to write on as he pleases.

Putting customer on sales force. Another human instinct that the sales-letter writer may legitimately take advantage of is *pride* of possession. John Doe buys a cabin on a nearby lake, and the next day begins to sell his best friend on doing the same. The cabin happens to be equipped with a Jones pump, and that makes John Doe eager to give it a boost. When he cures his ivy poisoning with some Jones lotion, he is eager to tell any other sufferer about it.

It is just natural for any individual to flatter his own judgment by believing his own choices and purchases are best; therefore, it's a sensible sales procedure to ask satisfied customers for the names of friends the company might approach. To be sure, there is one limitation to the use of the plan—the assurance of satisfaction. The unhappy customer is just as quick to attack as the happy one is to defend.

The following letter, signed by the advertising manager of the Williams Oil-O-Matic Heating Corporation, goes prospecting in a quite capable and tactful manner:

> Dear Mr. Doe:
> It's human nature to be proud of our possessions. From child-

hood on up we like to know that our coaster wagon—our bike—our car—is the best.

This letter is just to remind you that Williams Oil-O-Matic—the oil burner that heats your home—is still the leader in its field, just as it was when your Oil-O-Matic was installed.

As evidence of continued Oil-O-Matic leadership we cite these facts. Forty-eight different foreign countries—twenty-seven different climates—have sent to America for genuine Williams Oil-O-Matic. Oil-O-Matic users make up the largest single owner group in the oil-burner industry.

Naturally, we are proud of this world-wide preference for Williams Oil-O-Matic. It is a sure indication of the confidence which Oil-O-Matic performance has won and kept. Why not give us an opportunity to tell the Oil-O-Matic story to friends or relatives whose names come to mind as you read this letter? Write their names and addresses on the enclosed card and mail today—no stamp necessary. Your name will or will not be mentioned, as you wish. Thank you.

Very truly yours,

A companion letter to the foregoing uses about the same content, but the approach is different:

Dear Mr. Doe:

Since 1919 hundreds of oil burners have come and gone. But Williams Oil-O-Matic—the oil burner that heats your home—has come through these years with its position of leadership stronger than ever in sales, in performances, in prestige. On account of this marked preference for Oil-O-Matic you are a member of the largest owner group in the entire oil-burner industry.

Back of every Oil-O-Matic installation is the world's largest factory devoted exclusively to the manufacture of devices for temperature regulation and control. Back of every Oil-O-Matic is the famous Williams engineering staff and their patent-protected features that you will find on *no other oil burner*.

Aren't these the advantages—the protection—you want for friends and relatives who are now discussing a change to automatic heating? Whether these friends and relatives are making this important change right now—or will in the future—they should know the facts about Williams Oil-O-Matic.

We shall appreciate your taking the time to write on the enclosed card the names and addresses of parties who might be interested in learning more about Oil-O-Matic. Your name will not be mentioned. Just fill in the card and mail—no stamp necessary.

This generous cooperation will indeed be appreciated.

Very truly yours,

A final letter asking for the names of prospects is the one presented below. As a fine example of business writing, it is worthy of more than casual attention. Of course, we should expect something outstanding from the head of an advertising company, and in this case we are not disappointed. Note the good points.

Outstanding Appeal for Prospects

E. D. LeROY ASSOCIATES
ADVERTISING · THELKE BUILDING · APPLETON · WISCONSIN

Mr. J. C. Aspley,
Dartnell Corporation,
Chicago, Illinois

Dear Mr. Aspley:

Did you ever know an advertising man who wouldn't rather fish than work?

Neither did I.

But in order for me to do both I had to figure out a way to combine the two.

So I've bought Normandy Court, on Big St. Germain Lake -- which, according to Merritt Bacon, is the best fishin' hole in the state. Smith McLandress and Jim Whelan, agree that the beach, the woods, the cabins and the atmosphere are just about everything one could wish for.

Mrs. LeRoy, ably assisted, will be responsible for food and the complete comfort of the guests -- IF ANY. That is my job. Of course I'll get up there often enough to go fishing with you, I hope.

But to get back to the guests -- (and you can't run a resort without guests) -- here's where you can help! I want to build up a list of good people to whom I can send an invitation to spend their vacation, or a week end, at Normandy.

Will you trust me with the names of a few of your friends who like to fish or who go North on their vacation? I'll send them a guest card, like the one enclosed, and I'll not use your name unless you say so.

If it's O.K., please do it right now. It won't take but a minute and I can get my work started on time.

Cordially yours,

E. D. LeRoy

The design of the letterhead is excellent. It gives considerable prominence to the name of the company, without the billboard effect which so often characterizes letterheads of this type. In the original, the broad panel running up and down is in a light shade of blue.

The position of the letter on the page is perfect. The reader gets a fine impression of the entire ensemble before a word of the copy is read.

The content of the message is interesting from start to finish. The writer used the Star, the Chain, and the Hook—the formula which never lets a sales-letter writer down.

The language is bright, fresh, modern. There are no "whiskers" —no long and pompous words.

The argument is short but convincing. There could be no greater lure for a fisherman than "the best fishin' hole in the state." Also, the mention of two men known to the reader is a form of testimony that helps.

It is remarkable how a good letter-job always stands out among others of ordinary rank. Yet if you analyze the reason, it is usually because *all* of the factors that contribute to effective correspondence have been respected. And in this letter, that is what you find: pleasing appearance, natural language, expert carpentry, convincing argument; an interesting personality; and a friendly spirit.

6. Letters to Smooth Way for Salesmen

When he needs help most. It is much·easier for a salesman to work confidently with an old customer with whom he has attained a friendly relationship than to walk cold into a prospect's place of business and talk to him about a possible first order. Consequently, a letter of introduction preceding the call may help immensely in getting him off on the right foot. This letter may be mailed for the new man who has just been assigned to his territory, or it may simply be an ice-breaker for a veteran salesman who is about to call on a prospect he has not met before. In the first case, the letter goes to all customers and live prospects in the territory; in the second, to individual prospects as the salesman himself may direct.

Needless to say, some letters of introduction do a better job than others; the good ones do such an interesting job that the salesman is pleasantly remembered at the time when he appears on the scene and presents his card. The following letter gives salesman "Tom" such a fine build-up that some of the bankers who got it may even have looked forward to meeting him. If so, the effect on sales could hardly help being positive. The introduction was written by Carleton D. Beh, of Des Moines, Iowa, for the company that bears his name.

> Gentlemen:
>
> May we introduce our new representative in your territory—Mr. Thomas L. Ray.
>
> Tom is an Iowa product. He completed High School in his home town, Oelwein, Iowa, in 19..—graduated from Cornell College (and its football team), Mt. Vernon, Iowa, in 19..—served a year and a half in the School of Hard Knocks—then apprenticed himself to us and the Iowa Municipal Bond business.
>
> If you like industrious, ambitious young men of character, then you'll like Tom. He admits he doesn't know everything so he will be easy to get along with—except on Iowa Municipals—he's very enthusiastic about them. We are depending on Tom to get to know you as we know him, and are pledging our unqualified cooperation to him.
>
> So when a rather tall, dark and good-looking young fellow of about twenty-four summers' maturity appears in your Bank in the near future, a kind word and a little initial business will develop a friendship and trust with which we feel you will always be happy.
>
> > Very truly yours,

The part of this letter which is especially sound is that the spotlight is properly placed on the salesman, and not the company. The bankers who got the letter already knew about the Carleton D. Beh Co. and its services—they did *not* know salesman Ray. Furthermore, enough facts are supplied about the man to make him a personality, rather than just a name. He is an Iowa boy, went to an Iowa High School, and then to an Iowa college. At the latter he played football, a fact that would carry weight in the mind of any sports-minded reader.

Equally successful in setting up a personality for the reader to contemplate is the following introductory letter. The first paragraph is as deftly spun as one you might find in a bit of good fiction.

> Dear Mr. Doe:
>
> A light-complexioned man of medium build is about to enter your life. He is not a figment of some fortune teller's imagination, but a real, live man, who walks and talks. Incidentally, he talks about Smith's valves and he knows what he's talking about.

He's been with us about ten years now, and he likes his job as much as he does his golf. Because of his unusual knowledge of valves, and valve problems, we are putting him in your territory; where a man *has* to know valves.

Mr. Doe, may we introduce our new representative—Mr. J. W. "Jerry" Williamson.

You may expect a visit from Jerry next Thursday morning. In the meantime, you can reach him at Main 1-0123, should you need prices or information of any sort before his call.

Sincerely,

Using picture is a fine idea. Since one of the main purposes of the introduction letter is to get salesman and prospect or customer *acquainted* as quickly as possible, the attachment of a picture helps to make the presentation more effective. It doesn't need to be a fancy photograph—just an inexpensive "glossy" or a reproduction like those seen in trade or club bulletins. If the introduction of the same man is to continue frequently by letter, it may pay to have a special letterhead for him, with his picture printed in one corner. It is best that the job *not* be too elaborate. The object of the idea is to let the reader *see* the man talked about before he calls—it is not to promote a Hollywood star.

The United Autographic Register Co., Chicago, is responsible for the next letter of introduction. A small picture of the salesman appears in the upper right-hand corner.

Dear Mr. Doe:

Lately, we've told you a great deal about Uarco registers and manufacturing systems—but we haven't said much about Uarco's very valuable asset, the Uarco man who calls on you.

In some ways he's the most unusual salesman you've ever met. First, he's not a high-pressure salesman. He wouldn't sell you anything on a bet, if he thought for a minute that you wouldn't benefit by the installation.

Second, to use a slang phrase, "he knows his stuff." He knows records and record-writing machines thoroughly. He's trained and has had the experience of dealing with hundreds of different kinds of firms—especially manufacturing.

Third, he's the fellow who will service your registers. And when we say service, we really mean SERVICE. He'll not only help check your supplies, but he'll check your registers every call and see that they are working right. He'll oil them when necessary. And he won't charge a cent.

Finally, he's loyal to his customers and his "house." He's just as proud of Uarco as we are of him—and that's saying a lot.

He's glad to be working with a human firm which has been the leader in its line for half a century.

So when Carl Nutter calls on you, please make him welcome. Listen to his story. See what he has to offer. Ask questions and answer his. You'll learn a lot from him—and he, of course, will learn much from you.

Will you please write on this letter, "Sure, I'll be glad to talk with him," and return it in the enclosed envelope?

Cordially yours,

When the writer of the introduction and the reader are already acquainted in a business or personal way, the request that the salesman be received can be put as a favor—always a difficult appeal to deny. Wm. T. Summers, Jr., does this very well in the following letter written for Graham Brothers, Inc., Los Angeles.

Hello Mr. Briggs!

It has been some time since you and I exchanged greetings over the telephone. Frankly, I have missed hearing from you.

I just wanted to drop you a note to the effect that we have assigned Mr. George Tyson as our Ambassador of Good Will to your office. George is a newcomer to our Sales Department after two years' training in other departments here at the office. In fact, one of his positions with our company was in our own Purchasing Department. From this experience he has gained a true appreciation of your problems and will give them proper consideration in his visits with you.

I will consider your giving George a pleasant reception a personal favor. Do not hesitate at any time to call on me for anything I can do to repay your courtesy.

Yours very truly,

Helping overcome sales resistance. Unfortunately, a salesman is too often regarded as a necessary evil—a pest carrying a gold brick and blessed with lungs that never wear out. The prospect who holds such a notion is always on the defensive and determined not to be high-pressured. It is a false concept, for the average salesman is genuinely interested in the service he can render. Nevertheless, it's quite prevalent.

A letter which attempts to pass this barrier by displaying the salesman as a conscientious helper is one used by the Keystone Chemical Co., Inc., Cleveland. Notice, too, how the writer avoids a formal salutation.

When John Doe Calls on You—

Please don't feel that he's there to match wits with you and high-pressure you into placing an order. True, his job is to sell Keyspray and other products in our line, but his first obligation is to analyze your specific requirements and make intelligent recommendations.

We have found that this policy works to the advantage of all concerned. It has revealed and eliminated conditions that were a serious handicap to dealers' sales and profits. It has placed the purchasing and use of insecticides and sanitation supplies on a more efficient and economical basis. And in recognition of this helpful cooperation and the recognized value of Keystone products, it has favored us with preferred consideration.

So we say, when Mr. Doe calls on you, please feel free to take him into your confidence. He is a specialist in his particular line, sincere and conscientious, and will be only too glad to work with you if you will give him that opportunity.

Cordially yours,

When one salesman replaces another. You could scarcely ask for better examples of customer relations, conducted tactfully and with the sincere will-to-please, than two letters written by H. J. Cocking to handle a common problem in business—the death of a popular salesman, and the selling of the man selected to take his place. Too often in this situation there is a loss of business during the period of transition, but in this case the loss is avoided.

Letter About Salesman's Death

Gentlemen:

It is my sad duty to inform you that our Mr. John Doe, who has been calling on you for so many years, died very suddenly Tuesday night, February 13th.

Mr. Doe was with us for over 20 years and we are certainly going to miss him. His death will be a significant loss to the whole Quaker Organization.

He leaves a wife and daughter to mourn his loss, as well as a host of friends who will miss his regular calls and friendly co-operation.

You have done your job well, Mr. Doe, and the least we can do is to remember the thoughts of a brother worker, "God bless you, Mr. Doe...and happy landings."

But we must carry on. So may I ask, until we can replace Mr. Doe, that you kindly send us your inquiries and orders direct? You may rest assured we shall do everything possible to warrant a continuance of your friendship.

Sincerely,

Letter About the New Salesman

Gentlemen:

Since Mr. John Doe's sudden death, we have interviewed several men to carry on his good work. Now we are glad indeed to tell you that we have engaged Mr. Edward Jones who will call on you on behalf of this company.

You'll find Mr. Jones a likable chap and I'm sure he'll leave no stone unturned to help you in every way he can. He knows the Mechanical Rubber Goods line very well and has had a lot of hard selling experience.

At first, perhaps, you won't feel the same toward Mr. Jones as you did toward Mr. Doe...that's only natural. You knew Mr. Doe so well for so many years, and, like ourselves, had a world of confidence in him. But these changes cannot be helped, and we feel confident you will give Mr. Jones a break. You will help him all you can, won't you?

You know, it's pretty hard when a man first tackles a territory. A little encouragement goes a long way, so please extend him the glad hand. Breaking the ice is a bit tough, hence this letter.

I sincerely hope your business is good right now, and thanks a lot for the business you gave us through the late Mr. Doe. If there is anything we can do to help while Mr. Jones is getting into his stride, rest assured we'll be ever so glad to do it, and we mean every word of it, too.

Cordially indeed,

Of course, there are many other reasons why it is necessary to change sales representation—inefficiency, insubordination, promotion, resignation, and all the rest. But whatever the circumstances, the primary purpose of the announcement is usually to win goodwill for the new salesman, and thus help him get adjusted as quickly as possible. Turnover is always expensive to business; the problem is to hold the cost down as much as possible. The following letter, mailed by the Brunner Printing Co., Memphis, is typical of the sort that are satisfactory when no special problem is involved.

Gentlemen:

Mr. Bruce Bell, our salesman who solicited your business personally, is no longer connected with us.

Mr. Bell has entered business for himself and while we wish him every success, we want you to know that your orders are appreciated and noticed at Brunner's. We intend to give you the same service, quality, and reasonable prices as we have in the past.

Mr. Walton Wilder, who is taking Mr. Bell's place, will call on you at regular intervals. Although Mr. Wilder is not entirely familiar with the printing business, I know you will find him always on the job, ready to be of service to you. Any favors shown him will be highly appreciated by me.

I want you to feel free to call on me at any time that I can personally be of assistance to you.

Very truly yours,

When dealers take a hand. One of the most perplexing problems in customer relations is how to say "no" to the dealer who nominates an unqualified candidate for a sales vacancy. If the nominee happens to be a relative, then indeed must the sales manager be a good skater on thin ice. Another phase of the problem is when a number of dealers whose orders gross a considerable sum "gang up" for a salesman, or would-be salesman, who the sales manager has no idea or intention of placing in the territory.

The situation just described prompted the following letter. The former salesman, after considerable service in the territory, had died, and customers favored the joint appointment of his son-in-law and son to take over. Whether sentiment or wire-pulling governed their choice is inconsequential; the sales manager knew he would have to be careful about the way he explained the selection of an ʹoutsider. His solution was to stress the importance of the job and the several moves which the company had to make in order to assign a man who could adequately serve the dealers. In short, the moves were made for *them,* the dealers.

Dear Mr. Doe:

The sudden death of our former representative, Mr. Ben Richards, on April 15 was one of the saddest blows that ever fell on our organization. Ben was one of the leaders in our nation-wide sales force—a man with a host of friends because of his wonderful personality, trustworthiness and capability.

When we faced the problem of appointing his successor, we realized that it would take a real man to carry on where Ben left off. Consequently, we decided to remove an experienced man from another territory to take charge of the Davenport office.

To accomplish this, it was necessary to transfer three of our men in the field to bring Mr. Frank Williamson to Davenport from Milwaukee, Wisconsin. Perhaps Frank hasn't had an opportunity as yet to get around to see you. When he calls, won't you make him welcome and let him study your needs first hand?

You will like Frank as well as we do. In many ways he is just like

Ben Richards, especially in being conscientious and able in his work. If you will need to see him soon, send the enclosed card or get in touch with him direct at the following address:

> Telephone—ADams 4–1122
> Box 343, Davenport, Iowa.

You will be interested to know that Art Richards, Mr. Richard's son, and his son-in-law, Curt Dillon, are continuing as salesmen in the area. They are eager to follow in Ben's footsteps and succeed; and they will benefit greatly under Frank Williamson's seasoned leadership.

Should they call on you, your own assistance will help a great deal. Thanks a lot.

> Very truly yours,

The salesman announces himself. A letter from the newly assigned salesman to his customers and important prospects in the territory can also be made into an effective introduction. This permits a little more personal tone in the message, and if the latter is carefully worded to avoid the appearance of conceit or flippancy, it may have more influence than a more formal announcement from the company. Whether or not the new salesman actually writes his own letter need not enter into the picture, there being some things in business which from necessity must be confidential. A still better plan, which really gives the salesman a send-off, is the use of two letters—one from him, and one from his company.

7. LETTERS TO FOLLOW SALESMAN'S CALL

To keep the gate partly open. Very few sales are consummated on the salesman's first call, nor is such a happy event to be expected. There are numerous reasons to prevent it. The prospect may have in stock adequate supplies of all the merchandise of the kind being offered; he may be tied to a competitive company by many years of friendly dealing; he may have been too busy at the time of the call to give the merchandise fair consideration; he may have had previous relations with the salesman's company that were not satisfactory; he may have been impressed the wrong way by the salesman's approach; any of these reasons or numerous others may have kept the gate at least partly closed.

But so what? If selling were so easy that one call would usually win the order, good salesmen in business would not be needed. Closing a sale—especially with a new customer—is like winning a prize-fight. In the first round, prospect and salesman are sparring against each other: the salesman to discover what the opponent needs that matches what he has to offer; the prospect to form an opinion of the salesman and his line, so that he may know how to proceed in later rounds. The fight may be a draw for several rounds, but only a knockout can end it. The salesman may have to take considerable punishment for a while; his chances of victory may appear hopeless. But if he is a salesman and not an order-taker, he keeps on plugging. The harder the fight, the more he enjoys it. Victory is sweeter when hard-won. A good salesman never throws in the towel—but his trainers back in the office *can* help him.

Sales managers of the better sort do not turn their men loose to succeed or fail by their own efforts. Instead, they back them up with a barrage of sales helps direct from the home office. These helps include letters to the prospects that may add to the arguments already advanced by the salesman, or at least win a little goodwill for his next call.

Of course, the obstacles encountered by the salesman are never the same in two or more cases. He may report that the prospect was pleasant but non-cooperative; that objections were produced which he was not prepared to answer; or that the best he could get was a flat refusal with the pointed implication that any further calls would be a waste of time for both parties. In other words, after the first call, the gate may be partly open or it may be closed tight—and the follow-up letter from the office is dictated according to whatever situation may prevail.

Thanks for the interview. The simplest follow-up letter to write is the one in which the chances of getting an order are still considered good. There are no special complications, and the salesman is optimistic about eventually making the sale. Some sales managers seem to think that in such cases follow-up letters are unnecessary, but this is not straight thinking. A friendly letter of thanks for the interview may go a long way toward making the second call more productive; certainly, no sale can be hindered by an expression of goodwill from the home office. Instead, such a letter tends to create in the prospect's mind the idea that he has been contacted by a well-organized company, alive to sales opportunities, and eager to co-operate with its salesmen. Following are a few follow-ups of the salesman's interview that may be called typical and satisfactory.

The first of these letters has the added advantage of an enclosure which is both effective and unusual: a "Taxicab Pass", the prospect may use for trips to the plant. This is factual evidence of company appreciation used to supplement the words in the message. The idea is that of the Central Pattern & Foundry Co., Chicago.

Dear Mr. Connely:

William Zint, our representative in your territory, has told us about the interview you granted him. He appreciated your courtesy a lot, and so do we.

Although new in your territory, Bill is by no means a new man in the aluminum, brass and bronze casting business. He has been with our company for nearly nine years, in every department—through the factory, office, sales, and inspection units—and is thoroughly educated in the non-ferrous casting business.

After you have met him a couple of times, you will realize as we do that you can rely on his knowledge of castings and their uses —rely on his promises. He's a dependable, regular fellow.

And Bill knows, as we want you to know, that "Central" will back up any promise he makes, and every casting he sells.

Cordially yours,

A second neat follow-up of the salesman's interview is the following— used by Sellstrom Manufacturing Co., Chicago. Here it seems the salesman didn't get very far, so his efforts are supplemented by the offer of a catalog. It could have been mailed with the letter, but the psychologists tell us that it is better to make people *ask* for things, instead of offering unsolicited gifts. The request assured a closer inspection.

Dear Mr. Sweeney:

We are grateful to you for the courtesies that you extended to Mr. Rolfe when he called on you last Thursday.

He has told us of his talk with you and said that you were not quite ready to consider buying at the time of his call. It's not always possible for a representative to drop in at exactly the right time, but we want you to know that whenever you're ready, we're ready to serve you.

We have a new catalog that we shall be glad to send on if you wish. It lists many different styles of eye protectors for every purpose. Lenses can be had for any and every need. Along with the catalog we can send you prices so that you would find it convenient to select items you might be in need of before Mr. Rolfe's next call.

Feel free to call on us at any time that we may be able to render you a service. We shall welcome the opportunity to serve you.

Very truly yours,

"CENTRAL'S" TAXICAB PASS
====GOOD for BEARER and PARTY====
Mr.___Mr. Connely_____
YELLOW CAB COMPANY - CHICAGO
Kindly deliver the bearer and party from the loop . . . or any point in Chicago, to the main office and works
of
CENTRAL PATTERN & FOUNDRY CO.
3737 South Sacramento Ave. - Chicago
DRIVER:—Present the meter slip for payment, at the information window when delivering passengers.
Central Pattern & Foundry Co.

If the writer of the follow-up feels the need of an excuse for writing so that it may be something more than just a pat on the back, he can often confirm something told the prospect by the salesman. This is what happens in a letter used by Pfaelzer Brothers, Chicago meat packers.

(No salutation)

The courtesy and consideration you gave Mr. Hearst are sincerely appreciated. Thank you so much, too, for taking the time to discuss your requirements with him.

Mr. Hearst spoke very highly of your place and he also mentioned that you enjoy a very fine reputation for serving T-Bone, Porterhouse, and Sirloin steaks. The quotations he has asked us to confirm are as follows.

(Four items priced)

Mr. Hearst is confident—and so are we—that like many other leading night clubs throughout the country, you too will find that from Pfaelzer Brothers you can buy with confidence—knowing that your requirements will always be uniformly high in quality, consistent in weight, and properly aged. For economy's sake, you will find them always closely trimmed.

When you use our meats, Mr. Doe, you serve *steaks that won't come back to customers who will.* Give us a trial, won't you? The postage-free order card is for your convenience in ordering.

Kindest regards!

(No complimentary close)

A follow-up that smooths the way for another call is the letter sent by the Schuylkill Valley Mills, Inc., to a lady who retails hosiery.

Dear Miss Doe:

We were indeed pleased to learn that our representative, Mr. Oscar Meyers, had the pleasure of calling on you and of discussing our merchandise.

Apparently your stock was complete, but merely the fact that an order was not obtained on his first call does not discourage us; selling is not his entire mission. The important thing is that his visit brought Schuylkill Valley Mills to your attention.

As a keen buyer you know that hosiery retailing is gradually emerging from the destructive price market into which it had degenerated during the past few years, and is rapidly shaping into channels of carefully planned merchandising campaigns based on economically sound principles.

You know that profitable operation demands low stocks which turn frequently. Schuylkill has specifically designed its services to cater to the present day requirement of the retailer demanding maximum turnover on a minimum investment.

There is probably nothing we might add to what Mr. Meyers has already told you about the exceptional and unvarying quality of our hosiery and its possibilities from a sales and profit standpoint. Mr. Meyers will call on you at regular intervals and an opportunity to convince you of our ability to serve you promptly and efficiently will be indeed appreciated.

Yours very truly,

Also paving the way for another call of the salesman (this time the buyer was not in his store) is a friendly letter mailed by Mock, Judson, Voehringer Company, of Long Island City, New York. This message aptly attempts to approach the prospect as a seller rather than a buyer; the salesman is cast as a helper with sales ideas for the prospect's benefit.

Dear Mr. Harper:

You were away from the store when our representative, Mr. Walter Manning, was there a few days ago.

Since missing the folks who do the buying is not an unusual occurrence in a salesman's life, he left cheerfully with thoughts of better luck next time. But we'd like to leave just one thought with you, which perhaps will save some time for you and him on his next visit.

We referred above to "the folks who do the buying," but we really should have said, "the folks who do the selling," because when Mr. Manning calls again and presents the Mojud silk stockings and the profit-building plan behind it, he will talk to you about selling—your selling over the counter.

And he'll show you, among other things, the plan that helped build from scratch a hosiery volume of nearly $25,000 a year for a shop in Wyandotte, Michigan. We know you'll be interested. Here's hoping your latch-string will be out next time Mr. Manning comes to see you.

Yours for Sales and Profits,

Letter used with big order pending. When a salesman reports he has a chance to land a big order, the alert sales manager naturally hurries to lend a helping hand. In the following case, the writer of the assisting letter was somewhat favored by previous acquaintance with his reader. While the contact had been casual, it at least served to get the message off to a good start.

Dear Mr. Watkins:

When Carl Hite told me today that he had been talking to you about the College insurance, it reminded me that I haven't seen you since we met on a Chicago & Northwestern train about a year and a half ago. Do you remember that day?

We talked about the Lexington men with the Hardware Mutual —Masterson, Beggs, Westberg, Kohl, Bassett, Grove—and then about the Federal Companies and why they can return a 40% dividend on the Fire and Tornado Insurance for the Lexington College property.

When Carl mentioned the large line of insurance you have coming up soon, I decided to write you a personal letter expressing the hope that the business will be placed with us and offering to give you any information in which you may be interested.

My work is in the administrative branch of the Sales Department. From here it is possible to have a bird's-eye view of all of our operations. I wish that it were possible for you to spend some time with me so that I might show you the records of hundreds of schools, colleges, and public buildings that are turning to the Federal Companies for sound protection at the lowest cost consistent with such insurance.

I'm sorry. I started out to make this a short personal note, but it seems to be developing into a sales talk. Maybe this will sound like an attempt at subtle "high pressure," but I am honestly sincere when I express admiration and enthusiasm for the Federal Companies.

Mr. Hite can answer any questions you may put to him. However, if you want someone else's viewpoint, why not ask Masterson, Westberg, or any other of the many Lexington men with the Companies?

Cordially yours,

The above sales-helper was written by Rodney A. Kox for the Hardware Dealers Mutual Fire Insurance Company, Stevens Point, Wisconsin, and won him Gold Medal recognition by the Dartnell Corporation. Another fine attempt to help a salesman over a high barrier is a follow-up letter used by Graham Brothers, Inc., Los Angeles and Long Beach, California. It has that friendly and sincere tone that always adds distinction to a business contact.

Dear Mr. Doe:

I certainly thank you for the courtesies you have shown Mr. Lester Leach, our sales representative, during his recent visits with you. Les has just recently been transferred to the Sales Department after spending two years in other work with our company.

Naturally, he wants to make good and your pleasant reception has done much to build up his ambition and courage. It is our sincere desire that his calls result in a profit to your company.

We have asked our friends in Santa Barbara to furnish us with prices for you on the job you are figuring there. Just as soon as we get this information we will ask Mr. Leach to bring it to you. This should be in your hands not later than Wednesday.

Just a word in passing about Grahamixed Concrete. We realize that you have a considerable investment in mixing equipment and that naturally you want to derive a profit from your capital outlay. However, there may be times when the moving of a mixer from one job to another might cause inconvenience or a greater expense than by the use of Grahamixed Concrete.

In these or any other instances we will be glad to give you the best price possible on the quality of concrete you need. As almost every job is different in nature, we prefer to figure each one on its individual merits and quote accordingly.

Just as soon as possible, I want to thank you personally for your courtesy to Mr. Leach and our company. Until then, I wish you the best of success in all your undertakings.

Yours very truly,

How to follow hold-out prospect. Needless to say, no salesman can sell *all* of his prospects, and no amount of supplementary letters can achieve that miracle for him. But like the steady drops of water that eventually carve a channel in hard rock, consistent sales effort may often land what seemed to be an impossible victory. The sending of just one follow-up to a salesman's call may be totally inadequate. The man in the field and the man in the office may make many attempts before they reach the promised land, but sometimes they can and *do* get there.

The difficulty of writing the follow-ups to a specific prospect increases with the number that have to be mailed. The writer can't say the same thing over and over. This may be a good thing, even if it does add to his worries, since the need of new approaches may eventually bring forth the one that does the job. There is a case on record of one businessman who wrote a sales letter once a week for forty-nine weeks—all to the same prospect—before he got an order. But the order was big enough to pay for all the trouble.

It is a strange twist of human nature that sometimes a hold-out prospect may yield to some simple little appeal, although he couldn't be budged an inch by more elaborate and thorough prodding. For example, John M. Palmer, sales manager for the Lee Clay Products Company, Clearfield, Kentucky, strikes a new high in simplicity with the following successful gem of a letter.

Dear Mr. Andrews:

Did you ever know the source of that old expression, "an elephant never forgets"?

Somebody said it and it is a safe bet that in his spare time, apart from originating pat sayings, he was a Sewer Pipe Salesman.

Dale Boyd is no elephant...doesn't even own a trunk...but he keeps writing me to remind you that for the past year or more he has been expecting an order from you like nobody's business.

Why don't you give Dale a break and send us your next order for a mixed car of Sewer Pipe and Flues?

Cordially yours,

Yes, that's the whole of it, and the appeal is in the one question, "Why don't you give Dale a break?" But it may be a stronger appeal than some businessmen imagine. Any thoughtful person welcomes the opportunity to help somebody else—call it the feel of power, if you must. However, you will find that most follow-ups to a stubborn prospect run long and factual. The writer tries to review his major sales argument in the hope of giving it a new slant that may do the job better.

In a clear-headed, factual way, James Timmer, the Correspondence Manager for Federal Hardware & Implement Mutuals, replies to the objection which had cost one of their salesmen a sale—that the prospect had decided to stick with his local New York agent from whom he had gotten good service.

Dear Mr. Doe:

I want to express my thanks for the courtesies extended to our representative.

C. C. Jackson tells us that you are staying with your local agency for the present, at least, because you feel that they have been giving you good service. That certainly is a very commendable reason.

The Federal Mutuals realize that there is no substitute for service. That is why no Federal salesman, regardless of previous insurance experience, is permitted to enter the field until he has been thoroughly trained in property insurance coverages. Properly written insurance results in prompt and satisfactory settlement of losses. Over ninety per cent of our losses are settled within two weeks.

Then, too, we have fire protection engineers who periodically inspect all of our mercantile and manufacturing risks. If any hazards exist, recommendations are made for their removal. This minimizes the possibility of loss and frequently results in lower rates.

So you see, Mr. Doe, we are equipped to give you as good service as any other insurance carrier. In addition, we can save you thirty per cent of the premium on your Fire Insurance and forty per cent on your Windstorm Insurance, based on our present dividend schedule.

Before your next Property Insurance policy expires, we would like to demonstrate, with our Program Plan, what Hardware Mutual service is. The enclosed card will bring you this service without any obligation.

Sincerely,

The tone of the foregoing letter is extremely good. At no point does the writer seem to argue with the prospect, or to challenge his loyalty to the local agent. Instead, he begins by agreeing with him—"That certainly is a very commendable reason"—and that is always sound sales psychology. Then, after stressing the services rendered by his own company, he plays his ace of trumps—the respective savings of thirty and forty per cent, which it seems the prospect did *not* enjoy from his current protection. In the face of these circumstances, the average man would think twice before again renewing the old policy.

Thanking the old customer. A very delightful customer contact is a letter of appreciation written by M. H. Cable as Manager of the Sales Service Department for Roberts, Johnson & Rand, St. Louis. The occasion is the fine treatment given a new salesman by the customer, and the letter is a goodwill gesture that many a sales executive might easily overlook. The last paragraph especially should leave a pleasant impression not soon forgotten by the reader. This letter rates high as an example of the kind of customer appreciation which leads to more orders.

Dear Mr. Doe:

While Mr. John P. Sherman was getting ready to leave St. Louis for Kalamazoo and we were discussing the territory with him, we came across your name.

We told Mr. Sherman, of course, that you were one of the oldest and most faithful customers of ours in the entire southern Michigan district. He knew, therefore, that when he walked into your store for the first time, he could do it with the confidence that he would be meeting a man who thinks the same way we do about giving good values to his customers.

Mr. Sherman just reported his first visit with you the other day. He enjoyed it very much, Mr. Doe, and we want to thank you for being so cordial and courteous to a stranger and making him feel at home in your city.

It is nice to have some occasion to write you without discussing shipments, orders, prices, etc. Incidentally, Mr. Doe, we hope you end this year with a mighty fine volume of retail sales that will show you a healthy net profit.

Yours very truly,

The keynote of the above letter is the first sentence of the last paragraph—"It is nice to have some occasion to write you *without* discussing orders. . . ." A letter contact which has no motive except an expression of goodwill carries many times the weight of one where the writer is obviously seeking to feather his own nest. "Unnecessary" contacts of this sort build the friendship and respect that keep customers in the fold. Sales executives should take time to write more of them.

Follow-up of executive's call. Now and then every alert sales manager —sometimes the president—likes to rub shoulders with customers and important prospects in the field. These personal contacts are of great help to the salesmen, and they also tend to give the office executives a broader perspective on sales problems. In this connection, a letter from George J. Hughes, then Western Division Sales Manager of the Deltox Rug Company, is most enlightening.

Friend Frailey:

Sales managers, as you know, often make trips into the field to contact their salesmen, at which time important buyers are seen.

Good business policy suggests that the executive follow his visit with a letter to the buyer for the purpose of creating greater goodwill. Few of these letters, however, attempt to do a merchandising job.

I'm enclosing four letters which follow the executive's call on buyers which are far more productive than the usual kind. Note how they credit the buyer with freshening the executive's viewpoint. Note how they praise the buyer for some one thing he has accomplished. And then note how they seek to tie the line into the store's activity.

Most buyers, I find, have some pet business hobby. In retailing, it is usually some phase of merchandising, either sales training, store layout, display, or advertising.

A glance about the store, or a few minutes' talk with the buyer brings out the phase of selling in which he is particularly interested. A few pointed questions will get the buyer to talk about it. It is no trouble to note down afterward the high points of the talk or to write on these points after the return to the office.

Note that the paragraphs of the letters are formed, except the third and fourth. This method reduces dictation time to the absolute minimum. A new form can be prepared following every trip.

I think that the effectiveness of the letter lies in these facts: Ask a man—point-blank—to do a thing, and he balks like a mule. But give him a pat on the back first—then ask him to do that very same thing—and he goes to work with a will. Which just goes to prove that regardless of the size of our ego, we poor humans are starved for praise.

It's a shame, too, for it is so easy to praise when praise is merited —and makes a man work so much the harder.

I hope you like the letters—also, the philosophy. With best good wishes,

(No complimentary close)

Okay to the comments of this sales manager! He knows the philosophical undercurrents of selling. Let the buyer know, he says, that something in which he is particularly interested has captured the visitor's attention. This places buyer and customer on the same side of the fence—makes the former more receptive to the latter's suggestions. Following are two of the four messages that Mr. Hughes mentions; form letters *can be personalized* by changing one or more paragraphs.

Friend Godwin:

I can't resist the impulse to write and tell you how much I appreciated the talk I had with you when I was in your store several days ago.

Somehow or other—a fellow grows stale sitting at a desk on a job like mine, and all too often loses the retailer's viewpoint. But your clear merchandising ideas did a whale of a lot in giving me a fresh grasp of up-to-date retailing policies.

These two paragraphs changed to fit the conditions met in the respective retailer's store.

I was particularly impressed with the artistry of your newspaper advertising. I can easily understand why your ads have pulling power, and why they pay for themselves many times over.

I cannot help but feel that a Deltox Rug ad, used whenever you offer a suite for less than $400, would help a lot in making your fibre rug sales more profitable.

I don't get away from the office very often, but when I plan my next trip, I shall do so with the thought of meeting you again.

With best good wishes,

Friend Webber:

I can't resist the impulse to write and tell you how much I appreciated the talk I had with you when I was in your store several days ago.

Somehow or other—a fellow grows stale sitting at a desk on a job like mine, and all too often loses the retailer's viewpoint. But your clear merchandising ideas did a whale of a lot in giving me a fresh grasp of up-to-date retailing policies.

The other letter put finger on newspaper advertising. This one talks about furniture set-ups.

I was particularly impressed with your set-ups of furniture in the store to create the impression of model rooms. I can see why they would cause people to want to buy more things than they had planned to buy before entering the store.

I cannot help but think that a Delroyal Rug or two in those room set-ups would help a lot in speeding up the sale of Deltox Rugs.

I don't get away from the office very often, but when I plan my next trip, I shall do so with the thought of meeting you again.

With best good wishes,

Although, as Mr. Hughes explained, the use of the semi-form letter in making these dealer follow-ups cuts dictation time to a minimum, they still give the impression of being completely personalized. In every respect they are personal and friendly, and the plug for Deltox rugs is made in a way that could not offend. You can see, too, that this sales manager does not hesitate to start his letters with the intimate but pleasing, "Friend Godwin," "Friend Webber."

8. Letters for Other Needs Involving Salesmen

When the salesman is ill. Keeping the business of a popular salesman when he is off his beat is an ever-present sales problem. The man who pitches for him during his absence cannot be expected to know the respective needs of buyers, or be acquainted with their buying habits. But if he throws wild now and then, much loss to the company can be the result. Sometimes a buyer, looking forward to the time when the sick salesman will recover, holds up his orders. This loyalty speaks well for the salesman, but a customer not buying is never too safe under the fire of competitors.

Under these circumstances, a letter from the sales manager or president may be of considerable help to both the substitute salesman and the company. The best appeal is probably sympathy for the incapacitated salesman, with the assurance that he will receive full credit as before for orders sent direct to the office, or given to the substitute. Such a letter is the one used by Vernon S. Porter, Managing Director of S. Maw, Son & Sons, Ltd., London, England.

> Dear Sir:
>
> We are very sorry to advise you of the indisposition of our representative, Mr. A. K. Jones, which has resulted in his removal from his home to the County Hospital, Oldborough.
>
> It is still too early to give you any very definite news, except that the patient is relieved to be in the hospital with the benefits of specialized treatment.
>
> Mrs. Jones is, of course, keeping us posted with bulletins, and enquiries can be made to her home address (Telephone no. Hendon 9235), or to Miss Isherwood of our Telephone Department, Aldergate Street.
>
> During his indisposition, Mr. A. Sutherland is travelling the territory on his behalf. Mr. Sutherland is young, but we think you will find that he makes up for this in keenness and enthusiasm. He has been in training in the House for some six months, and has a thorough ground-work in our merchandise.
>
> We should like to explain that Mr. Jones receives full commission for all orders taken by Mr. Sutherland on his behalf. We hope you will be good enough to extend to Mr. Sutherland the courtesy always accorded the regular Maw representative.
>
> We ask for your valued support during this period.
>
> > Yours very truly,

Letters preceding salesman's call. All salesmen know that it is usually better to walk into a buyer's office or store at a previously announced date than to barge in on him without warning. An exception might be when the salesman knows he is not wanted, but in that case the call would probably be a waste of time anyway. Many salesmen handle their own announcements of future calls: some of them on their own initiative because they have found it worthwhile; others simply go as directed and announced by the sales manager, or some assistant. Unfortunately, many companies have no routine at all for announcing the calls of salesmen and leave them to sink or swim without this practical sales help.

A very simple practice where a salesman calls regularly on old customers is to supply him with postcards, to be mailed a few days ahead of his arrival. This works very well for the salesman who is detail-minded and can be trusted to carry out the assignment, but there are few sales forces blessed with men only of that type. Another weakness of the plan is that the card serves simply as an announcement, and cannot serve also to point out a sales feature or two that might be pertinent at the time of the call. The last purpose is best accomplished by a letter from the home office, although it involves a more systematic control and co-ordination of the salesman's time than some companies are willing or able to supply.

A typical letter is the one below, in which the salesman discusses the need of teamwork in selling, with a boost for himself and the way he plays the game.

> Dear Mr. Doe:
>
> At the start of the football season, I was watching two West Coast elevens battle.
>
> A back on one of the teams, a runt of a fellow, kept breaking through for long gains. The spectators were praising him to the skies—giving him all the credit for the yards gained.
>
> But I noticed that this little fellow had very little to do with evading tacklers. His teammates opened the holes for him, and all he had to do was grab the ball and run.
>
> As the score became topheavy, I lost interest. My thoughts turned to sales, but the subject of teamwork stuck in my mind.
>
> After all, selling is a 50-50 proposition. When I sell you a bill of goods, you still have the job of reselling. Conscious of this fact, I reason things out this way:
>
> > If I attempted to sell you certain merchandise knowing the goods would not resell easily, I would be a poor teammate.
> >
> > Yet, when other stores, similar to yours, are doing a good selling job in given lines, I feel I am practicing good teamwork in stressing these lines during visits with you.
>
> In other words, when I encourage the purchase of items I have good reason to believe will resell easily, and discourage the purchase of others, I feel I earn the right to continue playing on your team. And we both gain more ground!
>
> Incidentally, I shall be seeing you in a few days to show you a few things which will make me a better teammate of yours.
>
> > *(No complimentary close)*

At the end of a sales-letter campaign, the next logical step is a personal call. Such a situation is heralded quite cleverly by Roy Irvin in a letter once mailed by the Cargill Company, Grand Rapids, Michigan. Especially adroit is the introduction:

Dear Mr. Doe:

Courtships by mail are more or less satisfactory to both parties. But even an exchange of photographs may not reveal the fact that the bride-to-be stammers badly or that the prospective groom insists on eating pie with a knife.

It's much better to get well acquainted first.

For the past week or so, we have been conducting a little court-ship—all on our own part so far—and now we feel that the time has come to get better acquainted.

The writer is, therefore, planning to call on you during the next week, and he'd like mighty well to have the pleasure of meeting you and discussing with you those portions of your advertising and sales promotion activities which have to do with the printed word and picture.

To us, the term "printing" signifies a means to an end, the end being bigger sales and profits for our clients. We will appreciate the opportunity you may give us to explain further just what this means to you.

Sincerely yours,

When a sales manager knows his reader well enough to call him by first name, he can write more frankly than to customers with whom he has not had intimate contacts. In the following letter, no punches are pulled, but the closing words, "Thank you, Roy" indicate a relationship to justify the tone of the body content. The mailing was made for printers Hederman Brothers, Jackson, Mississippi, by C. B. Bardwell, Supervisor of Sales.

Dear Roy:

Down on the corner, just a block from where I am sitting, is a grocery store. Next Saturday, if you will send me the money, I'll step down there and buy your groceries for the next week, and then send them up to you.

What? You say that you have a grocery store in your own town, and that you prefer to buy at home and help your grocery man instead of the one in my town? I can hear you say "No" from here; and you are telling me that your first interest is to buy what you can where it will help build up your own community. That is exactly as it should be. Since your first interest is in your local community, then your next interest must be in the welfare of your State.

Our salesman has been calling on you regularly every five or six weeks and the records show that we have been favored with only a small portion of your business. We want you to know that we appreciate the portion that shows on our books, but we would like to have more. Our equipment is as good as money can buy, our product is as good as can be made anywhere, and our service is clicking with other customers. They buy regularly, so it must be good.

Mr. Walters is going up to call on you about November 5th, and before he gets there, what about looking over your stock, and jotting down a list of all that special ruling, lithographing, and other jobs that have been going to out-of-state firms? Just hand the list to Bob when he gets there. We'll get it in the next mail, and we'll do the work.

Thank you, Roy.

(*No complimentary close*)

The dramatized announcement. Showmanship is just as possible in paving the way for the calls of salesmen as for any other kind of business correspondence, but the expense is not warranted unless the announcement is going to a wide list of customers, or is to serve some special purpose where extra emphasis is desired.

Letters to those who won't see the salesman. Some salesmen are more gifted than others in slipping around the barriers that are set up to keep them from the individuals who have the authority to buy. The difficulty, of course, varies in different companies, depending on the amount of red tape in the purchasing department, the disposition of the buyer, and the general attitude of the company personnel toward the public. As a rule, business executives do not like to go over the head of the person who may be blocking a salesman, because the act is sure to be resented and may cause additional trouble. When a buyer simply will not talk to the salesman, and the latter has repeatedly failed to gain an interview, a letter to the proper executive may unravel the tangle; at least, it is worth trying on the assumption that there is everything to gain and nothing to lose.

The writing of such a letter is not a job for the novice, but one which the sales manager must do for himself. There is hardly any problem in business correspondence that provides a greater test of the writer's diplomacy. Here is how H. J. Cocking, when Sales Promotion Manager of the Quaker City Rubber Company, Philadelphia, matched his wits against those of the stubborn buyer.

Dear Mr. Doe:

Bill Robinson, our salesman in your territory, was at my desk this morning and told me he has never been able to get your ear for a single moment. He seemed a little hurt, too—you know how salesmen are.

Bill is a good fellow and a hard worker—knows the Mechanical Rubber Goods line as well as any fellow I know—so I told him I'd write to you to try to break the ice, as it were.

Of course, I explained to Bill that it isn't always convenient for a busy executive like yourself to see a salesman, especially when he drops in without any previous announcement.

I also told him that most officials are very liberal in granting interviews—because they expect the same courtesy to be extended their own salesmen—which is only right.

So with this little kink ironed out, Mr. Robinson will call on you November 10th, and if you can conveniently do so, I will certainly appreciate your giving him a few minutes. His story will be brief and to the point. He realizes your time is valuable.

Under another cover I am sending you a catalog. Should you desire samples and prices on anything enumerated therein, wire us at our expense.

For the courtesy extended Mr. Robinson, please accept our thanks.

Cordially yours,

Analyze that letter for a moment. What are the appeals that might get under the buyer's skin?

1. Mr. Cocking tries to arouse a little sympathy for the salesman —"He seemed a little hurt, too"—with the added compliment that the reader knows how salesmen are.

2. He refers to Bill as a good fellow, and as one who knows his line thoroughly.

3. He compliments the reader again with the words, "a busy executive like yourself."

4. He plays the trump card—you want *your* salesmen extended the same courtesy.

5. He announces Bill's next call with the confident tone of expectation that he will get his interview.

6. He says that Bill's story will be short, and adds another compliment—"He realizes your time is valuable."

7. He thanks the reader for his courtesy—again implying it will be forthcoming.

8. At no time does he appear to be angry, nor does he insinuate the reader has not been playing fair.

Measured by results, the letter was completely satisfactory; the salesman got his interview, and came out of it with a sizable order. Another letter to smoke out the recalcitrant buyer, with the added appeal that the reader cannot afford to disregard something important to his company, is one dictated by W. T. Quimby, Sales Manager of the Quimby Pump Co., Inc. Instead of setting a definite date for the interview, however, the writer says that the salesman will telephone for an appointment. This may be more tactful, but it gives the buyer another chance to dodge the issue.

The letter is addressed to the company, but carries an attention line— "Mr. John Doe, President."

> Gentlemen:
>
> I have before me a sales report from our Mr. R. R. Roberts, who has tried several times recently to talk to you on the subject of screw pumps.
>
> While we realize that an executive in your position is a very busy man and one whose time is exceedingly valuable, we also are confident that you would be one of the first to want to know if there were changes which could be made in your plant which would reduce maintenance and upkeep and save you money on your pumping equipment.
>
> Mr. Roberts reports that he has been very courteously received by certain of your employees with whom he has come in contact. He feels, however, that the message which he has is of sufficient importance to justify your personal attention, and has asked if I would write to you for an appointment so that he can lay the facts before you.
>
> In order not to inconvenience you, Mr. Roberts will call your office the early part of next week, and if you would leave instructions with your secretary as to what day and time is best for you, it will not be necessary to disturb you until the time of his arrival.
>
> > Yours very truly,

Mr. ——, writing for Prentice-Hall, Inc., uses rather different tactics. He devotes his letter to a summary of the reasons why the teachers were missing important help by not being allowed to see the salesman. Of course, he realizes that his reader is the man who refused the interview, but he is careful never to express that thought. The primary purpose of his message is to get a more favorable reception for the salesman on his next regular call.

> Dear Mr. Smith:
>
> Our representative, Mr. Stokes, has reported a most pleasant visit with you recently. Although I am sorry that it was not possible for him to meet your commercial teachers, I fully understand your inability to arrange a meeting at the time; increased enrollments have made many teachers' programs more than full.

However, our representatives come to you with a two-fold purpose—both service and sales. They are carefully chosen for their classroom teaching and supervisory experience, and their ability to present teaching materials.

In their daily contacts with hundreds of schools, they observe the latest methods in teaching procedures. Therefore, they come to you with both the newest and most up-to-date teaching aids—Prentice-Hall publications—and a sincere desire to present helpful teaching suggestions. With the present crowded schedules and bulging classrooms, your teachers need the best and most efficient aids in order to carry on.

Mr. Stokes plans to visit you again in about three months. He can help you and your teachers. Feel certain that the time you can afford to spend with him will prove worthwhile to your school.

Sincerely yours,

Letter aids for salesmen, and for the other purposes, are by no means limited to these illustrations. It is important that those responsible for sales in any company be continuously on the alert for special opportunities to contact customers and prospects. The effort must be made in a hit-and-miss manner, letting the chips fall where they may. A routine must be set up for the use of supplementary sales letters, and one or more persons delegated to make sure the schedule is carried out.

LETTERS TO REGAIN
LOST BUYERS

LETTERS
TO REGAIN
LOST BUYERS

1. WHY DO CUSTOMERS STOP BUYING?

Taking inventory of sales. As has been pointed out, the tendency in most sales departments is to place more emphasis on getting new customers than in holding old ones. This is understandable, as there is no greater thrill for a salesman or his chief than to land a new account, especially if the struggle for it has been long and difficult. Getting new business is one way to increase sales volume, but not the only way. Volume can also be increased by helping old customers to sell more. Remember, there is no gain at all if the amount of new business is offset by the *loss* of old business. Hence, the ideal sales program is the one that pays equal attention to both objectives—making new advances, but holding the ground already captured.

Certainly, the executives of any company should want at least an annual inventory of customers. For example, what percentage of sales last year went to newly acquired buyers, and what percentage went to customers carried over from previous years? They should want to know how many old customers stopped buying, *why* they stopped buying, and what can be done, if anything, to bring these lost sheep back to the company. Have the lost customers gone out of business? Not usually. Are they buying from other companies? Obviously. But what happened? Why *do* customers leave one company for another?

When the sales manager is reasonably sure of the answer to the last question—why customers run away—he is better qualified for two jobs. First, he can take steps to eliminate the faults which may have caused dissatisfaction; second, he can decide intelligently how to go about reclaiming some of the lost business.

Analysis made by retail store. To find out *why* customers quit buying, one of the nation's well-known retail stores selected a cross section of one hundred representative charge accounts that had not been active for more than one year. Personal calls were made on the one hundred lost customers, and they were asked to state frankly what had happened. The answers, tabulated in percentages, were most amazing.

Do customers leave a company because they are angry, because they can buy at a better price elsewhere, or because they have been influenced by friends or relatives? You would expect, perhaps, that those were major reasons, but none of them rated high in the survey just mentioned. In fact, more than two thirds of the one hundred inactive customers had *no special reason for not buying*—the retailer had simply *let them drift away.* Here are the figures:

68 of the hundred had no special reason
14 had grievances which were not adjusted
 9 were lured away by lower price or better service
 5 had been influenced to shop elsewhere by friends
 3 had moved and were shopping in other areas
 1 could give no answer—he was dead

To be sure, the figures just cited would vary for other groups of one hundred among customers of the same store, and in greater degree among customers for other types of business. But it seems fair to assume that the *indifference of the company* is the leading reason in the great majority of cases. People stop buying because they are *allowed* to stop. The company favored with their patronage forgets to show appreciation or does little or nothing to hold their goodwill. Often, the only check made of accounts is for credit purposes; no one bothers to notice that certain accounts are going stale; no one bothers to even ask the customer *why* when he stops buying. So he just drifts away, and *nobody seems to care.*

This is not true of all companies, for some watch their customers as a hen watches her chicks. But it is surely true of more companies than the simple principles of good business procedure seem to warrant. Of course, the company with strong field representation, and salesmen calling regularly on customers, has a more favorable opportunity to keep customers in the fold than the one that does a lot of business by mail, or the one in which personal contacts by salesmen are limited in number. Nevertheless, *NO* company, irrespective of salesmen and their calls, can afford to overlook any form of office co-operation which might help to keep customers satisfied and assured that they are considered *important* to the organization. And there is no better means of doing this office job than with letters!

Inactive customers still good prospects. The fact that a customer has stopped buying does not necessarily mean that he cannot be induced to buy again. A small percentage of the lost sheep may even wander back on their own initiative, but a far greater percentage need just a little encouragement—perhaps only the question, "We've missed you, where have you been?" It only takes a postage stamp, a piece of paper, and a little time to ask that question, and the payoff in revived business makes the effort worth many times the cost.

2. How to Approach Inactive Buyers

Easier to woo than strangers. One fact that makes neglect of inactive customers lamentable is the comparative ease with which many of them can be induced to buy again. There is no way to prove the figure, but some sales analysts maintain that a company spends twenty times as much getting a new customer as it takes to regain an old one. If that difference seems too large, at least it must be conceded that the cost of getting the old customer back is considerably less, whatever the exact figure may be. The mere prospect is a stranger to the company. He knows nothing of its services, and little about its products. He may have been buying a long time from a competitor, and has no reason for wanting to buy elsewhere. It takes hard, intensive effort to get his first order—when that happy end is finally reached.

But the old customer knows all about the company, its products and services; three-fourths of the usual sales program is already completed with him. The one-fourth that remains may be to adjust a complaint, or simply to give him a little attention—the attention that was lacking when he drifted away. We have already seen from the retailer's survey of one hundred lost customers that more than two-thirds of them had no real reason for leaving, and the ease with which they left suggests the ease with which they may be brought back. Of course, the inactive buyer likes to be *noticed,* and probably will *never* return if the company remains aloof. Not to be *asked* to buy again is damaging to his ego. Why should he go back to a place where he has not been missed?

But suppose *you* were the inactive customer, and you got a letter like the following one—what would be your reaction?

Dear Sir:

Away back in the early days of this business, I learned a very valuable lesson.

In those days we depended more on footwork—and less on head-work!

Well, here's what happened.

One day I was traveling thru the territory with one of our men, and we called on an old-time customer who had suddenly stopped buying. After exchanging the usual greetings I asked him why we weren't receiving any more of his orders. And this is what he said:

"There's really no reason at all. I just happened to give a couple of orders to another salesman who had been calling on me for a long time. Nice fellow, and I wanted to give him a break! But you folks have never made any effort to re-sell me so I just thought you weren't interested in my business. Never even got a letter from you asking why I quit, so I've been going along with this other firm."

Well, we *are* interested in *your* business.

And to prove it, we're writing to ask why we haven't been getting any of your orders. We don't want to make the same mistake we made years ago. We want you to know that your account is really valued, and that we'd like to keep it. If there's anything WE can do to restore our relationship, we'd appreciate it a lot if you would let us know.

Will you?

Thanks!

Sincerely yours,

That letter was used with considerable success by the Continental Coffee Company, Chicago. The approach is simple—"We appreciated your orders...Why have you stopped buying?" The story gave the letter length, but it was a good story and helped to convey the writer's thought. Here are three quite short contacts of the same sort.

Used by Hotel Fontenelle, Omaha

Dear Mr. Doe:

Do you realize that it has been all of six months since you and Hotel Fontenelle got together?

We enjoyed having you with us. When'll you be back? We miss you.

Watchfully yours,

Used by Rangecroft-Flotow Motors, Inc., Chicago

Dear Mr. Doe:

Just a short note to let you know that we have missed your coming in for service. The last time you were in was last July.

Anything wrong? If so, tell us, because you know we want to please in our service to you.

Won't you come in? Or better still, phone—the number is Longbeach 0-0000.

Thank you.

(No complimentary close)

Used by Allegheny Tube & Steel Co., St. Louis

Dear Mr. Doe:

Can you spare me two minutes?

One minute to read this—and one minute to say: "We haven't sent you our order for Nipples, because—

_____
_____"

Please fill in your answer and return this sheet to us in the stamped envelope enclosed.

This won't obligate you in the least and we'll surely thank you for your two minutes—and your courtesy.

Yours in anticipation,

The light, humorous touch can help you get the inactive customer back in the fold again. The letter having this touch will be read and enjoyed by its recipient, and it will certainly go a long way towards re-establishing a favorable image in the customers mind. The Plaza letter is an excellent example of this type of correspondence, and it is one that continues to be used most effectively.

How far should the letter go? When you reach the end of this section, you will have read many letters to inactive customers, letters actually used by business executives during recent years. Most of them can easily be adapted to the needs of any other company, although there is considerable variation in treatment and content. Some simply express appreciation of past business, and say the customer has been missed; some ask casually what is wrong; some assume a grievance, and lavishly promise to make things right.

These differences bring out the question of just how far the letter to lost sheep should go. For example, there are certain points that these contacts may develop; the use of one of them is a moot question among business-letter writers, as you will see momentarily.

How to recover lost sheep

1. Tell the customer his past orders were appreciated. If the

The Plaza

FIFTH AVENUE AT FIFTY-NINTH STREET, NEW YORK 19, N. Y. · PLAZA 9-3000

OFFICE OF THE
VICE PRESIDENT-MANAGING DIRECTOR

January 7, 1963

Dear Mr. Harris:

We looked in The Palm Court and The Oak Bar and behind the piano in The Edwardian Room. We even sent our best chambermaid to search the closets of all the guest rooms.

You aren't here.

We haven't seen you this year and frankly, we're worried. Several disastrous things could have happened to keep you from our doors. Perhaps our laundry starched your handkerchiefs on your last visit ... it actually happened twice last year! Or maybe The Persian Room was temporarily unable to supply your favorite champagne ... there is such a demand on the very great years! Worse yet, you may have been lured into another hotel and they've lost your IBM card and you can't check out. A prisoner! We shudder. You can understand our concern!

Seriously though, you may not have returned to The Plaza simply because you haven't returned to New York. If this is the case, don't hesitate another day. There are lots of new things to do here. The theater this year is superb. Philharmonic Hall is open at Lincoln Center. And, of course, The Plaza has added something since your last visit. You may have heard about The Plaza 9-. It's a new supper club under the aegis of Julius Monk. He's presenting his latest after dinner revue, "Dime a Dozen." I hope you read the reviews. They were wonderful! Don't miss it!

Please hurry back to New York and The Plaza. Or at least tell us how you are. We hate to lose touch with our friends!

Very sincerely yours,

Paul Sonnabend

Paul Sonnabend

HOTEL CORPORATION OF AMERICA

fact was not mentioned when he was buying, perhaps there should be some form of mild apology for the oversight.

2. Tell him how much he has been missed. *Don't* say you noticed his absence while "going over the records." No one is really missed if the fact is called to attention by a *record*. He wants to be missed as an *individual;* not as a name on the books.

3. Tell him you want to *serve* him again. That's better than asking him to *buy* again.

4. Tell him you are keenly interested in knowing *why* he stopped buying. Merely asking that question is *not* an assumption of dissatisfaction; it might be for some other purely normal reason.

5. Tell him about anything new and beneficial in service or product; things that have happened since he stopped buying. Or, mention some other inducement that might be interesting; a gift you want him to write or call for; any special thing you can do for him which would be fair to other customers.

6. Tell him you think something happened to displease him, and how eager you are to make things right.

It is point Number 6 that is questionable. Unless the writer has a guilty conscience and *knows* why the customer stopped, why should he invite trouble? Perhaps the mistake was inconsequential, and already has been forgiven if not forgotten. There is an old saying, "Let sleeping dogs alone." If something serious did happen, the customer will probably mention it in his reply; and remember, in the check made by the retailer of one hundred inactive customers, only *fourteen* had grievances. The odds, then, are better than 8 to 1 that the customer has no complaint to voice. Is it smart to play a long-shot?

No—not in the majority of cases. Let the storm clouds form as they may. Don't worry about them while the sun still shines. Go as far, if you think it wise, as to ask, "Why did you stop buying?" But don't do it fearfully, leaving the plain impression that you expect an unpleasant reply.

Of course, there are exceptions to all rules. A letter that handles the possibility of complaint in a very casual and adroit way is one dictated by C. W. Giller for the Shelby Salesbook Co., Shelby, Ohio. It demonstrates what has been mentioned so often in this Handbook—it isn't so much *WHAT* you say, as *HOW* you say it.

Dear "Old Customer":

Have you heard the saying, "Old friends are like the ticking of a clock"? You get so used to hearing the tick that you rarely notice it until it stops.

We get used to doing business with Old Customers, too. So much so that now and then we assume that everything is running along smoothly and we sometimes fail to express our appreciation as often as we should. And then—suddenly the clock stops and we find that an Old Customer has stopped buying.

That's just the position in which we find ourselves with you. Your orders have stopped and we are wondering if you would tell us frankly just what the trouble has been—whether there is something we did not do that we should have done, and whether there is anything we can do NOW to get you back on our list of regular customers. If there is, we surely want to do it.

If there is anything wrong with the works of our clock, let us see what is out of kilter. Of course, accidents will happen at times, and if one has happened in this case we hope you will tell us about it. We think we can fix it up the very day we receive your reply.

Like any successful business, our progress is largely dependent on satisfied customers. That's why we want you satisfied and that's why we earnestly request you to fill in the attached business reply card.

Let's see if we can't get the old clock to ticking again.

Sincerely,

3. Letters That Shun Possibility of Grievance

The most casual approach. You have now read a few letters that either made no reference to the possibility of the former customer being angry, or else did it so casually that he would pay little attention if in a good humor. This, as we have agreed, is probably the best approach in the majority of instances. The purpose of the more casual letter is chiefly to remind the lost buyer of the company, and to make him feel that he is important enough to be missed. His reaction is likely to be much the same as when a friend of former years calls him on the telephone and invites him out to dinner. If he has no reason to hold ill will against the friend, he is quite likely to accept.

The letters that follow are typical of the more or less casual group. Because of the importance to business of this form of correspondence, the number of examples is not stinted, and you may derive from them a reasonable concept of how various companies have seen fit to handle the problem.

The first consists almost entirely of a story which is both interesting and timely. Godchaux's of New Orleans, who used the letter, have had unusual success in reviving old accounts by this and similar methods—one mailing had the remarkable return of 45 per cent.

Dear Mr. Doe:

The day was warm and the milling crowd at the political rally stirred restlessly as the speaker left the platform. In an effort to swing the crowd, one of the candidates, a former General, had recounted his long experience.

His opponent arose and, laughingly addressing the crowd, said: "My fellow citizens, what General Smith said about having bivouacked in yonder clump of trees on yonder hill...is true. It is also true, my fellow citizens, that I...stood guard over him while he slept. Now all of you who were generals and had privates standing guard over you while you slept vote for General Smith, and all of you who were privates and stood guard over the generals while they slept vote for Private John Jones."

And so Private John Jones launched himself on a long and brilliant Congressional career.

At Godchaux's we have our "Generals" and we have our "Privates" too. We feel it to be an achievement that each account, large or small, receives the same meticulous service, the same prompt, efficient courtesy that one hundred and seven years in retail business have schooled us to give.

Recently you have not used your charge account. We hope that it was through no fault of ours. But if it was, won't you let us know. Meanwhile, your account remains open. When next you are in the store, won't you say "Charge it"?

Godchaux's

The sending of a stamped envelope with any kind of a sales letter should increase the chances of a reply; this is especially true of the more or less personal messages that reach out a hand to an old customer. Not many people will throw a stamped envelope away, and it doesn't seem honest to keep it. If the follow-up of the inactive customer is worth anything at all, it must be worth an additional cost of 5¢ to heighten its chance of success. This evidently was the opinion of the Cenol Company, Chicago, in using the letter below:

Dear Mr. Doe:

Did you ever look through an old Picture Album?

Today we have been looking through a most interesting album—one of our old sales ledgers. There, in clear precise figures, is the picture of the business we used to receive from you. It is almost a moving picture, for more than one transaction is shown.

Suddenly, the action stops.

Why?

We asked most everyone, but they don't know—the credit man's answer was, "Mister, I'll O.K. all the orders you can get from them." I thought that most interesting.

The order blanks enclosed show how Cenol and Lenwells have grown. Our policies haven't changed. We are still selling to independent drug stores only. Prices are maintained, profits assured.

May we have an answer to that big "Why" up above? The postage paid envelope will bring it to us—order, letter or whatever you send. The main thing is to hear from you.

A place for you has been reserved in our current sales album.

Yours truly,

Two letters with special play for attention. Just as for any other type of business correspondence, a good start in a letter to lost sheep may help to secure a happy ending. For example, consider the letter used by the Container Corporation of America (page 595) with the rubber-stamped "CREDIT O.K." This message, too, shuns the mention of a possible grievance, and simply asks *why* the customer has not reordered. The extra cost of a secretary's time in using the rubber stamp is inconsequential, and the idea does give the letter an effectiveness it would lack if the same words were merely typed in the line.

The following appeal to lost sheep has no mechanical device to attract attention, but it does start with a question of interest to almost any individual. Who does not remember his first door key, or how his mother always seemed to be awake when he got home? The letter did a reclaiming job for Anabolic Foods, Inc., Chicago.

Dear Doctor:

You remember that your mother always rested more comfortably after she heard the sound of your key in the lock? While you—proud in your possession of your first door key—laughed and told her there was no need to worry.

The Anabolic family is large and far flung. Yet we too feel better when all of the family "is in." Then we know we are successfully doing our part—that there is no call for any member "to leave home."

Since we have not heard from you for two months, we'd feel more comfortable if we heard you "come in" this month. The enclosed order blank is your key.

CONTAINER CORPORATION OF AMERICA

38 SOUTH DEARBORN STREET   CHICAGO 3   TELEPHONE FRANKLIN 2-6161

October 23, 19--

Rubinstein Can Company
P. O. Box 178
San Francisco, California

Gentlemen:

When your first order for containers was received and passed to
this department for **CREDIT O.K,** I commented that our salesman, Dunford, had landed a worthwile new account - the kind to
whom we'd like to sell lots of containers - just the kind that
our business needs.

Our opinion was correct - you discounted our invoice! But, as
anticipators - did we over-rate ourselves? We haven't had a
repeat order as yet, and we're wondering why.

You know how it is in your own business. There are many good
concerns who ought to be doing business with you. Their credit
is good and they buy frequently and in good volume. Maybe you
sold them once and they never came back for more. You wish they
would - but you don't know why they don't.

That's the way I was thinking about your account today - - just
that ONE order - -

                                        Yours very truly,

                                        Credit Manager

bs

Unusual Attempt to Regain Inactive Buyer

Anyway, will you drop a note "home" and let us hear from you? We'd like to know that at least you still feel like one of the family.

Cordially yours,

	Recipients	Replies	Sales
Letter 1	70	8	$308
Letter 2	62	12	$607
Letter 3	50	26	$74

Of course, deductions made from one limited test are not to be trusted completely, but insofar as these three letters are concerned, the second did a better job than the first. These two mailings together got most of the money, although the third letter developed far more replies. Probably a fourth letter would have been wasted. Three seems to have been exactly the right number.

(1)

Gentlemen:

We know that you will agree that old friends are the best friends. If an old friend suddenly seems to forget you, you're going to want the reason.

That's just the situation we are up against with regard to your company. Several months have passed since that last order, so, of course, we would like to know the reason "why?"

Won't you use the back of this letter and tell us why we haven't heard from you recently? It is our experience that a firmer friendship arises with a clearer understanding, and that is the reason we are asking you to write us today.

Yours very truly,

(2)

Gentlemen:

We are still wondering why we seem to have lost an old friend in you. A short time ago we wrote to ask why we aren't receiving your orders recently, but as yet we have had no reply.

This matter is of great importance to us. Frankly, we want to keep the business of old customers like you, and we are sure it can't be too late to restore the pleasant relations that we formerly enjoyed.

So once again we ask—won't you please take just a minute to jot down on the back of this letter the reason we haven't been hearing from you? We are enclosing a self-addressed envelope and will appreciate your reply.

Yours very truly,

(3)

Gentlemen:

It has been my experience that a frank discussion of any problem is the quickest and best route to a satisfactory solution.

Our problem right now is that we have not been getting your business, and I am greatly interested in finding out why. After all, we are dependent on firms like yours to distribute our products if we are to retain the place we enjoy in the field of competition today.

We want your business; we need your business; and if there is any complaint, be it a matter of service, policy, or quality of product, we want to know what it is so that we can make an honest effort to correct it to your satisfaction.

I would appreciate a personal note from you stating frankly why you are not buying our products, and what we can do to make you want to buy them.

Yours very truly,

The first and second of the above letters were mailed on regular company stationery, and the signature was identified with the Sales Department. The third letter was signed by the president, and reproduced on his personal stationery. The added pull of the president's name evidently caused the large number of replies, although the sales volume was very low. Evidently, the Sales Department had extracted most of the juice from the lemon before the president was allowed to squeeze it.

The letters you have just been reading tried hard to shun the possibility of a dissatisfied customer. They merely asked the former buyers where they had been; why had they been away; why didn't they come back home where the fatted calf was waiting for them. This is a fine approach to the customer who has wandered away for no particular reason; why look for trouble where no trouble is known to exist? However, many sales correspondents have taken other roads that lead to the same objective—we shall now see how.

4. LETTERS THAT ADMIT POSSIBILITY OF FAULT

The offer to adjust any mistake. Directly opposite in psychological appeal to those that assume *no* grievance, are the letters that carry the assumption of a mistake or fault, and ask the former customer what needs to be done to make things right again. The strategy, of course, is good when it happens to hit the truth; it may be so straightforward and sincere that even the reader who has no chip on his shoulder is favorably impressed by a company so eager to play fair. The approach, however, is often grossly misused, so that the writer seems too apologetic, too conscious of weaknesses in service or product.

Few would criticize the tone of a letter used by the Dennison Manufacturing Co., Framingham, Massachusetts. The writer frankly admits that he thinks something has happened to displease the former customer, and he seems very sincere in his desire to make reparation—but he doesn't overplay his hand or grovel at the feet of his reader.

> Dear Mr. Doe:
>
> Probably you have found yourself in the same position as I am now.
>
> You have wondered why folks you had been doing business with stopped abruptly and you heard no more from them. It caused you some concern. You began to wonder why you lost their business, because you did your best to keep them satisfied.
>
> It is possible that something we may have done—or did not do—has disturbed you, because we haven't had an order from you for a long time. Often it is just a misunderstanding, though I might make a thousand guesses. So all I can do is ask you "What happened?"
>
> In this old world we can't get anywhere by ourselves. We've got to have someone else's help, so won't you be good enough to tell me just why we haven't heard from you? Be absolutely frank. Don't be afraid of treading on anybody's toes—facts only can iron out a troublesome spot. Your goodwill is worth much to us, and we want to keep it.
>
> Please use the enclosed envelope for your reply.
>
> > Yours very truly,
>
> P.S.   Is there any service I could perform for you at this time— a catalog, prices, or just information?

Equally pleasing is a letter used by Lowe & Campbell Athletic Goods Company and signed by J. A. Browning, Manager for the Oklahoma Division. The very first sentence establishes the thought of a possible fault— the rest of the letter seeks the way to make up for it.

> Dear Mr. Doe:
> Is it our fault? Are we to blame?

You bought athletic equipment from us last year—so far this season we have not heard from you. We are naturally wondering why this should be. If we have mishandled any of your orders, we want to hear from you about it—a statement of the facts will enable us to correct any error we may have made, and to remove any misunderstanding that may now exist.

New customers are, of course, welcome at all times—but it is much more satisfying to know that our old friends are re-ordering. Will you not also look upon us as friends, and think of us as being here to see that you get immediate and satisfactory service on all your orders for athletic supplies?

Sincerely, Mr. Doe, we are anxious to find out why we haven't heard from you this year. Has our Fall Catalog failed to reach you? Have we fallen down on a previous order—or does it just happen that you haven't needed anything in our line this year?

Won't you use the back of this letter and the accompanying envelope in telling us just why we haven't heard from you? Better yet, just use the enclosed order blank.

Very sincerely,

Another neat attempt to bring back lost customers is one used by merchants T. W. Mather Co. Inc., Pasadena, California. It was written for this company by letter-expert Guy Burroughs.

Dear Mr. Doe:

When one of your good friends doesn't pay you a visit for a long time you first of all miss that friend very much—and then—

—you begin to wonder what keeps that friend away.

We've missed you for a long time now. And in trying to find the reason, we've thought perhaps we were at fault.

You know it's our constant desire to present only better quality merchandise that has been carefully selected as to style and service values. We've tried to merit your confidence by the nationally reputable merchandise, and by the attentive service of our salespeople.

If we've failed to please you some way, won't you give us another opportunity? We very much appreciate your patronage and it is our sincere hope that we may renew a relationship with you that has been most pleasant.

May we be favored by a visit from you soon?

Sincerely yours,

Letter for both sides of the story. A good letter idea, which may have lost some of its punch from too frequent usage, is the one that leaves half of the page vacant for the reader to fill in his side of the story. The idea is quite suitable for a call to lost sheep.

Dear Friend:

We are anxious to adjust whatever complaint you may have, or to know why you have ceased to order from us. But we can really do little until we hear *your side* of the story.

That's why we've arranged this letter to make it convenient for you to tell it.

Our side of the story	Your side of the story
The space on your order card is as white and clear as new-fallen snow.	
There is always a reason why a good customer stops buying, a reason we should like to know so we can remedy the difficulty if we have been at fault.	
That's your side of the story, the side we want you to tell us. Will you meet us half-way?	
Will you fill in and mail to us the other half of this letter in the enclosed postage-paid envelope?	
I will consider it a personal favor.	

Sincerely,

A questionnaire for reader to check. While the foregoing letters have varied in style and content, they all have contained the assumption of a fault that needs correction. Deltox Rug Company, in one of its follow-ups, goes even a step farther by attaching a questionnaire for the reader to check "Yes" or "No." You might also call it a disguised order blank, as the last two questions definitely probe for facts that could lead to sales.

Doe Furniture Company
El Dorado, Arkansas

You will agree, gentlemen, that it is poor business to permit a good paying customer to stray away.

So, as good and successful merchants, you follow old customers when, after a reasonable time, they do not return to buy again.

There is sound thinking behind such a practice. So sound, in fact, that we follow it ourselves.

Now it happens that we haven't had an order from you since early last year. A copy of our last invoice to you is enclosed. And for some reason we feel that this absence of your business is due to some fault of ours. If this is true we wouldn't be fair to you or to ourselves if we didn't take steps to remedy the situation.

So, will you do this for us? Look over the attached sheet. Answer the questions that have a bearing on the condition that keeps you from buying from us. Just a check mark will do. And we invite additional comments if you feel them necessary.

But please answer. A stamped air-mail envelope is enclosed to make this very easy.

With best wishes.

Check List of Questions From

Doe Furniture Company,
El Dorado, Arkansas.

1. Did you find our merchandise unsatisfactory in any way from a quality or workmanship standpoint? Check which:
   Yes ( )   No ( )

2. Did our merchandise fail to sell satisfactorily for you? Check which: Yes ( )   No ( )

3. Have you had customer complaints regarding our merchandise? Check which: Yes ( )   No ( )

4. Did our salesman fail to call on you regularly? Check which:
   Yes ( )   No ( )

5. Will you be in the market next Spring for summer rugs, such as fibre rugs? Check which: Yes ( )   No ( )

6. Are you in the market now for wool-surfaced rugs that you can sell at $26.50 and $35.50 in the 9×12 sizes, with smaller sizes selling for less? Check which: Yes ( )   No ( )

Added Comments_____

_____

_____

Letters with strong personal appeal. It is hard to hold ill will against an individual who says "I am sorry" as if he *means* it, and then asks for another chance. Explanations and apologies may help in some cases, but usually they only intensify the ugly situation, and the writer finds himself securely chained in the well-known "dog house." But regret, sincerely and simply expressed, is a great disarmer.

Some of the best letters to inactive customers are those that use the man-to-man approach—just one person talking to another. There are few people who will continue to hold a grudge against the man or company that seems concerned about any shortcomings, and eager to make things right. The letters that follow are good examples:

Used by Quaker City Rubber Company

Gentlemen:

New friends...new accounts and so-called big business deals are very alluring...but after all...the old friends of yester-year are the ones who count...those who made the grade with us...in good times as well as through the dim, dark days.

It becomes almost a habit to look for their business. In fact, we actually grow to expect it. Then...when one of them suddenly stops sending his orders, it's a severe jolt and we wake up to the fact we haven't a God-given right to the business of any concern.

But it isn't altogether a matter of dollars and cents...there's something deeper...something below the surface. Call it sentiment or whatever you will...I just can't explain it, but you know what I mean.

So...in this same spirit...if we slipped up or displeased you ...we are sorry. Tell us about it...don't send your business elsewhere...give us another chance...we'll do the right thing by you. We can't do more than that, can we? Less...we will not tolerate.

Our new bulletin just off the press is a humdinger...both interesting and helpful. Your copy will be mailed...just the very minute we know you want it.

There's a prepaid envelope attached for your reply. If you can slip an inquiry or order in it...well..."bully for you." Anyway, let's get together again...please.

Just for "Auld Lang Syne." Thank you.

Most sincerely,

The man-to-man thoughts expressed in the foregoing letter are not easy to resist. We all like to give the other fellow a break when he seems to deserve it. Note the impelling language in that letter.

"those who made the grade with us"
"something below the surface...you know what I mean"
"if we displeased you we are sorry"
"Tell us about it—give us another chance"

"we'll do the right thing by you"

"let's get together again...just for Auld Lang Syne...please."

In the next letter the writer even refers to past deficiencies, but in very human fashion he also reminds his reader of the other times when the best of service was rendered. The result of this man-to-man approach—the asking for another chance—was that the customer *did* return to the fold.

Used by Graham Brothers, Inc.

Dear Steve:

Jack Dempsey was my idea of what a real world's champion should be. I believe right now he could knock over most of these stiffs posing as top-notchers—if his legs would hold up. However, Jack was beaten—not once, but twice by the same man. Sooner or later, old man age bowls them all over.

Strange as it may seem, the rock, sand and cement business is something like the prize fighting game.

I like to remember Dempsey as a real guy. True, he was licked twice, but that's no reason I should be off him like a dirty shirt. Is it, Steve?

We were champions in the service with you for a long time. It is true that the "legs" we used failed to come through a couple of times. However, we often came out winners on tougher battles than those we lost.

Our experience on those two jobs of yours taught us a good lesson. Those trucks we had were champions in their day, but that day had passed. Jack Dempsey couldn't buy a new pair of legs—but we could and *did* buy new trucks. As you undoubtedly know, we have invested about a quarter of a million dollars in new delivery equipment, which again puts us on the winning side, and minimizes chances for delay to our customers.

Steve, we have really staged a successful comeback on our service. We are as near as your telephone, and will welcome your placing another bet on us like money from home.

Yours very truly,

The same strong personal appeal is found in a letter used by C. A. Winser to beat the bushes for customers lost by the Gates Rubber Company. According to Mr. Winser, this letter has never failed to bring back either an order or an explanation. A letter that pulls 100 per cent *must* be good.

Dear Mr. Doe:

We have always tried to look on our customers as friends as well. We want you to feel that we are every bit as much interested in serving you as we are in selling you. That is the idea upon which this company was founded.

But in spite of high ideals, we are all human—we *can* make mistakes, and we know that we sometimes do. Perhaps that is what has happened in your case, for it has been a long time since we heard from you, and we cannot help wondering why.

If we have made a mistake, handled an order in a way that did not meet with your full opproval, inadvertently sent you merchandise that wasn't up to the standard you have come to expect from us—then please give us a chance to make amends. You have our word that we will do everything humanly possible to prove that *you made no mistake* when you gave the Gates Rubber Company your business as in the past.

On the other hand, if there is some other reason why we have not heard from you, won't you please write us a letter and tell us about it? We want your business certainly, but if we cannot have it at present because of factors neither one of us can control, we still want your friendship. And with no word from you— neither orders nor letters—in the past six months, we have no way of knowing just exactly what has happened.

So please write to us—or better still, send us an order. Then we'll know everything is all right. We have missed you, and there is nothing that we would welcome more than the opportunity to take care of your automotive accessory requirements again.

We will be looking forward to hearing from you.

Cordially,

5. Letters That Offer Some Special Inducement

Appealing to reader's self-interest. So far, the letters we have been surveying have gone after inactive customers by recounting the friendly relationship of the past, and asking why it cannot be renewed. The reader has been told how much his orders were appreciated, even though the company may have neglected to say so sooner. "We miss you," most of the letters have said, "and if we were in any way at fault, we want to make things right."

You might say the major appeal in these letters has been to the reader's better self; to the tendency on the part of the average human being to forget a grudge when the other fellow meets him halfway; to that intangible urge to return to old places when he feels sure he is wanted. Few of the writers so far have offered any *special inducement* for the home-coming beyond general references to quality of products and services. Few of them have plainly and specifically asked for an immediate order. The writers tried instead to awaken the goodwill that once had existed toward the company; the assumption was that if that could be accomplished the orders would be forthcoming later.

The following letter uses different tactics. The reader is reminded that he hasn't bought for "quite a spell," and the story at the start implies that he has been missed. But he is not asked to tell *why* he stopped buying, and nothing is said about a possible mistake. Instead, the bulk of the message is devoted to three improvements in the product—all *beneficial to him* as a buyer. To prove these points, a sample of the new envelope is enclosed. The appeal is more to reason than emotion, because the idea is that the old customer will be interested in investigating a new product that solves some of his own problems.

> Dear Mr. Doe:
>
> Remember when you were a kid—when you were absent from Sunday School someone sent you a card telling you that you were missed? We are not accusing you of playing hookey but we have been doing a little checking up. Your name hasn't appeared on our order register for quite a spell. You have been away much too long.
>
> Since you last ordered from us we have made three important improvements in our envelopes that mean more sales and bigger profits to you.
>
> All the curl has been taken out of the flaps, which means up to 20% more production in your printing department.
>
> The gum is being applied to the flaps by means of a rubber roller. This means that there will be no dry lumps of gum to smash your type. No smashed type, more profit to you!
>
> The paper is watermarked. While this doesn't mean that the paper is better than it was, it does peg the grade as a definite standard. We find that our customers like it, therefore we believe this feature will help you sell more envelopes.
>
> You will find a sample of this cracker-jack envelope enclosed.
>
> You have our price list, so just write your order on the bottom of this letter if you like, slip it into the enclosed business reply envelope that requires no postage, and shipment will be made the same day your order is received.
>
> Sincerely yours,

This letter is signed by A. W. Peterson, Vice-President of the Berkowitz Envelope Company, Minneapolis. In similar fashion, H. N. Fisdale seeks to bring lost customers back to the Chocolate Products Company of Chicago,

Toronto, and London. Mr. Fisdale does not talk about missing the reader, or how much his business was appreciated in the past. On the contrary, his whole message is used to point out a benefit—the money to be made by buying a certain chocolate syrup. In effect, it is strictly a sales letter slanted at inactive buyers.

> Dear Mr. Doe:
>
> Spring is in the air! Birds singing, flowers sprouting, soft winds sighing, employees sleeping, and you—well, what are you doing? You should be getting ready for a bigger chocolate drink sales season.
>
> Are you?
>
> If you are, let's get started NOW.
>
> You haven't ordered any Stillicious Vitamin B Chocolate Syrup from us in a long time.
>
> Maybe you're figuring on waiting until the hot weather actually hits us before ordering.
>
> Don't wait.
>
> Like everything else in this world, if we want anything, we have to get out and work for it. The same with chocolate. Right now you should be paving the way for a big summer business on chocolate.
>
> Start putting it on your routes now; get your driver-salesmen enthused; let your customers know you are selling the best and richest chocolate drink on the market—STILLICIOUS.
>
> Use the enclosed envelope to send in your order. Overcome spring fever by acting at once. We'll be waiting.
>
> Very truly yours,

The above letter was mailed to 86 inactive buyers, and 24 replied with orders! Spring is also the motive of a Pfaelzer Brothers letter that takes a firm stand with the reader. He is told to order, or at least reply; otherwise his name will be removed from the mailing list. Of course, we wonder what the writer intends to do if the inactive buyer says, "take it off." It is not good sales psychology to pull an unloaded gun. However, the letter reads very well, and may have cleared the one hazard.

> Spring Cleaning
> Began Here At—
>
> Pfaelzer Brothers today, and among the many things that had our attention was our mailing list.
>
> When we found that your name was among the few that had not ordered for quite a long time, we were confronted with two

alternatives: one, to remove your name right away; the other, to drop you a line to find out just what the trouble seemed to be. And that explains this letter.

There must be a good reason for our not having heard from you —and surely, if it is important enough to keep you from sending us an order, it is worth our trying to find out what it is.

That is why we ask you to do us this favor. Look over the enclosed price list, use the postage-free blank to send us your order for 50 lbs. or more (beef, lamb, veal, corned beef, etc.)— or else use it to tell us to keep your name on our mailing list.

With the market as high as it is now, you will find our price lists even more interesting than before—because not only will they enable you to study the trend of the market, they will also help you to adjust your menu to meet current conditions. Our "Specials" which appear in every issue are timely and long on profit.

An order will be appreciated. Your reply will be most welcome. Either way, we'll know you are still interested. We'll be happy to hear from you again. Mail the blank TODAY.

Cordially yours,

A letter that had a remarkable pull. It is never possible to draw an exact line between active customers and inactive customers. *How long* must the company wait for an order before the customer can be called a lost sheep? The answer to this question depends partly, but not entirely, on the nature of the business. Certain products are sold more frequently, and must be ordered more frequently, than others. If Mrs. Flanigan has appeared almost every morning over a long period of time in Ryan's Grocery Store, and then does not appear for several weeks, the chances are she is buying her groceries at some other place. But the fact that Grocer Ryan has not bought wrapping paper for six weeks might mean nothing at all to the jobber that supplies him. He may have acquired a six-month's supply on his last order.

Nevertheless, it must be taken for granted that customers have been lost when they buy nothing for a period of three years. That would seem to be true of almost any kind of business. Furthermore, the longer an individual or company has gone without buying, the less can be expected of a letter that seeks to regain their business.

The following letter, written by N. Bjornson for the Cotan Corporation, went to customers who had not bought anything for three or more years, and yet 26.9 per cent replied. Because of this remarkable pull, the letter is worth your special study. *Why* did it do so well?

Gentlemen:

One of the ancient philosophers said that whenever he lost a friend he died a little.

We could not, I am sure, express our feelings at losing a business friend in a more appropriate manner. Nor need we try, for every man of seasoned business judgment knows that in the press of everyday duties, at times complicated by conditions beyond his control, things that should not happen sometimes do happen, and matters that should be taken care of are not always attended to.

In your case, was it something we did or was it perhaps something we did *not* do which caused you to drop out of sight as one of our business friends? Will you do me the favor of giving me your answer to that question?

I have a very definite and, in a sense, a personal reason for asking this favor.

In the first place, we have new management here, and frankly, we don't know all the facts about many former transactions. Secondly, we have now completed a thorough study of production costs and markets, and we believe we are fully equipped to meet all competition from a quality-service-price standpoint.

Besides that, we have fully improved facilities for research, much new equipment, several new lines, well scheduled service, and plenty of technical skill back of every job. And if I may add the personal angle, here it is: It is a part of my job to find out how we rate with former business friends, and what we can do to regain their confidence.

If you happen to be in the market right now, an order for even a roll or two of our materials would excite us, and so would a request for a quotation; but if that isn't in the cards, I shall just look forward to your answer to my question with sincere appreciation of your thoughtfulness.

There is no need to dictate a letter. Just jot down your reply in a word or two on the other side of this page. The enclosed envelope saves you further bother.

Very truly yours,

Well, what *did* make the letter pull? First, it starts with an interesting quotation that is peculiarly fitted to a letter to former customers. Second, it asks tolerance for any mistakes made in the past on the grounds that the reader himself probably has similar troubles in his own business. Third, it requests a reply as a favor to the writer—always a good appeal, for people like to feel they are able to do favors. Fourth, it renounces personal responsibility for past errors by referring to the new management. Fifth, it lists new facilities for serving the customer. Sixth, it asks for an order in a polite and casual way that is far remote from high-pressure. Seventh, it makes the reply easy. So you see, because of these seven points, the message has considerable persuasive power, and from start to finish is tactfully worded so as not to offend the reader.

Getting an answer for the boss. That the results attained by Mr. Bjornson were not accidental, or a "one-time" stroke of fortune, is proved by a similar pull attained by the following letter, which was prepared for the Dexter Folder Company, Pearl River, New York. This attempt to revive inactive business was mailed to 560 firms and produced 184 replies—a return of 32.8 per cent. The replies included several orders, and four prospects for new machines, as well as many assurances of future business.

To furnish a motive for the letter, a penciled note on scrap paper was attached—a copy of a memo which Mr. Bjornson had received from his superior officer.

The main argument in the body of the letter is the reminder that no company should be as well equipped to service a Dexter Folder as the one that made it. Again, we find the same technique in closing as in the first of Mr. Bjornson's letters—he simply asks that the reader scribble his answer on the back of the same sheet, and furnishes an addressed envelope to facilitate a reply.

Gentlemen:

Someone has said that excuses are but shabby patches with which people try to cover up their mistakes.

I should have known the answer to the question on this note— should have made it my business to find out *before* the Boss asked me—but I didn't. That was my mistake, and I had no valid excuse, nor did I try to invent one.

But now that the question is in my lap, I can think of no better way of getting the right answer than to rely on your generosity in helping me out.

Was it something we did or was it something we did *not* do which caused you to stop buying your machine parts from us? Or am I simply on the wrong track—am I assuming that you have bought parts elsewhere when in reality you may not have been in need of any?

Whatever the answer, I would warmly appreciate a brief reply. As you know, all Dexter parts are made to precision standards, and we feel that "the doctors" that brought your equipment into the world are better able than anyone else to supply the needed remedy in case of a strain or breakdown! We want your Dexter equipment to keep on making money for you as long as it is possible to keep it running fast and smoothly with the highest quality parts—the only kind we have to offer.

An order, no matter how large or small, would make us very happy—prove beyond any doubt that we're not in the "doghouse." But if that just isn't in the cards, I'm going to look hopefully for your reply telling me why we haven't enjoyed any parts business from you for several years, so that I can pass the answer to W. S. R.

No need to bother dictating a letter! Just jot your reply in a word or two at the bottom or on the other side of this sheet, and return it in the enclosed envelope.

Yours sincerely,

Trading gifts for replies. A very common device in letters to lost sheep is to offer a souvenir or gift as an inducement to those who will reply. The thing given away varies in value; the cost depends on what a customer is worth to the particular company. At least, it needs to be appreciated, or the effect is undesirable. Here are some letters of this type:

Used by Terry-Durin Company, Cedar Rapids

Dear Customer:

Here is the same fellow again, but wearing a new suit. About a year ago, we offered you a souvenir for an order. Several hundred of our good customers took us up and sent in orders.

Not a single one kicked about the souvenir, but a lot of fellows asked for, and received, another one.

Well, here I am again with a new gift. It's a peach of a little specialty that you can use at home or in your office. You'll like it, and it doesn't cost you a penny. Just an order for something you need...anything at all!

You're our friend and we'll give you service, and good value, as well as the souvenir. So mail the card within fifteen days... that's giving you time enough to really need something.

And thanks a lot for what you have already done for us.

Very truly yours,

Needless to say, the above letter went to regular customers as well as to those who had fallen by the wayside. The desire to get something for nothing has no limitations.

Used by Owatonna Tool Co., Owatonna, Minn.

Dear Mr. Doe:

You know, I just caught our file clerk throwing your old order card in the waste basket. Here's about the conversation which followed.

> "What are you doing that for?"
> "Oh, they haven't bought anything from us for three years, and probably never will again."

Maybe the first of what she said is true, but I certainly don't believe the last part. If you're still in business, there must be some reason why we haven't had more orders from you.

Would you like a copy of this year's OTC Hand Tool Catalog? I'll tell you what. If you'll write a short note about you and us on the back of this letter, and ask for a catalog, we'll send it to you pronto, and include a tool as a present.

Do it now, and send it back to us in the enclosed business reply envelope. O.K.?

Sincerely yours,

In that letter, D. H. Dyer told the inactive customer *what* he was going to get—a tool. But in the next one Jack Ruttenberg leaves the reader guessing. Only the psychologists could tell us which is the better procedure.

Used by Ruttenberg's, Reading, Pa.

Dear Mrs. Doe:

I have a very useful and attractive gift for you.

You don't have to purchase a penny's worth of merchandise in order to get it...we're not trying to get you in the store to sell you something. But we ARE trying to get you in just to have you say "hello" and tell us that you still think of Ruttenberg's as "your furniture store."

You see, we've MISSED you. My brother Lou and I have spoken of you several times since you were last in to see us and we certainly would hate to think that you were staying away because you were dissatisfied with either our merchandise or our service. And we're more than anxious to have you come in and have a friendly little chat with us.

Remember—you won't have to stay more than a minute; just as long as we see you again we'll feel satisfied. So call at the store on Thursday, Friday or Saturday of this week and ask either one of us for the little token of appreciation which we've put aside for you. If you can't get downtown during the day stop in on any of these three evenings. We'll both be here at the store working until around nine o'clock, and we'll gladly give it to you then.

It will seem good to see you again, so don't disappoint us... please.

Cordially yours,

The gift offered does not need to be something different from the usual item of sale. It can be an extra case free if a certain number of cases are ordered, a special discount for the one purchase only, or some other inducement equally attractive.

6. Showmanship in Letters to Lost Sheep

The problem of regaining attention. Dramatized letters are especially effective for rousing inactive customers, and especially so when they are mailed to long-dormant customers. In the latter case, the problem is not greatly different from writing a sales letter to a prospect who has never purchased—and we have seen in previous sections of this Handbook how showmanship, properly restrained and appropriate to the content, can win quick attention.

The principles, of course, in preparing a dramatized letter to inactive customers are no different than in preparing one for any other business purpose. No doubt you remember what they are.

1. The idea used must be really clever.
2. It should be fresh and original, as even a good idea grows stale when it has been used too often.
3. The point made should be the same as that in the body of the letter; otherwise the reader is likely to think you have tricked him into giving his attention.
4. The best ideas are those which do not involve a lot of expense or trouble. Remember the two strands of yarn in the rug letter.

With those simple but important principles in mind, we can now see how certain companies have used showmanship in letters to lost sheep; particularly, as to how well they meet the requirements. As nearly as possible, the examples that follow have been reproduced in their original form, although several of them were made more attractive by the use of two or more colors. However, this need not handicap your inspection, because you are interested in the *ideas* they contain, and how they might be adapted to your own correspondence.

The reply partly written for the customer. Boyd's of St. Louis are responsible for an unusual idea that contains considerable showmanship. To a letter saying the reader has been missed is attached a partly typed reply which he is supposed to complete and mail back to Boyd's.

WAUSAU MOTOR PARTS COMPANY

TELEPHONE 4494

WAUSAU, WISCONSIN

SAN FRANCISCO ... FT. LOUIS
LOS ANGELES ... CHICAGO
MINNEAPOLIS ... DALLAS
INDIANAPOLIS ... SEATTLE
KANSAS CITY ... NEW YORK

Holy Smokes, Miller Auto Supply !!

What a headache we got this morning ....

Then we went browsing through the ledger and found how many months it has been since you favored the WAUSAU MOTOR PARTS COMPANY with a bit of your patronage.

We haven't been "up to bat" when you have been "pitching" your piston ring purchases for a while of a long time. And golly, we'd like to know why we have been "benched".

Especially when those five "league leading" WAUSAU rings (Compression, Scraper, Savoil, Portoil, and Super-Portoil) are sure of a "hit" every time "up".

So here's asking "how come" you sent us to "the showers"?

It has been our pleasure to sell you rings in the past, and we can't tell you how much we'd appreciate it if you would tip us off as to why we have missed you these recent months.

WAUSAU rings are turning in unbroken "winning streaks" all over the country, and believe us, we'd certainly like to have them doing their stuff over your counter again, too.

How are chances for getting back up to bat? ...... SOON?

Cordially yours,

W.C.Landon
Inquiring for
THE WAUSAU MOTOR PARTS COMPANY

Your closest WAUSAU branch warehouse is checked in the heading above. A complete ring stock is maintained there at all times for jobbers' convenience in your territory.

[The Wausau Line]

WAUSAU COMPRESSION | WAUSAU SCRAPER COMPRESSION | WAUSAU SAVOIL—oil ring | WAUSAU PORTOIL—oil ring | WAUSAU SUPER PORTOIL—oil ring

Cartoon Follow-Up to Lost Sheep

AMERICAN TRADE EXCHANGE, INC.

MERCANTILE COLLECTIONS
A.T.E BUILDING · 1551 WEST LIBERTY AVENUE

PITTSBURGH, PA.

The Benton Stamp Company
43 Howard Avenue
Bridgeport, Connecticut

Gentlemen:

Died

November 20, 19

From Unknown

Causes

This is the epitaph we have on our records for your concern.

Seriously, we are interested in knowing why it is you stopped using our service, all of a sudden. If it was due to some fault of ours, you can appreciate it is to our advantage to know just what it is.

On the other hand, if you have just neglected sending us your delinquent accounts for no reason in particular, why not have your secretary fill in some "Free Direct Demands" now, when this letter is before you.

You are entitled to the best collection service available. Past performance proves that we offer it to you. Let us renew our relationship, today.

Yours very truly,

AMERICAN TRADE EXCHANGE, INC.
Edward J. Ott

In Mourning for the Departed

The Letter

Dear Mr. Doe:

On the attached sheet, we have taken the liberty of *starting* a letter written by you to us

Will.you finish it?

The reason for this unusual request is that we've missed you. And we'd like very much to know whether this is due to causes beyond our control—or to some situation which can be adjusted if we get together and talk it over.

There is another reason too. We are eager to show you some really exceptional values for all your Fall requirements. Skilled buying at the right time is bringing us a lot of new customers. But, it's old friends like yourself whom we are much more concerned about satisfying.

Won't you, therefore, tell us frankly why you haven't been in to see us lately by finishing the letter we started? A business reply envelope is enclosed for your reply.

Cordially,

The letter is signed by Louis Wellinghoff, Credit Manager—proving once again that in business there is no reason why the sales and credit departments cannot work together. In later sections of this Handbook you will find other examples of co-operation on the part of credit men—the answer to the myth that there is an unavoidable split in interests between credit men and salesmen.

And here is the attachment:

Reader's Reply

Dear Mr. Wellinghoff:

When a friend of mine—business, professional, or otherwise—passes me up, I always want to know why, just as you do in my case.

I believe as you do, that if a customer will give you his reasons frankly, it's often possible to adjust the situation with satisfaction to all concerned.

Therefore, I am willing to tell you why I have not used my charge account at Boyd's recently.

The reason is—

(Balance of the page left blank, for the customer to complete his reply.)

7. LETTERS THAT PULLED UNUSUALLY WELL

Orders amounting to $9760. Because of their importance to business,

United States Rubber Company

Rockefeller Center

1230 AVENUE OF THE AMERICAS
NEW YORK 20. N. Y.

TELEPHONE
CIRCLE 7-5000

November 8, 1962

Mr. Mark Olley
19 Ware Road
Upper Saddle River, New Jersey

Dear Mr. Olley:

I wish it were possible for me to step into your place and have a heart-to-heart talk with you. But as this is not possible, I am using this letter to keep up the contact between us.

The most unpleasant thing I have discovered in a long time is that we haven't had an order from you for more than sixty days.

There's a reason, of course. Won't you tell me what it is? If anything is wrong--whatever it is -- I'll fix it.

As you know, there isn't a more pleasant feeling than to know you have a pleased customer. A satisfied customer is the best asset any business can have. Errors cannot always be helped, but they can be corrected. That's what I am here for. If you're not satisfied with our service from every angle, then I'm not doing my job right.

Your account is always appreciated. We considered it so valuable that we will do whatever is necessary to keep it alive.

A stamped envelope is enclosed to make it easy for you to tell if anything is wrong -- and if you will send an order along at the same time, I'll personally see that you get special attention.

Yours sincerely,

(Signed) Allan R. Dodge
M A N A G E R

A R Dodge:MH

A "Heart-to-Heart" Letter

you have been promised tested examples of actual letters used to revive inactive customers. The contract is completed by those that follow—all bell-ringers of their type. The first was sent by Sales Promotion Manager H. J. Cocking of the Quaker City Rubber Company, Philadelphia, to only 300 inactive customers. The total cost of the mailing was about one hundred dollars—a trifling sum compared to sales amounting to $9760.

> Gentlemen:
>
> About the most interesting feature of my job is the writing of letters to good friends and customers like yourselves, from whom we haven't heard for some little time. Those who have fallen by the wayside, as it were! They bring forth so much sentiment and expression of goodwill.
>
> Besides, most of the replies I get are very interesting and encouraging. Many renew their acquaintance by sending me a nice order or by telling me when they will be in the market. So you see...it's worth the effort.
>
> Of course...once in a while...a great while...someone registers a "kick," but you know that's to be expected in a big family of 12,000 like ours. Anyway...we always manage to iron out satisfactorily any little difference that may exist. No half-way measures are tolerated. On that score my Company is adamant.
>
> Now...it's so long since you sent us an order that I am wondering if anything happened. If it did...which I hardly think is the case...then we'll make it right. Can't do more than that, can we?
>
> So, I'm going to bank on your giving me a break...just as I'd give you, were you in my position. Mind you...the enclosed prepaid envelope doesn't in any way obligate you, but I'd certainly appreciate a word from you. It will help me a lot. You'll do that much, I'm sure.
>
> And for your courtesy...one million thanks.
>
> > Sincerely,

The following letter, signed by E. C. Hopkins, Jr., went to 500 inactive customers of the Phillips Packing Company, Inc. It brought back 50 replies—not a spectacular return, but far above the average.

> Gentlemen:
>
> Ever had a customer suddenly stop buying? If so, what did you do? You asked him: "What, if anything, is the matter?"
>
> If his complaint was a just one and you had made a mistake, or had been wrong, you did your level best to make amends.

That is just the attitude in which I am writing you this morning We haven't had an order from you for some time and I would certainly appreciate it if you told me why not. If any department of this business has failed you I want to know it.

The fact that this business isn't perfect is surely not due to any lack of effort on our part, or because we aren't trying to make it so. Changing conditions have not as yet found us unprepared to take care of our trade. And, furthermore, never have we lost sight of our customers' interest.

I am looking forward to hearing from you with the keenest anticipation.

(No complimentary close)

One of the best. For a follow-up of lost business that makes no effort to do more than to contact the reader in a courteous way and ask why he has not been buying, you could hardly find a more effectively worded letter than one used by the Allen B. Wrisley Distributing Co., Chicago. The conclusion, especially, is business writing at its best.

Gentlemen:

Did you ever bump into an old friend on the street—one you hadn't seen for years? It's a real thrill, isn't it?

Something of that sort just happened to us. We were browsing through our old records when up popped your name. It was mighty nice to see it again—brought back old times— and incidentally started us to wondering why we had lost track of you.

Things have been going along pretty nicely with us—we've a lot of new products, and a lot of new customers—but somehow it's the old friends that we have made in our 75 years of business that really count. We don't want to lose them. And, if in some manner we have not served you properly, we'd certainly appreciate the opportunity to square ourselves.

The Wrisley Company is better equipped than ever to supply you with quality soaps and toiletries—we're extra proud of our Bath Crystals—and you'll be interested in the profit possibilities that every item in our "Complete Line" offers.

The envelope we're enclosing is to make it easy for you to turn this sheet over and write us—

> to have our representative call,
>
> to send you price lists,
>
> or, to say just what you think of us.

We hope it's good, but if it isn't—don't hold back; we can best correct our faults when we know exactly what they are.

Very truly yours,

And for sheer simplicity—courteous, friendly, to the point—here is another letter that rates a blue ribbon. It went out to look for customers lost by the Home Laundry Company, Inc., Washington, D. C.

> Dear Sir:
>
> There surely must be some reason why we have not received your bundle lately, and since it is important enough to cause you to stop using our service, it is certainly more important that I find out just what the reason is.
>
> It may be that the service you were getting was not exactly suited to your laundry needs. In this case, one of our other "Seven Superior Services" outlined in the enclosed pamphlet may appeal more strongly to you.
>
> At any rate, whatever the reason may be, won't you please tell me about it on the special form enclosed for your convenience, and send it back to me in the self-addressed, stamped envelope, also enclosed?
>
> Thank you, very much.
>
> Sincerely yours,

From the letters you have read in this section, perhaps you have gained a better idea of how wayward customers may be brought back to buy again. The cost of the effort is so small compared to the sales that may be gained. It is not nearly so difficult to revive an old customer as to get a brand new one. Most of those who stopped buying from your company had no special reason, except, perhaps, because nobody seemed to appreciate their patronage.

No company can afford to omit letters to lost sheep from their sales program. Doing so is a foolish waste of a sales opportunity and that means waste of profit. Contact at least twice a year the old customer-friends who have stopped buying. Tell them you want them back. You may be surprised at the number who accept your invitation.

LETTERS TO WIN GOODWILL

LETTERS TO
WIN GOODWILL

1. The Importance of Goodwill Letters

The company's biggest asset. It is doubtful if any business executive in his right mind would discount the importance of goodwill to sales. You can think of no company that could get along without goodwill unless it depends on a one-time sale, irrespective of quality or service, and has no thought of getting repeat business. But even such a company ceases to exist as soon as a sufficient number of disillusioned buyers can make themselves heard. There is no substitute for goodwill in business, and the company that fails to recognize its necessity is surely headed for failure.

> The most precious thing any man can have is the goodwill of
> others.
> It is something as fragile as an orchid—and as beautiful;
> As precious as gold nugget—and as hard to find;
> As powerful as a great turbine—and as hard to build;
> As wonderful as youth—and as hard to keep.
> —*Author unknown.*

In the broadest sense, everything that happens in business should be planned and carried out in a way to win and keep the favor of customers, prospects, and the general public. Wide awake executives know this to be a fact, and much of their thinking is directed to the promotion of what is rather loosely called "friendly public relations," and to the creation of a "favorable public image." Unfortunately, however, in many cases the effort made to gain goodwill is of the hit-and-miss variety, and many opportunities are either ignored or overlooked. Particularly is this true of the letters that *could* be written but never are. Because the writing of them is apart from

621

the actual operation of the business, they are not included in the planned sales program, and are pushed aside as something good enough if time permits, but not strictly necessary.

It is conceded that the "necessary" things in the operation of a business must claim first attention. Goods must be manufactured, sold, and shipped. Advertising must be planned and prepared. Credit terms must be established, and money must be collected. People must be hired, trained, supervised, and motivated. To these few examples, you can add many more—the things that must be done regularly, and under strict control, day in and day out.

Obviously, too, the *manner* in which these things are handled helps or hurts in the winning of goodwill. Prompt and efficient service, products of uniformly satisfactory quality, routine contacts conducted courteously in person or by mail—they all contribute to friendly customer and public relations. In this Handbook you have already seen how these routine matters, when handled in letters, can be made pleasing and helpful to the general sales program. You know that *every* letter written for business should do everything possible to win or to hold goodwill. Making the contact a pleasant experience for the reader is one of the primary obligations of the letter-writer, no matter what the news in the letter may happen to be. Under no circumstances, under no provocation, may a good business-letter writer be anything else than a friendly human being trying to do the best he can to serve his reader. Every business message can reflect company goodwill, even if it denies a customer request, or talks about the lawyers who are going to sue for an unpaid bill.

The difference, then, between all company letters and those you will see in this section is not so much in spirit as in purpose. The regular letters accomplish a double job—they sell, they collect, they adjust, *and* they win goodwill. But the winning of goodwill is the *only* job performed by the letters in this section. They can be ignored, and the routines of the business will continue. Maybe they are "unnecessary" but it is a mistake not to use them.

Goodwill letters receive special attention. The regular buyer is accustomed to getting certain types of letters from the supplying company—about his orders, his payments, and other routine matters. Even though they are friendly and help to keep the buyer satisfied, they are still more or less taken for granted. But when special letters, written for no other purpose than to carry goodwill, are received, they are certain to gain special attention. For example, a customer is complimented about his election to some civic office, he gets a letter of appreciation on the anniversary of his first purchase, or a letter of sympathy because some member of his family is in the hospital. None of these goodwill contacts would be expected; in a strict business sense none of them are necessary. But the mere fact that any one of them came in the mail one day would surely win special favor for the writer and his company.

The expression of goodwill does not need to be lengthy; it may or may not contain something more tangible than words—the effect is still a pleasant surprise to the reader. For illustration, here is a short note sent by the William E. Lyons Realty and Mortgage Company, Kansas City, to new tenants. With the note went a box of stationery, imprinted with the tenant's name and the address of the property into which he and his family have just moved.

> Dear Mr. and Mrs. Doe:
>
> Our sincere wish is that you find your new home as comfortable as you hoped it would be.
>
> This writing paper is with our compliments, and we trust it will help establish your new address with all of your many friends.
>
> > Sincerely,

Among those who think that landlords are hard to get along with, the receipt of such a goodwill gesture would be sure to soften their opinion toward at least this one firm. Furthermore, the favor created would help to smooth future landlord-tenant relations. Thus, the "unnecessary" letter and gift render a service to management that could well be worth many times its cost.

If the importance of the box of stationery in the idea just described seems greater than that of the message, consider next a letter mailed to customers by the Republic Engraving & Designing Co., Chicago. Here the message stands alone quite successfully.

> Gentlemen:
>
> One of the greatest assets of life, as I see it, is its true friendships. A friend is a valued possession.
>
> What is true of our personal lives is also true of our business lives. We like to have our customers feel that there is a warmth of friendship underlying each business transaction and that friendship in business is something more than just receiving your order.
>
> I have given this quite a bit of thought recently, and feel that those who respect their obligations promptly and abide by fair business ethics should have a word of praise now and then, and here it is—
>
> "Thank you good folks for allowing us to serve you, and for your loyal support in using our Readco Republic Rubber Printing

Plates, and most of all for your friendship and the pleasant business relations which we enjoy with you."

> Cordially yours,

From the point of view of necessary business operation, the writing of
the above letter was a pure waste of time; from the point of view of giving
a good customer a pleasant little surprise, it may have been the most productive letter mailed that day by the Republic Engraving and Designing Co.

The same may be said of the Ismert-Hincke Company's letter on
page 625. It appealingly combines picturesque prose with the gratitude of
"all the folks at I-H."

Something the reader may find useful. Speaking of the good that can
be accomplished by letters with no business purpose other than to carry a
little goodwill, R. W. Baxandall, Director of the Dean W. Geer Company,
once said: "For building goodwill and overcoming sales resistance, one of
the best ideas we ever have used is to send the customer or prospect some
idea or information he can use in his own business, saying that we are
sending it with our compliments, and hope that he will find it useful. Such
thoughtfulness, With No Strings Attached, is appreciated by the recipient.
It shows that the writer knows his problems, and is interested in helping
him."

After the above introduction, Mr. Baxandall illustrated his thought
with a number of pertinent examples.

> A bank sends business firms a reprint of a timely speech on cur-
> rent problems.
>
> A college sends to high school principals a "school calendar" with
> spaces for filling in the social and athletic activities for each day
> of the school year.
>
> A printer sends to business clients a football schedule for colleges
> in his state.
>
> A jeweler sends an inexpensive "Memory Book" to high school
> graduates.
>
> A department store sends a "Baby Book" to parents of newborn
> babies.
>
> A manufacturer sends his customers a mimeographed list of gov-
> ernment publications which may be helpful to them.
>
> A popcorn company in Iowa sends its customers ideas on how
> others are getting business—the best locations, etc.
>
> A company sends to customers and prospects copies of current
> legislation which might affect them.

The key words in Mr. Baxandall's comments are "With no strings

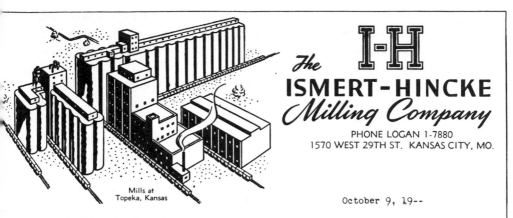

THE
I·H
ISMERT-HINCKE
Milling Company

PHONE LOGAN 1-7880
1570 WEST 29TH ST. KANSAS CITY, MO.

Mills at
Topeka, Kansas

October 9, 19--

Good Morning Friend:

On his trip around the world Mark Twain was entertained by Royalty
and the great of the time.

He was shown collections of glittering Jewels. He saw paintings
and sculpture done by famous talented artists. Everywhere he went
he was wined and dined. He was entertained by the leading singers
and dancers of the day. He saw the famous beauty spots of Europe,
Africa and Asia.

Upon his return someone asked which he considered the most beautiful
of all. Instantly he said "Missouri in October". That was nearly
one hundred years ago. 'Tis true today. Missouri is truly lovely
in October. It is really gorgeous.

This October the hills and valleys of Missouri are glorious with
their color. Nature, the Master Painter, is unfurling the ever
wonderful panarama. Painting a picture that no artist can duplicate. The vivid scarlet of the sumac. The gold of the oak and the
aspen. The deep green of the live oak. Shading from pastels to
the lively purple. Blended into an awe inspiring ever changing
picture.

We of Missouri are proud of our glorious scenery. It is our
heritage. Yet we often travel to distant places overlooking our
own beauties. As the Turk, of old. In his youth he dreamed of
diamonds. He found none and returned to the farm of his birth.
There he found diamonds - acres of diamonds.

Here at I.H. our customers and our friends are our diamond farm.
We value them more highly than diamonds. Throughout the years I.H.
has stood for integrity and High Quality - in flour, in service, in
value. This is our heritage and our constant aim.

We are always happy to serve you - that's for sure. This is why
we write you so often. We want you to know.

Yours Sincerely,

L.M. Lundgaard - writing for all
the folks at I-H

attached." Goodwill letters are not dictated to ask for orders. The best ones ask nothing at all except the privilege of a friendly contact with the reader; the chance, perhaps, to do him a little favor—something apart from the daily grind of business.

Goodwill works two ways. When the right relationship exists between public and company, goodwill flows back and forth on a two-way circuit. Although we are primarily interested in how a company may do its share of the job, the following letter, written by a customer of the Southwestern Bell Telephone Company, Kansas City, is the type that any company may expect to receive now and then if its own program for winning goodwill is in order. In business, as elsewhere, a company usually gets what it gives.

> Gentlemen:
>
> The joyousness which I feel this morning is boundless. I would be ungrateful, indeed, if I did not make some expression of thanks to your company—meaning more specifically the personnel from executive to operator; from cableman to local technician—for the part they played in producing this state of mind.
>
> Perhaps you have guessed. My son, whose voice I have not heard since he left the United States two years ago on a voluntary overseas assignment, called me and talked to me just a little while ago from London, England.
>
> I do not know what the charges for such a call are. What it meant to me cannot be expressed in monetary values.
>
> I am grateful for American industry and the American way of life—the "can-do" that surmounts all obstacles and makes possible the luxuries we enjoy, and such things as spanning half a world so that a son and mother may say "hello" to each other.
>
> I know an infinite number of people contributed to making this call possible. To each one of them I want to say with the warmth of personal friendship—
>
> "Thanks for a job well done."
>
> Sincerely yours,

There can be no problem in customer relations when the people served feel toward a company as did the mother who wrote the above letter. Moreover, the organization that receives few or no letters of appreciation from customers can well afford to examine its own efforts to build goodwill; it is almost certain that lack of friendliness on the one side of the business relationship indicates a similar lack on the other side. On the other hand, cordial contacts with customers—beyond the mere necessities of taking orders, shipping them, or collecting money—will build a reserve of respect and loyalty that tends to increase sales, reduce customer turnover, and eliminate misunderstanding. The letters you are going to examine in this section required no great outlay of time or money—just a little appreciation of the human equation in business, and the thoughtful application of the law which says that others will give to us what we give to them.

Types of goodwill letters. It would be an endless task to try to list all the kinds of letters that can be used in business to win and hold goodwill. Although the examples that follow do not begin to cover them all, they do reveal letter writers of friendly spirit at work; they show how easy it is to express the little courtesies of life in business as well as in social relationships. The executive who might question the value of these goodwill contacts would simply expose his own failure to keep in step with the modern tempo of business, which is no longer cold and impersonal.

The modern letter-writer goes out of his way to share (within reason) the experiences of those who favor his company with their orders. He seizes every opportunity to win the friendship of customers, along with their patronage. He lets them know that their buying is appreciated. He writes letters of congratulation when good things fall their way; he writes letters of sympathy when they suffer a business or personal loss. He remembers them on special occasions such as Christmas and birthdays, not with old platitudes, but with sincere expressions of goodwill. He treats them as members of the company family; explains new policies so that they will be understood; invites suggestions and criticisms. It all sums up to a concept of mutual dependence on each other—of the recognition that in every transaction *human beings* are involved. This is the modern trend of business—and it is good. Customers are not mere names on file in the order department. They are *people* whose friendship can be won for a company as easily as for an individual. Without that friendship, they are merely buyers—here today and gone tomorrow—with no ties to keep them in the fold.

Goodwill letters may be "unnecessary" in the narrow sense of routine business operations, but when viewed in the true perspective of helping to build faith and loyalty, they become of great importance to sales.

2. Letters to Show Appreciation

Unto Caesar what is Caesar's due. In this Handbook, you have seen many letters that let the reader know his support is appreciated. This recognition of what the customer means to the company seems to be a logical business procedure, although it has been too often overlooked until he has gone elsewhere to shop. As we discovered in Section 9, locking the stable after the horse is stolen is costly; it's much easier to hold than to regain a customer's goodwill.

The hardest customer to keep is the one you sell or service infrequently, or so efficiently that he is not apt to appreciate what you do for him. For example, if you are a fuel company and arrange with a customer to deliver oil or coal to his home, he may take good service for granted after a time. Your delivery truck probably arrives without having to be called, and there may be only a very few deliveries made during the entire heating season. When the next heating season comes around, another fuel company might not find it difficult to get the customer to switch—unless you have made an effort to keep his goodwill.

A good letter can be just the thing in this situation. For example, the Philadelphia and Reading Coal and Iron Company prepared the following three letters for their dealers to use in maintaining customers' goodwill. They were made available to each dealer, imprinted with his name, at cost.

(1)

Dear Mr. Doe:

In a few weeks memories of bitterly cold days, howling snow storms, and all the other untoward things brought us by this coldest of many a winter will melt before gentle spring breezes and a friendly, ascending sun.

But before this happens, we want you to know that we are happy to have been able to serve you with the finest fuel we know of—always-dependable Famous Reading Anthracite.

It is just such a winter as the one we've passed through which brings to mind the great importance of having fuel that delivers ample comfort and protection under all conditions. It makes us happy to be associated with a business which means so much to the families of our community.

So thank you heartily for permitting us to be of service. May the pleasant months to come prove to be a period of productive work and happy recreation for you.

Yours very truly,

(2)

Dear Mr. Doe:

Many a day we write letters asking for this and that, but this note asks nothing but that you accept our sincere thanks for the privilege of serving you.

It has been an unusually trying winter. There were times when we found it difficult to make deliveries. There were days when there were unavoidable delays. If you experienced any delays, we hope you'll not think of us too harshly. We did the best we could under the circumstances.

On the other hand, we are happy that we were able to supply you with the best fuel we know—comfort-packed Famous Reading Anthracite that can always be depended on to release an abundance of warmth whenever needed.

We hope this spring and summer will be pleasant seasons of work and relaxation for you and your family.

Cordially yours,

(3)

Dear Mr. Doe:

All the ghosts of the old-fashioned winters grandfather told us about came back to haunt us in this most modern of all years.

It was not pleasant for anyone, but we are happy that we were equipped to provide you with the one thing that kept them out of our homes—good fuel.

We were not always on the ball, but we tried hard, and so far as I know, no one of our customers actually suffered from lack of coal.

We are grateful for having been able to give adequate service, and we thank you warmly for the privilege of supplying you with Famous Reading Anthracite—the ever-dependable, heat-rich hard coal.

Now that we can once more smile a bit about winter's vicious onslaught, and look to pleasant months ahead, we ask you to accept our wishes for a happy spring and summer season of work and play.

Sincerely yours,

You noted, no doubt, that in none of these three letters did the writer ask for future business. Instead, he was content to thank the customer for the privilege of serving him—and on the goodwill thus created, he was willing to stake his chances of getting the next year's order. Had the writer, N. Bjornson, *asked* for the future business, the message in any of the three cases would have been just another sales letter, and much of the effectiveness would have been lost.

Appreciation with no strings attached. Telling a customer how much he is appreciated, and then putting the bite on him for more business, is not the best way to impress him with your sincerity. It is too much like using one hand to pat him on the back, and the other to reach for a favor, all the time saying to yourself, "If I say something nice to this fellow, maybe he will come across with another order." The customer recognizes the real purpose of the gesture, and it may do more harm than good.

In the following appreciation letters, no ulterior purpose is revealed. While they may ask for the goodwill of the reader, no strings are attached to the request. Sincerely, and without exaggeration or sweet wind, they thank the customer for his business favors and hope they may continue to merit his friendship. Naturally, any individual or group reacts favorably to a message which comes out of a clear sky—with no particular motive or necessity except the desire to say "Thanks."

Used by an Insurance Salesman

Dear Mr. Doe:

In the month of March, in the year 19—...

A young man set out in the earnest quest of earning a living. In the type of business which appealed most to him, he cast his lot.

It took but a very short time for this young man to learn that earning a living in terms of dollars and cents was not the primary requisite of employment.

He found in rubbing shoulders with a world of realities, that other things mattered far more—unselfishness, consideration of others, conscientious service, and above all, honesty.

He learned, too, that his most valuable asset was not his bank account, nor his worldly goods, nor things material, but rather his loyal friends.

Having personally played the role of this young man, I have learned these things, and learned them well.

I therefore want to express to you my sincere thanks for your loyal friendship and your genuine cooperation in these past years. They have made it possible for me to pass the milestones—one by one—and have contributed largely toward making my tenth anniversary in the insurance business possible.

Very sincerely yours,

Used by Killark Electric Manufacturing Company, St. Louis

Dear Mr. Doe:

BEFORE—a man marries—

He'll send the girl flowers and take her in a taxi to the theatre. AFTER—the only "flour" she gets is Gold Medal. And she has to lug it home from the shopping center in a twenty-four pound sack.

Business is a lot like that.

Firms spend much to make a man a customer. And then the best he gets is an invoice.

We believe a concern should tell a customer that his trade is appreciated—and tell him often. That's why we're writing this letter.

Not to sell you—but to tell you—it's always a real pleasure to serve you.

Cordially yours,

Used by Famous-Barr Co., St. Louis

Dear Mrs. Doe:

It is in a civic-minded mood, rather than a boastful one, that we point to our store's attainment in becoming "First in St. Louis ...Fifth in America."

We offer you our thanks and grateful appreciation for the role you have played in enabling us to reach this high place in the department store world. Your loyalty and confidence in our merchandise and service have contributed greatly to our success.

It has been a real pleasure to serve you, and we shall strive constantly to merit your friendship and patronage.

Please feel free to call on any executive of this store whenever he can be of assistance, for any of us will welcome an opportunity to further express our gratitude in terms of helpful service.

Very sincerely yours,

Used by the Palmer House, Chicago

Dear Mr. Doe:

This is the kind of letter that I am most happy to write, because I am taking this means of thanking you for your constant choice of the Palmer House as your home in Chicago.

Your name ranks high among those of our loyal and distinguished "repeat" clientele who, year after year, give us definite proof that we are setting the pace of hotel leadership in Chicago. It is to friends like you that we owe the success of the Palmer House.

And so I wish to express my sincere appreciation of your patronage, and to assure you that we shall continue to do everything within our power to maintain our present standards of service, cuisine, and furnishings.

Thank you again.

Very sincerely yours,

A little gift for good measure. The use of gifts with appreciation letters is more common at Christmas than at other times of the year, but the Miles Kimball Company of Oshkosh, Wisconsin, did NOT wait for any special occasion to present a goodwill token. In fact, as the letter tells us, the offering was made in the month of May.

> Great morning, Mr. Doe:
>
> There's something about a May day like this one up here in Wisconsin that gets into the blood of even an overweight letter-writer like myself.
>
> I got to thinking on the way to the office, ten minutes ago, how I spend most of my time trying to GET business, and precious little of it saying "thank you" to good folks like you who keep the wolf at our doorstep from having cubs.
>
> So this letter isn't to sell you a darned thing. It's just to tell you I appreciate your account, and that I'm sending you a little book I've enjoyed and think you may like.
>
> It's a sort of calendar—a timetable showing when and where to look for the various birds, flowers, and other actors in the pageant of nature. It isn't generally known by the cutthroats with whom he plays poker, but once in a while our Mr. Kimball likes to take himself a lone hike. This guidebook has made such occasions more interesting to him.
>
> It's coming in a separate wrapper. I'm hoping you will find it a little useful.
>
> > Cordially yours,

In the following letter, the first "birthday" of the thing purchased furnishes the motive for the goodwill gesture. To make the appreciation more tangible, a gift in the form of free service is offered.

> > Happy Birthday to you!
> > Happy Birthday to you!
>
> Well, maybe it isn't your birthday, Mr. Doe...but have you forgotten?...It's your car's birthday!
>
> Yes, just one year ago we delivered that smart, sparkling new automobile to you. We hope it's given you a full year of driving enjoyment and comfort...and that it will continue to.
>
> It seems fitting that today—on your car's first birthday—we should say "Thank you" once again for buying it from us. And because we are still just as much interested in your car's performance as we were the day you bought it—we have a birthday surprise for you.
>
> Drive in within thirty days, and we'll give your car a thorough factory-specified 20-point lubrication...FREE!

It won't cost you a cent. Just bring this letter along. We'll be looking forward to seeing you roll into our driveway soon.

Cordially yours,

The token sent with a goodwill letter does not need to be expensive, but it should serve some useful purpose. At one time or another, most men are bothered by the breaking of a shoe-lace, with no spare handy for replacement. Clarke's, of Tulsa, Oklahoma, use this annoyance as the basis for an appreciation message. Although at the end of the letter a play for another sale is made, it is not done in a way to offend the customer, or to detract from the cordiality of the contact. This letter is also very short, proving that appreciation can be aptly expressed without a book full of words.

Dear Mr. Doe:

Some morning soon, when you are dressing at a mile-a-minute rate, a shoelace might s-n-a-p. So we're sending you a new pair with our compliments.

We sincerely appreciate your patronage and want your purchases to be 100 per cent satisfactory—even to the laces.

It was a pleasure to sell you the shoes you're wearing now, and we hope for an "encore" when you need another pair.

Cordially yours,

Goodwill to the departing customer. Granted that those of cynical mind may question the motive behind a goodwill letter to customers— attributing to it the thought of future sales—the charge could not be made against a friendly expression of goodwill to the customer who has just been *lost*. Such a message is the one sent to those who have just sold their stock in the General Foods Corporation:

Dear Mr. Doe:

In a family of many thousands of stockholders, some new names appear and some drop out each week.

I have learned recently that your General Foods account has been closed. Possibly this may be due to a change in name or address, or to transfer of your stock to the name of some broker or other individual.

It is also possible that you have relinquished your General Foods stock. In this event, we sincerely hope to retain your friendship for General Foods, despite our regret in the loss of one of our family of stockholders.

Your frank comments would be sincerely appreciated if there has been any dissatisfaction with any of our products or policies.

If you would like, during the next year, to have us keep you on our mailing list for descriptive material about General Foods, such as we include in mailings of our dividend checks, please let us know.

Sincerely,

So much for these goodwill contacts of a general nature. When used with sincerity, and not as a "plug" for more orders, they can be a powerful help to any company. The best of the lot are those which are written for no special reason, except to let the customer know his business is appreciated. The cost of an occasional "Thank You" is small; the return may be abundantly large.

3. Appreciation Letters for the Holiday Season

A difficult letter job. Contrary to popular opinion, it is not easy to dash off a letter of appreciation for the New Year or Christmas. One difficulty is in making the message different from the many others the reader is likely to receive; another is conveying a sincere thought without having it take on the form of sentimentality. There is probably more pencil-chewing by businessmen at Christmas time than at any other period of the year. Many writers would like to get away from the expression, "A Merry Christmas and a Happy New Year," but nobody seems to come up with anything adequate to take its place. In view of these obstacles, perhaps the following suggestions may be helpful:

1. Don't try to be clever or spectacular in the preparation of a Christmas letter to customers and others.

2. Wait for a quiet moment when you can relax and write the message without interruption or pressure.

3. Think of something you would like to read if you were getting the letter instead of writing it. Then say that something in the simplest possible language.

4. Remember you can be a little more personal in a Christmas letter than in almost any other kind. People *expect* sentiment in a Christmas letter; they are in the mood to accept it at face value.

5. There is no limitation in length for a Christmas letter, but *as a rule,* the shorter ones seem best. At least, avoid too many adjectives, and try hard not to repeat.

6. Don't ask anyone else to write a Christmas letter for you. The sentiment you wish to express is *yours*—it suffers a loss of effectiveness when offered second-hand.

A "must" in the letter program. No matter how difficult the job may seem, there is no satisfactory reason for omitting a Christmas message to customers and friends of the company. It is a fallacy to argue that your mailing will not be missed among the great number of cards and letters the average person or organization receives. Neither is it fair to assume that it doesn't matter *what* you mail if you just mail something, since all Christmas messages are like peas in the pod, and few people read them anyway.

The right attitude, we think, is that the holiday season is one time during the year when the spirit of goodwill seems most in evidence, the time when people are in the mood to overlook past grievances, the time when they give and expect to receive appreciation. Thus, the Christmas message to customers is not just a formality to be gotten rid of as quickly as possible; it is a real opportunity to offer a friendly hand, to make up for former indifference, and to let the customer know that the company is sincerely grateful for his patronage.

If all the above is true, then surely there is no letter written for business that deserves a more serious effort in preparation. However, it is not a job that can be done by any set of rules or any formula. A good Christmas letter comes from the heart, and beyond the few simple suggestions already offered, no person can tell another *how* it should be written.

A few good Christmas letters. Instead, for your inspection and study— so that here and there you may find an adaptable idea or thought—some holiday messages have been culled from many times their number for this Handbook. They represent a fair cross section of the *best* letters of their type as used in American business during the past several years. Of course, there are many other letters that might deserve an equal rating, but here at least you have a dependable sample. You will find all of the letters sincere in tone—couched in simple language. They express appreciation in a way that would be accepted as real and genuine. They serve the purpose for which they are intended. They are *goodwill builders.*

Explaining the Origin of Christmas

Merry Christmas, folks!

Guess what! This gift-giving all started with a Saint named Nicholas throwing a purse of gold through a window each night for three successive night.

It happened that Saint Nicholas knew a poor nobleman in Lycia, Asia Minor. The fellow had three lovely daughters and he worried about their future, so Nick threw a purse of gold through their window, and returned the two following nights to do it again.

Well, you can imagine how happy that made them. And the news got 'round and folks all over Europe decided to make each other happy by giving gifts on a night called Saint Nicholas' Eve. For economy's sake they cut it down to one night, and dropped the gold purse idea—they just filled shoes and stockings with candy, cookies, and handmade toys and trinkets.

And that's how we got hold of the swell idea of giving Popeye dolls, scooters, trains, toasters, fur coats, and neckties during the grandest season of the year.

All I wish is that I could be the original Saint Nicholas this year —that I could be everyplace at one time. Then I'd be sure to visit *your* home, and I'd bring along that gold purse, too.

Anyway, I hope Santa brings you and yours all you want for Christmas, plus a New Year filled with all of the things that make life worth living.

Sincerely yours,

(Atlas Mineral Products Co.)

Giving Full Credit to the Customer

Dear Mr. Doe:

Christmas means more to us than holly cards and pretty sentiments neatly embossed. When, on Christmas morning, we find candy and candles on our cedar tree, we realize that there would not even be a cedar tree but for the goodwill and patronage of you and other good customers.

And we are grateful.

Just counting our own blessings leads us to wish you the most prosperous New Year you ever have known, and a Christmas as merry as ours.

In sincere appreciation,

(Ketterlinus Lithograph Manufacturing Company)

Just a Sincere "Merry Christmas"

Gentlemen:

MERRY CHRISTMAS—What other phrase can start the heart strings singing more quickly or more gladly than those two words? In them are wrapped all the best human emotions of the ages.

It's useless to try to improve on them for they form the perfect thought.

And so, as another year draws to a close, I want to say thank you for your part in making it a pleasant one, and again let me say right out of my heart—MERRY CHRISTMAS to you and yours!

Sincerely,

(The Washburn Company)

Distinguished by Its Simplicity

Gentlemen:

"Christmas" means a lot of things, but to our Organization this season centers chiefly around two of the finest things in life... home and friends.

Looking back over the years and thinking of Christmas Days gone by makes us realize just how empty life would be without the proper home life and good, true friends.

So at this season of the year we are thinking of you and your associates whose friendship has helped us along the way. We hope this will be a truly Merry Christmas for you and everyone at your house, and that the New Year will bless your home with all of the good things in life.

Sincerely yours,

(Dick Brothers, Inc.)

"Merry Christmas" in Rhyme

Greetings:

Once a year we drop things material—turn to matters even ethereal—wishes to all here and there—Xmas spirit fills the air—New Year's coming—just around the bend—may good luck—happiness—be yours—no end.

Cordially,

(Pacific Desk Company)

Mailed with a Calendar

Just in case—

you've lost the last lonely leaf on your calendar, we're sending you a new one to convince you that Christmas is about here and New Year will be right along too.

There was a time when all a man needed to know it was Christmas was for someone to give him a couple of loud neckties.

If a little girl was good, she got a box of handkerchiefs. Nowadays, if she's not so good she may get a real fur coat.

Yes sir, times have changed, and there's nothing much we can do about it.

Maybe we're just silly softies, as you might say, but we're still old-fashioned enough to believe there's some sentiment left in business, after all.

So not a single sentence about STENCILS. Just a single, sincere statement like this. . . .

May your Christmas be your Merriest and the New Year your most Prosperous.

Cheerfully yours,

(Marsh Stencil Machine Co.)

Showmanship in the Christmas message. Because so many holiday messages are likely to be received by the same individual or company, and because the things to be said are limited, any idea to attract special attention—if appropriate and in good taste—may give the Christmas letter an advantage over others of regular form. On the other hand, sentiment and showmanship are not easy to blend, and anyone using a dramatized mailing should be sure it is in keeping with the spirit of the season. Another factor, of course, in determining the fitness of the idea is the character of the group who will receive it; some firms are more conservative and critical in their reactions than others.

Advertising men, for example, would probably react favorably to a message which appeared in one of the business magazines a few years ago. It went like this. Be sure to read it aloud:

VROLIJKE KERSTMIS	BOAS FESTAS
SARBATORI FELICITE	FELICE NATALE
JOYEUX NOEL	CHRYSTOVJNA
FROELICHE WEIHNACHTEN	WESOLYCH SWIAT
TIN HAO NIAN	GLAEDELIG JUL
KINGA SHINNEN	FELICE PASCUAS
ICHOK YILARA	VESELE VANOCHE
GLAD JULEN	SRETAN BOZIC

BOLDOG KARACSONYI UNNEPEKET

All of which is by way of saying Merry Christmas, and (to which we add) a most excellent New Year.

Another Christmas message which gets out of the groove is adapted from an idea once used by the Florsheim Shoe Company. On the outside of a small folder is the drawing of a jewel box, and attached to the center of it is an imitation diamond. The caption says: "WE DO NOT ASK FOR DIAMONDS." Then on the inside of the folder appears the following message:

> As we pause in sober contemplation of the millions of people in other lands who cannot have happiness this Christmas, we are humbly grateful for the privilege of living in a country where spiritual values have not been subordinated to material things.
>
> So, in our letter to Santa Claus we do not ask for diamonds or other worldly possessions. Instead, we want only your goodwill —to so serve you that you will continue to think well of us, as surely we do of you.
>
> That you and yours will find happiness on Christmas day—that you will have good fortune during the coming year—is the sincere wish of myself and of all my associates.

Also impressive is a Christmas folder once mailed by "The Justin Boys," bootmakers of Fort Worth, Texas. On the outside, Santa Claus has just hand-lettered the recipient's name at the top of his list. The inside of the folder shows a picture of the plant, and Santa Claus holding a card on which is the message.

On the following pages, you will find additional dramatized Christmas messages. Most of the originals were in two or more colors, but at least you can gain a fair impression of the respective ideas, and how they might be adapted to your own use. The Rylander letter talks only about the New Year, but the two holidays have come to be more or less synonymous with respect to customer appreciation.

Showmanship in Christmas and New Year's messages is okay if you happen to like it; some will always prefer the more conventional and dignified greetings.

Letters for other holidays. Messages of appreciation need not be confined to Christmas and New Year's, although they are days which may come first in the company goodwill letter program. Certainly, a company is rather stingy that remembers to thank its customers only once a year. A letter mailed in connection with some other national event or day may carry the advantage of having less competition, too. Not uncommon in American business are goodwill gestures to tie in with Thanksgiving, the Fourth of July, Mother's Day, Father's Day, Easter, the birthdays of Washington and Lincoln, and other times held high in public esteem.

For certain types of business, the above days are particularly significant, and letters may be used either to gain goodwill or as sales helps. A florist

THE *Rylander* COMPANY · DIRECT MAIL ADVERTISING

216 WEST JACKSON BOULEVARD · CHICAGO 6, ILLINOIS · RANDOLPH 6-4760

December 31, 19

Dear "Customer" --

This letter is one of the very last to be mailed by our firm in 19 !

We hope it will be one of the first that you open in 19   so we can be among the first to wish you a Happy New Year.

Please accept our sincere thanks for our pleasant association together during the past year. Your orders have been most welcome and your many acts of cooperation are appreciated. We will strive hard to merit your patronage and good will for many years to come.

Sincerely yours,
THE RYLANDER COMPANY

Roy J. Rylander
S. E. Schmidt
Bob Rylander — at your personal service to
B.E. Heitmann   help you with your direct-mail
                    and letter service requirements.

Marilyn Mills — the "voice" who answers our phones.

Clara Rietock — who writes up your orders.

Lillian E. Strnad — she is our bookkeeper.

H. C. Hack — who ships and receives.

Cecil B. Smeeton, — our auditor, C.P.A. of course!

Charlotte Lewen — who are responsible for our good-
Esther Fait   looking (plug!) mimeographing.

J. Hennig - Printing Department Supervisor

Ed Norman — the "harmony" boys who multigraph
Ed McEvoy   your letters. They sing while they
                work.

Walter Retz - Mailing Supervisor

Wilbur A. Robinson - Typing Supervisor

Adeline Golojuch - Addressograph Supervisor

H. C. Stroud *James A. Traynor* - our dependable messengers.

And a couple of dozen other capable and friendly folks who are here to serve you.
(Wish we had room on this sheet for all their signatures too!)

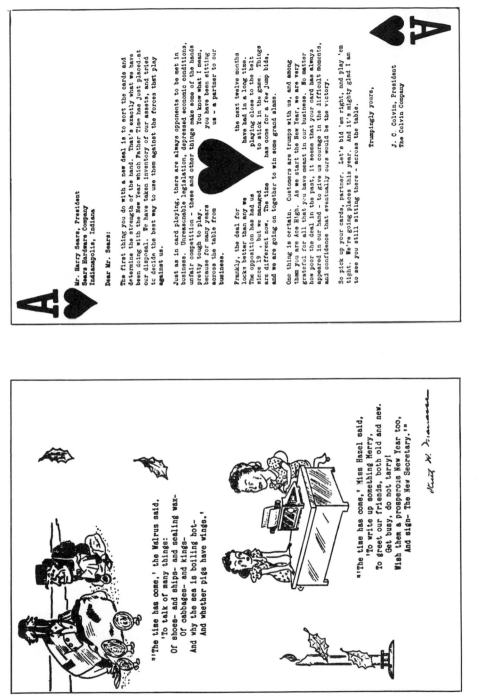

"'The time has come,' the Walrus said,
'To talk of many things:
Of shoes- and ships- and sealing wax-
Of cabbages- and kings-
And why the sea is boiling hot-
And whether pigs have wings.'"

"The time has come," Miss Hazel said,
'To write up something Merry,
To greet our friends, both old and new.
Get busy, do not tarry!
Wish them a prosperous New Year too,
And sign- The New Secretary.'"

A Mimeographed Message—Interesting and Inexpensive

Mr. Harry Sears, President
Sears Hardware Company
Indianapolis, Indiana

Dear Mr. Sears:

The first thing you do with a new deal is to sort the cards and determine the strength of the hand. That's exactly what we have been doing with the New Year which Father Time has just placed at our disposal. We have taken inventory of our assets, and tried to decide the best way to use them against the forces that play against us.

Just as in card playing, there are always opponents to be met in business. Unreasonable legislation, depressed economic conditions, unfair competition - these and other things make some of the hands pretty tough to play. You know what I mean, because for many years you have been sitting across the table from us - a partner to our business.

Frankly, the deal for the next twelve months looks better than any we have had in a long time. The opposition has had us playing close to the belt since 19 , but we managed to stick in the game. Things are different now. The time has come for a few jump bids, and we are going on together to win some grand slams.

One thing is certain. Customers are trumps with us, and among them you are Ace High. As we start the New Year, we are very grateful for all that you have meant in our business. No matter how poor the deal in the past, it seems that your card has always appeared in our hand - to give us courage in the difficult moments, and confidence that eventually ours would be the victory.

So pick up your cards, partner. Let's bid 'em right, and play 'em tight. We're going places this year. And it's mighty glad I am to see you still sitting there - across the table.

Trumpingly yours,

J. C. Colvin, President
The Colvin Company

The Customer Is Ace

naturally takes advantage of Mother's Day; a clothing merchant is equally interested in Father's Day; a sporting goods dealer finds the Fourth of July one of his booming sales periods. The Lincoln Life Insurance Company would hardly overlook Mr. Lincoln's birthday. And of course an expression of gratitude to customers is appropriate for any organization on Thanksgiving Day.

In this respect, a gesture made to Jewish customers by one company is especially interesting. The following letter, mailed by Hills, McLean & Haskins, Binghamton, New York, brought back many replies—and created a lot of goodwill.

> Gut Yom-Tov—
>
> and a joyous Pesach celebration to you and yours.
>
> As you and your family sit at the First Seder Wednesday evening, I am certain your thoughts will be along the same line as mine when this letter was written.
>
> We are all children of one Supreme Being and the trials and troubles of this world of ours only serve to emphasize the great truth of the universal Brotherhood of Man.
>
> And so, as a Gentile, I am taking the opportunity of offering sincere felicitations for the Passover Festival.
>
> We, here at McLean's, are proud of the fact that we number hundreds of Hebrew families among our customers and friends.
>
> Sincerely,

It doesn't matter so much on what occasions the goodwill letters are mailed; the important thing is that every company should use *enough of them* to keep the fire burning. Merely to mail a Christmas letter or card because the act is customary is a sad reflection on a short-sighted company. Customers need more attention than any one annual contact could possibly give. It is just as logical for a customer to *buy* only once a year, if that is as often as his purchases are appreciated.

4. LETTERS OF CONGRATULATION

People appreciate recognition. The individual who does not like to have his good deeds noticed is a rarity. The desire for praise when praise is due is a basic human craving. A man is proud not only of the honors he wins, but also of anything outstanding done by a member of his family, or an associate in his business. He is thrilled when his son earns a scholarship to college, when his daughter marries, when he first becomes a grandfather, or for no bigger reason than building a new factory or moving into more pretentious quarters. Anything that pleases him becomes doubly sweet when it is recognized by some other person or company. A letter of congratulation makes him feel important; adds a personal touch to a business relationship; can hardly fail to win a bit of his goodwill.

Hence, the astute businessman is ever on the lookout for *any opportunity* to write a letter of congratulation. He keeps in touch with the personal activities of his customers, and even of important prospects that he hopes to sell someday. His salesmen are instructed to report back to the home office about the honors and happy events incidental to the lives of customers. If a good dealer has recently been elected Mayor of his village, a letter of congratulation is forwarded promptly. If a purchasing agent is promoted to the rank of Vice-President, he is quickly commended. If a merchant has moved into a new and bigger store, that fact, too, is recognized.

It takes only a few minutes to dictate a letter of congratulation; the goodwill created may endure throughout the years. The executive who ignores an opportunity to render a word of praise to a customer is both thoughtless and negligent. It is not a form of hypocrisy to write these letters of congratulation—not when the writer is sincerely interested in the good deeds of others, and regards his customers in a friendly and personal way. To be sure, if the reader feels that his back is being scratched only in the hope of getting his orders, the result is negative; but the average business executive is really sincere about liking his customers. Naturally, he is glad to see them prosper.

Reasons are almost numberless. It is futile to attempt naming all the circumstances that might prompt congratulatory letters. The activities of mankind are too numerous—and interests too wide—for tabulation. However, if you were to tackle the endless job, you would probably include letters to cover the following types of situations.

> Congratulations to the customer or business friend who has received some form of promotion in business, in civic office, or in some social organization.
>
> Congratulations for any type of service which is of value to society, and for which the worker gives of his own time without recompense.
>
> Congratulations for election to office, or for service rendered in an office from which the recipient is retiring.
>
> Congratulations for some personal accomplishment: the winning of a golf tournament, the making of a speech, the writing of a magazine article, the solution of a business problem, or any similar achievement.

Congratulations for some business accomplishment: the building of a new plant, the opening of a branch office, the acquisition of another company, the announcement of a new product, the substantial increase in sales volume, the offering of a new service which will be of benefit to the community.

Congratulations for milestones reached in progress: the fiftieth anniversary of the company, a personal birthday, the anniversary of the opening of an account, the tenure of years in a business position.

Congratulations for honors won by members of the family: the winning of a varsity letter by a son, the election of a wife to some civic or social position of leadership, the graduation of a son or daughter from college, the winning of a scholarship, any one of a thousand achievements considered worthwhile by common agreement.

Congratulations for some happy event in the family circle: the birth of a baby, marriage, recovery from illness, return of a son from military duty.

Congratulations for some material advancement: the acquisition of a fine new home, the winning of a blue ribbon for "best dog of show," the gaining of control of some business enterprise.

Congratulations for some spiritual circumstance: the joining of a church, work done as Scoutmaster of a troop of Boy Scouts, the donation of a large sum to charity.

Congratulations for achievement in some personal hobby: acting in the little theatre, singing in a chorus or choir, public display of an oil painting, a poem published in the local newspaper, a display at a flower show.

You see, when such a list is started, there is no place to stop it. But no matter what the reason for the congratulatory letter, it is sure to win goodwill; not only because it flatters the ego of the reader, but also because it tells him that the writer takes a personal interest in what he is doing. We know of one business executive—tremendously popular and successful—who for thirty years has made it a point to start every working day with the dictation of a congratulatory letter. Each day, his secretary appears with her notebook, and asks the question: "Who is it today?" And surprising as it may seem, he has never once lacked a candidate.

Typical letters of congratulation. Because the circumstances that motivate congratulatory letters are never quite the same, we do not propose to suggest any forms to follow, or any letters that could be used word for word to cover respective situations. However, we will examine a few letters of the congratulatory type and catch, perhaps, the *spirit* with which they all are written. Here, for example, is a letter written by an executive of Curtiss 1000 Inc., to Miles Kimball, president of Direct Mail Associates, Inc., Oshkosh, Wisconsin:

> Dear Mr. Kimball:
>
> I take this opportunity to congratulate you on your letter announcing you have moved to larger quarters. This letter came to my attention through Dartnell Publications. It is a very interesting letter and worthy of the favorable comment which was given it.
>
> An extra tingle made a round trip on my spine when I read the fifth paragraph wherein you mention letterheads, envelopes and invoices, because I am keenly aware of the many fine envelope orders which we have had from you the past few years. This business is appreciated, I assure you.
>
> When I was a youngster I spent my summer vacation on a farm and my early recollections are closely associated with a pair of overalls which had conspicuously displayed across the shoulder straps, "Oshkosh B'gosh." However, in more recent years I find the name Oshkosh more closely associated with Direct Mail and envelopes than with blue denim and wide open spaces.
>
> I wish that I too might be in a position to climb up and inspect your new quarters. Naturally, I am interested in that sort of thing, and besides I have never had the pleasure of meeting up with one of those St. Bernard dogs.
>
> When you come to St. Paul, climb up and see us sometime. Our office is on the second floor.
>
> Yours very truly,

In that one letter, there are at least four things said that must have pleased the reader: first, the congratulations for the move to better quarters; second, the favorable comment about the letter in Dartnell Publications; third, the appreciation for past envelope orders; and fourth, the reference to a hobby, St. Bernard dogs. Then, at the end, comes the cordial invitation to call when the reader happens to be in St. Paul. You could not ask for a more generous, effective expression of goodwill.

It is only natural that a businessman of long experience should take pride in anniversaries, especially when they date back many years to the time of the company's founding. Using this pride as the basis for a goodwill letter-contact is both logical and appropriate. Following is the way the Deltox Rug Company recognized the fifty-sixth birthday of a retail furniture store.

> Mr. John Doe:
>
> What a thrill it must give you, Mr. Doe, to look back over your

many years in the retail furniture business. For each and every year testifies that you treated your customers fairly and squarely, and gave them full value for the money spent in your store.

Established 1888. Seventy-six years. That's a long, long time. And we'll gamble your records show that the children and the grandchildren of your original purchasers have bought from you.

There's something mighty comforting in a long record of service to the public. And we know that you are going to find, on the day that your business is seventy-six years *young,* that this spirit is particularly heart-warming.

As a comparative youngster, with only thirty-seven years of business life behind us, we congratulate you.

(No complimentary close)

A different type of birthday is that which marks the milestones of a business relationship. This event is recognized neatly in a letter used by the Wilkinson-Grey Company of New York.

Dear Mr. Doe:

"Good merchandise finds a ready buyer."—Plautus.

Year after year we become more interested in your wrapping problems, Mr. Doe. Each year we are *more* anxious to render a service which will meet with your highest approval.

This day marks another milestone in our business relations. Just sixteen years ago today you opened an account with us.

We are ever mindful of this day, and the writer personally wishes you to know that we are today even more interested in serving you than we were the first day we did business with you. And it is because you *are* a customer of long standing that we hope to continue to justify your confidence in us.

Is there anything that we can do to improve our service?—to make it more acceptable?—and to your greater satisfaction?

Wrappingly Speaking,

Other congratulatory letters. To illustrate further how businessmen of our time are building goodwill by letters of praise, a few more examples may be helpful. None of them offer much of a problem in the writing—a friendly hand extended in sincere commendation, and the job is done. The mere fact that the honor or deed *has been noticed* is more important to the person receiving the letter than the form in which the praise is worded. It takes so little time to dictate one of these goodwill messengers compared to that necessary for other kinds of business correspondence that it is difficult to understand why more of them are not written. Certainly, the trouble they involve is insignificant when set against their value in promoting better business relations.

Election to Office

Dear Mr. Doe:

It was a real pleasure to read in this morning's paper of your selection yesterday to be the next president of the Association of Retail Merchants. I can think of no one better qualified for this important position, and you have my heartiest congratulations.

Knowing, as well I should after the many years you have been a loyal customer, how thoroughly you have managed your own business, and what a great inspiration you have been to your employees, I am sure you will lead the Association in a way that will benefit every member, and be a real credit to yourself.

Please remember that all through the year while you are carrying the ball for many a touchdown, I will be up in the grandstand, rooting for you.

Sincerely yours,

Civic Service

Dear friend:

The fact that the Community Chest Drive has reached its quota two days before completion is only another evidence of your leadership ability and willingness to accept any obligation for the good of our community.

I have attended most of the noonday luncheons, and could tell from the first day that we had a Chairman who would direct the Drive successfully. It is not an easy job to control the efforts of so many volunteer workers, or to keep them happily united throughout the campaign.

Truly, you have held the torch high all the way, even though there must have been times when other men would have faltered.

There is little material reward for social or civic service, but I know you must feel amply recompensed by the thought of the good you have created for the unfortunate people in our city.

You have my sincere congratulations, added to all the others that you must have been receiving.

Very truly yours,

Personal Achievement

You old rascal!

Somewhere along life's way, you have discovered the Fountain of Youth—but you have never told me where it was. Is that the way to treat an old business friend?

I, too, was once a fairly good tennis player, but it has been at least ten years since I gave up the game because the old legs wouldn't take the punishment. But you are as old as I am, and now I read that you won the City Championship.

Today, I am going to ask for a new credit report on you, because I think you have been operating under false colors. Your name can't be Doe as it stands on our books. It must be Kramer or Parker or Talbert.

Seriously, I am both amazed and delighted about your victory. You have reminded me of something I forgot too soon—that a man is only as old as he *thinks* he is. Maybe I should have that racket of mine restrung.

Do you need a doubles partner?

Cordially,

Promotion

Dear Mr. Doe:

Congratulations—from all of us here at Armstrong's.

It is good to hear that you have been made Manager of the Jefferson. In a way, it's just like having one of our own family promoted, because all of these past ten years you have helped make so many of our conventions run smoothly.

According to the newspaper account, you started 23 years ago as a night clerk at the Jefferson. Somehow, it makes us feel good to contemplate the careers of ambitious young men who start from scratch and rise to the top—that can't happen in any other country.

Sincerely,

Good Fortune

Dear friend Doe:

I was deeply concerned a month ago when Tom Turner wrote that you had gone to the hospital for a major operation. While you and I have not met personally, the many letters we have written back and forth have developed a feeling of friendship which I know is mutual. It didn't seem right that you should suffer this misfortune.

But this morning word came from Tom that he saw you in your store a couple of days ago, and that you had set some kind of record for quick recovery.

This is indeed good news, and I congratulate you for being in such good physical condition after such an ordeal. Maybe I am like an old hen mothering her chicks, but I do hope you will take things easy for a while, and not bother too much about business.

Cordially yours,

The New Baby

Dear Mary Anne:

Welcome to our eventful world!

They tell me you arrived by air day before yesterday, via Stork Transcontinental. This, you know, is the oldest airline, and it has an unblemished record for safe transportation.

We could have written to your father—an old and loyal customer of ours—but no doubt he is too busy handing out cigars to even read his mail.

And of course your mother is just as proud and excited as he is. When you get older, Mary Anne, you will better understand what joy you have brought to your parents, and why we have hastened to congratulate them.

In the meantime, so that all the things now happening will be properly recorded, you are getting with this letter a Baby Book which we know you will cherish in the years when you become a grown-up.

Until then, best wishes to you, Mary Anne.

Cordially,

Marriage

Dear friend Doe:

She was a shy little girl with big blue eyes, and lovely blonde hair. It took a little while for her to accept me as a friend, but finally she climbed on my lap and we had a lot of fun together.

It's *your* little girl I am talking about, and the event was the night you had me up to dinner, after you gave me that first very much appreciated order. It seems only yesterday, but of course we both know that many years have passed over the dam since that pleasant evening.

If I had any doubt about that it would have been removed when I heard from salesman Gray that the little girl with the big blue eyes was married last week to a Captain in the United States Army.

This must have been both a sad and a happy occasion for you. It isn't easy to give up a daughter, and I know how devotedly you have worshipped her. But to have her marry so well must have been some compensation.

Congratulations? Why, I have a great store of them—for you, for your daughter, and especially for the lucky army officer.

This morning I had the extreme pleasure of spending an hour in our Gift Department—trying to find that one rare thing which might give the newly wedded couple something they would really cherish in future years together.

I think I made the right selection. At least, it is on its way to them with my best wishes.

Sincerely yours,

Birthday

Dear Mr. Doe:

Tomorrow will be an important day in your household, and I hope this letter arrives in time to include my congratulations with all the others you are sure to receive.

I have a friend who says he never wants to be reminded of a birthday. To me, that seems very foolish. It is not a misfortune to grow older, year by year—not when, as with yourself, each milestone represents additional progress.

More and more with the passing of time, you have become a vital force for good in your community. And that means more friends, more prestige, more to be thankful for each birthday.

It has been a great privilege to serve you these past thirty years. We have no customer who deserves more of our appreciation.

So a Happy Birthday to you tomorrow—and many, many more in the future.

Sincerely yours,

It is needless to continue with examples of congratulatory letters. As has been stated, they are easy enough to write; the chief problem is not to overlook their goodwill possibilities. Not all events in the life of a customer or friend are happy, however. There are times when condolences are in order rather than congratulations, and then the letter-writer faces a much more difficult job.

5. Letters of Condolence

A real evidence of goodwill. The old saying, "A friend in need is a friend indeed," has great significance in customer relations. Probably no business letter is so much appreciated as the one that expresses sincere sympathy for a reader in distress; in no other way can a few short sentences go farther in offering comfort and building goodwill that lasts. long after the shock of the misfortune has eased. Businessmen generally recognize the importance of this fact, but the majority approach the writing of a condolence letter with considerable dread. Their mental attitude in such cases is much the same as yours is likely to be when you visit a funeral parlor to console a friend. Your heart beats faster in sympathy, but you just don't know *what* to say.

The difficulty of the message varies, of course, with the nature of the misfortune. It is not nearly so hard to talk to a customer about an accident to himself or someone in his family, when the chances of recovery are promising, as about the death of a close relative. If the loss is material, the problem is comparatively simple; especially, when sympathy can be accompanied by some tangible help. But death is something nobody likes to think or talk about, perhaps because we instinctively fear it.

Unfortunately, this dread of writing the condolence letter too often leads to the omission of the task. We *mean* to express our sympathy, but put it off until the time has passed when it would be appropriate. Or, if the job is finally done, our thoughts are so frozen by the inhibition of not knowing what to say that the final form of the message is either too blunt and cold, or too "flowery" and exaggerated. In neither case is the result what we intended.

A few suggestions. True sympathy is not an emotion that can be expressed by following specific directions—as a woman may knit a sweater or bake a cake. The formula of the Star, the Chain, and the Hook, has little or no value in composing a message of condolence, and anyone who thought to use it for such an occasion would surely come out with a monstrous example of insincerity. However, a few flexible suggestions may be helpful to those who find the condolence letter a perplexing problem. Do *not* take them too literally, as the last thing you want to do is to make your message so mechanical that it lacks warmth.

First, mentally place yourself in the position of the person to whom you are about to write. What if *your* business had been wiped out by fire? What if *your* wife were dangerously ill in the hospital? What if *your* brother had been killed?

Forget you are writing a letter, and just say what you would face to face. The occasion is no time for a literary masterpiece; if you think you have written a good letter, it is probably very poor.

Resist the temptation to quote scripture or poetry, especially when talking about death. You are not delivering a sermon, and your reader is in no mood to hear one.

Use simple language, and not too much of it. Sympathy is not a thing that can be colored or expanded successfully; trying to make it so makes the message seem insincere.

Be sure the thought you are expressing is *genuine*. In other words, don't be hypocritical. If your motive is merely to gain goodwill for yourself or your company, you have no moral right to write the letter. The sympathy must be *real*.

A tangible offer of help—if help is possible—means a lot more to a person in trouble than mere words. For example, some form of material assistance will earn the everlasting appreciation of the customer who has suffered financial loss.

With the foregoing suggestions in mind, the best way to learn *how* to write an effective letter of condolence is to see how other businessmen have done the job.

Actual letters expressing sympathy. All of the letters which follow seem to have been dictated with genuine concern for those to whom they were directed. They have the saving grace of sincerity, although some of them would have done a better job in less words. However, they are representative of the better sort commonly seen in modern business correspondence.

First, it is enlightening to see how four different executives approached the same problem—the writing of a letter of sympathy to customers in an area devastated by flood. You will note that two of the letters add deeds to words by offering concrete forms of assistance.

For Safety Belt-Lacer Company,
By H. H. Stalker.

Dear Mr. Doe:

The words to express what we feel about the desperate situation through which you have been compelled to pass come with difficulty; such as do, seem futile and inadequate. What could one say that would in any way lessen your burden?

So in lieu of any words of the sympathy we feel and cannot express, we offer the following as perhaps being, in a small way, a practical demonstration.

Pending your flood insurance adjustment and your rehabilitation plans, we shall be glad to ship you such hooks and lacers as you may need to supply quick demand, on a ninety-day dating.

Sincerely yours,

For Quaker City Rubber Company,
By H. J. Cocking.

Dear Mr. Doe:

I have heard through our mutual friend, Frank Smith, about the big loss sustained by your family during the recent floods.

At a time like this it is hard to find words to express one's thoughts. But you must believe me when I tell you we, too, feel your loss.

To lose your home is sad. No matter how elegant or how humble it may be, it's always "Home Sweet Home" to you. The kindly thoughts associated with that home—especially, those of your boyhood days spent there—will linger long in your garden of memories. It can't be otherwise.

Yet, out of this catastrophe—from the mass of debris and ruins—bigger and better towns will arise. They generally do, you know —so don't despair.

Do you remember that Latin phrase, Mr. Doe? "Dum spiro, spero"—"Whilst I breathe, I hope." You know it's hope that pulls one through many a crisis.

It will pull you and yours through this one. As hard as it may seem, keep your courage, and don't lose faith.

Most sincerely,

For Curtiss 1000 Inc.,
By G. R. Allanson.

Gentlemen:

Our salesman, M. W. Prince, tells us you are in the locality most seriously affected by the flood. We realize there is very little help we can offer, but do wish to express our sympathy, and the hope that you have not suffered too great a loss.

If your envelope supply has been destroyed, we offer the complete facilities of our plant at Cleveland to rush supplies to you.

A letter outlining your needs will be given emergency attention. We shall also bend every effort to see that the most speedy delivery possible is made.

Sincerely yours,

When death is the reason for the letter. The most difficult to write of all condolence letters are those that deal with death. And yet, when death has visited the family of salesman, customer, or friend it would be an unforgivable discourtesy not to send some word of comfort. How other business executives—experts in letter writing—handle this trying situation is demonstrated in the following typical examples. The first was written by John A. Buxton, General Sales Manager for the Federal Hardware & Implement Mutuals, Owatonna, Minnesota:

Dear Malcolm:

As I stood and looked at your father yesterday, I thought of you and his immediate family and their natural sorrow in losing this man who had been father and counsellor for so many years.

But as I looked around me at the family and friends who were there, I knew that beneath your sorrow you were proud of your father and rightfully so.

No man is eternal. We all must face the last barrier, and the look of mild satisfaction on your father's face told me that he had accomplished a big job, honestly and well.

He has left behind him a fine heritage in sons and daughters, and in loyal friends. You will miss your father but you will never be entirely without him, for his spirit is incorporated in every one of you.

So in this inadequate letter, I tell you, Malcolm, that I am sorry you lost him, but let us believe that he has "Wrapped the draperies of his couch about him and lain down to pleasant dreams."

Yours sincerely,

You saw a moment ago how H. J. Cocking, Quaker City Rubber Company Sales Promotion Manager, wrote to a customer who had suffered damage to his business from flood. The letter below was mailed to a representative in New Zealand. The writer's beautiful thought in the next to the last paragraph might have been spoken for himself. He died suddenly only a short time after the letter was mailed.

Dear Mr. Royse:

The Quaker Organization was deeply moved upon hearing of the untimely death of your father, and hastens to extend its deep sympathy in this, your hour of trial.

While the privilege of knowing your father personally never fell to our lot, we realize the extent of the loss you have sustained.

At a time like this, mere words are empty and shallow, but yours is a suffering which is universal...which belongs to every human being in every corner of the world. A deep anguish which, sooner or later, cuts into every human heart...strong and weak.

Death is the inevitable goal, and there may be some small degree of consolation in the thought that death is but a narrow starlit strip between the companionship of yesterday and the happy reunion of tomorrow.

May this thought help you to carry on.

Sincerely,

George J. Hughes, writing for the Deltox Rug Company, also deserves commendation for writing a heartfelt note of condolence. Below he is talking to a dealer of long standing whose brother and partner had just died:

Friend Doe:

It was a shock to us to learn of the passing of your beloved brother and our good friend for many years. The loss to us is great.

But the greater loss is to Centralia itself.

We will never forget how you and he carried on courageously during the years of depression—how you two helped to restore confidence among merchants in your own and other towns by building a beautiful new store while others were still holding back through fear of the future.

These are but two of many things that the brothers Doe have done in a worthy way to make Centralia a better city, but their importance in general welfare in the most trying of times makes them worthy of particular mention.

We are as humble in our sorrow in the passing of this good man, your brother, as we know you to be.

> Yours sincerely,

Although it is true that words can do little to ease the sorrow that comes with death, there may be the possibility of a constructive thought in a condolence letter which will bring some inspiration. For example, the thought expressed in the fourth paragraph of the letter below would undoubtedly encourage some readers:

Dear James:

I just heard of the great calamity which visited you last week.

It is a hopeless task to try to express my feelings by mere words, but I do want you to know how much I sympathize with you in your time of sorrow.

Buildings, cities and even whole nations can be restored, but the untimely death of your beloved daughter is an irreparable loss. It brings home to me very forcibly the heartaches and sadness that are always with us.

But cruel as life can be, it is far better for we who carry on to put forth a little extra effort above and beyond what we would have ordinarily put forth—just as a slight token to ourselves of our determination to do our best, and that in memory of those for whom we care.

You can be sure, James, that your many, many friends are with you in spirit in this hour.

> Sincerely,

Shorter letters expressing sympathy. The foregoing letters are very fine in many respects; if they have any fault, it is that of unnecessary length. As we agreed in the beginning, the chief purpose of such contacts is to let the reader know he has a friend—individual or company—interested in what happens to him, and concerned when things go wrong. It is the act of expressing this concern that counts the most, and the sentiment offered needs no embellishment. Here are a few brief letters that were probably just as much appreciated as those ten times longer; in fact, stretching them might have made the letters less effective.

Illness

Dear Mr. Doe:

Salesman Brown tells me you went to the hospital a week ago for major repairs; that everything turned out fine, but you will be in bed another two or three weeks.

Knowing how strong you have been physically, I think you may fool these doctors, but just in case time passes slowly, I am mailing you today some books which I have read and liked.

The best of wishes for a quick recovery!

Cordially yours,

Accident

Dear Mr. Doe:

I hope the ruffian who smashed into your car buys from your competitor and loses his shirt. In the meantime, you have my sincere sympathy. I realize that kind words won't heal a broken leg, so if there is anything we can do to help in your store, just let me know.

That's not an idle gesture. We very much appreciate your loyalty in the past—tell me how we can now give you a lift. It will be a pleasure.

Sincerely yours,

Death

Dear Mrs. Drake:

Word has just reached me of your husband's passing, and I am both deeply shocked and saddened at this tragic news.

Throughout the twenty years I knew John, he had the respect and admiration of everyone who came into contact with him. To few are granted so warm a personality and so fine an intelligence.

Please accept my deepest and sincerest sympathy for you and your family in your bereavement.

Sincerely,

Fire

Dear Mr. Doe:

I have a friend in St. Louis whose business in the early days was twice destroyed by fire. But he never lost courage, and today he is the head of the biggest company of its kind in the world.

Somehow, out of this adversity you have suffered, good will come, because you are the kind of a merchant who will *make* it so.

In the meantime, if you need quick replacement of stock, longer terms—whatever it may be—please remember we appreciate past favors, and are standing by to help you.

Yours sincerely,

Financial Distress

Dear Mr. Doe:

I heard yesterday the true story of the incidents that forced you out of the business you worked so hard to build. Don't worry about what the newspapers said. You still have friends, character and ability.

When your plans are made to re-establish yourself, remember this company will go the limit to help you.

Sincerely,

Disappointment

Dear Mr. Doe:

I see the critics have had you on the fire. Forget it. The concert was splendid, and you deserve better treatment. Most of these critics think they must tear everything apart to prove how smart they are.

Rubbish! The concert was good. You are good. And we are proud that you come to our store for the things you need in what you are doing for the community.

Cordially yours,

Strive for simplicity in writing your messages of sympathy. Use short words. Use them sparingly. *Feel* what you are trying to say. You are not making a speech, writing an essay, or showing how kind you can be. You are just offering a friendly hand to a person in distress. Sentiment plays the part best when the stage is void of scenery.

6. Miscellaneous Goodwill Letters

About new quarters. Naturally a business leader feels good when he can present tangible evidence of growth or improvement—and the customers to whom he tells the story will share his pleasure, IF the progress is presented as a *benefit to them,* and not just something to crow about. For example, on page 645 you read a letter from an executive of Curtiss 1000 Inc. to Miles Kimball. It was a reply to an announcement of new quarters for Mr. Kimball's company, Direct Mail Associates, Inc.

Now you may read the announcement that impelled such a friendly letter. It must have developed considerable goodwill, if results are any measure. Mailed to a list of less than two hundred, the letter motivated many recipients to climb to the third floor to pay the writer a visit, and many more mentioned it to him later. And still better—four of the replies included what every business man loves—*orders*. Here's the letter:

Dear Mr. Doe:

Won't you eat a hearty breakfast some morning soon and make the climb up here to our new quarters?

It's a bit breathtaking (the climb) but the true adventurer won't mind that. Besides, we'll have our trusty St. Bernard Alpine rescue dog out on the stairs, with a cask of the best about this neck.

We're proud of our new home and want to show it off to you. There's more than twice the room we had over on the opposite corner, where we were born and spent the first eighteen years of our life. It's worth the climb just to see Joe Bubasta, our production manager, reveling in the increased efficiency he's getting now.

Then, too, when you visit us we'll have a chance to cough politely and call your attention to all the new equipment we've bought these last few months: the printing multigraphs, automatically fed, which deliver 7500 letters each hour...the new high-speed Baum folder...the nine new typewriters...the new automatic Gordon printing presses with Miller air feeders.

We'll hesitate—artfully—in front of these presses, because when you see the genuinely excellent color printing we're doing, you may make a mental note to call us in the next time you need letterheads, envelopes, invoices, or any other sort of printing.
The man in charge of this department is a master printer in the old Guild sense of the word. Enclosed is a sample of a job going through one of the presses today.

Then we'll take you to my own turreted office, where—immodestly enough—the bookcase is decorated with the silver cup presented to us (the cup itself says) "for excellence of letter copy," and with the gold medal we got last fortnight for another DMA letter.

Whereupon we shall realize at long last that these things which mean so much to us, couldn't possibly be quite THAT interesting to you...and for the rest of your stay we'll be well-mannered. We do want you to come. If there's a hurry-up job you need now, of course telephone us—at TR 0–0000.

But plan to visit us soon.

                                                    Cordially,

An equally interesting announcement of better facilities for service—disarming because of its candor—is one mailed by a letter shop in Chicago, the New Secretary. The writer doesn't offer the visitor a "cask of the best," as did Mr. Kimball, but perhaps it wouldn't have been appropriate. The writer is a lady.

> Dear Mr. Jones:
>
> Well, we've expanded! And here we are ready to do your work better than it was ever done before.
>
> You've probably been to formal openings where the men got mechanical pencils which didn't work, and the ladies, withered gardenias, with odor "Gone With the Wind."
>
> Well—we thought about having one like that too, and then we decided POSITIVELY NO.
>
> We've made a lot of new friends!
>
> And many of these have been kind enough to tell others about our services and reasonable costs. That's why we had to take the office next door.
>
> No flowers!
>
> We had no formal opening, gave away no souvenirs. Still, we'd like to have you come in and see our enlarged place, for we already have found it makes for increased efficiency. It's not the most beautiful office in Chicago—
>
> But it's ours and we like it!
>
> Cordially yours,

Dealers, too, can use appreciation letters to smooth relations with sources of supply. The one below was written by J. M. Busch for Busch-Tombal Co., Green Bay, Wisconsin. Reading this cordial letter no doubt made the shoe manufacturer feel better about the help extended to this merchant.

> Gentlemen:
>
> We're pretty busy these days, getting ready for the formal opening of our remodeled store. And it would take something pretty important to make us pause in these preparations.
>
> But that's what we think of your generous cooperation with us in the publicity for this event. It's important to us; has made us feel very good.
>
> But then we're not surprised, for in the period we have been doing business with you, we have found you always willing to go out of your way to be helpful to us. We might as well acknowledge, here and now, how much that spirit has been appreciated, and helped us enjoy our work.

Mineral, Va.
December, 1955

Mr. Walter J. Tuohy
President
Chesapeake & Ohio Railway
Cleveland, Ohio

Dear Mr. Tuohy,

We lived beside the railroad,
　　In a cottage small and white,
We loved to watch the trains go by,
　　At morning, noon and night.

We waved to all the engineers,
　　And called them all our friends,
But now there's been a tragedy,
　　That brought that to an end.

We had a dog we loved so well,
　　She was a big Great Dane,
We found her Monday by the tracks,
　　Killed by your speeding train.

We know you couldn't help it,
　　But she was our only pet,
If we could have another dog
　　It would help us to forget.

He wouldn't have to be so big,
　　Just one to love and feed,
A little fluffy puppy
　　Is all that we would need.

My daddy says that Santa
　　Is awfully poor this year;
There's five of us already
　　And another almost here.

But if he digs around his pouch,
　　And finds a little pup,
And leaves it here at our house,
　　We'll never give it up.

I'll love him, oh, so very much,
　　And keep him off the rail,
So please, if you see Santa,
　　Won't you tell him our tale?

Very truly yours,

Judy Mahone

⊛

THE CHESAPEAKE AND OHIO RAILWAY COMPANY
TERMINAL TOWER · CLEVELAND 1 OHIO

WALTER J. TUOHY
PRESIDENT

December 16, 1955

Dear Judy:

We're sorry that you lost your dog,
　　Your one and only pet,
But we have talked to Santa,
　　To see what we can get.

At Christmas-time it's not so nice,
　　To suffer such a loss,
Just when you should be happy,
　　You're saddened and you're cross.

We know how much a pet can mean,
　　Because we have one too,
A kitten we call "Chessie",
　　A little one like you.

Our Engineers are very sad,
　　They didn't see your Dane,
They didn't mean to hurt him,
　　And cause you all this pain.

So we have talked to Santa,
　　And told him what we did,
He said he'd look inside his pouch,
　　To see what he had hid.

We're sure he has a puppy,
　　(He hinted one was there)
We told him where to bring it--
　　To your cottage, white and fair.

To all of you at Mineral,
　　A Christmas full of cheer,
To your brother and your sisters,
　　To your Dad, and Mother Dear.

Judy, Merry Christmas,
　　Stay bright-eyed and dewy,
Take good care of the puppy,
　　Sincerely, Walter Tuohy.

Miss Judy Mahone
Mineral, Virginia

We, at this end, shall strive constantly to merit that consideration in the future. We think that your shoes are now in one of the finest stores in the state—anyway, positively the finest store of its kind in the city. We only wish that you could be with us Friday of this week for our formal opening.

Again, thanks sincerely. And now we'll resume trimming our windows.

Cordially yours,

A clever letter that attracted a great deal of goodwill was written by Mr. Walter J. Tuohy, President of the Chesapeake & Ohio Railway. It was sent in answer to an equally clever letter written by a young girl. Both letters are reproduced on page 660.

A dramatized announcement. In keeping with the nature of the announcement—the opening of "china and glassware headquarters" —Bechtel, Lutz & Jost, Inc., Reading, Pennsylvania, added showmanship to their invitation by using a cut-out in the form of a cup and saucer. The recipient's name was lettered on the outside to blend with the other copy. On the inside of the cut-out, to the left, was the formal invitation, showing date and time, and mentioning souvenirs; to the right, was a cordial letter, signed by one of the officials.

Dear Friend:

This is the engagement I hope you have kept open for us, because we want you to join our other customer friends at this grand opening of one of the finest, largest, and most complete china and glassware headquarters in the East.

You will enjoy your visit, and you are certain to go home with a lot of good, up-to-date ideas as a result of the interesting displays. . .and you will have an opportunity to talk things over personally with the representatives of some of America's best known manufacturers who will have special exhibits.

Make it a point to be here. We'll be LOOKING for you. . .and we'll be very much disappointed if you are not with us.

Cordially yours,

Letters of invitation. Most people like to be invited to see things, go places—especially when they are of a limited group to whom the invitation has been extended. A lot of goodwill can be created with such invitations if they are not too pointedly a sales effort.

It would be hard to resist, for example, the Bonwit Teller 721 Club invitation, or Warren Pipe's invitation to see the "famous Crown of The Andes." In the latter, Mr. Piper's postscript adds a personal touch that is both interesting and amusing.

Invitation to See Famous Crown of the Andes

BONWIT TELLER
fifth avenue · new york

Bonwit Teller
721
CLUB

This Card entitles you and all your friends
to Club privileges
NAME Mr. Richard R. Ettinger
721 FIFTH AVENUE

November 27, 19

Dear Mr. Ettinger:

On Thursday, December 2nd, we are having our Annual Stag Party in honor of the opening of our 721 Club for men, where we have assembled all the gifts that men like to give women.

It will start about 5:00 and will include such attractions as a fashion showing modeled by famous beauties of stage, screen and magazine.

I do hope you can be with us for the party at the 721 Club, Fourth Floor.

Sincerely,

W. M. Holmes

Mr. Richard P. Ettinger,
Prentice-Hall, Incorporated,
70 Fifth Avenue,
New York City.

·WARREN PIPER & COMPANY·
Importers of Diamonds
Manufacturers of Platinum Jewelry
31 NORTH STATE STREET
CHICAGO

September 21, 19

To my Friends, Patrons, Neighbors,
Rotarians, Club Mates . . . and to You in particular:

It is possible that you already know from the newspapers, radio or movies, that I have finally succeeded in buying the famous Crown of The Andes which contains the oldest and largest collection of emeralds in the world. I hesitate to place three superlatives in one paragraph, but it happens to be the largest jewel transaction in history.

I want my friends to see the famous Crown in all its glory while it is still in Chicago, because it is so magnificent that it is impossible to describe or illustrate its beauty. Also I am afraid it will be necessary to dismantle the lovely diadem and sell the jewels separately. The new owners are money-minded men who can hardly be expected to know that we who handle precious jewels are in the calm and proud possession of eternal things. There are 453 emeralds of superb quality in the famous Crown, and they have been offered $250,000 for one single stone.

I am enclosing two complimentary tickets for the exhibit of the Crown and other treasures which are now being shown on the 8th floor of The Fair Store, State and Adams Street corner, as a personal compliment to Mr. D. F. Kelly. The exhibit will be open from 9 A.M. to 5 P.M. daily until September 30th.

I hope you will enjoy the exhibit as my guests.

Sincerely,

Warren Piper

Please don't try to find me on September 24th, because that is my red-letter day, my forty-fifth birthday, my fifteenth wedding anniversary, and the twenty-sixth anniversary of my business. All three on one day, and the doctors have me on the water-wagon!

Letters of introduction. Although frequently used in business, letters of introduction are usually cold as ice, and far too formal. Obviously, this lack of warmth is a detriment to the person being introduced, since the success of his mission partly depends on the interest of the man who reads the letter.

The adequate letter of introduction should accomplish at least three things: first, give the full name of the person being introduced; second, give a satisfactory reason for the intrusion; and third, make the party who gets the letter really *want* to meet the person talked about. It is in the third of the purposes that the letter of introduction often falls short.

How personal the introduction may be depends on the relationship between writer and reader. If the two parties are friends, or if they have known each other in a business way for a long time, the tone of the message can be much more intimate than if they are comparative strangers. Here are three examples:

(1)

Dear Mr. Doe:

On the train returning from the National Convention, you will remember that we talked about the cold and lifeless letters commonly written by employees of insurance companies. We both thought something should be done to correct this condition.

Accordingly, we hired an outsider to conduct a Better Letter Course in our company. In a way, we stole a march on you, for the man in charge is a resident of your city.

His name is William Watson, and I am giving this letter to him with the suggestion that he present it to you personally. I am doing this as a sort of favor to you, because from the results gained here, I think you will want this man to do a similar job in your own company.

He is strictly okay, and approaches the job from a business point of view, rather than that of a college professor.

Cordially yours,

(2)

Dear friend Joe:

If you have ever doubted my appreciation of your many orders, here is proof of its reality.

During the past three years we have had a salesman who has been highly satisfactory in every way. Now, because of the illness of his wife, he is forced to move to your part of the country. You know, where men grow big and strong, and have plenty of hair on the chest.

Since we cannot use Jimmy Ware in Colorado, I am asking him to contact you. You'll like his red hair, and the way he brings in orders.

Regards,

(3)

Gentlemen:

One of the drawbacks in the size of our business family is the inability of many of our office men to get acquainted with dealers in distant territories.

Nevertheless, when one of them does get out on a trip, he tries to meet as many customer friends as possible. And that's what Russel Smith is going to do next month.

The name, of course, is already familiar to you, for he has written to you many times about matters pertaining to promotion and advertising. For example, he arranges the repainting of your signs, and often sends you reprints of ads, new promotional material, and other sales helps.

Russ and his wife are driving from here to Seattle and should pass through your city about the tenth of September. He won't have a lot of time, but you can be sure he'll spend an hour in your store, just to say "hello" and give you a preview of the new product you will hear a lot more about after the first of the year.

Don't plan any entertainment for Russ and his wife. They really won't have time for it. But it is good that you two should get to know each other personally.

Cordially yours,

The simplest forms of introduction are those written on the back of business cards. They serve the purpose when both parties are rather well acquainted, but are not appropriate if the relationship is more formal. The message on the card cannot be long, but it can at least say something to arouse interest in the person being introduced.

Any of the following might be adequate:

Joe: If you have wished for a really good secretary, wish no more. Introducing Virginia Browne. She's tops.

Hello, Mr. Doe. I want you to know Jack Smith. He has helped us no end—can do as much for you.

Jerry: This Irishman, Jim McNulty, wants to sell shoes. Take my word for it—he's okay.

Friend Doe: Shake hands with Henry Wilson. He has a story you will want to hear.

Walker Brothers: Give this new salesman a lift. You fellows can help him. I'll appreciate the favor.

In several of the sections that follow, you will find many additional illustrations to prove that goodwill may be woven into the fabric of all kinds of business correspondence. There is no reason for dividing letters into two groups, saying: "These are goodwill letters, and these are not." *All* letters should reflect a spirit of friendliness, irrespective of what they talk about. In this section, you simply have seen types of correspondence in which the emphasis on goodwill may be somewhat stronger; so strong at times, that the gaining of it was the only purpose in their mailing. Many of them could be ruled "unnecessary" from the viewpoint of actual operation of the business; but not from the viewpoint of cementing the bond of loyalty between company and customers. These so-called goodwill letters are *important,* and deserve most serious executive consideration. *Their omission is a direct loss to sales.*

HUMAN RELATIONS
IN LETTERS

HUMAN RELATIONS
IN LETTERS

1. LETTERS TO EXPRESS PERSONAL REGARD

The extra courtesies of business. Apart from company purposes, there are many letters written by businessmen that represent nothing more than good fellowship, and the will of the writer to be nice to those with whom he is acquainted. Indirectly, they may facilitate the transaction of business, but they are not mailed with that intention. Charles Hanson Towne's poem, "Around the Corner," perhaps points to the motive behind these letters. Do you remember it?

> Around the corner I have a friend,
> In this great city that knows no end;
> Yet days go by and weeks rush on,
> And before I know it year has gone,
> And I never see my old friend's face,
> For life is a swift and terrible race.
> He knows I like him just as well
> As in the days when I rang his bell
> And he rang mine. We were younger then,
> And now we are busy, tired men—
> Tired with playing a foolish game,
> Tired with trying to make a name.
>
> Tomorrow, say, I will call on Jim,
> Just to show that I'm thinking of him,
> But tomorrow comes—and tomorrow goes,
> Around the corner, yet miles away...
> 'Here's a telegram, sir'...'Jim died today!'
> And that's what we get and deserve in the end—
> Around the corner, a vanished friend.

669

The letters in this section were written by men who take their human relationships seriously. They like to pause now and then to dictate a personal letter to some business friend: sometimes, to reply when no reply is needed; sometimes, to comment on an incident of credit to the recipient. Without these human relationships business would be cold and uninviting, as indeed some people try to make it. But the men who get the most out of their business life do not agree that everything they do must be connected with the making of money. They *do* "remember Jim."

From the writing of these personal letters you can derive much enjoyment, and the replies that come back to you will more than make the effort worth while. Of course, they too are goodwill letters, if you want to call them that; but the writers speak not so much for their companies, as for *themselves*. For example, when Tim Thrift dictated the letter reproduced on the following page, he was replying to a compliment that had been paid to a booklet he had prepared for circulation among his business friends. He had written the copy, and set the type with his own hands, not for any special reason, except that it was his pleasure to keep in touch that way with those he knew and liked. Thus, the letter to Tim, and his reply, represented an *exchange* of mutual regard, 'and both men were warmed by the thought of it.

The format of this letter is also worth your attention. Most business executives have their own private stationery for use on semi-personal occasions. You would expect one of the masters of the letter-writing world to have something especially attractive, and Mr. Thrift does not disappoint you. The paper, a heavyweight, is buff color, with a deckled edge at the bottom. It is trimmed slightly smaller than the conventional $8\frac{1}{2} \times 11$ letter-head size. The two large t's are printed in a lively red, the rest in a solid black. The typist of the letter in question did her bit to complete the perfect whole with a neat job of blocking. The signature is bold and interesting. In its original colors, you could not imagine a more attractive ensemble.

Of course, a cordial letter contact does not need to be as pretentious as this sample. Personality and warmth may be just as conspicuous when offered in smaller doses. Note how one business executive made just two paragraphs interesting.

Dear Jim:

I have tried various means of putting myself in an Oriental mood in order to more fittingly accept your kind invitation for Thursday, June 28th, at 6:30 P.M.

However, my attempts have all been in vain, probably because

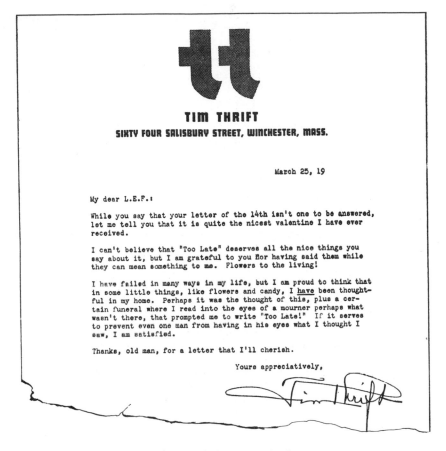

TIM THRIFT

SIXTY FOUR SALISBURY STREET, WINCHESTER, MASS.

March 25, 19

My dear L.E.F.:

While you say that your letter of the 14th isn't one to be answered, let me tell you that it is quite the nicest valentine I have ever received.

I can't believe that "Too Late" deserves all the nice things you say about it, but I am grateful to you for having said them while they can mean something to me. Flowers to the living!

I have failed in many ways in my life, but I am proud to think that in some little things, like flowers and candy, I _have_ been thoughtful in my home. Perhaps it was the thought of this, plus a certain funeral where I read into the eyes of a mourner perhaps what wasn't there, that prompted me to write "Too Late!" If it serves to prevent even one man from having in his eyes what I thought I saw, I am satisfied.

Thanks, old man, for a letter that I'll cherish.

Yours appreciatively,

Tim Thrift

Business Courtesy at Its Best

my Honorable Ancestors have imbued me with only an Occidental background. Therefore, I shall simply say "thank you" for including me, and I shall join you at 7 Mott Street at the appointed time.

Sincerely,

Jack Carr suggests more back-patting. Jack Carr, one of the small group of men who helped blaze the trail to better business letters has always seemed at his best when writing to a friend. Following, you have a sample of his man-to-man friendliness, and the light, humorous way in which he handles a more or less serious subject. Incidentally, in the longest paragraph, he pleads for more letters in business of the type we are considering in this section.

Presenting Jack Carr!

It's too bad, friend Doe—

there seem to be so few men in the world like you—fine fellows who will take the time and trouble to write a little letter like yours of the 11th.

I wish I had Tom Dreier's gift of expressing my emotion when I read your marvelous message. Imagine what a wonderful thing is the mail...capable of conveying across a continent a warm, human handclasp like you put into that letter.

We've never met personally, I don't believe. And still as I read your message here on my desk I feel we've got much in common...besides tonsils.

Here's an idea!

Nothing new about it. Men like yourself and Dreier and any number of other word-wielders have been doing it for years. Perhaps not consciously. Let's start this New Year with a resolution to write more letters like yours. Do a little more verbal back-patting. God knows the world is hungry today for a bit of sympathy and understanding and encouragement.

Billy B. Van has the right idea. As a spreader of sunshine that man merits a monument. There's a place in the sun, under my Palm Tree, any old time he's ready to sit there. And if you'll just say the word, we'll move over and make room for you too.

A heap o' happiness to you always and if you ever keep a woman may her name be Lady Luck.

Cordially yours,

Recognizing a business friend's birthday. E. O. Fenton, former president of the American Institute of Business, Des Moines, Iowa, was a top-flight letter-writer who frequently took time from routine responsibilities to extend a business courtesy. On page 671 is a card used by him (he is leading the elephant) to commemorate the birthday of a business friend and associate. The use of his own face in the cartoon helps to personalize the greeting.

Contacts like these are much simpler to make than those that appear in the form of a letter; when the idea is clever, as in this case, they may be even more effective. Thus, the executive who says he hasn't time to recognize birthdays really means he hasn't hit on an idea that would do the job without too much trouble.

A tribute from a former employee. Not long ago, the papers carried the story of the 100th birthday of a well-known and greatly loved State Street merchant in Chicago. Hundreds of letters and telegrams were sent by business friends to celebrate the occasion. The recognition of service anniversaries is a much appreciated act of business courtesy, especially when the event represents a great many years in the harness.

The following letter was mailed to the head of a Midwest company on his 50th service birthday. The writer was a former employee.

> My dear Mr. Doe:
>
> I don't know of any letter I would rather write than this one about your 50th service birthday. And yet it seems impossible to put in words how I feel toward you and the company which you have led to so many victories. You know how it is with the thoughts which are deepest in the heart—like people caught in a burning building, they all rush out together.
>
> So often we hear it said, "If I could only live my life again, how different it would be." I, too, have wished I could do that, but there is very little I would change in the ten years I spent in your company.
>
> All that I have managed to do since dates back to what *you* gave me—the will to work with enthusiasm, to plan ahead, to make every accomplishment only the beginning of another step forward, to encourage others to make the most of their opportunities, to live for God, and *with* God, realizing that this earthly stay is only a preparation for His kingdom.
>
> All of these precious values you gave me, and I shall ever be grateful. A lot of water has passed over the dam, but not a day comes that I do not feel the influence of your inspired leadership.
>
> God bless you on this 50th anniversary. You will never really grow old, Mr. Doe, for yours is the spirit of youth, and all that you have taught others will live on eternally.
>
> Yours sincerely,

Reply to letter of congratulation. Sometimes a letter of appreciation may give the recipient an opportunity to reply in the same spirit. A selfish or egotistical person will accept praise as fully deserved, and never think of returning the favor; but not the business man who dictated the letter below:

> Dear Henry:
>
> Among the letters in my possession is one written by a merchant in Florida to a credit manager "up North." He said, "I don't see why you pester me about a bill which is only two months past due—down here in our state that's considered about the same as cash."
>
> I thought of that a minute ago when, after working all day on a pile of unanswered letters, the one you wrote to me a month ago came to the surface. It looks as if replying in thirty days is considered about the same as by return mail—by yours truly.
>
> Nevertheless, I can't ever remember getting a letter which I appreciated so much, and I shall always prize it highly.
>
> Of course, what you said wasn't the whole story, because everybody knows (unless it's you) who is responsible for the progress in your Department—who trained and inspired all the fine people working there.
>
> But it's nice to know a man like you who takes the praise that rightfully is all his own, and says to a friend, "Come share with us lest we be selfish." It's been a long time—too long, Henry—since I have read the Bible, but I think it talks a lot about sharing our honors with others.
>
> I don't know exactly how to say it—maybe I shouldn't even try. But I think you are the salt of the earth, Henry, and I am very grateful to have had a little bit of your business friendship.
>
> Sincerely,

A letter mailed at Christmas time by Harold Pitcairn McQueen is another evidence that business correspondence may at rare moments rise to exalted levels. This message, too, is an expression of personal regard for the reader.

> Dear Mr. Doe:
>
> Always at this time of year I take inventory...
>
> ...not of merchandise on dusty shelves or in gloomy store rooms, but of friends.
>
> I seat them before me in a comfortable group and through clouds of smoke from a much used pipe, I look them over carefully and ask myself, "What have I done to make their lives happier—and what have they done for me?" For friendship is a two-way road.

And I see that I have received much—and given but little!

Sweet people, these, for their hearts are molded to the proposition that it is better to give than to receive.

Are some outstanding? Yes! For some men hand out priceless gifts like encouragement and inspiration. They stimulate the mind. They help tremendously in smoothing over the rough spots...with no thought of reward.

And I pause—to gaze upon a kindly countenance—the smiling face of one of my outstanding friends. I would chat with him. The group withdraws—and I am left alone with this one man. I offer him my pouch and point to a glass. We drink a toast, of my proposing...to "My friend, John Doe!"

Sincerely,

Follow-up of time spent together. Some businessmen are more thoughtful than others in writing a thank-you or appreciation letter after personal contacts in which some service or courtesy was extended. The situations that call for such letters are numerous—failure to take advantage of them means loss of goodwill that easily could have been salvaged, and in some cases, an act of rudeness. The speaker who has been well-treated by a business organization, the executive who has been the guest of a friend at the latter's golf club, the man who has been taken out to dinner by a business acquaintance in another city, any recipient of a business courtesy, should take time to send a little letter of appreciation.

A typical illustration is a letter written to a business friend in Chicago by shoe-man "Bert" Fisch of Fort Worth, Texas.

Dear John and Josephine:

One of my most enjoyable evenings was spent with you folks in Chicago. It will always be a pleasant memory to me, and all along I shall be hopeful that you will make the trip to Mexico, and arrange to spend some time here with us in Fort Worth.

Gosh all fishhooks! It's hard for a country boy like me to find words to express myself properly. Not having the command of the English language like you do, it's possible that in such a case the less one tries to say, the better off he is. Silence would, no doubt, be golden, but I just can't help talking, even in a business letter. So I must say that I am grateful to you for your hospitality.

Here's one of those long-distance handshakes from down in Texas, and although you may not hear from me very often, I want you to remember throughout the year that I will have pleasant thoughts of you two.

My love to both of you!

Cordially,

Following is a letter sent by a speaker to the secretary of a business association. This man had collected his fee, and was not forced to continue the contact, but wanted to express his appreciation for the courtesies he had received.

> Dear Willard:
>
> Here I am back home again after a day which was really tops for fellowship and interest. I could see that you have built an unusual spirit among the members of your association.
>
> That is no exaggeration. You know a speaker compares and rates audiences, just as audiences compare and rate speakers. I don't know when I have talked to a group as "ready, willing, and able" as yours.
>
> Particularly, did I enjoy the trip to John Doe's farm. From now on I'll get more pleasure out of watching the horses run—because I can bet on his stable. It may cost me some money, but it will be worth the gamble. I saw one black colt that should win a big race someday. I'd like to *see* it happen.
>
> Here's hoping our paths cross again, my friend—until then, get plenty of that old sunshine.
>
> > Cordially yours,

2. Letters to Applaud Performance or Service

Recognizing good work. As we go through the daily grind of business, now and then we are favored by exceptional service or a special courtesy on the part of some worker. He may be the filling station attendant who takes particular pains to wash the windows and check the battery, a clerk who makes a helpful suggestion, a railroad conductor who tries to make his passengers comfortable, or any other individual who gives to his job that "something more" which the average worker never even thinks to give. The business man who stops to write a letter of appreciation for such outstanding service is not only performing an act of courtesy but he is also helping to encourage the kind of public relations we all want, but seldom encounter, in the business world.

A bouquet of orchids, then, to Vice-President H. Clay Jackson, of the Southwestern Petroleum Co., Inc., who took the trouble to commend the good work of a telephone operator in Fort Worth, Texas. Evidently, Mr. Jackson was well acquainted with the executive to whom he wrote, for he addresses him as "Dear Ed."

> Dear Ed:
>
> It is a long cry from that curious instrument exhibited by Alex-

ander Graham Bell at the Philadelphia Centennial in 1876 to the intricate and marvelous System of today; from that first New York exchange, noisy as the Board of Trade in a Bull Market to the almost noiseless automatic service. Truly the history of the telephone is the history of the Nation.

Before we hear the last "number please", due to your mechanical gadgets that will rob us of that lull where we might put our feet up on the desk and wait for "her" to do the work, let me take time out today and pin a bouquet on the lapel of one of your splendid operators whose willing service is appreciated very much by the writer.

A few days ago, I was trying to locate one of our salesmen traveling in Ohio . . . this young lady in your office worked very hard on the call, and though we did not locate the party, it was not her fault. She stayed right on the call for at least half an hour, and it was a very pleasant visit for me to listen to her as she had Chicago, Detroit and many other large cities helping her with her work.

I do not know her name, but I did get her number (30) . . . and I know this fine girl is writing her name in kindness, love, and mercy on the hearts of thousands with whom she must come in contact year by year. Her name and her deeds are building a monument for The Southwestern Bell Telephone Company that storms of Time can never destroy.

I have "kicked" about telephone service when I thought a kick was coming. Not many kicks, however, on your Fort Worth service . . . and since this was a most unusual case of service well performed, I most heartily commend this young lady to you, and would appreciate your conveying my good wishes and thanks to her.

Very cordially yours,

It is true that letters of the above variety take a little time to write, and when they are not written nobody knows the difference. However, it seems that the bigger the man in business, the more thoughtful he is likely to be in passing along such courtesies. Perhaps the reason is that the leader in business best knows the importance of praise in motivating employees. Just as he appreciates a good word for one of his own workers, he tries to speak favorably for those in other companies that serve him well. An outstanding example was the late L. A. Downs, president of the Illinois Central System, whose letters helped in many ways to develop friendly public relations for his railroad. When Mr. Downs consented to an article about himself in *American Business,* he had no further obligation to either the editor of this magazine, or the author. Nevertheless, he took time to write the following note of appreciation:

Dear Mr. Frailey:

Mr. Whitmore has sent me a copy of American Business for March, and I have read with more pleasure than I can possibly express here your exceedingly generous article about my letters.

Please accept this note as a sincere statement of my deep appreciation.

With the kindest regards,

Sincerely yours,

Later on, you will have the opportunity of reading more of the goodwill letters written by L. A. Downs. How he found time to write them was a puzzle to his associates, but thousands of individuals in all walks of life were favored with his cordial, human messages.

Letters to men retiring from business. A heart-warming exchange of business courtesies is found in the two letters next offered: one sent to an executive retiring after fifty years of service, and the other, his reply.

The Letter

My dear John Doe:

As I contemplate your resignation as Vice-President, my emotions are split two ways. I know how abundantly you have contributed to the reputation of the Blank Company, and certainly 50 years is a long time to remain steadfastly in the service. For all of that you have my sincere congratulations.

And yet, as I think of the company *without* your quiet, rugged leadership, there comes a feeling of great loss, and the wish that you could always be there in your office; ready as in the past to help your boys when in distress, or to share the joy of their good deeds.

Knowing the modesty of your personality, I doubt if you realize how much the boys have leaned on you—or how often they have spoken your name to me with genuine appreciation of the interest you have taken in them. You may be sure, Mr. Doe, that your name has been written too deeply in their hearts to ever be erased by the passing years.

I do not know what plans you have made for the future. I only know that I wish you a period of great happiness, and perhaps the opportunity to do some of the things you have been denied under the pressure of work obligations. I can think, too, of no greater pleasure than to pause at the end of 50 years to review old accomplishments—to take inventory of your many friends.

And so, old friend, I salute you! May God bring you many more happy years—the reward for all that you have done for others.

Sincerely,

The Reply

Dear Joe:

> "Do you turn from your work with a smile
> and feel that it's all been worthwhile?"

These words seem to sum up my feelings, Joe. Do you remember them? They are from that old favorite, "The End of a Perfect Day."

To me, the 50 years I have spent with this wonderful organization have been like a perfect day. I am leaving with the same feeling I would have if I were sitting on a bluff watching a beautiful sunset. My heart is full of thanks for all this day has brought me

Yes—it's been worthwhile.

The day to come will not be as long as the day gone by, but it will be enriched by the memories of my association with men like you. Your letter, with its good wishes, will be kept among my most valued treasures.

And so, old friend, adios.

May God bring you good fortune, good health, and a full life of happiness—just things you so justly deserve.

Most sincerely,

Letter from Justice Owen J. Roberts. When Justice Owen J. Roberts retired from the Supreme Court of the United States, he received many letters of regret—more than he would have been expected to answer. But cheerfully, and with appreciation of their intent, he answered them all—in longhand. Here is one of the congratulatory but regretful letters; his reply is shown on page 680.

Dear Justice Roberts:

I was indeed sorry to read of your retirement from the United States Supreme Court. During my studies at Harvard Law School and thereafter in the practice of law, I followed your opinions carefully. I have always admired your sound reasoning and the excellence of your decisions.

Your retirement will be a great loss to the country. It will be difficult to replace the dignity which you lent to the Supreme Court.

With all best wishes,

Cordially yours,

Letter to the man promoted. Recognition of good performance includes the friendly "amen" for the individual who has just climbed a step higher

Supreme Court of the United States.
Justice's Chambers.

Chester Springs R.D.#

Dear Mr. Powers,

It was good of you to write me concerning my resignation and I am grateful for your generous expression.

Sincerely yours,
Owen J. Roberts

To John G. Powers, Esqr.

Courtesy of a Great Jurist

on the business ladder. He may be a business associate of the man who writes the letter, or connected with some other company. In either case, congratulations in writing are likely to be more appreciated than those extended on the telephone or in person. A letter may be taken home for family inspection, or filed for safekeeping. You may think that the average businessman attaches no importance to the compliments he may receive on "the way up," but this opinion is contradicted by the many successful executives who keep scrap books, or some other record forms, to mark the pleasant incidents in their careers. One business leader, known from coast to coast and often quoted in the newspapers, has two letter files to which he alone has access. One is labeled "Bouquets," and the other "Brickbats." These two collections, he claims, have helped to keep his Ego in proper adjustment.

Be that as it may, a letter of the following type—sincerely motivated, and so accepted—is a certain goodwill builder.

> Dear "Vice-President"—
>
> It was a great pleasure to hear of your promotion. At the banquet where the good news was announced I tried to congratulate you personally, but I cannot resist the urge to place in print how I feel about your good fortune, which surely you so much deserve.
>
> It must be a challenge to take the place of one who has been both your leader and your friend. I know that you have prayed for the strength to carry on his good work—and to add, as you surely will, to all that he accomplished.
>
> It always has seemed to me that you and Mr. Doe were like brothers united in one common purpose. I know how often the two of you were mentioned by employees in your company—as if you were a team pulling them over a rough road.
>
> Now, my friend, the load is yours to pull alone, and we who know your power have no doubt of the result.
>
> It must be, too, a great satisfaction for you to start this new responsibility with the hearty approval of those in the ranks, as well as that of the board members who selected you for the job. You have always gone out of your way to be decent and helpful in contacts with workers—now the seed you planted is bearing fruit. There isn't a man or woman in your company who isn't glad to see you made Vice-President.
>
> In the mental image of the many who are pleased over your promotion, look at the man in the back row, second from the right. Yes, that's *me*. The old boy is tickled pink.
>
> Sincerely,

A friendly gesture to employee's parents. An idea that seems unusually good for the company that can use it is the tendering of appreciation for good work to the parents of an employee. It is illustrated in the following letter used by an organization that often has the need of part-time workers, mostly girls. The purpose is to win as much goodwill as possible, and make it easier to rehire those who were satisfactory.

> Dear Mr. and Mrs. Doe:
>
> Your daughter, Marjory, has just completed a short term of employment in our Transcription Department.
>
> I thought you would like to know that we were well pleased with her work and attitude, and we were sincerely sorry to see her go. When she again looks for a position, I hope we will have something which will appeal to her.
>
> Marjory has been a credit to your home, and I know you must be proud of her.
>
> > Sincerely,

The idea of paying tribute to *someone else* who has had a hand in the success of an individual can be adapted in many ways, and since this other person is usually left in the background, the goodwill created by an unexpected letter of praise is sure to be more than worth the effort. Here are two examples:

To Wife of Salesman

> Dear Mrs. Doe:
>
> Of course, at the sales party the other night you were proud to sit with your husband at the table of champions.
>
> And you had a good right to be. An increase of 68% in volume over last year is something to brag about. I am proud of Harvey, too.
>
> But the purpose of this personal note is to let you in on a secret. It concerns *you.*
>
> One of the biggest reasons for Harvey's success is the cooperation and encouragement which he gets from his *wife.* I know this is true, because he himself has told me so.
>
> You know, as a sales manager I have seen some salesmen held back by wives, and others pushed ahead. You are one of those that *inspires.*
>
> Harvey and I are very grateful for your fine understanding of a salesman's problems—for all the help in making him a success.
>
> I thought you ought to know.
>
> > Cordially,

To Secretary

Marjorie:

Since I saw Mr. Doe this morning, I have been thinking about the many years you have been my efficient secretary.

The reason is that Mr. Doe was very complimentary about the report you typed on the new Training Plan. He said it was not only logical in content (my part) but the best looking report, and easiest to read (your part) he had received in his 40 years with the company.

You see he wanted it to be a perfect job, because now it goes to the Chairman of the Board.

I could have told you all this, but it occurs to me that I have been thoughtless in not always giving you credit for your loyalty and good work. This time, I wanted to make my appreciation a matter of record.

We have worked together as a team for a long time. You really have done a swell job, although many times I must have tried your patience.

Sincerely,

A letter such as this last one, if the writer wanted to think of it selfishly, should be worth many times its weight in gold, for surely the girl who got it would be inspired to extra effort. And the same is true with respect to any down-the-line employee, whose work is too seldom given proper recognition.

3. Other Letters to Improve Human Relations

An intricate pattern. As you no doubt realize, the threads woven and embroidered into the cloth of human relations run in many directions. The letters you have been reading touch only a small number of the activities common to business. They do, however, have one common attribute—the reflection of the writer's personality, and his feeling of brotherhood with other human beings. No man is properly trusted with human relations unless he has a genuine *liking* for people—all people, irrespective of their station in life, or their work level in the business world.

The letters that follow were obviously written by individuals who enjoy human contacts. Always you see a *man talking* sympathetically to his reader —understanding the latter's emotions and eager to share them, good or bad. Every company needs workers of this calibre, for the goodwill they win is an asset too great for calculation.

Delivery of a Job

Dear Bill:

I won't give you any excuses for the delay, except to say I am sorry. But with this note, you are getting the booklet, and I hope it proves worth waiting for.

Also, kind sir, I thank you for the privilege of doing this work for you. I trust your client appreciates the bargain you engineered for him, as I really spent more time than I had anticipated. But Grandma always said it is more blessed to give than to receive—and who would argue with Grandma?

Until the bell rings again,

> "Begging to remain,"

Explanation of Delay

Dear Cy:

Thanks for your impatient letter. I don't blame you for wondering about the book. But really, I'm helpless.

I spent one afternoon last week with the printers, but they are in an awful mess, due to labor pains. The situation in the whole Chicago area is lousy. If fist fights would help, we would be in there swinging.

At least while out there, I saw the plates coming through. And I promise to keep after everybody who has a hand in the job.

I don't know what you mean by that "Casanova" stuff, but I could retaliate by saying, "Look at the pot who's calling the kettle black."

> Sincerely,

Follow-Up of Visit

Dear Wallace:

Isn't it a doggone shame when some nice guy drops into your office to say "hello" and finds that you are out on a Welfare, Chamber of Commerce, Y.M.C.A., Boy Scouts, or what-have-you Drive? Apparently that is what I was doing last week. I am so sorry I missed you.

I did check on your speech to the Ad Club, and am told you did yourself proud.

Now please do not forget the address, and when you are in town again, drop in for a good chat.

My best wishes to you and Mrs. Smith.

> Yours very truly,

Personal letters about death. The difference between the following letters and those in Section 11 is in the relationship between reader and writer. Here, the letter is more personal—quite separate from business affiliations. The nature of the problem, however, is the same—what can be said that might bring some comfort to a person so saddened by death?

To the Wife of a Business Friend

My dear Mrs. Doe:

I was shocked to hear of Bill's passing. Mrs. Smith and I wish we could do something to make things easier for you.

You and Bill were so nice to us at the Charlotte Convention. It will always be a pleasing memory.

On December 31, Bill wrote to me that he had just returned to the city from a fishing trip. I think this must have been one of his last letters to a friend. I shall prize it highly.

Should you and your lovely daughters ever come to Cleveland, please remember our home is your own.

Sincerely yours,

When the Wife of a Friend Dies

Dear Walker:

A letter came from Miss Jones yesterday, with the word of Mrs. Doe's death. I was deeply saddened.

Probably others would expect me now to know what to say that might help a little bit to soften your sorrow. Instead, it all seems so futile, there being experiences in this patch-quilt world of ours that simply will not yield to words.

You know, however, my good friend, that I feel deeply for you in this time of adversity, and the many miles between us cannot lessen my feeling of being *close* to you—or the wish that I *could* help.

Faithfully yours,

Trying to salvage a wayward employee. We implied a moment ago that there is no telling for what strange purpose a human relations letter may be used. Here is one that surely wanders far from the beaten paths in business.

Dear Mr. Doe:

About eight years ago, I hired a young man from Arkansas. He was eager, impetuous, and friendly—in our office of about five hundred there wasn't a man or woman who did not like him.

When later he wanted to go to college, I was instrumental in arranging financial help, because I though he was an unusual boy, and that he would come back to our company after graduation, better equipped to make a name for himself.

That boy—John Smith—is now No. 15633 in the penitentiary of which you are the head.

What happened in this boy's life, I do not know—only that a letter from his mother tells me an older man led him astray. I could understand that, because John was the kind of a lad who would give the utmost in loyalty and faith to any man he admired.

But this lad isn't really *bad*. Like a lot of other country boys, he probably found the big city too much for him. He went to work for a man who was not honest, trusted him, and now he is paying the penalty.

Mr. Doe, isn't there some way we can get this boy back into society under the right influences? Can't he have one more chance? I know how it is with hardened criminals—we have to keep them behind locked doors. But there is a tremendous amount of potential good in John Smith—in many ways he would make a good citizen in any community.

I am willing to go before the Parole Board and testify for this boy. Who among us all can really afford to throw stones at a youngster who has made one mistake? I know that once out of prison, he will go straight.

This letter is not an idle gesture. A business friend on the coast is willing to give John his second chance. What can we do to get it for him?

Sincerely,

A typical example. Lawrence A. Downs started with the Illinois Central System as a rodman. Step by step he became roadmaster, assistant chief engineer, division superintendent, and finally, president. Throughout his business career, Mr. Downs never lost interest in human relations. He did everything that might be expected of a business executive to win and hold the friendship of those who even remotely had any contact with his railroad. His own circle of friends reached far and wide into all walks of life. He had an uncanny sense of human relationships, and could talk with sympathy and understanding to any individual, on any subject.

In his letters, Mr. Downs practiced the principles and spirit which are upheld in this Handbook. You saw one of his shortest messages earlier in this section; now you are going to see more. He is our choice as the typical executive among many who use letters to win goodwill and to maintain public esteem. Thousands of people in and out of the Illinois Central System remember the sincere friendliness of his personality; thousands have been touched by fellowship, which was neither forced nor limited to a select group. Mr. Downs *liked people*. He went out of his way to extend those little extra courtesies—usually by letter—that are so often overlooked in business life.

You will like the letters of "Larry" Downs; you will be sorry that his last message has been typed. He proved beyond any question that friendly letters can be an asset to any business. From even the few examples of his work that follow, you may gain a better concept of human relations—ideas for your own use.

Ambassador of Goodwill. These letters were originally printed in the magazine, *American Business*. They were taken almost at random from the many carbon copies available. It would have been wasted effort to try to cull the "Best" for Mr. Downs wrote on the same high level of friendly effectiveness, day in and day out. He wrote no letters that held any reasons to offend. He was what every business letter writer *can* be—an Ambassador of Goodwill.

To a Fellow Executive

The one purpose of this letter is to tell you how well I think you deserve the splendid compliment that is paid you in the N. W. Ayer & Son brochure, "Who Are the Leaders?"

If I were asked to name one man to represent what I consider the finest and best in our American tradition, whose life and work would stand as a refutation of the abuses that are heaped upon American business by some social and political agitators, you would be the man.

I am proud that the railroads can be represented in this fine tribute to America's industrial high command by one of its own leaders, and one who so well deserves that honor.

With assurance of my genuine affection and esteem,

About "Preacher" Walker

Your editorial of February 5 in commendation of "Preacher" Walker is one of the finest tributes to a member of his race that I have ever read. As president of the company of which he is a faithful and conscientious employee, I thank you for this tribute to him.

The Illinois Central System has some 5700 Negro employees engaged in various kinds of work. Wherever they are employed in sufficient numbers to permit of group action, they have organized themselves into booster clubs. Their clubs are doing splendid work among the Negro employees and among the members of their race on the outside.

I am glad to join you in a tribute to "Preacher" Walker and to the other members of his race who are faithful to their trust.

To a Friend

I would not be frank with you if I did not say that your letter May 7 touched me. I like to believe that the railroad has made progress during my administration, and the things you say bolster that belief.

We have been through some difficult times, as you know, and it is only natural to wish for smoother going in order to make the best possible showing for the Illinois Central. In all sincerity, I say that I am dedicated to that purpose.

I thoroughly enjoyed your verses and appreciate your birthday greetings.

With best wishes.

About the New Baby

The announcement of the birth of Larry Downs Cavender on May 24 was received some time ago. I have delayed acknowledging the very nice compliment you pay me in giving the baby my name until I could secure a little gift for him. It is going forward today.

My wish for the boy is that he grow up to be a fine young man, a useful and worthy citizen, and a joy to his mother and dad.

With kind personal regards,

Appreciation

Your letter pays me the finest compliment that one in my position could receive. I want you to know that I very much appreciate the sincerity and frankness of it.

Looking backward, it does not seem like forty years since I started working for the Illinois Central at a spot which I can see from the windows of my office.

However, the calendar tells me that it has been forty years, and my heart tells me that they have been happy years, notwithstanding the disappointments which have been an inevitable part of the difficult times we all have experienced recently.

I thank you most cordially for your letter and your good wishes.

To a Customer

On Saturday morning I received your letter and answered it immediately. I suppose you got my answer on Monday.

On Saturday evening we received your car of lumber from our connection at Winona, Miss. At 7 o'clock Sunday evening we had it in Robinson, 500 miles away.

If I do say so myself, that was pretty good service. We are always glad to look after our friends.

Loss from Fire

As a neighbor, the Illinois Central is mighty sorry over the loss which your company suffered through fire yesterday. I hope that the property destroyed was fully protected and that you will soon be able to rebuild.

With kindest regards,

Death of Child

On my desk this morning is the report of the death of your baby boy while attempting to cross our tracks yesterday afternoon.

I know how little my words mean to you in this situation, but I want you to know that you have my sincere sympathy.

To Retiring Director

Your decision to retire as a director of the Illinois Central has been received by the directors and also by the officers of the railroad with very keen regret. For myself, I regard your retirement as a deep personal loss.

The ties of nearly half a century are not easily broken in any case, and in the case of a man of your accustomed vigor and devotion to duty I know this decision was a hard one to make. As compensation for the sacrifice, however, you have the knowledge of an extraordinary length of responsibility conscientiously performed. Your service as a director has covered more than half the history of our railroad, and you have participated in decisions which have more than doubled its mileage, and have multiplied its capacity and efficiency many times.

Your faithfulness in attendance upon the annual inspection trips has endeared you to the many members of our organization, few of whom have rendered longer service than your own. They, too, will regret your retirement.

My own work as officer and director has benefited from the example and counsel derived from your seniority in years and experience. For that I thank you. It is my earnest wish that the relinquishment of the cares which you have borne so faithfully may result in your improved health.

To Another Executive

I do not undertake to read everything Arthur Brisbane writes, but I do not miss what he writes on any subject of as much interest to me as your birthday.

I read the piece about your birthday while on the train, and this is my first day in the office since then, and the first opportunity to send you a personal word of greeting.

I hope that you have a great many more anniversaries and that all of them will be happy ones.

Apology for Mistake

I don't know how to answer your letter. Our error was a piece of bad work, the like of which has never before occurred in my experience and I am sure will not occur again. Our people feel keenly over it; so much so, that they unburdened themselves to me, and I was told about it immediately.

I feel now that this is a belated apology and expression of regret —nevertheless, it is sincere.

To a Young Employee

It is true that my first job on the Illinois Central was in the position of rodman. That was in 1896. I was a graduate of Purdue University, having completed the general academic work and also the course in civil engineering.

While I was a rodman the thought never occurred to me that I might some day be president of the railroad. My immediate concern was to be a good rodman, and after I had mastered that job I began figuring on what I might do next. The usual line of promotion in that department is from rodman to instrumentman, so I began to prepare myself to be an instrumentman.

After awhile my chance came, and I was promoted. With each advancement in the organization, I went through the same experience—first endeavoring to do my immediate work thoroughly and later undertaking to prepare myself for the next step.

There are several thousand employees in our organization, and only one of them can hold my present position at any one time. However, every position in the organization is worth any man's best efforts.

Of course, the same is true of every other organization.

I send you my best wishes.

To a Fellow Official

The years pass swiftly. It seeems only yesterday that we first met, when you and I were youngsters in the service. Today marks your fortieth anniversary with the Illinois Central. I am happy to present you and Mrs. Doe with lifetime passes.

On such an occasion, I could say much regarding your splendid record, your faithfulness to the railroad, your loyalty as a personal friend, but I need not do so.

You know what is in my heart. It is my earnest wish that you
and those dear to you will have many happy years together.

A genuine love for his railroad. When you meet an executive interested
in people, writing friendly letters to them, extending out-of-the-ordinary
courtesies, you are almost sure to discover also that he is motivated by
enthusiasm for his company, its products, and its personnel. Enthusiasm is
not a quality that can be bottled; instead, it flows in ever-widening circles.
Naturally, the person who *enjoys* his business connection is better able to
scatter goodwill in his letters than the one who goes about with a long face
and is at heart a malcontent.

Certainly, in all of the letters written by L. A. Downs, you catch a feeling of enthusiasm for the Illinois Central. He wanted others to respect his
company as much as he did; perhaps, subconsciously, he felt a connection
between his own goodwill contacts and the reactions of his readers to his
beloved railroad. We do not think for a moment that friendly letters are
written for that ulterior purpose, but we *do* believe that goodwill is a thing
that inevitably bounces back to the individual or company that expresses it.
Hence, one test of the fitness of a worker to handle correspondence is the
extent of his own loyalty to his company. Note these paragraphs from other
letters by Mr. Downs that reveal his enthusiasm for Illinois Central:

> Some of my friends may think I do a good deal of bragging
> about the Illinois Central, and I guess I do, but all that I could
> say in that regard is nothing compared with the compliments of
> those who have given us a chance to show our stuff.
>
> .   .   .   .   .
>
> I am also grateful for the compliment you pay our suburban
> service. I am certain you would like our passenger train service
> equally as well, and I hope that before long you may have an
> opportunity to make a long trip south on one of our fine trains.
>
> .   .   .   .   .
>
> You make it plain that the Illinois Central is a progressive rail-
> road, and I do not think I am immodest to admit the allegation.

In short, goodwill is largely a matter of mental attitude. Normally, the
happy, satisfied worker will find more opportunities to make friendly letter
contacts than the person not sold on his job or his company.

4. LETTERS TO MOTIVATE EMPLOYEES

An obligation of leadership. In the small company, with just a handful of workers, the president or manager can keep in touch with each employee personally. This, of course, is the most desirable form of supervision and motivation, but it is not practical in the larger corporations. The president of a flock of one thousand, for example, seldom knows all of his workers by name, and he couldn't possibly sit down and talk to each one of them at necessary intervals. To be sure, part of this leadership responsibility is delegated to department heads, but the head of a company is properly reluctant to lose all contact with those he should, by right of office, be the most qualified to encourage and direct.

In this predicament, the majority of chief executives and other leading officials usually fall back on personally dictated messages in which their thoughts for the mutual good of company and personnel are set forth. In some cases, the distribution takes place at regular intervals; in others, only when the business leader has something on his mind which he considers worth passing down the line. No matter in what form, or how often, the letters are sent to employees, it is highly important that they be written in simple language every employee will understand, and in such an interesting and convincing manner that they gain favorable acceptance. To make his messages effective, the chief executive obviously needs acquaintance with the principles of letter construction; he is no more immune to improvement than any humble correspondent who may be a member of his clan.

Unfortunately, some of the executive letters you may have seen or received do not do the job intended. The cause may be just one fault or a combination of several. The writer may forget that he is talking to folks of less experience or knowledge, so that what he says goes "over their heads." He may lack the ability to unbend and talk the language of the common man; or he may "preach" instead of point the way. He may write with the false notion that anything coming from the president is sure to be carefully read, and make no attempt to make his words interesting or his suggestions impelling. In the latter case, he ignores the formula of the Star, the Chain, and the Hook, although what he writes is an attempt to influence human behavior. In that sense his message is just as much a sales letter as one sent by the sales manager to customers or prospects.

We think the one man in a company who should know the most about business letters and how to write them is the chief executive; of course, this is sometimes true. You have just examined some of the letters written by L. A. Downs, and there are other presidents who write just as well. Certainly, the president has the best chance to motivate his employees—*if* he approaches them in the right way.

Letter of Jewel Tea Company executive. A personal letter to employees of the Jewel Tea Company, Barrington, Illinois, is duplicated below. It was written by William D. Smith, Vice-President, in a way that wins attention and respect.

Dear John:

I am about to celebrate my thirtieth Thanksgiving Day with Jewel. And I am happy. A question is on my mind; it is one which may interest you as well as me. What profit for a man to spend thirty years in one occupation, while his youth slips away?

Young men are impatient. Things, they feel, must happen for them, and happen quick. If they don't happen in one spot, the urge is to try a new spot, and then maybe another. Natural, yes. But what the young man possibly does not yet know is that the only happenings which can really count are those which happen within himself.

Luck, he says, I must have; I must place myself where I will get the breaks. He has not yet learned that a good man makes his own luck. He does not realize that in shifting about in search of BREAKS he may actually be applying BRAKES to his career; leaving him, when youth is gone, just where he started.

So I think these years have been well spent. And as for the vanished youth—I wonder. Health I still have; it has been a healthy life. And I wonder if, when we speak so yearningly of vanished youth, we do not really mean that bodily health which, largely through indifference or ignorance, we so often abuse. For true youth is a thing of the spirit. And in spirit I do not feel a day older than I did thirty years ago. That, I think, is my grand Good Luck; that and the friends I have made these many years in this one spot. And I am thankful.

But you should be interested in my life only to the extent to which you can use the fruits of my experience to guide better your own course in your life. Here are a few simple suggestions of things worthwhile which I have learned, and which may appeal to you as good.

I have learned that one is laying up trouble for himself if he neglects the simple things that make for good health. Yet men are prone to do just that—and regret it later. Moderation in all things, and immediate heed to danger signals, will preserve that priceless possession of good health, the lack of which is a most serious handicap. Never forget it.

Teach yourself to like people and to like work. Take your job seriously—but don't take yourself too seriously. Believe that HOW you work is more important than WHERE you work. Cultivate a sense of humor—laugh. To keep young you must play and you must have fun; make your job and your life a game —and play the game to win. Learn to get entertainment out of your work and out of your contacts with people. Be a good loser, but never quit.

Read—and keep an open mind. Just as stiff joints mark an aging body, so fixed ideas mark a mind in its dotage. Question your own opinions continually, and invite new ideas. You will never be old as long as you can say truthfully: The only thing I really know is that I don't know—but I propose to learn.

And quit worrying about yourself and your success. The men the world remembers best are those who forget themselves—and work for their fellow men. Center your interest not in yourself, but in your job, your family, your fellow workers. Study and strive for their success—and you will wake up some morning to find yourself a success.

Good health; interesting work; the satisfaction of accomplishment; the respect and love of your associates. For these be thankful

Sincerely,

Making the worker a partner in progress. Another message full of "meat" for any employee with a serious attitude toward himself and his career is one signed by President G. D. Colborn, of Century Metalcraft Corporation, Chicago. You feel that this executive is full of fight, and that his spirit must penetrate throughout the organization. Evidently, in the Metalcraft program, strong emphasis is placed on the position of each employee as a *partner* in the business. Also, the fact is made quite plain that the idea of partnership is not a mere slogan—each worker is expected to make his contribution to the team.

Dear Partner in Progress:

I have always been tremendously proud of the high type of men and women who represent this Company. That you have dedicated March as National Colborn month is but another indication of the splendid loyalty and co-operation with which you have always backed me up.

March closes the fiscal year, and all of us are naturally anxious to have it represent the best year by far in the history of our organization. I greatly appreciate the extra effort you are putting forth to make this month outstanding.

During periods of economic readjustment, many businessmen and salesmen blame their lack of success on "conditions." I know, however, that the real Century Crusader is much like Napoleon. When asked how he intended to combat seemingly unsurmountable circumstances, he replied: "Circumstances?... I *make* circumstances."

General business conditions today mean little to the wide-awake salesman. He capitalizes on them, whatever they may be. Remember—when people are most interested in conserving money, "Silver-Seal" offers a real investment in economy.

Time and time again in the early days of this business, when others were spending their time "harmonizing the blues," my Fighting Partners were proving the old saying that "Good pilots are made in stormy waters." These men doubled their efforts; did some constructive thinking; and made their own circumstances. *They* GOT THE BUSINESS.

Although there is absolutely no comparison between *then* and *now*, some salesmen are licked by a few newspaper headlines. We remember, however, that this business enjoyed a successful inception during the toughest times this country has ever seen. We are privileged to draw aside the curtain of recession's "fog" and look forward to personal prosperity and continued success. We, of Century, have never made a compromise with "conditions"—we never intend to. We are concentrating our efforts. We *are* getting the business.

During the coming year, I want to see you keep in step with the progress of the Company by being prepared to take ever-increased responsibilities. More high-type men and women are joining our organization today than at any other time in our history. New opportunities for advancement are arising daily for those who demonstrate their ability to lead.

The outlook for the coming fiscal year is exceedingly bright. Brookmire's forecast of consumer incomes—the best index of future business activity—places the estimated consumer income for the next six months at 6% *over* the average for the past three years. Capitalize on this *fact*. Shove aside "recession talk" with POSITIVE THINKING, POSITIVE ACTING, and POSITIVE SELLING.

Now is the time to act. Get going—and keep going, with

Your Fighting Partner,

Thanking employees who carried on. Before his courageous spirit finally yielded to Death, Carl Wollner, President of the Panther Oil & Grease Manufacturing Company, Fort Worth, Texas, had several periods of illness. Returning from one of them, he dictated the following message to his employees.

To All My PANTHER Friends
In Office, Factory and Field—
As I return after an absence of more than six months, my thoughts for you all can best be expressed in the words of a poet . . .

A rose to the living is more
Than sumptuous wreaths to the dead;
In filling love's infinite store
A rose to the living is more
If graciously given before
The hungering spirit is fled.

Let me thus hand a rose to all Members of the Panther Organization who have so nobly carried on, and have done such a fine job during my stay in the hospital, and subsequent convalescence out West. It was all along a wonderful inspiration to me to watch from the background how well the Panther Organization kept on functioning.

Space does not permit individual mention of those whose work has been particularly outstanding during this year. Fact is, everybody must have done a good job for the *result* to be so gratifying. I wish I had the command of words to express adequately my gratitude to each and every one of you.

Things are topsy-turvy in the world across the seas. We are mighty fortunate to be AMERICANS—let us all be proud of that. Let use realize anew what the grand old American Way of doing business, and the matchless American Way of living has done for us all. Let us appreciate it enough to be willing to do our part to always keep this country sane and safe, as it has been.

Above all, let us pledge ourselves once again to do our part, to the utmost of our ability, to continue to make good on our respective jobs, so that the Company we love may continue to prosper as an important part of the greatest country on earth.

Amazing as it may seem, it's only 110 days till Christmas, and those days will pass rapidly. With them the year will be gone. There is still much work to be accomplished between now and the dawn of another year. We'll all have to get busy to find ourselves in anywhere near as good position as we hoped to be by Christmas.

Again, Heartfelt Thanks to all of you for the good work you have done—and every good wish to you all.

Sincerely,

A message from "Uncle Jake." Employees of the Kalamazoo Vegetable Parchment Company, Kalamazoo, Michigan, received the following Christmas message a few years ago from their president. It is one of the many pages from the philosophy of a business leader, a philosophy never smeared by the thought that money is the only thing to be derived from business.

WHAT A CHRISTMAS GIFT!

A Christmas in 1920 still remains the most memorable one to me.

It was made so by a gift received from a business man and a good woman at a Sunday School Christmas Service.

This good man came up to me, squeezed my hand, and with a hand on my shoulder, said, "My boy, I perceive that God will make of you a force for good in the world. Never refuse an opportunity to take part in all such services!"

The woman came up and said, "Jacob, you said your piece beautifully!"

These were the sweetest words I have ever heard. I did not sleep that night. Something happened inside of me. My candle of hope was lighted—and ambition sprouted. It wasn't true what so many had said to me—"You are just a dumb, good-for-nothing kid."

My heart still beats fast with a profuse gratitude for the Gift of those two good folks.

It lies within our power and will to create such a memorable Christmas for many a poor soul—discouraged, hope and faith burning low, possessed with an inferiority complex, and ambition waiting to be lighted.

Maybe just a word or a friendly glance from you or from me will make this Christmas a most important and joyous one. I know it will be to the giver, as well as to the poor soul who is in need of inspiration.

My wishes for this year are that every day will be Christmas in Spirit. Now and forever!

Uncle Jake

A letter based on an inspiring story. Sometimes the precepts for getting ahead in business are more acceptable when presented in story form. Here, the reader is left to make his own deductions, except for one short paragraph near the end.

To the Thoroughbreds in our Company:

Sportsmen the world over will never forget Black Gold, winner of the Kentucky Derby in 1924. In size, he was little more than a pony, but there never ran a horse with a heart so big.

And yet, it isn't his victory in the Derby that gave Black Gold immortality. Many years have passed since that chunk of black dynamite went to the post for the last time, but strong men who were at the track that day are not ashamed of tears when they tell you what happened.

A true thoroughbred never quits. His body may be broken, he may even be matched against unconquerable Death, but his spirit still laughs, and his brave heart carries on. And so it was that last day in the life of Black Gold.

They took their places and soon they were off—a fine field of blooded horses—and many in the grandstand had placed their bets on Black Gold. But somehow, they didn't mind losing those bets—it was like paying tribute to the great soul of a noble friend.

You see, coming down the stretch Black Gold stumbled—some said he was kicked by another horse—and his leg snapped. The other horses thundered past him, and he was left helpless in the rear.

But the race wasn't over for Black Gold. Long after the others had gone under the wire, he came hobbling home—finishing his last race on the three good legs that were left to him. No Victor's Wreath for Black Gold when that race was done—only a bullet to end his life. But bless that little horse for teaching us what it means to be a thoroughbred.

We need thoroughbreds in this business, too—products that will stand any test, salesmen who will finish each day's work as that horse finished his race, workers who will face the public with an honest will to serve.

"John Doe, Thoroughbred"—better to possess that title, than to be called a king.

Sincerely,

Those New Year's resolutions. At the beginning of each new year, most people decide they are going to do better; some of them wisely set specific goals to be accomplished. Naturally, the good business leader encourages this practice; a gain for the individual is a gain for the company —if he wants to look at it selfishly. The man who wrote the following letter, however, knows how easily New Year's resolutions are forgotten. He hopes this follow-up may help to keep them alive.

"Those Grand Resolutions!"

Along with the rest of you, on New Year's Day I made a few resolutions. I felt good about them too—kind of satisfied with myself. But here it is the end of January, and some of these resolutions are already beginning to crack. And I looked for the reason.

I think I found it. We can't create new habits—destroy old ones—by simply resolving. Only indomitable persistence, trying and failing, trying again and failing not so soon, will make resolutions a reality.

I have certain tasks to accomplish—a contract with myself. I will eat moderately, play moderately, save more money—I will have a passion to overcome every influence that keeps me from being my *best*. I won't be a flower that blooms on January first, and dies a month later. Not for a few days only, but all through the year, I'll fight to make my life really count.

Get out your resolution, your aims, your quota, or whatever you said to yourself that you *would do*. Then say, "I'll make the flame of my resolution just as hot today as it was on January 1. I set myself a goal, and by the Eternal, I'm going to *make* it."

Persistently yours,

5. LETTERS FROM THE PERSONNEL DEPARTMENT

A delicate phase of human relations. When a person applies to a certain company for a job, he expects to be received in a courteous manner, even if his application is rejected. The employment manager who simply says "no work today," or tacks a sign on his door to that effect, is not functioning in a way to win goodwill for his company. Neither is it considered good business practice, irrespective of the discourtesy involved, to have the secretary of the personnel man or the girl at the information desk turn away applicants. Any man or woman who comes to a business office looking for employment is entitled to courteous *attention*. After all, no person need apply for a job with his head hanging down. He is offering what he has to *sell* to a company that *buys* personnel. If the sale is not made, it is still possible to retain the applicant's good will, and surely from the point of view of public relations, the good will of one person may be as important as that of another.

Human relations with respect to employment are usually pretty well organized in the larger companies, and letters play their part in the program. In these companies a Personnel Manager or Director conducts the interviews and writes such letters as are considered necessary or desirable. Of course, he may have one or more assistants, but they all work toward the same end —to make the applicant feel that the company appreciates his interest, and to handle the application in such a manner that goodwill is created. Even if the company is small and has no personnel department, some individual, on a part-time assignment, is filling the shoes of an Employment Manager. He may be the head of the business, a bookkeeper, or any other worker with the delegated responsibility, but his functions and duties are no different from those who give full time to employment.

Naturally, the person looking for a job is more or less on the defensive, and if he has been rudely received other places, he is quite likely to have a chip on his shoulder. To handle him tactfully is a delicate job for which some people are better qualified than others. This is especially true of the letters written to the applicant, as there must be nothing in them that might cause ill will, or bring trouble back to the company. On the other hand, if these letters are friendly and encouraging, they may win goodwill that could prove fruitful at some later time.

Kinds of letters used. The following letter-uses are not intended to apply to the applicants for work in a factory or plant. Such prospective employees are usually hired or rejected "on the spot," and the decision is made by the foreman or superintendent. However, if an application form is filled out and left for future disposition, the would-be worker is entitled to a written notice if the decision is unfavorable. The information needs to be worded just as carefully as the notice sent to an office or sales applicant. We admit that this courtesy is not always extended; in fact, it is probably the exception rather than the rule. But mere frequency of a fault in business practice does not in any way justify it.

The first of the letters used in connection with employment is quite often written by the applicant: either in answer to an "ad," or because he has selected the company as a place where he would like to work. Strictly speaking, the application letter is not a form of business correspondence, although it may serve the purpose of benefiting business by bringing applicant and company together. In many cases, however, the job-hunter simply calls at the employment office, and the contact begins with the interview.

If the first interview develops the certainty that the applicant is not to be hired, the employment routine stops right there. Tactfully but plainly, the applicant should be told that the decision is unfavorable; it's an injustice to let him go away thinking he has a good chance of getting the job. However, this still permits a business courtesy that will help to retain goodwill:

> Send a letter to the rejected applicant, thanking him for having
> called, and wishing him good fortune in finding a job.

Assuming that the applicant passes the first interview, the second step is usually to have him fill out the company form that supplies information needed, a record of past jobs, and the names of people to whom the company may write as references. Very few employment managers hire "on sight." There may be others that they hope to interview for a particular position, and they wish to guard against the dangers of a first impression. A valuable opinion of the applicant may be gained, too, from the neatness and accuracy with which the form is filled out. Hence, with the question of employment not settled, another form of business courtesy may be rendered:

> Send a letter to the applicant still under consideration, saying
> that the company appreciates his interest, and that he will be
> notified as soon as possible whether or not he will be hired.

Often it happens that the person applying for work has brought a letter of introduction from some other businessman, from a teacher or minister, or from some other individual who thinks he has an "in" with the employment manager. In such a situation, common courtesy again comes to the front with a suggestion:

> Send a letter to the individual making the introduction, thanking him for his interest, and assuring him that the "candidate" will receive special consideration.

With the application form on file, the next step is to make use of it. Certain information is required from the persons whose names were given as references, and from the companies listed as previous places of employment. The problem in either case is to get *all the facts,* and not a build-up for the applicant with the worst side of the story withheld. The letters written for these purposes are not special business courtesies, but the way they are worded may decide the result. Anyway, two jobs are at hand:

> Send a letter to one or more of the places where the applicant has worked—preferably addressed to an official—asking in confidence a frank opinion of his ability and character.
>
> Send a letter to those given as references, trying to get an impartial evaluation. This is difficult, since the applicant has given the names of people he is sure will speak only well of him.

There are, of course, other sources of information the employment manager can use, and he may turn to them if the position to be filled is considered important:

> Send a letter to the Dean of Men at the applicant's college, asking for a report on his studies, activities, and conduct. Or, the letter might go to the Principal of his high school, the Minister of his church—or to both.

Once the decision is made—to hire or not to hire—the applicant should be notified. If he is to be hired, the word may reach him by telephone, telegram, or by letter. If not, the letter is adequate. Here, unfortunately, is where Courtesy usually stubs her toe. The application is left in the file, and the applicant is left in doubt. Eventually he realizes that he is not getting the job, but the fact that he was kept in the dark is irritating—goodwill is lost. In keeping with good human relations, the employment manager has another obligation:

Send a letter to the successful applicant, congratulating him and saying when to report. Or...

Send a letter to the rejected applicant, trying not to discourage or offend him. This, too, is difficult, but it can be done.

You might think that the cycle of employment letters is now complete, but there remains at least one more important step. The first day on a new job is always the hardest, with new people to meet, new policies to learn, new methods to master. One thing may help to cushion the adjustment:

Send a letter of welcome to the new employee, signed by the president. As a matter of routine, this message should be delivered the morning of the first day by a messenger—or mailed by special delivery to the employee's home.

The above, then, are some of the most important letters the employment manager may write as his contribution to friendly public relations. Some are necessary to the handling of the application; others are just acts of courtesy that help to win goodwill.

Examples. The letters below are typical of the kinds used by the modern personnel director to cover the situations mentioned. None of them need be long, or take much time to dictate. When one proves to be adequate, it may become a standard to follow, and can be used over and over again without revision.

When First Impression Is Negative

Dear Mr. Doe:

Thanks for calling on us yesterday about employment. It was nice of you to think of our company as a place where you would like to work.

We are sorry that we could not offer you any encouragement, but this is no reflection on your attitude or ability, and we are sure that you will find a place where you can demonstrate your worth.

You know the work needs of different companies are never the same. Your problem is to find the place that *fits* your combination of experience and training—as of course you will.

The best of fortune to you, both in finding the right job, and in making the most of it.

Sincerely,

The aim of a letter such as the above is two-fold: to remove any resentment the applicant might have toward the company, and to offer the encouragement that she may need. That second objective is not so much a business necessity as a moral obligation held by any person who handles employment. Of course, if the applicant is left feeling good toward the company, a benefit to human relations is also gained.

When the Decision Is Pending

Dear Mr. Doe:

We appreciate the time you took yesterday to fill out our application for employment. The fact that you were asked to do so is evidence of the good impression you made in our little visit together.

Of course, you realize that filling out the blank does not mean for sure that you will be hired, but it does mean that we will give you every possible consideration. Also, if the job does not work out this time, we will still have a record of your experience and training when something else turns up.

Because of the importance of the position for which you are being considered, and the fact that other applications must be studied along with yours, it will be about two weeks before we can give you the final decision.

In the meantime, thanks for coming in to see us.

Sincerely,

There is no problem at all in dictating a letter like the one you have just read, and the reaction of the recipient is sure to be good. It tells him that the filling out of the application was not a mere formality, or an excuse for getting rid of him; also, he learns that the company is systematic in handling details of employment. Another purpose accomplished is paving the way for a possible rejection, so that the applicant will not feel so discouraged in the event he doesn't get the job.

As previously stated, if the applicant brought a letter of introduction, the personnel man now has another letter to write. He usually has several versions already prepared to fit different situations, as the introduction may have come from a friend, a business or professional man, a dealer, or just from some other company. Here is what might be said in two of these cases:

When an Individual Makes the Introduction

Dear Colonel Doe:

It was good of you to send young Perkins in to see us. Many of our best employees owe their jobs to people like yourself who take a friendly interest in our company. You can be sure that, with your stamp of approval, this lad will receive very special consideration.

In the event that we are unable to find an opening now that would challenge your protégé, we will surely keep his application in mind for a future possibility.

Thanks again for your cooperation, which we are very happy to regard as evidence of your goodwill.

                                                                        Sincerely,

Dear Colonel Doe:

It was good of you to send young Perkins in to see us. Many of our best employees owe their jobs to people like yourself who take a friendly interest in our company. Please always feel free to recommend any person of whom you approve, as we value your judgment highly.

As it happens, we had nothing to offer Mr. Perkins yesterday, but we did make some suggestions that may lead to his employment elsewhere.

Thanks again for your cooperation, which we are very happy to regard as evidence of your goodwill.

                                                                        Sincerely,

When a Company Makes the Introduction

Gentlemen:

A lad named Perkins called on us yesterday, saying you had given him a list of good companies to check about employment. We consider it a fine compliment that you included us in the list.

Mr. Perkins told us he had held a temporary position with your company, and he seemed quite eager that we should investigate his record while with you. Of course, we would have done this, except that there just wasn't any job open for which he could be considered.

Nevertheless, it speaks very well for the good feeling between our two companies that you tried to give us a new employee. We thank you for doing this, and shall do as much for you when the opportunity develops.

                                                                        Sincerely,

The letter sent to companies where the applicant has worked is more difficult to write. Even if an employee has been discharged for some good reason, the average personnel manager hates to tell the truth—it goes against the grain to "kick a fellow when he is down." Unless the letter can in some way break through this barrier of compassion, the reply is quite likely to be noncommittal, and of no value to the company that wants the facts.

Certain companies send out a questionnaire, and sometimes request a letter, too, but the reception is not always favorable. It seems an imposition to ask a busy man in some other company to take the time and trouble to answer a lot of questions. Since no two men are likely to interpret a questionnaire in the same way, the answers to a specific question are hard to compare. A short letter that puts the shoe on the other fellow's foot—asking him to be as frank as he would want the writer to be with him—is more likely to produce a fair and impartial report.

Asking Former Employer for Information

Gentlemen:

John Doe, a former employee of yours, has applied to us for a job in our bookkeeping department, and we will greatly appreciate your frank opinion as to his ability and conduct.

Probably, what we are after all adds up to answering one question: Was your experience with Mr. Doe such that you would be glad to hire him again?

Knowing by reputation the high standard of your personnel, we think anyone considered good enough for your organization is plenty good enough for us.

On the other hand, should there be some reason why this applicant is not likely to make good with us, it is far better for him not to start him out, as nothing is more damaging to a man's morale than to fail on a job.

So, as a favor to him as well as to us, won't you please give us the information you would want if you were now in our shoes? Anything you say will be strictly in confidence, and we shall be very happy to do as much for you when our positions are reversed.

Sincerely,

If the preceding letter is tough to write so that the truth will be obtained, the one for securing full information from a character reference is even tougher. Obviously, the applicant has offered only the names of people he is sure will say nice things about him. He has probably gone to the trouble of finding out if the opinion will be in his favor *before* he supplies the name. This, indeed, puts the writer "behind the eight-ball," and for that reason many personnel managers do not even bother to follow up these character references, unless they have some friendly relationship with one or more of the references.

The chief hope, it seems, in this predicament is to put the request in such a way that the reader feels he would be unfair to the applicant and himself by giving a distorted report. In some cases, this appeal works; in some, it does not. For lack of a better one, it has to be used.

Asking Character Reference for Information

Dear Mr. Doe:

It seems that Fred Jones leans heavily on your judgment, for he has given your name as that of one who will help me decide whether or not it is best for him to go to work for our company.

First, I will place my cards on top of the table, and then ask for yours. Fred strikes me as a young man who may make a name for himself in some company, and in fairness to him I would not want to employ him unless what we have to offer *fits* his pattern of abilities, his disposition, and what he really *likes* to do.

It is a great injustice to hire a young man with some doubt of his making good, and then have to let him go later. I know you wouldn't want that to happen to Fred.

Now, that's how *I* feel—and I very much need to know what *you* can add so that the right decision will be made.

Will you do me the favor—and Fred the favor—of telling me what you know about this young man? Particularly, will he be happy working on a routine job? Is he dependable? Are his friends a *help* to him? Would *you* hire him if you were in my place?

Please be assured that everything you say will be considered confidential. All we are after is to put our two older heads together and come up with what is best for Fred.

Thanks, Mr. Doe, for your help. I shall hope in some way to have the privilege some day of doing as much for you.

Sincerely,

A much easier letter for the personnel manager to write is the one to an individual *not* named by the applicant as a work or character reference. In this situation, the man to whom the letter goes has no personal obligation toward the applicant, although he may still be reluctant to give a detrimental opinion. Here, for example, is how a letter might be written to a former teacher or principal of the applicant:

Checking the Applicant's School Record

Dear Miss Doe:

I know you must be busy with the new school term just starting, but I have a favor to ask which I hope is not too great an imposition.

Sally Smith, who graduated from your fine high school two years ago, would like a secretarial job with our company. You can help me a lot in deciding what our reply should be.

I can't think of any individual so well qualified to know the real ability and character of Miss Smith as the Principal of her high school. You have watched her in and out of the classroom for four long years, and indeed your opinion should be absolutely impartial.

Of course, there is also the question of her work as a student, although we are not so narrow-minded as to think high grades are all that counts in determining the fitness of an applicant.

Miss Doe, I don't want to hire Sally Smith unless the association will work out right for her and our company. I very much need your impartial judgment. Won't you please drop me a line during the next few days, telling what you think we should know about this young lady?

It will all be treated in confidence—and my appreciation will be great.

Sincerely,

When the final decision is made, only one of two letters is needed. The applicant gets the job, or he does not; but in either case, he should be told. There is no doubt about sending the good news if the decision is favorable; but even if it's negative, the company owes the applicant the courtesy of a letter.

Telling Applicant to Report

Dear Mr. Doe:

You win. Your application for the position in our Advertising Department has been accepted. Can you report for work Tuesday morning at eight-thirty, September 17th?

It will interest you to know that you are getting this job in competition with 38 other applicants, a vote of confidence which I know will challenge you to prove we picked the right man.

Sincerely,

Giving Applicant the Bad News

Dear Mr. Doe:

I promised to let you know when a decision had been reached about the position in our Advertising Department. This happened yesterday.

Picking the right man out of 39 applicants was not easy, and I want you to know that you were one of four after all the others had been eliminated. However, the final choice was an older man who had had considerable experience in writing our type of copy.

Otherwise, everything about your application was fine, and it would please you a lot to read all the complimentary things that some very important people said about you.

With your permission, we will keep your application in our active file, looking forward to some other opening that may develop.

Thanks, Mr. Doe, for your interest. I predict considerable success for you in the business world.

Sincerely,

The last letter of the series is the all-important message of welcome received by the applicant the first day on his now job. The length may vary according to the set-up of the organization. There is certain information about the rules and policies of the company that the new employee needs to know. It may be given to him personally by the personnel manager—the best way when expedient—or included in the letter of welcome. But the primary purpose is to make the individual feel at home—to ease the shock of that first difficult day when everything seems strange, and the simple things appear complex.

Dear Miss Doe:

As president of the company of which you are now a very important part, I extend a hearty welcome and the hope that you will like all of us as much as I am sure we are going to like you.

Today will be the hardest you will ever spend in our organization. I know that is true, because I still remember my first day on my first job. Things will seem strange, and some of the work you are asked to do will seem much more difficult than it really is.

However, there isn't a worker in our office who doesn't want to be your friend, and help you get adjusted to the job. If you have questions to ask, see Mr. Jones. He is a lot more interested in you now as a member of our business family than when he hired you.

You are going to enjoy your work here, Miss Doe; more, I think, than you can possibly realize as a beginner. Our company is the biggest and best of its kind in the world, and that's something for you to be proud of. We work as a team, and not as individuals, and everybody in your department *wants* you to make good.

What may be even more important to you, and to your parents, is that you'll find things around our office pretty much as in your own home. It's a fine place for a young lady to be—with all the consideration and courtesies you have the right to expect.

So congratulations, and my best wishes! There are lots of others who wanted your job. I know you feel challenged—and will give your best.

Sincerely,

A letter such as this one signed by the company's president, is a great morale-builder, and it arrives at the time when the new employee most needs encouragement. The attitude of a worker throughout his whole period of employment may be influenced by his experiences the first day. He reads the letter, and he takes it home to the family. It is a simple, easily tendered business courtesy that should never be omitted in the letter program.

Letters of application. Whether or not a Handbook of Business Letters should pause to discuss the letters written by individuals seeking employment is a question of some doubt. Businessmen do not write these letters—they *read* them. On the other hand, the application letter does serve a business purpose, because it brings together the company which may need a worker and the worker who does want a job. For the benefit of those in business who are not employers, it will do no harm to pass along a few helpful suggestions.

1. Do not waste the time of a business executive—or your own—answering an "ad" about a job, unless what you have to offer the company *matches* the specifications listed.

It may be tempting to the person badly in need of work to disregard facts mentioned in the "ad," in the hope that a letter may make the sale in spite of these deficiencies, but the chances of success are not one in ten thousand. If the advertisement reads, "Man not over 30, with college education," it does not open the gate to a person 40 years old who didn't finish high-school. Unless the individual fits the pattern of the job, the finest letter ever written would no doubt be futile.

2. The application letter is one evidence of the writer's ability. It is a *sample* of his work, and he is sure to be judged by the care and intelligence with which the job is done.

This fact seems to be overlooked frequently by job hunters. They don't put their best foot forward. The letter asking for the interview is dashed off with an inane disregard of appearance, spelling, and correct English. Sometimes it is written with a pencil on soiled paper—with fingerprints for added decoration. How any person could expect to make a favorable first impression with such a letter is difficult to understand. A letter asking for a job is a *sales* letter—perhaps the most important ever to be mailed by the writer.

3. A few employment managers like to receive letters written in longhand, but the great majority prefer them typed. If the applicant is forced to use a pen, great care should be taken to write plainly. A letter hard to read goes into the wastebasket. That's where it belongs.

If you feel inclined to argue about the last assertion, consider the position of the man in the big company who gets letters asking for employment. At times, he is literally beset with them. They swarm in upon him in every mail. Why should he extend the courtesy of trying to read a sloppily prepared letter, when the writer himself was discourteous in making it so hard to read?

4. The problem of attracting special attention is very great in the application letter. If the writer is able to make his letter favorably different from the others, he has given himself an advantage.

Any businessman who handles application letters knows how much they follow the same old groove. They start with "The writer would like to apply for a position with your company," or "With reference to your advertisement in this morning's *Star,* the writer wishes to apply for said position." Then they follow with a monotonous description of personal characteristics, jobs previously held, educational institutions attended, throw in some references, and end with, "Hoping to receive the courtesy of an interview," or something equally as colorless. Naturally, any executive is bored with reading these letters, and turns with relief to one which is done in a more interesting style.

5. As is the case in all types of sales letters, the person applying for a job should avoid generalities, and try to advance specific points to his credit.

Just to state that you graduated from the University of Illinois means nothing. The fact becomes more interesting if you say, "During my four years at the University of Illinois, my lowest grade was B. I won varsity letters in football and track, was captain of the debating team my senior year, and the president of my fraternity, Chi Psi." Those are *reasons* why the reader of the application letter should be interested—actual *proofs* of outstanding accomplishment.

6. Attaching a picture of the writer is a good way to attract attention, since it helps the reader of the letter to visualize the individual and catch some idea of his personality.

The picture used need not be an expensive or large photograph; a small snapshot in some informal pose is much more effective. It costs very little to have "glossies" made from a negative, and one attached to the letter will surely be a point in its favor.

7. Don't try to describe your history since birth; concentrate on a few points especially in your favor, and leave the rest of the story for the interview.

A good way to avoid the necessity of a long two or three page letter, is to prepare an information sheet that gives the details of education, age, experience, and the like, and save two or three of the strongest points about yourself to include in the letter. Thus, the letter first wins the attention of the reader, after which he can turn to the information sheet for additional details.

8. The principles of good letter-carpentry are just as important in the preparation of an application letter as in any other form of written salesmanship. The old formula of the Star, the Chain, and the Hook, is the one to follow.

The foregoing suggestions are by no means the whole of the story, but the person who tries them will soon find that his application letters are having a better "pull" than before. Employment managers are human and react like anybody else to an approach that is interesting, convincing, and different from the daily run-of-the-mill. Actually, there is no reason why any individual should have a feeling of inferiority or dread in asking for a job. The man who reads the letter is a buyer of work hours; the man who writes it has work hours for sale. It is a fifty-fifty proposition, like any other business deal.

A few good examples. Each of the following application letters won an interview for the writer. That is all that any similar letter may hope to accomplish. It has done its job if the writer is called to the company office to meet the employment manager. Some people are good at getting interviews, but poor, unfortunately, when it comes to taking advantage of them, but that is a problem in personal selling, and need not be discussed in this Handbook.

Here is an application letter written by a young lady in Atlanta, Georgia, to a paper mill. It won an interview—and she got the job!

Gentlemen:

I figured it out this way:

(1) Every firm uses one or more stenographers. They are, so to speak, "Standard equipment" in every office.

(2) Most firms have occasional use for a commercial artist to illustrate a product, to design a label or package, to sketch an attention-getter for a sales letter, etc.

(3) A stenographer who can do commercial art work should be valuable to her employers in a number of ways, especially in connection with sales work.

So I learned shorthand and typewriting, and combined this with commercial art training.

For some two years or more I have done most of the art work for the Blank Rubber Company of this city, filling out my time by writing sales letters.

I could continue to do their work, but the fact that my father is one of the department heads places me at a disadvantage so far as advancement is concerned. Also, I believe that a connection with another firm would broaden my experience and make me more efficient.

I am twenty-one years old and have a high-school education.

I am what might be called an "experienced beginner," and have no exaggerated ideas as to what I should expect as a starting salary.

If you believe it possible that you could find a place for me in your organization, I will appreciate an opportunity to show you samples of my work, and to give you any information you may wish.

Please do tell me when I may see you.

> Yours very truly,

The foregoing letter is in no sense remarkable, but it does reveal an individual intelligent enough to plan her education to fit a specific business purpose. Furthermore, it does not bore the reader with a long drawn-out exposition of details. It is certainly a far better application letter than the average ones received by those who "hire and fire."

The next letter was sent by a young man to the managers of 25 large hotels. It produced several interviews—and the job he wanted. It is done in a simple, natural style, sure to impress more favorably than the typical stilted messages frequently mailed by job-hunters.

Dear Mr. Doe:

My name is Smith—William Smith. I am itching to work in your hotel.

I am 23 years old, six feet tall, and run to the lean side with a weight of only 150 pounds. For the past four years I have been connected with the Blank Feed Company. General office work, advertising service, and some selling have taken most of my time there.

My record is okay plus. You can verify that. Telephone Mr. A. B. Jones, Personnel Director, and he will tell you it is so.

I have had considerable training in connection with conventions and much of my life to date has been spent in hotels. I know the atmosphere. I know people. What I don't know about the hotel business is plenty, but it is nothing that hard work and study will not supply.

I am not afraid of hard work. I like it.

All my life I have had the secret desire to be in the hotel business. All I want is a toe-hold. I'll do the climbing after that.

I have no high-hat ideas about salary. I wouldn't be worth much at first. A man must *prove* his worth as he goes along. I want to start on that basis.

Will you dig up some place for William Smith to hang up his hat, roll up his sleeves, and show his stuff? Give me just that chance, and you have my promise you will never be sorry.

Tell me when I can come and talk to you. It's the biggest favor I have ever asked.

Sincerely yours,

The young lady who prepared the following application letter understood the formula of the Star, the Chain, and the Hook. She gets quick attention, using a beloved name as the lure, arouses interest and desire, and then closes with a positive, confident request for action. Attached to the page in the upper right-hand corner is a small picture. She is plainly dressed, looks pretty and intelligent, and has a slight smile for the reader—the kind of a person businessmen like to see in their employ. And here is her letter!

Dear Mr. Doe:

Why did Abraham Lincoln win rail-splitting contests so easily?

You've heard the reason: He knew exactly where to place his wedge to give his blows the most power. The scene of Lincoln's youth—Springfield, Illinois—is where I was born, where I lived through the school years. When Lincoln won these contests, he was the same age as I am now; and I, too, want to enter a log-splitting contest.

I have a good, strong wedge and a sturdy hammer, but I need a log.

In the first place, I want to get into dress designing or any allied field of women's ready-to-wear. I have creative ability which has been fostered by art courses—water-color, life, art appreciation, clay modeling stage and costume design, one summer at the Traphagen School of Dress Design in New York City. I taught stage and costume design for one year.

In 1961, I received a degree in English from the University of Chicago. Since then I have been molding my wedge: working as a stenographer until I am now capable of answering letters independently.

This, then, is my wedge into the field of women's wear: to be a stenographer to a buyer, to a designer of clothing or window displays; to the art staff, or to an advertising director. Your store and its opportunities can be my log.

Will you let me enter the contest?

You may reach me by calling Englewood—0000. Or, just jot down the time you'll see me on the postal card I'm enclosing, and toss it in tonight's mail.

Sincerely yours,

He was too old to hire. A very appealing letter asking for work is one written by an older man who refused to accept the verdict that he was ready for rocking chair and slippers. His problem was one faced by many an older man in business. Perhaps this letter may suggest a way out for someone else whose "gray hair tops gray matter."

Gentlemen:

Will you give work to a man aged fifty=two?

In December, I lost a job as Advertising and Sales Promotion Manager. The reason did not concern my ability or character.

A shock came when applications for other positions were turned down with the comment "too old."

A man in perfect health, with twenty-five years experience and a very special ability for advertising and sales work was to stay idle and watch the "cubs" go by—perhaps to become a shabby down-at-heel, cadging nickels and chased by cops.

I was beginning to see *red* and then I saw the truth. No real advertising man need ever be out of work. He certainly should be able to sell his services.

That is why I am establishing my own business, to supply real, honest advertising, sales promotion and research service to non-conflicting clients for a reasonable monthly retainer.

This service covers every phase of sales publicity and research. No assignment is too small or too large to be given proper attention. I can work with your executives, advertising agency —or alone.

And as far as age goes, what does it matter as long as gray hair tops gray matter?

I ask *your* help. May I have a talk with you?

You can leave a message at PEnn 0-0000, or write—and I'll come running.

Cordially,

P.S. This letter is multigraphed on plain paper and mailed in a plain envelope because I won't run into debt.

The application letters you have just read have at least two common characteristics: first, the approach is out-of-the-groove, and therefore interesting; second, they reveal the personality of a pleasing person. The writers just *talk* to their readers about their problems and their ambitions, and that is the secret of their pulling power.

Pinch-hitting for the job-hunter. The businessman who writes a letter of introduction for someone seeking employment is in no different position than if the latter "rolls his own." He must strive to place his candidate before the reader in such a way as to arouse interest. Here is an example:

Dear Mr. Doe:

The bearer of this letter, Eddie Smith, has one trait which I believe will carry him far in business . . .

He is burning with ambition.

Having been a personnel director, and having observed thousands of young men—green as grass and just starting out—I decided long ago that the first essential to success is the *craving* to be a "somebody."

Eddie has it.

I don't know a darned thing about his specific abilities—where he is weak or where he is strong. But he has been working around our office for about six months or so, and I have noticed that he is willing to do anything for anybody—always with a smile.

He told me that he was going to see you about a job—wanted me to play a blue chip for him.

I do believe that Eddie will tackle any assignment you give him with more than the average get-up-and-go.

He *wants* to get ahead—so I think he *will*.

Cordially,

SALES MANAGER LETTERS

SALES MANAGER LETTERS

1. Importance to Business

Between the devil and the deep blue sea. The best sales supervision is that which takes place in the field. Since the assumption is that the sales manager knows more about the company products and how to sell them than any of his men, it must follow that he should be able to give them more help personally than by mail. But no sales manager can spend all of his time out of the office, and even if this were possible, only a small part of it could be spent with any one of his men. Thus, he is forced to do most of the job with letters.

In facing this fact, however, many a sales executive finds himself between the devil and the deep blue sea. He must either furnish the salesman with more letters than he will want to read, or take the chance of letting him run amuck for lack of proper motivation and control. One fact that adds to the problem is that the average salesman gets a vast amount of mail from other departments and individuals in the company. After a hard day's work, he is expected to open a bulky envelope and wade through a lot of correspondence that he often feels has little connection with sales; and sometimes, unfortunately, he is correct.

The person who has never worked as a salesman probably does not realize how many letters flow from the office to the field, and apparently some sales managers are just as much in the dark or they would do some constructive streamlining. This does not mean that necessary letters can be omitted; it means that the salesman should not be bothered with details which could be handled just as well in some other way.

A tabulation made by one company. In an effort to find out just how many letters the salesmen of his company were expected to read, the vice-president of one large corporation had them counted for one week. The actual figures were as amazing to him as they probably will be to you:

Number of salesmen receiving mail 900
Letters sent to them in one week . . . 23,405
Most letters received by one man 87
Fewest letters received by one man 19
Average number per man that week . . . 26

Whether or not the above figures furnish a fair estimate of what goes on in other companies we do not know, but for the organization with this many salesmen they no doubt come close. Hence, we must concede that a serious encroachment is taking place on time that could better be devoted to selling.

Obviously, where the problem does exist the solution seems clear. First, some form of control should be established over the salesmen's mail to keep the amount of it no greater than is reasonable and necessary. Members of other departments should not be allowed to write to salesmen unless the necessity is understood and approved. Second, writers in the sales department should take pains to make sure that their own letters are necessary, and promote the general objective of using the salesman's time to the best possible advantage. Third, letters used to motivate salesmen—inspire them to greater effort—should be so constructive and interesting that the salesmen *want* to read them.

The sales manager who assumes that this third point does not apply to his own letters and bulletins might very easily be fooling himself. It is no exaggeration to say that many men in the field—perhaps the majority of them—do not look with special favor on the word-lashings they get regularly from headquarters. They are meant to inspire but they only *tire*. They call on the salesman to give the old college "try," but they don't include the *"how."* Too often, the salesman's reaction is something like this: "Another shot in the arm from the Boss! He thinks I need a sermon once a week." He may quickly scan the message to see if it contains any fact he must know, but that's about all the attention it gets.

Of course, these disparaging remarks do not, by any means, apply to all sales-manager letters meant to inspire. None need wear the shoe unless it fits. But let's face it—anyone knows that salesmen in general look with cynicism on some of the letters they receive. For this attitude they are not entirely to blame. They are tired of "pep" talks when what they need are solid, workable sales ideas. They have been getting the sauce without the meat. The sales manager who supplies *both* is the one whose letters are read.

How the letters may be classified. Practically all of the letters mailed to salesmen serve one of two general purposes—to challenge or to control. From the point of view of better business correspondence, you are more concerned with the first group than the second. Letters to control include all the matters of a routine nature that must be planned and supervised—in them, the salesman is told what to do and how. Letters to challenge are just what the word implies. If successful, they inspire greater effort—produce more sales. They include letters of constructive criticism, since a man may be challenged to correct a fault as well as to multiply a virtue. Of course, some sales manager letters do a double job; they tell the salesman what to do, and make him want to do it better than ever before.

As we have discovered in other sections of this Handbook, there is nothing about a generality to impress or challenge the reader of a business letter. This is perhaps even more true with respect to letters to salesmen than of any other type. Contrary to general opinion, the average salesman is not thin-skinned nor overly sensitive. He is a fighting man with plenty of scars. If he were squeamish and highly imaginative, he would listen to the objections of his prospect, and be swayed by them. Instead, he overrides objections. He has only one point of view—his own. The prospect should buy. His ego is strong, as it must be or he could not sell. He appreciates a compliment when he thinks it is sincere. He is *not* responsive to inspirational patter that merely says, "You can do it, old boy, you can do it."

Advantage of letters based on experience. The most effective letters to salesmen are written by individuals who have been through the fire themselves. The man who has rung doorbells, walked the streets with a sample kit, pleaded with merchants for orders, is the man who can talk the salesman's language. He knows from experience what he is talking about. He, too, has gone to a shabby hotel room at night, sat on a rickety chair, and opened the inevitable brown envelope from the home office. He knows the difference between real help and platitudes. This is not a treatise on personnel procedure, but it must be evident that the best-equipped sales managers come up from the ranks. There are exceptions to this rule, but they are only exceptions. The man who himself has sold is best able to tell others how to sell.

For example, the sales manager who wrote the following letter did not deal in generalities. He wanted to drive home one sales point—that every call made by a salesman costs the company money. He gave the exact figure to prove his point, but he didn't preach to his reader, or exhort him to "do better." He presented the facts, and let the salesman draw his own conclusions.

Dear J. D.

Suppose every one of your dealers had a ticket booth and cashier at his front door and required you to purchase admission. And suppose that admission cost you $8.85 plus 10% tax, or a total of $9.74.

If it were an actual cash outlay out of your own pocket, I'll gamble you would insist on your money's worth. "Buyer out," "Come back tomorrow," "Stocked," "Too busy," "Haven't received last order," "Turnover too slow," would fall on deaf ears. And, further, I'll gamble you would have a very definite message someone would have to hear; you would have a real proposition ready before you opened your pocketbook.

I am not putting a premium on the number of calls you make. But I do emphasize the necessity for making as many productive calls as possible—making every call count. A dealer sold today does not require your time later.

It costs this company just $9.74 to put you in a dealer's store; not for each order but for each call; just YOUR salary and expenses.

Our only possible dividend is an *order*.

Sincerely,

Selling the need for letters. The sales manager who dictated the following letter evidently believed that the best defense is to attack. Or it may be that the grumbling about letters on the part of some salesman had reached his ears. Anyway, he tries to make his men see the *reason* for letters—a smart move, but still not as good as making the letters so interesting that the salesman liked to get them.

To all SALESMEN:

During the war the boys in the front line used to feel that the general, remaining behind the lines, ordering them into combat, had a soft cinch, and did not appreciate their troubles.

Sometimes salesmen get to feeling the same way about their sales manager. We all think our own troubles are bigger than any one else's. We magnify our discouragement and forget that a sales manager has discouragements too, and that there are many times when he envies the salesman on the firing line who has only his own troubles to worry about.

No, this isn't written to take it out on you because I have troubles of my own, or because the Chief is egging me on to produce more sales. It is written to *help you* keep the right viewpoint about every letter that you get from the office. The object of every one of them is to HELP YOU.

The general is useless without the men in the field. And no one knows so well as he that no plan he makes can be successful unless he gives most careful thought and preparation toward giving his men all possible help in making the plan work.

The sales manager is in the same boat. He must have his men know that he is giving them all possible help; that he repeatedly goes to the front for them; that he is their friend in court, and will back them up to the limit in their hour of need.

And in doing that, he expects equal loyalty from his men. We are working together—each doing *his part of* the same job. How to help you is the biggest part of my work; and I think you fellows feel I'm trying hard to make good there.

Yours for real cooperation,

The foregoing letter is good enough, but a specific incident to prove a salesman should give careful attention to the letters he gets carries a lot more weight. Here's a sales manager who believes in putting teeth in every bite.

Dear John:

Sometimes, I wonder if you fellows in the field really read all of the letters I write to you. I'm not kidding myself about the answer, for I spent ten years of my life doing exactly what you are—and two of them in YOUR territory.

Anyway, let this be a lesson to you, my buckaroo!

Two months ago, I wrote to you about a company, Blank & Blank, which seemed to be doing a lot of business, and I suggested that a call might land you a nice order.

When none of your daily reports showed that this call had been made, I wrote again—and a third time just two weeks ago.

I wouldn't for the world want to jump to wrong conclusions, but there were only two things that might explain why you didn't see Blank & Blank; either you didn't read my letters, or you had lost faith in my nose for orders.

Anyway, we got an order yesterday from this company by mail, and it totalled $505.50. Of course, you'll get commission on this order, but a personal call—with all your persuasive power— might have doubled the size of it.

Yes, I know. Letters are a nuisance after a hard day's work. But it could cost you real dough not to read them carefully, as I'm sure it did in the case of Blank & Blank.

All of this is said in the best of spirits, old fellow. You know I appreciate your efforts, and anything I suggest is for your good as much as the company's.

Sincerely,

P.S. By the way, did you read *this* one?

"Don'ts" when writing to salesmen. One of the Sales Letter Bulletins distributed by the Dartnell Corporation of Chicago, listed ten "don'ts" for handling salesmen by mail. They are worthy of your consideration.

1. Don't pick on them [the salesmen]. If you must write unpleasantly, put it all in one letter.
2. Try to make the letter that your men will receive on a Monday morning as cheery and helpful as possible. Give them a running start for a big week.
3. Don't preach to your men. Teach as though you taught not.
4. Don't write unnecessary letters about trivial things and ask salesmen to answer them.
5. Don't be forever talking about what some other salesman did or is doing. It's just like talking about pies mother used to make.
6. Insist that every letter going to salesmen should pass over your desk. Otherwise, some sour bookkeeper may send a man a letter which will put him off his feed for a week.
7. Don't be forever telling the boys what you used to do when you were a salesman. They don't give a damn.
8. Praise for doing something well is usually more effective than bawling a man out for doing something wrong. This is especially true in correcting faults.
9. Don't write white-blooded letters to red-blooded salesmen. Put some pep and vinegar in them. Write to a man as though he sat across from you at lunch.
10. Whatever else you do, don't write when you are mad. Madness is a mild form of insanity. If you write at white heat you will surely regret it. Give your anger a chance to cool.

Although the above admonitions are quite sound, one fact needs to be remembered—and all great leaders recognize it. No "don't" or "do" can be made broad enough to cover all individuals. What can and should be said to one salesman, may be the wrong thing to say to another. Not that there is any logic in the notion that salesmen are different from other human beings—that they have to be coddled and handled with gloves. This is nonsense. Once in a while, one meets a salesman who seems to enjoy the pose of being temperamental, but it is only a pose. Men do differ in mental stability and emotional reactions, but this is true of all human beings—not just salesmen.

2. LETTERS OFFERING SPECIFIC SALES SUGGESTIONS

Ballast better than ballyhoo. The best letters to salesmen are those that do more than root for better performance; they carry to their readers specific information, ideas, or suggestions that can be *put to work*. We have small liking for the message that merely prods the salesman without showing one or more ways to "run faster." Surely, one of the obligations of any manager is to show HOW. No man in the field is assumed to know as much about selling as his manager. Why, then, should the latter not pass along the benefit of his knowledge and experience?

In the letter that follows, the importance of getting new accounts is given the spotlight, and then the salesman receives a *concrete suggestion* for doing the job—*concentrate on brewing demonstrations.*

Dear Larry:

You are running first in the current campaign, but I hope you won't let that go to your head. From what I hear from many of our other men, they are out to get your scalp. It won't surprise me if some of them start climbing up very close to first position. You'll have to work doggone hard to hold first place, but I'm counting on you to be there when the campaign is over.

New accounts are going to play a big part in winning, because additional new customers will help push up volume. Of course, converting split business into exclusive accounts will help tremendously too, but in the final analysis, you cannot deny the importance of those new accounts.

[Now comes the concrete suggestion]

Most of the men who have been doing exceptionally fine work in securing new business tell me they are making demonstrations frequently because they find that it helps not only to secure orders but to build steady business. I am passing this along to you because I believe that you, too, should be able to use this suggestion to good advantage.

Why not run a little two weeks' campaign of your own in which you concentrate all your time on brewing demonstrations? Instead of trying to sell by mere words, simply brew coffee with every prospect possible; emphasize that there is no obligation involved, and that you just want to show the kind of blends we are now producing.

There is no doubt in my mind but that the results you will secure will be beyond your own expectations. Try it and see.

Sincerely yours,

Illustrating what service means. One of the most frequently used words in business is *service,* and nobody questions its right to that prominence, but *service* is merely a generality unless explained and interpreted. You might write to ten salesmen about giving dealers better service, and no two of them would come up with the same notion of what you meant by service, since every individual defines a generality according to his own inclination and thinking. Sales manager H. N. Fisch knew better than to fall into that trap. Here's his letter—with *service* so clearly explained that no one could mistake his meaning.

Dear John:

Walking down the street with Abe Davis, who operates one of Fort Worth's finest exclusive men's stores, was Bill Morgan (not his real name). Abe said to Bill: "You know, Mr. Morgan, I have my house insured with your organization, and ten days ago that heavy wind we had blew several tiles off the roof. I've been forgetting to notify your office."

Bill said, "That's too bad."

Then Abe sort of stuttered a bit, and finally asked, "Well, whom should I call down there about it?"

And Bill replied, "Just call the complaint department."

What a splendid opportunity Morgan had to render a real service to one of his customers! And how he muffed it! Abe left an opening for Bill to say, "Well, Abe, let me make a note of that right away. Don't worry about it. I'll take care of it just as soon as I get back to the office."

But what did he do? He simply referred Abe to the complaint department—after Abe had already said he had been forgetting to report the damage.

That is what we mean when we talk about service in selling. Service isn't giving a dealer an extra discount. It isn't giving him thirty or sixty days extra dating. It's doing the things for him that are *not included* in the regular duties of selling. Service is the first person in the trinity of modern selling.

To increase your sales, John, observe and watch for every opportunity for *Service*.

Servingly yours,

Suggesting a call-back. In Section 9, we put our heads together to see how lost business might be regained. We agreed that it is sometimes easier to revive an old customer than to get a brand new one. The truth of this contention is demonstrated in a sales bulletin used by the Sinclair Oil Company.

The Lost Legion

Business is a battle. During the past year you have called on a lot of accounts from whom you secured no business. They are the lost soldiers of your industrial army. Why not make a list of each of these accounts which might again be open for business during the coming year, and go after it?

The sales manager of a large concern tells of a salesman who had made a splendid showing during a sales contest. After it was over, he wrote his manager, "I have scratched the bottom of the barrel to make a showing in this contest. There simply isn't any more business in sight right now."

No sooner had the letter been mailed than a prospect called the salesman, asking him to come and see him. The salesman had tried hard to sell this prospect during the contest but had been turned down so emphatically that the account seemed hopeless.

But the prospect had been thinking over some things the salesman had said. Now he had gotten around to where he gave the salesman another hearing, and an order.

That gave the salesman an idea. He called on all the prospects who had turned him down during the contest and soon had a nice month's business booked.

One of the oldest and most successful oil companies used the following plan for years. Every six months the accounting department made a list of all accounts who hadn't bought anything for two years. Then the salesmen went out and tried to get them started again.

Because an account was lost last year, or turned you down on your last call, doesn't mean that it may not be available in the future.

Perhaps, because of your former experience, you can play your cards a little more intelligently this time—and present just the argument that will land him.

Very truly yours,

Emphasizing planned use of time. Getting on an elevator the other day, a businessman said to the operator, "Good morning, Tom, and how are you today?" The aged elevator man, with a broad smile, replied, "Well, I feel mighty good. The Lord has given me a *new* day, and I mean to make the most of it. Yes, sir, old Tom has a new day for himself, just the same as everybody else."

In his remark was a suggestion often used by sales managers in letters to their men—forget the past, take the time that is yours, and plan your work to make every hour as productive as possible. It's a good suggestion, too, for many salesmen jump around like grasshoppers—"Good on distance, but hell on direction." If the salesmen are willing to profit by good advice, the two letters below bring them constructive help.

Dear Al:

How would you handle your deposits in a bank that goes broke every day?

If you put $864 in a bank every morning, and if every night when that bank closed its doors. the president took whatever amount you had not used during the day and put it in his own pocket . . .

WHAT WOULD YOU DO?

Why, you would draw out every cent just before time to close, wouldn't you?

Well, you have just such a bank and its name is the "Time Bank." Every morning the Time Bank credits you with 86,400 seconds. Every night it takes away from you every second that you have not used during the day. It carries over no balance— it accepts no "I'll do it tomorrow" checks. Each day it opens a new account for you with a deposit of 86,400 seconds.

IF YOU FAIL TO USE THE DAY'S DEPOSIT, THE LOSS IS YOURS. There is no going back. There are no left-over seconds to be credited to your tomorrow's account. You've got to use up all of the 86,400 seconds on the day they are deposited for you.

BUT HERE IS WHAT YOU CAN DO—

You can begin to draw out and use your 86,400 seconds on any day that you wish. Even though you have wasted yours—even though you have never cashed in on one cent's worth of time— still you can start tomorrow and you'll find the cashier of the Time Bank ready and willing to pay you money for each and every minute you give him in exchange.

DON'T WASTE TIME, FOR TIME IS MONEY.

Yours sincerely,

The weakness in the foregoing letter—even though it dramatizes rather well the abundance of a day's time—is that no concrete suggestions are offered to show the salesmen HOW to make the best use of the 86,400 seconds. George Hughes, writing for Deltox Rug Company, is more specific.

Friend Jimmie:

Ever since Tuesday I've been a happy man.

For it was on Tuesday we received your first orders of the week— which proved that you had knocked Old Man Slump for a row. And the several orders you secured since then show that you have what I said in my last letter—a winning heart.

What pleased me more than anything else was that the dollar value of the orders you secured was far above the average For that you get a hearty slap on the back—and an invitation to get yourself a big Italian dinner in that old New Orleans restaurant we both know so well.

You remember the place. I certainly shall not forget it. The place where the waiter, when I asked for more dressing for my salad, told me: "You eat that salad the way she is fix. The chef he know better than you how to fix a salad." Remember?

Well, I remember the time we were in the midst of a seller's market, and could talk to buyers in much the same way.

Today, though, the better plan is to counsel with buyers. Show them why we feel certain lines will sell well for them. And indicate by everything we say and do that our sincere purpose is to do for them what we, were we in their shoes, would do for ourselves.

Tonight, Jimmie, when you return to your room, get out your book of customers and qualified prospects—and *plan for tomorrow*. Make a list of all the well-rated stores in New Orleans, and then decide on the order in which you will contact them tomorrow. This process—which I have mentioned many times before—will help you get a quick and profitable start in the morning.

Lay this letter on your dresser, so you won't forget.

More power to you!

(*No complimentary close*)

More calls per day. Closely allied to suggestions for planned use of time are those that remind the salesman how he can make the law of averages work for him. These letters point out that it takes a certain number of calls to get one order—that any man can increase his volume of sales by simply making more calls. This is true, but the lazy salesman likes to ignore it.

The following letter suggests ten calls each day—a reasonable quota.

Dear Jack:

I have just finished writing three pep letters, and have just finished tossing them all into the waste-basket.

I figure that soft soap and smooth talk from me won't help to pull you out of your sales slump. That's something you ought to talk over with yourself. And if you feel you need a lecture, then start in on yourself right away, because I don't want to lecture you—I want to help you.

Really, this should be our best season—but like any other time, we'll have to go after the business in order to get it. We know people are eating popcorn—we know it takes machines to pop the corn—we know some one has to sell the machines. That's our job. And we are going to do it.

You know, Jack, we have a successful distributor who says he never yet has failed to make a sale when he picked out, called on, and conscientiously worked on, ten good prospects.

So here is my suggestion. Every day without fail pick out ten good prospects, put the sales kit under your arm, and go after the orders—and remember that neither you nor I is going to be satisfied with anything less than that—ORDERS.

There is plenty of business waiting for us—let's *get* it.

Very truly yours,

[*A Dartnell presentation*]

And here's a second of the same type.

TO ALL SALESMEN:

An old plainsman once taught a young chap a lesson that would do a great many agents some good if they applied the principles of that lesson to their daily work. As the story goes, the young chap became anxious to hunt sage-hens after he noticed that the veteran of the plains returned with a full game-bag each evening.

Granting his request, the plainsman gave the enthusiastic but inexperienced youngster a gun the following day and directed him to one of the best hunting spots. Nothing was heard of him until he came plodding back to the ranch-house toward evening —tired, hungry, and empty-handed. He complained that he saw no game, salving his disappointment with what he considered a good alibi.

The experienced plainsman listened patiently, and then explained that the young hunter was at fault because he had showed a lack of intelligent aggressiveness. The young man was told to go out the next day and try disturbing each clump of sage-brush by walking through it.

Those directions were carried out, and the next evening found the hunter proudly exhibiting his game.

Of course, not every clump of sage walked through disclosed the presence of a sage-hen, but being a known haunt, it was merely a matter of *walking through enough of them* before finding a fowl.

Just so it is with prospects; see not just a FEW people, but LOTS of them. You can't walk through the sage-brush without finding a hen. And the more brush—the more hens.

Very sincerely yours,

Be sure the buyer understands. A lot of trouble could be spared their companies if salesmen would adhere to the suggestion offered in the following message. When a buyer gets his order and it isn't as he expected—when the terms turn out to be different from what he understood—the company is left holding the bag.

BE SURE THAT YOU UNDERSTAND EACH OTHER.

A clear-cut understanding in a business deal saves both time and money. Definiteness and frankness are necessary to conclude any sale in the right way.

We are constantly forced to write to salesmen asking them what was their understanding regarding certain deals. We constantly get letters from customers saying, "Your salesman told us we could do so-and-so."

The best salesman knows that the worst thing he can do is to assume a weak-kneed attitude with a buyer. There's nothing that creates confidence so quickly as to snap right out what your price is, what the terms are, and what your house will and won't do.

You don't have to take an apologetic attitude about anything. You are rendering your customer a service by calling on him. Every sale must bring a fair profit. There must be terms which must be respected. Then why be mealy-mouthed about it? Get your profit. Your trade knows you are not giving away goods.

When your customer mentions cheaper goods, tell him we can make them at half our price, if he doesn't want *quality*. If he makes a general statement about other prices, get something *specific*. Don't take generalities about prices, complaints, or anything else.

It's the easiest thing in the world to speak in generalities. Many a complaint or opposition to your proposal fades away when you ask for *facts*.

Never leave a customer in doubt as to what you or the house proposes to do. Never leave any part of a transaction up in the air.

Lay every card on the table. Be definite. Be frank. Be thorough.

Sincerely yours,

[*A Dartnell presentation*]

When the prospect says "not interested." Suggestions to offset objections are particularly valuable to salesmen. Your next exhibit is a letter which seeks to tell the salesman what to say when the only negative reason he can get out of the prospect is "not interested"—a difficult situation to overcome, because the statement can mean everything or nothing.

Dear Mike:

A new member of our sales organization was "talking shop" with me when I was spending a day in the field with him. "It's my first week out," he said, "and I haven't done so badly; but there's one thing that stumps me. What do YOU reply when the prospect says, 'I'm not interested'?" This is a problem that has floored many an oldster. Well, what DO you say?

The prospect who says, "Not interested," may really mean that YOU are not interesting. You have failed to dramatize your approach in a way that commands consideration.

"Not interested" is really no answer at all. That's why it is the most difficult of all responses to combat. It may be a cloak to disguise any one of a dozen more or less valid objections, such as, "I haven't the money," "I don't need it," or "I don't believe it will do what you claim."

"Not interested" is always an indication of weakness. The prospect is AFRAID to reveal the REAL reason for fear his objection will be broken down. Always counter with a question that can only be answered in the affirmative.

"Aren't you interested in having your business under complete control?" or "Wouldn't you like to know how to get the highest percentage of profit from your business?" have always proved effective for many of us in this business.

But, of course, the very best solution of the problem is to make your talk so INTERESTING that the prospect will have no chance to say, "I'm not interested."

Try out the suggestions I have given you. They have worked for me, and I am sure they will work for you.

Cordially,

How to overcome objection of "high price." Probably the most common obstacle confronting salesmen is the prospect's retort, "Oh, your stuff seems all right, but your price is too high." Either the objection must be removed, or the sale is sure to be lost. The letter below tries to tell the readers how this very important problem may be solved.

Dear Fellow-workers:

KNOW YOUR POTATOES.

The farm wagons stood in a public market. Both were loaded with potatoes in bags. A customer stopped before the first wagon.

"How much are potatoes today?" she asked the farmer's wife.

"Two-fifty a bag," the wife replied.

"Oh, my," protested the woman, "that is pretty high. I paid only two dollars for the last bag I bought."

" 'Tators has gone up," was the only thing the farmer's wife had to say.

So the housewife went to the next wagon and asked the same

question. But Ma McGuire "knew her potatoes." Instead of treating her customer with indifference, she replied:

"These are Wisconsin white potatoes, Madam. They are the best potatoes grown. In the first place, we only raise the kind with small eyes so that there will be no waste in peeling. Then we sort them by sizes. In each bag you will find a large size for boiling and cutting up; a medium size for baking. The baking size cook quicker and are all done at the same time, which means a big saving in electricity or gas. Then we wash all our potatoes clean before sacking them, as you can see. You can put one of these bags in your parlor without soiling the carpet—you don't pay for a lot of dirt. I'm getting $3.00 a bag for them—shall I put the bag in your car or deliver them?"

Ma McGuire sold *two* bags, at a higher price than her competitor had asked, in spite of the fact that the customer had refused to buy at the first wagon because she thought the price was "too high."

All of which proves that a customer's idea of price depends entirely on *ideas in his own mind*. When YOU put the right ideas there, the sale is not far away.

The more you know about what you are selling—regardless of whether it is some highly technical product or just potatoes—the better able you will be to overcome price objections. Customers should not be allowed to think that a price is too high. They won't think so if you know the fine points of what you are selling —as well as the farmer's wife knew the good points about her potatoes.

Study your product—then you can *sell* it.

Sincerely,

Ask him to buy it. It seems foolish that any salesman would talk to a prospect about his product or service and NOT ASK FOR AN ORDER. Nevertheless, there has never been a sales convention at which those attending were not reminded, "You can't get an order unless you ask for it." Perhaps it is a feeling of fear that makes the salesman hesitate. He has told his story, and now he is face to face with the decision. Unless the attitude of the listener has been encouraging, he hates to pop the question for fear of a negative answer.

Be that as it may, the letter that follows is built around the precept, "Ask and ye shall receive."

Dear Joe:

After calling on a butcher five or six times, a salesman selling a special meat cutter decided to give him a demonstration. The following conversation took place.

Salesman: It's a nice machine, isn't it?

Butcher: Yes.

Salesman: It saves time and labor, doesn't it?

Butcher: It sure does.

Salesman: Do you like it?

Butcher: Yes.

Salesman: It will be easy to keep clean.

Butcher: I think you're right.

The salesman continued to slice the meat without saying anything further. The butcher became impatient and asked if he might try to work the machine. The salesman let him do so, but was at the end of his rope. He felt no further on with the sale than when he had started his demonstration.

Finally, he asked, "If you like the machine, why not let me have the order?" To this, the butcher frankly replied, "You haven't asked me."

How many salesmen go out and call on prospects day after day, giving one talk after another, and never mention the order? You'd be surprised. Salesmen time and time again wail about the merits of their products—and never once ask for the order. The prospect listens politely and finally the interview ends with the salesman asking permission to come and tell his little story over again another day.

Fellows, the business is here. Somebody is going to ask for the order if you don't. When you tell your story and forget to ASK FOR THE ORDER, you are giving your competitor a chance to walk in on what is to him a "Cold Turkey Prospect," and he gets the order on his first call.

Beat him to it: ASK FOR THE ORDER.

Very truly yours,

So much for the sales manager letters that try to pass along specific help in getting the order. Of course, hundreds of other examples could be added to those you have just read, but the purpose of them all is to hand out tools with which the salesman may do his job better. They are not emotional in their appeal. They simply say, "Here is a good idea—USE it."

3. Inspirational Letters to Salesmen

They must be interesting. A great many letters to salesmen are purely inspirational in nature. The manager who uses this type of letter is content to leave more specific facts about selling to instructional bulletins, to sales meetings, and to personal conferences in field and office. In these particular messages he wants to get under the salesman's skin, to appeal to his better self, to challenge him to greater effort.

The tone of an inspirational letter must obviously be quite different from that of a factual letter. The former aims to stir the emotions of the salesman; to make him alert to his shortcomings, and eager to do better. The factual letter aims to make him think more intelligently about his sales efforts and provides him with actual ideas he can use to improve them. Both types can be effective, but the inspirational letter has one special obligation to meet. It *must be interesting.*

We have discussed the natural tendency of the average salesman to look with a cold and critical eye on his mail from the home office. He feels—sometimes rightfully—that much of it could be omitted, and that it is an imposition on his time to clutter his evenings with unnecessary correspondence. There is always the danger that a purely inspirational message will not be taken seriously—that it will be pushed aside as just another "pep talk."

The mention of this danger is not meant to imply that inspirational sales messages should be discarded. Not at all; but to do the job they must be bright and interesting, so that the salesman will really look forward to getting them—never fail to read them. This puts a premium on the skill of the sales manager which is not nearly so evident when he composes a brass-tack idea or a practical suggestion memo. In the latter case, he can be prosaic and still get attention. But not so in writing the inspirational letter. If dry and dull, it is tossed aside with a yawn or a shrug.

Some sales leaders have the gift of writing topnotch inspirational copy, just as some ministers are better able to inspire their congregations; some coaches better able to inspire their teams between halves; some politicians better able to inspire their listeners. There is hardly any way that the "gift" may be explained or copied. The man who lacks the personal magnetism, the imagination, or whatever it may be, to challenge others should simply not attempt this type of motivation. He may try very hard, and mean everything he says, but the message just won't play on the heart-strings, or accomplish its purpose. The result is "pip," not "pep."

As a rule, it is not a wise practice to set up a routine under which a challenging letter must be mailed at regular intervals, weekly or otherwise. The obligation of coming up, week in and week out, with an inspirational thought that really clicks, is far too heavy a burden on the average sales manager. Often he is busy and cannot get to the writing of his "Saturday Sales Special" until shortly before it must be sent to the printing department for multigraphing. Working under pressure, and lacking a really good idea, he is likely to dictate a message that *drips* more than it *drives.* When not forced to meet a mailing date, he may wait until something really worth talking about turns up—and the message is sure to be better.

A few better-than-average inspirational letters. Because the nature and purpose of the inspirational letter to salesmen is easily understood in the reading, it is hardly necessary that we comment on any of the following examples. Instead, they are presented as typical of the better sort that you encounter in sales correspondence. Their individual effectiveness you may judge from your own personal reactions. If *you* were a salesman, would these letters, some or all of them, inspire you to greater effort? The answer to that question is probably the only index to their value.

> The Best People
> In the World!
>
> The other night, after seeing the show at the Hollywood Theatre, we went over to Renfro's Drug Store—just for a little ice-cream before going home. While seated there, I noticed a large sign over the door on the inside of the store. The words impressed me so strongly, I wrote them down.
>
> > "The best people in the world pass through
> > this door—OUR CUSTOMERS"
>
> I wondered then, as I often have before, if these Drug Store clerks realize that their customers are to them the best people in the world.
>
> And I wonder today if Panther folks everywhere—out on the Firing Line, in the Office, in the Mailing Room, in the Order Department, in the Bookkeeping Department, at the Factory, everywhere—realize that the best people in the world to us are our customers?
>
> If we realize that, we can't help doing our jobs better.
>
> With a heart full of appreciation to our customers for their goodness to us, how can we help treating an Order with even more care? Filling a drum over at the Factory with thought of the customer's needs, to make that package look prettier than any that ever left the Panther factory? Rush the credit information with double care that we might give this customer, our best friend, better Service than ever? To write that letter to the customer with every consideration due him, yet carry out our purpose? And if we're in the field, realizing that the best people in the world are our customers—sell each and every order so that there be no misunderstanding, no friction.
>
> In the retail field throughout the country, there's a pronounced scarcity of genuine Salesmanship. Everybody will admit that. While it isn't true in the wholesale end of business generally, yet here too, there's need for more EXPERT SALESMANSHIP, so that the BEST PEOPLE IN THE WORLD may be served still better.

Do *we* realize that *our* customers are the "best people in the world"?

Yours for the BEST PEOPLE in the world,

(Panther Oil & Grease Manufacturing Co.)

Good Morning, Jim:

"Do you know what I consider the secret of successful accomplishment?" a prominent executive once asked me, supplying the answer himself: "It is singleness of purpose."

Since then I have thought of that a good many times. I have found myself starting enthusiastically to develop one idea, only to leave it half carried out, while I turned to another. On the golf course, for example, I have driven from the first tee, determined that day to concentrate on keeping my right elbow in. But by the time I reached number 9, I found I was directing my attention to keeping my left arm straight, or to keeping my head down or my eyes on the ball. I did not continue to work to one end, and therefore I did not improve in any direction.

The father of that great French ace in World War I, Guynemer, who brought down sixty German planes, said to his son, who had applied again and again for admission to the aviation corps: "The dog waiting at the door to get in always in the end gets what he wants. His one thought is to get in, while people's minds cannot continually be concentrated on keeping him out."

It is almost a certainty that the businessman of average intelligence can accomplish just about what he sets out to accomplish, if he will concentrate all his efforts on that *one thing* and stick to it, working for it, and believing in it.

If there is one prospect you particularly want to sell, one company or family whose business you are anxious to get, concentrate on that one and *persist*—and you will, almost inevitably win that patronage. If you are right there with the persistent SINGLE PURPOSE, you will one day find resistance weak—and the door will open to you.

Cordially,

(Central Produce Company)

A FIGHTER!

Many years ago he came up to the big leagues—with the Baltimore Orioles. He was slight in build and not tall but he was an Irishman and made up for lack of physique with a spirit that tackled everything in sight and never backed up.

He fought all the way. He had few soft words for opponents. When they licked him, he politely offered congratulations, but he always had his fingers crossed. He fought the umpires. He kept his men fighting all the time. Even when his team was in the cellar, they drew great crowds, for the fans knew they were going to see a fight—and probably a fist fight.

He never thought about losing and neither was he satisfied with a·tie. He went out to WIN. He was scrapping every minute. He was a FIGHTER.

When the little Irish Napoleon stepped aside after over 30 years in the arena, he had to his credit ten National League Championships and three World Championships. But all the other years he was in the fight. He knew baseball, but most of all, he knew the value of fighting every inch of the way.

Today YOU are in a real fight. How is your pulse today? Are you coasting along, waiting for the breaks? Have you settled back in a resigned attitude, figuring out your alibis—or are you in there every minute, burning up the paths?

Tell me how much it burns you up to lose and I'll measure how high you will go. I commend to you John J. McGraw, and his spirit. He was out to win every day. Catch his fighting spirit this week and step out ahead of the crowd.

Sincerely yours,

(Air-Way Electric Appliance Corporation)

Dear Jim:

It's a dirty trick!

I read competitors' letters. Yes, I'm on their mailing lists with a phony name and address. Every so often I get a letter that just about sells me.

When I get one that shaves our prices, I say, "The dirty bums, they're unfair competition."

When I get one quoting prices that are higher, I purr to myself, and if anybody asks about that concern, I tell 'em that they are a fine bunch of fellows. Real gentlemen, in fact.

Now, it would be fine if we didn't have to face facts in this world, but when we do face them, we find that the "dirty bums" do us the most good. They make us *hustle*.

If it were not for concerns that give us a run for our money, fellows like you and me wouldn't have jobs. The company hires us to do battle with competitors, and begorra, it's good we've got some real ones.

We can't and won't cut prices, but there are other ways to outsmart the other fellow, and that's the thing we get paid for in this organization.

No, you wouldn't get a bonus for cutting the throat of that fellow who took a big order away from you.

However, you'll get real recognition for selling where competition is toughest, and it isn't necessary to tell me where it's toughest.

That's my job, watching competitors. Your job is outselling them, and every time you do it, you chalk up another score here in the office.

I was pleased to put that Wharton sale you made on my report to the president this morning.

Cordially yours,

Letters for special occasions. Messages to motivate salesmen are sometimes more effective, and probably easier to write, when connected with some special occasion—a holiday, a campaign, an anniversary, or some similar event to which the salesmen already attach importance. This is particularly true of contests, since the men are already urged by the incentive to win and are thus in the mood to accept encouragement and suggestions. In the following letter the salesman gets a good "shot in the arm," plus the fact that he is supposed to state definitely what he will accomplish the following month. A question that must be answered increases the pull of such a letter.

Keeping Interest in Contest Alive

WHAT NEXT?

You have just passed the halfway mark in the Campaign. In March all previous records were broken. You have every reason to be proud of your efforts.

But in April...WHAT NEXT?

There is always one danger in a good beginning—the temptation to "coast" to the finish. Once a man lets down, it is almost impossible to regain the same high level. What seems to be sure victory slumps off to defeat.

You have seen this happen in football games, in prize-fights, and on the baseball diamond. Sometimes you see it happen in business. "The time I bear down the hardest," says the world's greatest golfer, "is when several holes up on my opponent."

Neither you nor I want to lose any of the momentum already gained in this sales contest. We can't afford to look backward, or feel too satisfied over what has been done. There's plenty of hard work ahead—no time to waste in a too-hasty celebration.

Records are made to be broken. March was good, but April comes as a new challenge. This contest is as important to you as to the company. It's your bread and butter. As you help to increase sales, you strengthen your own security.

Congratulations? Sure. In all sincerity, you have them. But again...WHAT NEXT? By how much in April will you *exceed* your March record?

Knowing you as I do, I am not afraid to ask that question. You are not the kind to dodge a specific question. Jot down on the bottom of this page the answer—and send it back to me in your next report to the home office.

Make it worthy of the best you have to give. By how *much* will *your* April sales beat those you made in March? Ten percent? That's too little. Twenty percent? Fine enough, if that's your level.

Come on now—seriously—because you mean to DO it . . .

In April, WHAT NEXT?

> Sincerely,

To take advantage of the spirit of competition that most human beings seem to possess, sales managers hold sales contests frequently; usually they last from one to three months, and are accompanied by many devices to keep interest at a high pitch. One of the common features is the use of special letterheads that tie in with the idea on which the contest is based. The aim may be to see which of the salesmen can score the most runs in an imaginary baseball game, cover the most miles in a trip around the world, or win the most rounds in the padded ring. In each case, the letterheads are designed to fit the motif of the contest.

The letters reproduced on pages 742 and 743 are examples of this form of showmanship. In the one contest, the salesmen are playing the role of cowboys out for a big "Round-Up of Orders"; in the other, they are striving for a "Knockout." While such games may seem childish to certain individuals, sales managers know that they help to stimulate sales, but their success depends considerably on the originality of the idea and the way it is promoted. Merely to announce a contest, and say nothing more about it until the winners are decided, would be a very foolish procedure. Letters, bulletins, standings—frequently distributed—are necessary to keep the salesmen interested.

Drive to honor popular executive. Material prizes are not the only incentive to better sales performance. The joy of winning, if properly applauded, may be just as potent a reward for the average person, and many a successful campaign for orders has been based on nothing more tangible. Sometimes, too, people may be induced to work harder just to honor someone else, and that is the idea used in the following letter written by Glenn Stewart of the Kalamazoo Vegetable Parchment Company. The idea works effectively in proportion to the popularity of the individual being honored; it may backfire if that popularity is not a reality.

Dear Bob:

On the night of August 12, forty-five years ago, a big, raw-boned youngster swung off of a Michigan Central day-coach at Kalamazoo, and for the first time in his life, set foot on United States soil. There was no band to welcome him; no one to give him the keys to the city. Even the hack drivers hardly gave him a glance. They knew there would not be enough money in the boy's pockets to make it worthwhile...he was too obviously "from the country."

And they were right about that. The smell of the cow barns was still on his clothes and his hands were covered with the callouses that come only from the handles of pitchforks and the "faucets" of cows.

Early the next morning found this boy trudging along a dusty road to a spot three miles north of Kalamazoo where, in the middle of a corn field, another immigrant boy was dreaming and sweating—trying to make a little converting plant into a gigantic paper mill. The boy had heard there might be a job. And that is how Doc Southern, at seven o'clock in the morning of August 13, met Jacob Kindleberger and went to work for KVP.

I think you know much of what had happened before...how, discouraged by two years of looking for work in his native London and not finding it, he borrowed money and sailed by steerage for Canada ... landed in Halifax ... was sent to Leamington, Ontario, by an employment agency with the promise of a job waiting...found it a false report...walked the streets all night in the snow with only 6¢ in his pockets...hired out to a farmer the next morning although he had never had a farm tool in his hands before...milked cows and tended tobacco crops for two and a half years.

Then the trip to Kalamazoo on the hearsay evidence there might be a job. First, a job as a clerk...but that was only a title. In those days, everyone from J. K. down pushed trucks, shoveled coal, tied bundles...did whatever had to be done. Next, a road job, selling ice blankets. Before long, production. Then a hand in sales, General Sales Manager and 3rd Vice-President in '25. First Vice-President and director in '36.

That's pretty sketchy, but it gives the high spots—some mighty low ones, too, for that matter.

Forty-five years of Doc's kind of Hard Work and Loyalty call for some real recognition. Now don't reach for your check book ...this is something a darned sight more important than golf bags and loving cups...something that will please him a thousand times more.

Dear Pardner:

Just got a letter from "Bob" - the foreman, in
which he was telling me that the BORN RANCH is
figurin' to pull off the biggest Round-Up of orders ever staged in these parts.

Yessir, I'm Going to Town to help the old boy
shoot off his long range, high power, big caliber ammunition.

Cinch up your saddle, old timer, and ride along with the
bunch. We want real chaps who can go out, rope, throw and
tie 'em. Don't forget, old top, that I'm leanin' on you
for an order or two a day. It's the orders received at
.the BORN RANCH May 17th to May 22nd, you know, that count.

Man - there's a power of persuasion in that BORN Spring
line. All-wool fabrics by the hundreds. Not a maverick
in the whole bunch. If there ever was a time to sell -
it's now.

Don't let me down. Get your dander up. Some good hard
ridin' and order getting, will put you headin' the herd.

There's good profit in it for you on every order - - and
listen to this - to the chap who sends in the most business in dollars and cents from May 17th to May 22nd goes
a DOUBLE-BARRELED SHOT GUN or a SCHICK ELECTRIC SHAVER -
and a STETSON HAT to the chap who takes second place.

And get this - we will send an AUTOMATIC PENCIL to every
dealer "Going to Town" with orders.

I know your envelopes containing your orders will be
fatter than Stuffy Williams, who was built when meat was
cheap.

                          Yours - rarin' to go!

              (Signed) Duncan Campbell
                       M. BORN & COMPANY

A Dartnell Presentation

Dear _____

And now, with just a few days left for the windup of The Battle
of a Century, let's make it a KNOCKOUT!

The crowd is roaring, nerves are tense, everybody's sitting on
the edge of his chair in this breath-taking moment of suspense,
waiting impatiently for that final blow which means victory or
defeat. Which will it be? Only you can answer!

This is no time for sparring or explaining -- it's F I G H T !
-- in capital letters. Don't be satisfied with anything but a
KNOCKOUT.

Here's the way to get it   You know the Old Man's weak spot --
keep hammering it. You know your strongest attack -- use it.
You know what it takes to put him to sleep -- give it to him.
You know the crowd is cheering for you -- are you going to
disappoint them?

Not if we know Bill Jones. He's been in some mighty tough
spots before and came out on top. He'll do it again. Every
man has reserve that he can draw on in case of emergency. Now
is the time to bring it into action and hand this fellow a
haymaker that will make Rip Van Winkle look like a piker.

You can always tell a sailor in a storm, a jockey on the
home stretch, a ball player in the last of the ninth, a football star on the last down, and a FIGHTER IN THE LAST ROUND!

This is it, man -- let him have it and listen to the crowd
yell -- "IT'S A KNOCKOUT!" Two more New Accounts will
do it!

                              Yours for the Winning Wallop,

A Dartnell Presentation

Just send him some ORDERS.

Don't think I'm crazy. I know just as well as you do that you have orders in here since last May that are unshipped...that you are afraid to face some of your customers without a bodyguard...that you are scared to call on others for fear that they will make you take an order.

That condition, however, does not apply on two lines—PARCHMENT and SPECIALTY. We can still handle BIG increases in both. And both can be highly profitable.

So what we are asking is this...will you go out every day between now and Labor Day, determined to make the next five weeks the greatest for PARCHMENT and SPECIALTY orders in the mill's history?

You will? That's great. Not that I had any doubt about it... in fact, I was all prepared. For in this mail, you should also find a packet of stickers like the one attached...ONE FOR DOC. Put a sticker on every PARCHMENT and SPECIALTY order you send in between now and Labor Day. Put one on the envelope, too.

Let's pile them in until the bloody h'Englishman yells for 'elp!

ONE FOR DOC,

P.S. He started work on the morning of the 13th. I'll bet a little personal note arriving that morning (it's on Friday) would make him feel like a million...yes, TWO million.

4. Telling Salesmen About Their Faults

A supreme test of leadership. It is much easier to praise a salesman in a letter than to point out one of his faults. Criticism, even though well-intended and constructive, is often taken in the wrong way, especially when directed to a man whose general record is good, and whose connection with the company covers a considerable period of time. There is hardly any kind of letter writing that requires more tact—more sympathetic understanding of the particular individual—more knowledge of human nature. Nevertheless, letters of criticism must be written, for it is a function of leadership to *improve* as well as to *inspire*. In the larger sense, the overlooking of a weakness for fear of hurting the feelings of the salesman is not a favor to him. If the fault is pointed out and corrected, the salesman is benefited as much as his company. But the problem of making him believe that is not simple. Many good salesmen are lost to their companies because of tactless letters of criticism.

As every capable sales manager knows, no two salesmen are likely to react in the same way to the same treatment. Some skins are thick; others are thin. One man discounts a criticism as only an attempt to push up his sales; another magnifies it so that a mole-hill becomes a mountain in his mind. One man knows he must have faults, and appreciates help in correcting them; another thinks he is just about perfect, and that anyone correcting him must be prejudiced.

The sales manager's formula. For writing to salesmen who have faults needing correction, one sales executive of national reputation has a formula that is both simple and interesting. "When I face the problem of pointing out a weakness to one of my men," he says, "I do three things. First, I build him up by saying something true about his work which is a compliment. Second, I tear him down by pointing out the weakness. Third, I try to build him up again with another complimentary remark, or some words of encouragement." This plan, the executive says, is used invariably, whether the criticism is presented in a personal interview or in a letter. How the plan would work for others, we cannot testify, but it seems logical in principle:

> Build him up,
> Tear him down,
> Build him up again!

Another sales executive, equally well known for his success in handling men, is not nearly so considerate. His philosophy is much more rugged. "I am willing to work hard with any salesman who can take my suggestions in the right spirit," he says. "I will overlook mistakes, hang on to him longer perhaps than would the average sales manager; but when I find out he is super-sensitive to criticism, I am through. Selling is a tough game. There is no room in it for the man who is soft and can't take the bad with the good."

How various sales managers do the job. The letters that follow have been selected as representative of those being written in modern business, and to show how different sales executives handle criticism. In each case, the man who has dictated the letter is a tested leader of salesmen. It is well to remember, however, that each letter is for a particular individual; a different approach might have been used for some other man.

Blunt Letters to the Negative Thinker*

Look Here, John:

Sit square in your seat for a few minutes and keep your shirt on. You're going to hear a few things that maybe you won't like to hear. And the more you resent them, the more I'm going to say, "fine."

---

* Because of the personal content of these letters to salesmen, none of the writers' names are given. For the same reason, they are all addressed to "John."

I *might* start off by telling you that you're a good boy, and we like you fine, and you're doing a good job. But what good would it do you if I did tell you that? It would just flatter you into a favorable opinion of yourself and you'd continue to knock along, getting about as many orders as I could put in my eye, and without making any money for yourself or the company.

So...brace yourself. You're going to get mad. So what? So you're going to get that torpid liver stirred up and break into more action than you've shown in months. Results? You're going to do yourself some good. Now ...here goes.

You are doing too much *negative thinking.* You know what I mean by that. I mean that even before you call on a prospect you're thinking up an excuse for not getting his order. You've got a first-class array of "if's, and's, and but's" that never did get you anywhere...never got you one signed order. You lie in bed too late of a morning. Don't tell me you don't because I know. If you were getting up at a decent time you'd be making more calls, but instead of that you're piddling around, letting the fresh, cool part of the day go by before you stir out. You're not even running around in circles—you are just leisurely *walking.*

Does this make you mad? Okay, keep your seat. There's more coming.

You're wasting more time and energy thinking about how poor times are, and what you would do "if," than is good for you or your pocketbook.

Yes, I know. You and I were successful back in the old days when we had time for leisure, and could tilt a chair back in some shady corner and gossip. But that method of living went out with Model T Fords. We can't fiddle-faddle like we used to. The rocking-chair days are gone.

Nobody gives a hoot whether you or I like the present day's speed. We've got to keep pace with it or fall behind. For my part, I have no intention of falling behind, and ultimately going on relief. And YOU'RE not either, if I can do anything to jar you out of your rocking chair.

To begin with, you're a salesman. If you weren't, you couldn't get *any* orders. You have sold merchandise, and therefore you can sell more. What's the reason that you're not doing it? You haven't a salesman's personality? We know that's the bunk. People aren't buying like they used to? Other salesmen are getting plenty of orders, without much trouble. Your personal worries are getting you down? Skip it. We all have personal worries, but we don't have to let them whip us.

So, it all adds up to this, John. The bugaboos that are keeping you from being a success exist only *in your own mind*. And what's more, you're going to get rid of them. Starting right now, you're under doctor's orders. You're going to bed with the chickens, and you're going to get up with them, too.

Then, you're going out and make more effective calls before ten o'clock in the morning than you have been making in two days.

> You're still mad, aren't you? Good! That's fine. When you get up in the morning, read this letter again, and get mad all over again.

And when next Saturday rolls around with the biggest commission check you've enjoyed yet, we'll see who is right. Hold off writing that nasty letter you're planning on sending me—until we see who *is* right.

Yours for a change in thinking,

Well, no question about it, the foregoing letter contained a lot of blunt talking. No doubt "John" was mad, as the writer predicted he would be. But what happened? Did this salesman follow instructions, and go to bed with the chickens? Did he get that big commission check? That depends, we think, on how he accepted the criticism. Many salesmen would have resigned on the spot, but the writer must have known this fellow could "take it," or he wouldn't have been so outspoken.

Here is a letter quite different in tone, and yet the circumstances seem to have been about the same. Which of these two letters would *you* have accepted in the best spirit? Which would have done *you* the most good?

Dear John:

It's easy for me to appreciate just how you feel. The big Eastern houses are jittery. That's the reason they are only talking about lower prices but haven't really issued a new price list. Of course, that has caused some of your customers to wait—to lose confidence, and make you the goat.

The very same thing that is happening to your customers is happening to YOU. You are commencing to LACK CONFIDENCE.

Don't overlook that you are not in direct competition with these folks—in product, price, or quality. You are like a runaway horse headed in the wrong direction. Jerk yourself back just as you would the horse if you got hold of its bit. Give yourself a good, hard yank.

You have been basing your sales arguments on price, and price alone. Naturally, that has always been a weak-kneed argument. Today, it's worth less than ever. If you, yourself, are afraid of the price situation, how the devil could you inspire a prospect to put his name on the dotted line?

Mine is just a hunch that you are trying too darn hard to sell your goods. I say this because I've noticed how you report calling on this or that good customer, not getting an order, and then calling on a half dozen poorly-rated, slow-pay fellows in the same town.

Some guy a whale of a lot smarter than I am said: "THE GOLD MINE of any company is its list of present customers." That's truer now than ever before. These customers *know* that your price has ALWAYS been right, and they *know* it's right NOW. It's to them you want to go with CONFIDENCE. Be at ease, be friendly, and leave the impression you are there to serve. To check up his stock! To suggest needed sizes and new styles! To stimulate HIS customers' interest in what HE has to sell! Not in what YOU have to sell.

For crying out loud, John. You can't let this thing get you down. You are just as good a salesman as any man I know. You've got personality, a heart, a soul, a body, and your Creator endowed you with plenty of brains. Is there any reason under the shining sun why you cannot sell?

Don't forget that there are plenty of WANTED goods. It's your job to demonstrate to your customer that your company makes these wanted goods. Plenty of people have money. Just look at the people who haven't lost a day's pay in years. In any community, no matter how small, you can point them out to your prospect by the dozens.

All you need, John, is a good shot of CONFIDENCE that will restore in you mountain-moving FAITH in yourself.

Suppose tomorrow morning while you're shaving you memorize this little creed, and then, each morning as you pick up your order book, repeat it.

> I believe in myself.
> I believe in my work.
> I believe in my company.
> I believe in the quality of the goods I am selling.
> I believe my goods are priced right.
> I believe I'm going to have a good day.

It's been a long time since I mentioned the "third vest button." There's something in it, though, so I'm suggesting that TO-MORROW when you have picked up your brief case, after reciting the above creed, you STICK OUT YOUR THIRD VEST BUTTON, square your shoulders, get that fighting light in your eyes—and doggone it, John, you just can't help but sell.

                                                    Cordially,

The circumstances behind the next letter happen over and over again in the life of a sales manager. A young and inexperienced salesman had become convinced that he was working in a poor territory. He was doing as well as the company expected him to do, but in his own mind he had failed. The letter is a reply to one in which the salesman had offered to resign. The last, and most pleasing, chapter in the story is that the salesman was encouraged to carry on, and became a better-than-average success.

To Salesman Who Thought Territory No Good

Dear John:

I have read your letter, and think the fellow giving you the most trouble in your territory is a cuss by the name of John. Until we either regulate his liver or clear his mind, he will continue to bother you a lot.

Now, in talking this over with you frankly, John, I don't want you to get the idea that we don't realize that you have had a hard proposition over there. Neither do I want you to feel that we have been critical about your work. We think you have been doing fine, and the fact that we gave you a better contract this year should convince you that our feeling is sincere.

The experiences you have been having are not much different from those of many other salesmen in your Division. For instance, I consider the territory north of you, the one held by Brown, harder than your own. The same applies to Smith's territory, east of you. South of you is Jones. He took the worst scolding of any man in our Division for the first six months he was in that territory, but he is now sitting on top, laughing at conditions

Did you check the standings at the end of the last quarter? If you did, you know that Brown, Smith, and Jones got over the quota line. So did White who was in a territory that looks about as prolific as the desert of Sahara. Now, get me right, John. This isn't a criticism, but simply a comparison of territories and men. These are results brought about by men who have been absolutely determined that nothing in God's green world is going to hold them back.

The reason I am making this point so strongly to you is because I am sincerely convinced that your territory trouble is really trouble with yourself. If you are absolutely sure in your own mind that our proposition is not profitable for your dealers and consumers, then I would have very little respect for you if you continued with the work. No salesman ever becomes gifted enough to make a success selling goods in which *he* does not believe.

Of course, you'll always have some trouble. There are some consumers that will insist our price is too high, that other products are better. But don't let that kind of talk get your goat. You can't please everybody with one religion, or any one kind of politics. Neither will you ever be able to sell and satisfy every prospect. But the breaks are in your favor. Also, here is a little secret I will let you in on. If our competitors are having such a walk-away, why do I have seven applications received this week from salesmen now selling competitive lines?

You know, John, it's a mighty good thing for a salesman that we do have these conditions that build up sales resistance. Otherwise, there would be no need of salesmen. Most sales conditions, however, are a matter of mind, and our most successful salesmen are the fellows who generally make their own conditions.

Now, as for your resigning, John, it's entirely up to you. You are over 21 and you know your own business. What we want you to understand is that we have found no fault with the work you have done. We'd like to have you stay if *you* think you are the man for the job. I am willing to back any of our men to the limit as long as he "thinks he can." When he tells me he *can't* then it's time for him to quit.

We are going to stay in your territory, and we are going to build up a real business there which will be mighty profitable for the dealers who stick with us. Some salesman is going to collect on this business. You have the first chance.

I expect to be up in Smith's territory next week. If you want me to drop off and talk this matter over with you, I'll be mighty glad to do so. Just tell me where you want me to meet you.

Yours very truly,

A mischief worker on any sales force is quite likely to be Self-Satisfaction. In the following letter, the sales manager seems to think his man is coasting too much on his father's reputation—perhaps not laboring as hard as he might, although serious enough in attitude. The letter is long, but we think any salesman would read it with appreciation and respect. One that didn't would hardly be worth his salt.

Dear John:

This is not a "pep" letter. It's a straight-from-the-shoulder, heart-to-heart talk.

You want to make money, John. Everybody does. That's our burning ambition, and there is no need to be ashamed of it, in spite of what some folks refer to as being mercenary.

You've always had a lot of ambition to succeed. The flames of that ambition increased when you married, and then again when your baby came. But somehow or other you just haven't been able to hit your stride. It must be in you, because your father is one of the most successful salesmen on the Coast. You can follow in his footsteps.

Suppose, for a minute, we be brutally frank and compare father and son. Your father has a wonderful personality that radiates confidence. He approaches his prospect with ease, but of course, he's a veteran at it.

Your personality, John, is equally pleasing, but you approach your prospect very tensely. Responsibilities have come to you rapidly and have caused you to be a bit overserious. Of course, selling is a serious business, but contacts must be friendly and human. I would urge you, therefore, to forget your worries, and lose yourself in the job at hand.

It often has been said that the best way to learn is to watch successful men. You could find no better man to watch than your father, and being of the same blood, you could readily adapt yourself to his ways. *Cultivate a spirit of confidence.*

Your territory is pretty well centered around your home town. Your work keeps you there a great deal, and I'm wondering if you find it a bit difficult to get started on Monday and other mornings. When a man is a salesman he is on his own hook. It's up to him to manage his own time.

Eight o'clock is the time I'm supposed to be at the office, and I don't get here at eight-thirty or nine. That's easy for me, because I'm *supposed* to be here at eight. Plenty of people would comment if I were late regularly. But there is no one to watch your movements, so if you find it difficult to get started in the mornings, make up your mind to be in some prospect's store at eight o'clock.

Let's look at Bill, over in West Texas, for a moment. Bill is making money. He told me not so long ago that he had 10,000 round American dollars salted away. But Bill is not satisfied with even being on the job at eight o'clock. I know if there's a store open at seven, Bill will be there. I've seen him write an order at ten o'clock at night.

Now, there's Jack, up in Oklahoma. I happen to know that he's got a nice block of oil stock which he bought with money earned selling our products. Not only that, but he has a few thousand dollars in government bonds as a nest egg. Jack's on the sidewalks at the crack of dawn, and he helps his customers turn off the lights at night.

I could tell you how Smith is paying for a beautiful home, earned from territory uncuitivated before he took it over and made a success of it. Or how Jones has paid out a farm in Oak County with the money he has saved above his living expenses.

Not one of these men had anything on the ball that you don't have. The fact is, you've had wider retail experience than any of them.

And now I'm going to turn the spotlight in our direction. Is there, in your opinion, anything wrong with the company's product—with our prices, service, or quality? If there is anything wrong in our set-up that has caused your sales to slump, we'd surely appreciate knowing about it. Knowing what is wrong would enable us to correct it, and in that way, help you.

No, John, we are not thinking of making a change in your territory. We have a man whom we know is honest and sincere—who needs only to *find himself,* and that's what I wish we could help you do.

This letter is not intended to criticize your efforts, or to belittle you. We just want to be helpful.

Next year, we celebrate our sixtieth anniversary. You joined this big family of ours with the intention of staying, and stay you will, so long as I have anything to say about it.

I mentioned before that you could look around a long time before you could find a better man to study than your own father. You'll never find a finer product to sell. So why not buck right down into it, like the true westerner does when he is bulldogging a steer?

Stick to it tenaciously, John, and remember that your house offers opportunities which are *proved* by the successful men who represent it.

Encouragingly,

Every football coach knows the danger of winning several consecutive games. The team becomes so smug that the fighting spirit wanes. Along comes an inferior team with more enthusiasm and another "upset" is written in sports history. This is the thought, no doubt, in the mind of the sales manager who writes to an old and successful member of his team.

To the Salesman Who Has Become Too Complacent

Dear John:

Is length of service an asset or a liability?

Practically all of the men in our division have been with the company over ten years. The average is eleven years, and you are the Dean of Service College with twenty successful years behind you.

What a wonderful asset this should be for you. On the other hand, it could be a liability. Twenty years of service in the same sales organization is a tremendous asset only if it has built a rich background of broadening experience. If it has deepened the rut of personal satisfaction—lulled you into a false feeling of security—then it's a great liability.

Regardless of how the company may feel about you or me in a

personal way, they would be unfair to allow this feeling to have any influence in their judgment of future value. When we get down to brass tacks, John, it is FUTURE performance that will determine your progress—not the victories of past years.

What brought this up? Well, I will tell you.

Yesterday, from the statistical department, I received an analysis of the sales for every salesman in our division, starting from the first year of his employment. If you could see your own chart, I think it might surprise you.

No, your sales volume hasn't dropped sharply in recent years, and your commissions are still running better than $600 a month. But the curve *is* dropping, John, and the decline began four years ago, just after you were crowned champion of the division.

I know that a good salesman doesn't bother a lot about figures, or to compare them one year with another. So maybe you didn't realize that each of the last four years your monthly average has been a little less than the one before.

This wouldn't worry me if you were an old man—up in the sixties —but if my record is straight, you are only 44, with at least another span of twenty years ahead of you. Right now, you have one boy in college, and another soon out of high-school. The three girls are younger, but in the years coming up they, too, will need to be educated.

In other words, you just can't afford to let your income gradually slip downward, and the time to reverse the direction is while you are still making good money.

I'm not sure *why* your sales curve has been going down, but the reason *could* be the one I mentioned in the beginning of this letter. Success breeds self-satisfaction—sometimes too much of it for our own good.

Please, old fellow, don't think I am preaching or criticizing. You are one of our best salesmen, and you know how much I admire all that you have done, and are doing. But that sales chart with your name on it...well, somehow, it made me think about the both of us, and how easy it would be for success to become a liability.

One thing I am rather sure of. Your curve has dipped as low as it will ever be. You are smart. You'll see the common sense in what I've said. You'll be on the way back to the champion's spot for the rest of this year, and for all the years to come.

I'll bet my last shirt on that, John. And you know it wouldn't look so good for me to go around the office without a shirt.

> Sincerely yours,

In the foregoing letters, you have witnessed various sales managers in more or less critical moods. Some spoke bluntly; some tried to correct the fault with gentle reasoning. Each letter was slanted at a different individual, which helps, no doubt, to explain the variations in tone and content.

Of course, there are other situations that would require a sales manager to reprimand members of his sales team; for example, an instance in which a salesman had an argument with a customer, or otherwise incurred ill will. Or, the case of a salesman who turned in excuses and alibis for not making good, rather than bringing in revenue from closed deals. However, the illustrations given above seem to apply to the most common situations in this area, and will serve as a valuable reference to any sales manager who finds it necessary to stir a salesman into productive action and to keep him moving at a profitable speed:

ADJUSTMENT LETTERS

ADJUSTMENTS
LETTERS

1. How to Correct and Avoid Misunderstandings

Majority not serious. No company can be expected to attain perfection in production, performance of personnel, or in any of the other parts which together we call a *business*. Even if such a state ever did exist, misunderstandings would surely occur now and then between company and customer. Hence, in any well-regulated organization, you will find experienced "trouble-shooters" whose job it is to investigate, adjust, and even anticipate any interruption in pleasant customer relations. One of their primary qualifications is the ability to write courteous, satisfying, persuasive adjustment letters.

Meeting this obligation is often a difficult and exacting problem, for an angry person is seldom in the mood to listen to reason, or to accept any explanation which conflicts with his own preconceived ideas. It is not easy to apologize in such a way that a mistake will be understood and forgiven; to refuse a special request from an old and faithful customer without incurring his displeasure; to make an impatient buyer understand why the shipment of his order has been delayed; or to handle tactfully any other of the thousand and one situations which complicate customer relations.

Fortunately, the majority of the complaints received in the routine operations of a company are not so serious that they cannot be pleasantly and quickly adjusted. One company, for example, after analyzing several thousand complaints in an effort to discover the causes, came out with some rather surprising figures. The percentages would probably vary for other individual companies, and for business as a whole, but there is no reason to doubt their approximate correctness. This company found that:

22.5 per cent of all complaints they received were sincerely made, and with just causes.

41 per cent were motivated by impulse rather than deliberate reasoning.

23.7 per cent were pretended abuses: usually a defense for lack of funds, or some other inability to go through with the purchase.

12.8 per cent were totally unwarranted, and caused by downright cussedness.

Insofar as the above percentages are accurate, they lend considerable encouragement to the man who writes adjustment letters. With proper tact and understanding, he may hope to handle with reasonable success all customers with chips on their shoulders except the last group. The latter *know* at heart that they have no just cause for complaint, and for that reason will resist to the last ditch any attempt to smooth their self-ruffled feathers. No amount of reasoning or fair play will change their attitude, since they are *looking* for trouble and are not to be satisfied unless they get it.

The troublemakers, of course, deserve no special consideration; letters to them may be short, firm, and courteous. The others *mean* well toward the company, even though their claims are unwarranted. With a little tact and patience, letters may be devised which will restore their goodwill and leave them still friends of the company. To show how these folks are handled by the experienced "trouble-shooter," is the purpose of this section.

Complaints are blessings. In spite of the trouble they cause, complaints are not resented by the modern business executive. Instead, he views them as a means of finding out what things are wrong in the operation of his business, in the quality of his products, in the attitude and performance of his personnel. It is seldom pleasant to discover a fault, but much better than to let it continue unsuspected.

The proper reaction toward customer misunderstandings is very adequately presented in this bulletin that was sent to Montgomery Ward's correspondents:

HOW DO WE REGARD A COMPLAINT?

In answering complaints, sometimes I wonder just what the correspondent thinks—what his attitude is when he starts to write.

There are two ways to look at complaints—the right way and the wrong way. If we, as correspondents, take the attitude that each letter is just another complaint to be handled, and tackle it in a routine way without regard to the thoughts and feelings of the customer, is it fair to Ward's or to us that we stay on the job? We are not fitted for adjustment work or any work that puts us in contact with customers, if we think that way.

The real correspondent is the one who deep down in his heart is thankful to the customer for having made the complaint, because it may show us where we are weak in our merchandise or service. And it also offers us a splendid opportunity to prove that Ward's is really anxious to please.

It is seldom that a complaint is wholly unjustified—there is usually some ground for the customer writing, and the "kicks" we receive should not be considered as an annoyance. Few are from grouchy old customers who are trying to get something for nothing—ninety percent of them are legitimate complaints which we should welcome with open arms.

They open the way for an investigation. And we must all admit that if no one complained about our merchandise, or the handling of his order, Ward's would have been out of business years ago.

These remarks are made to give you a little better idea of what complaints really mean to Ward's. Let's adopt the right attitude. Let's show more tolerance and a sincere effort to run complaints down. After all, they are a barometer because they point out our weak spots.

We should be glad the customer writes to us instead of remaining silent or broadcasting his complaints to his neighbors and not giving us a chance to make things right.

Understanding the customer's point of view. Success in handling an angry or dissatisfied customer depends partly on the reader's ability to look on the letter of complaint as if he himself had written it. Then, and then only, is the correspondent in the Adjustment Department in the right position to reply. From the correspondent's point of view, the complaint may be just another worry, and the letter, an unreasonable tirade which deserves to be answered, tit for tat. From the customer's point of view, the complaint represents something he paid for and didn't get; his letter is a warranted appeal for justice. Just what the complaint really is—what the letter stands for—depends on the circumstances of the particular incident and the honesty of the individual. But right or wrong, the customer must have first consideration, and the letter needs to be interpreted *his* way, not the correspondent's.

Another important point made in the bulletin above is the necessity of *investigating the facts* before attempting to write the adjustment letter. Several workers in a Chicago store did *not* take time to know the facts, or the following customer's letter would not have been necessary.

Gentlemen:

Enclosed find check for $6.63 to settle balance shown on your books as due you. Of this sum, $3.50 plus 13 cents postage is for one copy of O. Henry. That's okay. I ordered the O. Henry I now pay for the O. Henry.

The remainder pays for the second of two cigarette cases, satin-covered, initialed E. T.

I ordered one cigarette case in December.

You sent two.

I returned one.

You sent it back to me.

I wrote to you, saying I'd ordered only one.

You wrote to me, saying I could send it back.

You returned it, saying that on account of the initials you couldn't accept it. . . I'm tired of paying postage on the doggone thing. . . so here's your money.

But that isn't the last straw. My wife ordered an egg poacher. You sent a cookie-dough squirter. We have a cookie-dough squirter. We don't have an egg poacher. We don't want a cookie-dough squirter. We do want an egg poacher. I hesitate to return the cookie-dough squirter lest it start on a series of travels similar to those of the cigarette case.

Now personally, I like to buy from your store, but if there is any more of this monkey business, I'll trade somewhere else. After all, a customer likes to get what he ordered—no more, no less, no different.

Yours very truly

The mystery of the second cigarette case! The cookie squirter that turned out to be an egg poacher! What a mess of trouble for the correspondent before he can qualify himself to answer that complaint letter. But he can't do it adequately until he finds out what happened. And finding out may bring to light faults in the store's routine for handling mail orders. But that's not the only benefit to be gained. There's a customer at stake. He likes the store, but he doesn't like the "monkey business." His wife still wants an egg poacher—not a cookie squirter. Here's a customer to be saved or lost by what the adjustment correspondent says and does. It's a chance to render a service to customer and company—nothing to be annoyed about.

Strange as it may seem, a customer *does* want "what he ordered—no more, no less, no different." Maybe he shouldn't be so finicky, but he wants what he wants. Here's another letter that proves it.

Nuts to you!

I received a letter from you (initialed JD) which started with this sentence, "I would like to send you a copy of the *March* issue for free examination." And then it read, "Simply sign the enclosed card and we will mail you the *March* issue."

So I sent a dollar. Did I get the March issue? No. Instead, I received a postal card telling me the March issue was no more, but that you were sending a copy of the April issue.

Now that isn't what I wanted. I was willing to pay a dollar to read the articles in the March issue, and then decide if I wanted to be a subscriber or have my dollar returned.

The March issue is what you offered. The March issue is what I wanted. If you can't supply it, return my dollar and I will return your new 64-page book, "Answers to Health Questions."

Maybe I am unreasonable, but I am rather tired of being offered one thing in a mail solicitation, and then being disappointed by receiving another. I feel that I have had enough.

Either I get what you offered and I ordered or there is no sale.

Phooey from me to you,

If you like to know how stories end, you'll be interested to know that the above letter was a success. The writer got the March issue.

Procedure in writing the adjustment letter. It is foolish to say that all letters answering complaints should be prepared in the same mold. The proper procedure depends on the nature of the particular case and the personal inclination of the correspondent. However, there are certain steps that seem logical, and unless you can improve on them, it is better to follow them rather than to write in a hit-and-miss manner.

1. Say something in the beginning to make the customer feel you are really glad to know about his complaint—*thank* him for telling you.

2. Tell him in a friendly way what you can do, or can't do, to make things right with him.

3. Justify the decision. Don't argue, if it is not favorable, but lay the facts on the table, so he will know *why* you are refusing.

4. Try to regain his goodwill—perhaps, by doing something else that might please him.

5. Assure him that he is appreciated as a customer—imply confidently that he is *still* a buyer.

When a clash is inevitable between customer and company points of view, and the writer of the adjustment letter faces the necessity of a complete turn-down or of a compromise which he knows the customer is not likely to approve, there is always the grave danger that the continued correspondence exchange will develop into a first-class dog-fight. That means, of course, the end of the business relationship. Hence, no matter how incorrect the customer may be in stating his side of the case—no matter how insistent and argumentative—the company representative cannot properly let himself be drawn into a heated argument.

Benjamin Franklin once gave some sage advice on "How to win an argument," which some business letter writers could follow to their own advantage. Here it is:

> The way to convince another is to state your case moderately and accurately. Then scratch your head, or shake it a little, and say that is the way it seems to you, but of course you may be mistaken about it; which causes your listener to receive what you have to say, and as like as not, turn about and try to convince you of it, since you are in doubt. But if you go at him in a tone of positiveness and arrogance you only make an opponent of him.

It may be a little difficult to scratch your head in a letter, but you can go along with the idea of not being too aggressive or arrogant. Winning an argument at the cost of a customer is hardly a good investment. A famous football coach always said, "We aim to win but not humiliate." Deny the customer's request if you must, but in a way that says, "I know exactly how you feel, and I wish we could do as you wish, because there is a lot to be said in your favor."

Mistakes to avoid. Before we examine actual letters used to handle complaints and special requests from customers, a few *Don't signs* will be useful guides to those who aspire to success in this important field of business correspondence.

1. When the customer is right, admit the fault frankly. Don't try to cover up or alibi.

2. Say you are sorry, but don't cry all over the carpet. Profuse apology is a sign of fear and weakness. Sincere regret is all that the customer expects.

3. In general, it does no good to explain all the gory details of an error. The customer wants to know that the error will be *adjusted;* not how it happened. Keep that skeleton in your own closet.

4. Never grant a concession or make an adjustment with an air

of condescension—as if you are doing it merely out of the goodness of your heart, and not because it is the right thing to do. This belittles the customer—he resents it.

5. Never refer to the "complaint" of a customer as such. Not when writing to *him*. Call it a "request" or a "misunderstanding." Complainers are not liked in this world. The customer is asking for justice—not making a *complaint*.

6. Avoid the use of any word or phrase which might imply suspicion of the customer's integrity or truthfulness. For example: "We have your letter in which you *claim* one case was missing."

7. Never delay the reply to the customer's letter. If it takes time to investigate, write and thank him immediately—tell him how soon he may expect your final decision.

8. Never go back at a customer in a spirit of anger, no matter how unjust or unreasonable or discourteous he may have been in his letter to you. A business letter writer is an Ambassador of Goodwill. He may never play any other role, even though the customer is the villain.

9. Never try to dodge responsibility by placing the blame for a mistake on some other party. People do not admire buck-passers. Above all, protect the salesman if you can. He needs the respect and confidence of the customer.

10. Never repeat the details of a fault. For example: "We have your letter about finding two dead roaches in one box of our flakes." Let the customer forget such things as fast as he can. Make the adjustment, but talk about something more pleasant.

11. Never pretend great surprise over a mistake. This implies you doubt it really happened. For example: "Never in all our thirty years in business, has such a mistake been made in our factory." Who will believe you?

12. Don't hide behind the word "policy" in refusing a claim or request. The customer has the right to know *why* he is denied.

13. Treat a complaint with just as much respect as an order. Let the customer know you are just as eager to serve as to sell him

14. If the matter at hand seems important to the customer, don't try to change his opinion. Join *with* him. Attach an airmail stamp to your reply or send it special delivery. For the cost of a few pennies, you may make your company stand first for service in his mind.

15. If the customer addressed his letter to you, never turn it over to someone else for reply unless company organization makes it necessary. In that case, write to him anyway, and tell him he will be hearing from the other party.

To the above cautions might be added one trite but very true axiom—"An ounce of prevention is worth a pound of cure." A certain number of errors is unavoidable in any company, but there is little reason why the *same one* must happen over and over again. The individual handling a complaint should be sure that a report is made to *all* departments and workers who may have been involved. A faulty routine can be changed; an inefficient employee can be fired. Certainly, the salesman in the area should get news of the complaint, and how it was handled. This is also true of any request made by the customer which requires special decision: a variation in regular terms, permission to return goods not selling as anticipated, or any other dispensation apart from the usual custom or policy.

Types of adjustment letters. The most logical way to classify adjustment letters, so that each type may be considered as a separate problem, is to think of them in relation to the action which the company intends to take. This action is influenced by several factors: the circumstances which provoked the customer's complaint or request, the determination of responsibility if an error has been made, the relative importance of the customer as a buyer of the company's products, and other conditions which make it impossible to set up a rigid, unbreakable policy. For example, a company may insist that all customers are treated alike, and an honest effort may be made to live up to that intention, but the brutal fact remains that, for the sake of keeping his goodwill, a big buyer is more likely to receive special concessions than is the small buyer. Be that as it may, these company letters that seek to smooth out the wrinkles in customer relations may be grouped in the following ways:

1. Letters of regret and apology—chiefly used in situations where the damage has been done, and the main objective is to salvage as much goodwill as possible.

2. Letters in which the answer to the customer is "Yes"—he gets what he wants, completely and without reservation. In the case of a mistake, a letter of this type means that the company is assuming full responsibility.

3. Letters in which the answer to the customer is "No"—he gets nothing that he wants, or a compromise which may or may not be satisfactory. This type of reply places the fault in the lap of the customer, provided a complaint has been filed.

4. Letters in which objections are *anticipated* and explanations are offered *before* the customer has had the chance to complain or be displeased. Thus, one of these letters may announce and justify a change in policy, an increase in price, the discontinuation of a service or product, or some other step the customer might be expected to resent.

The above classification demands a broader interpretation of the word *adjustment* than when it is used merely with reference to a customer's complaint about an order, or how it has been handled. But all of the conditions covered in the broader interpretation need to be "adjusted" if pleasant customer relations are to be maintained; in that sense, the letters which talk about them *are* adjustment letters.

2. Letters of Apology and Regret

Attempt to salvage goodwill. Things may happen in business which interfere with cordial customer relations, but by the time they are brought to the surface it is too late to repair the damage. You can think of numerous illustrations: a dealer wants some goods for a special sale on a specified date, but they are shipped to Jackson, Mississippi, instead of Jackson, Michigan; the president of a trade association makes much ado about the luscious steaks to be served at the annual banquet, and they turn out to be very tough; a gift shop orders goods for the holiday season and they arrive after Christmas; an important guest is treated rudely by the night clerk, and the fact does not come out until the former takes an important convention to another hotel. These and many other slips occur in business; their number and kind defy count or description. Sometimes, a partial reparation may be made; usually not. The only adjustment left is a letter of regret and apology, which may or may not heal the wound.

Examples taken from business. There is, of course, no *one* way that a correspondent may best write a letter expressing regret when some service or product has gone sour. It is useless to offer a lengthy explanation which to the reader is only a confession of weakness, an alibi for something that never should have happened. Instead, it seems better to just express the regret—simply, sincerely, and without weeping on the customer's shoulder.

Here are three examples:

(1)

Dear Mr. Doe:

There is a saying that "Even a monkey falls out of a tree once in a while."

But we certainly have gone the monkeys one better by making a mistake twice on your order. We're having the printer try again today, with instructions to "double check the imprint." Shipment will be rushed tonight.

We surely appreciate your good nature under these exasperating circumstances. We hope you will believe that our printers are usually not so dumb.

Cordially yours,

(2)

Dear Mrs. Doe:

Thank you for your card which reports the second dish broken. I·don't blame you for saying what you did about us. If I were in your shoes, I'd probably say a lot more.

This premium business is very new to us. We are still experimenting, but hope to find the right way to pack these refrigerator dishes so that they will arrive in perfect condition.

I am sorry you have been put to so much trouble, but another dish is being mailed, and we have made some further changes in the way of packing.

One thing you can count on, Mrs. Doe. We will see that you get a dish all in one piece, if it takes all winter.

Very truly yours,

(3)

Dear Mr. Doe:

Dealer Smith sent us the overalls which pulled out at the seams, and we wrote and told him he did the right thing by replacing them immediately. Of course, we have made good with Mr. Smith.

Whatever you do, don't blame Mr. Smith for your trouble with this pair of overalls. It really wasn't his fault. We are the ones to blame, and you can be sure we regret the unpleasant experience you have had.

What we want now is to know if the new garment proves to be all that you have the right to expect. Mr. Smith would like to know, too. Will you please tell him?

Thank you.

Very truly yours,

How a mail order house did the job. There are no better systems for handling orders than those used by the big mail order companies, but in spite of all the care taken to avoid mistakes, they do happen occasionally. Since the success of these companies depends so much on contacts by mail, you would expect especially good adjustment letters from them. The following exchange of letters shows how the job of soothing an angry customer is handled by an expert.

Letter from Customer

Gentlemen:

I am a customer of long standing—my home being almost completely furnished with your appliances, such as electric refrigerator, washing machine, etc. I have always felt that your merchandise was thoroughly reliable, and still do. But unless the mistakes that have been so common in my orders lately are eliminated, I will be forced to take my business to some other concern.

The nuisance of having to send things back is getting to be just a little too much. The last three orders have all had mistakes made in articles sent.

The first was a Prophylactic tooth brush instead of Pepsodent Tooth Powder. This I sent back and it was corrected. The second was ¼ pint of enamel in place of the ½ pint I ordered and paid for. I needed the paint so gave you the 49¢ rather than wait for the adjustment. The last mistake was sending 2 table forks instead of the 2 oyster forks ordered.

These were three successive shipments. Your percentage of error seems to be too high.

For your own information, you have already lost several accounts in this region because of similar mistakes. So it might be wise to eliminate the cause of these mistakes, and save more of your customers—including *me*.

Yours very truly,

The Reply

Dear Mr. Doe:

It would be a great disappointment to lose your business but an even keener one to lose your friendship and faith in our firm. So I want to thank you for your letter which I feel was written in friendliness to give us another chance.

It is a bother to send things back, Mr. Doe, and I am sorry you had to do this. I don't wonder that you didn't return the enamel when we sent the wrong quantity, but even though the amount involved is trifling, we want to make it right. Here is our check for the ½ pint you didn't receive.

If you wish the forks exchanged, let me know the article number and pattern you selected. The correct forks will be sent at once and then you can return the others when convenient. A check will be sent for postage, as we certainly don't want you to have extra postage expense because of our mistake.

Your orders should all be filled promptly and completely, and I am going to see that a more careful check is made to prevent those things you bring to our attention. You see, letters like yours have a real value—they help us to know just where we are slipping.

You have been a good customer for a long time, Mr. Doe. From past experience, I am sure you know that our aim is to please—both by our goods and our service.

Sincerely yours,

Four gallons of gas and 85¢. The two-act drama below actually happened, word for word. In Act I you have the customer's letter. "Don't bother to answer," he says, but of course, the manager of the hotel couldn't be indifferent to a long-time guest who was "all through." He had to make the best he could out of an unhappy situation. His reply is Act II.

The Customer's Letter

Dear Sir:

I used to think that the Doe House was a good hotel. I have changed my mind.

Not that my opinion matters much to you, because one customer won't make or break the Doe House. And not that the Doe House matters much to me, either, because there are a lot of other hotels in Chicago. But when one of your employees is unnecessarily antagonizing customers, you may like to know it. So here's the story.

My wife and I drove to Chicago on a business trip on the morning of October 16—a trip of only 200 miles. We intended to drive back the same evening.

While I was having a conference at a studio on Erie Street, my wife spent the afternoon at Field's. I met her there shortly after five o'clock. She had selected a dress, and by the time I paid for it, my purse was flat. However, I had a government check for $74.25 in my pocket, which I thought would be as good as cash. So I said, "We will turn in this check at the Doe House when we go there for dinner."

When I presented this check, your credit man asked if I had a rating card, and if I was registered at the hotel. I told him I had no card, and was not registered, but that we had stayed at the Doe House many times. I gave him the date of our last visit (in August) and suggested that he look up the card I signed then.

He refused to take any further interest in the matter. I then went to one of your assistant managers, and he stated he could not go over the head of the credit man.

So there we stood in your lobby, 200 miles from home, with four gallons of gas in our car, with 85¢ in our pockets, and with nothing to eat since noon. We had to start driving North.

At a filling station near Waukegan, we stopped, and told the man we wanted some gas, but had nothing but a check to pay for it. The boy at the station said he would see what he could do for us, and took the check inside. A motor policeman came out and offered to help.

The officer looked at my auto registration card, and made a telephone call. He came out and said the check was O.K. We got the gas, and the balance of our check in cash. Quite a contrast, wasn't it, with the helpfulness at the Doe House?

Your credit man either lacked the resourcefulness to know his business or the desire to be of service—and I feel sure that the desire to be of service is what he lacked. I realize that hotels are imposed on, and must have rigid rules, but that is no reason for treating old customers like crooks.

Don't bother to answer this letter. We are all through with the Doe House.

Yours truly,

The Reply

Dear Mr. Jones:

I am grateful for your letter. You have done the Doe House a big favor in telling me of your experience.

Our credit manager, the assistant manager you speak of, and I have just had a talk—a serious one. I did most of the talking.

Thanks to your thoughtfulness, other guests of this hotel will not be treated with the same heedlessness. Of that I am sure.

Somebody has said that excuses are shabby patches with which we try to cover our failures; so rather than try to explain away our conduct, I prefer to rely on your generosity.

My associates and I are genuinely sorry. We ask you also to convey our apologies to Mrs. Jones.

I said no excuses. I shall try to stick to that. But may I leave this thought with you? We are all human. A sleepless night, or some personal worry, can at times throw the steadiest nature off balance. Has that ever happened to you or someone close to you?

I suspect that something was amiss with my associates the day you were here. However, neither one tried to cover his mistake, and for that I give them credit. Can you—will you look at it in that light?

When you folks are again in Chicago, I will be happy to have you step over to the Doe House and have dinner with us. Your consent will show me that you have decided to overlook the incident, and this simple gesture on our part may help to let you know how sorry we are.

Drop me a line when you are coming, and a table in the Gold Room will be reserved for you and your party. Of course, there will be no check.

Sincerely yours,

A promise to do better. The management of a cemetery is somewhat off the beaten paths of business, but the same principles prevail there as in any other line of business when it comes to handling a disgruntled customer. Notice that in the following letter the cemetery superintendent gets off to a good start by *agreeing* with the customer—then tries patiently to regain her goodwill. The lady who got the letter was well pleased.

> Dear Mrs. Doe:
>
> We are very sorry that you had any reason not to be pleased regarding your flowers, but we realize that the bed has not looked as it should, in spite of the care we have given it.
>
> The geraniums all over the cemetery have not done well this year, and the colas have been better than usual. Just why this should be so, we do not know.
>
> The grave you mention is certainly lovely, and it has had only the care our men have given it, which was no more than yours received. As to the difference in price of a bed filled with colas instead of geraniums, there would not be much difference, but the geraniums can be planted before Memorial Day, and they bloom until late in the Fall, while colas are usually planted the second week of June, and are gone at the first touch of frost.
>
> However, we wish to assure you again that we are sorry for the failure this year, and whatever you plan for the bed next year, we shall try to make it the very best. If it fails again, it won't be because of lack of effort on our part.
>
> Yours very truly,

Mystery of the bobby-pin. Sometimes the circumstances behind a customer's complaint are so unexplainable that even the adjustment letter writer is stymied in knowing how to handle it. In the case that follows—the mystery of the bobby-pin—the reply was, to say the least, unorthodox. The writer took the chance of matching wit with the customer—always a dangerous procedure. In explaining how he happened to write such an unusual letter, the writer said: "Well, from reading *his* letter, I sensed that he was a chap who didn't take anything too seriously, and that he might react more favorably if I joked with him, than if I remained serious and apologetic. That was the way I figured him, but I'll admit his second letter took a load off my mind. I had my fingers crossed, because I knew he had to be the kind of a fellow I surmised, or my letter to him would be a dud."

The remarks of this experienced adjustor take us back to the section devoted to Letter Carpentry. You will remember that one of the steps in planning a letter is to *visualize your reader*. That is exactly what this letter writer did, and he was willing to stake his reputation and twenty years experience in handling claims on the assumption that the reply in jocular language would be the right approach for this particular individual. You can see for yourself, in the customer's second letter, whether or not the analysis was correct.

And now—the strange mystery of the bobby-pin.

The Letter of Complaint

Gentlemen:

Heretofore, I have been a great exponent of your cereal as the perfect breakfast food. But imagine my chagrin when this morning I opened one of your beautiful packages and saw in all its ugliness the enclosed bobby-pin.

Though I have served in the army of my country where at times filth was of necessity thrust upon me, yet there is to my mind nothing more disgusting in food than the tubular growth that covers our heads. Next to it, I class all appurtenances that are deemed a necessity by the fairer sex to keep their tresses in order.

To find a bobby-pin in one's breakfast food is, to say the least, quite disconcerting.

I may be able to live it down, but never again will I be able to look a choice portion of your cereal in the face without seeing this crinkled, unappetizing bit of foreign substance.

Once a booster for your cereal,

The Letter of Conciliation

Dear Mr. Doe:

You've got me, Mr. Doe, if you saw a bobby-pin in a box of our biscuits. I haven't a thing to say, and I know most of the answers.

You can bet the factory superintendent will hear about your report and every precaution will be taken to prevent the possibility of repetition. You showed a mighty fine spirit in reporting the incident, but believe me, it is a serious matter to us.

> [*Until now the letter is conventional in content*
> *—here the writer begins to skate on thin ice*]

I can readily understand how one might feel at a time like that— if his mind just ran to bobby-pins without any of the trimmings. However, consider for a moment, the romantic side.

You should see some of the "snappy numbers" working in our modern, sanitary plant. Nearly all of them are good for an extra heart-beat or two, and a second look from any live wire—and who cares about the dead ones? Can you honestly say you felt any offensive revolt any time you ever got your face all tangled up in lovely tresses, and whispered sweet nothings into a shell-like, receptive ear?

Even a bobby-pin wasn't so offensive at a time like that, and I'll bet there have been moments when you thought that even hair would make a good breakfast food, if properly treated with a little sugar and cream.

Ah me; those days have gone forever—possibly; but our biscuits (barring unfortunate accidents) are still delightful morsels. I am having another package sent direct to you from the mill.

Here's hoping the evening before was not too strenuous, and the sun is shining brightly, the first time you try this replacement package of —— —— for breakfast.

Sincerely yours,

The Customer's Second Letter

Dear Mr. Smith:

Your "apology" relative to bobby-pins has been received, and appreciated. Thanks for the ride. Mrs. Doe and I were hoping for one, and you didn't disappoint us.

Since your softness of heart will not permit the proper chastisement of your beauty chorus, I hope that the lash of criticism will be laid lightly upon the shoulders of the Simon Legree that superintends your factory. Your use of the word "if" burns me up—however, we will skip it, and get down to cases.

Being an exponent of hair as a breakfast food when treated with sugar and cream, you must be the person about whom it was written—"He stood on a bridge at midnight, his head was in a whirl; his eyes and mouth were full of hair, his arms were full of girl." Be that as it may, your attempt at evasion was delightful, and your description of pulchritude quite inviting.

I was sorry to hear that for you "those days are gone forever," but I am glad to know that one who could at least talk about such things had the privilege of replying to my letter. I am still waiting for the replacement package, and if it is not filled with gold plated bobby-pins, or a round-trip ticket to your city for the purpose of giving your beauty chorus the onceover, I shall be greatly disappointed.

Appreciatively yours,

The tip-off in the adjustment story just reviewed comes in the way the customer ended his first and second letters. The one closed with "Once a booster for your cereal," and the other, "Appreciatively yours." You might accuse the writer who brought this change about as being "unbusinesslike" or "not dignified," but his letter hit the jackpot. It is difficult to find fault with success.

How another adjustment letter made a friend. One of the joys of being an adjustment correspondent is the fact that it is possible to measure the results of a letter by the reader's reaction to it. You saw this fact illustrated in the case of the bobby-pin, and it happens again in the following exchange of correspondence between a gentleman living in Santa Ana, California, and Wm. T. Summers, Jr., writing for Graham Brothers, Inc., Los Angeles.

1. *Complaint*

Gentlemen:

On February 3, I sent your truck driver, A. B. Smith, a repair bill for $15.50, the amount of damage he did when he collided with my auto in front of the school house on E. Chapman Ave. I had signalled a left turn, which he admits.

Up to now he has ignored the bill. If not paid in 5 days, I shall begin suit in the small claims court, to recover same with costs.

Very truly yours,

2. *Adjustment*

Dear Mr. Doe:

Needless to say, we sincerely regret that your claim for damages in the amount of $15.50 has not been adjusted to your satisfaction before this time.

During the twenty-seven years we have been in business we have been extremely jealous of the reputation we have acquired for courtesy, not only from our office executives but from our drivers as well.

We are sorry the accident occurred but hope that our driver conducted himself in a courteous manner. We have instructed Mr. L. B. Long, manager of our operations at Orange, to pay you immediately the $15.50 in full settlement of the claim.

Again we apologize for our delay in taking care of this matter and will appreciate your not holding this unfortunate experience against our record for carefulness and courtesy.

If at any time we can be of service to you, you have only to let us know.

Yours very truly,

3. *Appreciation*

Dear Mr. Summers:

Your most courteous letter was received, and Mr. Long gave me his check for $15.50 in full settlement for the damage done to my auto by your truck driver.

I owe you people an apology for my hasty action and hope you will forgive me. It has been many years since I received so courteous a letter. It has impressed me greatly, and my wife and I often speak about it. . . .

Very truly yours,

It must be conceded "a job well done" when one short letter such as Mr. Summers' can change an angry man threatening to sue, to a smiling man who says, "I owe you people an apology."

3. Telling the Customer "Yes"

Not a difficult letter to write. It requires no particular skill to grant a customer's request, or to adjust a misunderstanding his way. The big thing he is after is satisfaction, and if he gets it, the letter telling him so is comparatively easy to dictate. However, there are two things the correspondent should keep in mind so that the situation may be turned to the best advantage of the company.

One, as already noted, is taking care to grant the request or make the adjustment cheerfully without implying that the customer is getting something to which he is not really entitled. A favor extended grudgingly or with an air of patient condescension is little better than a favor denied. The recipient naturally resents the insinuation that he has been unreasonable, or that he is being humored as a matter of policy.

The second is the complement of the first. If the implication of coddling is carefully avoided, and the adjustment or concession is offered in the light of a *service* which the writer and his company are happy to render, then the time is propitious for the winning of considerable goodwill. Usually the person filing a complaint or asking some special service is on the defensive. He may even present his case more belligerently than the circumstances warrant, hoping in that way to force a favorable reply. If money is involved, he fears that an argument may develop, and worries about a possible loss. Then back comes the letter from the company —sympathetic, agreeable, cheerfully accepting the customer's viewpoint, and asking only the *privilege* of making things right. Under such circumstances, the customer's reaction is highly favorable: he feels that he is dealing with a fine, dependable company; his attitude is one of goodwill. Many a lasting business relationship dates back to a complaint properly handled. The individual who writes adjustment letters can be a *salesman,* even though he never leaves the office.

Make it a big YES. There are a lot of words in our language that people especially like to hear, and surely one of the first ten is *yes*. Of course, it can't always be used in business letters, but when it is possible its use is sure to please.

> Yes, Mr. Doe, you can have another thirty days to pay this bill, and we are very glad to do you this favor.

> Yes, you are right, Mr. Doe. A dealer cannot always anticipate the exact volume of his Christmas sales, and we certainly don't want a fine customer like yourself to be without any of our goods when he has the chance to sell them. We stopped taking orders four weeks ago, but don't worry. You'll get your five cases not later than Wednesday of next week.

> . . . . .

> Yes, Mrs. Doe, what you say in your letter is true. We were late in making the shipment, and we are sorry.

> . . . . .

> Yes, Reverend Doe, your July bill for gas used in your home is somewhat higher than usual—but did you notice that the two preceding bills were averaged?

> . . . . .

> Yes, indeed, Mr. Doe. We will be glad to exchange the sizes, and we consider it a privilege to render you this little service.

Yes is a fine word, isn't it? Well, then, as a business correspondent, use it at every possible opportunity. The reader smiles when you *agree* with him; he frowns when you do not. Even if you are not going to do all that he has asked, it is usually possible to say "yes" about some little part of it. If that is so, *start* with the part that says *yes;* then, reluctantly, swing to the *no.* Even a turndown letter can be dictated in such a way that the reader feels you are sorry it couldn't be otherwise. *Be happy to say yes— be sorry to say no.* The writer who takes pains to follow that simple slogan will make many customers friends.

Consider, for example:

A Happy Yes

Dear Mr. Doe:

Yes, of course. It makes us feel right good to have this chance to give you a lift. You have been a loyal customer for many years; why shouldn't we do something for you once in a while?

Jack Smith, during his call next week, will help you pack the china and see that it is shipped. In the meantime, the numbers that you want will be rushed right out to you.

Best regards, Mr. Doe, and thanks for putting this problem of yours where it belongs—in our lap.

Cordially,

A Sour Yes

Dear Mr. Doe:

It seems a little unreasonable that you should ask us to take back china which you have had in your store for almost a year. We urge our buyers to anticipate their sales carefully, and not to overstock, and while we are pleased to grant you this concession this one time, we must go on record that we are not setting any precedent to follow when you find yourself in a similar predicament in the future.

We might say, also, that several dealers in your territory have been reordering the same numbers you wish to exchange, and if they can sell them, we believe a little push would do as much for you.

Please pack the china very carefully, as we will not be responsible for breakage.

Yours very truly,

A Sad No

Dear Mr. Doe:

Yes, how well we know what a good customer you have been, and you have every right to ask any favor within our power to grant. We do appreciate your business, and like to prove it when we can.

The candy business, as you know, is difficult. We try hard to package our line in the best possible way to withstand the condition you describe. We think you must have found that our candy *does* stay fresh longer than any other brand.

But when we ship an order, and it is accepted by the buyer, about all we can do is sit back and hope he sells it within a reasonable period of time. We just couldn't guarantee it to keep fresh indefinitely—if we did, we would soon be out of the candy business.

The lot you mention has been in your store eight months, and that is a long time for any candy to stay in the condition it left the factory. Of course, as an old candy dealer you know how true that is.

There is one bright side to your problem. You bought 144 of the one pound boxes, and have sold 123. On the latter you have made a substantial profit, and more than enough to offset any loss on those still unsold.

Please understand, Mr. Doe, we feel very badly that we can't take the 21 boxes back. But some other time, we surely will go out of our way to do you a favor—something that the rules of our business will allow.

I think you know how hard it was for me to write this letter, for we are proud to have you sell our fine candies, and surely wish you well.

Sincerely yours,

A Sour No

Dear Mr. Doe:

As a good businessman, and one who has handled package candy for many years, we think you must understand how unreasonable it is to ask any maker to accept the return of goods which are eight months old.

You know that no other firm would do this for you, and you certainly can't ask, in any spirit of fairness, that we be the exception.

Another time, we suggest that you give our packages a better display on your counters and push them harder. Also, it may sound strange for us to say so, but we would much rather you ordered in smaller quantities, than to overshoot the mark and then ask us to hold the bag.

Our answer has to be no, Mr. Doe. We cannot, and will not, allow any dealer to return candy which he has accepted and found to be in good condition. We make it—you sell it. That's the only way we can both realize a fair profit.

Yours very truly,

The letters you have just read need no comment. Two were written by friendly businessmen who really did appreciate their customers. The other two were the misguided efforts of men who have never learned how to say *happy yes* or a *sad no*. Their letters kill business, rather than build it.

Living up to guarantee. The customers receiving the following two letters must have felt kindly toward the writers and their organizations. Both say "Yes" without quibbling. The first letter was mailed for rose growers Jackson & Perkins Co., of New York; the second for Hecker Products Corporation, Indianapolis, makers of Shinola shoe polishes.

From the Rose Growers

Dear Customer:

We are sorry the plants you received from us did not prove satisfactory. In spite of our best efforts, plants sometimes fail to grow properly. We know this has caused you extra work and disappointment.

We want our plants to be satisfactory, and are glad to replace them as we guarantee.

We have, therefore, entered a replacement order for fresh stock to be shipped to you this fall. We are sure this shipment will increase the beauty of your garden.

Yours very truly,

From the Shoe Polish Company

Dear Mr. Doe:

We have received the tin of 2-in-1 Black Paste which you returned—with the key opener broken.

We maintain a rigid inspection crew whose job it is to detect even the slightest imperfection in our tins. Occasionally, one does get by, but it's very rare; nevertheless, you have been unfortunate in receiving one of these imperfect tins, and we are sending you double the purchase price and another tin of 2-in-1 Black Paste.

We want you to be convinced that 2-in-1 Shoe Polishes are the finest you can buy, both in package and contents. Please continue to use 2-in-1—we know you will be satisfied.

Yours very truly,

Cooling a hot-headed customer. It is indeed an unusual trend of events when a customer demands an adjustment, gets it, and then relents and gives the money back. All of this was brought about by the fine letter written by the company correspondent. You could hardly find a more satisfying example of well-handled customer relations than the following— an adjustment drama in three acts.

Act I—Customer's First Letter

Gentlemen:

Your letter of January 8th asks about an order we made for goods in November. This order was mailed with two one-dollar bills and forty cents enclosed.

I note what you say in regard to receiving the 40¢ remittance only. I want to ask again as I did in my former letter, why did you send the goods, if there was only 40¢ in the envelope? Please answer this.

We have never established a credit with you. We have always paid cash. It is very unreasonable for you to have sent goods when you received only about one-sixth of the cost. I don't believe the head of your company tolerates that kind of business. Furthermore, I believe if a clerk filled an order that way, you would release him from your service.

Please give me the name of the clerk that filled the order in this way. Also his address.

I am sorry after so many years of dealing with you that such a thing as this should interrupt our friendship. But it would be an easy matter for your clerk who handled this order to take the two one-dollar bills.

We have a neighbor who had the entire amount of money for his order taken, but the order was filled later—by either you or Sears Roebuck.

Kindly give the above information, so it will be easier to trace the thief.

Yours truly,

Act II—Company Reply

Dear Mr. Doe:

I am sorry there has been a misunderstanding about your remittance. But there was only 40 cents with the order when we received it, Mr. Doe. We looked carefully and are still holding the piece of cardboard in which the coins were wrapped.

And now I will explain why we sent the goods without the full amount to pay for them. Evidently, Mrs. Doe forgot to put a stamp on the envelope, for the El Dorado postmaster wrote us for the postage. We sent it at once, and the letter was delivered to us on November 12. Although you have never had an open account with us, there had already been quite a delay and thinking you were in a hurry for the goods, we sent them on and wrote you for the balance due us.

Our mail is opened by bonded clerks and each one is under the strictest supervision, so it is hardly probable that the two one-dollar bills were taken after the order reached us. As we have a number of these clerks, it is impossible to give you the name of the one opening your letter.

As you perhaps know, it is not safe to send money through the mail in any form except by express or post office money order, bank draft or personal check. If for any reason silver or currency must be used, the letter should be registered. Otherwise, the money goes at the sender's risk, and we can hardly be expected to make good any loss that may occur.

But you have been such a good customer for so many years that we wouldn't risk having a misunderstanding come between us, so we are marking the $1.99 account paid. So, if you will use one of the safe ways when sending your future remittance, we can promise you prompt and efficient service.

Yours very truly,

Act III—Customer's Second Letter

Dear Sir:

Your kind and explanatory letter of January 15 received. I assure you such a fine letter is thankfully received.

I am sorry indeed this trouble has occurred between us. I have repeatedly cautioned my wife about sending cash through the mail, as the weight of the coins would signify there was money inside, and by taking out the currency and leaving the coins, the next postal clerk might swear the coins were still in the envelope when he handled it.

We understood cash is sent at our risk. My wife has sent much cash in this way and refuses to buy a money order.

I am sure the two one-dollar bills were placed in the envelope with the coins as our oldest son saw his mother place them there and seal the envelope. He did not see her mail the letter, however, so doesn't know whether she stamped it or not. She doesn't remember stamping it.

I note your explanation about your clerks and I hope they are not guilty of stealing the money.

I am sending my personal check to the amount of $1.99 to cover this account. I will ask you to re-enter the account on your books and then balance it with this check. I am enclosing two five-cent stamps for the postage you sent to El Dorado as you mentioned in your letter.

I assure you again I am very sorry about this trouble and appreciate your attention, and the kindness you have shown, and I believe you are correct all the way through.

My wife says she is through sending cash in this way.

                                        Very truly yours,

P.S. I placed an order through your store at Nevada to your house for $11.07 last Monday.

When shipment is larger than ordered. Among the most common and annoying mistakes in business is the shipping of goods not ordered, or sometimes just a larger amount than ordered. In such cases the customer must be satisfied, of course, even at the cost of having the unwanted goods returned. In the following letter, you see how this problem is handled by E. C. Carlson, writing for McKesson & Robbins, Minneapolis wholesale druggists.

Friend Doe:

Jim Hopkins reported with the nice order given him yesterday that we shipped five cases of soap on an order written for one case.

Since it's expensive soap and a sixty-day or more supply, it's entirely up to you as to the return of the overshipment, but that involves trouble to you and expense to us, so I thought if thirty days extra for discounting the bill is O.K. with you, I'd mark the account accordingly.

I talked with the operator in the Entry Department about the error and can see where she could easily have read the one for a five, but I know Jim intended it as one case and that's that. The Adjustment Department is ready to pass credit if you return it, so you can just do as you like. I'll make notation on the account card that the dating will apply if no return is made.

Very sorry about the mistake, Mr. Doe. You know we try hard to avoid such things, and thank you for today's order which is on its way.

Yours very truly,

Of course, the letters you have been reading are only a small sample of the many that must be written by the Adjustment Manager, or someone in his department, when different circumstances justify telling the customer that what he wants will be granted. You will see more of them in the following section devoted to Credit and Collection letters. As previously stated, the writing of such letters involves no particular problem, since the reader is sure to be pleased with the "Yes" which they contain.

4. Letters That Must Say "No"

A much more exacting job. When the customer's request must be denied, completely or in part, the man telling him so faces a rather difficult situation. The only bright side of the problem is that in many cases the customer's request is based on a misunderstanding of the circumstances, and being fair-minded, as most people are, he may listen favorably to reason. If, however, the appeal to reason fails—from lack of tact on the part of the correspondent or stubbornness on the part of the customer—future business may be wiped out.

Certainly, the job of refusing the customer should not be left to an inexperienced clerk, or to one not well-regarded as a writer of friendly letters. It is a task requiring the highest type of diplomacy, and should be delegated to one of the best letter writers in the company, and of course, one who is closely allied to sales.

The letters which follow cover a few of the circumstances in business which involve trying to deny the customer what he wants and at the same time keeping his goodwill. The number of these situations is almost countless, but the method of handling them is pretty much the same. They all seek tactfully to make the customer *understand* why the company cannot go along with him—they appeal to the customer's sense of fairness when he is acquainted with the company's point of view.

Turning down request for advertising help. Every advertising manager is beset with the problem of what to say to customers who ask special advertising helps. The request may take any one of a thousand forms, but whatever its nature, if granted it has little or no value to the company, and becomes an unwarranted drain on the coordinated advertising budget. A dealer wants free goods for sampling at a local business show, money for participation in some special advertising scheme promoted by his home-town newspaper, prizes to contribute to a church bazaar, permission to sponsor an athletic team which means paying the entry fee and buying the uniforms, or for some other purpose which in his mind is worthwhile promotion for the company and his own store. Or, the request may be a contribution to some civic or charitable enterprise—money for the Community Chest, a batch of tickets to the Firemen's Ball, or for food donations to the poor.

In many cases the cause is worthy, but what the individual dealer does not realize is that the city involved is only *one* of *many* in which the company's goods are sold. If the bars are let down in one instance, a precedent is established for similar action in all other instances of the same type. An enormous amount of money can be spent by any company for such purposes, and yet none of them are connected with the general advertising plan for the year, nor has any money been included in the annual budget to cover them.

The letter which follows covers one of the situations just described. It is evidently a follow-up of a previous denial which had aroused considerable anger.

> Dear Mr. Doe:
>
> That was a sizzling response you gave to our last letter. Please accept my apology for not making our position clear.
>
> You, as a director of promotional work, must have the problem of deciding where your advertising money is to be spent. From the many very desirable advertising media available, you must select a few. When advertising dollars are scarce, good management demands that you concentrate them on a few lines that have proved most effective for you.
>
> Well, we're in the same boat. Our budget this year just would not cover booth space and premium-list advertising, although we know it is valuable.

This year, as usual, we are receiving requests to advertise with hundreds of show secretaries, county agents, and association men who are our good friends. We can't advertise with them all, and you'll agree, I know, that it would be unfair to play favorites.

Our wish for your success was not as empty as it may have seemed. Our men know the value of good shows. They also know good stock and have helped many a feeder to select and develop prize winners. Many of the entries in your show this year will be made by owners who were encouraged by our salesmen to send them to you.

So we believe our relations thus far have been mutually helpful. We want them to continue that way.

Sincerely yours,

Sometimes a dealer takes the bull by the horns and spends company money without the slightest authority. Of course, it turns out later that he has spent *his own* money, but the problem of telling him so is a little difficult. A typical situation of this kind is covered by the two letters below: first, the dealer's letter assuming the expense will be approved, and then the company's letter which sets him right.

Dealer's Letter About Unapproved Advertising

Gentlemen:

The first lot of your radios is more than half sold. You can see that you made no mistake in giving me the account. On the very first day we hit the ball for nine of the Super-Tones, six of the Miniatures, and had three auto installations. Here's how we did it:

We put on a grand opening two weeks ago last Saturday. Every woman who came to our store that day got a present of a fine potted flower, and we passed out thirty-cent cigars to all the men. This cost me some dough, but I'm not a piker when it comes to doing things right. Also, we gave balloons to all the kids.

Of course, I had to let the public know what was going on, so I ran a half-page ad in the Gazette for two days before the grand opening. The owner of this paper is a lodge brother of mine, and he gave me a special rate of $100 for the two insertions.

I asked your salesman, Tim Murphy, about your paying for this ad, but he said he had no authority to approve it. So I went ahead anyway, knowing you would be glad to cooperate. If there is any question about it, I'll meet you halfway and split the bill, but I imagine you'll pay it all, now that you know how much we sold the first day.

Don't worry about your account here. Your account is in good hands, as you'll have more reason to know as the year goes on.

Very truly yours,

The Company Says "No"

Dear Mr. Doe:

When Mr. Murphy sent us your initial order he remarked, "If Mr. Doe doesn't lead any other dealer in this part of the country, I'll eat my hat." And from the start you have made, it looks as if he will escape indigestion.

We can see you are a merchandiser from the word go. That you rightfully look on local advertising as an *investment* is evident from all the things you did on your opening day.

You appreciate that the only sound relationship between dealer and manufacturer is an unselfish partnership—each partner accepting a fair share of the responsibilities. Our advertising responsibility is to plan and pay for a big, successful *national* program; yours is to support this program locally, as you have so well started out to do.

If we tried to advertise locally for nearly three thousand distributors, we couldn't do the right job nationally. We know you would rather have the benefits of a desire-creating national campaign, running month after month, building sales for you, minimizing the strength of competition, increasing the power of your own advertising, than receive a petty allowance, and be left to fight a lone battle.

Your opening advertising showed you a profit on actual sales, and gave you contacts which should lead to many more sales in the days ahead. And we know you say, "Any advertising expense that makes a profit for me is all to the good."

You can count on us to do our part always—with the greatest radio value on the market; with prompt, careful service—with a continuation of our national advertising. And we know we can count on you in the same way to do *your* part—with your usual force and enthusiasm.

Sincerely yours,

Refusing a big order at a lower price. More thorns in the flesh of business are the requests from customers who think a big order should bring them a concession in price. Often, they are difficult to refuse because an order may be lost, but most executives are agreed that price-cutting is a practice which in the long run does not pay. He who can write the letter which makes the order stick without any concession is a favored son in his company—and here's how one man did the job.

Dear Mr. Doe:

John Smith submitted to us your order for 10 dozen of our style No. 190 at $12.50 each, and I am forced to grip the arms of my chair with super-strength to resist his arguments, which are the embodiment of logic and common sense.

But the man whose example I want to follow—the man whose business principles I admire and try to emulate—is none other than yourself. I know for a fact that if the Beau Brummel of your city came into your store he could not buy his clothing one cent cheaper than the lowliest habitue of your Main Street, despite the fact that the selection of your clothing by this Beau Brummel could influence countless others to trade at your store.

If your business had not been built on the principle of *one price to all,* your store never could have achieved the success it has, nor would it be recognized today as *first* in your city.

By no other policy could it have won the confidence of your community, and what is just as important, even the confidence of your competitors.

And the same principle of one price for all, Mr. Doe, is the one that can build also for me. So you need only to look into your own heart to know why I must at all costs adhere to the same policy on which your own store's business was built, for if I waive I should surely be a failure.

I know that you, above all, will give me credit for this desire to succeed in the right way. I am also sure you will be the last one to refuse to give me business simply because of my determination to stick to the path you yourself have followed.

I enclose a little booklet which explains style No. 190 fully, and I wish there were some way by which I could have you know, just as well as I do, that every statement in this booklet is a correct statement of facts—with nothing "dolled up" to make it sound good.

Should you care to compare our No. 190 with any other competing number you can easily get the facts by having a pair of each tested by a reputable testing firm. We have had tests made of all the numbers that compete with ours and we can say with honest conviction that we have not found its equal yet.

Sincerely yours,

Refusing to sell direct. We don't suppose a day passes in the life of the average manufacturing company that one or more letters are not received from people who are trying, either from ignorance or intent, to bypass authorized distributors. No company of reputable rating, however, will compete with its own dealers by selling direct to a consumer; in fact, no company would long have any dealers if it followed such a practice. Under such circumstances, the logical procedure is a friendly letter to the ambitious buyer which holds his interest in the product, but sends him to the nearest distributor to get it. A very good letter to handle this situation is one which appears in the *Business Executive's Handbook,* published by Prentice-Hall, Inc. It uses the line of thought which would fit almost any similar need.

Dear Mrs. Doe:

Thank you very much for your order for one of our new ELEC-TRA electric irons.

We sincerely appreciate this evidence of your interest in the new ELECTRA, and wish that we could fill your order. However, as manufacturers, we sell through retail dealers, and our arrangement with the dealers throughout the country does not permit our selling direct from the factory.

We regret, therefore, that we must return your check with the request that you either visit or telephone the ELECTRA dealer in your city, who will be glad to deliver your iron at the price advertised. In buying from the dealer, you will have the advantage of choosing from a large stock and will avoid the annoyance of possible delay in shipment.

The name, address, and telephone number of the ELECTRA dealer in your city is:

> Polk Electrical Supply Company,
> 4422 East Main Street,
> Telephone, YOrk 8–3330.

Every ELECTRA is guaranteed by us, and also by the dealer, to be in perfect condition.

We hope that you will soon be numbered among the many thousands of women who have found that with the new ELECTRA ironing is no longer a drudgery. The ELECTRA is very easy to handle. It saves 30% of the time needed when you use any other electric iron now on the market.

To bring an ELECTRA to your home, simply pick up the telephone and call:

> YOrk 8–3330.

Sincerely yours,

With this suggested letter, the *Business Executive's Handbook* supplies an outline which can be followed by any person faced with the same problem of telling a would-be direct buyer to see the authorized dealer.

1. Start by thanking the buyer.
2. Explain that you sell only through dealers.

3. Say that check is enclosed.

4. Give name, address, and telephone number of dealer.

5. Mention guarantee of the product.

6. Re-sell the product to hold the buyer in line.

We think the above outline might contain two more points. These would be:

2½. Explain *advantages* of buying from a dealer.

4½. Notify dealer of a prospective customer in his town.

When *true,* as it may be of certain products and services, point 2½ can be made quite convincing in the turn-down letter. The person buying from a local dealer or agent can conveniently turn to the latter for repairs and get quick attention for any justified complaint. People who buy automobiles at the factory, for example, sometimes have more trouble in getting them serviced than do those who buy their cars "at home." An alert dealer would appreciate point 4½—the *service* from the factory, the customer-lead.

Explaining damage in transit. A considerable number of the complaints that must be adjusted in business are based on customer dissatisfaction with the *condition* of the delivered goods. Some of these causes for complaint are purely imaginary, and must be handled with a firm but polite *no.* An example was the case of the merchant who wanted to return candy which had been in his store eight months. Other times, the damage claimed is so slight that the buyer is only looking for trouble in mentioning it. Even if the trouble is so slight as a tiny scratch on the leg of a chair, no company can afford to brush it off too brusquely. The concern of the buyer may seem petty and foolish, but it is still important to *him.*

In the great majority of damage claims, the common carrier is at fault and not the company. The goods are carefully packed and delivered in perfect condition to the carrier, and the damage occurs between that time and delivery. In such cases, the carrier is responsible, but not unless the condition is declared before the goods are taken away and stored or displayed in the buyer's place of business. Not all claims may be approved by the carrier, and when one isn't, the shipper is likely to feel the full blast of the buyer's displeasure.

Experienced buyers—retail and wholesale—understand the obligations of the carrier, and how to handle claims for damage in transit. All the seller has to do after learning of the damage is to supply the date of shipment, the bill of lading number, and the name of the transportation company. With this information, the buyer is content to present his claim direct to the carrier; this is the procedure usually followed.

However, as a goodwill service some companies prefer to adjust the buyer's complaint and look to the carrier for compensation. This plan is especially favored in dealing with small or inexperienced buyers who seldom get a shipment and do not understand how to present a claim to a carrier. It involves trouble and some small expense for the company, but both are more than offset by the goodwill to be won by the special service. A good illustration of such service is found in the book, *Modern Business English,** by Babenroth and Parkhurst. You will agree that any person who received a letter like the following one would feel cordial toward the company sending it.

Dear Sir:

We are very sorry to know from your letter of March 15 that the mahogany desk you ordered as a birthday gift for your son arrived so badly marred that you cannot accept it.

As the Chicago, Milwaukee and St. Paul Railroad gave us a receipt acknowledging that the desk was received perfectly crated, it must have been damaged in transit. Although our responsibility ends when the railroad has accepted the desk, we know how much interest you have in this beautiful and useful gift for your son. We are, therefore, sending you today, by pre-paid express, another desk exactly like the one you ordered. It should reach you promptly.

If you will please telephone the express company to make a special delivery immediately on the arrival of the desk at their receiving station, you should have it not later than the day of your son's birthday.

Please leave the damaged desk in the hands of the railroad. We shall enter a claim with them, so that you will not be troubled further.

We thank you for writing promptly, and assure you that our only desire is that you receive the desk promptly, and in perfect condition.

Sincerely yours,

The man who dictated the above letter demonstrated both his own keen knowledge of human nature and a fine spirit of service on the part of his company. First, he made plain to the customer that the company's responsibility ended with delivery of the desk to the carrier. Hence, he made it clear that the company was going out of its way to make the son's birthday a pleasant one, and to spare the customer the necessity of filing

---

* Publishers: Prentice-Hall, Inc., Englewood Cliffs, N.J.

his own claim against the railroad. In other words, the writer made sure that the goodwill services rendered by his company would be understood and fully appreciated.

5. LETTERS THAT DEAL WITH PRICE ADVANCES

How to announce higher prices. Naturally, no individual or company likes to hear that the price of a commodity or service has gone up. Unless the news is presented tactfully, the buyer may turn to other sources of supply in an effort to escape the increase, and even though unsuccessful, may place his order with another firm. Businessmen do not like to see their customers in a shopping mood, and they realize the importance of making the announcement of a price increase as painless as possible. Unfortunately, this objective often tends to make the announcement letter too apologetic, as if the writer *feared* an unpleasant reaction from his customer. Note the almost guilty tone of the opening paragraph of a letter used by one sales manager.

> For months, against a steadily rising market, we have stoutly battled to maintain our present price levels, but we are now reluctantly forced to advise increases which we hope you will accept as necessary, and without any loss of your valued business.

It is obvious that the writer of the above paragraph was trembling in his boots, and fearful that the reader would resent the increases and take his orders elsewhere. Because of his own mental attitude toward the price changes, the very thing he fears is likely to happen. The customer says to himself: "The writer of this letter must· know his company is taking advantage of a higher market, or he would not be so apologetic—he isn't pulling any wool over my eyes."

Of course, it is also possible to make the announcement of higher prices too blunt or casual. No doubt you have seen letters of this type, in which the writer seems to gloat over the fact that at last the company can reap a greater profit. He makes it plain that business is brisk, and that the orders of the customer are not especially needed. For example:

> We are pleased to send you our new price list, with the under-standing that all of the quotations are subject to change without notice. We might add that our factory is now operating around the clock, and orders on hand are ample to keep us on that schedule indefinitely.

There is plenty to irritate the customer in such a tactless announcement. The writer is "pleased" to send it. He says in a rather domineering way that the quotations will be changed at the will of his company. Then he boasts about the number of orders on hand, and how the factory is running twenty-four hours a day. He plainly implies: "Here are the new prices. You may take them or leave them. It makes no difference to us." In assuming such a devil-may-care attitude, the writer forgets that the time may come when his company will again be begging for orders. He creates a spectre of ill will which later will come back to haunt him.

Another illustration of the same short-sighted business practice, is supplied by the experience of a purchasing agent representing a large Midwestern corporation. He wrote to a furniture manufacturer, seeking to contract for a considerable number of items to be used in sales contests. His first letter, and a second, were ignored but finally the third attempt produced the following reply.

> Dear Sir:
>
> We note your comment with respect to previous letters which you have written to us, but you must understand that we are under great pressure, and we cannot favor correspondence to the detriment of important operations incidental to the filling of orders.
>
> We do not care to sell on the basis outlined in your letters. For the past three months we have been running our plant day and night, and without another order we would still keep busy for the next six months.
>
> Frankly, we prefer to concentrate on serving customers already on our books, rather than negotiate any new business.
>
> Yours very truly,

Not only is the above letter discourteous, even insulting, but it also demonstrates how differently a prospect may be regarded in good times and bad. For several years, the purchasing agent who wanted to buy the furniture had been beset by salesmen of the company who needed his business.

One of the simplest ways to announce higher prices is to send the new list without special comment, while trying to put into the letter something else that may be encouraging to the buyer. The latter is well aware, usually, of any general trend in the market, and he is not likely to be surprised when a particular company follows the trend. If the buyer is a merchant, his own sales prices have been advanced, anyway.

When it seems best to *explain* the price changes, figures carry much more conviction than mere generalities, such as "in keeping with the advancing cost of raw materials," or "because of the stiffening market in all lines of business." The figures used in the next letter make the price advances seem quite necessary and reasonable.

Gentlemen:

As you no doubt expected, the enclosed new price list reveals a number of increases. A few figures will quickly tell you why these quotations leave us only a reasonable margin of profit.

Today we are paying 40 per cent more for burlap bags than we did a year ago. Of the more than one hundred ingredients that we mix to put in them, not a single one has failed to advance in cost to us. The range of these increases runs from 20 to 160 per cent.

So, to keep in step with these widespread improvements in business conditions, we have had to change our own prices accordingly. Probably you have had to do the same thing in your own business.

Sincerely yours,

The psychological approach used in the concluding paragraph of the above announcement is particularly good. In a rather casual way, the increase in prices is connected with something pleasing to the dealer— "improvements in business conditions." Then the idea is pleasingly advanced that the dealer has also advanced his own prices. Thus, the customer and the company are placed in the same boat, and the chance of mutual understanding is good.

Although it is not possible to set forth any "one right way" to announce higher prices, certain general principles seem to emerge from the comments already made:

1. Don't apologize. Prices must go up and down with the business market. The seller is always entitled to a reasonable profit.

2. On the other hand, don't be callous or indifferent if the announcement happens to be made when orders are easy to get. The customer is entitled to as much courtesy and consideration in good times as in bad times.

3. In a general rising market, it is usually unnecessary to *justify* the advance. Don't weaken your position with explanations.

4. If, for some special reason, an explanation does seem desirable, be specific. Figures that prove increased cost of production are far more convincing than generalities.

5. When possible, accompany the announcement with some comment or fact that points to more favorable business conditions. Make the buyer realize that higher prices are only an indication of better times for *him*.

Breaking the news optimistically. The letter containing the announcement of higher prices should never indicate fear or doubt in the mind of the writer as to how the news may be received. The tone of the letter needs to be confident, unconcerned, and as optimistic as it can possibly be made. This is the tone in the following letter written by D. H. Dyer for the Owatonna Tool Co., Owatonna, Minnesota. First, he talks about the many new "specials" brought out for the benefit of customers, and then he minimizes the extent and number of the price increases—he makes *good news* of the fact for his customers.

Dear Mr. Doe:

Your copy of the OTC Hand Tool Catalog is in the other compartment of this envelope.

Because of new machinery design, you now require many more special tools than ever before, and we are happy to tell you that over 100 of these "specials" were brought out for you during the last year. They're all in this pocket edition catalog, along with the 800 other items in the OTC line, so look it over carefully. (If you hurry, you might skip a page which shows just what you have been wishing for.)

Since the cost of everything from soup to nuts has been skyrocketing, you'll be surprised when you see that not all of the items have been advanced; that many were raised only a little; and that some are still the same. We had to scratch our heads to do it, but conditions like we are going through are good for all of us because we keep on our toes.

One thing you can be sure of is: OTC quality is still tops. So, when you need anything, shoot your order in to us on one of the postage-free cards, and we'll see that you get what you want, when you want it.

Thanks for readin'.

Sincerely yours,

In a letter written for the Menasha Products Company by B. T. Hoffmaster, the edge of higher prices is dulled by reminding the jobber of the extra profit to be made from stock already on hand, or that ordered before the advance. The emphasis is placed on sales to be made, and the mention of prices is secondary.

COLD CUT TIME IS
KABNET WAX TIME

And, with temperatures ranging from 70 to 100 degrees, THIS IS COLD CUT TIME!

Butchers everywhere are appealing to jaded summer appetites by featuring luncheon meats and other hot weather foods. Most of them are wrapped in waxed paper. To help your salesmen make it KABNET WAX, a full page ad is appearing directly inside the front cover in the August issue of *Meat Merchandising,* the Business Paper of the Retail Industry. Reprints will be mailed to your salesmen in a week. Cash in on this KABNET WAX season.

More good news for you is the fact that your present inventory of KABNET WAX, plus any orders placed prior to August 2nd, will make you some extra profit. Attached are the slightly higher prices effective as of that date. Higher retail schedules are also attached. Regardless of what floor stock you may have, may we ask that you advise your sales force of these new prices and put them into effect with your trade at once? We are making this request of all KABNET WAX distributors.

Your co-operation in capitalizing on the summer KABNET WAX season, and in putting these slightly increased prices into effect at once, will be sincerely appreciated.

Yours very truly,

Using price advance as sales lever. An old sales stimulator—and it works, as you know—is the offer to accept orders at prevailing prices until a given date, when an advance is to be made. In fact, salesmen frequently are accused of dating orders back in the misguided attempt to get the old prices for their customers; but when the company makes the offer and adheres to the announced date, there is nothing unethical in the practice. H. M. Sossaman, in the following message to customers who have not ordered, used the lever to pry up business for the Quaker City Rubber Company.

Gentlemen:

This morning the robins were chirping at a great rate—so loud, in fact—that I got up half an hour earlier than usual.

Now—if you ever saw any person uneasier than a commuter in the morning with more than five minutes to spare—I'd like to meet him. That's what the robins did to me.

Five minutes to kill! "When the robins come, the lawn must be sprinkled." So down to the cellar I went and pulled out the hose —a fifty-foot section of Wonderful Garden Hose—that had already seen ten seasons' service. It may last another!

That's the kind of hose we want you to be selling. Quaker Garden Hose makes and keeps customers. We missed your order greatly this year. Kinda nice to fill it last year—we want to do it again.

And here's the offer—

Prices are advancing! If you will send us your order before May 1st for shipment as soon as possible, we will accept it at the before-the-advance price. A clear-cut saving of 10 per cent to you. Sorry—but orders for future delivery cannot be accepted.

You know Quaker products—Quaker goods have a margin that is interesting. The order form is for your convenience. Fill out NOW—insert in envelope and mail—no stamp necessary.

Very truly yours,

Using the same weapon in less romantic fashion—without the robins —is an announcement mailed by the Moncrief Lenoir Manufacturing Company, Houston, Texas.

TO THE SHEET METAL TRADE:

Prices on Galvanized Steel and Copper Bearing Flat Sheets will advance 25¢ per 100# on August first.

Save money! Send us your order for your needs during the next few weeks. Our complete stock is ready for immediate shipment.

Orders will be accepted at present prices until August 1st. Shipment or delivery will have to be made by August 10th.

TERMS: 2% ten days or thirty days net, subject to the approval of our credit department.

Protect yourself against this advance.

Send us your order now.

Yours very truly,

Letter to customer of long standing. The preceding announcement presented no special problem to the writer. It was a form letter sent to the trade and could be strictly impersonal. Many notices of higher prices fall in the same class. An entirely different problem confronts the executive who must break the news to an important distributor with whom he is well acquainted after years of business relationship. In the latter case, the letter goes to *one* man, instead of a group, and the plea for understanding can be made in a personal way, as one friend talks to another.

A very fine example of this kind of business writing is a letter once sent to a business friend and customer by President Jim Shirreffs, of the S & M Light Co., Los Angeles.

Dear Ernie:

Everywhere we go, we notice that prices are increasing. It makes no difference whether this is soup or nuts—in the average meal we eat, shoes, clothing, or perhaps the price of liquor. Inasmuch as you read the newspapers, it will be no news to you that the price of labor and materials has advanced rapidly and consistently.

Higher labor costs have increased material costs, or vice versa. In any event, finished goods are commanding higher figures today than they have for many months. These higher wages mean more prosperity for the working man, which in turn reflects back to the capital goods industry, and sooner or later affects Ernie Doe and Jim Shirreffs.

All of which means that, effective June 15, there will be an increase in the price of finished goods for your company. This increase is not very material, and no doubt can be easily absorbed without making any change in your cost setup, at least temporarily, and can later be passed on to your dealers and consuming public.

I am outlining the various items which we make for you, with a comparison of your old cost and the new. This is covered by the attached sheet. You will note that in three cases there have been no changes. The sum total, considering all these items as component parts of one unit, shows a net increase of 11 per cent. This covers labor and material.

As you know, Ernie, material and labor costs have been advancing. We have preferred to absorb these costs for the past several months, rather than to pass them on to you, but it can't be done any more—hence, all new shipments are being billed at these new prices, the first batch of which are covered by the enclosed invoices.

I look for these prices to be stable for some time to come, but in the present labor and metal market, anybody's guess is good.

Best regards from Bill and "Yours Truly,"

Yours for "Better Lite-ing,"

The above letter follows the line of thought suggested earlier in this discussion. It is not in any sense apologetic. Mr. Shirreffs simply puts his cards upward on the table and asks for cooperation. His letter is friendly and convincing. It accomplished its purpose.

Answering price objections. There is considerable difference between *announcing* a higher price and *defending* it when some customer files an objection. The reply to the latter must take time to answer every point, and to change the unfavorable opinion. Unless this job is fully performed, the danger of a breach in the business relationship is present.

The writing of such a letter is not to be taken lightly. Great care must be used not to *argue* with the customer, or to scoff at any reason he may have advanced in support of his opinion. On the other hand, the writer must firmly support his own position, and prove the price is *not* too high. Obviously, the job requires both skill and patience; it is one of the most difficult in the field of business correspondence, as well as in the field of personal selling. The following letter shows how one sales manager handled the "too high" objection.

Dear Mr. Doe:

I certainly appreciated your letter, even though I cannot agree with you that our prices are too high. While it is true that some commodities are cheaper today than they were a year ago, this does not apply to our particular line.

In fact, Mr. Doe, we are paying 10 per cent more, on an average, for our raw materials.

Prices, after all, are relatively unimportant. Except in one or two rare instances, no manufacturer and no merchant has ever developed a permanent business or made any money selling "price goods." We cannot afford to do business on a price basis, and I do not believe you can either.

When both sides of the ledger have been added, and a balance struck, isn't it a fact that our biggest and most important asset is our good name? In that respect, we are all like Tom Smith of Big Bend, Kansas.

One day Tom was the richest and best beloved man in his town. The next morning he was a homeless pauper—house and store scattered to the four winds by a tornado.

In six months he was on his feet again and almost as well off as before. Why? Because Tom had one valuable asset. People trusted him. We wired him to order what he needed and pay when he could—and so did every other house with whom he was doing business. A tornado might destroy his house and his store —but it could not damage his good name.

Your good name, too, is worth more to you than anything you own, just as ours is to us. Your name and our name stand for the goods we carry and the business methods we use. Neither of us can afford to sell poor goods at cut prices.

Considering the cost of our raw materials and labor, our prices are fair. Our overhead is the lowest in the industry. The only way we could reduce prices, and continue to make normal profits, would be to cheapen the product. If we did, it would destroy our good name as a manufacturer, and yours as a merchant, if you continued to sell our line.

Do you believe that either of us can afford to do this?

                                     Yours very truly,

The foregoing letter has several points in its favor. It starts with a word of appreciation for the customer's letter, and cleverly avoids any semblance of irritation or resentment. It compliments the customer as a high-grade merchant, and leads him gently to the thought that he could not afford to handle cut-price goods. It wins agreement by asking questions which must be answered in the affirmative.

Another very excellent letter of the same type, is the one below—written for the Gates Rubber Company, Denver, Colorado, by C. A. Winser. The situation facing this writer was critical, for the buyer had refused to renew a contract because of a 5 per cent increase in price. On Mr. Winser's letter depended whether the business would be lost or saved. The letter triumphed; the contract was signed.

> (*No salutation*)
>
> Last year, Mr. Doe, you gave us $5,533 worth of business—and believe me, we appreciated it. We tried to show this appreciation by giving you the finest service we could, and what is more important perhaps, we did supply you with the finest V-belts that you could possibly buy.
>
> I am not going to say anything about Gates quality to you, because you are familiar with it.
>
> But you know, Mr. Doe, *quality* is an odd commodity. The sincere manufacturer buys it by the pound and by the hour; he builds his factory with it; he makes his engineers use it to design his products; he surrounds his salesmen with it; and lastly, he stuffs it into his products until it reaches the bursting point. Gates products are built that way.
>
> It would have been very easy to leave that 5 per cent out of our manufacturing cost, Mr. Doe. I don't think anybody could ever detect a 5 per cent loss in quality. However, if we did leave it out, Gates Vulco Ropes wouldn't be the *best* we could manufacture—not by 5 per cent they wouldn't.
>
> We didn't like raising our prices, but *every single item* that goes into our belts has gone up in price during the last few months. We *had* to.
>
> If you do the same amount of business with us this year as you did last, that change in discount only comes to $285 for the entire year. *One* set of cheaper ropes that fail can cost you many times that much in lost time alone.
>
> We are very proud of that agreement with your company, Mr. Doe. It means a lot to us. Won't you send it along—and be sure of getting the finest belts on the market for another year?
>
> (*No complimentary close*)

In the last two letters, you have seen an adroit use of the only argument that seems to hold water against the customer's lament, "Your price is too high." Price is a relative condition, determined by prevailing cost of materials and labor, plus a reasonable profit for the seller. Assuming that methods of production are efficient, there seems to be no way to reduce a price except by the sacrifice of quality. Both of the writers presented this thought effectively.

The high cost of advertising. The average consumer may look suspiciously on various forms of national advertising—television and radio programs on chain hook-ups, full page insertions in the magazines, and all the other media used to tell him about some product or service. He knows that all these things cost a lot of money, and he thinks that they add to the cost of what he is asked to buy. Dealers, too, with their local viewpoint, often question the value of national advertising, and a very common problem in business correspondence is answering a letter like the one that follows.

> Gentlemen:
>
> Maybe you do not care to have your dealers tell you how to run your business, but the comment is frequently heard in our store that your goods are too expensive, and that a cut in the cost could be made if you would not spend so much on advertising. Printer's ink will sell any article, good or bad, but meritorious articles sell themselves.
>
> Painted signs at every country crossroad, expensive booklets scattered all over the country where half of them are never read at all, and T.V. radio programs, cost a heap of money.
>
> The writer cannot help suggesting that if you would advertise sufficiently but not so extravagantly, and give your buyers the benefit of the saving, it would be a contribution to your firm, and to ours as well.
>
> If your products are anything like as good as you claim they are, you do not need all these extravagant advertisements—both in cost and expression—to sell them. Why not put your prices where people can afford to buy, and remember that "the best advertisement is a pleased customer?"
>
> Yours truly,

The above letter was written to the sales manager of a well-known corporation that sells from coast to coast. It is typical of the many similar complaints received by companies that spend a lot of money advertising their products.

These complaints, like any of the others that come to a business organization, need to be adjusted. The explanation, of course, is that advertising *reduces* price of product by stimulating greater sales volume; the greater the volume, the lower the cost of production. Any major business executive understands this fact, even though it is not understood by the average man of the street, or by down-the-line dealers.

The following letter shows how two business executives handle the complaint of high cost advertising:

Dear Mr. Doe:

I know a man who owns ten suits of clothes. I mentioned it to a friend not long ago. "Ten suits!" he exclaimed, almost angrily, "Why, no man needs ten suits. I only have two."

I told him that the man was one of the most successful securities salesmen in the Middle West, and that his clothes were just as necessary in meeting customers as was his car in taking him to their places of business. But my friend couldn't see it. He still insisted that ten suits was an extravagance. He never has sold anything and never will; he needs only one suit for work days, and one for "Sunday best."

Our advertising is like those ten suits of clothes. We don't advertise to preen ourselves. We do it because advertising is necessary—vitally necessary to our business. We manufacture a tremendous number of tires each month. In order to maintain this volume we must advertise heavily to practically every man and woman in America through as many mediums as we find profitable. It is our aim to keep you conscious of our tires from the time you leave your house in the morning until you switch off your radio at night.

Years of careful checking have shown us that we are on the right track. After all, the million dollars we spend annually for advertising represents only a small percentage of our sales cost— a few cents per tire. But it is these few cents per tire which keep up our volume and hold down our costs. We are building a better tire today than we have ever built, and we're selling it to you for less money.

Advertising has done it. We pre-invest a few cents in each tire to guarantee its sale so that you save dollars when you buy. If we didn't advertise at all, our sales would drop to the point where production costs would increase—and up would go our prices. Eventually we would be out of business.

About extravagant expression. Advertising is only a reflection of current thought. We try to keep in step with the times. It is just impossible to make people buy nowadays with side-whiskered advertising. We'd like to be modest and soft-spoken, but if we were in times like these, we'd perish. No girl ever won a beau staying shut up in her own home. She's got to advertise; and if she has a pretty knee, it's no mortal sin to show it off occasionally.

Our advertising is like that.

We're highly pleased that you have written to us so frankly. We appreciate your interest, and thank you most heartily for your goodwill.

Yours very truly,

A fair cross-section. The things that may cause complaints or misunderstandings in business are as numerous as the people who are bothered by them. In this section, you have surveyed some of the more common irritation points, but far from all of them. A fair cross-section of the *causes* which make adjustment letters necessary has been presented with actual samples taken from business to show *how* the letters may be written. Behind the writing of any effective adjustment letter, there must exist on the part of the writer and his company a genuine desire to meet the customer half-way and, if possible, to make the adjustment that will retain his goodwill.

Viewed in the right perspective, complaints are a blessing to the company that receives them. They bring to the surface errors and faults that need to be corrected, conditions of which the company has not been conscious. A mistake cheerfully adjusted may lead to a long and pleasant relationship with the satisfied customer. Even if the customer is at fault, and his complaint must be denied, it may be possible to put the company in the right light, and still retain the customer's friendship.

A great many of the misunderstandings—the causes of friction between customer and company—are connected with credit or collection incidents, and their adjustment falls properly into the hands of the Credit Manager. What they are, and how they may be handled, you will find out in the next section of this Handbook.

CREDIT AND COLLECTION LETTERS

CREDIT AND COLLECTION LETTERS

1. COLLECTION LETTER PRINCIPLES

Relation to sales. To do the job completely, a collection letter has two objectives to reach. The first is to get the money; the second, to retain the customer's goodwill. Some credit men seem to concentrate so hard on the first objective that they overlook the second. If we remember our premise, however, that every individual in a company is a member of the sales department, and that everything he does may help or hinder order-getting, there remains no other conclusion except that the Credit Manager and those who write letters for him must do everything possible to build customer friendship.

The actual attainment of this ideal is not as easy as it may seem. The matters discussed in a credit or collection letter are often irritating and controversial, and no amount of diplomacy or understanding on the part of the writer can make them otherwise. Sometimes, the credit man is poised like a boy on a fence between two pastures, with a bull on either side. No matter which way he jumps, he may be in trouble. If he is too lax in approving credit or collecting a bill, the company may end up with a sour account and the treasurer then puts him through the wringer. If he rejects a doubtful applicant for credit, or insists on the payment of a bill, a customer may be lost and the sales manager accuses him of lack of co-operation. Even the average customer looks suspiciously on his best efforts, and is ready to fly off the handle on the slightest provocation. No business correspondent requires a larger bump of diplomacy, or a greater knowledge of human nature, than does the credit man.

In spite of all the difficulties, the writer of a credit or collection letter to meet his company obligations must be able to co-ordinate his activities successfully with those of the sales department. He is not expected to ask for orders, although some of the letters in this section do that very thing, but he is expected to *sell* goodwill—to make the news in his letter as painless as possible. In other words, he should be order-minded as well as money-minded—not to the extent of being too lenient—always remembering the value of a customer.

The following letter, for example, is signed "Credit Manager," but the writer hardly deserves the title.

> Dear Sir:
>
> We refuse to have further expense writing you letters.
>
> We take the position that you have treated us in an unjust and unfair manner in view of the definite promise you made when you requested us to ship goods to you.
>
> You promised if you did not pay for the goods within ten days you would send them back to us. You have not paid for them and you have not returned them.
>
> We have had considerable expense writing you during the past many weeks, and still we do not find the matter brought to a conclusion.
>
> Therefore, be advised and informed that we have definite legal rights in a matter of this kind. We assume you are aware of the action we can take if this matter is not completed at once and by return mail.
>
> Therefore, without further delay you are to immediately and at once pay for the goods in question.
>
> We are not interested in any excuses. We demand and insist that the matter be completed at once. We will expect your remittance within one week of the date of this letter. If we fail to receive it we will reserve our legal right to take further action WITHOUT ANY ADVANCE NOTICE being sent to you.
>
> We have been fair. We have been reasonable. In return we have not received what we consider proper consideration from you. If the condition were reversed, how would you like to be treated as you have treated us?
>
> We are marking in our records that the matter will be settled within one week. We will not assume responsibility for any action that may be taken if there is a delay beyond that time. You will therefore see to it that remittance is sent to us at once.
>
> Very truly yours,

The foregoing letter is not only extremely ugly in tone, but verbose to the point of being silly. I wonder just what position the writer means he will take? If a man is advised, is he not informed? If he expects a reply by return mail, why does he later give the reader one week? Why demand, and then insist? It's obvious that this fellow feels more important when he uses a lot of words and threats.

This is not, however, the attitude of a sales-minded credit man. The word of a company's discourtesy spreads fast, and no customer good or bad is without influence in his circle of friends. Enemies are never an asset to a company, no matter what the circumstances. As you will see later, it is possible to notify a stubborn customer that a lawsuit is about to be filed, and still do the job in a courteous and sympathetic manner.

Collection letter carpentry. The principles to be followed in the construction of a collection letter vary little from those that apply to other forms of business correspondence. You have surveyed these principles in the section devoted to Business Letter Carpentry. The purpose of a letter may be to sell goods, to adjust a misunderstanding, or to collect money, but in any case the main objective is to gain a favorable reaction from the reader. The attempt is to *influence human behavior*—to plant in the reader's mind a flow of thought which passes from *Attention* to *Interest* to *Desire,* and finally to the *Action* wanted. This formula of the Star, the Chain, and the Hook may seldom be disregarded.

Particularly important is the *planning* of the collection letter and using the steps with which you are already acquainted. Form letters are not too effective in persuading people to pay their bills, since the circumstances holding up the payment are rarely the same with different customers. The best appeal to use in one situation might well be the worst in another. Only by careful analysis of the particular account, its history and present condition, and of the particular individual, who may be acting for himself or for his firm, can the writer of the collection letter select what seems to be the most promising approach.

Another factor influencing the letter is the *credit policy* of the writer's company, to which of course, he must usually adhere. In some companies, and in certain types of business, the terms may be more lenient than others; but whatever they are, the credit manager must be governed accordingly. No policy is so inflexible, however, that it cannot be bent a little to fit the need and inclination of respective customers—in method of handling, if not in change of terms.

In his *Handbook of Modern Retailing,* produced by the Rice-Stix Merchants Service Bureau, Sidney Carter supplies a useful analysis of customer paying characteristics. In all, he lists twenty different types of buyers—any one of which might be visualized by the credit correspondent while handling a particular case.

1. Pays promptly and prides himself on it.
2. Takes all the time possible because he has other uses for his money.
3. Buys the limit on credit, then pays cash—sometimes to other merchants.
4. Easy going—needs to be reminded a number of times.
5. Hates to let the money go or likes to keep it in the bank as long as possible.
6. Sickness or other unusual circumstances prevent prompt payment.
7. Will pay to keep from losing his credit standing.
8. Will pay only when convinced he must to avoid trouble.
9. Unfortunate or indulgent. He wishes to do the right thing but cannot control his family's buying.
10. Withholds payment because he has a grudge against the store.
11. Thinks because he gives the store virtually all of his business, he is entitled to take more time to pay.
12. Never did intend to pay. This buyer does not succeed so well in getting credit established because of the organization of the modern credit structure.
13. Lives in the future, post-dates checks, thus buying on "cash-credit."
14. Reckless.
15. Installment contracts use up a large portion of his income, making it difficult for him to pay on due date.
16. Poor financier. Honest enough but simply cannot get his affairs untangled. Always more or less in "hot water."
17. Lives beyond his means. Will pay in time but will take all the time he can get.
18. Has old debts which interfere with prompt payment of current obligations.
19. Out of town. Has plenty of money and cannot believe there are any people or institutions who need money to run their businesses. Goes to Europe for six months and leaves the caretaker to file the bills away.
20. Carelessness or oversight. Not systematic. Forgetful, interested in other things, does not keep records.

Having listed his twenty types, Mr. Carter says: "There may be other kinds of people. It is important to understand them before sending out collection letters. It ought to be possible to figure out the reason why the money has not been paid. No man with a bad temper should be in the credit business, just as no man who is too easy and sympathetic can succeed in making a deadbeat pay promptly. The essential thing is that each account is to be treated as a special case and should have individual attention."

Foremost, then, in the carpentry of a collection letter is *analysis* of the particular customer and his account—what are his personal characteristics, and how has he previously paid his bills? With this concept formed, the selection of the right approach is simplified.

The spotlighting of analysis does not, however, mean that any of the more general factors in letter construction may be overlooked by the credit correspondent. You will remember these factors as they are set forth in the Rating Scale for business letters. Each has something to say about the effectiveness of a letter, no matter what the purpose. A neatly typed message on an attractive letterhead will always be regarded with more favor than one which looks cheap and shoddy. Natural language—short words—will always make a better impression than ancient stiff and stilted expressions. People who owe money are just as receptive as any others to the man who can "Relax—be natural—just talk." Any letter which reveals the personality of the writer and reflects the spirit of his company, will out-pull one of the cold, colorless, conventional sort.

From first reminder to notice of suit. Until now, the collection letter has been mentioned as if it were a single unit expected to do the whole job. But you know better than that. In many cases, it takes more than one request to get the money—and sometimes, a pack of lawyers. Most credit managers, therefore, have a series of letters ready to fire at the customer as long as there is a reasonable chance that he may be induced to pay his bill. The first of the series is merely a gentle reminder based on the assumption that the customer has overlooked the mailing of his check. Each letter thereafter increases the pressure, and various appeals are used in the hope that one of them may rub a soft spot.

Naturally, all collection efforts begin when the payment is due, although a short period may be allowed before the first shot is fired. The same efforts end—if they stretch that far—when legal action is filed. Between these two points, the credit manager's feeling about the account also passes through a number of changes. At first he is only mildly concerned, and the tone of the first reminder is casual. As time goes on, and successive letters fail, he begins to worry, and to talk more firmly to the delinquent customer. It is during these later stages that some credit men break down and begin to say things which only cause more trouble. This loss of control is understandable for the provocation is great; nevertheless, it is not in keeping with the goodwill objectives of the company, and it seldom helps in making the collection.

The actual number of letters in the series varies among companies and industries. One company may attempt to make the collection in a short span of time; another may not turn to legal action for six months or even a year. Despite these differences, the appeals used seem to travel over about the same course. One sequence may consist of a dozen letters, another of only six, but the same ground is covered up to the unhappy day when defeat is conceded and the file is sent to the legal department. A psychological procedure seems to have been developed among credit men for the collection of past-due accounts, and almost any collection letter that you encounter can easily be placed somewhere in this established procedure. This is what happens:

1. The customer is simply reminded that the bill should have been paid on a certain date. The reminder may be a statement, or a short letter very casual in tone.

2. The first reminder, unheeded, is followed by another; perhaps a second statement with a pencil notation or sticker to gain special attention. Or, it may be a letter, still friendly, but not quite so unconcerned.

3. With two ineffectual attempts washed out, the approach stiffens considerably. The writer of the letter no longer suggests that the customer has forgotten to pay; he is more likely to ask *what's wrong*. The customer is told that in the event of some difficulty which is holding up the payment, the company will do its best to help, but can't do anything if left in the dark.

4. Now the attack shifts to a new front. The writer knows the account is in danger; he looks for some special appeal that may arouse the customer's better self. He asks for *fair play*. He may enclose a note for the customer to sign.

5. Since the customer has not responded to the Golden Rule, the writer tries to touch *self-interest*. The customer is reminded of the importance of his credit rating. The legal clouds are forming—a hint of court action may appear in the letter.

6. The sand is running out. It is time for the final appeal. It may be written by the credit manager, or by a major executive. The customer is reminded of the expense and embarrassment to him, if a suit is filed. He is told that the company still wants to co-operate with him, but cannot let the matter drag out any longer. It is what you might call the *last resort* letter.

7. Success now hangs by a thread. There remains the one hope that the customer may be frightened into action. A specific number of days is given him to pay. He is told there will be no more letters. He either pays or the suit will be filed.

Logically the above psychological process blends with the reasons why people do not pay their bills. It is not hypocritical for the credit man to ask in the beginning, "Have you forgotten to pay this bill?" Lots of people are careless about money matters. They do forget to pay, and only need a reminder to be spurred into action. Others are poor managers. They are honest, but frequently find themselves burdened with financial problems. Why isn't it natural for the credit men to ask, "Is anything wrong? Can we help?"

Then there are those irresponsible people who do not take their financial obligations as seriously as they should. They write a few checks this month, and some more the next. At heart, they mean very well, and sometimes are governed by a sense of sportsmanship. Some of these folks may respond favorably when the credit man asks, "Don't you want to play fair with us, as we have played fair with you?"

You see, each of the appeals used in the collection letter series may smoke out a different class of buyers, and when in turn they are all applied to the same customer the *right* one may induce him to pay. Finally, as the series runs its course, the credit man is forced to the conclusion that he is dealing with a very selfish individual—a chiseler who has no intention of paying unless forced to do so. Such a fellow may value his credit rating, and the mention of it is worth trying, but the chances are that he will pay no attention to any letter until he is told, "Pay or be sued." If he has the money, he will probably pay to escape the lawyers. If he hasn't, there is nothing left for the credit manager to do personally to save the account.

Faults to avoid. Later in this section you will inspect letters that illustrate each step on the chart; meanwhile, there are certain common faults in collection-letter writing that need to be avoided, and you should know what they are. A writer may be guilty, though unintentionally, of one or more of these faults, and find that his efforts have been frustrated.

The customer's reaction to these faults is purely psychological. He may be left indifferent, humiliated, or annoyed, but in any case the result is the same—he is *not* moved to pay the bill. Thus, we remind ourselves once again that a letter of any sort is a *personal contact,* and to make it pleasant and effective, the writer must rely heavily on his knowledge of human nature. Only when we are able to subordinate our own emotional reactions to those of our readers are we able to win their confidence, and have some chance of getting what we want from them.

The first of the faults that you should recognize, so that it will never handicap your own efforts, is the use of an *obvious* form letter. Even if the message is going to a large group of poor-pay customers, it can still be personalized in such a way that each recipient thinks it was specially written for him. This involves perfect matching of multigraph and typewriter ribbon, and very careful work on the part of the typist. No doubt you have seen many collection letters where the fill-in of name, address, and salutation did not match the body of the letter. To such an apparent form message, the average recipient is likely to be indifferent. He says: "The writer of this letter isn't really worried about my account, because he is saying the same thing to a lot of others." So he pushes the letter aside, and *doesn't* pay the bill.

We are not advocating that all collection letters should be personally dictated and typed, although that would be a fine practice if the cost were

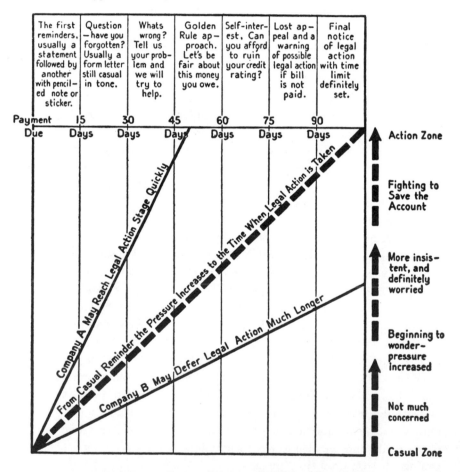

**The Number of Letters Used or the Time Allowed May
Vary, but the Cycle Is from Casual to Action Zone**
From *Effective Credit and Collection Letters,* by L. E. Frailey.
Prentice-Hall, Inc., Englewood Cliffs, N.J.

not too prohibitive, but the same effect can be attained by intelligent planning to avoid give-away insertions, by the use of the right equipment, and by perfect secretarial co-operation. The personal letter will always out-pull the form letter, and since the purpose is getting the money, it seems foolish not to use the best possible method.

The fault of insincerity. It is never smart for a letter-writer to say anything he does not really mean. The average reader is not easily deceived by flattery, extravagant statements, or any other kind of insincerity. He considers an attempt to pull the wool over his eyes as a reflection on his intelligence, and rightfully he resents the implication. For example, how would you have reacted to the following collection letter?

> Dear Mr. Doe:
>
> Out of the thousands of men and boys who have taken my course, only a few have ever attempted to beat me out of the payments. My boys are a mighty fine bunch of fellows as a whole. You are one of the bunch and I can't help but feel that you are as square and honest and proud as any of them.
>
> If you didn't get that last letter I wrote, or those before, you couldn't answer them. I'm sure you haven't been getting your mail. Someone must be opening it, and I want you to make an investigation. I am really getting worried and if I do not hear from you soon, I will ask the Postal Authorities why mail is not being delivered to you.
>
> As I said before, 97% of my students are square shooters. It is only once in a while that some little weasel-faced skin-flint, smart aleck, sneaky crook, tries to get my course and not pay for it. I don't care to know such fellows, and I let the law take care of them.
>
> It would be mighty hard to prove to me that you don't want to treat me white. I know down deep in my heart the reason why you haven't answered is that you have not received my letters.
>
> But even if you are hard up when you get this letter, don't be afraid or ashamed to tell your old friend. I, too, have gone through the leanest kind of poverty. I had to wear cheap suits, cheap shirts, cheap shoes—everything I wore had to be cheap. That's why I take such an everlasting joy in helping young men like yourself to better things in life.
>
> But remember that if you do remain silent—if you let the next ten days go by without choosing the path of friendship between you and me—I shall feel the same way toward you. I shall feel that you have misunderstood me, that you have chosen to go

into a lawsuit with your eyes open, in spite of my kindly efforts.

Of course, I shall stand up for my rights under our agreement. Even you wouldn't think of me any more as a MAN, if I were to back down now. No. I must ask that you pay as agreed.

But I repeat, when our attorney sues you, it will only be because you left me no other way out. I'll still want you for a friend, just as much as I ever have.

Good-bye,

It is difficult to comprehend how any businessman could expect such a conglomeration of insincerity to fool his reader, or how he could forget his own self-respect in taking the pose of a friend when he obviously intends to have his pound of flesh.

Granted that the above letter is an extreme example of the fault of insincerity, it is unfortunately true that similar letters are by no means uncommon in everyday business. The letter below, for example, spreads the honey too thickly. By the time you get through reading it you may be a bit nauseated. Maybe the writer did not mean to sound so insincere, but that's how he comes across on paper.

Dear Mr. Doe:

Please excuse me for writing to you personally. It has been my experience that there are mighty few difficulties that can't be overcome, mighty few difficulties that can't be adjusted, when the two parties sit down and talk things over.

I would love to walk into your store this morning and have a chat with you. I know you would greet me courteously and treat me fairly, but since I can't see you personally, let's talk it over.

What I want to talk about is your account of $125.00. Before I do so, however, excuse me please, while I talk for just a little bit about myself. I am living in New York, but I am not a New Yorker. I am from "Down South" myself. I have traveled in every Southern State; yes, I guess I have been in every Southern county. I have made my home in the South; I have even followed a mule, plowing corn on an Alabama plantation. I have managed a commissary, have owned and operated my own retail business. In fact, I have done pretty much the same thing that you are doing. I know your business problems and your local conditions.

When your order was received, it was I who put O.K. on it—I have always insisted that the folks down South were sometimes poor, sometimes a little slow, but always honest.

Now I am in bad. The Company has sent you statements, they have written you letters, but so far they don't seem to be getting very far in collecting your account. Just what is the matter? Can't we get together? The company wants to do the right thing by you, and I wish you would look on me as your friend and believe me when I tell you that if there is anything you want done that is fair to good business principles, I am here to help you.

I would be mighty well pleased if you would send me a check by the next mail. If you can't pay all your account, send a part payment and see if we can't get everything fixed up. We will advertise for you if your goods aren't selling well; we will make an exchange for you if you have something that doesn't sell as well as some other item.

I am counting on your reply and I am sure you won't disappoint me.

Cordially yours,

Humiliating the customer. Almost as unwarranted as insincerity in a collection letter is the unsavory, and equally ineffectual, use of ugly names and insinuations which humiliate and anger the reader. In this connection, we are reminded of a description in verse of credit manager, John Itellum.

Now John Itellum was a hard-boiled baby,
He respected neither man or lady;
His letters were sharp and to the mark,
No roaming dog could claim a better bark.

At collecting money he was truly great,
He made them pay on the discount date;
He boasted with pride no payment was lost,
Itellum could collect at any cost.

"This son of a crook," he'd snort and roar,
"Would take an inch, and then want more,
I'll mince no words in letting him know
No monkey business with me will go."

"So come, Miss Green, and take a letter,
We'll make it sizzle, the hotter the better;
He'll settle in full, and within ten days,
Or the Judge will cure his dead-beat ways."

Thus every day, and hot under the collar,
Itellum chased the almighty dollar;
But here's the truth, and it isn't funny—
'Twas customers he lost instead of money.

It seems a queer and perverted kind of reasoning that motivates a letter writer to bully and scold his reader, when the purpose is to win co-operation. Why should the humiliated customer be expected to run for his checkbook? Is he not more likely to defer his payment until the last possible moment, or even endure a lawsuit rather than favor a credit manager who has goaded him so unmercifully? What would be *your* reaction to the following choice sample of business discourtesy?

> Dear Mr. Doe:
>
> It is now obvious to us that you will never pay the money you owe our firm until we have resorted to court action. This is after all the only way to deal with people who shirk their obligations.
>
> We have given you more than a reasonable time to settle this bill; we have been fair to you every step of the way. Unfortunately, it is useless to be decent to a dead beat.
>
> In three days we shall begin legal action. Be assured that this will cost you far more than the amount of our bill. Wouldn't it be much easier for you to begin acting like a responsible citizen and pay us what is rightfully ours?
>
> Yours truly,

One of the best tests of a collection letter is the customer's reply, especially if it contains a smile and a check. However, the reply may turn out to be embarrassing. It is hoped that few credit men are forced by their own mistakes to read replies such as the following.

> Dear Mr. Doe:
>
> We acknowledge your remarkable letter of July 16.
>
> We think, Mr. Doe, that you are a hell of a credit manager.
> We owe your house, due July 10, $462.02.
>
> We sent you July 10, $242.06, and on July 18, $129.64. Today, July 18, we are sending $90.32, which pays all invoices due this month.
>
> A glance through your ledger will convince you that we always have paid our bills from 5 to 10 days before the 10th of the month due.
>
> Where do you get the idea we asked for any favors, Mr. Doe, and where do you get the brain storm that you are handing us any favors? We think you are a hell of a credit manager, Mr. Doe.

What we said, Mr. Doe, was that we would pay the balance, which was $219.96, in 10 days or less. Well, we sent you $129.64 in 5 days and the balance in 10 days. Now in view of the fact that for 5 years we have paid you from 5 to 10 days before the dates due, are you handing us any favor? Mr. Doe, you are a hell of a credit manager.

And where, Mr. Doe, do you get the brain storm that you can ask us to pay our August bills which are not due for 25 days yet? Mr. Doe, we think you are a hell of a credit manager, and the kind of a credit manager, Mr. Doe, that makes it tough for the sales department.

And furthermore, Mr. Doe, we think you are a hell of a credit manager, and in conclusion, Mr. Doe, we think you are a hell of a credit manager, Mr. Doe.

Respectfully, Mr. J. Smith,

P.S. We still think you are a hell of a credit manager, Mr. Doe.

In spite of the repetition of the above letter, the writer manages very well to make clear what he thinks of Credit Manager Doe. Another irate customer, speaking below, is equally frank.

Dear Mr. Doe:

You must be a very lucky man indeed. It's not every company that will hire such a blockhead as you for a credit manager. Such stupidity in business is rare these days.

Two days after I received goods from your firm, you began dunning me. Before the end of two weeks, I had received no less than three statements from you. Had you checked my credit record you would have noticed that for the past four years I have been paying my bills to your firm promptly on the first of each month. Now you can pay the penalty. You may either wait one more month for your money or enter suit.

Sincerely,

We assume the two customers whose letters you have just read had cause to be angry; at least, they had not been handled tactfully by the credit managers. Right or wrong, the good credit manager manages to keep his boat on an even keel. With a sympathetic understanding of the customer's problems, he performs his collection duties without arousing resentment, even though at times he may have to demand payment of a delinquent bill. Such an understanding must have existed between Credit Manager Samuelson and the customer who wrote to her as follows.

Dear Miss Samuelson:

Somehow or other I cannot imagine your zeal in attempting to collect our account. Surely you know that it is only a matter of 120 days or so past due. In the state of Florida this is considered practically cash.

But last week Stanley came in and I gave him an order. Now when the bill gets to the point where WE think it's getting too big and too old, we pay it. Therefore, you are no doubt speechless at the enclosed check in full—and well you may be—we are, too.

So now be a good girl and run around and show this to Ralph and all the others with a real big "Look what I did" smile. And after this don't scowl when our firm's name is mentioned in your presence.

So dry your tears and perhaps some day I'll buy you a nice big balloon—like Ralph's—and gee, wouldn't that be a dandy?

May your mascara never run,

It speaks well for the public relations of a company when a customer will take time to joke with the credit manager as happens in the above check transmittal. Obviously, the lady c. m. had written several collection letters to the customer, but they must have been tactful or he would not have replied so good-naturedly.

Other faults to side-step. In earlier sections of this Handbook, you have encountered principles of letter writing which apply with equal force to the work of the credit correspondent. The old-time "whiskers" may deaden and defeat a collection letter as easily as they do one which seeks to sell or accomplish any other business purpose. The best collection letters are friendly and personal in tone; they reveal the human qualities of a man who merely asks and expects the money due his company. Such a tone is, of course, impossible in a letter couched in formal, stilted language.

The fault of self-pity. Especially obnoxious are the collection letters which whine for co-operation. In them, the writer appears as a very much abused person. He paints a nice halo around his own head, and then tries to shame the ignoble reader into paying his bill. The latter resents the injured tone of the message and the inference that he is most unreliable compared to the man with the halo.

It is true that good business relations depend on mutual understanding and co-operation. The appeal to fair play is often used adroitly in collection letters, but the result is opposite to that intended when the writer wears his heart on his sleeve, and reproaches the customer as might the sweetheart of a wayward lover. Sad, sweet souls are never popular in business correspondence. There is one talking in the following letter.

Dear Mr. Doe:

I think you know that I'm your friend. And now because I was your friend, because I went to bat for you many times, I find that I'm in trouble.

When you said last year that you needed the goods, I saw that you received them even before I was able to see your credit repor . When you were late with your payments on several occasions, you received no dunning from me. I went out of my way to show you that I wanted to help you all I could. I wanted you to see for yourself that all credit managers aren't callous to other folks' troubles. Some of us have a heart, Mr. Doe. But your last bill is now six months overdue, and they are asking me here why I let you alone for so long. They are blaming me for being too easy on you.

I know that you will agree that one favor deserves another. There is no better way you can show your appreciation for what I've done for you than by paying this last bill immediately.

Very sincerely yours,

You know, also, the importance of avoiding certain insinuating words which imply deficiencies of character in the reader—red-pepper words which dig in and sting. You know what these words are—neglect, failed, ignore, claim, should, and others innocent enough in the dictionary but troublemakers in a business letter. These words are just as destructive in a message asking for payment of a bill, as in one with some other intent. The second purpose of a collection letter, you will remember, is to retain *goodwill*. Insinuating words irritate—they are never goodwill builders.

Dated action also has an important part to play in the construction of a collection letter. When a specific time is set for payment, the chances are increased that it will be forthcoming. This is a tested fact, and you may prove it by using *dated action* in your own correspondence.

Avoiding the divided urge is another plank in the platform of the collection-letter writer. When people are given their choice of several things to do, they are likely to do nothing. Don't say:

We ask that you send us immediately a payment on your account of not less than $100, or if you don't feel able to do that now, send us a post-dated check for the same amount. Certainly, the very least you can do is to write and tell us when we may expect our money.

The credit manager should decide what *one* card is most likely to win the trick, and not mention any others. The customer is then impelled to action with greater force than he is when offered several choices.

So that you may begin to get your account with us in better shape, we must ask for a payment of not less than $100. Please mail this payment to arrive at our office within five days, which means by Saturday.

The *divided urge* is a serious fault in any collection letter. Do not use it.

2. Casual Reminders

What the name implies. As a matter of routine, most companies mail a casual reminder to the customer a few days after he has failed to pay a bill on the agreed date. This is the first in the sequence of collection letters, and of course, if the payment is made, the last. The period of time allowed before the first reminder is mailed depends largely on the nature of the business, and the judgment of the credit manager. Irrespective of the number of days before the reminder is sent out, its tone is almost always casual and gentle. No attempt is made to put pressure on the customer, since the implication is that the payment has been overlooked, and that it will now be forthcoming. The credit manager is not worried about the account; he knows that for one reason or another people and companies do put off the payment of their bills.

Instead of a letter a statement is often used, but in either case the purpose of the mailing is the same—to bring to the customer's attention the fact of non-payment. If the nature of the business is such that a rather long time is allowed before any pressure is applied, a second and even a third statement or short letter may be used before the credit manager shifts into high gear and makes a more determined effort to collect the bill.

Because a bare statement showing the date of the purchase and the amount due is at best a cold and impersonal contact with the customer, some credit managers personalize one or more of the statements—usually the second—with some special device to gain attention. It may be a handwritten notation, as shown on page 820. A similar effect is gained, perhaps less effective, by typing the notation on the statement in red ink, or by using a rubber stamp to high-light a word such as "Please." Here is a personalized statement of the latter type.

Personalizing statement with sticker. Another rather common idea used to attract special attention to a statement is to attach a sticker, often of a semi-humorous nature. To avoid repetition where statements are mailed several times to the same customer, the company may have several on hand—adding new ones at regular intervals. This is a necessary procedure, as no sticker is likely to attract as much attention when exposed to a customer the second time.

As with any other idea to gain attention, the success of a sticker on a statement depends on how clever or unusual it may seem to the recipient. For example, John T. Heyward, of the Michie Company, Charlottesville, Virginia, has used a number of out-of-the-groove stickers, and reports a better return with them than from the more conventional letter reminders. The one below was especially effective in bringing home the checks.

Perhaps you think a reminder in verse is far removed from the dignity of business, but Mr. Heyward tells us that numerous customers sent friendly comments about the sticker along with their checks. Some of them were in the same humorous vein, and one came back with another verse.

> Here's a check for $18.00,
> Never mind receipt,
> My bills come so thick and fast,
> They're hard as h—to meet.

We recommend the use of stickers to add pull to statements. Many credit managers will testify that the combination of sticker and statement does a better job than the statement does alone. Some users, however, save

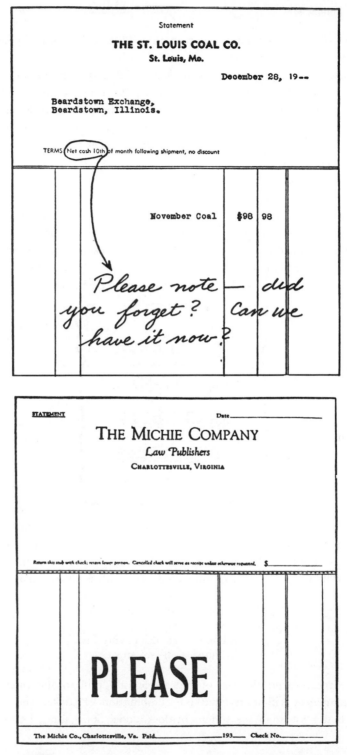

the sticker for the second mailing. The procedure which works best for you can only be determined by test and comparison over a considerable stretch of time.

The first reminder letter. Whether or not statements are used as reminders, the time eventually comes when letters become necessary. In either case, the tone of the letter is usually casual, although a little pressure may be found when one or more statements have already failed. You will see from the following examples that letters of this type fall into one of three classes.

1. Those which simply tell the customer that the bill is past due.
2. Those which "save face" for the customer by suggesting that no doubt he has overlooked the payment.
3. Those which advance some reason why the customer should not be indifferent to his obligation.

Letters of the third class are commonly used where collection of the account is pressed to a conclusion in a comparatively short period of time; only a few requests are made before talk of legal action is heard. The credit manager in the case is anxious to hasten the payment, and does not propose to wait very long before cracking the whip.

Although you are not likely to find the writing of the first reminder letter difficult or arduous, you may discover in the following letters an approach which is adaptable to your own needs. They all fall in the first class—simply telling the customer that the bill is past due.

Dear Mr. Doe:

Your payment has not yet arrived.

There is a reason, we know, why you haven't sent us your check. But. . .you haven't let us know what that reason is.

Won't you take the few moments necessary now to send us your payment and bring your account up-to-date.

We'll appreciate your prompt cooperation.

Cordially,

. . . . .

Dear Mr. Doe:

Just a friendly reminder that your check for $25.00 will be warmly appreciated.

If your check is in the mail. . ."thank you." If not, will you please give this account your usual prompt attention?

Cordially yours,

. . . . .

Gentlemen:

We have not received the payment due on your Budget Account in accordance with your agreement.

If your remittance has not yet gone forward, your prompt attention will be greatly appreciated.

Very truly yours,

．　　　．　　　．　　　．　　　．

Gentlemen:

It isn't going to take much to balance your account—you owe so little.

That's why I'm so sure this reminder will bring us your check by return mail.

Am I right?

Very truly yours,

．　　　．　　　．　　　．　　　．

Gentlemen:

Will you please do us a favor?

Our annual audit will take place this month. Can we count on your cooperation in making sure your account will not appear among those showing past-due balances?

If your check is already in the mail, please disregard this reminder.

If not, your cooperation in mailing your check by return mail will be appreciated.

Cordially,

．　　　．　　　．　　　．　　　．

Dear Mr. Doe:

This letter calls your attention to an overdue account of $24.63.

May we expect your check before the end of this month?

Yours cordially,

And here are some examples of reminder letters of the second class—those that "save face" for the customer by suggesting that he has overlooked the payment.

Dear Mr. Doe:

IT'S SO SMALL...

we wouldn't be surprised if you had forgotten all about the balance due on the attached statement.

But as a lot of these small accounts can add up to a truly sizable sum, won't you please take a minute right now to send us your check. Then we won't have to trouble you again.

Cordially,

. . . . .

Dear Mr. Doe:

You are usually so prompt in sending your payments that I wonder if you realize your account is past due. Since this is undoubtedly an oversight, won't you please send us your check to cover the overdue balance of $54.00?

We appreciate the splendid cooperation you have always given us and shall look forward to hearing from you soon.

Sincerely yours

. . . . .

Gentlemen:

You will note from the attached statement that a number of charges have run beyond our regular terms.

We realize that it is sometimes difficult to process for payment invoices from all suppliers on their due dates. But now that our monthly statement is before you, won't you please put through our overdue items for payment?

You can be assured that we will appreciate your cooperation.

Cordially,

. . . . .

Gentlemen:

May we remind you in a friendly way that your payment of $101.50 is past due?

We are not in the least worried about your account—test us with another order—but it does take money to pay *our* bills.

You can help us by sending your check.

Sincerely,

Dear Mr. Doe:

This letter is being sent to you just as a reminder of your account with us.

Under the terms of sale, the amount shown on the endorsed statement is now due for payment.

May we expect to receive your check in the next few days.

Very truly yours,

. . . . .

Dear Mr. Doe:

When you opened this letter, it reminded you of a good intention—something you forgot to do.

It was to send us a check.

Will you do it please, right now? Then you'll be sure it won't be overlooked again.

Cordially yours,

·   ·   ·   ·   ·

Dear Mr. Doe:

Undoubtedly, you've forgotten. The amount of $11.63 now owing on your account is so small...

We feel sure, however, that you will want to clear this matter up as quickly as possible.

Yours truly,

·   ·   ·   ·   ·

Dear Mr. Doe:

With all the things you have to do, it is easy now and then to forget to pay a bill.

We know that; also, that you won't mind our asking for the check which is due us.

Just slip it in the enclosed envelope which needs no postage. And at the same time, why not send us another order?

Very truly yours,

·   ·   ·   ·   ·

Gentlemen:

The majority of our customers pay us promptly, and when they do not, it is usually because they have just overlooked the fact that rental payments are due monthly in advance.

I am sure this must be true of your account, and I know you will accept this request for payment in the same friendly spirit in which I am sending it.

Yours very truly,

·   ·   ·   ·   ·

Dear Mr. Doe:

Sometimes matters such as this are easy to overlook. Frequently, they are delayed for other reasons.

We refer to your account. We do not want to seem too insistent, but the amount is now overdue. Since our terms are thirty days, we necessarily look for the payment of our accounts promptly each month when due.

We feel sure we may depend on your immediate response.

Cordially,

The third class of first-reminder letters consists of those in which some reason is given the customer why he should not be indifferent to his credit obligation. Unlike the first two groups, these letters contain a little pressure.

Dear Mr. Doe:

You surely know...

it's not HOW MUCH a person owes that determines his credit rating...but rather HOW PROMPTLY he pays his bills that really counts.

Take the amount you owe us. It is not large. But it *is* long overdue and should, for the above reason, be given your immediate attention.

Won't you send us a check today?

Cordially,

.   .   .   .   .

Gentlemen:

You will agree, we feel certain, after checking the overdue amount as shown on the enclosed statement, that our terms of NET 30 DAYS have been lost "somewhere in the shuffle."

Your remittance by return mail will enable us to continue to serve you on an uninterrupted basis. By the same token, you will also be in a position to take care of your customers' immediate requirements. We'll both profit by this arrangement, won't we?

Please send us your payment today! This action on your part will pay dividends and will be mutually beneficial.

Thank you.

Cordially,

.   .   .   .   .

Dear Mr. Doe:

We'll be the first to admit...

that the amount you owe us is small. Possibly, for this reason you do not consider it a pressing obligation.

This premise would be all right if a customer's credit standing were based on how little he owed, rather than how promptly he paid.

Actually, we both know that this is not the case, and your unpaid balance is so small that you certainly would not want it to adversely affect your credit standing with us or with others.

Can we count on your cooperation in bringing your account up-to-date? We sincerely hope so as it is a pleasure to number you among our many thousands of valued customers.

Sincerely,

Dear Mr. Doe:

Our fiscal year ends February 28. As your ledger card will be audited, I know you want it to reflect the utmost of credit for you, as well as to me. This can only be accomplished with your full cooperation.

If your check is not in the mail—here is a self-addressed envelope. Use it to send your check for the above amount to reach us before February 28.

Sincerely yours,

.   .   .   .   .

Dear Mr. Doe:

Have you had an opportunity to check the statement we sent you recently? Part of the balance is now past our 90 day terms, and it is important to have your account brought up-to-date without delay.

If there is a question about any of the items, please let us know. Otherwise, won't you kindly send us your payment.

Very truly yours,

.   .   .   .   .

Dear Mr. Doe:

The privilege of serving you is certainly our pleasure. For this, we extend our sincere thanks.

However, the enclosed statement of your account as of the end of last month lists an amount that became due some time ago.

We feel certain that you understand how important and necessary it is that every successful business organization keep its receivables up-to-date, and you can help us in this respect by sending us your payment within the next week.

If this is not possible, will you kindly tell us at the bottom of this letter the approximate date on which we can expect payment and return the letter to us.

Your cooperation will be greatly appreciated and will, above all, enable us to continue to give you the high type of service to which you are entitled.

Cordially,

.   .   .   .   .

Dear Mr. Doe:

Enclosed is a statement showing how your account stands on our books.

It has always been your custom to pay such accounts promptly, and we wonder if there is some confusion about these items which causes you to delay making payment.

If these charges agree with your records, will you please send your remittance by return mail?

> Very truly yours,

.   .   .   .   .

Dear Mr. Doe:

It is always a pleasure to do business with a customer who meets his obligations as you have done. We like to see you earning for yourself the two percent discount, which over a period of time amounts to quite a saving.

We are wondering, therefore, why we have not received your check. No doubt it was an oversight and needs only this reminder.

It is always difficult to get back to a normal paying basis once you have let a month's purchases go over into the next—and of course the result is a real loss to you.

We shall be looking for a check by return mail. We hope you will not disappoint us.

> Cordially yours,

.   .   .   .   .

Dear Mr. Doe:

It's such a small amount that you probably haven't bothered about it—neither have we. But as long as it is on the books our bookkeeper has to carry it over at the end of each month.

With thousands of small accounts on our books this causes a lot of extra work. And the cost of sending reminders on such small amounts is out of proportion to the amounts involved.

So won't you please enclose your check, stamps, or coins for this amount—before you lay this letter aside?

> Very truly yours,

.   .   .   .   .

Gentlemen:

Will you help us?

We're in a quandary as to what to say in a so-called collection letter that will make it effective when an account has "lost track" of the fact that our terms are NET 30 DAYS.

If it is a mildly worded letter...we are "easy" and can wait for our money. Conversely, if it is harsh and demanding, we can still wait for our money, and, in addition, stand the chance of losing the goodwill of a valued customer.

We're in a dilemma, aren't we? If you have the magic formula, won't you please pass it on to us. Better yet, send us payment for your overdue account today.

Then, speaking in the vernacular, we'll both be taken "off the hook."

Cordially,

3. Follow-Ups When First Reminders Fail

End of the first stage. The common approach in the letters you have just been reading was the assumption that the customer had overlooked paying his bill. While this may be said (with reasonable doubt in the mind of the credit manager) it is still a strong enough possibility to preclude the charge of hypocrisy. Besides, it is only a form of courtesy that the customer should have the benefit of the doubt.

But when the casual first reminder has been mailed and several days later the customer still remains silent, the credit manager faces the probability that the account is not in as good shape as he hoped, and that it is going to take more pressure to make the collection. He may try again to probe gently for the money; or perhaps he may stiffen his attack and go more bluntly at his customer. Usually, the decision of which approach to use depends on the type of business, the trade customs in the field of operation, and the credit manager's analysis of the particular customer.

Certainly, when a second letter is necessary following the first and one or more statements, stage one in the bill collection procedure is nearing an end. It is no longer reasonable to assume that the customer has forgotten to pay his bill. There may be some cause, unknown to the credit manager, which is holding up the remittance. It may or may not be a serious obstruction, but it does exist and dilatory collection letters are no longer advisable. If the requests for payment continue to be mild and casual, the customer may take them too lightly. He must be jarred loose from the complacent attitude that he can wait as long as he wishes, or that the company will continue to dance as long as he plays the fiddle.

Thus, while we may call the letters which follow "Second Reminders," or "Follow-Ups" of the first letters, they are written in a far more serious mood, and with a far different psychological background. The credit manager is no longer viewing the account with unconcern. He may hide his doubt for the sake of policy, and try to keep the second letter on the same friendly plane as the first, but inwardly he is probably looking at the customer with considerable suspicion.

Examples from credit correspondence. In the letters below, you will sense the change which has taken place in the attitude of the various credit managers who wrote them. Some exert more pressure than others, but they all begin to tighten the screws which, with the last turn, will lead to talk of the lawyers, and finally to court action. The latter stage in the collection sequence may still be several letters ahead, but the stagehands are beginning to set the scenery.

Dear Mr. Doe:

A DOLLAR WON'T DO AS MUCH AS IT ONCE DID... because people won't do as much for a dollar.

That's pretty descriptive of these modern so-called easy days. But it hasn't been easy for us to induce you to part with some of those "WON'T DO AS MUCH DOLLARS."

What we're trying to say is that we've been patient and friendly in asking you to send us your check for the amount above.

Once again, then, please send your check by return mail. The enclosed addressed envelope will simplify matters.

Cordially,

· · · · ·

Dear Mr. Doe:

It's hard to believe, but another 30 days have gone by and still no check from you for the overdue charges on your account.

As you have not questioned any of the items on our monthly statement, we assume our records agree with yours. Won't you, therefore, let us have your check to bring your account up-to-date?

We'll appreciate your prompt cooperation. May we hear from you by return Air Mail?

Cordially,

· · · · ·

Gentlemen:

We are at a loss to understand why we have had no acknowledgment of our reminders concerning the past-due balance on your account.

Since your firm has not questioned this balance, we presume that it is correct.

Perhaps our mail has not been directed to the proper office. If so, will you please bring this unpaid balance to the attention of the person authorized to make payment.

We'll appreciate your cooperation. An envelope is enclosed for your convenience.

Sincerely yours,

· · · · ·

Gentlemen:

To keep your goodwill is always our first consideration. That's the reason we have let your balance run far beyond our regular 90-day terms.

Surely, though, you must realize that this cannot go on indefinitely—no matter how much we want to cooperate with you.

So won't you please take the time to send us a check AIR MAIL today?

> Cordially,

.   .   .   .   .

Dear Mr. Doe:

NO NEWS IS GOOD NEWS...

doesn't always hold true. Especially, so, when we have sent you a number of reminders about your past-due account, and have received no response.

And certainly not, when the absence of any word from you could adversely affect your CREDIT STANDING—ONE OF YOUR MOST VALUABLE ASSETS.

It is our earnest wish to cooperate with you in every possible way, but you make it difficult to do so by not answering any of our reminders.

May we expect some good news...by return mail?

> Cordially,

.   .   .   .   .

Dear Mr. Doe:

At the outset...

we want you to know that we appreciate having the pleasure of numbering you among our many thousands of satisfied customers.

However, as the several reminders mailed to you have brought no response, may we again call to your attention that your account became due for payment some time ago.

You'll agree, we feel certain, that our request for payment is not unreasonable. Won't you respond to this friendly reminder by sending us your remittance by return mail?

Your cooperation will, in all sincerity, be appreciated.

> Yours very truly,

.   .   .   .   .

Dear Mr. Doe:

Just why you didn't answer my recent letter with a check, I don't know.

I am confident that you have not intentionally ignored your account.

Surely, this second reminder will start your check on its way—TODAY. Don't bother to write, for I understand that we all forget now and then.

Just obey that impulse which says: "I'll send my check now before it's forgotten again."

.   .   .   .   .

Gentlemen:

I've been playing a game with you, although you didn't know it. The game was who could keep silent the longest.

You win.

May I have a remittance of some kind on your account?

Yours truly,

.   .   .   .   .

Dear Mr. Doe:

I hesitate to send you this second reminder about your past due account. Still, it *is* past due and it should have been paid before now.

Won't you please oblige me by sending along your check of $78.61 by return mail? We'll appreciate it.

Cordially,

.   .   .   .   .

Dear Mr. Doe:

Reluctantly, I must once again bring to your attention the $472.50 open on your account, and 45 days past due. I say "reluctantly" because I dislike writing letters like this as much as you must dislike receiving them.

Your check will give me a chance to write you a letter you'll enjoy receiving, and one that will be a pleasure for me to write. Won't you send the check today?

Sincerely,

Follow-ups using the story approach. In the past it was probably true that credit and collection correspondence was the driest and dullest of all the letters written for business purposes. One of the reasons may have been the great importance attributed to money matters, with the resulting notion that anything said about money must be in the most austere and dignified manner. Be that as it may, many credit men of the modern school have discovered that sometimes more money can be collected in a shorter time with an *interesting* letter than with one which bores the reader with rigid formality. Many a collection letter has clicked in a big way because of a story or an unusual approach which would not have been tolerated in the past.

In this Handbook, you have already discovered that it is quite all right to use a story to gain *special* attention provided it does not backfire for want of any logical connection with the main thought of the letter.

The story idea must add emphasis to the thought content which follows; if not, it merely gains temporary attention. It may even distract the reader from the central theme of the letter. In some way, perhaps subconsciously, the reader is made to feel that he was *tricked* into giving attention, and so his initial interest is turned into resentment.

Another thing worth remembering about a story introduction is that it must be *really* as interesting to the reader as the writer *thinks* it will be. In speech or writing there is nothing less likely to attract favorable attention than a story which falls flat in the telling.

When contemplating the use of a story in a collection letter two "musts" need to be remembered: first, that the story is not too shopworn; second, that its connection with the central theme of the letter is not too thin. In short, it must be a good story appropriate to the occasion. People do like stories, there can be no doubt of that. Otherwise, why are they told so frequently at all the places where folks get together? The use of one which is to the point and interesting may add life and pulling power to a collection letter. But don't drag one into the message unless it *fits*.

The story approach is usually more suitable for letters in the early stage of the collection sequence. Later, when the tone can no longer be so chatty or casual, a story may tend to soften the seriousness of the situation, leaving with the customer the impression that he may continue to dilly-dally about the payment. The letters which follow were mostly second reminders—the writers were still trying to maintain a warm and human tone without too much pressure.

> Dear Mr. Doe:
>
> Thousands of people sit on the porch of the Inn at Yellowstone National Park watching for the eruption of "Old Faithful." The traveller is never disappointed. "Old Faithful" spouts with the regularity of the sun, moon, or tide.
>
> The credit man at his desk is not so fortunate. Payments are not always made on agreed terms. Perhaps there should be a little elasticity to terms, but to stretch them on and on indefinitely is merely to place a burden on the company that must base sales prices on anticipated sales revenues.
>
> So, how about playing "Old Faithful" to us today by placing a check for the above amount in an envelope and starting it on its way.
>
> Yours truly,

.   .   .   .   .

> Dear Mr. Doe:
>
> Once when Lincoln was poor and hungry, a stranger approached him and requested change for a twenty dollar bill.

Being without a cent, and seeing the humor of the situation, Lincoln stooped down and confided: "Sorry, I can't oblige you stranger, but I thank you for the compliment just the same."

Some of our friends pay us the same compliment that this stranger paid Lincoln. They let their account stand on the books, thinking no doubt that we don't need the money. But we do. You would be surprised.

So won't you please give this little account of yours the necessary attention, and let us have a check for $620 within the week?

Very truly yours,

. . . . .

Dear Mr. Doe:

Here is a good story they tell of Uncle Joe Cannon.

One member, making his first speech in the House, found its members listless under his oratory. After adjournment, he sought out Mr. Cannon and asked him what he thought of the speech.

"Well maybe what you said was all right," replied Uncle Joe, "but it seemed to me that you did not make the most of your opportunities."

"My opportunities?"

"Yes. You had several chances to sit down before you did."

Lest we be accused of making too long a speech about the $50 you owe us, we will make just one remark, and then sit down to wait for your answer.

PLEASE SEND US A CHECK.

Now, we're sitting.

Sincerely yours,

. . . . .

Dear Mr. Doe:

Did you know that we Americans use 22,978,828,252 postage stamps a year?

That over 61 billion pieces of mail—316 per citizen—were sent out last year, more mail than is handled by all the rest of the post offices of the world put together?

Who else sends so many greeting cards? The number of Christmas cards that go ASTRAY each year because of mistakes in postage or address is over two million.

Where else do kids eat so much and accumulate so many box tops?

Well now, we're not offering any prizes for box tops. But in exchange for the enclosed postage paid envelope, we'd like to have your prompt check for your past due account.

Fair enough?

Cordially yours,

Dear Mr. Doe:

Very few persons, even those in the country, know whether a cow's ears are above, below, behind, or in front of her horns. Others do not know whether cats descend trees head first or tail first.

Very few people can distinguish between the leaves of the various kinds of trees in their neighborhood, and comparatively few are able to describe their own houses, beyond the most general features.

Persons who pass the same traffic signals every day cannot tell whether the green light is at the top or the bottom.

It's fascinating to notice and analyze the things you see and hear in your daily routine; to notice the faces of people, their walk, their characteristics. If you look for interesting and odd things, you will find them.

Incidentally, have you misplaced our bill covering charges of $54.00, dated September 20th?

Cordially,

Dear Mr. Doe:

"What do you do with your beard when you go to bed at night?" a little girl asked her grandfather. "Do you put it on top of the covers, under the covers, or in your nightshirt pocket?"

Grandpa had never thought about his beard at night, so he couldn't answer the little girl's question. But when he went to bed that night, he tried putting his beard on top of the covers, under the covers, and in his night-shirt pocket. But no way seemed right.

All night long, Grandpa tumbled and tossed. He lay on his back, he lay on his side, and he lay on his stomach. He couldn't get comfortable with that beard—he couldn't go to sleep.

You see, the little girl's question had made him beard-conscious. I wonder what question I could ask you to make you CHECK CONSCIOUS?

Your account is long past due, you know—since June 10th.

Sincerely,

4. MIDDLE STAGE—USE OF SPECIAL APPEALS

Increasing the pressure. Assuming that statements and reminder letters have failed to collect the delinquent account, the credit manager steps into the middle stage of the collection procedure. He can no longer afford to regard the situation lightly, or to continue with more or less casual requests for payment. He knows that something has happened which is keeping the customer silent, or that the latter is simply the kind who will not pay until he feels lawyers breathing on his neck. He still hopes that the money can be collected without recourse to legal action, and wonders what appeal he might use to stir the customer into meeting his obligation.

From long experience in dealing with human beings, the credit manager knows that unless the customer is totally without funds he may be receptive to some special reason for paying, but he also knows that different appeals vary in effectiveness with different individuals. Thus, in the effort to collect a particular account, he may use a sequence of letters, each one going at the reader in a different way. In one, he may in man-to-man fashion encourage the customer to tell what is wrong, and stress the desire of the company to *help* solve the problem. In a second, he may appeal to the customer's sense of fair play—the Golden Rule approach. In a third, he may talk about the value of good credit rating, and how the customer cannot afford to lose it. In each case he is probing for a "soft spot"—the one reason for paying which may have greatest weight in the customer's mind.

This is the middle stage, and it may drag out or be very short, depending on the willingness of the credit manager to match his wits against the stubbornness of the customer. In either case, the casual tone of the reminder letters is gone. These new letters may still be friendly, and should be, but they must be more insistent. The screw is being turned— the pressure is increasing.

Appeal to reason—what's wrong? Credit men realize that all customers cannot be expected to pay their bills regularly and when due without an occasional slip. When the emergency is real, and the customer's intentions are honest, the average company is more than willing to *help* the customer solve his problem. But no help is possible when the latter keeps his troubles to himself, as frequently he does. The reason, of course, is pride. The average individual is embarrassed when he gets in a financial jam. He wants to keep up appearances. Instead of placing the facts before the company to which he is indebted, he ignores the collection letters which come to him, hoping for a turn in fortune that will permit him to pay.

The experienced credit manager understands the reluctance of his customer to explain a financial difficulty, so he seeks to write the letter which will break down this reserve and produce the facts. It has to be a tactful letter, with nothing in it to injure the reader's pride, for if the latter feels humiliated or belittled he is not likely to reply. The appeal is to *reason*—how can we help unless we know what's wrong? Here's a very good example of the appeal to reason. The desire to *help* the customer is strongly stressed.

Dear Mr. Doe:

We know just as definitely as though we were a partner in your business that something out of the ordinary has made it impossible for you to settle our invoice of June 1st.

The reason we know this is that in all our previous dealings with you you have always made it a point to meet your obligations at maturity.

If you will only acquaint us with the details of this apparent difficulty, you can be assured of our wholehearted cooperation. Just let us know what we can do to help you.

We feel confident that we will have some word from you along these lines by return mail.

Very truly yours,

We think almost any honest-minded customer would appreciate the foregoing letter. Here's another one of the same type.

Dear Mr. Doe:

In an experience of more than fifty years, we have found that when people do not pay their bills promptly there is usually some good reason for it, such as sickness, dearth of funds, disagreement about terms, dissatisfaction with the goods, or failure to receive them.

Therefore, it seems very probable that there has been some such reason for your failure to pay the amount below.

But why do you keep us in the dark?

We do not want you to feel that we are inconsiderate if there is good reason for non-payment, but we cannot know the reason for your failure to pay unless you tell us.

So will you not, as the very minimum of fairness to us, write on the back of this letter just what the trouble is? Or better still, if the amount is correct and it is at all possible, send us your check and have this matter off your mind and ours.

Very truly yours,

The point, "We can't help you unless you tell us," is very neatly expressed in a brief letter written by another well-known credit manager.

Dear Mr. Doe:

You must have a good reason for not having paid anything on your account since October—we're sure of that. But you don't tell us what the reason is.

If we only knew the facts, no doubt some arrangement could be made that would relieve your mind of the worry of an overdue debt, and satisfy us, too.

If you can, send in a part payment with your answer. But whether you do that or not, at least tell us what's wrong. Give us a chance to help.

What do you say?

Yours sincerely,

In the following letter, the writer talks about the importance of preserving mutual goodwill, but his main purpose in writing is to find out *why* the customer has not replied to previous letters.

Dear Mr. Doe:

Our goodwill for each other is a real asset to us both. It costs each of us something to build it up. Neither of us can afford to let it be destroyed.

We are trying all the time to deserve and to keep your goodwill, and we believe that you feel and act in the same way toward us.

Your account being overdue $324.87 need not of itself disturb our mutual good feeling. But continued silence on your side, instead of frank response to our letters about the account, does really endanger it. From experience we know that it may cause you to feel a constraint that will make it hard to write us for help on your advertising and other selling problems or to order more goods when you need them.

So let's protect this mutual asset, which we have built up and shared together. Sit down now and write us just what the trouble is. We'll gladly make any needed corrections or adjustments. And if you will send us a part payment now, we'll go just as far as circumstances will allow to make it easy to meet the rest.

Sincerely yours,

Here's how another credit manager tries to find out why his letters have not been answered. Notice that again in this letter, as in the foregoing one, the writer makes a point of the previous good relationship between the two firms.

Dear Mr. Doe:

I wish that I were able to sit down and talk to you for about ten minutes about your account. I would like very much to know the circumstances that have caused you to delay your payment of January and February charges.

Without this information, I have to sit back and look at such factors as past experience, ratings, and credit information, in an effort to determine why your account has not been paid. Now the surprising thing is that all these factors point to your having a very satisfactory credit standing, but for some reason or other we have been waiting five months without even a partial payment.

At present, there is a balance of $196.23 on shipments that were made last January and February. Ordinarily, we would be very much alarmed about an account as old as yours and would seriously consider taking other steps to protect our interests. But our attitude about your account is quite to the contrary. In view of the very satisfactory manner in which invoices have been taken care of in the past, we do not feel at all concerned about ultimate payment.

The thing that does bother us, however, is that you have not at any time written, explaining the reason for the delay. I know you will understand that it would be a lot easier for us if we did have an explanation, and it would make us feel that you are not abusing the confidence we have in you.

To avoid the possibility of any misunderstanding, we will appreciate your either making immediate arrangements for taking care of this overdue balance, or dropping us a note today telling us just what we can expect.

Surely, you will agree that we are entitled to this consideration.

Yours very truly,

The letter that comes next is cleverly designed to "save face" for the customer. In speaking of financial difficulties, the writer places himself and the customer in the same boat with the sentence, "Every business, large or small, meets with difficulties at some time or other." Then, to sharpen the comparison, reference is made to losses incurred by the company in the recent flood. It is a very good letter of its class.

Dear Mr. Doe:

Among our outstanding accounts is yours of $120.00, which dates back to March 11.

All of us like to see the checks rolling in regularly, and when a customer gets behind, we wonder why. Usually there is a good reason for a delay in payment, and our company has always tried to see the other side of it as well as our own.

Now, if it is impossible for you to send us a check, write and tell us so—we like to hear from you. Maybe we can help you. If we can, all you have to do is to let us know.

Every business, large or small, meets with difficulties at some time or other. If it weren't for the assistance of business associates—if the business world operated on the principle of every man for himself—none of us would survive for long.

At present, our company is making a strong fight to make up for losses incurred in the recent flood. Anyone who escaped this disaster is, indeed, fortunate.

Back to your account—if you can possibly help us out with a check now, we certainly would appreciate it. A part payment will do.

May we hear from you by June 1?

Cordially yours,

Sometimes people are more willing to check the answers to a few questions than they are to talk in detail about themselves or their unpaid bills. The following letter uses the question method, but lacks most of the warmth found in the preceding examples.

Dear Mr. Doe:

May I ask a favor of you?

Your account for September has not been paid, and we have had no explanation of the reason. Will you please check the blank below, and return it to us in the enclosed envelope?

This will help us no end to co-operate with you.

Yours very truly,

I have not paid my account because:

1. Of oversight ———
2. Of the rush of work ———
3. Of error or overcharge ———
4. Of disagreement as to price or terms ———
5. I will remit in ——— days
6. Payment is in the mail ———
7. Check is enclosed ———

A hint to the wise. Not all credit men are as mild and gentle at this stage of the collection as were the writers of the letters you have just read. Some manage to put a little "stinger" in the letter—a hint that patience is wearing thin, and that the customer may soon expect more drastic action if he continues to remain silent. They do not *talk* about legal action, but unless the customer is very dumb he can read between the lines that it's not far off.

The following examples show how this hint of impending doom can be incorporated in a collection letter without damaging the friendly tone which should be present up to the last notice that suit is being filed. The words in italics are those that contain the hint.

Dear Mr. Doe:

Until you let us know why your matured account of $290.00 is unpaid and what you expect to be able to do with it, it will be impossible for us to decide how to handle the matter with fairness to you. *Every day of silence on your part adds to the difficulty.*

If we are to help you, fairness requires that you must help us. We, as well as you, have many obligations to meet. By pulling together, we can help each other through this period of temporary difficulty.

The first thing we must do is to reach a clear understanding. To that end, we urgently ask you to do three things **NOW**.

First—write us frankly if you cannot pay us in full.

Second—let us know when and how and in what amounts you expect to be able to pay.

Third—mail us a check on account now for as much as you can spare.

When you have done these things, we will have a basis on which to suggest an arrangement equitable to both of us.

Our ability to help delinquent customers has its limits. We must necessarily conserve it for the benefit of those who show a willingness to clear their accounts. Please let us hear from you.

> Yours most sincerely,

·   ·   ·   ·   ·

Dear Mr. Doe:

For some time now we have been writing to you about the outstanding balance on your account. We must know your intentions before we go any further.

Collecting long overdue accounts leads to many problems, most of them unpleasant for us and for you. If you'll tell us your situation now, perhaps we can still settle amicably. Certainly we'll do what we can to make it as easy as possible for you.

Please send us something today. A check if you can, but some statement of your intentions at the very least. If we don't hear from you, we'll have no choice but to go ahead with collection measures we prefer not to use.

> Sincerely,

Dear Mr. Doe:

We are trying to be as calm and collected about your past due account as the late Calvin Coolidge when he was caught napping in the middle of a busy day. He opened his eyes, grinned, and asked, "Is the country still here?"

We just can't all be Calvin Coolidges, and we do need the money. We have gone along with you for some time, expecting each day to see your account balanced, but this has never happened.

There must be some reason for this but since you have not written, we are at a loss to understand why all the silence. We like to do all we can to aid our good customers when they find it tough going, but we have to be told how we can help. There must be something we can do, Mr. Doe.

Won't you please send us some word *before your account passes out of our hands?* This postage-paid envelope is for your letter or, preferably, your check.

Very truly yours,

Applying the Golden Rule. Having written without success to ask *why* the customer has not paid his bill and to offer the help of the company in removing whatever obstacle may exist, the credit manager is still reluctant to drag the delinquent into court. He wonders what other appeal might do a better job. He knows there is a decent streak in the average human being which makes him want to play fair with others—that the Golden Rule is not entirely obsolete in human affairs. This is reflected in the spirit of sportsmanship seen in athletic contests, in the commonly shared contempt for any person who double-crosses another, in the often heard remark, "oh, give the fellow a break." In fact, it is said that there is honor even among thieves.

Probably very few individuals or companies accept the privilege of credit without feeling a moral obligation to pay when due. They don't pay because some unexpected obstacle turns up, or because optimism led them to overshoot the mark. When caught in one of these predicaments, they still feel a little bit ashamed for having violated the other party's confidence. Hence, there is power in the credit manager's question, "We tried our best to do right by you—don't you think you should do as much for us?"

The next letter makes use of the fair-play appeal in a way that only a hardened rascal could resist. It does not shed crocodile tears, or wear a halo of holiness, or rant about the customer's lack of appreciation. Instead it tries to put the reader in the company's shoes.

Dear Mr. Doe:

You have read collection letters where a fellow tries to kid himself and you too about "oversight" and so on; well, we want to be different.

If we deal with just the facts, our conclusion is that the reason you have not paid is because you haven't had enough money to go all the way round.

Sometimes the fellow who makes the biggest howl is the one who gets his money first, but this plan would not work with us, and we are placing you in the position we would take, taking it for granted you feel as we do.

Instead of worrying you with "duns" we just want to appeal to your sense of fairness. If you owe other bills that are older than ours, then we guess it is up to us to wait our turn; but if not, don't you think it would be only fair to let us have our money next?

Let us have a few lines from you today, will you, so that we may know how to figure on our collections. If you just can't send us a check in the mail tonight, give us an idea when you can send it. We certainly will appreciate this courtesy. It won't take much of your time and it will help us a lot.

Sincerely yours,

Equally effective in the use of the Golden Rule is the next letter. It puts more pressure on the customer than the foregoing message, but the tone is still that of one man pointing out to another in a friendly manner that fairness works both ways.

Gentlemen:

If our positions were reversed, and we owed you a bill like the one enclosed—two months overdue—how would you feel, and what would you do? Wouldn't you feel justified in writing a sharp demand for your money? We do...*almost*.

If there is a good reason for your delay in paying this bill, let us hear from you. We want to be fair. Otherwise, do what we think we'd do if our positions were reversed—sit right down and write out and mail a check.

Yours very truly,

Letters using the fair-play appeal do not have to be long and over-padded. Here is one which does the job, and does it well, in a few short sentences.

Dear Mr. Doe:

We were glad to cooperate with you and grant extra dating on a number of invoices covering shipment of your Fall requirements, as listed on the enclosed statement.

In all fairness, don't you believe that you in turn should reciprocate by taking care of the past-due items now?

We'll greatly appreciate your prompt cooperation.

> Cordially,

An interesting introduction may be just as helpful to a collection letter as to a sales letter. If the reader is placed in a good humor at the beginning, he is likely to be in the same mood later. The definition of "dun" in the message below would be of interest to almost any individual.

> Gentlemen:
>
> They tell us the word "dun" comes originally from the middle English word "dunnen," meaning to make a loud noise.
>
> Now, if there is any one thing we dislike to do it is to "make a loud noise" about an overdue account. In fact, we dislike to write a dunning letter just as much as you might dislike to receive it.
>
> However, because of the age of our February 10 invoice amount, $116.00, and as we have written you several times, we are getting near the end of our rope and are being pressed for something definite from the higher-ups. As we have gladly carried these items for you, it seems to us that it would be only fair to depend on your best efforts to help us out.
>
> In your good judgment, are we asking too much for you to send us your check, or tell us when you will do so, by return mail, using the attached, self-addressed envelope?
>
> > Yours very truly,

And here's another short one!

> Dear Mr. Doe:
> Since you received
> > Good salable merchandise,
> > Fair treatment,
> > A reasonable extension of time,
> Isn't it only fair that we should receive
> > YOUR CHECK?
>
> > Yours truly,

When the Golden Rule turns to brass. It is hardly consistent to talk about fair play, while at the same time calling the customer ugly names. Nor does it arouse goodwill to assume an attitude of smug holiness, the inference being that the writer is a very fine fellow, and his reader a skunk. On the contrary, the success of the letter appeal depends on a sincere man-to-man assumption that the customer is an upright fellow, and that the company still has faith in his good intentions. This assumption cannot be created by insincere exaggeration, or by statements that humiliate and anger the reader.

Consider the following examples:

Customer Has Deliberately Ignored Bill

Dear Mr. Doe:

We've written you twice now to remind you that you've owed us $117.42 since last November.

If this item was at first unpaid because of an oversight, surely you've had ample time to put a check through. Or if there's something wrong with the invoice itself, you've had plenty of time to write us about it.

But you haven't written...or sent a check! Instead, you've seen fit to deliberately ignore the matter.

We've been doing business with you for many years, Mr. Doe. We'd like to cooperate with you if it's a temporary cash shortage or some other equally good reason that prevents you from paying this bill. We'd certainly hate to throw your credit rating in the waste basket for $117.42.

It seems reasonable, though, that we should know what the reason is...doesn't it?

Cordially yours,

Silly Exaggeration

Dear Mr. Doe:

Right over our desk we have a little motto—you know the one about "the man with a smile."

Well, we try awfully hard to keep on smiling, but just the same it's mighty hard when we write letters and letters about your account, and can't get even a reply. Not the slightest indication that you have understood our pleading—that you want to play fair.

But we'll keep on smiling and watching the mail, because we have faith that you will do your part. Yes, we honestly believe you will sit down and write us a check—right NOW.

Cordially yours,

Just Another Pep Talk

Dear Mr. Doe:

Paying a bill, Mr. Doe, is just like climbing a hill or mountain. Lots of times it's a tough job before you reach the top, but it can be done step by step, and finally the rocky road is all behind you.

You were doing a great job of clearing the old debt, and the part payments were appreciated. Then, just as you were about ready to get on top and put this obligation behind you, something happened!

Just one more step would have turned the trick and you'd have had this old bill licked to a frazzle. Seems a shame, doesn't it, that the sum of only $25 stands between you and your goal?

Surely though, you have overcome much bigger obstacles than this before now. Just as surely, you can lick this problem and reach the point where this rocky road is all below and behind you.

Just one more step and you have made it! That step is the final $25 payment about which we have written so many, many times. In justice to your own past efforts, will you please mail the check for $25 right away.

Yours truly,

In none of the three preceding letters is the tone pleasing. You feel in each case that the reader was regarded as a puppet, with the writer pulling the strings. But the average human being is not so gullible; he can tell the difference between a sincere smile and the mere showing of false teeth.

A grocer to his customers. You could not find a better use of the fair-play appeal than that in a collection letter sent to his customers by a Pennsylvania grocer. It was prepared for him by Mabel Dill, Editor of the *Quality Grocer,* who knew that the customers of a village merchant are his friends and neighbors, who take advantage of his goodwill, but seldom intend to cheat him in the end. Thus, the letter stresses appreciation of their business, and asks only their help in return. Fair play is never mentioned, but that is the theme of the message.

Dear Friend:

I know you will take this letter in the friendly spirit in which it is meant. Here's what it's all about.

Due to my desire to be as helpful as possible during these recent years, I have extended the credit privilege until now I have thousands of dollars outstanding. Some of you, no doubt, feel that you could pay me something, but would rather wait until you could send me a substantial amount.

However, small sums paid regularly from many sources would make a total which would be of real assistance to me.

So I am asking you to let me have a little every week if possible to apply on your account, which I know you are just as anxious to whittle down as I am. I don't want you to feel embarrassed over this request. I know you will do the best you can.

With best regards, I promise you the same faithful service in the future that I have tried to give in the past.

Very truly yours,

If you were in our shoes. The essence of fair play is mutual understanding, and the lack of it is usually caused by the failure of one party to see the other's point of view. The paying of many a bill is put off because the debtor assumes his one account cannot be of any great consequence to a big company; the latter, he thinks, can easily afford to wait for the money. Understanding this kind of reasoning very well, the credit manager often uses a question, "What would you do if you were in our shoes?" to start the customer thinking with the right perspective. Because the approach is a very good one, and may perhaps be effective in your own credit correspondence, you may wish to study the letters below. All were written by experienced credit managers; all were successful in producing a better-than-average return.

Starting Off with a Story

Dear Mr. Doe:

Do you remember the story of Midas, the great king of ancient days? You know he was said to have the magic touch—that everything he touched turned to gold.

Now if we had the Midas touch, we wouldn't be writing this letter. We wouldn't be insisting on payment of your overdue account.

Nevertheless, a contract is a contract and should be lived up to. If we give our word to the bank to pay, we have to be right there with the money at the proper time. If we're not, the bank takes legal action against us.

Frankly, if someone owed you the amount of money you owe us, for as long a time, and you needed it just as much as we do, —wouldn't you go after it with all the power you could use? To be sure you would. Then please treat us as fairly as you expect to be treated. Give us a square deal.

We will expect your prompt remittance.

Sincerely yours,

Asking for a Square Deal

Dear Mr. Doe:

If someone owed you $150 and seemingly made no effort to pay it, how would you feel?

But now suppose you had put yourself in the place of the customer, assumed that perhaps he had been hard pushed for money, and had decided to wait rather than appeal to the law to collect your money.

Then later, suppose you wrote him a friendly letter, asking him to treat you fairly as you had treated him. Wouldn't you feel certain that you could expect a prompt response?

Although there are laws that regulate business, Mr. Doe, the biggest reason that almost all business transactions are completed smoothly is that most people believe in the square deal. Business would go to pieces if we couldn't depend upon the sacredness of an agreement.

That is all we ask from you—a square deal. You believe in that just as we do, don't you? Then let's settle this matter. A check from you by return mail will keep us friends.

Sincerely,

With a Hint of Things to Come

Dear Mr. Doe:

What would you do if...
you had written a customer several times about his overdue account?

He did not pay.

He offered no explanation for non-payment.

We think you would consider taking effective action to collect the account immediately.

Must we do the same?

Cordially,

A nice world it would be for credit managers if the appeal to fair play could always be counted on to bring back the money; unfortunately, it cannot. There are some debtors whose better self seems strangely calloused, and for them some other more potent approach must be found. The end of the search is easy to guess; people who seldom play fair with others may be judged as thinking only about themselves. Perhaps the obdurate customer needs to be told how by not paying he is hurting *himself*.

Letters that appeal to self-interest. The value of a good credit rating is well understood in business, although some buyers do not seem to realize that the only way to be sure of one is to pay their bills promptly. No individual or company wants to lose the privilege of credit and a letter which points to that possibility may get attention when others have failed. The appeal in such a letter is to self-protection; its success depends on the *fear* it can arouse in the mind of the reader.

By the time the credit manager gets around to this letter he is nearing the end of the middle stage. Not so far ahead, the lawyers are waiting to take over, and the chances that the bill can be collected without their aid have lessened. Nevertheless, the c. m. wants to try.

It may seem illogical to talk to a man about protecting his credit standing when he has already indicated an inability to pay or a disregard for the consequences if he doesn't. On the other hand, many slow-pay customers are not out of funds; for one reason or another they simply wait to be properly forced—and the most convincing argument seems to be the threat of what will happen to them or to their business if the delay continues.

It is obvious that the tone of a collection letter under such circumstances cannot be as casual or as personal as that found in earlier letters to the same customer. The credit manager still tries to be courteous and friendly, but he knows he is, in most cases, dealing with a hard-boiled customer who is not receptive to sentiment.

The customer's interest in his credit standing is usually manifested in two ways: he wants credit for the material reason that it is necessary in the operation of his business; he also has a certain personal pride in its possession. We sometimes encounter the paradox of an individual who neglects his bills as long as he can but regards his ability to buy on credit as proof of his own integrity. This fact influences some of the collection letters that stress the value of credit rating, since they also seek to stir the pride of the reader, but we doubt if the addition carries much weight.

Collection letters appealing to self-interest are usually shorter than the others you have been reading in this section, except for the first reminders with which the credit manager begins the chase. The length depends on the inclination of the writer, and whether or not he thinks it worth while to reason or argue with his reader. The examples that follow illustrate both types; you may decide for yourself which seem to be the better.

Short and to the Point

Dear Mr. Doe:

Your credit is one of your most valuable assets.

Prompt payment of accounts is the foundation of a high credit record.

You can assist us in maintaining your rating by giving your account your attention NOW.

We'll appreciate your prompt cooperation.

Yours very truly,

Short but More Interesting

Dear Mr. Doe:

HERE'S AN ENVELOPE!

It looks like any other envelope, doesn't it? But it isn't!

It's the envelope that is going to keep your credit good.

Put your check in it and mail it now to take care of your overdue installment.

> Yours very truly,

Establishing a Credit Reputation

Dear Mr. Doe:

Your installment, long overdue, has not been received by this office.

Insurance of your credit reputation and the payment of honest debts are reflected in the manner in which you pay this account.

A REPUTATION CANNOT BE BOUGHT.
IT MUST BE ESTABLISHED.

You can establish yourself by paying this indebtedness NOW and your future payments when due.

> Yours sincerely,

Credit Is a Convenience

Dear Mrs. Doe:

CHARGE IT TO MY ACCOUNT!

Haven't you enjoyed the feeling of pride when you have said these words? It's wonderful to be trusted; heartwarming when merchants have faith in your integrity.

Credit is a great convenience; it comes to your rescue when you need it most. It is an emblem of citizenship.

Of course, like everything else in life, credit carries responsibility. You have to protect your credit by prompt payment to have it protect you.

So...please pay your past-due bill with us now...$36.00, and you can continue to say:

CHARGE IT TO MY ACCOUNT!

> Cordially yours,

Quoting from Agency Report

Dear Mr. Doe:

A reputation for honest and fair business dealings is a wonderful asset.

It was that asset—and not cash—which induced us to fill your order for twenty raincoats. We had never dealt with you before. We had never had the pleasure of seeing your place of business. But when the agencies reported you as "honest, capable, and bears a reputation of paying bills promptly," we sent the raincoats to you that very same day.

Why are you holding back on your remittance to us? That "pays promptly" is a big asset to you. It got credit from us; it will help you get goods from us again—and from others, too.

But *it won't* if you *don't live up to it.* Have your bookkeeper make out the check for $54.98 now before you do another thing. *Don't abuse or lose that asset.*

I shall look for your remittance by return mail.

Yours truly,

Mentioning the possibility of legal action. The majority of the letters that stress the value of a good credit rating do not bring up the subject of possible legal action. They save that card for use in the last stage of the collection procedure. There are exceptions, however, as you can see in the following examples.

There's Trouble Ahead!

Dear Mr. Doe:

Is it worth it. . .

to jeopardize your credit standing—one of your most valuable assets—over the amount shown above? If you will give this question the serious consideration it deserves, we believe that you will agree with us that it isn't.

The last thing we want to do is to take any step which would impair your credit standing, but the amount you owe us is long overdue, and we have received no response to our many reminders. So unless we hear from you promptly, we'll have no choice but to turn your account over to our attorney for collection.

Neither of us will gain from this action—and the needless expense and embarrassment can be avoided. But only if you send us a check for the full amount within the next 10 days.

We shall expect your prompt reply,

Cordially,

"We Hate to Do This, but . . ."

Dear Mr. Doe:

It has been our desire to avoid placing on you an unnecessary burden of costs and expense. If you do not pay your account, however, no other course is open to us. We will have to take the necessary steps to enforce collection.

We hate to do this. A lawsuit over an uncollectible account becomes a part of your permanent credit record, and is always a reflection on the debtor's willingness and ability to pay his bills.

We shall expect to hear from you no later than February 14.

Yours very truly,

You have now examined representative letters taken from American business showing how collections are handled in the first and middle stages. You have witnessed the tightening of the screw as the credit manager passes from casual reminders to the more serious letters in which various appeals are used that might stir the delinquent customers to favorable action. Finally the sand runs low, and the credit manager is forced to admit reluctantly that nothing is left but the threat of legal action.

5. Letters Preceding Legal Action

The end of the rope. No credit manager reaches the last stage in his collection efforts without considerable regret. He wonders what he might have said in his previous letters that would have secured favorable results. Although the circumstances may have been beyond his control, he feels deeply the responsibility of having accepted an open account which is about to sour, with loss of profit and the additional expense of legal action. He therefore tries one final plea which might avert the catastrophe.

Obviously, this last collection letter in the series must be firm and positive. But no matter how the writer may feel toward the customer who has given him so much trouble, he must still be courteous and considerate. He may be tempted to call the customer what he probably is, but that would certainly defeat the purpose of this last important effort to get the money. Sarcasm, reproach, ugly names—all are futile in a collection letter. Only the shysters and the quacks have any faith in browbeating a wayward debtor.

In the writing of this "last resort" collection letter, one fact needs to be remembered. It is a serious mistake to cry "Wolf" unless the wolf is there. To tell a customer that he is getting the last chance to pay before turning the account over to the lawyers, and then later to write to him again with the same threat, is an indication of weakness and insincerity which the customer is quick to sense. There is no point in pulling a gun unless you mean to shoot exactly as and when promised. The custom of trying to frighten the customer with one letter after another that merely *talks* about legal action is common enough in certain types of business, none too savory or reputable, but good companies of established reputation do not stoop to such methods.

Usually, three letters are considered adequate in this last stage. The first is a plea that the customer pay the bill and save himself the trouble and expense of legal action. The latter is mentioned as impending, but no date is set. The second sets the date, but still leaves a period of time during which the payment may be made. The third is more of a notice than a letter, and sometimes is omitted. It simply tells the customer that the lawyers have taken over.

Right and wrong way. There is no accepted formula to follow in dictating the final-stage collection letters. Some credit managers make them short, the assumption being that it does no good to rehash circumstances or to repeat arguments advanced in previous messages. Others plead their case at greater length, repeating freely in the hope that a spark might cause fire even though it failed the first time. Then, there are those who seek an entirely new approach—a last minute telegram, a dramatized idea, or a story which is particularly appropriate.

Whatever the method or content, the only true measure of effectiveness is the percentage of success—in one hundred cases, how many times does the letter induce the customer to pay his bill and avoid legal action? There is one way, however, that a collection letter of this type may be tagged "right" or "wrong," without argument or equivocation. This is the distinction between the letter which disregards courtesy, and the one which still approaches the customer as a business friend.

The Wrong Way

Dear Mr. Doe:

You do not answer our letters. What is more serious, you do not pay your bills.

Matters of courtesy and honor are important to us, if not to you.

You will either pay this bill, or take the consequences. If the latter, it's your fault, not ours. We at least have acted like gentlemen in this transaction.

In ten days, we shall send this bill to our attorneys for collection. You will not find them as easy and lenient as we have been.

Yours truly,

The Right Way

Dear Mr. Doe:

Our collection manager just came to my desk with a statement of your account; he was about to send it to our attorney. I have asked him to postpone action for a few days, because I don't want to collect money in this manner if I can help it.

It will be much easier for both of us if you'll simply send your check, today.

Let's get this matter straightened out in a spirit of mutual consideration.

Sincerely yours,

No doubt the difference between the above letters is plain enough to require little explanation. In the "Wrong" letter, the writer is petulant, sarcastic, and insulting. In the "Right" letter, the writer is a decent fellow who doesn't want to take legal action, but will if he has to. Notice the tone of the letter. It's frank, but friendly throughout. The credit manager shows a willingness to assist the customer in whatever way he can.

Here are some other examples of "Right" letters. They are somewhat stronger letters than the foregoing, but they manage to make an unpleasant point without being rude.

Dear Mr. Doe:

Unfortunately, we have not received a satisfactory reply to our many requests for the payment of the account mentioned below. As you know, this account is now considerably overdue.

We are sure you understand that at our present wholesale prices we cannot afford to allow accounts to remain outstanding for a long period.

Therefore, if we do not receive a remittance within seven days from the above date, we shall be reluctantly compelled to place the matter in the hands of our attorneys without further notice to you.

We sincerely hope that this will not be necessary and that you will send us your check by return mail, so that we can continue to be of service to you.

Cordially,

. . . . .

Your balance is many, many months overdue, and we've had no answers to any of our letters. Therefore, unless we hear from you within the next 10 days, we'll have no other choice but to turn your account over to our attorneys for immediate collection.

It is our sincere hope that this will not be necessary, since it would cause us both needless expense and embarrassment. To avoid this unpleasant action, do let us have your check by return mail.

. . . . .

Dear Mr. Doe:

It is with regret that we find it necessary to send this fourth letter, our last REQUEST that you forward a check in payment of your note.

This obligation was incurred a considerable time ago on the basis of its being paid when due, and it seems reasonable to believe that ample time has elapsed for you to comply with the terms mutually agreed on when you purchased your policy.

If your remittance for the full amount of this note is not received within the next week, we shall assume that it will be in order for us to take such steps as circumstances warrant.

Yours very truly,

.   .   .   .   .

Dear Mr. Doe:

Although we have written you a number of times about your December 16th bill amounting to $55.00, we have received no response whatever.

Your references spoke well of you and we were glad to give you the benefit of the regular 30 day accommodation. However, further correspondence now seems to be useless, and we have decided to place the account with our attorneys for collection unless it is paid in full by May 1st.

We urge you to take care of this account without further delay.

Very truly yours,

.   .   .   .   .

Dear Mr. Doe:

Ninety per cent of the accounts we collect through attorneys are handled that way because the customers will not answer our letters.

We are forced to sue because friendly requests bring neither payment nor explanations.

Your account of $407.98 is long past due. We must assume that the amount is correct, for you have never questioned it.

We both want to keep away from the courts if possible. So before sending the account to our attorney, we will wait ten days for your letter and check.

Yours very truly,

.   .   .   .   .

Dear Mr. Doe:

Do we sue?

Indian summer has turned to winter. Winter has dissolved before the warm spring sun. Now summer is about ready to take over where spring leaves off...and we still have heard nothing from you since that November day when you authorized us to place your $25 ad in our paper.

We published that ad in good faith, and you know how patiently we've been waiting for our money. At first we thought our turn hadn't come around as yet. Then we wondered if anything had gone wrong that prevented you from paying. We even offered you a small gift and told you how non-payment of this small debt would hurt your credit standing.

The time for further warnings is now past. You really have left us no other course but to turn your account over to our attorneys for collection.

We really don't want to do this, Mr. Doe, so we're giving you three more days of grace. This is your last warning, however. Your account is *scheduled for the attorneys on May 5.* Save it by doing the right thing and mailing us your check today. A handy envelope is enclosed. Use it at once.

Yours truly,

Letters seasoned with humor. You might think that nothing but a serious tone would be appropriate for the final stage of the collection procedure, and in general this is true. However, some credit managers have had considerable success with letters that talk in a lighter vein, even though the news in them may not be so pleasant. In using this approach, the writer skates on thin ice, for if what he says seems too superficial, the customer may not take the message seriously. Humor has power to influence human behavior, but unless it "rings true" it tends to do more harm than good. For example, who would be favorably impressed by the following letter?

Superficial and Insincere

Gentlemen:

A young man by the name of Jones—one of the Jones boys— came to me today with the sad story of your account. He says that up to now his letters have brought no reply, no check, "no nothin'."

I told him he'd better have one of our cute numbers type a nice, fresh statement, and I'd send it direct to you with a special letter. I still think Jones has been missing the mark, and that none of his reminders have reached the man who writes the checks.

Now that you know the facts, I know you'll have a check made out for your signature. Put it in the enclosed stamped envelope and let it go rejoicing to me here in Chicago. Then I can call Jones over and say:

> "Here it is, My Boy. I knew these good folks would come across for the Old Credit Man and justify my faith and confidence."

Here's hoping your business is good. You can prove it by sending an order along with that important piece of paper.

Confidently yours,

There is a certain dignity to be maintained in business, even though many writers of the stiff-shirt variety over-emphasize its importance. The tone of the following letter is neither convincing nor sincere. The hard-boiled customer who has ignored all previous collection efforts is not likely to believe such a conversation actually took place, nor is he likely to be moved by a "cute number" who types a fresh statement.

Nevertheless, it is possible to season a collection letter with a sprinkling of humor, and at the same time preserve the dignity which is expected of business relationships. The following letters might or might not get the money, but at least their approach is interesting and sincere.

Immaterial, Irrelevant, and Irregular

Dear Mr. Doe:

The lawyer said, "The question is immaterial, irrelevant, and irregular," and because the witness did not have to answer the question the case had to be dismissed.

YOU have been sent five notices requesting payments of $65.40 which is due us. The notices were sent to you on the following dates:

> January   5
> January 10
> January 15
> January 22
> January 29

NOW, we are sending you the final notice. If we do not hear from you, we will have to place your account in the hands of a collection agency. Let us hear from you, and please send your check so we can dismiss these letters as "immaterial, irrelevant, and irregular."

Yours truly,

"Our Collection Department Is Fixin' to Kill"

Dear Mr. Doe:

Slick Johnson was sentenced to the gallows for the excessive use of an exceedingly sharp razor.

Sitting in his cell, he struggled to find words that would explain his predicament to the Governor and win a pardon. The next morning the Governor received this message in his mail:

Dear Guvenor

They are fixin to hang me friday and here it is tuesday.

Respectfully
Slick Johnson

Like Slick, we too are in a predicament. Our collection department is fixin' to "kill" your policy next Friday because the payment hasn't come in.

One of those printed forms in your check book is ideal for arranging a prompt pardon for a friend, who for only $20 a year can serve you both faithfully and well.

Most respectfully,

"Pay or We'll Shoot"

Gentlemen:

An interesting story is told of Benvenuto Cellini, the celebrated 16th Century goldsmith.

It seems that Cellini, after months of painstaking labor upon a cunningly wrought gold vase which he had been commissioned to make for the Bishop of Salamanca, was unable to collect his fee. Exasperated and in- need of funds, Cellini called on the debtor and pointing his pistol at him cried, "Pay or I shoot!" The Bishop paid and Cellini went his way rejoicing.

This simple and direct method of collection is not used today, but there is a similar one that has similar characteristics. When every other friendly means of getting our money has been used and our customer, like the Bishop, simply refuses to pay, we say, "Pay or we'll shoot."

And we are serious about it. We have no pistol, it is true. Our "gun" is the Cooperative Adjustment and Collection Service— and it has a mighty fine reputation for hitting the mark.

Don't make us unlimber this weapon to collect your account. We don't like to shoot it off because it makes a big noise and scares everybody—and you know how it is, there is always the likelihood that someone will get hurt.

Very truly yours,

Pinch-hitting for the Credit Manager. A common practice in collection procedure, when the time for legal action is near, is to send the customer a final appeal signed by some other important executive—the treasurer, a vice-president, or even the head of the company. Such a letter not only carries the weight of coming from a top executive, but it may also have a new approach which gets better results than those already used

Office of
CARL WOLLNER
President

Wednesday

Dear Sirs: Doggonit! Have I lost my ability to write a customer a letter friendly enough to get an answer? You got my letter — didn't you? Why the heck didn't we get an answer? That account of yours is old enough to have whiskers on it and we really need our money. You've got no right to keep it.

Maybe the Credit Mgr. was right after all when he said you wouldn't answer my friendly letter.

Do I have to pass the buck back to him and let him get the money any way he can — friendly or otherwise?

Before I do, here's postage and envelope to mail that check right now, please sir!

Still Friendly,
Carl Wollner

A Chief Executive Writes a Collection Letter

by the credit manager. At least, the game is worth the effort, and some-times it does the job.

For example, a check was promptly gained with the following letter written in long-hand by the late Carl Wollner, then president of Panther Oil & Grease Manufacturing Co. You will note that the customer is handled without gloves, although the spirit of the message is summarized in the complimentary close, "Still Friendly."

Here are five more "last resort" collection letters in which top executives pinch-hit for their credit managers.

The Company President Writes a Letter

Gentlemen:

The effort of Mr. Clark to bring about a friendly settlement of your long overdue account was referred to my attention this morning along with the file of correspondence for review and decision. As you know, there is an unpaid balance of $96.43 and this has been explained in our many letters and statements. I feel sure that if there were any question regarding it you would have taken it up with us some time ago.

There comes a time in the collection of a long delinquent account when it seems that there is nothing left to do but to place it with our collection attorney. When that happens we both lose something. We lose your good will and the opportunity for a continued friendly business relationship, and you lose your valuable credit reputation. Isn't that worth your serious consideration?

I have instructed Mr. Clark to delay action on this for ten days, which will give you time to get your check to us. You will be glad, I know, if you take this opportunity to prevent an unpleasant situation. We have tried to be considerate in handling your account and any action that we may be forced to take will be your responsibility.

Cordially,

A Treasurer Delivers an Ultimatum

Gentlemen:

Our Credit Manager has just handed me the enclosed statement of your account, with the recommendation that it be referred to our attorneys for collection. After carefully going over our Collection Department records, it looks as though you have ignored the terms of your agreement.

Invoices covering your rental installments have been sent to you promptly each month; letters written to you requesting payment have not resulted in settlement.

Nothing can be inferred from your inaction save a violation of the terms of your subscription, to which we invite your attention. There is no question as to the validity of your contract. There is no question of our good faith in carrying out our part of the agreement. The next step is up to you. What do you intend to do?

If for any reason settlement will be delayed longer, I suggest that you wire me immediately. If I do not hear from you promptly, I shall be forced to assume that you are prepared to defend the action that will be started immediately, involving the entire amount of your contract, plus attorney's fees.

Very truly yours,

Granting an Extra Five Days

Dear Mr. Doe:

Our Collection Manager has placed before me a statement of

your long overdue account and informed me that his repeated efforts to collect have had no effect.

He also asked for my instructions as to whether he should place your account with our attorneys for collection. I have instructed him to hold this matter in abeyance for five days until I could write to you.

If you cannot pay the full amount overdue, send me half of it at once, and tell me when you can pay the balance.

If you fail to answer this letter promptly, I will be forced to conclude that it is best for the Collection Department to proceed with legal action.

I am enclosing a stamped envelope, addressed to me, and I ask that you let me hear from you by return mail.

> Very truly yours,

Citing the Golden Rule

Dear Mr. Doe:

Our collection manager tells me that we must take legal action against you. He says that you owe us $73.00, that the bill was past due after September 15, that he wrote to you without reply on September 25, October 10, October 20, November 1, and November 15.

I have asked him to hold the law in check for a few days. Speaking as man to man, I don't want to get our money by force. As a business man, I don't relish the idea of paying out money to collect an account. This, in my opinion, is a step to be taken only when the other party refused to sit down at the council table with me.

I have been frank with you, Mr. Doe. Won't you be the same with me? Write and let me know what is the matter. Even though your account has reached the ultimatum stage, I may be able to help you.

Just sit down now. Write that letter. Use the enclosed envelope which has been addressed to insure my personal attention. The Golden Rule that you and I learned in school may be considered an outmoded, overworked idea by some people, but I believe, if we both apply it, we can straighten out this matter to our mutual satisfaction.

> Sincerely yours,

To the Point But Not Unfriendly

Gentlemen:

This morning our collection manager suggested to me that we turn your account over to Dun's. He placed before me copies of the five letters which have been mailed to you since April 5.

I do not wish to authorize such action before taking up the account with you personally. You understand that I want to give you every opportunity to settle your account without reporting it to Dun's.

To speak frankly, I am inclined to think you have some good reason for not writing to us. I shall retain this correspondence on my desk ten days to give you an opportunity to send your check, or to tell us what to expect.

You must realize that this debt is a matter of real importance to you. Please let me hear from you.

Sincerely,

When very old accounts go haywire. An especially difficult problem for the credit manager is how to handle the old and honored customer who for some unknown reason has recently stopped paying his bills. Naturally, he does not want to throw over the business which might still be salvaged, but any account old or new reaches the stage of legal action when all other collection efforts have failed. Nevertheless, the tone of the "last resort" letter to one of these older customers is usually less stringent than if sent to a customer not deserving the same consideration. The writer wants to get the account back on the right basis if he possibly can. Consider this example:

Dear Mr. Doe:

Frankly, we are reluctant to send your account to our lawyer for collection. You have done business with us for some time, and we believe in your good intentions. After all, lawyers do have a way of getting the money, but in the end it costs you more and often leads to many unpleasant consequences. So, we are going to give you every chance to avoid outside collection of your account.

It will be necessary, though, for you to do your part. A payment of a part of the account by March 10 and satisfactory assurance on the balance is what we consider your part now.

It is entirely up to you.

Yours very truly,

The foregoing letter is relatively short and to the point. In no way, though, is the tone unfriendly or abrupt. The writer is quite clearly anxious to be helpful and to give the customer special consideration. The next letter is very similar, but for some reason it seems a little warmer.

Dear Mr. Doe:

Isn't there some time during the day that you have a few moments to spare? Will you do me this favor? Use a few of those moments to sit down and write a letter about your present financial condition and how things will be for the next few months.

We dislike to talk about such a delicate subject as payments and credits, but it has become necessary to be very frank with you. I know that you will be equally frank with us.

We have had to delay shipments because of the condition of your account, which has always been past due during the last few months. Balances, and rather sizable ones, too, have been carried forward to the next month. That, considering that you have an opportunity to make your sales before we require payment, is a condition that should not exist.

And so, I am asking you, as I believe you would ask me, to tell us the whole story. You have been a customer of ours for a number of years, and we want to continue serving you. Taking legal action on this account is really the very last thing we want to do.

You will find us ready to work with you on any plan that will help you to get on a better basis.

We want to see you earn the two per cent discount we allow for prompt payment. With billings the size of yours, this would amount to quite a sum over a year's time.

So, won't you do me that favor? Just tell me the story. And, with your letter, can you send me a check?

Very truly yours,

Another excellent letter, we think, is the final one in this series of "last resort" letters. It is somewhat hard hitting—but not ugly. There are no angry words, only a simple and polite statement of the situation. The solution is left clearly up to the customer.

Dear Mr. Doe:

Your balance is still $123.90, and our patience is still holding out. We have enjoyed our business relationship with you for several years, and we are reluctant to end it in unpleasantness. However, your silence is putting us into an uncompromising position.

The problem is simply that we have been unable to collect by our usual, friendly methods. Good business policy demands that we do collect. The solution, you see, is squarely up to you.

We must ask now that you remit a substantial payment on your account immediately. Unless you do, we shall have no choice but to turn the account over to our attorneys ten days from now.

Let's solve this problem today, and stay friends.

Sincerely,

Curtain . . . end of the play. When the final appeal fails, the credit manager has reached the end of his personal efforts to collect the past due account. He may or may not send a final note, saying that legal action has started. It doesn't matter so much—the customer soon finds out that he is in hot water.

Throughout the many preceding pages, you have watched this three act drama.

> In Act I, you saw the letters used in the first stage of the struggle —nice, easygoing letters, containing no pressure. They were mostly reminders—nobody was much worried.

> In Act II, the plot thickened. Doubt was beginning to form. The letters were longer—more intense. Various appeals were tried to stir the debtor into action—the plea for co-operation, to fair play, to pride, to self interest.

> In Act III, came the climax. By then all in the audience knew the customer's intentions were not good. Could he be driven to pay by threat of legal action? In the wings, new characters waited for their cues—the lawyers. One last appeal. Unhappy ending. Curtain!

So now we turn from the somewhat regimented letters used in the collection procedure to those that serve special purposes, and are out-of-the-groove.

6. Out-of-the-Groove Collection Letters

The pro and con of showmanship. You're well aware by now that the dramatized letter may sometimes out-pull others of more conventional style. The reason is that people tend to give special attention to things which are *different*. This is a psychological fact. If it were not true, all automobiles would probably still be painted black, and the various makers would not try so hard to bring out new, more strikingly designed models. Few of us like to do the same things in the same old way; we seek different forms of amusement; we buy different types of clothing; we rush to try a new cereal for breakfast; we may even go to a different church now and then to see if salvation is being offered in different ways.

Hence, there can be no logical argument against the use of an occasional collection letter based on a different approach, or prepared in some special way to gain attention. The dramatized collection letter is okay, provided it conforms with the rules for showmanship in any other kind of business correspondence. The idea must be original and really clever and it must be appropriate to the purpose and thought of the message in the body of the letter. As you know, it is a mistake to gain attention by some spectacular device, only to have the reader realize later that there is little or no connection between the idea and letter-content. In such a case, the showmanship turns out to be an insult to the reader's intelligence, and does more harm than good.

Certain disadvantages limit the extent to which the dramatized collection letter may be used. If a special letterhead has been prepared, the reader knows that the message is not for him alone—that it is a form letter sent to numerous customers who have not paid their bills. A form letter is seldom taken as seriously as one pointed directly at a particular customer. Moreover, a dramatized message must sacrifice some dignity for effect, and may not be regarded too favorably by conservative readers who never wander from the conventional path. Highly original collection letters are not for general use, although we know that they often out-pull the cut-and-dried ones.

When only the copy is different. A collection letter may get out of the groove merely in thought-content or the way it is typed. It may travel on the regular company letterhead, and not involve the expense of a separately printed form or of some special gadget that has to be attached. Here, for example, is one that displays an unusual bit of typing.

Dear Mr. Doe:

Regarding the ALMIGHTY $.

There i$ a little matter that one of our cu$tomer$ ha$ $eemingly forgotten entirely. $ome make u$ promi$e$ but do not keep them. To u$ it i$ an important matter—it'$ nece$$ary in our bu$ine$$.

We don't like to $peak about $uch remi$$ne$$. NUF $ED.

Very truly your$

Ordinarily, letters in code are not effective, because it's an imposition on a reader's time to expect him to decipher such a message. The next, however, is simple enough to offset the objection.

Good morning, Mr. Doe:

Here is a little Secret Code Writing. Can you solve it?

rof kcehc evah ew yaM
stnec evlewt dna srallod owt-yteniN
?liam nruter yb

Please let us have your answer immediately. Thank you.

Yours very truly,

P.S. Solution: Just read it backwards.

Because business letters are commonly written in prose, it is obviously a form of showmanship when a collection message is put in rhyme. These attempts can be very good or very bad, depending largely on the quality of the verse, and since business men are not poets, the result is usually not so good. The following letter used by the Moore Fuel Corporation is one of the better sort.

Dear Mr. Doe:

It's easy to remember,
That back in mid December,
Your mind from coal and oil was never free.
When winter winds were howling,
And snow-filled skies were scowling,
Your first thought was to telephone one three.

But now that winter's over,
And you've started mowing clover,
There's one more little bill you have to pay.
We know you wouldn't let us,
Even think you might forget us,
So we hope your check will soon be on its way.

Thanks,

We don't think that Mr. William Shakespeare would have envied the credit man who devised the above rhyme; nevertheless it must have been sufficiently appealing to get favorable attention, for the letter proved to be a potent collector for the Moore Fuel Corporation.

Letters built around attachments. Often you encounter collection letters with some attachment which dramatizes the thought of the message. Such a letter can be very successful if the point is not too far-fetched and the gadget not too elaborate. One popular letter had a feather attached. The letter read: "A feather is not very heavy, but have you ever carried a feather-bed upstairs? One small unpaid account does not burden us, but hundreds of them can make a tremendous load." Obviously, the feather itself adds a little punch to the message and is quite appropriate.

Unfortunately, the idea is sometimes overdone. An illustration of how far from the path of common sense a writer may wander is a collection letter on which was attached a small cigar in a cellophane bag, a safety match, and a small strip of sandpaper. The idea, of course, is: "Have a cigar on us, and please send your check." But you can imagine in what shape the cigar arrived after its journey in the mail. Furthermore, any smoker would regard with suspicion the obvious cheapness of the tobacco even had there been no damage in transit. This type of attachment is plainly in very poor taste. The credit manager who uses this kind of gimmick succeeds only in offending the conservative customer.

On the other hand, some very effective collection letters have been built around attachments selected for their interest value and with good taste. The following idea used by Vic Knight in the Dartnell Business Letter Service is both amusing and original. Across the top of the letterhead in big type is the caption, "WE'RE GIVING YOU THE WHOLE WORKS." Attached is a packet of seven miniature letters. The normal eye would need a glass to read them, but this doesn't matter as they are intended only to dramatize the following copy.

Dear Mr. Doe:

Once upon a time we thought we could write good collection letters. They started off with the mild hooey of, "Perhaps you overlooked last month's statement, isn't it lovely weather, and how are all the folks?"

Then they worked up to grand finale and in the last letter, we said something like this: "Now see here, you yellow-livered deadbeat, if you do not lay the cash on the line by day after tomorrow, we will have you clapped in the hoosegow—if not sooner."

For quite a while, we thought that was about the world's best series of collection letters. Then it just so happened there came a time when we were slow about paying one of our own bills, and we began getting that same bunch of letters back—one every ten days.

That experience cured us of the notion we could write collection letters. Our best efforts are reproduced above—not so you will waste any time reading them, but so you won't feel slighted. Yes, with this letter you are getting "The Whole Works."

But all we are now attempting to do is to keep some cash coming in by telling good customers like yourself the truth. We need the $67.95 that you owe us, and it will please us a lot if somehow you can manage a check.

Hopefully yours,

The packet of miniature letters attached to the above message recalls another written on a small letterhead about one-fourth the usual size. The copy reads: "Your overdue account is so small that we are using as little space as possible to write to you about it. Please send your check today. Thank you." Then, of course, you think of the "BIG" collection letters—blow-ups four times as large as a standard letter, with the copy reading: "Since all of our regular-sized letters have somehow escaped your attention, we think this BIG one may do a better job."

Attached to a letter written by Canadian R. G. D. Anderson for the North American Lubrication Co., was an artificial forget-me-not; here is how this blue flower is used as the theme of Mr. Anderson's letter.

Dear Mr. Doe:

This little Forget-me-not is sent you so that you may know that even though we do not send you a lot of high-powered letters, do not send collectors, or make it unpleasant for you because you happen to owe this company an account, we do expect you to pay that bill—when and as you can.

Another year has brought tremendously disappointing crop returns to many parts of the West. There will be many good people in distress again this year. But even in the worst districts, crops have been spotty; here and there, a good one to be found. And wherever a reasonable crop is harvested, the much better prices will make actual returns quite good.

We ask that you do one of these things—

1. Pay your account in full if you possibly can.
2. Pay something at least—$5.00, $10.00, or some definite sum.
3. If you honestly cannot spare one dollar, just turn this letter over and tell me so in confidence—entirely between you and me.

So may my Forget-me-not remind you that we are still very much your friends here, and as friends we ask your help in doing one, two, or three.

Sincerely,

Illustrations and special letterheads. There is much truth in the Chinese saying that one picture is worth a thousand words. You know how profusely advertising men use illustrations and color to enliven their copy—in magazines, in booklets, on billboards, and in other forms of publicity. In the same way, a business letter may gain favored attention because of a colorful letterhead or an interesting picture or heading. The two letters on pages 868 and 869—one written for *Gentlemen's Quarterly* and the other for the Elgin Watch Company—show how cleverly-illustrated ideas may add effectiveness to collection letters.

The easiest way to illustrate a collection letter, although it may not be the most effective, is to attach a sticker. A number of the companies offering business services carry a wide selection of stickers designed for use in sales, collection, and other forms of business correspondence. An advantage of these stickers is that one may be used for a short while and then discarded in favor of another before repetition has destroyed its interest value.

GENTLEMEN'S QUARTERLY

1255 PORTLAND PLACE / BOULDER, COLORADO

I MUST PAY FOR MY GQ SUBSCRIPTION

Dear Sir:

Gentlemen's Quarterly subscribers use this reminder in different ways.   Some paste it up on their shaving mirrors.   Others clip it to tomorrow's calendar leaf.   Still others put it in a pocket of their newest one, two, or three button business suits, or give it to their wives for "processing," or . . .

Whatever system they use seems to work.   Payment reaches us; GQs keep reaching them.

Now if you're too busy to bother with systems or reminders (or if you're too considerate to burden your wife), just make out your check, mail it, forget the "business" part of your GQ subscription and concentrate on the fashions.

But do it soon, please, so there'll be no break in service.

Cordially,

M. A. Pfenninger

M. A. Pfenninger
Subscription Accounts Manager

MAP:kd

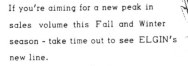

If you're aiming for a new peak in
sales volume this Fall and Winter
season - take time out to see ELGIN's
new line.

We're just loaded with style and feature
ideas to make your sales climb - ideas that
have sell-appeal and profit that's real.

But first - let's get last seasons account out
of the way. Send your check today and we'll
"yodel" for your salesman.

Cordially Yours,

EFWiehrdt

Assistant Credit Manager

EFWiehrdt/ls

ELGIN NATIONAL WATCH COMPANY
ELGIN, ILLINOIS   TEL. SHerwood 2-3300

Special letterheads for collection letter purposes also may be obtained from the Carr Speirs Corporation in Waterford, Connecticut, and from other similar organizations, which means that any credit manager may have a fling at showmanship without too much trouble or expense. Although we do not recommend these special letterheads as a standard item, there is no question but that now and then, if inserted in the regular run of letters, one of them may do a surprisingly good job in collecting unpaid bills.

Collection letters for specific days. If we assume that *anything* out of the ordinary may be called of particular interest to mankind, we can agree that a collection letter may successfully get out of the groove even *without* the use of special letterheads, cartoons, gadgets, or any of the other devices we have been reviewing. In the examples that follow you will see how various credit correspondents have written effective collection letters in connection with certain days or events to which the average man attributes importance.

The reasoning that prompts such letters is that the customer's respect for the day will in some intangible way make him receptive to a letter that talks about it. To what degree this reasoning is sound, no one knows, but we cannot deny the prevalent emotional reactions displayed at certain times of the year—a feeling of good will and tolerance during Christmas week, of patriotism on the 4th of July, of renewed ambition at the start of a new year. Hence, a collection letter which touches one of these impulses often has a better chance of success than the usual run-of-the-office variety.

In connection with the use of these special-day letters, however, one caution needs to be mentioned. The writer must guard against insincerity and exaggeration; unless he himself feels the same emotional reaction which he is trying to arouse in his reader, the message will fall flat. With this reservation in mind, examine the following examples.

Keeping Things in a Christmas Spirit

Dear Mr. Doe:

When the holiday season comes around, we do not like to change the atmosphere of pleasant tidings...so we won't.

We are postponing further correspondence about your account until after the first of the year, when we will review all accounts again.

In the meantime, we would like to wish you a joyous holiday season.

                                    With best wishes,

A More Conventional Letter

Gentlemen:

We take this opportunity to extend our sincere wishes for a Happy Holiday Season.

We sincerely hope that your sales during this season will far exceed those of previous years.

We realize that you are busy at this time, but our calendar year is drawing to a close and we are anxious to have our receivables as up-to-date as possible.

Won't you please take a few minutes to send us your payment now, as your account is considerably past due.

Your cooperation will be greatly appreciated.

Cordially,

First of the Year Letter

Dear Mr. Doe:

We should like, at the outset, to extend our sincere wishes to you for a most successful 19__. And we thank you for having granted us the privilege of serving you during the past year.

Judging from all reports, most businesses enjoyed a substantial increase in holiday sales as compared with the same period for the past several years.

We hope that you, too, shared in this increase and that the added sales will enable you to start the new year right by bringing your account as shown on the enclosed statement up-to-date.

We will appreciate your cooperation.

Cordially,

Beginning the New Year on the Right Foot

Dear Mr. Doe:

For a special reason we make this request now. Inasmuch as this is the last month of the year, we are anxious to have our accounts paid up-to-date before we make our annual reports.

On the enclosed statement, we list your purchases that are past due, and the months in which you sent us these orders.

Since part of your account has been extended quite a while, we feel certain that we can depend on you to send us your payment in the next few days.

Cordially,

Doing Things the Chinese Way

Dear Mr. Doe:

IT'S AN OLD CHINESE CUSTOM!

In China, the celebration of New Year's is a great event. The custom for all good Chinese is to go among their creditors and settle their obligations.

This starts a chain because with the money received, one man pays another and the second pays a third, and so it goes—THEN they all celebrate with a lot of noise, the burning of redfire and the shooting of fireworks.

If you could start the chain, we could close our books with our obligations paid to others. Just an old Chinese custom, but a pretty good way to start the New Year in ANY country.

You'd be surprised, too, how loudly we can shout—

"HAP ... PY NEW YEAR-R-R!!!!"

The amount is $18.00. Do we get it?

Cordially yours,

End of Fiscal Year

Dear Mr. Doe:

Although a month's time has elapsed...

there is still time to mail us your remittance so that it will be received before our annual audit starts on the fifteenth. We are naturally anxious to have our overdue accounts reduced to the absolute minimum before this date.

Also, this action on your part will prevent your account from appearing among those showing past-due balances in the auditors' report to our management. It is our belief that you would not want your name to appear on this "Past-Due List," and we certainly wouldn't want it either.

Now that this second request is before you, won't you please send us your check in payment of the overdue items by return mail.

You can be sure that we will greatly appreciate your cooperation.

Cordially,

A Red Letter Day

Gentlemen:

October 31 may seem like just another "Blue Monday," but to us it's a red letter day, since it marks the close of our fiscal year. There is no reason in particular why that should be of any significance to you, but believe me, it's really an important matter to us.

That is the time when we have an annual reckoning on what's happened for the past twelve months in sales, profits or losses, and collections. That last word is a big one in this department— and we're naturally anxious to have our overdue accounts reduced to the absolute minimum before the end of the month.

We can't accomplish this without the co-operation of all our good customers. Will you do your part by paying your account before the end of this month? Thank you.

The amount is $103.75.

Yours very truly,

Lincoln's Birthday

Dear Mr. Doe:

This coin is only a penny. But the character of Abraham Lincoln is an inspiration worth millions to any American.

When he was an Illinois country storekeeper, Lincoln once innocently overcharged a customer a few pennies—then walked three miles through rain and mud to refund them.

Deep down inside of us, we all want to be as fair as Lincoln was. His birthday is a good time for you to show your fairness. And what better way than by paying your overdue account?

That's fair, isn't it?

Yours very truly,

(*Lincoln penny attached*)

Washington's Birthday

One hundred and fifty years ago this month, Washington's troops suffered untold hardships at Valley Forge because the Colonies couldn't raise the money to feed and clothe them. Their credit was mighty poor.

We may not be walking over the snow with bare and bleeeding feet like Washington's soldiers, but like the Colonies, you do owe us some money.

Don't wait for warmer weather to get into action. Unlimber that fountain pen and fire us a volley of $274.00 while you grin and bear it like the boys at Valley Forge.

Duty calls!

Yours until Cornwallis falls,

Saint Patrick's Day

Dear Mr. Doe:

If some mysteriously powerful individual started to do a good turn for business, as Saint Patrick did a good turn for Ireland, do you know what he would do first?

He would drive the past due accounts out of your business and ours.

Now, it is our duty to ourselves and to our customers to keep the past due accounts from accumulating on our books. As there is no chance of our being visited by a patron saint, we have to call on you to assist us.

Won't you please send a check for $341.00, remembering how much better we'll both feel in celebrating March 17?

Yours truly,

The Pilgrim Fathers

Gentlemen:

The Pilgrim Fathers *came across* in the Mayflower.

Of course, your account isn't quite as old as that, but you'll admit it's a long time since you "came across" with some cash.

Suppose you have your bookkeeper look into our statement of charges NOW. (I'll wager you'll find it O.K.) Then the next thing to do is to instruct him to fix a check for you to sign and send it to us TODAY.

In other words—do as the Pilgrim Fathers did.

COME ACROSS.

Sincerely yours,

The Early Settlers

Dear Mr. Doe:

Our hats are off to the early settlers!

And I don't mean this time those courageous pioneers of covered-wagon days.

I refer to those grand people who settle their subscription accounts early.

Of course, the enclosed statement does not come under the heading of "big business" so far as you're concerned. But when you have thousands of these little items on your books as we have, it's certainly "big business" to us.

So, won't you take a minute now and write your check for $4.00—and join the ranks of the EARLY SETTLERS. To bring it back to us, we enclose a postage-paid envelope.

Thank you.

Cordially yours,

Time for House Cleaning

Gentlemen:

Spring is finally here. The air is warm and fresh; the grass is green; lilacs are in bloom. It's the season for fishing, maple sugar, green onions, and a lot of other pleasant anticipations. Some, also, not so pleasant—House Cleaning, for example!

Which suggests our problem!

Not that we need to clean house here, but it will contribute a good deal to our security if we can persuade our customers to clean up old balances still due from last year.

In fact, last year will soon be only a memory. Won't you kindly cooperate to make it a pleasant one by sending your check for $95.00—using the enclosed envelope?

It's all we need to make Spring wonderful. Please don't let us down.

Yours sincerely,

The number and kinds of these out-of-the-groove collection letters are limited only by the imagination of those who write them, but those you have seen are fair samples of the run. And just for good measure, here are twelve "shorts"—one for each month of the year.

January

Well, the little fellow arrived on time this year. Sorry we can't say as much for your check that was expected in our office on January 5.

February

February, the month of holidays! Lincoln's and Washington's birthday...and Valentine's Day. We hope that your check for $25 has not taken a holiday. You know it was due on the 10th. What's that—it's on its way? Thank you.

March

March, they say, comes in as a lion—goes out as a lamb. Not roaring like a lion, but gently reminding you, comes this little notice to tell you that your payment of $40 was due last week.

April

April showers bring summer's flowers. But not yet, alas, your payment of $15 which was due on April 3. In anticipation... thank you.

May

Now comes the merry May

When shines the sun each day...

Not much as poetry, I realize, but then poetry is not my line. What I really want is to remind you that your payment of $10 was due on the 14th.

June

Summer—time for vacations—jolly blossom-scented days, moon-mad nights ... No wonder, perhaps, that your payment of $55, due the 21st, is A.W.O.L.

Won't you send it, please?

July

Month of the 4th—much noise! Thoughts of shade, ice-cold lemonade, a fishing trip in the North Woods. And no thought at all, it seems, of your payment of $32 which was due on the 8th.

Too hot to worry much ... but won't you send it, please?

August

Ever hear of pore ol' Pete? He weighed a good 400 pounds. Then along came August. Up went the thermometer and with each degree of heat pore ol' Pete got thinner. Seemed like he jest began to melt. And as it got no cooler, Pete plumb faded away. Pore ol' Pete.

But what about your check for $17, due on the 15th? We hope it ain't like Pete.

September

Throughout the land the school bells toll. Well do we remember the way we scampered to avoid getting in after the tardy bell rang. Maybe that payment of yours for $105 hasn't been to school, and didn't try to beat the bell.

Before we send for the truant officer, we'll try again. There. Did you hear it?

October

Boooo-oooo-oooo ...

'Tis the month of Ghosts, Witches 'n' Goblins—time of Hallow-een! But we don't really mean to frighten you: only to remind you that your payment of $20 was due on the 10th.

November

Ye olde Thanksgiving is almost at ye hande. Yea, verily, all men rejoiceth. We hope.

May there be bounty at thy home and much feasting—without ye stomach ache to follow.

And may thee please hurry thy payment of $44, due on ye 17th ... so that we too may rejoiceth.

We thanketh thee.

December

'Twas the night before Christmas . . .

And as you well know, throughout the house no one was stirring. To your house, we hope Santa Claus will come, making all your dreams come true.

But desolate is our house, for to it your payment due on December 3rd has NOT come. Play Santa, won't you please, and see that we are not forgotten any longer?

The merriest Christmas to you!

7. THE CREDIT MANAGER HELPS TO SELL

No reason for lack of teamwork. It is not unusual to find a company in which the credit and sales departments stand apart. Of course, this is understandable since the nature of their work may often cause differences of opinion. However, there is no basic reason why the salesman should not be interested in the financial security of an account, or why the credit man should not be interested in helping the account to grow as much as possible. Both conditions contribute to the customer's value to the company, and as the company prospers so do all its employees.

Consequently, the credit correspondent who thinks only about money matters is not making the most of his opportunity to serve and help his company. Granted that his major responsibility is to extend credit privileges wisely and to make sure they are not abused, he still has another responsibility, that of maintaining goodwill and helping as best he can in the general sales program.

Note, for example, how all these responsibilities are well met in this short letter.

Dear Mr. Doe:

Thank you for bringing your account so nearly up to date. Another small check this month, and you'll be current again.

With the spring rush coming up soon, wouldn't you like to stock our new line of gardening tools now?

Sincerely,

The credit manager who wrote that letter deserves master rating: first, because he firmly asked for the money due his company; second, because he did it in the nicest possible way; and third, because he also asked for another order. Thus, he served as a business builder as well as a money protector.

There are many ways in which the alert credit and collection letter-writer can help to win goodwill and increase sales. Some of the more important ways are illustrated in the following letters.

It collected the money and got an order. A rather serious credit problem confronted Howard Pope when he dictated this letter for the Menasha Products Company, of Menasha, Wisconsin. The customer had allowed his account to fall so far behind that he dared not send in any more orders. This meant a double loss to the company until the money could be collected. Accordingly, Mr. Pope as credit man suggests a solution to the problem—as a salesman he invites additional purchases.

> Gentlemen:
>
> Your orders have been missed. For many years you have sent in each month a number of orders which have been appreciated, and have had our prompt attention.
>
> You have not told us the reason why you have not favored us with any business recently, but we are inclined to believe it is because you owe us a past due account.
>
> We want your business, and we want to provide as convenient a manner for handling payment of your account as is possible. There is no reason why it should be necessary for you to turn to some other source of supply, for we are sure you have been well pleased with the quality of Menasha merchandise.
>
> Let's start out on a clean slate again.
>
> Attached are two notes of $112.81 and one of $112.80 dated today, and falling due on November 20, December 10, and December 30. Will you kindly sign and return the notes which will take care of the balance on your account? Then, having deferred the charges now outstanding, you undoubtedly will be in a position to handle current charges promptly. In fact, you can take advantage of the 2 per cent which we offer for payment in ten days.
>
> Your consideration of the settlement that we have offered will be appreciated. Why not sign the notes and send them along with a nice order for merchandise to be billed on our regular terms?
>
> > Very truly yours,

As so often stated in this Handbook, the only dependable test of a particular letter is whether or not it *does the intended job*. The customer who got the letter you have just read promptly complied with both of Mr. Pope's requests. He did sign and return the notes. He did include an order.

Here's another good collection letter that sells.

Gentlemen:

The old saying, "no news is good news," is no doubt true in many cases, but we cannot share that attitude when we are waiting to hear from a good customer.

You may not have realized it, but it has been over three months since we shipped your last order. So, before you lay this letter aside, won't you please start a check for $87.60 on its way, thereby saving yourself the time and trouble of reading more of this kind of letter from us in the future?

By the way, we have a large stock of the new colors in paint all ready for shipment, so any orders you have in mind for us will receive our usual prompt attention.

Very truly yours,

Telling the customer how to sell the order. When a merchant does not pay promptly for a shipment of goods, the reason is sometimes that they are not selling as he anticipated. To offset this possible objection, the writer of the following collection letter comes up with specific sales suggestions. Thus, he not only functions as a collector, but also may accomplish a double purpose for the sales department: first, to help move the stock now on the merchant's shelves; second, to pave the way for another order.

Dear Mr. Doe:

So far we have not received your check for the ten cases of Pet Milk delivered on June 10.

When you bought this Pet Milk, you didn't intend simply to add merchandise to your inventory. You bought it to increase your sales and your profit—and you selected the ideal brand for that purpose.

"Company Coming?" is the title of a Pet Milk advertisement that has been read by practically every woman in your neighborhood. This advertisement suggests a tempting and delicious dinner to be served to the company that evening. It starts in with cream of tomato soup, baked veal, sweet potatoes, and down the line to pineapple mousse, spice cake with caramel frosting, coffee, and candies.

How many women in your neighborhood have company coming today? How many will come into your store in a quandary as to what to serve? And what will you do to help them solve their problem?

Every one of these women is a golden opportunity for you—an opportunity to make suggestions, to make sales, to make profits. We want to help you to make these suggestions. We want to help you increase your sales not only of Pet Milk, but also of other things as well. If you are at a loss as to what to suggest, please return this letter to us and we will send you a supply of recipe leaflets that will help you do the job.

For your own good, for your own profit, we urge you to use these leaflets. It takes more than just a store with a stock of merchandise to make a successful and profitable business. Your success depends upon the salesmanship you put behind the merchandise —and salesmanship is largely suggestion.

Pet Milk, plus *your* salesmanship, equals profit. Try it. You will find that it works.

In the meantime, won't you please send us your check to cover our invoice of June 15?

Yours very truly,

Introducing new product or service. Because of the many letters ordinarily written by the credit manager, they can be made a useful means of spreading the news about new products and services. A splendid illustration of this possibility is a letter prepared by Credit Manager J. H. Winchester for the Ohio Rubber Company. At the top of the page is pasted a two-inch square of a new safety flooring offered by the company. In reality, the letter does more selling than collecting, for a check is not requested until near the end.

Gentlemen:

That small square you see above is a sample of Orco Safety Flooring.

Try rubbing your thumb over it. Do you notice the resistance it gives? Well, imagine walking on an area covered with this material—you'd feel safe, and it would be comfortable, too.

Your rubber heels have taught you that rubber is resilient— comfortable. You also know that you feel safe with them on. We combine those natural qualities of rubber with wear-resisting abrasive Norton Alundum for extra safety, add an attractive color, and we get Orco Safety Flooring.

It is the best insurance against accidents due to falls that we know of.

And speaking of falls, I hope that this request for payment of your past-due account, amounting to $25.00, does not fall into the discard. We imagine that our first request for payment slipped your attention. This bit of Orco Safety Flooring is to prevent that, and to perhaps establish your interest in our new material.

May we expect your check soon and an inquiry regarding our new product?

Very truly yours,

To remove any doubt with respect to the effectiveness of a combined sales and collection letter, we hasten to tell you that 68 per cent of the recipients sent checks within two weeks, and a round dozen sent orders for the new flooring. Here's a similar collection letter which takes time to sell a new product, although a sample could not be attached.

Gentlemen:

It is not only because we want to see this account paid that we ask you to send a check today, but also because we want to do more business with you, and we're afraid that the overdue account, amounting to $35.67, is keeping you away.

The popularity of our new ELECTRA model warrants your stocking it. A circular is enclosed. Although introduced only two months ago, the ELECTRA is already demanded in preference to all others. It is advertised in all the leading magazines.

We have not received an order from you for several months, and doubtless you are now in need of some of our line.

Just add ELECTRA to your next order, and, at the same time, let us have your check.

Thank you.

Yours very truly,

An improved service is just as much worth selling to a customer as is a new product. The credit manager who dictated the following message proves the point.

Dear Mr. Doe:

Many of our customers call at the yard for their own supplies. To speed our end of the affair, we have just installed the very latest loading equipment, and also have put extra men in the warehouse. Your trucks can now reduce their loading time here by from 30 to 50 per cent—a very substantial saving.

We haven't seen any of your drivers for some time. We hope, however, that you will soon give us an order, and test for yourself the efficiency and economy of our new loading system.

Stop in at our office some day next week, and we will be glad to show you the new equipment. At the same time, we would like to talk over your account, $77.65, now past due. We think that you will want to give us at least a substantial payment.

Please do drop in next week. We will be glad to see you.

Yours very truly,

Three more letters asking for orders. Before we lower the curtain on the pleasing picture of the sales-minded credit manager, here are three more letters actually used in business to ask for orders as well as checks.

Dear Mr. Doe:

The check you were to send us has not been received. If you have overlooked it, won't you kindly see that it goes out in the next mail?

Send us an order at the same time; it's always a pleasure to see new bills taking the place of old ones.

Very truly yours,

.   .   .   .   .

Dear Mr. Doe:

We don't mind admitting that we get a lot more fun out of selling materials than we do out of writing letters asking for money. But, as you well know, getting in the money is an important part of any business.

The balance of your account has now been due for several weeks, and we really ought to have your check for it. Won't you give this matter your immediate attention?

And if you need anything else that we can supply, send us an order along with that check. We are always at your service.

Cordially,

Dear Mr. Doe:

Have you overlooked our previous letters regarding your account? We expected your check before now, but as your payment has not been received we believe that something must be wrong.

We'd like to help you, Mr. Doe. If there is any reason you cannot pay at this time, won't you do the next best thing and tell us what the reason is? Then we can have a common ground for understanding.

Perhaps you are now able to make payment. We sincerely hope so. We have a complete line of Fall merchandise awaiting your appraisal.

Very truly yours,

Thanking those who pay promptly. A growing tendency among credit managers, and one sure to win goodwill, is the occasional recognition of those to whom it is never necessary to send collection letters. This, we think, has been in the past a too-often neglected courtesy. The customer who never causes any trouble deserves applause—for the selfish purpose of holding his favor if for no more commendable reason. If you concede the connection between goodwill and sales, you will agree it is no exaggeration to call the following message of appreciation a *sales* letter.

Dear Mr. Doe:

When you send us an order, we receive it with appreciation and try to fill it promptly with the highest quality merchandise.

Then we send you an invoice or statement and you promptly send us your check. We also appreciate that. But sometimes we forget to tell you about it.

We just want you to know that we genuinely thank you for your orders, and I, in particular, thank you for your prompt payments.

Yours very truly,

The next letter probably only took a couple of minutes to dictate and a postage stamp to place it in the hands of the customer, but it should/go a long way toward building goodwill and increasing sales.

Dear Mr. Doe:

Your account with us is now paid up-to-date.

If, in the course of transactions, we have left some doubt in your mind as to the policy we have maintained, please be assured that our deepest concern has been to strengthen our business relationship.

The personal touch is too often overlooked in the handling of large volumes of correspondence; therefore, if we have not thanked you for your cooperation, let us do so now.

We will look forward to the opportunity of serving you once again.

Cordially,

It is especially gratifying to see a similar letter of thanks coming from the Collection Department of an insurance company, for few of the big insurance organizations take advantage of such opportunities to win customer goodwill. For example, the policyholder who pays his premium regularly year after year usually gets only a receipt from the agent or home office—couched in stiff language and bearing no evidence of goodwill. In a different light, however, you see O. A. Moyer expressing appreciation for The Central Manufacturers' Mutual Insurance Company, of Van Wert, Ohio.

Dear Mr. Doe:

Did you ever have the feeling that you were failing to do something important, and could not think what it was? I have—but today I thought of it.

The writer who is responsible for collections has spent most of his time with a list of names that does not include such good agents as you. The most familiar names are those to whom we write many letters. When we glance at your account, we pass on with a genuine glow of satisfaction, knowing that your remit-

Then, with the o.k. of our credit department, we can ship your order as soon as it is received.

Cordially yours,

. . . . .

Dear Mr. Doe:

We have just received the order you gave our sales representative, Mr. Jones, for 10,000 cartons. It is a pleasure to welcome you cordially to the rapidly growing number of our customers.

Mr. Jones has asked us to ship your order on a "RUSH" basis. We would like to do so, for we want you to have the satisfaction of using our cartons at the earliest possible moment.

We and all other reputable members of the cardboard carton industry follow the practice of making a credit inquiry about new customers to confirm their good credit standing. This inquiry will take about a week to complete.

To avoid a delay on your first order, will you authorize us to ship it immediately on a C.O.D. basis? If you will send us a wire collect to that effect immediately upon receipt of this letter, your order will be on its way to you before the close of business tomorrow. If we do not receive a wire from you, we will ship your order on regular terms as soon as our credit records are complete.

Will you help us complete our inquiry by filling out the enclosed financial statement form and mailing it back to us at your earliest convenience?

Very truly yours,

Asking the wrong way. All of the preceding letters were friendly in tone, with nothing in them to cause resentment. We cannot, however, compliment another credit manager who handled the same situation for a furniture company. You will hardly feel inclined to do so either, after reading his insulting letter.

Dear Sir:

In your application for credit, looking up to a charge account with us, you failed to include sufficient intelligible information to enable us to make a decision in your favor.

We have to be very careful in granting credit, for there are so many irresponsible customers who are willing to take advantage of us and abuse their credit privilege.

In order to compensate for your deficiencies, we are asking you to fill out the enclosed form, furnish us a TRUE balance sheet

tances follow from month to month like clock-work without even a reminder from us.

When we consider all the letters we have been compelled to write during the year, it is a pleasure to write one voluntarily to an agent who has, even in this present day stress, maintained such a high standard. Perhaps it has never occurred to you what a joy such an account as yours is to the credit department.

Now my conscience feels better. With sincere appreciation and cordial good wishes to you,

Sincerely yours,

You know, of course, what an enormous amount of business is transacted on the time-payment basis. Some of the letters you have read in this section were undoubtedly sent to installment plan purchasers who failed to keep up with their contracts. Yet there are many thousands of people who never fail to make their payments regularly until the obligations are cancelled. These conscientious customers are a joy to the companies that deal with them—but this joy is seldom expressed in a letter of appreciation as it should be.

Consider the things that you may have bought "on time." How often have you received a friendly note such as the following?

Dear Mr. Doe:

The play has ended and the stage is dark.

This does not mean, however, that the memory of a good performance is forgotten, or that the principal actors, whose work made the play a memorable thing, are unappreciated.

On the contrary, we do appreciate the fine manner in which you paid your notes on the fan account, and it is with real pleasure that we return the original note and mortgage to you, cancelled with recorder's release.

This one play is over. That is true, but the show of business continues and we want to have a part in that big performance by helping you either with our equipment or suggestions.

Again that word of thanks for your choice of our equipment, and your promptness in making the payments. We hope, too, that we shall soon rise to the curtain call for serving you again.

Cordially yours,

8. LETTERS FOR OTHER CREDIT PROBLEMS

Need of judgment, skill, and diplomacy. So far, most of the letters in this section have revealed how various credit managers, or their assistants, go about the job of collecting money from customers who for one reason or another have not paid their bills as agreed in the terms of sale. These letters are of great importance since no company can afford to treat collections lightly. There are, however, many other situations connected with the allocation and control of credit which the credit manager usually handles by mail, and some of them may require the highest degree of judgment, skill and diplomacy.

Ordinarily, people expect to be reminded when they have not paid their bills. They are not as "touchy" about a collection letter as about one that asks for a financial report, one that refuses to allow an unearned discount, or one that insists on cash in full before the shipment of an order. Any one of these or other similar problems may turn out to be as difficult for the credit manager to solve as the collection of a troublesome account. It is not easy, for example, to write the letter which tells a prospective customer that available information does not justify credit privileges, and which nevertheless tries to salvage both the order and goodwill. But this is part of the credit manager's job, and he must know how to go about it with a reasonable percentage of success.

Another bothersome angle to these .special credit problems is the natural tendency of persons in the sales department to resent the loss of orders which the credit manager will not approve for credit. As a result, the c. m. is accused of lack of co-operation when he is really only performing his duty to the company by not taking on dangerous accounts. He stands on the point of a needle, wanting to please both customer and salesman, but still mindful of the fact that he will be held responsible for errors in judgment. At best, he can only play his cards as he sees them, trying to make the customer understand the *reason* for any action considered necessary, and being always as friendly and tactful as is humanly possible.

Asking for credit information. Obviously, any decision with respect to the credit privilege depends on the information which the credit manager is able to get about the customer. It may come from one of the agencies that furnish credit reports, from other companies that have had experience with the same party or firm, or from any other source considered reliable. Supplementing this assembly of facts, the credit manager in many cases also requests the buyer himself for a financial statement. All this takes time, and if the order-shipment is held up pending the final decision, the credit manager may quickly find himself in hot water with the new customer. That such a situation can be handled tactfully is illustrated by the following letters.

Dear Mr. Doe:

To me the high spot in any business day is the arrival of the first order from a new customer, and I want to tell you personally how much I appreciate your order.

Concerning the rather delicate question of terms and credit, I do not like to see a new customer receive the usual cold and formal request for credit information without some personal word from me on the subject.

It is our policy to extend every possible accommodation to our customers, and we realize that a friendly credit policy is just as important as the maintenance of quality in our product. These two services make for a permanent and happy relationship between manufacturer and customer.

Will you, therefore, kindly send me some information on which our credit manager can base his records? The name of your bank, together with the names of several suppliers with whom you have already established credit, will be satisfactory.

There will, of course, be some delay in our receiving this information. For prompt delivery, perhaps you would prefer to send a check for the first order so that we can make immediate shipment.

Please accept my thanks once more for this order.

Yours very truly,

• • • • •

Gentlemen:

It was a pleasure to receive your recent order which was entered for immediate shipment at our regular thirty-day terms.

To enable us to extend the line of credit you may need, will you send us the usual credit information? For your convenience, we enclose a simplified financial statement form.

Thank you again for your order, and we hope that this is the beginning of a long and mutually pleasant business relationship.

Cordially,

• • • • •

Gentlemen:

Our representative has just written to us the good news of your decision to distribute our products. He tells us to expect your initial stock order soon.

We want to be sure that you will receive your stock without delay, and, as our credit department requiries that we furnish them with information on all new accounts, we ask that you assist us by filling in the enclosed form.

of your business, and to give us more detailed information concerning the possibilities of your present location. This is required of all applicants.

If you do not do this, it will mean further delay and may result in a refusal on our part to consider your application any further.

Yours truly,

The letters we have just inspected were by no means final with respect to credit classification. The writers were simply trying to save the initial order and at the same time secure information to guide them in handling future business. But a much more serious problem confronts the credit manager when finally he has to *refuse* the credit privilege. When he can do that and still make the order stick, he is really at his best.

Letters that refuse open terms. When the financial picture of a new customer does not warrant his buying on credit, it is indeed difficult to tell him so and still retain his goodwill. Some credit managers do not seem to worry much over this problem, for their letters are displeasingly blunt. Others, more sales-minded, try nobly to break the news gently, and to make the order stick on cash terms. The latter is frequently possible, as many of the best credit men will agree. In fact, they say it should be the rule rather than the exception.

Consider what one prominent credit manager says about salvaging orders in spite of credit obstacles. The speaker is C. G. Beardsley, of the Taylor Instrument Co., Rochester, New York.

We do not turn down orders. We accept them.

Then, we try to sell the customer on our terms instead of his. Moreover, the job cannot be done with a form letter. The reply must meet each case and show a thorough understanding of the buyer's problem. If that can be done then our proposition is half sold. We discuss the matter frankly, though politely.

We approach the customer by saying that since he is a newcomer, or is not rated, it is only natural that we should make credit inquiries, which we have done. We then discuss with him what the reports show, always making allowances for the fact that the reports may be wrong, and that there may have been improvement in the customer's business not reflected by the reports.

We tell the customer the reason why we must have our bill paid promptly, or why it would not be wise for us to supply him with added credit, and why we must have cash.

That this plan works is proved by the fact that we rarely have to cancel an order for credit reasons.

A disputed question among credit men is how far the letter should go in telling the customer exactly *why* he cannot enjoy the privilege of buying on open terms. Some think the truth only tends to anger the customer, and so they do as little explaining as possible. Others, as in the case in the letter below, put the cards face-up on the table.

Dear Mr. Doe:

Thank you for sending us your business statement and references so promptly. All your references spoke very highly of you, as a businessman and as a member of the community. We feel sure that you are going to make a very profitable business out of the Arcade Shop, and we want to do everything we can to help you do so.

We have studied your business very carefully, and we want to make one or two friendly suggestions. We do not believe it would be to your advantage for us to fill your order on the open terms you asked for. Frankly, Mr. Doe, you are somewhat under-capitalized, and for you to assume additional current liabilities just now might seriously jeopardize your prospects. If you possibly can, you should obtain at least $3,000 additional capital. With your personal ability and your favorable location, you should have little difficulty in doing so.

We also recommend that you allow us to halve your order and ship to you on cash terms. You will save the 2 per cent discount, which will mean a lot to you right now. We can ship the other half of the order on a moment's notice if you find you need it, and you will avoid tying up more capital in inventory if you do not.

Very soon—in a few weeks, perhaps—you should be in a position to command our most favorable credit terms. We hope that our suggestions will help you to do so. We will ship the first half of your order the moment we get your approval.

Sincerely yours,

When a large retail company declines to open a charge account, there is no way of knowing the reaction of the applicant. He may continue to buy for cash or, disgruntled, he may go elsewhere with his business. Probably, what he actually does depends a lot on the tone and content of the letter in which he is denied credit. The letter below does the job in a nice way, inviting the customer to call and discuss the matter if he is not satisfied with the credit manager's decision.

Dear Mrs. Doe:

Thank you for your application for a charge account. We sincerely appreciate your interest in our store.

It has always been our policy to accommodate our customers in all matters as well as we can. Unfortunately, there are times when temporary circumstances prevent us from offering certain services to everyone.

Your application has been very carefully considered, and we regret that it seems inadvisable, from your standpoint as well as ours, for you to open a charge account with us just now. This, of course, in no way prohibits you from making another application at some future date. And if you should feel that our decision is in any way unjustified, we would be very happy to have you come in and discuss the matter with us.

In the meanwhile, we hope you will take advantage of our other services. You may reserve any article in our store on the lay-away plan, and you may, of course, order any advertised item by telephone for C.O.D. delivery.

Sincerely yours,

The circumstances of the following letter are perhaps somewhat special, making it possible for the credit manager to suggest alternative means of obtaining credit. All the same, the writer has made a commendable effort to be particularly polite and gracious about his refusal. A less tactful credit manager might easily have alienated a customer of long standing.

Dear Mr. Doe:

I do wish we could arrange a time payment order for you, but owing to our small margin of profit, our requirements for credit are quite strict. To qualify, one must have a regular, established income.

This being the case, there isn't any way in which we can fill an order in your name alone. I regret this more than I can say, for we always like to help our customers, especially the old friends of our firm.

You mention that your sons contribute to your support. Perhaps one, of legal age, can qualify, and would be glad to order the things you want, in his name. Or he might sign the contract with you and guarantee the payments.

If so, the order should be sent in the usual way on one of our order blanks that you'll find in the back of our catalog. All questions should be answered carefully, and the contract signed as specified, so we can make our regular credit investigation and establish the proper credit rating.

I do hope you will understand the reasons behind this decision, Mr. Doe. We want you to know you are one of our valued customers, and we want to continue serving you.

Yours respectfully,

In contrast, what would have been your reaction had you received the following goodwill-buster? "Dear Sir: We cannot do business with you for obvious credit reasons. Perhaps one of our competitors will not be so particular, as we do not lean backward when it comes to risking questionable accounts." Decidedly, that is NOT a good way to refuse the credit privilege.

Second attempt to make order stick. It is refreshing to see a credit manager who fights for orders, even though it may be his unpleasant duty to restrict the terms. In the next case, the would-be buyer had been refused credit in a previous letter. Presumably, he has gone shopping elsewhere, but the credit manager is determined to make the order stick if he possibly can.

> Dear Mr. Doe:
>
> We are sorry not to have heard from you in answer to our letter of May 16, which asked for your confirmation of cash-in-advance terms on our proposed manufacture for you of wringer rolls, channel rubber, and the die to make the channel rubber.
>
> You may think we are unduly aggressive, but since there is a die to be made before we can manufacture your rubber, we will need sufficient time to make this die if we are to ship exactly on schedule as you tell us your needs.
>
> We are very anxious to have your business, Mr. Doe, and regret that conditions will not permit us to allow you open account terms. But I know that you, as a man of good business judgment, will not take this as a personal affront; nor can it be construed as such, because every company, unless it has a large working capital in the beginning, starts business the same way—on a cash-in-advance basis.
>
> Later, after we have had a chance to assist in a company's growth, and to observe its habits, we quite often allow open account credit. So that is always a possibility, Mr. Doe, and we want you to feel just that way about it.
>
> Why not, then, give us the business on a cash basis and see what kind of work we can do, and just what kind of people we are to do business with? You will surely not regret it. More often than not you will find us "leaning over backward" to please you.
>
> We are dating your file ahead ten days. Please let us hear from you within that time.
>
> Very truly yours,

What to say when credit is approved. Although no problem confronts the credit manager when he tells a customer that a charge account has been approved, he has an excellent opportunity to win goodwill by making the letter something more than just a cut-and-dried confirmation. In other words, the credit privilege should be extended cheerfully, and with a hand of welcome. It may also explain the credit policy of the company in order to get the new account off on the right foot, and to discourage any infractions which the customer might be tempted to make later. However, such explanations tend to mar the friendly tone of the letter, and usually they have been clearly made at the time the application was taken. We like best the type of letter which simply welcomes and thanks the customer, and promises to serve him well. Here is an example:

Dear Mrs. Doe:

Like making friends, there is a real satisfaction in adding your name to our growing list of charge account customers.

We hope that this may be the beginning of a long and pleasant business relationship—profitable to you and to us—and that we may enjoy one another's confidence, friendship, and respect.

Please call on us at any time. We look forward to serving you.

Cordially yours,

The two notes that follow are somewhat less demonstrative, and are perhaps more typical of the common run. Both, you will observe, mention terms.

Dear Mr. Doe:

We are happy to tell you that your application for a charge account has been approved. This is only the beginning of what we hope will be a long and pleasant association.

Your account has been opened on a monthly basis. You may take advantage of the discount for payment within ten days after delivery, as explained, or you may pay the gross bill during the month following your purchase. We mail our regular monthly statement about the first of the month.

We sincerely hope you will enjoy the convenience of your new charge account. If you have any question or suggestion that might enable us to serve you better, please feel free to get in touch with us.

Cordially yours,

.   .   .   .   .

Dear Mr. Doe:

It is our pleasure to notify you that a charge account has been approved in your name. We will constantly endeavor to serve you courteously and to your complete satisfaction.

Arrangements have been made to place at your disposal credit amounting to $250. When you wish to exceed this sum, I will be happy to discuss the matter with you.

Bills will be rendered on the first of each month, and are to be paid in full by the tenth.

An identification plate is enclosed, and a booklet that tells you how to use it. We know that you will find this new charge account a great convenience.

Cordially yours,

Offering the credit privilege. In many types of business, charge accounts—properly controlled—are considered a real asset: first, because customers are more likely to consolidate their purchases where they enjoy the privilege of credit; and second, because they tend to create goodwill. Thus, the charge account encourages more spending (as many husbands know) and keeps it in the same store. It is, therefore, not uncommon for the credit manager of a company to *offer* the credit privilege to those who have been buying with cash and are thought to be dependable. Like this:

Dear Mr. Doe:

When we cashed a check for you the other day, it occurred to us that you might enjoy the convenience of a charge account with us.

This credit privilege does away with the need of paying for each purchase separately, and allows you to order by telephone when you are too busy to call at the store. It also brings to you the news of special services that we arrange from time to time only for charge customers.

We will be very happy to extend our credit service to you, and for the time alone saved you will find it a real convenience.

Just fill out the enclosed credit card and return it in the enclosed envelope which requires no postage. Twenty-four hours after the card is received, your charge account will be cleared and ready for you to use.

Cordially yours,

Dear Mr. Doe:

We are happy to extend to you our cordial invitation that you open a charge account.

All you have to do is to sign and return the enclosed card, so that we can have a charge-plate made for you to use. With this plate in your purse you may buy anything you want from us without any bother or fuss. You don't need any cash—the charge-plate tells our clerks that you are a preferred customer, and entitled to credit privileges.

Another great convenience, of course, in having a Blank charge account, is that you can order anything you need by telephone or mail. For the busy modern woman, this privilege is indeed often a blessing.

Each month you will receive an itemized statement, and you then have ten days to pay the bill. Sales tax tokens are not used when charging a purchase—the amount of the tax is simply added to the monthly bill.

There are other special privileges that our charge account customers enjoy. What they are you will pleasantly find out after your account has been made a matter of record.

So, please do return the card the day you receive this letter.

                              Very cordially yours,

Putting the brakes on a charge account. One thing that makes the life of a credit manager interesting is the way seemingly stable accounts will all of a sudden begin to turn sour. Over a long period of time, for example, a customer may promptly discount his bills, so that the credit manager never has the slightest worry about him; then, month by month the unpaid balance carried over gets larger and larger until finally it is necessary to suspend the credit privilege.

It is not easy, as any credit manager knows, to tell an old and loyal customer that future shipments must be made C.O.D., even though the change in terms is presented as a temporary means of helping the customer to get his house in order. If the letter is not extremely tactful, the writer may bring two evils on his head: first, the complete loss of the customer's business; second, the problem of having to fight for the collection of the unpaid balance.

Here is how one prominent credit manager went about the job.

Dear Mr. Doe:

Your recent letter of explanation about your past-due account and your order amounting to an additional $400 forces me to write to you frankly, as I would want you to write to me if the conditions were reversed.

Of all the companies who have accounts with us, there is not a one in which we have greater confidence than yours. But like yourself, we too have allowed many of our old accounts to become much larger than we would have in less trying times. However, we cannot continue to be so lenient, and we must watch collections closely if we are to stay in business and continue to offer quality services and merchandise.

In substance, Mr. Doe, this means we are in the same boat with you—our creditors depend on us to keep their business solvent, just as we depend on you, and you in turn depend on your customers. It's a sort of moving chain of credit, and no link can be broken without injury to all.

In view of the fact that the amount of your account has steadily increased during the past 12 months (with a present balance of almost three thousand dollars) we believe you will understand why it is best for both your company and ours that your last order be shipped C.O.D.

In fact, we are so sure that you will be in sympathy with this decision—it being the same that you will have to make with some of your own customers—that we are going ahead with the shipment so as not to delay the customary prompt service.

A substantial payment on your account will in the meantime be a great help. We can ask our manufacturers for more credit when you and other good customers are able to reduce the total of their past due payments. And this means eventually we can resume shipments to you on the old basis.

For the present, you will realize why your own account must be considerably reduced before any more credit can be extended.

With our very best wishes,

Yours very truly,

The letter below is similar in purpose, but there is one important difference in circumstances. In this case, the customer is comparatively new.

Dear Mr. Doe:

You ask, "Why C.O.D. terms?" Here is the explanation, and we want you to see it our way, so that we may work together to make the C.O.D. basis only temporary.

Back in August we approved credit terms for you although reports indicated that your obligations were not always promptly settled. We told you then that we did not want to be guided entirely by records, and that we would do our best to assist you in rebuilding a credit rating. That is why open account terms were approved, and we expected you would promptly discount our various invoices.

Since you did not do this, the past-due account raised the question of continued credit, for such delays in payment often point to business difficulties. Consequently, in order to collect this old account and prevent invoices from piling up, we had to suspend credit terms.

This necessity is regretted by us, but we honestly believe that you will gain by our action. You now have the opportunity to catch up on the past-due account, to clarify this credit problem, and to earn your 2 per cent cash discount on current shipments —all by paying C.O.D.

We do not want to stress the 2 per cent discount too much, but after all the purpose of any business is to make money—and discounting bills is one of the easiest ways. There is no need to tell you that competition is very keen nowadays—generally, your margin has to be small, and it is important that you use every possible advantage to put yourself ahead of your competitors. When you earn cash discount and your competitor loses it, you strengthen your business and he weakens his.

Past-due accounts are expensive—for both of us! It costs you money because you lose the 2 per cent discount and jeopardize your credit rating. It costs us money because of additional bookkeeping work, collection costs, and extra office time.

So that's the answer, Mr. Doe, to your question—"Why C.O.D. terms?" and we think you must understand we have tried to do the fair thing, in the right way.

Sincerely yours,

Asking the customer to sign notes. That credit managers are not so hard to get along with as some people suppose, is proved by the two friendly letters below. In both cases, the customer has already placed the facts on the table—an act of frankness which would eliminate a lot of credit troubles if only carried out more frequently. Credit men, as a rule, are willing to go along with a customer who seems honest and sincere; it is lack of explanation—continued silence—that forces them to be "tough."

Gentlemen:

The writer wants to thank you personally for your very frank letter. Everybody is up against it at one time or another. We have been ourselves. And that is exactly why we are going to help you.

Don't worry about that account with us, even if it is past due. Forget it for ninety days. We are going to ask you to sign a note covering that period. By that time, things will undoubtedly look better.

We wouldn't do this for everybody, but from your letter we get the idea you are strictly all right. We want you to build up a good business, and we will help you all we can. It's a pleasure to have folks know that we sell service as well as quality.

Just sign the note and return it to us promptly.

Cordially yours,

Dear Mr. Doe:

We are glad to read of your intention of paying as soon as possible our bill of June 3, amounting to $77.63. We realize of course, that the farmers have been having a difficult time. But that, of course, makes hard sledding for us, as a large share of our merchandise goes to farmers.

Now, we try to make things easy for everyone, but we have to ask our friends to pull with us—not against us. For this reason, we are enclosing a note for the amount due. This note is dated August 1 and is due September 1—in other words, in two months.

Just please sign the note, and return it to us.

Yours very truly,

You will recall that the same plan of getting notes signed was used by Howard Pope (page 879) although the amount involved was much larger.

Letters that explain value of discounts. In many sales contracts a special discount—usually 2 per cent—is offered the customer who pays the bill within a stated period, commonly ten days from the date of invoice. This "bonus plan" can be either a blessing or a curse to the credit manager, the former when it speeds collections as it of course does in many cases, the latter when it leads to an argument with some customer who thinks he should have the discount even though the stipulated date is past. On the whole, the good of the plan undoubtedly outweighs the bad, although the proportion may vary in specific companies or types of business.

When a buyer does not take advantage of the discount privilege, one of two reasons is likely to be the cause: first, he does not understand how much money could be saved; or second, he simply hasn't enough liquid cash to meet all obligations promptly. There isn't a lot that a credit manager may do to offset the second reason, but he *can* educate the buyer who doesn't realize what discounts may amount to over a year's time. Here are a couple of examples to show how this education job may be done.

Gentlemen:

Yesterday we uncovered something that we think will interest you.

On last year's purchases, you neglected to earn discounts amounting to $127.80.

It occurs to us that perhaps you are unaware that it is possible, in a year's time, to save 24 per cent on your average monthly purchases from us by deducting 2 per cent from the face amount of our monthly bill, providing you pay it by the 10th of the month following delivery.

No, there's no trick to it. Suppose your average monthly purchases come to $500. If you send us your check in full payment by the 10th of each month following your purchase, you can deduct 2 per cent, or $10, from the total bill. By doing this every month, your annual savings will amount to $120, or 24 per cent of your average monthly purchases of $500.

Isn't that surprising? It's a grand idea if you can do it. And that brings us to the point of our letter. We don't want to seem to be telling you what to do. It's your business and you know best what can be done, but we do hope that in bringing these facts to your attention, perhaps you can finish the year with a sizable "discount earned" account.

We hope that you will buy frequently from us and that it will be possible for you to discount your purchases when you do. However, please be sure that discounting or not, we have enjoyed doing business with you and will continue to do so.

Very truly yours,

Dear Mr. Doe:

This is an explanation of how we can help your profits. Some of our dealers do not know that we give them a discount of 2 per cent if they pay their accounts within 10 days.

Six weeks ago, you gave us a $206 order. Had you paid this bill in full within 10 days, you would have saved $4.12. In other words, by waiting the full 30 days to remit payment, you paid, in effect, an interest of $4.12 on $206 for 20 days. Since there are eighteen 20-day periods a year, this is the equivalent of paying an annual interest rate of 36%.

This savings is so important that many of our customers who are pressed for cash find it profitable to borrow from a bank—at 6%—to take advantage of this service.

It's entirely up to you, of course, whether you avail yourself of our discount privilege. I just want to make sure that you know of this savings we offer our customers—a savings that means many vital dollars to you in a year's time.

Cordially,

Letters such as these just read present no particular problem for the credit manager. He really has a strong sales point to develop, and can write with the good of his customer at heart. But the negative side of the picture is not nearly so pleasant.

Collecting discounts taken but not earned. It may seem very simple to say that no discount will be allowed after the stipulated date, but *getting the money back* from a customer who has abused the privilege is not as easy as it sounds. Particularly, if the amount of the sale is large, and the customer an old friend of the company, the credit manager is up against it when forced to write: "Since the ten day period expired before your check was mailed, may we ask that you kindly forward the amount of the discount which you inadvertently deducted?" He may say "inadvertently," but he is not fooling either himself or his customer. And the latter, called on the carpet, is quite likely to fight back. The temptation, of course, is for the credit manager to yield, but this is not fair to other customers who play the game according to the rules.

Possibly business would be better off without the discount privilege which came into being shortly after the Civil War. This was during a period of depression, and merchants said: "Send us the money which we need badly and in return for the favor you may deduct 2% from the face amount." They probably had no thought of starting a custom which now exists in most lines of business.

Be that as it may, here are letters in which credit managers of today seek to handle the problem of collecting discounts not earned.

Must the Seller Beware?

Gentlemen:

Terms of sales should be considered more binding than seems to be common these days. *"Let the seller beware"* is apparently the policy under which many payments are mailed out.

Some concerns evidently have one policy for payment of their purchases and quite another and different policy which they expect their customers to follow in paying their bills, but they cannot justly take unearned discounts and generally ignore the terms of the houses they buy from and expect their own customers to do anything different.

It is time that every business house of standing and reputation started a housecleaning in this regard and spread the word along the way that the present looseness and disregard of terms is a thing of the past, and that buyer and seller must "eventually" conform to a high standard of practice—*"so why not now?"*

In calling your attention to this situation we have in mind the fact that several payments have been returned to you because of the expiration of the cash discount period before the check was mailed. In each case a letter has been written to you explaining the matter and requesting your cooperation. Nevertheless, we do not seem to make any headway; so we request that you give proper attention to this letter and to this subject, advising us at your earliest convenience of your cooperation along these lines.

Yours very truly,

"We Are Within Our Rights"

Dear Mr. Doe:

Although you say that you will quit doing business with us if we insist that you pay the unearned discount deducted from our invoice of April 10th, I honestly believe it would be the other way around. I say this because few of us have any respect for those who do not stand for their rights. And we are within our rights, else I wouldn't write.

Let's suppose a man came to you and bought a bill of goods. Upon buying, he asked for the cash price and the term price. Then, suppose he waits until long after the term period had expired, and then pays you the cash price. Wouldn't you go to him and say he still owed you the difference? I believe that you would.

Now, that is our position exactly. When we offered our proposition, we, in effect, said to your buyer: "If you pay our invoice within 70 days, you may deduct 4% as a cash discount. But if the bill is not paid after 70 days, then the invoice is net. The discount privilege is lost!" This term proposition was accepted when you bought $101.60 worth of rugs on April 10th. The last day for discounting was June 20th. But your accountant didn't mail the check until August 6th—or 47 days after the last discount date. When he did, he deducted a discount that was no longer available.

What would you do were you in our place? Would you ask for the $40.64 erroneously deducted? If you wouldn't say anything, then we'll write it off this time. But if you would, then you will know what to do with the stamped envelope I enclose.

With best wishes.

Sincerely yours,

It Is Not a Crime

Gentlemen:

It is not a crime to take unearned discount.

Our only purpose in writing at all is to remind you of our terms, which are 2% in 10 days, net thirty days.

The last letter, written to you on March 18, mentioned the amount of $1.29 which was charged against your account. This meant, to our way of thinking, that you still owed that small amount.

However, while we would like you to pay what is due us, nevertheless, we realize that in demanding it we might cause some ill feeling, and we can assure you that no discount is large enough to cause us to do that.

So we're leaving it up to you. Pay it if you think we are right—don't pay it if you think we are wrong. But above all, let us remain good friends, both of us remembering...

It is not a crime to take unearned discount.

Very truly yours,

Refusing special terms. A thorn in the side of the credit manager is the customer who makes what appears to him as a sensible request, although from the point of view of the company it is another exception to established routine and cannot be granted. A policy not adhered to strictly becomes no policy at all, and there is no reason why one special favor should be allowed unless the company is prepared to do as much for others. For example, a common request is that the discount be conceded if bills are paid on the tenth of the month, instead of within the ten days following date of invoice. Or the customer has some other time of the month when it is more convenient for him to pay his bills, and sees no harm in the practice provided the date is understood and he adheres to it faithfully. But no matter what the request, or how reasonable it may seem to the customer, it is still an exception to the established credit policy and only under very special circumstances can it be considered.

Saying "no" to these requests is, of course, a task requiring considerable diplomacy. The credit manager must take time to explain the company point of view, and do his best to make the customer accept it as fair and necessary. This job is done rather well in the following two letters.

Gentlemen:

Mr. Doe of our Cleveland office has referred your letter to us regarding our regular terms of sale. We certainly appreciate the opportunity to discuss these terms with you.

In your position as Purchasing Agent, you no doubt have a much better understanding of terms than does the average person. Consequently, you know that the best terms are those which permit the retention of working capital for the longest period of time. Conversely, it is also true that from the selling standpoint, it is best to have short terms which will bring in working capital within the shortest period of time.

To get a balance between these two is indeed difficult, particularly when one considers that he buys from hundreds of different concerns and perhaps sells as many different ones.

Our terms of sale are 2% tenth prox., net thirty days. These are standard in the Rubber Industry, and we like to think that we treat all of our customers alike. Obviously, if a good customer like yourself said that you would not give us any more business unless we changed our terms, it would be foolish to think that we wouldn't give you the terms you wanted, but our experience has been that customers are willing to co-operate and as a rule do not ask for special preference.

We think of you as being like that, and we would appreciate very much your adhering to our terms of sale. We don't want to be arbitrary and we assure you we aren't. But if at all possible, we hope you will buy from us in the future on our regular terms.

Yours very truly,

Gentlemen:

We refer to your letter of May 30, in which you suggest a change of terms on our merchandise from 2% 10 days from date of invoice, to 2% if paid prior to the 10th of the calendar month.

We can see a great deal of justice in your request that some change be made in the discount period. From our standpoint, however, we are in somewhat of a dilemma because we are anxious to accede to the view of our customers, and while leaning in that direction, our sources of supply have tightened up their terms, as against becoming more lenient.

Thus, we are somewhat in the position of a tight-rope walker trying to maintain a balance—trying to favor our good friends on one hand, and take care of our invoices within the terms as laid down by our sources of supply.

As I have intimated, our sources of supply, instead of becoming more lenient, have tightened up on us to the extent that instead of giving 2% for remittance in 10 days from date of invoice, it is now one half of one per cent, and on some commodities, such as pig tin, of which we use a lot, we must pay upon receipt of shipping document. So, there are times when the goods have been paid for many days before we receive them.

With this explanation, I know you can see our position, and that you will be willing to pay our invoices according to the terms which for so long a time have prevailed.

Believe me, this co-operation on your part will be greatly appreciated.

Sincerely yours,

We think the extremely pleasant tone of the two foregoing letters could hardly fail to strike a receptive chord in the mind of the customers. Thus, as this section comes to a close, you have seen two credit managers meeting fully their obligations to company needs, but at the same time approaching their customers with courteous appreciation of their viewpoint.

These examples may be accepted as the one and only basis on which any sales-minded and sincere credit manager may handle his responsibilities completely, and with credit to himself. There are, of course, any number of situations not illustrated which may from day to day confront the "watch-dog" of the company's money. But so long as he continues to adhere to company policy without causing unnecessary friction in customer relations, no situation can be so difficult that no satisfactory solution can be found. The credit manager is a very important executive in the average company. On the whole, he is doing his job in a way that deserves our commendation.

INDEX